solutions@syngress.com

With over 1,500,000 copies of our MCSE, MCSD, CompTIA, and Cisco study guides in print, we have come to know many of you personally. By listening, we've learned what you like and dislike about typical computer books. The most requested item has been for a web-based service that keeps you current on the topic of the book and related technologies. In response, we have created solutions@syngress.com, a service that includes the following features:

- A one-year warranty against content obsolescence that occurs as the result of vendor product upgrades. We will provide regular web updates for affected chapters.

- Monthly mailings that respond to customer FAQs and provide detailed explanations of the most difficult topics, written by content experts exclusively for solutions@syngress.com.

- Regularly updated links to sites that our editors have determined offer valuable additional information on key topics.

- Access to "Ask the Author"™ customer query forms that allow readers to post questions to be addressed by our authors and editors.

Once you've purchased this book, browse to

www.syngress.com/solutions.

To register, you will need to have the book handy to verify your purchase.

Thank you for giving us the opportunity to serve you.

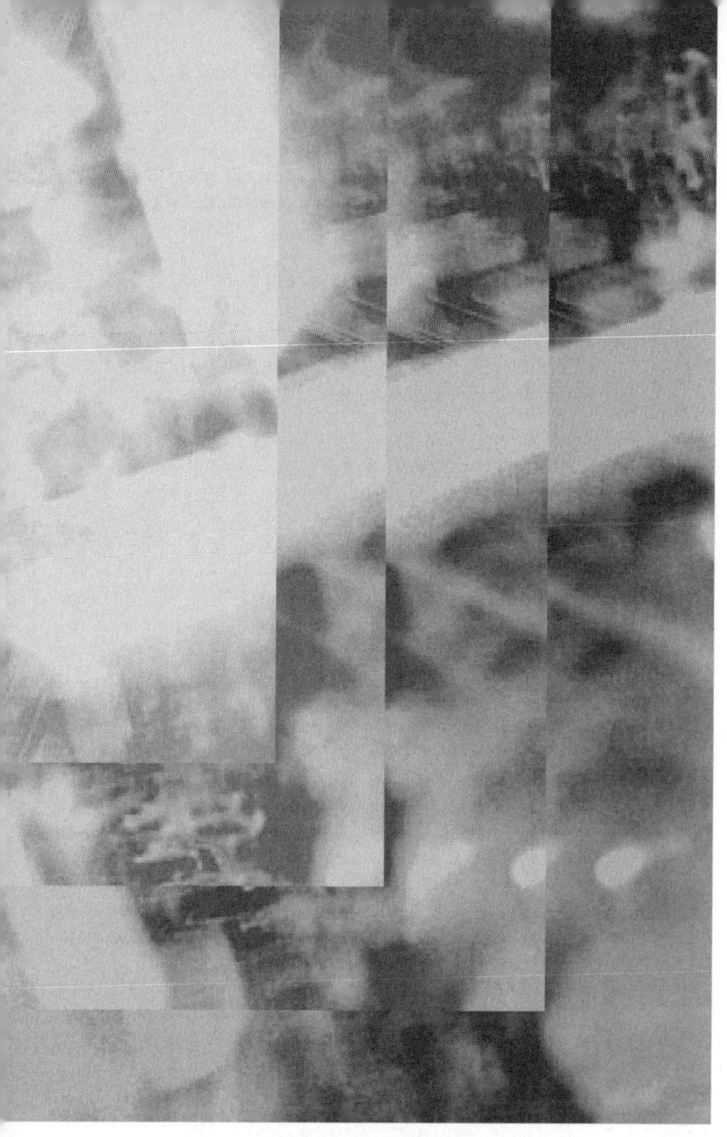

CONFIGURING

EXCHANGE 2000 SERVER

SYNGRESS®

KEY	SERIAL NUMBER
001	58P6DNSDSE
002	XPSPPL35C4
003	C3NMCF6FV7
004	P95C87BC2W
005	A4PCA94D55
006	6762RALTHG
007	Z7P8K522Q5
008	KUDJKE3427
009	7HSW2E947J
010	36GRMPS272

PUBLISHED BY
Syngress Publishing, Inc.
800 Hingham Street
Rockland, MA 02370

Configuring Exchange 2000 Server

Copy edit by: Joeth Barlas, Darlene Bordwell, and Nancy Hannigan
Technical edit by: Liz Mason and Bill Wade
Technical review by: Neil Hobson
Co-Publisher: Richard Kristof

Developmental Editor: Kate Glennon
Freelance Editorial Manager: Maribeth Corona-Evans
Acquisitions Editor: Catherine Nolan
Index by: Robert Saigh
Page Layout and Art by: Shannon Tozier

Distributed by Publishers Group West

Acknowledgments

We would like to acknowledge the following people for their kindness and support in making this book possible.

Richard Kristof, Duncan Anderson, David Marini, Jennifer Gould, Kevin Murray, Dale Leatherwood, Laura Cervoni, and Rhonda Harmon of Global Knowledge, for their generous access to the IT industry's best courses, instructors, and training facilities.

Ralph Troupe, Rhonda St. John, and the team at Callisma for their invaluable insight into the challenges of designing, deploying and supporting world-class enterprise networks.

Karen Cross, Lance Tilford, Meaghan Cunningham, Kim Wylie, Harry Kirchner, Bill Richter, Kevin Votel, Brittin Clark, and Sarah MacLachlan of Publishers Group West for sharing their incredible marketing experience and expertise.

Mary Ging, Caroline Hird, Simon Beale, Caroline Wheeler, Victoria Fuller, Jonathan Bunkell, and Klaus Beran of Harcourt International for making certain that our vision remains worldwide in scope.

Anneke Baeten, Annabel Dent, and Laurie Giles of Harcourt Australia for all their help.

David Buckland, Wendi Wong, Daniel Loh, Marie Chieng, Lucy Chong, Leslie Lim, Audrey Gan, and Joseph Chan of Transquest Publishers for the enthusiasm with which they receive our books.

Kwon Sung June at Acorn Publishing for his support.

Ethan Atkin at Cranbury International for his help in expanding the Syngress program.

Joe Pisco, Helen Moyer, and the great folks at InterCity Press for all their help.

Stephen Chetcuti at www.msexchange.org.

From Liz Mason, Contributor and Technical Editor

I would like to thank Syngress Publishing, especially Kate Glennon, Catherine Nolan, and Andrew Williams for their professionalism, patience, and assistance. You are a quality team of publishers.

I would also like to thank Bill Wade for his reviewing skills and Paul Salas for his insight and moral support.

The authors of this book worked very hard and produced some great content. Congratulations on a job well done.

A special thank you goes to the MicroStaffers that helped out during writing and editing days: Mickey Owens, Tan McGill, and Gale Porterfield, Ken Meece (MCSE, MCT) and Alex Cook (MCSE, MCT) for their clustering and Exchange assistance and David Smith (MCSE, MCT) for his time diagramming and editing.

Thank you to Trevor and Michelle for your support over the holidays. Thank you to Mom and Dad for your love. Thank you to Flossie for your kindness, consideration, and willingness to help. Most importantly, all my love and appreciation to my understanding and supportive husband Geoff and our wonderful son Liam.

From Global Knowledge

At Global Knowledge we strive to support the multiplicity of learning styles required by our students to achieve success as technical professionals. As the world's largest IT training company, Global Knowledge is uniquely positioned to offer these books. The expertise gained each year from providing instructor-led training to hundreds of thousands of students worldwide has been captured in book form to enhance your learning experience. We hope that the quality of these books demonstrates our commitment to your lifelong learning success. Whether you choose to learn through the written word, computer based training, Web delivery, or instructor-led training, Global Knowledge is committed to providing you with the very best in each of these categories. For those of you who know Global Knowledge, or those of you who have just found us for the first time, our goal is to be your lifelong competency partner.

Thank your for the opportunity to serve you. We look forward to serving your needs again in the future.

Warmest regards,

Duncan Anderson
President and Chief Executive Officer, Global Knowledge

Contributor and Technical Editor

Liz Mason (MCSE, MCT, CTT) is founder and CEO of MicroStaff Information Technology (www.microstaffit.com), a consulting and training firm specializing in Microsoft BackOffice services. Liz has not strayed far from the server room in the past 18 years: She worked for NCR Corporation, starting in 1984, where she did development on MailReady, a C/UNIX messaging product. At NCR, she performed a variety of technical functions, from developing and maintaining NCR's UNIX SVRV.4 operating system, utilities, and applications, to international support for LAN/WAN communications. When Microsoft introduced Windows NT, NCR assigned a team to the BackOffice products, and Liz was given EMS/Exchange. She has worked closely with the Exchange performance team at Microsoft for nearly two years on understanding server scalability and performance issues.

In 1995, Liz founded MicroStaff, a Microsoft Solution Provider and Certified Technical Education Center. From her first project in Exchange migration at Shell Oil, to supporting and training the military, various government agencies, and Fortune 500 companies, Liz has continued to take on roles of support analyst, trainer, author, administrator, and consultant for Exchange and clustering. Liz was co-author for *Exchange Administrator Survival Guide* (Exchange 4.0). She has also developed three courses on Clustering for Windows NT utilizing Exchange and SQL, two administrator courses on Exchange 5.0 and 5.5, as well as end-user manuals for Microsoft Outlook. She, and the team at MicroStaff, has focused on supporting and educating their clients on Exchange, clustering, Windows NT/2000, IIS, SMS, and disaster recovery.

Contributors

William Lefkovics (MCSE, A+) is currently employed as a
Systems Analyst and Messaging Solution Developer at AscentrA,
a group of innovative healthcare companies in the Southwestern
US. He is the Microsoft specialist on an IT team supporting a
diverse multi-platform environment. Williams has previously
worked in data retrieval in an AS/400 environment for a large
retailer, as well as in Information Systems and inventory control
in a manufacturing environment. William holds an Associate
Certificate in Network Engineering from the British Columbia
Institute of Technology and hosts an Exchange website, which
can be found at www.exchange2000admin.com. William is active
in many Exchange-related newsgroups and can be reached at
william@lefkovics.net. William started with computers composing
ASCII adventure games in Basic on a Commodore 64 in 1982 in
his home town of 100 Mile House, BC, Canada. He is currently a
resident of Las Vegas, NV, and grateful to share his life with his
wife, Bertina.

Melissa Craft (CCNA, MCSE, Network+, MCNE, Citrix CCA) is
Director of e-Business Offering Development for CompuCom.
CompuCom provides IT design, project management, and support for distributed computing systems. Melissa is a key contrib-
utor to the business development and implementation of
e-business services. As such, she develops enterprise-wide technology solutions and methodologies focused on client organizations. These technology solutions touch every part of a system's
lifecycle—from network design, testing and implementation to
operational management and strategic planning.

Melissa holds a bachelor's degree from the University of
Michigan and is a member of the IEEE, the Society of Women
Engineers, and American MENSA, Ltd. Melissa currently resides

in Glendale, AZ with her family, Dan, Justine, and Taylor. Melissa is the author of Syngress Publishing's best-selling *Managing Active Directory for Windows 2000 Server* (ISBN: 1-928994-07-5).

Brian Barber (MCSE, MCP+I, MCNE, CNE-5, CNE-4, CAN-3, CNA-GW) is a Senior Technology Consultant with Sierra Systems Consultants Inc. in Ottawa, Canada. He provides technical architecture consulting and analysis to public and private sector clients in the National Capital Region. Brian specializes in Internet, intranet, and extranet technologies, focusing on Web-enabled service delivery through directory services and messaging. His background includes positions as Senior Technical Analyst at MetLife and Senior Technical Coordinator at the LGS Group Inc. (now a part of IBM Global Services). He would like to thank his beautiful wife, Rosemary, and daughter, Miranda, for all of their love and support, Hugh for encouraging him to tackle this project, and Blair Cribb and Scott Fraser at Microsoft Canda for providing everything he needed to set up his lab.

Neil Hobson (MCSE, CLP) is a Senior Messaging Consultant with Silversands, a UK-based Microsoft Solutions Provider Partner, and has been in the messaging field for over six years. Neil is responsible for the design, implementation, and support of corporate messaging systems across the UK and Europe and is primarily focused on implementing Microsoft Exchange solutions. His clients include Barclays Bank plc, Hays plc, and the Royal Borough of Kensington & Chelsea. Neil currently resides in Weymouth, England, with his family Sally, Corinna, and Amber.

Steve Schwartz (MCSE, MCT) is the founder and Principal Engineer of Implement.com, LLC, a consulting and training company based in Seattle, WA. Steve was one of the first MCSEs, obtaining his certification in April, 1994 and has been an MCT since 1993. He has over 12 years of experience implementing enterprise scale systems and training individuals and companies to do the same. He has a broad range of consulting and teaching experience, including training internal Microsoft support and consulting personnel in Europe, South America, Asia, the Middle East, and the United States. He can be reached at sschwartz@implement.com. Steve resides in Seattle, WA.

Keith Boesel (MCSE+I, CCNA) is a Technical Professional with TEKsystems in Phoenix, AZ. He specializes in designing and deploying business solutions based on Windows NT/2000, Exchange, and Cisco. Keith has also worked with IKON Office Solutions, MicroAge, and General Electric. He has a BS degree in Computer Engineering from The Ohio State University. He lives in Chandler, AZ with his very patient wife, Dorothy.

William C. Wade III (MCSE, MCT) has been a Networking and Systems Consultant for ten years. He has worked for several solution providers, where he gained experience implementing Microsoft solutions for organizations of all shapes and sizes. Today, as a principle of Wadeware LLC, Bill works closely with Microsoft and other companies on Windows 2000 and Exchange 2000 projects. On these subjects he has written numerous articles, white papers, and MOC courses. He is also the author of two books, including *Implementing Exchange Server*. He resides in Issaquah, WA.

Contents

Chapter 2 Active Directory Integration with Exchange 2000

Chapter 3 Security Applications that Enhance Exchange 2000   **91**

Chapter 4 Basic Administration 145

Chapter 5 Client Access to Exchange 2000 for E-Mail   223

Chapter 6 Deploying Exchange 2000 Server   279

Chapter 7 Defending Exchange 2000 from Attack   329

Chapter 12 Basic Monitoring and Troubleshooting Methodology

Foreword

I think it's a fairly obvious statement to say that Exchange 2000 is vastly different to any previous version. The sheer amount of new features and capabilities provided by Exchange 2000 will undoubtedly lead to the quest for the knowledge required to successfully deploy and support the product.

As someone who has been involved in designing, implementing, and supporting Microsoft Exchange server systems since the product was first released, I can safely say that having the right information available is of paramount importance. And that's where *Configuring Exchange 2000 Server* comes in. This is not a book for beginners; it's a book for experienced Windows NT administrators who are either upgrading from an existing Exchange 5.5 environment, or who are deploying Exchange 2000 as their first messaging system. It's a book written by authors who are not theorists—each and every author is actively working with Exchange, giving you practical information gained from experience in the field. Simply, it's a book for those of us responsible for designing, deploying, and supporting a reliable and scalable Exchange 2000 messaging system.

Exchange has come a long way since version 4.0 first made its appearance in 1996, when the main focus of the product was migrating from Microsoft Mail. In early 1997, Exchange Server 5.0 embraced the Internet protocols, such as Post Office Protocol v3 (POP3) and Hypertext Transfer Protocol (HTTP), the latter forming the basis for the introduction of Outlook Web Access (OWA). Then, in late 1997, Exchange Server 5.5 was released, giving significantly increased performance and scalability.

Some three years on, we now have Exchange 2000, architecturally very different from the previous versions. Exchange 2000 Server has been designed to meet the needs of businesses that range from small organizations to global enterprises, and as a result is available in three editions. First, there's Exchange 2000 Server, providing the messaging and collaboration features that a small to medium organization will require. Second, there's Exchange 2000 Enterprise Server, offering reliability and scalability features such as clustering and multiple database support, elements that are required for today's largest enterprises. And finally, there's Exchange 2000 Conferencing Server, in essence a separate product that gives the ability to implement data, voice, and video-conferencing solutions.

The feature list for Exchange 2000 is impressive. Let's briefly discuss some of these features, to give you a glimpse of what is to be covered in the chapters of this book.

Perhaps the first thing you realize about Exchange 2000 is the fact that it relies upon an underlying Windows 2000 operating system, primarily because there is no longer a separate Exchange directory service. Exchange 2000 takes full advantage of the Windows 2000 Active Directory, a highly scalable enterprise-class directory service. In previous versions of Exchange, the link between the Exchange directory service and the Windows NT Security Account Manager (SAM) was minimal—a Windows NT account was an attribute of an Exchange mailbox. Now, the roles have been reversed, whereby the Exchange mailbox is an attribute of the Active Directory user account. The Active Directory therefore gives administrators the benefit of unified administration. The strong link between Windows 2000 and Exchange 2000 incorporates the Windows 2000 security model, giving administrators the ability to use Windows 2000 access control lists for messaging resources. This extends to the ability to implement permissions at the item or document level, allowing for new levels of security.

Exchange is now tightly integrated with Microsoft Internet Information Server (IIS), providing the Internet protocols that were previously bundled into the Store process in earlier versions of Exchange. Therefore, a new requirement exists in that IIS must now be installed and operational prior to the installation of Exchange 2000, to allow access via protocols such as POP3, Internet Message Access Protocol v4 (IMAP4), and HTTP. Clients play a big part in an Exchange 2000 system; there wouldn't be much point in operating a messaging system without any end clients. Fortunately, *Configuring Exchange 2000 Server* has an excellent chapter on client access to Exchange 2000, which is rather handy when you consider that there's now such a wide choice of client options available.

Take OWA, for instance. As I stated earlier, OWA first appeared with Exchange 5.0, allowing browser-based access to Exchange. It became progressively better through Exchange 5.5 and the subsequent service packs, but overall it still proved to be somewhat difficult to scale upwards. The Exchange 2000 implementation of OWA has been significantly enhanced—after all, the code base was developed again from scratch. Scalability has now significantly improved, with early indications that the new OWA will be able to support somewhere near the equivalent number of MAPI users per server. From a user perspective, you'll notice right away that the look and feel of the new OWA is more like Outlook than ever before, with features such as drag-and-drop and right-click shortcut menus. It's interesting to note that data such as e-mail messages and documents can now be accessed through a Web browser via a friendly URL. (Remember the complex public folder URLs from previous versions of Exchange.)

Those of you familiar with previous versions of Exchange will know that the messaging databases in Exchange versions 4.0 and 5.0 were limited to 16 GB. This limit was removed in Exchange 5.5, when the "unlimited" store was introduced. (The theoretical limit was actually 16 TB, unlimited as far as most people were concerned.) But this removal of the previous limits brought with it other problems and challenges for Exchange administrators. Some databases were getting large enough to cause backup and restore issues, and database errors resulted in outages that affected all users. Exchange 2000 addresses these scalability issues with the introduction of multiple database support, giving us several key advantages. For example, one key advantage is that individual database failures no longer affect all users on the server, as failed databases can be repaired offline.

Over the years that I've been involved with messaging, I've seen e-mail systems go from the "nice to have" category, to becoming business critical applications. Let's face it, e-mail messages now contain important business decisions; if e-mail is unavailable, money is lost. Although the introduction of multiple databases significantly increases system reliability, businesses that require the best end-user availability can now implement Active/Active Clustering in Exchange 2000. All servers in a cluster can now be used to actively perform work, and when a failure occurs in a server cluster, the responsibilities of the failed server transfer to another server within the cluster. I personally believe that more and more businesses will implement clustering than ever before, so now's a good time to evaluate the importance of clustering within the pages of this book.

However, hardware failure isn't always the perpetrator of messaging system outages, as anyone who's experienced viruses such as Melissa will testify. This is why *Configuring Exchange 2000 Server* covers the topic of anti-virus within Exchange 2000, a topic that comes around again and again, usually after the latest outbreak! Traditional anti-virus products have been based on MAPI, with the notable exception of Sybari Antigen, which uses an innovative method to monitor the attachments table before any attachments are delivered to mailboxes. Microsoft released the new AntiVirus Application Programming Interface (AVAPI) feature in Exchange 5.5 Service Pack 3 and, of course, this feature is still available in Exchange 2000. The AVAPI was Microsoft's offering to allow software vendors to develop their products to scan attachments before the client accesses them. When taking into consideration the impact that viruses can cause on a messaging system, it's good to know that books such as this one cover such important topics.

Perhaps a phrase that you've seen and heard numerous times when researching Exchange 2000 is the "Web Store," arguably one of the biggest developments in Exchange 2000. The Web Store provides for the integration of knowledge sources by providing a single database for managing messaging, collaboration, and rich document storage within one infrastructure. One of the most interesting aspects of the Web Store is the fact that it can be accessed by such a wide variety of client software, including Outlook, Outlook Express, Office 2000, Windows Explorer, Web browsers and even the MSDOS prompt. The Installable File System (IFS) allows for the integration between Exchange and the Windows file system, mapping drive M on the Exchange server to give direct Win32 API access to the Web Store. Those that have used Microsoft Mail will sympathize with me when I mention that I thought we were returning to Microsoft Mail technology when I discovered the drive M mapping! The Web Store also incorporates built-in content indexing, allowing for high-speed full text searches. Importantly, users can continue to use the familiar search facility within Outlook, but the searches are much faster and can include documents attached to e-mail messages.

Message routing in Exchange 2000 has taken a giant step forward with the introduction of Link State routing. Previous versions of Exchange used the Gateway Address Routing Table (GWART), which gave us a consolidated map of the Exchange Organization, but it lacked downstream link intelligence and dynamic updates. The new Link State routing system is designed to allow for the immediate propagation of link status around the Exchange Organization. When there's a link failure, the new link information is published immediately to the entire Exchange Organization, allowing intelligent routing to take place at once. The Link State propagation protocol is based on Dijkstra's algorithm from 1959, which has been used for many years in the format of Open Shortest Path First (OSPF) routers.

Configuring Exchange 2000 Server covers the new Instant Messaging and Conferencing Server offerings, as well as the Chat service that has existed since Exchange 5.5. These three features all demonstrate the advances made for real-time communication in Exchange 2000. Take Instant Messaging for example. It allows fast and simple communications over Transmission Control Protocol/Internet Protocol (TCP/IP), on a one-to-one basis. But when you need to have a discussion with your entire team, that's where Chat comes in, particularly if people are in different geographical areas. However, if you're looking for a full multi-media resourced meeting, then Conferencing Server is for you. This excellent new product allows for the sharing of video, audio, data, whiteboards, and chat. Perhaps the biggest challenge with these new solutions will be to understand the business requirements for implementing them.

Over the last few years, you've probably heard a lot more of the term Application Service Providers (ASPs). ASPs are successfully providing managed Exchange messaging services, among many other software applications, to businesses of all sizes. Although hosted messaging services have been possible with Exchange 5.5, it is anticipated that using Exchange 2000 for these services will allow ASPs to provide even more functionality. Using Exchange 2000 Server as an ASP platform will allow ASPs to reach more businesses and provide a more reliable service that also encompasses areas such as Instant Messaging and Knowledge Management. There can be no doubt that together, the Active Directory and Exchange 2000 make an excellent platform for hosted messaging systems. This book covers the steps necessary to implement Exchange 2000 as an ASP platform, from security considerations to configuring virtual servers and address lists.

You've probably read the last few paragraphs and come to realize that with such a vast array of new features and technology, it's not difficult to see why *Configuring Exchange 2000 Server* is a vital tool for the Exchange 2000 professional. I've been impressed with the book's no-nonsense approach, clearly and concisely providing the information required by anyone faced with implementing Exchange 2000. I've also been impressed by the book's approach to covering some of the vital areas of Exchange that can be overlooked, such as anti-virus solutions and clustering, as well as some of the new technologies such as Instant Messaging, Conferencing, and the Application Service Provider market. Also, each chapter covers useful troubleshooting points, along with a selection of Frequently Asked Questions (FAQs), and Tip, Note, and Warning sidebars to help guide you through the information. All of these elements help to place *Configuring Exchange 2000 Server* as a must-have book for those who want to be in the know. As you will see, Exchange 2000 is an incredibly complex product, but *Configuring Exchange 2000 Server* allows you to understand the key principles you'll need.

Read and enjoy, safe in the knowledge that this book has been written by real-world Exchange administrators, for real-world Exchange administrators.

—Neil Hobson, MCSE, CLP
Senior Messaging Consultant, Silversands, Ltd.

What's New in Exchange 2000

Solutions in this chapter:

- Introducing Microsoft Exchange 2000 Features
- Exchange 2000 CD Components
- Exchange 2000 Resource Requirements
- Exchange 2000 Licensing

Introduction

To say that Microsoft Exchange 2000 is a major release is an understatement. Exchange 2000 has demonstrated the mantra of messaging anytime, anywhere, in any form. When you say Exchange is the messaging backbone for your infrastructure, you should change your vision from the backbone of a person to an image of pure immenseness and complexity, such as how democracy is the backbone of a country. Microsoft Exchange (version 4.0, 5.0, 5.5, and now 2000) is being implemented in organizations that directly affect the lifeblood of our civilization—the economy, civic rights and politics, health care, transportation, the arts, and so on. So, let's move on from this mantra of Exchange and begin to review the product.

If you are new to Exchange and reading this as your first introduction to messaging, here is quick summary: In brief, Exchange 2000 is a messaging architecture that delivers server, client, and networking components with industry standard application programming interfaces (APIs) and protocols that provide, retain, and deliver various methods of instant, time-delayed, and scheduled communication. The Exchange 2000 server components can store, index, and search personal and publicly shared e-mail messages and attachments, voice mail messages, telefax messages and attachments, and almost any form of electronic information. The Exchange 2000 client components (Outlook 2000, Outlook Web Access or OWA, and Instant Messaging or IM), interfaces, and supported protocols allow a wide variety of methods to utilize these data and messaging services. Exchange 2000 networking components allow the transfer of e-mail between different messaging systems and the synchronization and replication of address book and directory information within and to similar messaging environments. These components also allow the scheduling, management, and delivery of voice, data, and audio conferencing among thousands of participants. The Exchange 2000 APIs and interfaces enable clients, tools, and third-party applications to utilize Post Office Protocol v3 (POP3), Simple Mail Transfer Protocol (SMTP), Messaging Application Program Interface (MAPI), Hypertext Transfer Protocol (HTTP), and more to access, synchronize, and manipulate this data. Most of these messaging objects and services are controlled and integrated in the Windows 2000 network operating system.

Product Versions and Components

Microsoft Exchange 2000 is not one product, but three. Microsoft has packaged Exchange 2000 into three product sets based on feature functionality, which will be explained in detail throughout this book.

- Exchange 2000 Server

- Exchange 2000 Enterprise Server
- Exchange 2000 Conferencing Server

The end of this chapter reviews resource requirements for each of these products as well current licensing programs.

Exchange 2000 Server

This product is best utilized by small organizations. It has all of the improvements and new features of Exchange 2000, but with just a few exceptions. For one, Exchange 2000 Server has a limitation of a 16GB information store, and it can have only one private and one public database per server. If you believe your e-mail storage requirements will exceed 16GB on one server, then you need to choose the Exchange 2000 Enterprise Server edition. Exchange 2000 Server does not include clustering technology, and it does not allow the front-end/back-end configurations that allow for more efficient service distribution. These two features are not typically required in a small organization, so the product is sized and priced appropriately for smaller businesses. The Exchange 2000 Server product contains the following components:

- Exchange 2000 Server
- Exchange Server 5.5 with Service Pack 3 (SP3)
- Outlook 2000 Service Release 1
- Outlook for the Macintosh 8.2.2
- Office Developer Tools 2000
- cc:Mail connector
- MS Mail Connector
- Notes/Domino Connector
- GroupWise Connector
- X.400 connectors
- Instant Messaging

NOTE

Exchange Server 5.5 is distributed on the Exchange 2000 CD because a required migration step to convert existing Exchange 4.0 and Exchange 5.0 environments to Exchange 2000 is to first upgrade to Exchange 5.5.

Exchange 2000 Enterprise Server

This is the product that most Exchange administrators reading this book should and will be deploying. It is delivered with all the components mentioned previously, and it has greater functionality than the Exchange 2000 Server product. The Enterprise product is targeted for medium to large enterprises. These larger organizations require information stores greater than 16GB. The Exchange 2000 Enterprise product allows the creation of multiple information stores on one Exchange Server. Exchange 2000 Enterprise Server allows clustering of Exchange resources for higher availability as well as distributed configurations to allow for front-end/back-end optimizations.

Exchange 2000 Conferencing Server

Exchange 2000 Conferencing Server is a unique product that complements Exchange 2000. It works with Exchange 2000 Server or Exchange 2000 Enterprise Server. It provides audio, video, and data conference resources, as well as conference scheduling and conference management. When purchasing the Exchange 2000 Conferencing Server, you get the following components:

- Outlook 2000 Service Release 1
- Outlook for the Macintosh 8.2.2
- Data conferencing and applications sharing
- Multicast video teleconferencing

Overview of Features

Exchange 2000 is not just a feature upgrade from Exchange 5.5. The movement from running on Windows NT 4.0 to Windows 2000 has caused a tremendous change in the internal architecture and implementation of Exchange. This section divides the total body of Exchange 2000 into six subsections and reviews the architectural changes, the key improvements, and the upgrades:

- Windows 2000 and Active Directory Integration
- Server Features
- Routing and Networking Features
- Client Features

- Development Changes and Features
- Advanced Concepts and Implementations

Windows 2000 and Active Directory Integration

Exchange Server has always incorporated an integrated directory, which stored address information, messaging data, and details about the system configuration. In Exchange 2000 there is no independent directory as such—it is tightly integrated with Windows 2000 Active Directory (AD). Exchange 2000 can query, modify, and even extend Active Directory when necessary. User and group information and Exchange system and routing information are stored and updated in Active Directory. Exchange 2000 can be managed and monitored by Active Directory tools. Concepts such as Forests, Domains, Organizational Units, and Routing Groups are integral to the planning and installation of Exchange. We'll briefly review the impact of Windows 2000 security, Active Directory Connector, Microsoft Management Console (MMC), and online help, but for more on the integration of Windows 2000 and Exchange 2000, see Chapters 2 and 3.

Windows 2000 Security

One of the benefits of Windows 2000 integration is that administrators do not have to learn two methods to apply security. In Windows 2000 you modify the Access Control Lists (ACLs) of objects that you wish to secure. You do the same with Exchange 2000. You can set security permissions on users, containers, and most objects within the Exchange organization. You do not have to create your own user group and user accounts. You would use the groupings in Active Directory Users and Computers. The beauty of Windows 2000 and Exchange 2000 integration is that the security groups and distribution groups are both mail-enabled. Figure 1.1 shows the security ACL for an Exchange object. For more information on Windows 2000 Security and Exchange, see Chapter 3.

Active Directory Connector

The Active Directory Connector (ADC) is a component that, when installed and configured, synchronizes the Exchange Server 5.5 directory with Active Directory. There are two versions of the ADC—one that is included with Windows 2000 and another that is included with Exchange 2000. Both versions synchronize recipient objects between directories. This synchronization includes users to mailboxes, groups to distribution lists, and custom recipients to contacts. The Exchange 2000 version of the ADC, however, does more. It also synchronizes the configuration objects between

Figure 1.1 Exchange 2000 Security Utilizing Windows Access Control Lists

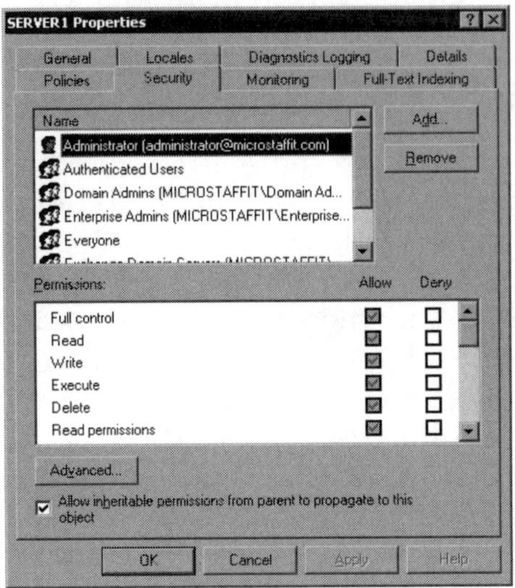

the Exchange 5.5 directory and Active Directory. This gives Exchange 2000 and Exchange Server 5.5 insight into each other's configuration, which allows the two to coexist. For more information on Active Directory and Exchange, see Chapter 2; for more information on deploying Exchange 2000 in an existing or new environment, see Chapter 6.

Microsoft Management Console Integration

The Microsoft Management Console (MMC) is the new interface to administering your Exchange 2000 server. Administration is detailed in Chapter 4. In legacy Exchange you would run Exchange Administrator on local or remote Exchange servers to manage the Exchange environment, and you would then use Windows NT User Manager to add users. When required, you would switch back to Exchange Administrator to add distribution lists and more.

In Exchange 2000 you have two new tools to perform these functions. Think of them as one for system management and one for user management.

- **Exchange System Manager** This tool is similar to Exchange Administrator in functionality. It will be used by your key administrators responsible for managing the Exchange system components (such as administrative groups, routing groups, connectors, templates, policies, server settings, etc.). This is a snap-in to the MMC. See Figure 1.2 for a quick look at what the Exchange System Manager looks like.

Figure 1.2 Exchange 2000 System Manager

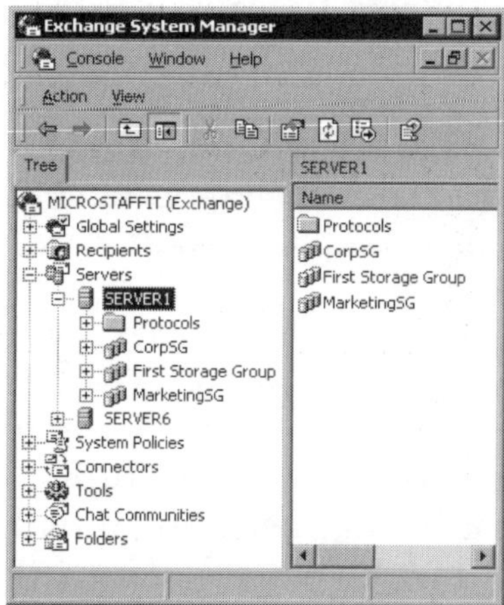

■ **Active Directory Users and Computers** You will use this tool to add, delete, and modify mailbox-enabled users and mail-enabled users. Exchange 2000 adds extensions to the Windows 2000 version of Active Directory Users and Computers. Until you install the Exchange Server Administration Tools, as described in Chapter 4, you will not see these additional features such as e-mail address and Exchange mailbox store. Figure 1.3 shows you the Properties of a user account in Active Directory Users and Computers.

Figure 1.3 User Properties

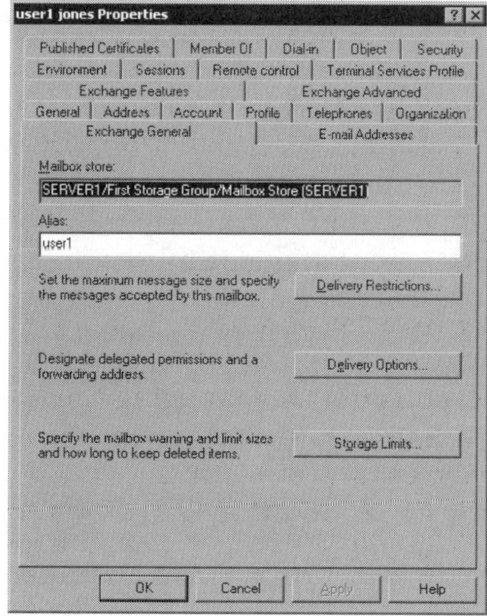

Using the Help Files

Help is normally an overlooked product feature, but no more. The Help functionality delivered with Exchange 2000 really makes it an integrated support tool. When I've exalted the improvements and usability of Help in Windows 2000 and Exchange 2000 to administrators and developers they don't believe me until they use it. Help is *really* useful. Each Help subsection has a How To and a Concepts section. The How To section explains basic administration procedures with overviews, checklists, and references to other material in Help. The Concepts section explains the concept of the topic, discusses why it is important and when appropriate, and includes links to Microsoft subject matter. In some sections, tips on troubleshooting and maintenance are given. The Help feature in Windows 2000 and Exchange 2000 gives you enough starting information so that you don't have to browse through myriad Microsoft TechNet articles or Exchange manuals the first time you have a question. Figure 1.4 shows "Using Firewalls with Outlook Web Access," a typical section in Help.

Figure 1.4 Using Exchange 2000 Help

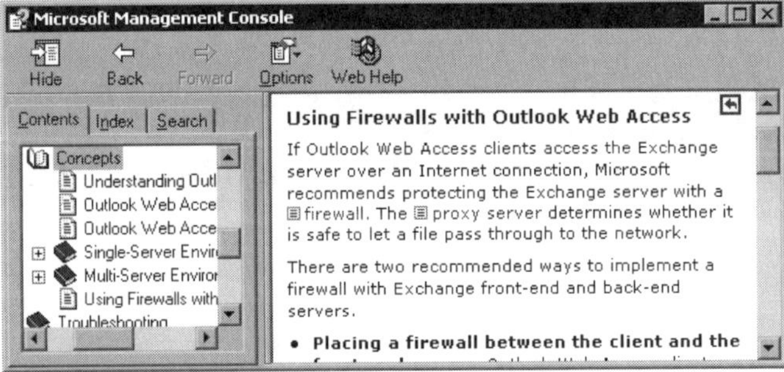

Server Features

Now, let's move on to Exchange server components. If you understand how the Exchange database components worked in legacy Exchange, you'll see that the basic functionality has stayed within the storage components, but each component has been tweaked and improved to increase functionality and interoperability. There is more architectural information on the database components in Chapters 10 and 12.

Multiple Information Stores

Previously in legacy Exchange products, such as Exchange 4.0, Exchange 5.0, and Exchange 5.5, messages were kept in database files called priv.edb and pub.edb. *Priv.edb* contains private, personal, and individual e-mail that normally has a user account associated with the mailbox. *Pub.edb* contains public information that is secured by the administrator, who defines which user or groups of users can view the data. In Exchange 2000 these two files are now called priv1.edb and pub1.edb (by default). The concept of single instance store (SIS) applies, in that a message is stored once and the database has pointers to those mailboxes that reference that message.

Exchange 2000 includes priv1.edb, but it also has a companion file, priv1.stm. Priv1.edb files contain Rich Text Formatted (RTF) content messages. A priv1.stm file contains non-RTF messages. The .stm suffix comes from the word *streaming* and is utilized for containing Internet Multipurpose Internet Mail Extension (MIME) data. Typical .stm would be audio, video, and any streaming MIME data. Note that the two files contain different content but that both files store data in the same format, called the Extensible Storage Engine (ESE) database format. As you can see in Figure 1.5, the pub1.edb file also has a companion pub1.stm file.

Figure 1.5 Exchange 2000 Default Objects for c:\Program Files\exchsrvr\ MDBDATA

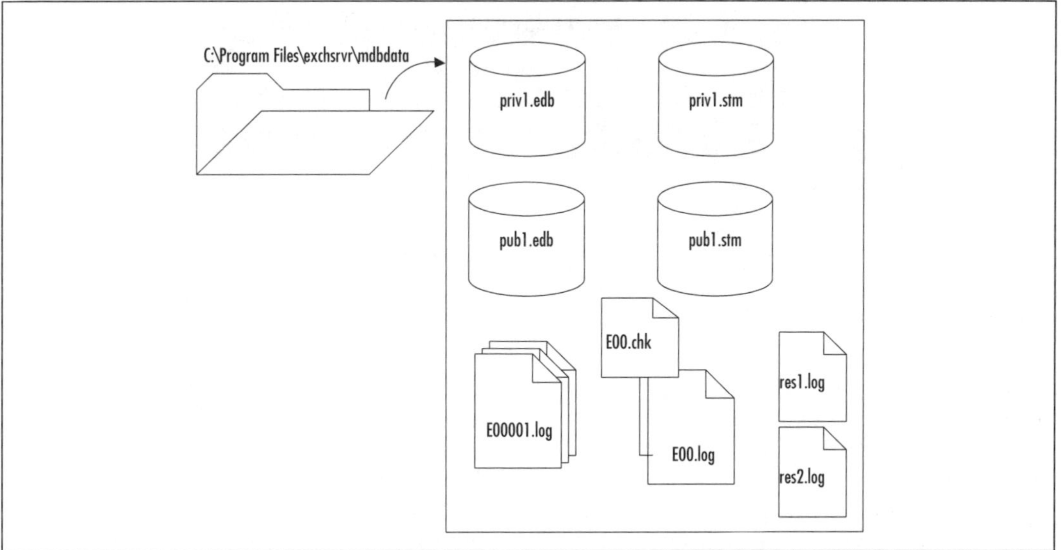

Transaction Logs

The private and public databases are not complete without the inclusion of transaction logs. The transaction logs function basically the same as in legacy Exchange. You have one active transaction log and then multiple, sequentially numbered transaction logs that contain past Exchange database transactions. Refer to Chapter 10 and Chapter 12 for more information on the importance of transaction logs.

Installable File System

The Installable File System (IFS) exposes Exchange 2000 information stores to the file system. Exchange 2000 automatically creates an M: drive on the local Exchange server that will allow you to share the mailbox or public folder that is the root level of the default public folder tree, the root level of all mailboxes, and a domain folder for each accessible domain. Previously, in Exchange 5.5, clients could access data in the stores via MAPI, Lightweight Directory Access Protocol (LDAP), Network News Transport Protocol (NNTP), HTTP, POP3, and Internet Message Access Protocol v4 (IMAP4) clients. Exchange 2000 clients can now use Explorer, My Computer, or other file access applications/tools to open, read, write, and save data on the Exchange Server information stores. Figure 1.6 gives you an idea of how this looks in Explorer. The purpose of this feature is to allow applications to interoperate with the Exchange data.

Figure 1.6 View of the Administrator's Mailbox from Explorer

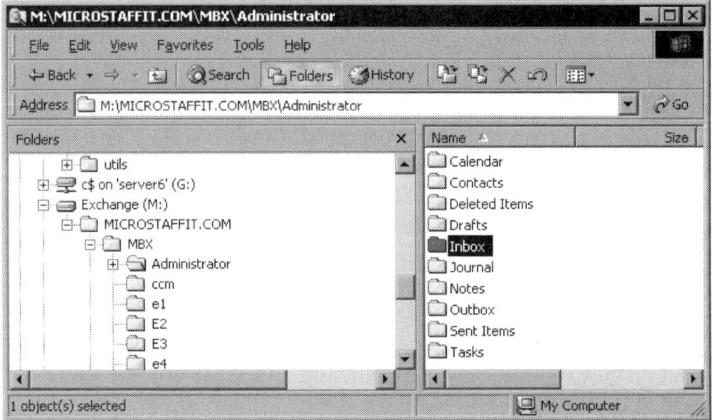

The Web Store

Making the Exchange information store accessible from the Internet was a major contribution to making the data available, anytime, anywhere, in any form. The changes to the information stores allow end users to access contents of the stores via browsers, Outlook, Office 2000 applications, wireless devices, conferencing solutions, and more. View the Web Store as an Internet-capable wrapper around the Information Stores, exposing well-known objects to properly authenticated users or applications.

Storage Groups and Multiple Message Stores

Legacy Exchange had one private and one public information store per Exchange server. Exchange 2000 now allows multiple stores per Exchange server. They are grouped in an object called a Storage Group. You can have up to four Storage Groups per server, with a maximum of five databases per Storage Group, so you could theoretically have 20 databases per server. Also, each Storage Group is maintained by its own instance of the Extensible Storage Engine (ESE), which ensures that all databases within a Storage Group are consistent. Within a Storage Group, there is one set of transaction logs. Operations within a transaction log can apply to any of the databases defined in the Storage Group. See Figure 1.7 for an example of multiple Storage Groups and stores. We have the first Storage Group that was installed with Exchange, called First Storage Group. It contains three different pairs of databases (private data, public data, and Company Infrastructure data). The second Storage Group is the Corporate Storage Group, CorpSG. It contains just one pair of databases. The third Storage Group, MarketingSG, has two pairs of database (Marketing and MarketingFax). Look to Chapter 12 for more details.

Figure 1.7 Multiple Storage Groups and Stores

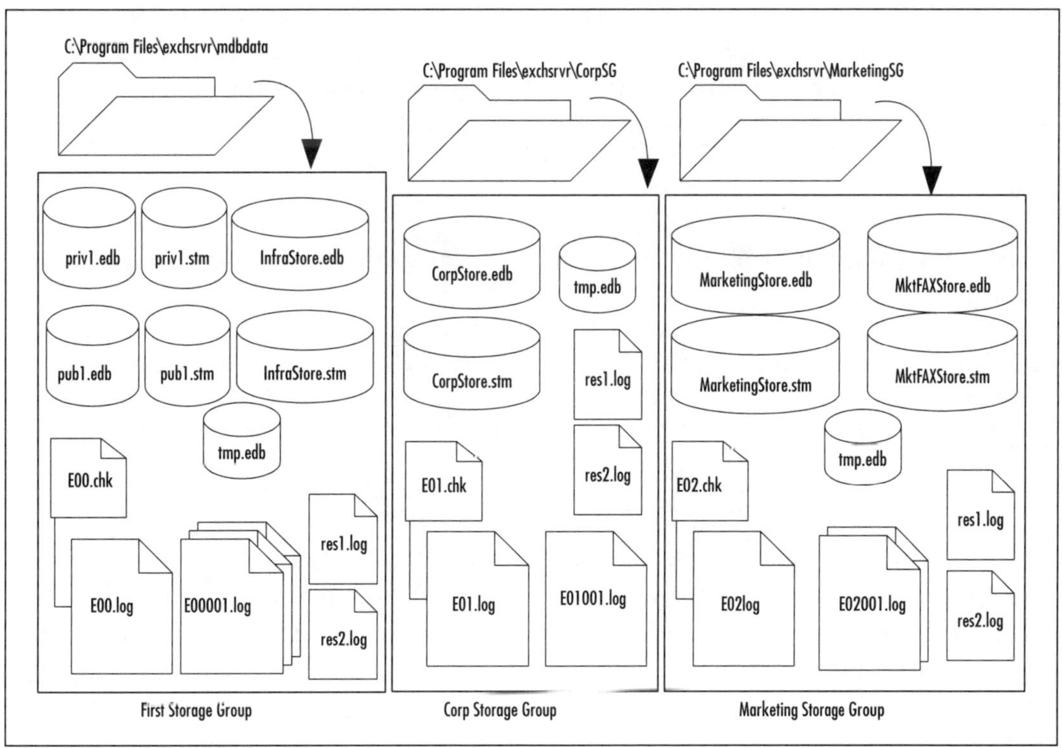

You would utilize Storage Groups and multiple databases for ease of administration, flexibility in configuration, and optimization of your backup and recovery strategies. Also, it is possible to configure a unique set of policies for each storage group. We might put more restrictive policies on First Storage Group, and then loosen up requirements on CorpSG and MarketingSG. You may want to have four information stores with a maximum file size of 50GB each, rather than one information store at 200GB. This would allow faster restores if just one database became corrupt. (Note that if a drive fails and all the stores are on that drive, then they would all have to be restored.) Another reason for multiple stores is that when you are performing maintenance operations, you would have to take offline only one set of users at a time. As an application service provider (ASP), you may want to create storage groups based on the companies you are hosting as well. Administering these servers and securing the environment will be much easier with a clear delineation between Storage Groups.

Also key to the Storage Group concept is that you affiliate one transaction log to one Storage Group, not one per database. A family of transaction logs contains the active transaction log (E00.log), past sequentially numbered transaction logs (E0000001.log, E000000x.log), and the res.logs (res1.log, res2.log) in that same folder path. If you had one Storage Group with five Exchange databases, you would have just one transaction log family. If you had three Storage Groups, each group would have its own family of transaction logs that would be specifically applied to it. As an example, we've created three Storage Groups on our Exchange server. We have a Storage Group for the users in Corporate Headquarters, Marketing, and the rest of the company. See Table 1.1 for details about these components.

Table 1.1 Multiple Storage Groups and Stores with Associated Transaction Logs

Storage Group Name	First Storage Group	CorpSG	MarketingSG
Use	First/Default Storage Group. Everyone not in Corporate or Marketing.	Everyone reporting to Corporate Office.	Everyone reporting to Marketing.
Stores	Mailbox Store Public Folder Store Infrastructure Store	CorpStore	MarketingStore MktFAXStore

Continued

Table 1.1 Continued

Storage Group Name	First Storage Group	CorpSG	MarketingSG
Storage Group Folder Path and Files	C:\Program Files\exchsrvr\MDBDATA	C:\Program Files\exchsrvr\CorpSG	C:\Program Files\exchsrvr\MarketingSG
Private Stores	Priv1.edb Priv1.stm InfraStore.edb InfraStore.stm	CorpStore.edb CorpStore.stm	MarketingStore.edb MarketingStore.stm MktFAXStore.edb MktFAXStore.stm
Public Stores	Pub1.edb Pub1.stm		
Transaction Log Path and Names	E00.log E0000001.log E0000002.log	E01.log E0100001.log	E02.log E0200001.log E0200002.log
Other Files	Res1.log Res2.log Tmp.edb E00.chk	Res1.log Res2.log Tmp.edb E01.chk	Res1.log Res2.log Tmp.edb E02.chk

Within these Storage Groups you can see that we have two private stores within both the default **First Storage Group** and the **MarketingSG**. The **CorpSG** Storage Group has one private information store. There is only one public information store on the Exchange server, and this is the default public store for all the other private information stores. For the Storage Groups with multiple stores, you will notice that we do not have a set of transaction logs per store. There is one set of transaction logs per Storage Group. Any transactions for the **MarketingStore** and the **MktFAXStore** will be both committed to the E02.log file. Then the transactions will be applied to the individual stores as appropriate. Also note that in the **First Storage Group** we have two private and one public set of stores. All transactions for these stores will be committed to the same log family.

NOTE

Key to understanding Exchange storage benefits is the concept of Single Instance Store (SIS). When a message is received, it is stored once and the database creates internal pointers to reference which users' mailboxes contain this message. Movement of the message within a single Exchange store (intact) will still keep one instance of the message. Modification of the message or copying of the message will create a second message entity.

If a message is sent to two users in the *same* Storage Group, but on different stores, Single Instance Store is not maintained—there are two copies of the message. If a message is sent to two users in *different* Storage Groups, Single Instance Store is also not maintained.

Multiple Public Folder Trees

Legacy Exchange allowed only one public information store per server. Public stores contain messaging content that can be exposed to the entire Exchange organization. (User mailboxes are stored in the priv1.edb file, and the users that typically own the mailbox are the only viewers.) Public folders are stored in the pub1.edb file and are created with the intent of sharing all their data to all Exchange users. The Exchange 5.5 design and the default installation of Exchange 2000 install one public information store. This is known as the equivalent of having one public folder tree. Exchange 2000 allows the creation of multiple public folder trees that can be secured and exposed in a finer detail. You may want to have the default public folder tree designated for your organization's public information, and you may then create a second public folder tree that will be populated with information just for one department—for example, Human Resources or Marketing.

On-Demand Content Conversion

As mentioned earlier, the .edb and .stm files contain different content. This content will need to be converted if it is being read by different client types. For instance, an Internet client may not be able to read RTF messages, and it will need the message converted before opening. Exchange 2000 will convert the message to the client's requested format, which is known as *on-demand content conversion*. This feature is not evident to the administrator or to the end user, as it is an internal architectural improvement.

Policy Settings for Information Stores

Now that we have multiple stores and storage groups, Exchange 2000 has a better way to manage them. In Exchange System Manager, you will choose an administrative group. Under that group you have System Policies. Here you can set policies that can be applied to one information store or sets of information stores. Also, you can layer the policies. If you have two private information stores, you may want to archive all the e-mail on store1 and then set two different storage quota limits on store1 and store2. Figure 1.8 shows that we have a storage group with multiple stores within it; you can also see some of the system policies defined.

Figure 1.8 Setting Multiple Policies on Information Stores

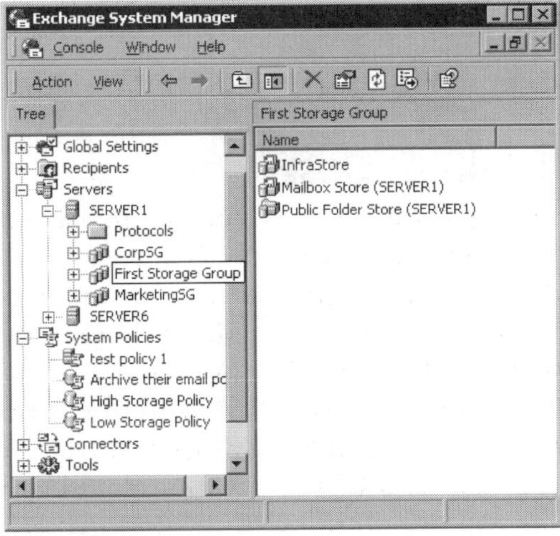

Clustering

Exchange's previous implementation of clustering was active/passive. This meant that you could have one Exchange virtual server hosted/configured between two nodes. Exchange 2000's implementation is active/active. This means, in brief, that you can run Exchange on both nodes of a cluster, and if one server fails, the remaining server will host both Exchange virtual servers. Also, depending on the version of Windows 2000, you can have two nodes in a cluster (Windows 2000 Advanced Server) or four nodes in a cluster (Windows 2000 Data Center).

Routing and Networking Features

Networking protocol functions and processing that were resident in the legacy Exchange server have been moved to the Internet Information

Service (IIS). Directory functions that were in the legacy Exchange directory service, such as maintaining the routing table and replicating directory information, have been moved to Windows 2000 Active Directory. Let's take a look at how these changes have improved Exchange 2000.

SMTP Routing of Messages between Servers

Start saying goodbye to Remote Procedure Call (RPC) message transfer in Microsoft Exchange environments. In legacy Exchange, RPCs were used to transfer or route messages between servers in an Exchange site. Now SMTP is the default transport protocol to transfer or route messages. A more extensive version of SMTP is installed in Windows 2000 when Exchange 2000 is installed. SMTP has many advantages over RPCs: better end-to-end performance over poor communication lines, lower utilization of bandwidth, and less overhead, for example.

Integration with Internet Information Services

You will need to have at least version 5.0 of IIS installed on your Exchange 2000 Server if you wish to utilize some of the new features in Exchange 2000. This is the version included in Windows 2000. Exchange 5.5 handled many of the protocols required to enable messages. In Exchange 2000, much of this protocol handling has been taken out, and now Exchange 2000 relies on IIS to handle SMTP, HTTP, POP3, IMAP4, and NNTP access. Exchange depends on IIS to perform required message routing functions and to enable Instant Messaging. Exchange creates *virtual roots* (IIS terminology) for mailboxes, public folders, and administration tools. These virtual roots can be accessed via standard browsers. Finally, IIS integration with Exchange 2000 enables developers to create Web content that is message enabled.

Improved System Monitoring of Exchange

Monitoring of your Exchange server, services, and links has matured in Exchange 2000. There are at least three new ways you can monitor services and objects in Exchange 2000. In Exchange System Manager you can set monitors on the queues for SMTP and X.400 connectors to alert you when messages on the queues are growing, as in Figure 1.9. You can enable diagnostics logging on all protocols and on many of the objects in Exchange.

You can monitor the Exchange-related services on local and remote Exchange servers to ensure they are up and will be restarted if they fail. You can also monitor disk space to alert you when the drives are filling up. Figure 1.9 shows you objects that you can monitor on an Exchange server.

Figure 1.9 Properties to Monitor on Server1

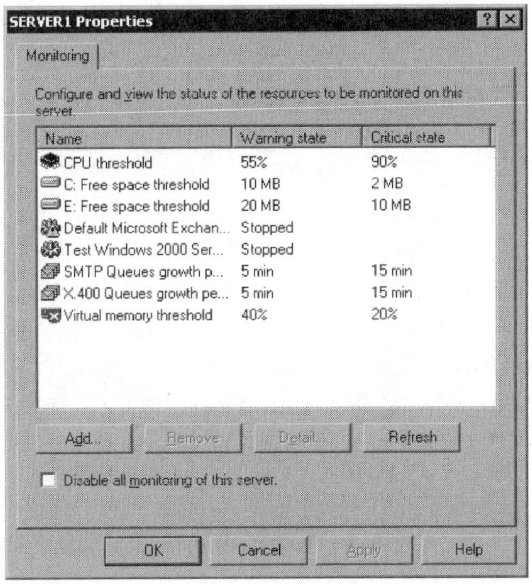

Message Restrictions to Reduce Spamming

The development team has made it easier for administrators to get a handle on junk e-mail and spamming. The Exchange System Manager in Exchange 2000 will now let you set limits on the number of recipients a user can send to at one time on a per-virtual-server basis. For example, if you decide that you are not going to let users send out e-mails to more than 100 people at a time, they can not send out more than 20 e-mails in a session, and they are limited to messages smaller than 8MB. Figure 1.10 demonstrates this requirement in the Messages tab on the SMTP Protocol for the Default SMTP Virtual Server. For more information on protecting your Exchange server against spamming and other attacks, see Chapter 7.

Client Features

The architectural changes in Exchange 2000 and in the Web store allow more Microsoft and non-Microsoft client products to access and utilize the Exchange resources. You need to stop thinking of clients as name brands, such as Microsoft Outlook or Netscape Navigator, and start thinking of them in terms of protocols. Are they MAPI-compliant? Do they support POP3, SMTP, or HTTP? You will see more HTTP clients in the coming years.Look to Chapter 5 for details on the following features.

Figure 1.10 Exchange 2000 and Message Restrictions

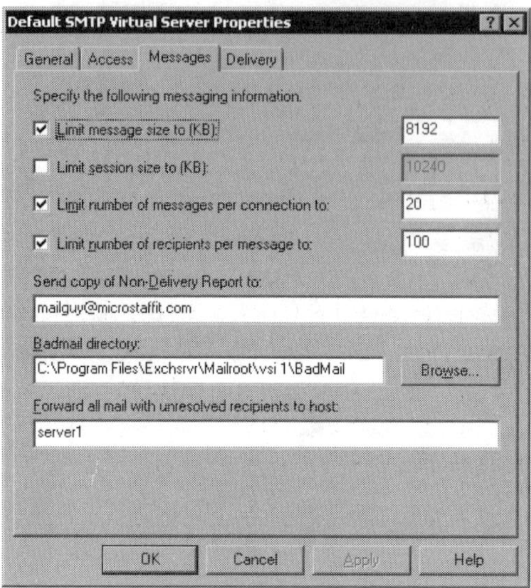

Increased Protocol Support

The Exchange 2000 Server product allows clients and applications using the following protocols to access its data and perform sends and receives of messages and information:

- MAPI
- POP3
- SMTP
- IMAP4
- HTTP
- WebDAV
- NNTP

Outlook 2000 and Outlook for Macintosh 8.2.2

Outlook 2000 comes on the Exchange 2000 Server CD. Outlook 2000 can be installed on systems running Windows, Windows 95, Windows 98, Windows Millennium Edition, Windows NT 3.51 and 4.0, and Windows 2000 systems. A version of Outlook 2000 to run on Macintosh 8.2.2 is also supplied. Outlook 2000 is a fully functioning contact management and universal inbox for all your communications. It provides e-mail, calendaring, contact management, journaling, and more. See Chapter 5 on Clients for more information on Outlook 2000. Outlook 2000 is not new to running on Exchange, but it is now being delivered on the Exchange product CD.

Accessing the Exchange Store from Microsoft Office and Win32-Compliant Utilities

We mentioned the basis of this in the previous section on servers, but I'm mentioning it again as this is a feature to really brag about. With the changes in Exchange system and server architecture, it is now possible to access your Exchange server data from within a Microsoft Office application. With the administrator sharing on the Exchange server M: drive, you can perform a File ? Save As, and save a Microsoft Word document as \\servername\MBX\user1\inbox\\marketing_material.doc. It will then appear in the designated mailbox folder, as in Figure 1.11.

Figure 1.11 Saving an Office Document Directly to the Exchange Store

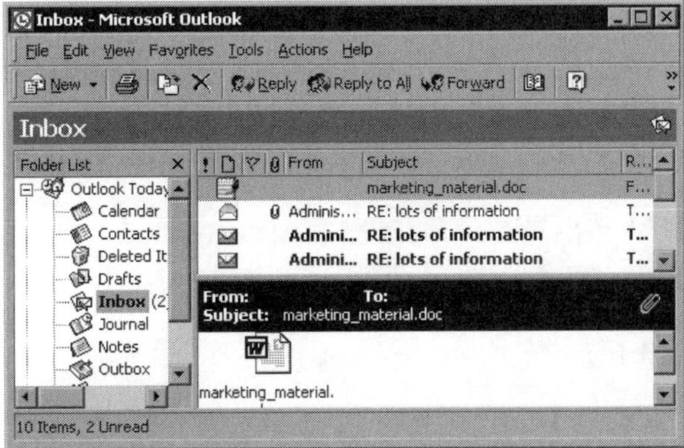

Accessing the Exchange Store from Browsers

An equally exciting feature is the ability to access your Exchange store directly from a browser. Whether you use Microsoft Explorer, Netscape Navigator, or Bill's Browsenet, if your organization exposes your Exchange server data to the Internet, you can access your personal and public data from anywhere in the world. For example, by typing in http://owa .syngress.com/exchange, I could access someone's e-mail (if I was authenticated correctly); I could also access our public folders by typing in http://owa.syngress.com/public, as well as Exchange administration features by typing in http://owa.syngress.com/exadmin. Figure 1.12 shows how a typical mailbox view of your Outlook Calendar will look in Internet Explorer. We'll cover the Client browsing feature again in Chapter 5.

Figure 1.12 Viewing Your Calendar in a Browser by a URL

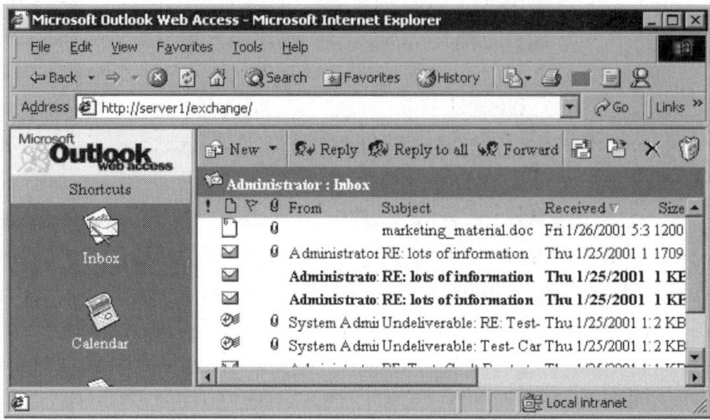

Searching the Exchange Store Faster

The indexing feature is disabled by default on the Exchange server. This feature will traverse every object in an Exchange server store and create an index to allow for faster searches. Once you turn this feature on, your clients will notice a much faster search response time. Also, by enabling this feature, you will notice that there is a small impact to performance on your Exchange server when indexing is run. The good news is that once the first full index is run, Microsoft has architected indexing to base subsequent indexing off incremental changes from the first full index. You can schedule indexing to occur at your convenience. This is configured per Exchange server store, not storage group.

Development Changes and Features

Exchange 2000 is a technology that wants to enable third-party vendors to develop personal devices to synchronize and communicate with the Exchange server objects. Exchange 2000 has openly documented APIs that allow companies to develop anti-virus solutions that integrate completely with the server and the client-side-messaging component. For example, third-party vendors can add connectors, monitoring objects, and client snap-ins to allow mass faxing of documents out to distribution lists and to configure PBX systems to route incoming faxes to Exchange users' personal mailboxes. There are many products that integrate with Exchange. For a full list, check out third-party products on www.microsoft.com/exchange.

Application Development

Exchange 2000 provides an object library, Collaboration Data Objects (CDO), which allows access and manipulation of calendaring, contact management information, and messaging. A library of workflow services based on event processing is included with this CDO library. Third-party vendors can use these objects and APIs to create generic and workflow applications.

OLE DB 2.5 Support

OLE DB is *Object Linking and Embedding Databases*. Supporting this allows third-party vendors to develop applications that can query the Exchange 2000 database without coding specifically for Exchange 2000. As OLE DB 2.5 can also be used to query SQL 2000, your development staff should be able to leverage their SQL knowledge into developing queries and applications to navigate the Web Storage system.

Utilization of Web Store Content in Web Sites

The development of the Web Store technology, or the exposing of the Information Stores to authenticated uses and applications, allows Web sites to integrate the Exchange store as a dynamic and integrated component. Web sites can directly access Exchange server objects and integrate their results into the Web pages.

Event Modeling and Workflow Improvements

When creating a workflow process you want an application to initiate one or multiple routines based on various conditions. Exchange 2000 allows routines, also known as *events*, to be initiated in a few different methods. An event can be initiated at the arrival of SMTP and NNTP messages, it can be initiated when a condition occurs, and it can be initiated after a condition occurs. For example, when an SMTP message comes in, you may want to trigger your anti-virus product to scan the SMTP message before it is passed on to the Exchange server store. You could also create a process to trigger once a message is delivered to a mailbox, such as a customer support help desk.

Advanced Concepts and Implementations

Once you move beyond basic messaging concepts, you see that Exchange 2000 has the features and foundation to build advanced solutions and implementations. The use of real-time communications in Instant Messaging, Chat Services, and Conferencing enables you to structure business communications beyond store-and-forward e-mail. ASPs can leverage the power of Windows 2000 and Exchange 2000 through hosting messaging services at basic and premium service levels. In addition, ASPs can enhance their service offerings with collaborative services and development opportunities. Look to Chapter 8 for more information on Instant Messaging, Chat Services, and Data and Video Conferencing.

Instant Messaging

When you want to know if someone is on his or her computer, you can use Instant Messaging. Instant Messaging requires that there be some service running in the background that knows you are on your computer and that can communicate your status to outsiders who are looking for you. This is known as *presence information*, and Exchange 2000 Server provides this feature with rendezvous protocol (RVP). With Instant Messaging you can send an instant message to a predefined contact. An instant message is not saved in the Exchange store. Exchange Instant Messaging uses a combination of Active Directory, Domain Name System (DNS), and IIS to provide this feature.

Chat Services

Chat Services allow one person to communicate to many users on a virtual text-based conference call or a discussion group, by the user typing in his or her comments and forwarding them to a central sharing point for all to see. Exchange 2000 uses the Internet Relay Chat (IRC) protocol and IRC Extensions (IRCX) over TCP/IP. Exchange first supported Chat Services in Exchange 5.5; enhancements in Exchange 2000 enable multiple levels of users, administrators, servers, channels, and communities.

Data and Video Conferencing

The Exchange 2000 Conferencing Server allows you to share video (cameras on your desktop), audio (desktop microphones or any telephone), Chat Services (for nonvideo/audio transmission), file transfer services (for communication of documents, presentations, etc.), application sharing, and whiteboard usage (the electronic version of a conference room whiteboard or easel). On the server side, the Exchange 2000 Conferencing Server is T.120 and H.323 compliant, which enables other T.120 clients to use the Exchange Server as a conferencing back-end. This conferencing implementation allows users to connect to the conference, both internal and external to a firewall, and it is possible to do scheduling and joining of the conferences through Outlook 2000. The H.323 compliance allows a Quality of Service component to the transfer of video, audio, and voice between the Exchange server and other computers not running Windows 2000. The inclusion of IP Multicast transmissions allows directed broadcasts to specific computers, thereby reducing the multidestination video and audio traffic on the network.

Conferencing and Real-Time Communication Clients

The Instant Messaging client will work within the Exchange 2000 environment; it can be also be used to connect to the MSN messaging back-end. The IM client is available as a download from Microsoft's Web site, as well as on the Exchange 2000 install media. With regard to the Chat feature, if your clients are using Chat 2.0, they will have to upgrade to Chat 2.1, which can be found on Exchange 5.5 Service Pack 3. And finally, with regard to a client for conferencing, all three Exchange products have the Outlook 2000 client on the CD. Outlook 2000 is the full-featured product to schedule resources, invite attendees, and join the conferences. Look to Chapter 8 for more information on the features and implementation steps for Exchange 2000 Real-Time Communication features.

Application Service Provider and Internet Service Provider Solutions

Application service providers and Internet service providers can offer a core messaging service that allows the customer to send and receive messages, store messages, and access Exchange 2000 data using a Web client. Basic service offerings can include accessing and storing messages using MAPI and a MAPI client such as Outlook 2000, POP3, IMAP4, and the Web interface that is built into Exchange 2000: Outlook Web Access.

An advanced service offering would be to provide MAPI client premium features, such as access to calendar and contact data. Other opportunities include using Exchange 2000 to provide real-time services such as Instant Messaging, Chat conference rooms, and data, video, and audio conferencing. Look to Chapter 9 for more information on the basic architecture of hosting Exchange 2000 and configuring Active Directory and Exchange 2000 for an ASP environment.

Exchange 2000 Resource Requirements

It is not possible to provide definitive system resource requirements for an Exchange server environment, but we can provide minimum and recommended requirements for servers running Windows 2000 and Exchange 2000. It is up to the Exchange administrator to determine the resource requirements.

Exchange 2000 Resource Minimum Requirements

As a starting point, Microsoft recommends the following minimum requirements:

Exchange 2000 Server and Exchange 20000 Enterprise Server

- Pentium 133 MHz with 128 MB RAM

- Windows 2000 Service Pack 1

- 700 MB hard disk space (200 MB is required for the system disk, and 500 MB is required for the disk where you install Exchange)

Exchange 2000 Conference Server. This product can be installed on a system with or without the Exchange 2000 (Server or Enterprise Server) installed. Microsoft minimally recommends the following:

- Pentium 133 MHz with 128 MB RAM

- Windows 2000 Service Pack 1

- 15 MB of hard disk space (5 MB is required on the system disk and 10 MB is required on the disk where you install Exchange)

Exchange 2000 Resource Recommended Requirements

Server sizing is an art form that comes from years of working with servers, understanding their architecture, working with operating systems, characterizing transactions, and more. In lieu of performance analysis and server sizing, you are advised to have at least the following for your Exchange 2000 Servers.

- Pentium 300MHz or higher

- 256MB RAM for a small Exchange server, 512MB RAM for up to a few hundred users, and 1GB RAM for larger Exchange servers. Windows 2000 will require the first 128MB at a minimum.

- Review of OEM and industry benchmark reports for external peripheral subsystems as well as for dual or quad CPU systems.

- Utilization of multiple SCSI drives (internal and external).

- Log of performance numbers against RAM, CPU, and IO on your Exchange 2000 Server for a while. If appropriate, consider getting a dual or quad CPU system.

Exchange 2000 Licensing

Refer to your local Microsoft representative for exact licensing requirements. When purchasing Exchange Server, you need to purchase a license for each server on which you are going to install Exchange 2000. Next, you must purchase a license for every client that is going to access the Exchange Server. The client license is called a Client Access License (CAL). If you are going to install Exchange on five Exchange servers to support 2,000 users, you need to purchase five Exchange 2000 Server licenses and 2,000 CALs. Please note that it is possible to purchase the Exchange 2000 Server product with no CALs or with five or 25 CALs. Make sure you understand which product you are purchasing so that you can subsequently purchase the correct number of CALs. Currently, the philosophy for CAL licensing is that you purchase a CAL for every user who is going to access the Exchange server. Please investigate with your Microsoft representative the best licensing program for your environment. He or she will help make sure that you buy the correct number of licenses.

Also, by checking with your Microsoft representative, you may be eligible for a free upgrade. Those who purchased Exchange 5.5 server or CAL products between June 15, 2000 and August 30, 2000 should receive a free upgrade for the equivalent Exchange Servers and CALS.

Summary

This chapter introduced you to the new products of Exchange 2000, and it gave you an overview of the features of Exchange 2000. It is easy to see that the feature enhancements in Exchange 2000 appeal to large corporations, application service providers, and even small businesses. The integration of Active Directory and Windows 2000 allows Exchange Server to focus on messaging features. The enhancements in the database components and the introduction of the Installable File System and the Web Store allow greater interoperability and use of the messaging data. The SMTP routing of messages between servers allows better end-to-end performance over poor communication lines, lower utilization of bandwidth, and less overhead. The real-time communication features are easy to install and may help your organization communicate more effectively. Clustering and all the other improvements in development features will help your organization reach higher levels of productivity.

FAQs Visit www.syngress.com/solutions to have your questions about this chapter answered by the author.

Q: What is the difference between Exchange 2000 Server and Exchange 2000 Enterprise Server? Which product should I purchase?

A: If your organization is small, and if it doesn't use large amounts of disk space for e-mail, then consider Exchange 2000 Server. The information store is limited to grow no larger than 16GB. Exchange 2000 Server does not include clustering technology or the front-end/back-end configurations in Enterprise Server, so it is sized and priced appropriately for smaller businesses.

Q: What Windows 2000 components will help me administer Exchange 2000?

A: The Active Directory Users and Computers snap-in to the MMC will be a key tool in managing your Exchange environment and users. You will be adding users, managing them, moving their mailboxes, and executing various Exchange tasks on the users. Check out Chapter 4 for more information.

Q: I have Windows NT 4.0 and Exchange 5.5. What should I do to implement Exchange 2000?

A: In this book, look to Chapter 6 for details regarding migrating to Windows 2000—it is important that you understand the Windows 2000 environment to take this step.

Q: If I have just one domain in Windows NT 4.0 and one or two Exchange servers, what should I focus on in this book?

A: Focus on chapters 2 and 3 on Active Directory and security, Chapter 4 on administration, Chapter 5 on client access, Chapter 6 on deploying Exchange, Chapter 7 on preventing attacks on your Exchange server, Chapter 10 on backup and restore, and finally Chapter 12 on troubleshooting.

Q: Where can I get more information on Exchange 2000?

A: Try these Web sites:

www.microsoft.com

www.mcpmag.com

www.swynk.com/exchange

www.slipstick.com/exs/exs2000.htm

www.exchangeadmin.com

www.win2000mag.com

www.syngress.com/solutions

Active Directory Integration with Exchange 2000

Solutions in this chapter:

- Why Use Exchange 2000 on Active Directory

- Understanding Active Directory Architecture

- Planning for Active Directory

- Implementing Active Directory and Exchange 2000

- Troubleshooting Exchange 2000 During Implementation

Introduction

Few electronic messaging programs thrive without some sort of address list to store mailbox names and address information. In fact, an address list becomes a rather critical component for people who need to manage many e-mail recipients' names and addresses. Without that address list, there is no way to look up the information needed.

Looking up addresses is only one of the functions that an address list fulfills. It also organizes other information about recipients and helps administration by enabling the application of automated functions and scripts. A directory service, which is typically used by a network operating system, performs the exact same service.

Microsoft realized that merely connecting the legacy Exchange Server 5.5 directory service to the legacy Windows NT directory service (the Service Account Manager—or SAM) was not enough. The Windows NT SAM had limitations that led to its replacement by the Active Directory in the Windows 2000 Server operating system. The Active Directory is so similar in nature to the Exchange Server directory service that using the two on the same network leads to two directory service stores representing the same or similar subsets of information. Microsoft chose the solution of integrating the subsequent version of Exchange Server (Exchange 2000 Server) with Windows 2000's Active Directory.

Why Use Exchange 2000 on Active Directory

In order to secure any network host, there must be a mechanism for managing identities of end users and mapping them in some form of relationship to the resources available on the network. A directory service may store information about:

- Applications
- Computers
- Files
- Policies
- Printers and other peripherals
- Relationships, such as roles and group memberships
- Resources, such as backup systems and routers
- User accounts

The Organization within the directory service provides a consistent method for listing, locating, managing, and securing the network data.

Microsoft made the decision to design Exchange 2000 as an extension of the Active Directory for Windows 2000. They had several reasons for using the Active Directory as the directory service for Exchange 2000 Server:

- It uses the same type of storage system as used in Exchange 5.5 (Extensible Storage Engine database).

- It scales to millions of objects.

- It removes the confusion of Exchange sites versus NT domains— now it is a single architecture.

- It provides a single point of administration and a common interface for administrative tools.

- It strengthens security with single sign-on.

Because Exchange Server had always incorporated an integrated directory that stored address information, messaging data, and details about the Exchange Server system configuration, it provided the template upon which to base the Active Directory. The Active Directory had the same goals; as a result, Microsoft based its architecture on the same type of store used by Exchange Server—the Extensible Storage Engine (ESE). A Windows 2000 domain controller holds a copy of the domain database file within the ESE database. The database is both fault-tolerant and transaction-based. The database itself is distributed among multiple domain controllers. Each domain controller is considered a master, and synchronization of changes is executed through multimaster replication.

In legacy Windows NT, a domain was based on a Security Account Manager (SAM), and was limited to approximately 40,000 objects. Because Active Directory uses a much more robust data structure (the ESE database), it is capable of scaling to millions of objects. In addition, the Active Directory uses a hierarchical naming system based on the Domain Name System (DNS). This enables the creation of *trees* of domains, with a parent domain being named "domain.com" and a child domain being "sub.domain.com" and grandchild domain being "next.sub.domain.com". Each of these is called a *namespace*. Multiple namespaces, or trees, create a *forest*. Within a forest, all domains trust each other using Kerberos, an Internet-standard authentication protocol that specifies bidirectional, transitive trust relationships between domains. A forest can grow to multiple millions of objects.

In the legacy Windows NT system, network designers faced a dilemma of how to match up Exchange sites and Windows NT domains. With the

Active Directory providing the directory service for Exchange, there is no need for a secondary design for the messaging system.

The Microsoft Management Console (MMC) is used to administer the network. An administrator can customize the MMC to access any network component, including each Active Directory domain or site. The Active Directory itself provides a single point of administration for user accounts, workstations, member servers, and applications. Between the MMC and the Active Directory, there is a single point of administration.

The Active Directory facilitates a relationship between each user account and network resource. The network administrator can establish rules regarding these relationships, such as permission for a user to access a resource. Security features of Active Directory extend into policies. Group policies can be distributed throughout the Active Directory domains, sites, and organizational units.

The Role of Active Directory in Exchange 2000

Every version of Exchange Server had integrated with the underlying Windows NT operating system in some form. Windows NT provided authentication by mapping the Exchange Server mailboxes within the Exchange Server directory service to user accounts existing in the Windows NT SAM. There was also some basic administration including event logging.

In Exchange 2000 Server, there is no longer an independent Exchange directory service that lists mailboxes. Instead, Exchange 2000 Server *must* depend upon the Active Directory in Windows 2000 for a directory service. Exchange 2000 extends the Active Directory to incorporate the types of objects and attributes needed for messaging. Other applications can also extend the Active Directory. When this occurs, a relationship can be established between messaging and applications through the directory service. In fact, an organization can apply standardized business rules to Exchange and other distributed applications without requiring a specialized method of administration.

Exchange Server's Need for a Directory Service

A directory service is absolutely essential for an enterprise-capable messaging service. It provides an index of mailboxes, distribution lists, messaging servers, and connectors. Because of the flexibility of a hierarchical organization, the directory service can group various objects into relevant subsets. When an Exchange administrator applies a rule to one level in the hierarchy, the lower levels can inherit the rule.

Understanding Active Directory Architecture

A directory service is a structure that stores information about objects existing on the network. These objects include user accounts and network resources, as well as other information. The directory service provides both a source of information and the service to make that information available on the network. The first step in understanding how Exchange Server benefits from the Active Directory is in examining the Active Directory architecture. There are several aspects worth exploring:

- Hierarchical structure
- Storage
- Internet standard protocols
- Replication
- Policies

Hierarchical Structure

The largest unit of an Active Directory structure is the forest. You can have multiple forests within a network, if you need to have more than one. A forest can have one or more domains within it. The first domain installed into the forest is called the *root domain*, as shown in Figure 2.1. The domains within a forest have the following characteristics:

- They share the same schema.
- They share the replication and configuration.
- They share a single global catalog.
- They own transitive trust relationships with domains within the forest.

Figure 2.1 Root Domain in an Active Directory Forest

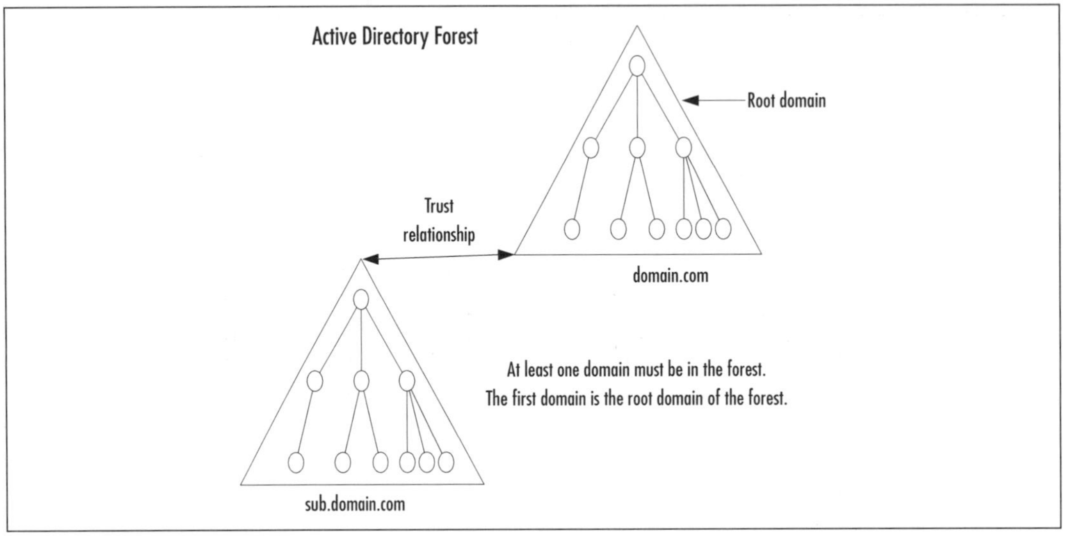

Domain Trees

Domains that join a forest form *trees*. They all use the domain name system (DNS) for naming; as a result, each tree of domains shares a namespace. For example, a holding corporation owns several businesses. One arm of the business manages subsidiaries in landscaping—Right Lighting, Breezy Trees, Urban Curbing, and Winkler's Sprinklers. The other arm of the business deals in clothing manufacturing—Drew's Shoes and Better Sweaters. In the Active Directory forest, the company has decided to create a namespace for landscaping and another for clothing—landscape.biz and clothing.biz. Below landscape.biz, each subsidiary has a domain— trees.landscape.biz, lights.landscape.biz, curb.landscape.biz and sprinkler .landscape.biz. The Breezy Trees company has decided to spin off a part of its nursery to the cultivation of shrubbery. They add a domain for this, in anticipation of a corporate spin-off, and call it shrubs.trees.landscape.biz. This entire set of domains becomes the landscape.biz namespace tree, and is illustrated in Figure 2.2.

The second namespace that the holding company creates is clothing.biz, with child domains of shoes.clothing.biz and sweaters.clothing.biz. This namespace tree—combined with the landscape.biz namespace tree—both exist in the same forest, as shown in Figure 2.3. Note that since the land-scape.biz domain was installed first, it is the root domain, which is why it is depicted at a somewhat higher level than that of clothing.biz. Also note that the lines shown in Figures 2.2 and 2.3 each depict a bidirectional, transitive trust based on the Kerberos authentication protocol. A bidirectional trust

Figure 2.2 Landscape.biz Namespace Tree

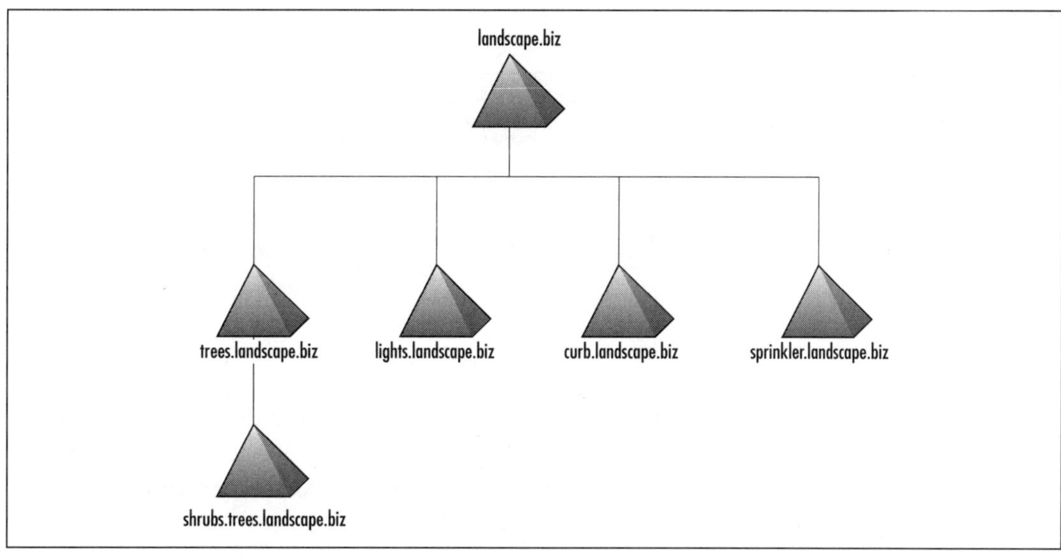

Figure 2.3 Forest with Two Namespaces

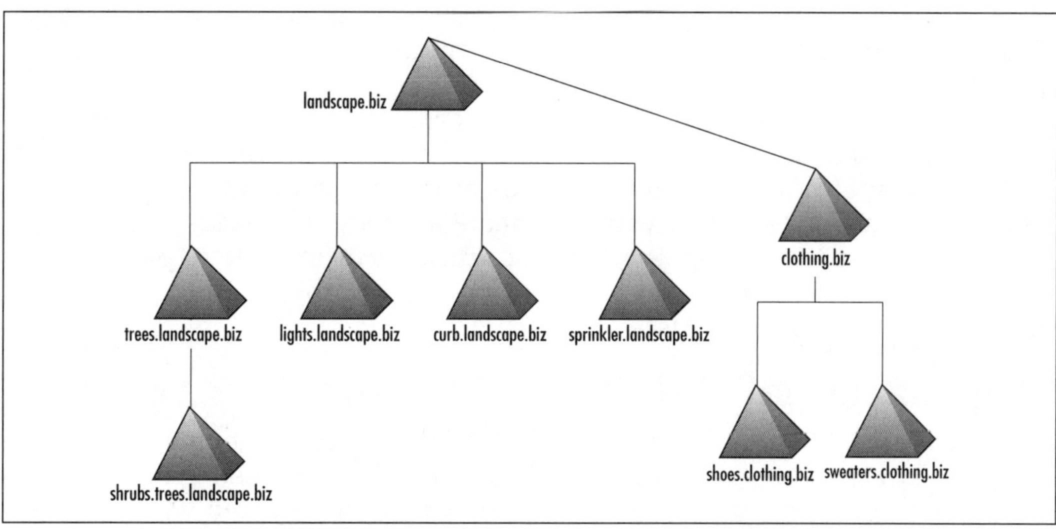

means that if trees.landscape.biz trusts landscape.biz, then landscape.biz trusts trees.landscape.biz in return. The transitive nature of the trust means that since landscape.biz trusts clothing.biz, and clothing.biz trusts shoes.clothing.biz, then landscape.biz trusts shoes.clothing.biz, as shown in Figure 2.4. This is a significant change from the way that trusts were handled in Windows NT.

Figure 2.4 Kerberos BiDirectional, Transitive Trust Relationships

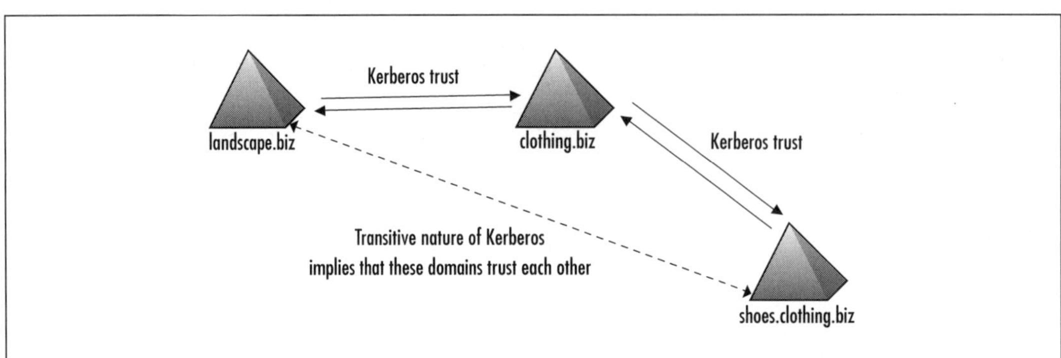

Unidirectional, nontransitive trusts still exist when a domain in one forest must trust a domain outside of the forest—either another Windows 2000 domain in a different Active Directory forest, a Kerberos realm, or a legacy Windows NT domain. These are all external trusts that enable authentication to an external domain or realm.

The reason that a trust relationship is created in the first place is to enable users in one domain to be recognized in another domain, and if granted access to resources, to be able to access them. With trust relationships, an administrator can manage user rights for users in other trusted domains.

When a user in one domain wants to access a resource domain in another domain, the resolution of trusts follow the path up the path to the root and down to the other domain. This authentication path can become long and involved. However, you can create a *shortcut trust* (also known as cross-link trusts) to reduce the time for authentication to take place. This can only be done between non-adjacent domains through the Active Directory Domains and Trusts MMC.

Organizational Unit Tree Structure

The hierarchical organization within the Active Directory does not stop at the way that domains are named and placed within a forest. The true strength of the hierarchy is found in a tree structure created within each domain. If you have ever worked with Novell Directory Services (NDS) or Banyan StreetTalk, this hierarchy will look very familiar.

First of all, the Active Directory specifies objects to represent user accounts, groups, computers, servers, applications, and network devices. The Active Directory also specifies containers to organize the network resources. A container can contain other containers, which creates a tree structure. And it can contain objects that represent the network resources.

The main type of container used in the Active Directory is called an organizational unit (OU). At the top of the hierarchy resides the domain container, below it are OUs that can contain other OUs (effectively nesting the OUs), as designated by the administrator. The Active Directory OU structure is so flexible, you can configure the OU hierarchy in any way that works best for your organization. A sample OU structure is shown in Figure 2.5.

Figure 2.5 The Active Directory OU Hierarchy

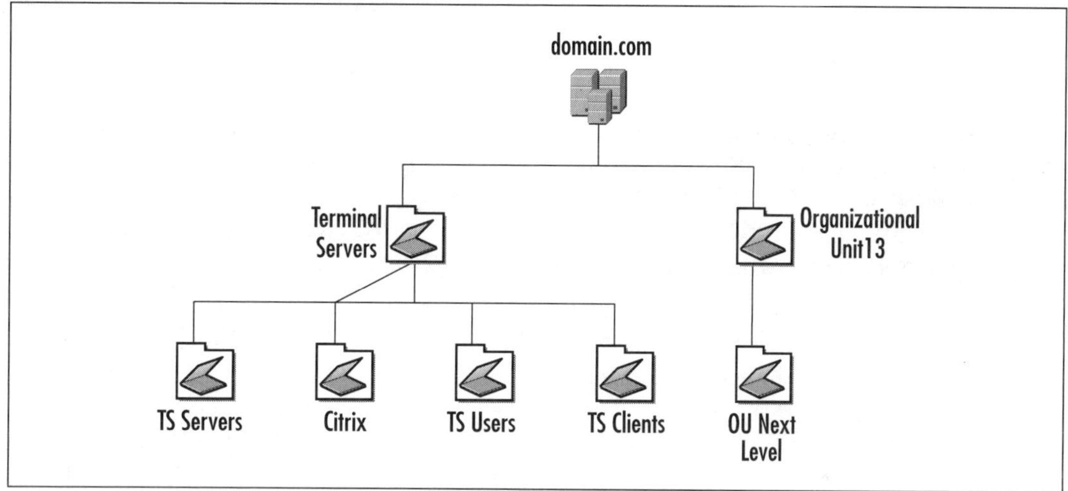

Global Catalog

The Active Directory provides for a Global Catalog (GC). The GC is essentially a database that is stored on one or more domain controllers. The GC database includes a partial copy of objects in each domain. The GC provides an index for all the objects in the Active Directory, regardless of where they are placed in the hierarchy, so that they can be located. There is only one GC per forest. The GC is used for queries and logon authentication. It is a critical directory service component for Exchange 2000, as we will discuss further on.

When a user searches for a network resource, the GC removes the domain boundaries and allows that user to find a network resource anywhere within the forest. This is in contrast to having to search each domain separately.

TIP

Once the Active Directory has been deployed, finding network resources becomes much easier for users and for administrators. They can use the Search command on the Start menu (or the Find command, if an older version of Windows), as well as the Active Directory Users and Computers in the MMC. The user can search for user accounts based on details such as a person's office location or e-mail name. The user can search for resources such as finding a printer based on its printing capabilities. These searches query the Global Catalog so any object within the Active Directory forest can be located.

Logons must be executed with help from the GC because it stores the information for universal group memberships. Universal groups are only available in native mode, so the GC is only required when the domain has been changed from mixed mode (a Windows 2000 domain that can have legacy NT backup domain controllers) to native mode (a Windows 2000 domain that will not support any legacy NT backup domain controllers.). The GC also helps with logons that use User Principal Names (UPN). A UPN uses the same format as an Internet e-mail address. UPNs can be configured so that every user in the forest has an identical domain suffix. For example, if Mary was a user account located in the Sub.domain.com domain, she could still have a UPN of mary@domain.com. The logon process uses the GC to resolve the actual domain location for Mary if she uses the UPN form to log on to the network.

The Five FSMOs

There are five flexible single-master operations (FSMO) roles that are automatically assigned to the first domain controller installed in a forest. When you add new domain controllers to the forest, you can move these roles around.

Of the five FSMOs, the following two must be unique within a forest:

- **Schema Master** This FSMO role controls the modifications that can be made to the schema. The schema defines the

Continued

> types of objects and their attributes that can exist within the Active Directory forest.
>
> - **Domain Naming Master** This FSMO role controls whether domains can be added to or removed from the forest.
>
> The three remaining FSMO roles must be unique within each domain of the forest.
>
> - **Relative Identifier (RID) Master** The RID master provides the portion of each object's unique security identifier (SID) that represents the domain security information. A domain controller requests pools of RIDs from the RID Master to use when new objects are created on it.
>
> - **Primary Domain Controller (PDC) Emulator** The PDC Emulator acts as though it is a legacy Windows NT PDC when there are NT BDCs in the domain running in mixed mode. Once the BDCs are removed and the domain has been changed to native mode, the PDC Emulator is still used to handle password changes. With replication, it is possible for a user to change a password and that change might not be replicated to another location when the user tries to logon. To handle this issue, before denying access, all password changes are preferentially replicated to the PDC Emulator, which is checked to ensure that the password has not been changed.
>
> - **Infrastructure Master** This FSMO role handles the object references for a domain object whenever those referenced objects are moved. For example, if a user object is renamed or moved, the infrastructure master updates the groups that the user object belongs to with the new name or location.

Storage

A domain controller can contain the database portion of only one single domain. For a server to become a domain controller, an installer must run the dcpromo.exe program, also called the Active Directory Installation Wizard, which configures the directory service components. Each domain controller contains a copy of its own domain's data. All domain controllers also contain a copy of the configuration information for the forest and of the schema information of the forest. If a domain controller has been designated as a Global Catalog server, it also contains a copy of the Global Catalog.

The actual file structure located on a domain controller is a fault-tolerant transaction-based database, which is based on Extensible Storage Engine (ESE) technology. Active Directory transactions occur in a short sequence:

1. The administrator creates or changes an object or attribute, which initiates the transaction.

2. The transaction is written to a log file.

3. The transaction is then committed to a database buffer.

4. The database on the disk is written and completes the transaction.

As you can see, there are several files involved in this process. The ntds.dit file is the database file that stores all the objects for that domain controller's partition of the Active Directory (plus there are some log and patch files).

Transaction log files can reach 10 MB in size. The currently used transaction log is edb.log, and is used until it reaches the 10 MB limit. At that point the log is saved as a separate file, edb00001.log—where the numerical portion of the filename is incremented as new full log files are saved—and the edb.log is emptied for new transactions.

Circular logging will not create the past transaction log files. Instead, it will rewrite over the current transaction log. Unlike the legacy and current versions of Exchange Server, circular logging is automatically turned on in Windows 2000 Active Directory to reduce the number of log files on the hard drive. When there are multiple domain controllers in a domain, replication will execute and bring the Active Directory files up to date, regardless of whether there are log files. Therefore, log files are less necessary to server recovery than in other database systems.

Another file used is a checkpoint file named edb.chk. This file contains pointers to the transactions in the transaction logs that have actually been written to the database. The file literally checks the point at which the log file and the database are consistent.

Two reserved log files, res1.log and res2.log, are each 10 MB in size and will become log files if there is not enough space on the disk to create a new edb.log file. Any outstanding transactions are copied from memory into the reserved logs and then the Active Directory will shut down with an out-of-disk-space error.

Patch files are used to track transactions written to the Active Directory database during backup. Split transactions are those that are written across multiple database pages. A split transaction can be written to a portion of the Active Directory database that has already been backed up. The backup process is:

1. A patch file with a .pat extension is created for the current database written to disk.

2. Backup begins.

3. Active Directory split transactions are written both to the database and to the patch file.

4. The backup writes the patch file to tape.

5. The patch file is deleted.

The Active Directory will automatically run a garbage collection process to delete unused objects, delete unused files, and defragment the database. When files are manually deleted, the Active Directory can become corrupted, so it is best not to delete log files. Garbage collection will take place on a 12-hour interval basis, but is configurable. Deleted objects exist in the Active Directory as tombstones for a period of time before they are actually purged from the directory. *Tombstoning*, or marking an object for deletion, will remove the item from view, but will make all replicas agree to delete the object. If this method was not used, there could be spontaneous reappearances of previously deleted objects. If you wish to change the tombstone lifetime (the number of hours that a deleted item lives in the database before it is permanently eradicated) or the garbage collection interval (how often the garbage collection takes place), you can make these changes in the ADSIEdit console:

1. Click Start | Run, type **mmc**, and press Enter.

2. Select Add/Remove Snap-in from the Console menu.

3. Click Add.

4. Select AdsiEdit from the available consoles and click Add.

5. Navigate to cn=Directory Service,cn=WindowsNT,cn=Services,cn= Configuration,dc=rootdomain,dc=com and edit the Properties where you will see the tombstone lifetime and the garbage collection interval attributes.

WARNING

When you restore deleted objects from the Active Directory, those objects will be deleted (actually become tombstones) the next time that replication takes place. The reason that this takes place is that the objects have been marked for deletion in another domain controller's replica of the Active Directory and replication will re-delete them in the database you just restored. This is normally the behavior you want to have take place, except in the case of accidents. In those cases, you want to perform an authoritative restore with NTDSUTIL.

Offline database management is performed with the ntdsutil.exe program. To run this offline database tool:

1. Boot the server.
2. At the initial boot menu screen, press the F8 key.
3. Select the Directory Services Repair Mode option.
4. Run the ntdsutil.exe tool.

WARNING

Using ntdsutil can be just as dangerous to your Active Directory database as editing the registry with regedit. All it takes to create a disaster is to hit the wrong key. Before you use it, read up on it and, if possible, test your procedure on a lab machine first.

Internet Standard Protocols

With the popularity of the Internet, and in making every type of system able to connect to it, multiprotocol networks are quickly becoming a thing of the past. Nowadays, everyone uses Transmission Control Protocol/ Internet Protocol (TCP/IP) and the Internet standard protocols that work with TCP/IP. Windows 2000 and Active Directory use TCP/IP and Internet standard protocols as the requirements for functionality, so it is Internet-ready. Some of the protocols that directly affect how the Active Directory functions are:

- Domain Name System (DNS)
- Lightweight Directory Access Protocol (LDAP)
- Kerberos Version 5

Domain Name System

DNS is a standard Internet service whose primary purpose is name resolution. Name resolution is the process of translating a computer's name, in the form of computer.domain.com, to its Internet Protocol (IP) address, in the form of a 32-bit number represented by four octets (numbers) separated by periods, e.g., 191.100.200.121. While a computer's name is fairly easy for a human to remember, the IP address is very difficult. However, the IP address is the unique identifier for a computer on the Internet. So, in order to reach a destination computer, a message must include the IP address.

Before DNS came about, users either had to remember the IP address, or create hosts files on their computers to remember the hosts that they commonly accessed. These hosts files became unwieldy, both because they grew to enormous sizes and because they had to be updated on many computers whenever a single computer name or IP address changed. DNS grew out of the need for a globally accessible system of remembering IP addresses.

The DNS system was built in a hierarchy so that it could be distributed globally. The root of DNS is represented by a dot (.). There are several copies of the DNS root servers and they include pointers to the top-level domain names. Top-level domain names include:

- **.com** commercial enterprises
- **.edu** educational facilities
- **.net** Internet-related
- **.org** non-profit organizations
- **.gov** non-military United States government
- **.mil** United States military
- **.us**, **.uk**, **.au** and other two-letter country abbreviations

The next level of DNS domains includes those that have been registered with InterNIC. These domains are typically the organization's name or some meaningful word or phrase. Under DNS, this name is followed by a period and then the top-level domain. For example, Syngress Publishing's domain name is syngress.com. Organizations can further subdivide their DNS name by adding child domains. Syngress could create a subdomain called corp.syngress.com, for instance. This hierarchy is illustrated in Figure 2.6.

When a user types in a Uniform Resource Locator (URL) into a browser, or attempts to access another host on the Internet with its host name, the request needs to be in the form of a 32-bit IP address in order for the other host to actually be contacted. So, as a DNS client, the workstation sends the user's request to the DNS server. The DNS server, if it is not authoritative for that domain address, sends the request upstream towards a DNS server that can refer to a server that has the authority for that domain address. For example, if the user is located in syngress.com and requests an address for Microsoft.com, the syngress.com DNS server refers the request to the .com DNS server, which then refers the request to the

Microsoft.com DNS server. The Microsoft.com server can supply the IP address back to the syngress.com DNS server, and subsequently the IP address is supplied to the client. Now, if the user had requested an address for ieee.org, the request would have been sent all the way up the hierarchy to the root [.] DNS server and then down to the ieee.org DNS server.

Figure 2.6 DNS Hierarchy

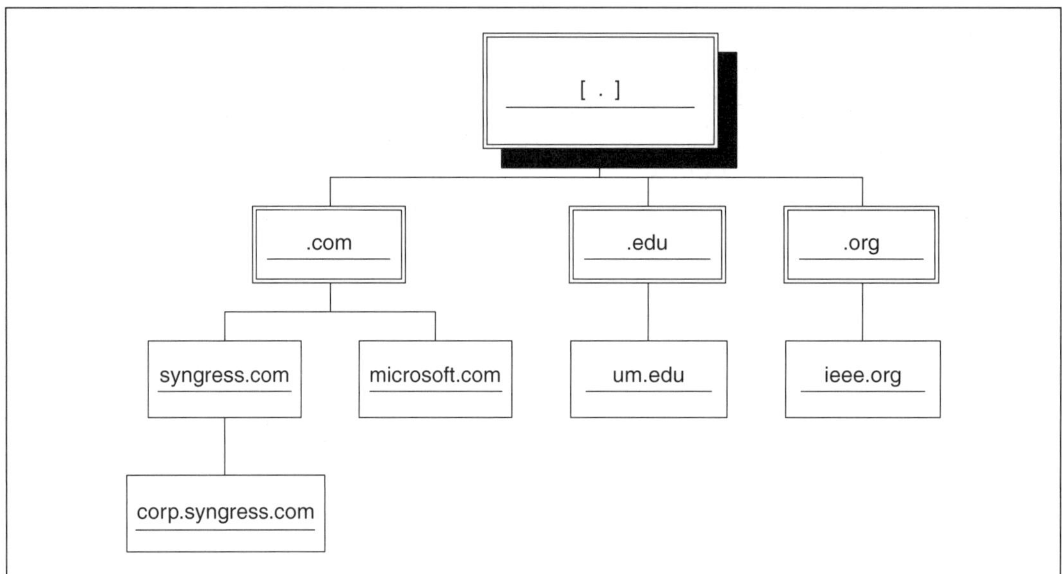

The DNS database is stored in zones. A *zone* is the information for a domain stored on a single computer. Some zones include information for child domains, too. Zones can be copied, or replicated, to other servers. One of the DNS servers is considered *primary* and handles all the updates for the zone. The remaining servers with copies of the same zone are considered *secondary* and merely resolve requests for IP address-to-name mapping. The Active Directory provides for an Active Directory integrated zone, a type of zone that uses multimaster replication.

DNS information is in the form of *resource records* (RRs). Each RR represents the resource and its associated IP address, as well as other details depending on the type of RR. The most common RR types are address (A) records and pointer (PTR) records. The Active Directory requires a newer type of RR: service (SRV) resource records. These records are used to locate the services that are running on the Internet, including the Active Directory service. This is defined in RFC 2052.

One of the most important things to remember is that the Active Directory cannot function without a correctly configured DNS. DNS provides the means for a domain controller to locate other domain controllers and for a client computer to find a domain controller for logons and queries. All of the Active Directory domains use a DNS name, and every Windows 2000 Server and Active Directory client has a DNS name. However, the Active Directory domain data and the DNS domain data are different sets.

TIP

If you want to greatly simplify administration of DNS, you should implement Dynamic Domain Name System (DDNS), also known as Dynamic Updates. As the name implies, DDNS enables DNS clients to dynamically update the DNS server with their name and IP address mapping. Otherwise, an administrator must manually enter each computer's name and IP address into the DNS database.

Lightweight Directory Access Protocol (LDAP)

When the Active Directory is queried, the requests are sent from clients via LDAP. LDAP is an Internet protocol used specifically for access to directory services. The protocol specifies what operations can be performed on the directory service and which information can be accessed. Because it is a standard protocol, LDAP provides a level of interoperability with other directory services that also employ LDAP, and any LDAP-compliant client applications. Active Directory supports LDAP versions 2 and 3.

LDAP provides a naming convention for the objects within the Active Directory. Distinguished Names (DNs) use attribute types and then the actual value of each component of a name in order to locate it within the directory service. The attribute types that the Active Directory uses are:

dc domain component (denotes a domain)

ou organizational unit (denotes an organizational unit container within a domain)

cn common name (denotes a network resource object)

Using these attribute types, a user account named Justine located in the jang.com domain under the Sixth OU, which is located in the AllUsers OU, would have the DN of:

```
Cn=Justine,ou=Sixth,ou=AllUsers,dc=jang,dc=com
```

When you use an Active Directory tool, it will not display the LDAP abbreviations. The LDAP naming is only required when using an LDAP-compliant script or application. LDAP URLs are used to access an object when using LDAP in a script. An example of an LDAP URL is:

```
LDAP://server.jang.com/cn=Justine,ou=Sixth,ou=AllUsers,dc=jang,dc=com
```

Windows 2000 incorporates a command-line utility called LDAP Data Interchange Format (LDIFDE). LDIFDE can be used to import directory information into the Active Directory from another directory service. It can also perform batch operations to add, delete, rename, and modify objects in the Active Directory. Most administrators will find LDIFDE useful for batch files, especially when making a large number of similar changes to a group of objects. For example, if a company merges with another company, they will probably consider merging users into a single forest to take advantage of the reduced administrative requirements. One of the tools that they can use to migrate those users is LDIFDE.

Kerberos Version 5

The authentication provided by Windows 2000 Active Directory is based on Kerberos version 5 (V5), an Internet standard. All trust relationships between the domains within an Active Directory forest are also based on the Kerberos V5 authentication protocol.

Kerberos lends itself to the interoperability of Windows 2000 with UNIX systems, being able to authenticate UNIX clients as well as enabling a trust relationship between a Kerberos realm and a Windows 2000 domain. When there is a trust relationship between a Kerberos realm and a Windows 2000 domain, a client in that Kerberos realm can authenticate to the Active Directory and use network resources within that domain.

Replication

The whole concept of replication within the Active Directory is entirely different from that used by legacy Windows NT domains. In Windows NT, there was no information exchanged between domains; the flow of domain information between domain controllers simply copied all of the information within the PDC to the backup domain controllers (BDCs). The Active Directory specifies each domain controller (DC) as a peer to all other DCs. Information can be updated on any DC. Then, changes are replicated to all the other DCs, constituting a process of *multimaster replication*.

Multimaster replication provides the Active Directory with a method of fault tolerance and load balancing. If one DC fails, another DC can respond to the Active Directory request. Replication is profoundly tied to sites. A site is defined as a set of well-connected IP subnets. *Well-connected* refers to the fact that the subnets should be linked by highly available and reliable networks. This will most likely be local area network (LAN) links.

Replication uses Update Sequence Numbers (USNs) rather than time for propagation of updates. Domain controllers maintain USNs, which are 64-bit numbers, to track updates. As new updates are made to objects, the USN is advanced and stored with the changed attribute, along with an attribute that indicates which domain controller the change was made on. Each domain controller maintains a table listing the USNs that it has received from its replication partners (those other domain controllers with which it exchanges information directly). Actually, this table lists the highest USN. At the time that replication is made, only the USNs that are greater than the last, highest USN listed in the table, are requested. As a result, replication is more granular and not dependent upon the clock of a server.

NOTE

Sites are a significant improvement over the way that Windows NT performed. I recall working on a global network in Miami FL a few years ago. Sometimes I would log on and be authenticated by a BDC located in Miami. But most of the time, I'd be authenticated by a BDC in Sydney, Australia, or Atlanta, Georgia, or Phoenix, Arizona and so on. It was not an efficient system. Windows 2000 sites end this random chance authentication process. When a client requests a service, it knows which site it belongs to by its own IP subnet and automatically directs its request to a DC in the same site.

All replication only consists of updates that have been made to the Active Directory. For example, if a user account named Mjones has had its office phone number changed, the only information that will travel across the wire will be the location information for the Mjones object and the new telephone number.

When discussing replication, it is important to understand there are two types of replication:

- Intrasite replication
- Intersite replication

Intrasite replication is the exchange of directory data within a site. This type of replication occurs frequently (approximately every five minutes between DCs), using uncompressed traffic; it travels a replication topology of Connection Objects created by the Knowledge Consistency Checker (KCC). The KCC ensures that there are no more than three hops (or four DCs) in a replication ring, so that replication can completely synchronize the DCs within a site in a maximum of 15 minutes. Figure 2.7 illustrates a replication topology within a site.

Figure 2.7 Intrasite Replication Topology

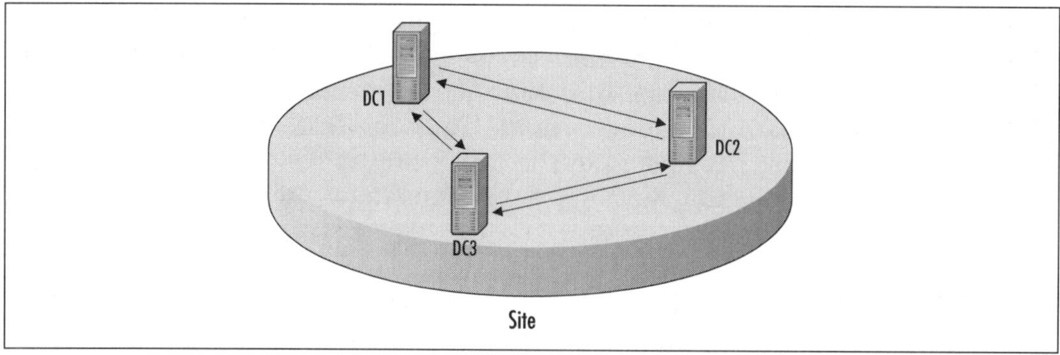

Intersite replication constitutes the exchange of directory data between sites. This type of replication occurs only on the periodic basis that the administrator has configured. It uses compressed traffic to optimize transmission over slow or unreliable network links. Intersite replication requires additional components—Site Links and Site Link Bridges—to be configured by the administrator. Figure 2.8 illustrates a sample intersite replication topology.

Figure 2.8 Intersite Replication Topology

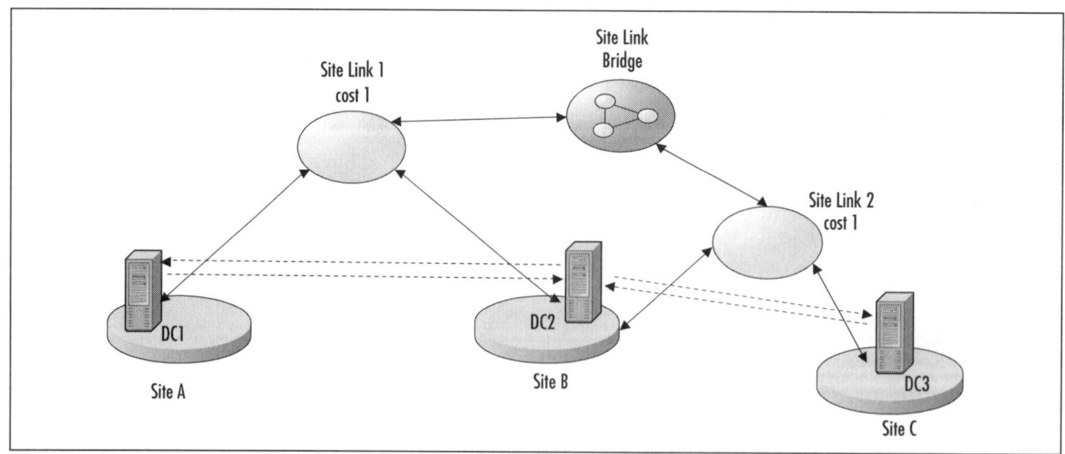

Policies

One of the major benefits of Windows 2000 Active Directory is the ability to apply Group Policy to user accounts and computers in order to control the environment. Under Windows NT 4.0, System Policies were available for defining some environmental information, and those policies were stored in the registry. The Windows 2000 Group Policy, by contrast, defines a larger set of environmental components and stores them in the Active Directory.

When a computer starts up, it first applies any local group Policies. Then it checks the Active Directory Site for any site-connected Group Policies. Next, it checks the domain for domain Group Policies. And finally, it checks each organizational unit, from the top of the domain to its containing OU, and executes each of those Group Policies. When multiple group policies are used, the logon process lengthens, so it is best to keep the number of Group Policies to a minimum. In addition, later Group Policies can override the policies that previously executed, though an administrator may block this inheritance. So again, to reduce time-consuming logons and complex troubleshooting, an administrator should keep the number of Group Policies to a minimum.

There are a great number of options available in Group Policies for managing a user's environment. An administrator can use Group Policies to deploy applications, to lock down access to desktop icons, or to configure the appearance of a user's desktop.

An administrator uses the Group Policy Editor to create or edit Group Policies. The Group Policy Editor can be accessed as a custom MMC, or through the Active Directory Users and Computers MMC.

In the Group Policy Editor, navigate below the Users node to edit policies that will affect users regardless of where they log on, or navigate below the Computers node to edit policies that will affect specific computers regardless of who logs on to them. You will see a screen similar to Figure 2.9.

Working with the Architectural Details

Legacy Exchange Server's directory service had a similar architecture to the Active Directory because they both use an ESE database structure. However, there are some changes in the way the two have been implemented. These changes are detailed in Table 2.1.

Figure 2.9 Group Policies

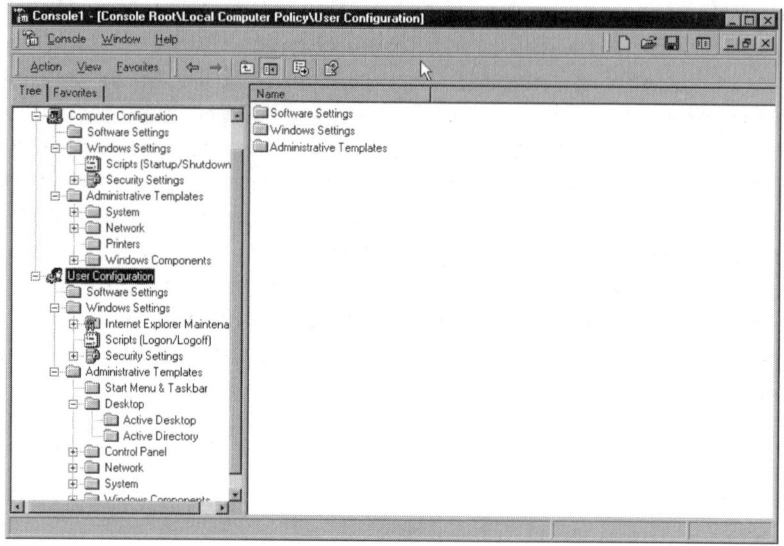

Table 2.1 Differences between Active Directory and Legacy Exchange Server

Active Directory	Legacy Exchange Server	Function
LSASS.EXE	DSAMAIN.EXE	Manages transactions
NTDS.DIT	DIR.EDB	Directory database
10 MB log files changes	5 MB log files	Contains transaction
Per-attribute replication	Entire object replication	Optimizes replication traffic
Mailbox-enabled user	Mailbox	Provides mail functions to a user
Mail-enabled contact	Custom recipient	Provides external mail recipients without a user account
Mail-enabled group	Distribution list	Provides a group of mail accounts to simplify e-mail addressing

The fourth item in Table 2.1 mentions per-attribute replication. There is a huge performance enhancement in using per-attribute replication as opposed to entire object replication (see Figure 2.10). In the Active Directory, a user object contains much more information than the information held in a legacy Exchange Server mailbox. Plus, the Active Directory user object can be extended to contain more information, so the size of the object is not necessarily static. In per-attribute replication, the Active Directory only replicates the change that was made, plus the location information for the object that was changed. (Location information is simply an indicator of which object was changed and where it can be found in the Active Directory hierarchy.) The difference in traffic size can be several kilobytes of information for each object that has changed. When many objects change in a short period of time, this can be a tremendous performance enhancement.

Figure 2.10 Performance Difference between Full Object Replication and Attribute Replication

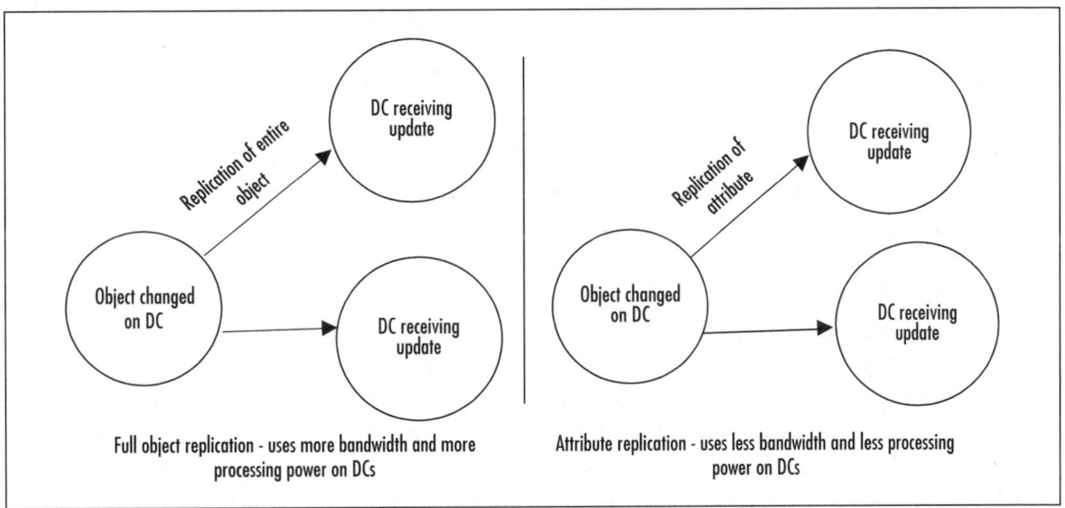

Windows 2000 does not support X.400 connections between sites. It only supports Remote Procedure Calls (RPCs), which is the default protocol used, and Simple Mail Transfer Protocol (SMTP), which is only used in certain configurations.

When you first implement Windows 2000, you may notice that the Active Directory only supports one e-mail address for user accounts. You shouldn't worry, however, because when you install Exchange Server and extend the Active Directory schema, you will find that more e-mail addresses are added to each user account.

How Exchange Connects to Active Directory

The Exchange 2000 Server application connects to the Active Directory through a software layer called the Directory Store Access Application Programming Interface (DS API). This layer sits on top of LDAP. The DS API enables Exchange 2000 Server services to query the Active Directory for information.

Exchange 2000 Server will query the Active Directory to look up addresses and to validate configuration data. The Global Catalog is used to discover information about e-mail addresses, since a simple domain controller will not have information about *all* user accounts, merely those that exist in the domain controller's own domain.

Exchange Servers are not necessarily installed on Active Directory domain controllers. Because of this fact, the Exchange Server must query the Active Directory to gain access to information. In order to reduce the time it takes to access information, Exchange Server maintains a reserve of information called the Directory Access Cache. This cache lists the results of Global Catalog queries. The Directory Access Cache optimizes performance, since performing a query to the Global Catalog takes more time than to hit the cache on the local server. If information is not available within the Directory Access Cache, then the query is made to the Global Catalog.

You can adjust the amount of information that is held in the cache through the HKLM\SYSTEM\CurrentControlSet\Services\ MSExchangeDSAccess\Instance0\MaxMemory registry key. The value that you place in this area will be the number of kilobytes (KB) that the cache will hold. If you want to hold 10 megabytes (MB) of information, then change the reg_dword value to 10240. If you decide to make changes to this registry key, you will likely be increasing the value. You should increase the Directory Access Cache on all your Exchange Servers when your Global Catalog servers are suffering performance woes. You should also increase the Directory Access Cache on Exchange Servers that sit closer to users than their nearest Global Catalog server. Try incrementing the amount of cache by 1 MB at a time, and if performance is still unsatisfactory, then add or move your Global Catalog servers around the network.

Exchange Servers also need to look up routing information in the configuration data of the Active Directory. To do this, the Exchange Server does not need to connect to a Global Catalog server, but to any domain controller. All domain controllers hold a copy of the forest's configuration data. When an Exchange Server connects to a domain controller, it continues to try to use the same domain controller each time it needs to read configuration data. This type of query is performed using LDAP over TCP port 389.

When older client applications access the Global Address List (GAL), they will look for a Directory Store on the Exchange Server. Client queries are executed using either MAPI or LDAP over TCP port 3268. Since there is no directory store on Exchange 2000 Server, there needs to be some conduit to the Active Directory. What Exchange 2000 Server has is a Directory Store proxy service. This proxy intercepts the requests from these older clients and forwards them to the nearest Global Catalog server. By contrast, Outlook 2000 works seamlessly with Exchange 2000 Server by writing the name of the Global Catalog server it was directed to last by Exchange Server into its own Registry. The Outlook 2000 client then uses that information to connect to the Global Catalog directly to access the GAL. To direct requests to a specific Global Catalog server, you can edit the registry keys at HKLM\SYSTEM\CurrentControlSet\Services\MSExchangeSA\Parameters—editing both the NSPI Target Server key and the RFR Target Server key by entering the name of the Global Catalog server as the value. The NSPI Target Server key will set the proxy for older client applications, while the RFR Target Server key will set the referral for Outlook 2000 clients to a specific Global Catalog server.

Administrative Tools

When you begin using the Active Directory, you will administer it using new administrative tools based in the Microsoft Management Console (MMC). To start up the MMC and choose consoles:

1. Click Start | Run and type **mmc**.
2. Click the Console menu and select the Add/Remove Snap-In option.
3. Click Add and then select the console(s) from the dialog box.
4. Click Add for each console you want to include in your custom console.

The following list explains the role of each console:

- **Active Directory Users and Computers** Manages the user objects, computer objects, and domain controllers that are part of a single domain. The majority of administration will happen in this console.

- **Active Directory Domains and Trusts** Manages the relationships between the domains within the forest.

- **Active Directory Sites and Services** Manages the site configuration, IP subnets, and replication topology.

- **Group Policy Editor** Manages the Group Policies to be applied to users and computers.

The Active Directory Users and Computers is the place where mail-enabled user accounts are administered. Other than the Active Directory Users and Computers MMC, you will probably conduct most of the administration of Exchange through the Exchange System Manager MMC. Once Exchange Server has been installed, there are additional dialog boxes available for user accounts and their mailboxes.

You can execute advanced operations using some additional graphical and command-line tools available with Windows 2000 and with the Windows 2000 Resource Kit, which can be downloaded from www.microsoft.com/windows2000/library/resources/reskit. These include:

- **ADSIEdit** Views or modifies directory service object information. This tool is most useful when you need to change an object and can't find the object in the standard Active Directory consoles.

- **DSACLS** Views or modifies the Access Control Lists (ACLs) on objects. When you migrate objects from one domain to another, DSACLS is useful for making certain that the access is correct.

- **DSAStat** Compares directory service data on different domain controllers to check status and detect inconsistencies. If you have to troubleshoot replication, this utility offers some helpful information.

- **MoveTree** Moves objects from one domain to another domain. Use this tool for migrations.

- **NetDOM** Manages domain operations such as trust relationships and domain membership. This command-line utility is great for batch files used on workstations in migrations.

- **REPAdmin** Manages site replication. Replication is critical to maintain consistent and up-to-date information, and this tool can assist you in managing it.

- **REPLMon** Monitors and displays replication information. REPLMon should be used daily by an Active Directory administrator to monitor the way that replication takes place.

- **SIDWalker** Fixes SIDHistory on migrated accounts. SIDWalker is best used after a migration from legacy Windows NT to Windows 2000 in order to handle SIDHistory issues.

Planning for Active Directory

Planning is crucial to the successful implementation of Windows 2000, Active Directory and Exchange 2000 Server. These systems are complex and have an impact on the underlying infrastructure and on each other. The interdependencies of these systems will affect your designs as well. You will need to create four designs for the Active Directory itself.

1. Forest plan
2. DNS and domain plan
3. Organizational unit plan
4. Site plan

Sizing Domain Controllers

Exchange administrators are somewhat better prepared for the size of servers used to house the directory service than standard Windows NT administrators. The legacy Windows NT SAM did not support more than 40,000 objects. The Windows 2000 Active Directory can support millions of objects in a more complex database structure. Exchange Servers have always demanded a great deal of resources to house the directory store and information stores, so this resource demand is nothing new to the Exchange Server administrator.

When sizing a domain controller, you should specify a hardware-based Redundant Array of Inexpensive Disks (RAID) array. You could use a mirrored configuration, known as RAID 1, and place the transaction logs on a separate physical disk. Or you could use a RAID 5 array that provides fault tolerance should any single disk within the array fail. In any case, you should ensure that your server has enough disk space to grow with your network.

Your domain controller will need enough random access memory (RAM) to operate the server operating system as well as perform Active Directory operations. At a minimum, you should consider at least 256 MB or more of RAM. However, you can never have too much RAM, so don't skimp on your domain controllers.

Finally, you should select a server-class machine for your domain controller that offers fault-tolerant features. Consider using redundant power supplies and failover Network Interface Cards (NICs) to ensure that your domain controller can remain online even if another component in your server fails.

Exchange Server's Impact on Design

When you upgrade to Exchange 2000 Server, you will have new capabilities available to you. For example, in the sizing of domain controllers, you will need to consider the extensions that Exchange Server brings to the directory service. These extensions will have a small impact on the size of the hard drive you will need. The likelihood is that the network will have more traffic resulting from the extensions and greater usage of the directory service. However, this traffic increase for the Active Directory is balanced by a significant reduction of traffic from the legacy Exchange Server directory store replication that no longer needs to be executed.

Active Directory domains have two possible modes of operation:

- Mixed mode
- Native mode

Domains are installed for the first time in mixed mode. *Mixed mode* means that the domain will support Windows NT BDCs. *Native mode* will not. Exchange Server requires that the domain it is installed into be in native mode. In order to change a domain to native mode:

1. Make sure that there are no more legacy Windows NT BDCs in the domain.
2. Click Start | Programs | Administrative Tools | Active Directory Users and Computers.
3. Right-click the domain object.
4. Select Properties.
5. Click Change Mode. Once changed to native mode, the domain cannot be changed back.

Exchange uses the type of groups that are only available in a native mode domain—the universal group. Exchange 2000 Server automatically creates administrative groups and routing groups in Active Directory. All the Exchange Servers join the default groups until configured otherwise.

- Administrative groups are used to establish groups of servers for administrators with specific management capabilities.
- Routing groups specify the message topology and how messages are exchanged between the Exchange Servers.

Administrative groups contain Exchange Servers for a certain group of administrators to manage. Routing groups contain Exchange Servers to replicate messaging information. Routing groups are the equivalent of

Exchange 5.5 sites, except that routing groups do not include the same administrative boundary. In fact, the administrative boundaries are set by the administrative groups. If you place the same Exchange Servers into an administrative group as you do into a routing group, then you will have the exact same functionality as an Exchange 5.5 site. If you migrate from a legacy Exchange 5.5 system, you should create an administrative group and a routing group to correspond to each existing Exchange site and then migrate the servers into them. Once they have been migrated, you can move the Exchange Servers into the routing or administrative groups that would better suit your needs. For more information on migration from legacy Exchange systems to Exchange 2000, see Chapter 6, Deploying Exchange 2000.

One of the main impacts on the Active Directory design will be in the area of Global Catalog servers. The majority of the queries that Exchange makes to the Active Directory are made to Global Catalog servers. You should make certain that at least one Global Catalog server exists in each Active Directory site (remember the physical location) where Exchange Servers are located. In order to accelerate performance from the end-user's perspective, you should place more than one Global Catalog server in each of those Exchange Server locations. However, too many Global Catalog servers will cause excessive replication traffic, so you should consider carefully where to place them.

There is no rule of thumb for the number of GC servers when using Exchange. For example, if your network only has a single domain, a single physical location without WAN links between sites, and 500 or fewer users, using more than two GCs is unnecessary. You should place at least one GC in each site, and possibly two or more if there are a lot of users in a particular location. To determine when to add another GC server, you should monitor the performance of the GC servers that are located in each site; from that performance data (looking at the CPU and memory utilization), you can determine at which points to install additional GC servers.

DNS is a consideration during the planning process. Whereas the Active Directory requires SRV RRs (server resource records), Exchange Server requires Mail Exchanger (MX) records for each Internet messaging server and Address (A) records for every server. Exchange Server will look to SRV RRs to locate Active Directory domain controllers and global catalog servers, too.

One final factor that you need to review is the impact that Exchange Server clients have on the network. The following process takes place when a client performs an address book lookup via the Directory Service Proxy:

1. The client sends a packet containing a plain-text name to query to the Exchange 2000 server where its mailbox is located.

2. The Directory Service Proxy on the Exchange Server forwards the request to a Global Catalog server located in the same site.

3. The Global Catalog server sends the query response back to the Exchange Server.

4. The Exchange Server forwards the response back to the client. This process up to this point is shown in Figure 2.11.

Figure 2.11 Address Lookups through DSProxy

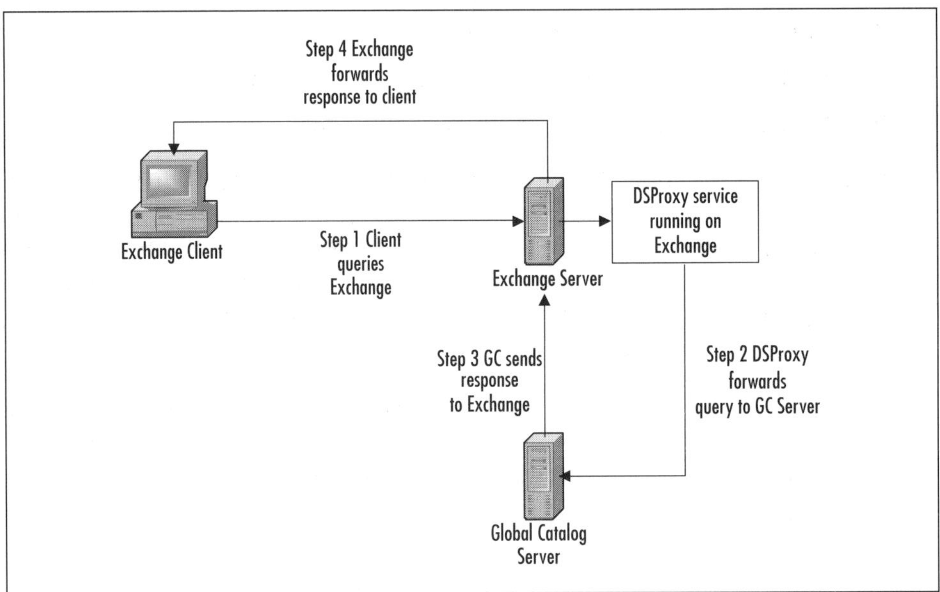

5. The client sends an acknowledgement to the Exchange Server.

6. The Exchange Server's Directory Service Proxy forwards the acknowledgement to the Global Catalog server.

Legacy clients produce more traffic on the network than Outlook 2000 clients. The first time the Outlook 2000 client queries, it uses the Directory Service Proxy on the Exchange Server in the same way that the legacy client does. However, after that point, when an Outlook 2000 client queries for a name, it contacts the Global Catalog server that it was referred to directly. Therefore, you should use Outlook 2000 as the mail client if you want to reduce traffic on the network, reduce the load on the Exchange Server, and reduce the latency for address book lookups.

Forest

The forest is an Active Directory database that has the following traits:

- A common schema
- A single shared Global Catalog database (although there may be multiple Global Catalog servers that replicate the Global Catalog database)
- A shared configuration, which includes the forest's site topology
- One or more domains
- It cannot be split into more than one forest.
- It cannot be merged with another forest.

Your forest plan consists of the number of forests that you will maintain on your network and the root domain for each forest. Since additional forests add incremental administrative overhead and network traffic, you should keep the number of forests to a minimum. If at all possible, try to keep the number of forests to one. There are only a few reasons for designing multiple forests:

- You need to have separate schemas. For example, if one group of users (developers) needs to create custom extensions to the schema that you do not want used on the rest of your production network, then you will need two separate forests—one with schema extensions, one without.

- You want to have separate Global Catalogs. For example, if you are providing the directory service on an extranet and wish to keep internal employee information from being listed in the extranet's Global Catalog, but available to internal employees, then you will need two separate forests—one for extranet users, the other for internal users.

- You want to have a test network where you can test applications before placing them into production. In this case, applications may extend the schema or cause network traffic problems for the Active Directory forest replication, so if you have a separate forest for testing you will have less impact on the production network.

- You want to separate your production network domains from the ones serving the Internet. All the domains in a forest have an implied trust relationship with all the other domains. As a result, the optimal way to secure your network domains is to use separate forests for the production network and the Internet network.

Remember, the first domain installed into the forest is the root domain. The root domain can not be removed, changed, or renamed. For instance, if you have a forest with a root domain of root.domain.com, and you want to make the root domain mydomain.com, your only option is to create an entirely new forest and migrate each domain controller, server, network resource, user account, and member computer to the new forest.

You should plan the root domain namespace carefully, as well as every other namespace root in the forest. Consider a forest with the root domain of root.domain.com. If you wanted to add the domain namespace domain.com to the forest, you could not. You can only add child or grandchild domains to a namespace once it has been installed into a forest. Your forest plan will list the number of forests, their function, and the root domain for each forest. When you create your forest plan, it will look similar to Figure 2.12.

Figure 2.12 Forest Plan

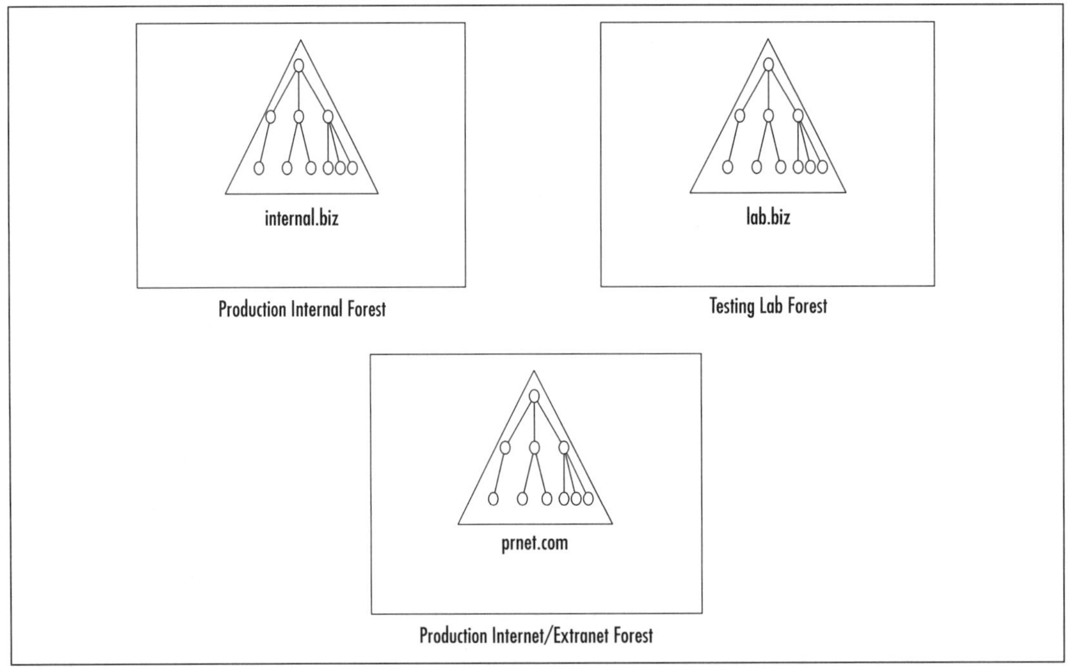

TIP

Think about what you plan to expose to the Internet. It may make sense for you to use a domain.local name, or a more generic name for your root domain, and then only later on, you can create alias (yet live on the Internet) domain names for Web sites or e-mail systems.

Using Exchange 2000 as an Application Service Provider (ASP)

ASPs host applications for clients. A business will hire an ASP to host an application such as Exchange Server for end users to access over the Internet. An Active Directory forest easily functions as a directory service for a single business running Exchange Server. But how do you work this system as an ASP, and still gain efficiencies from sharing physical hardware even though there are multiple businesses using them?

The main issue you need to consider is the forest boundary. While you may find that most businesses do not need to have a separate forest, there may be a few that do. These businesses will be distinguished by their need for:

- A separate schema
- Full administrative control over the forest
- Extremely rigid security requirements

You can design a shared Active Directory forest where multiple businesses each have their own domain within the forest. This method reduces the ASP's administrative overhead somewhat. However, since a domain controller cannot host more than a single domain partition of the database, each hosted business will require at least one dedicated server. For those individuals (not businesses) who subscribe to a hosted application, you may create another domain. You will find that a business will require a separate domain if it has a specific domain security policy.

Your optimal solution is to design a shared Active Directory forest where each business is granted its own Organizational Unit tree, which is then delegated to the appropriate administrator or administrative group. The business's OU tree can be customized to match the business' requirements, such as delegated administration. You can also create an OU to contain the individual subscribers. When you configure the OU tree, you should pay special attention to how users see their Exchange 2000 Global Address List entries.A Windows 2000 forest can support one, and only one, Exchange 2000 Server Organization. This adds another reason for creating additional forests—if you need more than one Exchange Organization, you will automatically need more than one Windows 2000 forest. An Exchange 2000 Server Organization cannot span more than one forest. This means that you may need to revisit your forest plans if you intend to have a single Exchange Organization to support messaging in your network.

When there are two forests, and subsequently, two Exchange 2000 Server Organizations, you face some challenges:

- You cannot use a single configuration for message routing, even if both forests span the same physical network.

- You cannot use the same administrative and routing groups.

- You cannot have a single Global Catalog with a cohesive address book. Instead, a connector must be used to link up the organizations so that their users are seen as external mail-enabled contacts (equivalent to custom recipients in a legacy Exchange 5.5 environment).

- You cannot allow access to calendar information between forests.

As you can see, the fewer number of forests and Exchange Organizations that you have, the better your network will perform. While the Exchange 2000 Server impact will not change the original reasons for having separate forests, it should make you think twice about having more than one forest before establishing a final design.

Domains/DNS

Domains and the DNS namespaces are so intertwined that they are generally consolidated into a single plan. This denotes the next level of detail for the Active Directory plan. DNS is the naming structure for the Active Directory. Each domain is given a DNS name, and is organized into a hierarchical namespace based on the name that it is given.

You must create a domain plan for each forest that you designated in your forest plan. Since you cannot easily move, change, or rename domains, you should carefully consider whether you need more than one domain. There are very few reasons to have more than one domain.

- You want to have more than one DNS namespace. A domain can only have a single DNS name, so multiple DNS namespaces requires multiple domains.

- You want to provide services on the Internet from within your forest but you want to keep your production domain separate.

- You need a different domain password or security policy for a group of people.

- You have a group of people who are not directly connected to the corporate network and must use SMTP to transmit replication traffic from their site to the rest of the forest. SMTP-based replication can only occur if there is no common domain spanning the site link. A configuration using SMTP-based replication is depicted in Figure 2.13.

Figure 2.13 SMTP Replication Only Occurs between Sites

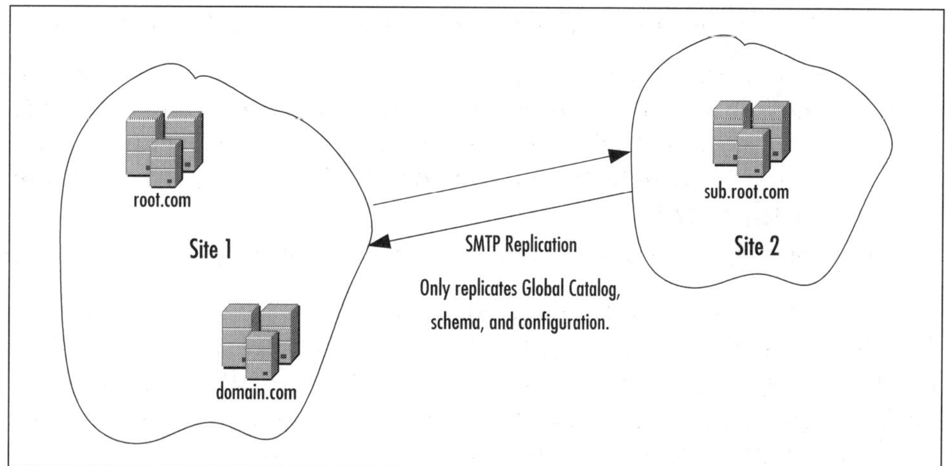

- You want to maintain an empty root domain in order to house the schema and keep it secure from the curious. The root domain of the forest is where the Schema Master FSMO is placed originally. In this domain, there is a group called Schema Administrators. Any member of the Domain Administrators group can add themselves to the Schema Administrators group, seize control of the Schema Master FSMO, and extend the schema. To reduce this possibility, you can create a root domain with no users except for a few trusted administrators.

You should try to keep your Internet domain name separate from the corporate domain namespace. You should also avoid too many domains within the forest because they will bring incremental traffic during replication. If at all possible, you should use a single domain.

One of the Windows NT practices was to create additional domains for administrative separation. Under Windows 2000, an administrator can delegate administration for a subsection of the domain to other administrators so there is no longer any need to create additional domains.

TIP

Windows NT 4.0 and past versions of DNS do not support SRV RRs. If you are using one of these past versions of DNS (or another version that does not support SRV RRs), then before you install your first Windows 2000 domain controller, you *must* install a DNS version that does support SRV RRs. Your DNS should support RFC 2052.

When you create your DNS and Domain plan, you will designate the number of domains in each forest and assign them a name. The plan may specify functions for the domains as well as the names for them. Your domain plan will look similar to Figure 2.14.

Figure 2.14 Domain Plan

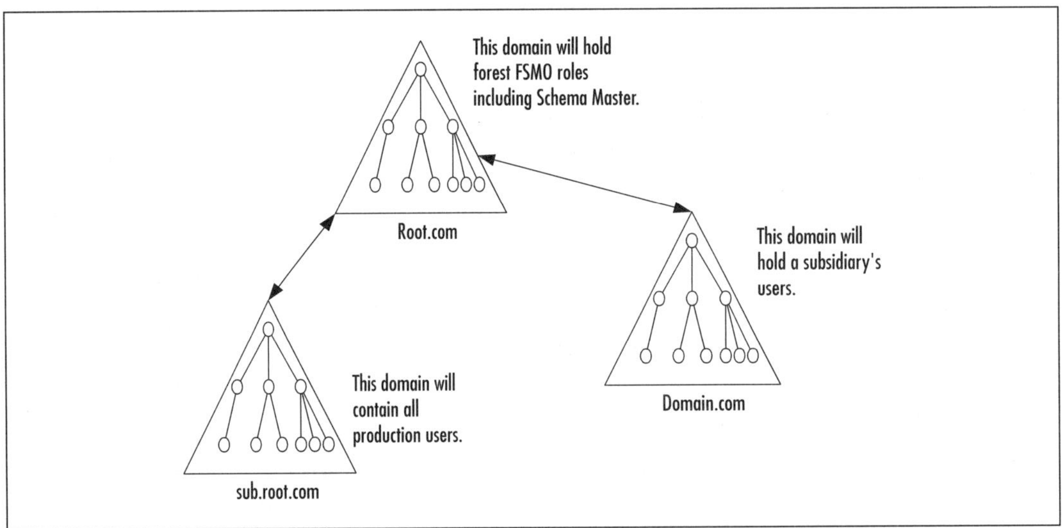

You will also organize a plan for DNS at this point in time. First, you must validate that the current DNS version used will support SRV RRs. If not, then you must decide on a new version of DNS. You may use Windows 2000 DNS if you don't wish to upgrade an existing DNS system, or if you do not have DNS currently on your network.

DNS is critical to the functionality of Active Directory. If a domain controller or client cannot access a DNS server, then there is a failure on the network. Your DNS plan should ensure that there are sufficient DNS servers in each location.

You should look at the DNS services that are provided for Internet users and for the production users. Then you should determine if there is a need to separate the DNS services for Internet users from the DNS services for production users. In many organizations, DNS already exists and works properly. You may not need to make any changes to an existing DNS service unless you are adding new domains.

NOTE

There are some limitations to the way that you configure domains. You cannot move a Windows 2000 Active Directory domain from one forest to another forest. You cannot change the root domain to a different domain in the forest. You cannot add a domain that has a higher level domain name to a forest that already contains a child-level domain (such as trying to add domain.com if sub.domain.com already exists in the forest).

Organizational Units

An Organizational Unit plan will be needed for each domain that you have designated in each forest. OUs are containers for user accounts and resources within the Active Directory domains. An OU can be nested into a hierarchy. There are some common rules that can help guide your OU design:

- You should designate the top-level OUs for administrative delegation.

- You can hide entire containers full of objects. If you wish to hide containers, you should place those containers just below the administrative delegation level.

- The next level of OUs can be designed for the application of Group Policies. And below that, you can add further levels of OUs if the business requires them.

- You should select short, descriptive names for your OUs.

- Even though you can create many levels of OUs, you should try to keep the OU hierarchy flat and simple for ease of use.

- You should try to apply Group Policies only at the OU levels that contain users because the more Group Policies that you apply, the longer the logon process takes.

When you design your OU hierarchy, you can test a design on the production network and change the design later. Unlike domains and forests, you can move, change, rename, and delete OUs at any time with little impact to the network. You will want to use OUs to group Exchange users or clients or servers and then delegate administration for those OUs to the appropriate administrators. The resulting OU design should resemble Figure 2.15.

Figure 2.15 OU Hierarchy

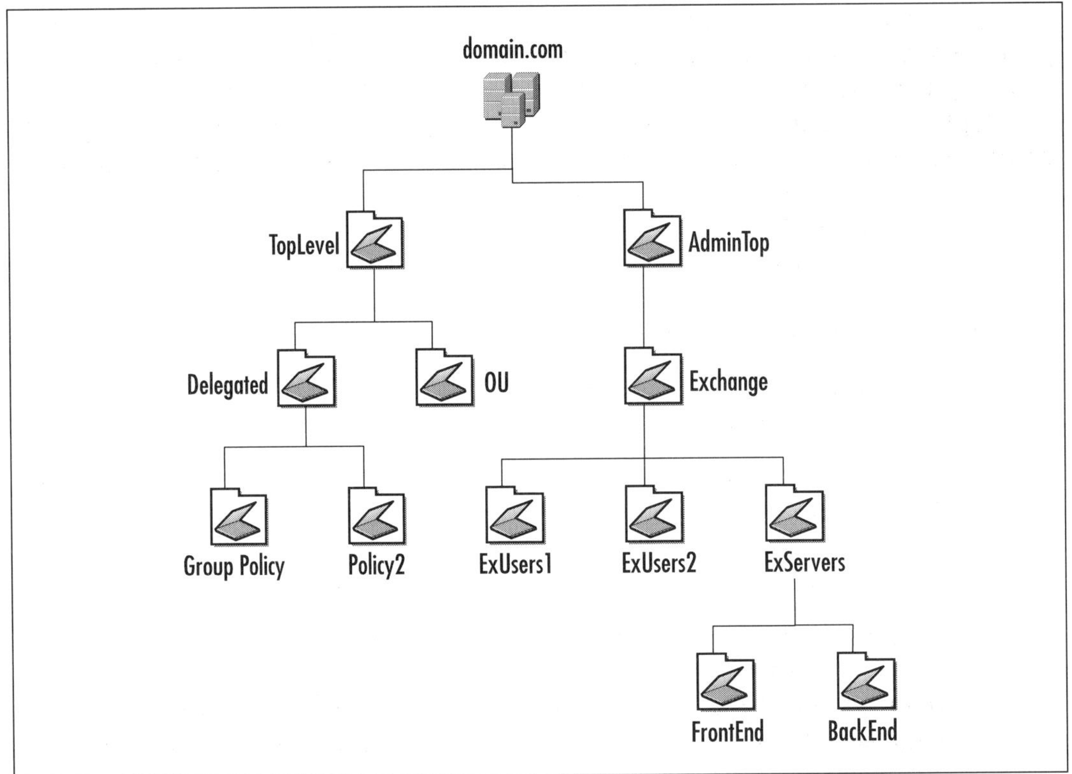

Sites

The Active Directory site is defined as a set of well-connected IP subnets. The difference between an Active Directory site and a legacy Exchange 5.5 site is that the Active Directory site does not contain a unit of the namespace, nor is the Active Directory site a part of the hierarchy of domains (or OUs for that matter). In the Active Directory, multiple domains can exist within a single site. In addition, a domain can span multiple sites.

Sites define the topology for replication to take place, and they direct how RPC communications can act. For example, a client workstation determines which site it belongs to from its own IP address. Then, when it contacts a domain controller, it sends its RPC traffic to a domain controller within its own site. Therefore, if you designate a site boundary at a wide area network (WAN) link, you can be assured that RPC logon and query traffic will not be randomly transmitted across it.

Replication traffic within a site occurs frequently (about every five minutes) and uses uncompressed traffic over RPCs. The Knowledge Consistency Checker (KCC) automatically creates connection objects between domain controllers for replication traffic to follow. The KCC also periodically checks the replication topology and makes changes to ensure that replication will always fully synchronize a site within fifteen minutes.

Replication traffic between sites can be either via RPCs or SMTP, and is compressed and can be configured to occur on a periodic basis to optimize the network's traffic. The KCC does not calculate a replication topology for the network. Instead, an administrator must define the connection objects, IP subnets, sites, site links, and site link bridges to create the replication topology.

When you create your site design, you can use the following guidelines:

- You can simplify your task by reviewing all the network connections (especially WAN links) that exist in your network.

- You can take advantage of traffic management by designating sites to be equivalent to a LAN and bounded by WAN links.

- You should place at least one domain controller, one Global Catalog server, and one DNS server within a site.

- If you will not be placing a domain controller, DNS server and Global Catalog server within a site that has a small number of users, even if it is located across a WAN link, you can incorporate that smaller site into a larger site that is directly connected to it.

- You should designate a set of IP subnets to each site in your plan.

- You must create a site boundary when you cannot use RPC traffic between two networks, and must rely on SMTP traffic instead.

Since a site can easily be created, renamed, changed, or deleted, you can easily make changes as your network grows and changes. Exchange 2000 Server uses the sites in Active Directory as a way to localize the queries for a local domain controller or Global Catalog server. Exchange 2000 Conference Manager will also use Active Directory sites to redirect clients to Exchange 2000 Conference servers that are located nearby. Note that Exchange Server does *not* use sites for messaging traffic—that is the job of routing groups. When you have finished creating a site topology plan, it will resemble Figure 2.16.

For more information on Exchange 2000 Conferencing Server see Chapter 8, Knowledge Management.

Figure 2.16 Site Topology Plan

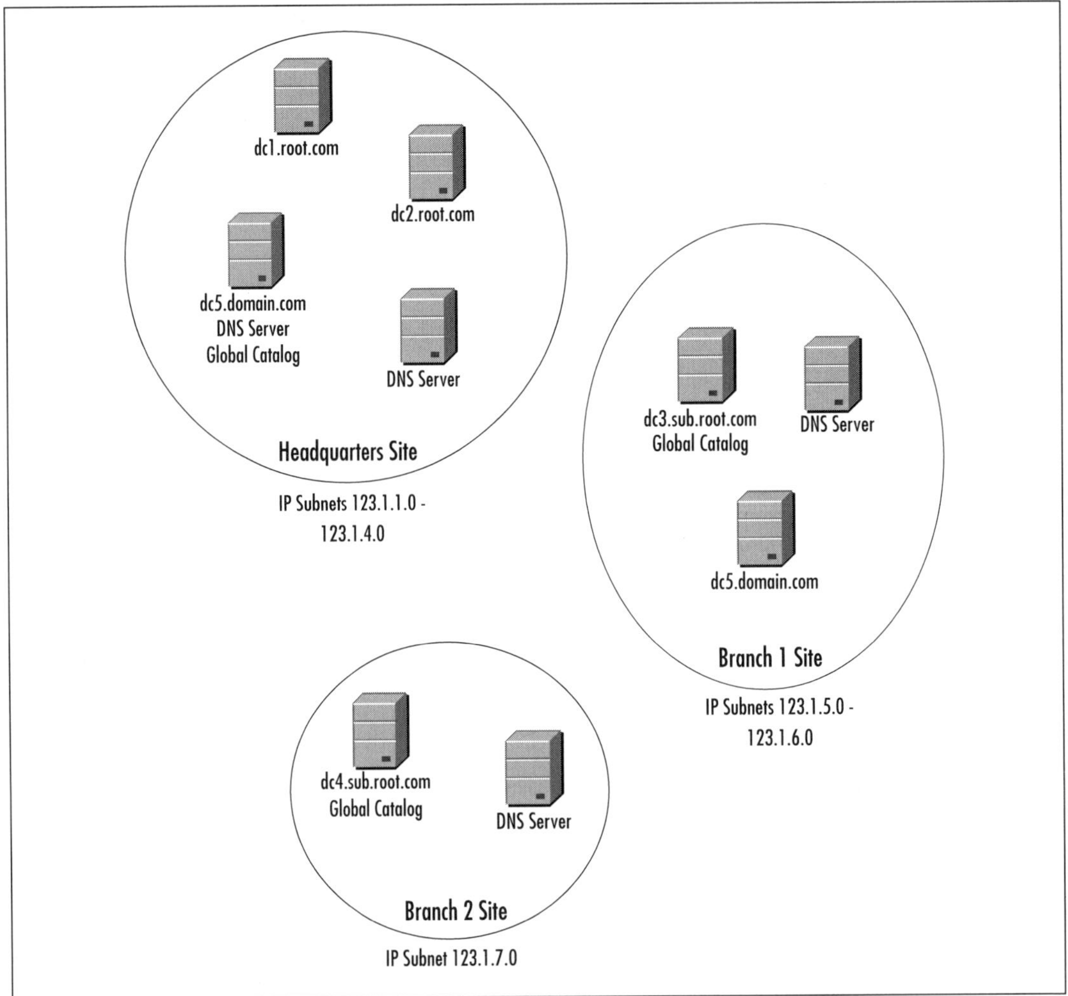

Implementing Active Directory and Exchange 2000

When you start to implement a new operating system, directory service and messaging system, you will be faced with hundreds of details. These details can take you off course and delay your implementation, if you are not careful. One way to stay on track is to remind yourself of the next major step in the implementation process. Those steps are:

1. Design your Active Directory: forest, domains, OUs and sites.
2. Develop a plan for installation of Windows 2000, DNS, Active Directory, and Exchange 2000 Server.
3. Install Windows 2000.
4. Install Active Directory and configure it.
5. Prepare the Active Directory for Exchange 2000 Server.
6. If legacy Exchange Server systems will be migrated or upgraded, prepare the legacy systems.
7. Install Exchange 2000 Server.
8. If upgrading a legacy Exchange Server system, upgrade the servers and their components.

The major processes of implementation that we will explore are steps 4 and 5—installing Active Directory and preparing it for Exchange Server. (Steps 5 to 8 are covered in Chapter 4 "Basic Administration" and Chapter 6 "Deploying Exchange 2000 Server," if you would like more information.) This process involves three applications:

- dcpromo.exe, also known as the Active Directory Installation Wizard
- ForestPrep
- DomainPrep

DCPromo

When you want to install a new Active Directory forest, you simply install the first domain controller for the root domain of the forest. A domain controller is a server that contains a copy of the Active Directory database, so that it is capable of authenticating users for the domain. To install that domain controller, you run an application called dcpromo.exe. This application is also called the Active Directory Installation Wizard. When you run dcpromo, you will need to know what role the DC will be playing in the Active Directory forest and other information.

- Is this the first DC in the domain?

- Is this the root domain for a domain namespace?

- Is this the first domain in the forest (e.g., the root domain)?

- Will this server be a DNS server?

- Is the server a DNS client?

- If a new domain, what is its DNS domain name?

- If a new domain, what will be the NetBIOS name?

- Where will the Active Directory files be located?

- Where will the system volume be located?

- Will security be relaxed for NT RAS backward compatibility?

- What is the password to be used on this server to restore Active Directory?

Table 2.2 shows the dialog screens for the Active Directory Installation Wizard, and the actions that you may select.

Table 2.2 Active Directory Installation Wizard Options

Dialog Screen	Your Options	Comments
Welcome Screen	None	Click Next to bypass this screen.
Domain Controller Type	First domain controller in new domain. Domain controller in existing domain.	If you are creating a new forest or a new domain, select the first domain controller option.
Create tree or child domain	First domain in a domain tree. Child domain of a domain tree.	You will only see this dialog screen if you selected First domain controller in a new domain.
Create or join forest	Create a new forest. Place this domain tree in an existing forest.	You will only reach this screen if you selected to Create a new domain tree.

Continued

Table 2.2 Continued

Dialog Screen	Your Options	Comments
DNS Configuration	Configure this computer as a DNS Client. Install this server as a DNS Server.	If you reach this screen, your DNS configuration is not functioning. You should bail out of the application, configure DNS, and then start all over again.
DNS Domain Name	Enter the domain name.	Use the format "domain.com" for this name.
NETBIOS Domain Name	Enter the domain name.	Use the legacy NT format "DOMAIN." This will automatically default to the first 15 characters of the DNS domain name before reaching a period.
Active Directory Files location	Enter the location for the database and logging files for Active Directory.	The default location is the C:\WINNT directory. The best practice is to place the transaction logging files on a separate physical disk from the database files.
System Volume	Enter the location for SYSVOL.	Place the SYSVOL in a location that has plenty of room to grow. SYSVOL is replicated to every DC in the domain. It holds the logon scripts, Group Policies, and File Replication Service (FRS) information. It grows over time as new items are added.

Continued

Table 2.2 Continued

Dialog Screen	Your Options	Comments
Security	Standard Windows 2000 Security. Relaxed permissions for backward compatibility with Windows NT 4.0 Remote Access Service (RAS).	You only need to select the relaxed permissions option if you are going to be using Windows NT 4.0 RAS servers.
Directory Services Restore Password	Enter and confirm the administrative password that you will use to restore the domain controller in the event of a failure.	This password will not change on the DC. Each DC has its own restore password. You should not make this the same as your administrator's password, since that will change. You should write down the password for each DC and place the list in a secure location.
Summary Page	None	Click Next to install the Active Directory on your server.

Active Directory Connector

If you are intending to interoperate Exchange 2000 Servers with Exchange 5.5 servers, you will need to use the Active Director Connector (ADC). The Active Directory should already be installed on the designated domain controllers from your plan. Before using the Active Directory Connector, at least one domain in your forest must be in native mode so that universal groups can be supported. You should also ensure that all the Windows 2000 domain controllers are at the latest service pack level—currently Service Pack 1 (SP1), which is available for download from www.microsoft.com/download.

In Exchange 5.5, you will need to make some changes if you have user objects that have been granted multiple mailbox accounts. This configuration is incompatible with Exchange 2000 and Active Directory, because Active Directory supports a single mailbox attribute for each user account in the directory service. If you have any users that have multiple mailboxes, you can delete the mailboxes, create new accounts and attach it to the extra mailboxes, or mark the additional mailboxes as resource mailboxes so that when they are connected to the Active Directory, new accounts are created for them in the Active Directory. If you don't do one of these things, you may experience problems: for example, a user with two mailboxes will lose the connection to one of the mailboxes when the ADC runs—and it may be the user's personal mailbox, in which case the user will not be able to receive his own e-mail after executing the ADC.

It may be difficult to determine which user accounts have more than one mailbox associated with them in a large messaging environment. You can identify user accounts that have multiple mailboxes by running the MultiMB utility. You can find the MultiMB utility on the Exchange 2000 Server CD.

When confronted with a user account that has more than one mailbox, your first task is to mark the mailbox that the user account should be linked to. Then you will mark the additional mailboxes as resources by placing the value **NTDSNoMatch** in Custom Attribute 10 of each of those mailboxes.

Before running the ADC, you will also want to make certain that servers are located in the sites where you really want them to be. Once both Exchange 2000 Server and Exchange Server 5.5 are running in the same organization, you will not be able to move servers between sites. You will have to wait until all the Exchange 5.5 servers have been upgraded or migrated to Exchange 2000.

ADC will connect the Exchange 5.5 directory store to the Global Catalog in Active Directory. The ADC does the following:

- Extends the schema with mail-related attributes

- Populates the Active Directory with mail-related attributes and values

- Adds Exchange directory information to Windows 2000 security accounts, or if no accounts, creates the Windows 2000 security accounts

- Synchronizes the information between the Active Directory and the Exchange 5.5 Directory store

Once you install the ADC, you need to create *connection agreements.* Connection agreements are used to synchronize objects. The type of connection agreement used determines the information that is synchronized.

- **Recipient Connection Agreement** synchronizes mailboxes, distribution lists, and custom recipients. Recipient synchronization is simplified if you synchronize an entire Exchange 5.5 site rather than individual recipient containers.

- **Public Folder Connection Agreement** synchronizes public folder attributes used for sending mail to those public folders.

- **Configuration Connection Agreement** synchronizes the information about message mechanics, such as connectors between sites and other mail systems, monitors, protocols, and topology. Site information is synchronized with Active Directory routing and administrative groups.

You will need to create a recipient connection agreement to every Exchange 5.5 site, and a public folder agreement to every Exchange 5.5 site. When you create the connection agreements, you can define the direction in which the data will flow. For instance, you can create a one-way connection agreement from an Exchange 5.5 site to Active Directory, and the data will flow from Exchange 5.5 to Active Directory, but not vice versa. If an object does not exist in the Active Directory and it does in Exchange, the ADC will create it. Otherwise the ADC does not add new objects.

You may run into a condition where two accounts have access to the same Exchange Server mailbox. One account exists when the ADC creates it in the Active Directory. The other account exists in Windows NT 4. The ADC will copy the NT 4.0 SID to the msExchMasterAccountSid attribute of the new Active Directory user account. Users can still access their Exchange mailbox from the NT 4.0 user account, even if that mailbox has been upgraded to Exchange 2000 Server. However, if you upgrade the NT 4.0 domain to Windows 2000, you will have two Active Directory accounts attached to the same mailbox. At this point, you must merge the accounts so that the mailbox can be used. You can merge the accounts using the Active Directory Account Cleanup Wizard. The only time you will need to run this wizard is after a Windows NT 4.0 domain has been upgraded to Windows 2000 and users in that domain have Exchange accounts connected with the ADC. For more information see Chapter 6, and the resources mentioned at the end of this chapter.

ForestPrep

Even though the Active Directory is running on your network, you still have work to do before installing your first Exchange 2000 Server. The forest must be prepared for the Exchange Server-related information to be added to it.

The Exchange 2000 Server setup program includes the utility for this process. ForestPrep is the Exchange Server setup program that is executed with the /forestprep switch. For example, you would run D:\setup\i386\ setup /forestprep to run ForestPrep if D:\ is your CD-ROM drive and you are running the Exchange 2000 Server CD-ROM.

If you are upgrading an existing Exchange 5.5 organization to Exchange 2000 Server, you will need to run ForestPrep after running ADC, although you have the option of running ForestPrep before ADC. If you are creating a brand new installation of Exchange 2000 Server, you do not need to run ADC, but you must run ForestPrep.

One of the challenges organizations face is distributing appropriate permissions to various administrative groups. Windows 2000 Active Directory enables these organizations to distribute rights and permissions to the appropriate administrative personnel. For example, one Windows 2000 administrator may be allowed to create user accounts, while another administrator may only be granted the ability to change passwords. When Exchange Server administrators are added to the mix, an organization may not wish to have these administrators create user accounts. However, the organization will probably want the Exchange Server administrators to be able to install Exchange Servers into the Active Directory.

ForestPrep creates an account with the appropriate permissions to install an Exchange 2000 server into the Active Directory, but does not grant that account any permissions to manage user accounts. If you wish this account to have user administration rights, you can make the account a member of the Account Operators group or use the Active Directory Delegation of Control Wizard to grant custom rights. ForestPrep will give this account the Exchange Full Administrator rights for the Exchange Organization. To create more Exchange Administrators, you should run the Exchange Administration Delegation Wizard.

ForestPrep also extends the Active Directory schema, so you will only need to run it one time per forest. In order to extend the schema, the account that runs ForestPrep must be a member of the Enterprise Administrators and Schema Administrators groups. The ForestPrep utility must also be run in the domain that has the Schema Master FSMO, which is usually the root domain of the forest.

ForestPrep will update the Display Specifiers in the Active Directory. Display Specifiers are the components that make information visible in Active Directory consoles. The Exchange information is displayed on the Exchange General, Exchange Features and Exchange Advanced tabs of user objects and group objects in the Active Directory Users and Computers MMC.

Before you run ForestPrep, you should have the following information available:

- The name of the Exchange 2000 Organization you are creating. ForestPrep actually creates this Organization in the Active Directory. You can only have one Exchange 2000 Organization per Active Directory forest.

- The name of the account that will be granted the Exchange Full Administrator rights.

NOTE

You can use ForestPrep to install an Exchange 2000 Server that will join an Exchange 5.5 Organization. You will first need to have the Active Directory Connector (ADC) from the Exchange 2000 Server CD installed in your forest and your Exchange 5.5 Servers should be installed with the latest service pack—at a minimum Service Pack 3. The user account that runs ForestPrep requires Admin permissions within the configuration naming context of the site as well as the site name context. ForestPrep will tell you this if you haven't entered the correct permissions.

To execute ForestPrep:

1. Use a domain controller that exists within the forest in a domain that has the Schema Master FSMO role.

2. Place the Exchange 2000 Server CD in your CD-ROM, or be able to access its files from some place on your network.

3. Logon as a user with Schema Administrator and Enterprise Administrator group membership.

4. Click Start.

5. Click Run.

6. Type **D:\setup\i386\setup /forestprep** in the run dialog box and press Enter.

7. The Exchange Installation Wizard will start. Click Next.

8. At the license agreement screen click I agree and then click Next. You will see the screen shown in Figure 2.17. Note that *ForestPrep* appears in the Action column.

9. The following screen will prompt you to either create a new Exchange Organization or join an existing Exchange 5.5 Organization. After making the selection, click Next.

10. If you select to create a new Organization, you will be shown the dialog screen in Figure 2.18, where you are asked to type the name of the new Exchange Organization, and then click Next.

11. The following dialog screen allows you to type in the name of an account that will be given Full Exchange Administrator privileges. Click Next.

12. Click Finish.

Figure 2.17 ForestPrep

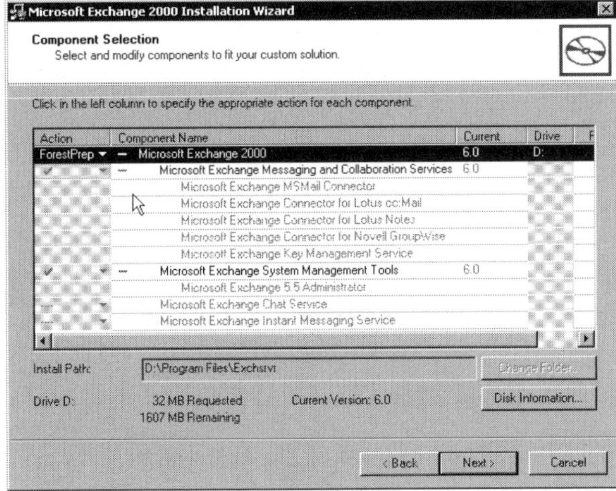

Figure 2.18 Exchange Organization Name

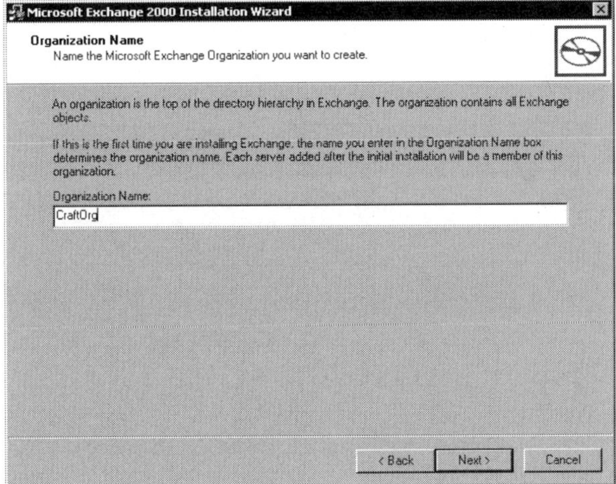

After you've finished running ForestPrep, the Active Directory schema will need to replicate throughout the entire forest. Depending on the number of your domain controllers and domains, you may want to wait a couple of hours (up to days) for replication to occur. In addition, the Global Catalog will be rebuilt to include the new objects and attributes that the schema extensions add to it. The Global Catalog literally becomes a new database and the entire GC database will also need to replicate throughout the forest to all Global Catalog servers. You can force replication to occur through the Active Directory Sites and Services MMC. If you prefer, you can also force replication using either of the REPAdmin or REPLMon utilities. To use the Active Directory Sites and Services method:

1. Click Start | Programs | Administrative Tools | Active Directory Sites and Services.

2. Navigate to the server that you wish to replicate.

3. Below the server, navigate to the NTDS Site Settings object.

4. Right-click the Connection Object that exists below the NTDS Site Settings of that server. If you do not see a Connection Object, you can right-click NTDS Site Settings and select New Active Directory Connection. This is shown in Figure 2.19.

5. Select Replicate Now.

Figure 2.19 Active Directory Sites and Services MMC

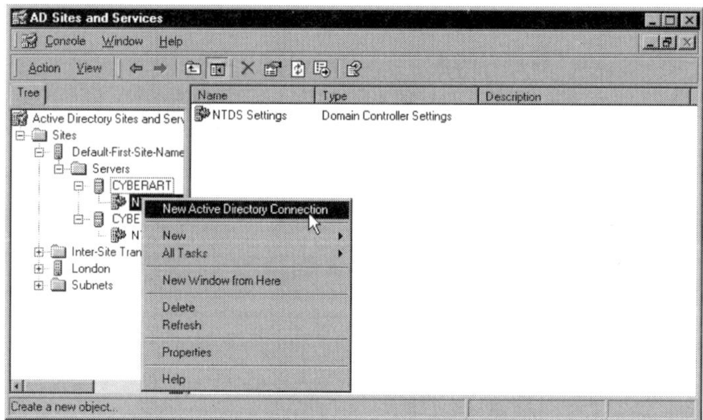

DomainPrep

DomainPrep is a similar utility to ForestPrep, however it does not perform forest-wide operations such as extending the schema. Instead, it performs domain-wide operations for any domain that will either host an Exchange Server or host an Exchange user. In many organizations, this scope includes every domain in the forest, but for some it does not. For example, if you had a forest with an "empty" root domain and did not intend to put either Exchange Servers or Exchange users in that domain, then you would not need to run DomainPrep on the root domain.

To run the DomainPrep utility, you must be using an account that is a member of the Domain Administrators group. Only a Domain Administrator member has the permissions required to execute the DomainPrep changes to the domain. DomainPrep will:

- **Create a Windows 2000 Global security group** called Exchange Domain Servers. This group contains the computer objects for all the Exchange Servers in the domain. This group is empty. As Exchange Servers are installed into the domain, they will populate this group. The Recipient Update Service uses the Exchange Domain Servers group to generate and update address lists, and to update recipient policy changes.

- **Create a Windows 2000 Domain Local security group** called Exchange Enterprise Servers. The Exchange Enterprise Servers group contains every Exchange Domain Servers global group from each domain. As soon as DomainPrep runs, it adds the Exchange Domain Servers group as a member to the Exchange Enterprise Servers group.

- **Create a Public Folder proxy container** in the Active Directory.

Before you execute the DomainPrep utility, you must first have completed the ForestPrep process on the Active Directory forest. Also, the changes made by ForestPrep must be replicated throughout the forest so that the schema and Global Catalog are fully synchronized with the new Exchange information. You must run DomainPrep before installing the first Exchange 2000 server in a domain or when you want the Recipient Update Service to run on a domain that hosts Exchange mail users.

To execute DomainPrep:

1. Select a domain controller within the domain where you are planning on installing Exchange Server or hosting Exchange users.

2. Place the Exchange 2000 Server CD in the CD-ROM, or ensure that the Exchange 2000 Server setup files are accessible over the network.

3. Click Start.

4. Click Run.

5. Type **D:\Setup\i386\setup /domainprep** and press Enter. The Exchange 2000 Installation Wizard will begin. Click Next.

6. Click the I agree radio button and then click Next.

7. In the Component Selection dialog screen, you will see that the word *DomainPrep* appears in the Action column, as illustrated in Figure 2.20. Make certain that all options are selected and click Next.

8. The final dialog screen completes the wizard. Click the Finish button.

Figure 2.20 DomainPrep

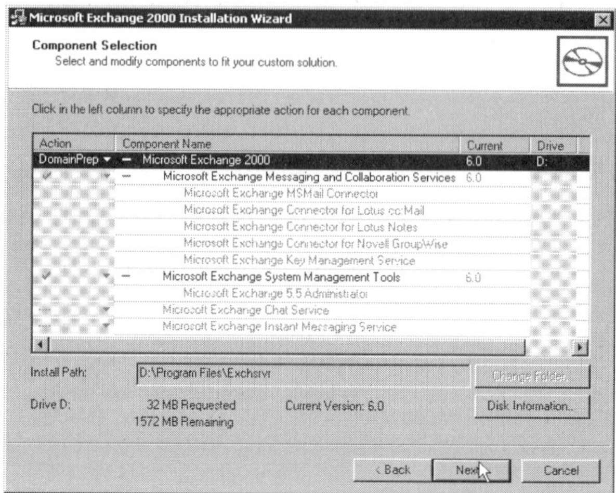

Once you have completed DomainPrep, you can now install your first Exchange 2000 server, or upgrade an existing Exchange 5.5 server. For further information about Exchange 2000 Server installations and upgrades, see Chapters 4 and 6.

TIP

If you are using an account that is a member of the Schema Administrators and Enterprise Administrators group, and you are installing the first Exchange 2000 Server into the domain that has the Schema Master FSMO, then ForestPrep and DomainPrep will execute automatically as part of the Exchange Server installation.

Setting Up your Active Directory

When you set up your Active Directory, one of the crucial tasks is to create a site. To do so:

1. In the Active Directory Sites and Services console, right-click the Sites container and select New Site.

2. Type in the name for your site, select a Site Link (DEFAULTIP-SITELINK is fine for now, since you may edit the site links later).

3. Click OK.

4. Repeat this procedure for your remaining sites.

This does not complete the site creation, however. You must also add the correct IP subnets to the site. Even the Default-First-Site-Name site will not have any IP subnets assigned to it.

To add a subnet:

1. Right-click the Subnets container and select New Subnet.

2. In the New Object-Subnet dialog box, type in the address and subnet mask.

3. In the Site Name box, click the name of the site to which this IP subnet should be assigned and click OK.

When you have multiple sites, you must create a site link between adjacent sites. You can apply a cost and replication frequency to these site links to manage how they are used. The higher the cost, the less likely a site link will be selected when there are multiple routes to the same destination.

To create a site link:

1. In the Active Directory Sites and Services console expand the Sites container, then expand the Inter-Site Transports container.

2. Right-click the IP container and select New Site Link.

3. In the dialog box, select the appropriate sites and click Add to incorporate them into the site link..

4. At the top of this dialog box, name the site link, and then click OK.

5. To change the cost and frequency of each site link, double-click it to display the properties and make the changes to those attributes.

If you have non-adjacent sites, you can create a site link bridge to enable replication between them. The site link bridge connects non-adjacent sites through a commonly shared site. This process is nearly identical to creating a site link.

1. In the same IP container below the Inter-Site Transports container, right-click the IP container and select New Site Link Bridge.

2. In the resulting dialog box, select each of the new Site Link objects in the left-hand pane and click Add to move them to the right pane.

3. Give the Site Link Bridge a name and click OK.

After you have created sites and populated them with IP subnets, you can create a hierarchical organization by generating each Organizational Unit you specified in your OU plan. To create an OU:

1. Open the Active Directory Users and Computers console

2. Right-click the domain or container within which you will place the OU.

3. Select New | Organizational Unit from the pop-up menu.

4. Give the OU a name and click OK.

With the hierarchy in place, you can now fill it with user accounts. To create a user account,:

1. In the Active Directory Users and Computers console, right-click the container that will hold the account and select New | User.

2. Complete the information for the user in the first dialog box.

3. Complete the remaining information in the second dialog box.

4. Click OK to save the user information.

5. To add more detailed information about the user, you can right-click the new user object and select Properties.

Troubleshooting Exchange 2000 during Implementation

Sometimes it seems that the only troubleshooting you really need to do is to shoot the computer that is causing you trouble. This section covers the peaceful alternative. There are a few areas in the implementation of the Active Directory with Exchange where you may run into some problems.

Problems with the DNS

The Active Directory will not function without DNS running properly. Any number of problems can occur. Even if your network has a fully functioning DNS service, you may find that there are problems caused by DNS. Many of these problems will show up as "Cannot locate..." a server, a Global Catalog server, a forest or some other network element. These are the items you should look for if you suspect that you have a DNS problem:

- Your DNS version does not support SRV RRs. Or a DNS server on the network does not support SRV RRs and is primary for your Windows 2000 domain. Both of these problems will cause the

Active Directory to fail. No one will be able to log on or use the Windows 2000 network. Please note that Windows NT 4.0 DNS is not compatible with Windows 2000. You can fix this problem by installing a compatible DNS server and making certain all zones are compatible.

■ Records needed by the Active Directory are not available in DNS. You can fix this problem easily by configuring DDNS for each Active Directory domain, deleting the existing information about the domain controllers, then bringing down the servers and bringing them back online or forcing a DNS refresh. This will create the correct records in the DNS database, and you can disable DDNS if you no longer want it to run. This can be configured in Windows 2000 DNS by right-clicking on the zone and selecting Properties from the pop-up menu. Then, where the drop-down box asks whether to Allow dynamic updates, you should select Yes, as displayed in Figure 2.21.

Figure 2.21 Enabling DDNS in Windows 2000 DNS

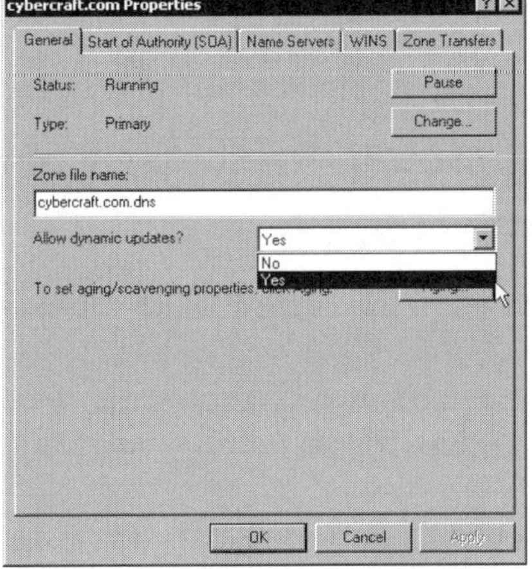

■ A network link between your current computer and the DNS server (or between the DNS server and an Active Directory domain controller) is not functioning. A DNS Server should always be available to client workstations, to member servers, and to every Active Directory domain controller. If the network does not function, or is unreliable, you should adjust your DNS design to include additional DNS servers in those locations.

TIP

You can check if your DNS supports SRV by doing the following at the command line:

```
nslookup [enter]

set type=SRV [enter]

_ldap._tcp.<your active directory domain> [enter]
```

Then you should see your SRV entries.
For example:

```
_ldap._tcp.syngress.com [enter]

Server: server1.syngresss.com

Address:10.0.0.3

_ldap._tcp.syngress.com          SRV service location:

    priority    = 0

    weight      = 100

    port        = 389

    svr hostname = server1.syngress.com
```

And so on.

Active Directory Connector

The ADC can cause considerable problems if the connection agreements are not configured properly. To configure a one-way connection agreement in the ADC:

1. Click Start | Programs | Administrative Tools | Active Directory Connector.

2. Right-click the Active Directory Connector.

3. Select New.

4. Select Recipient Connection Agreement.

5. The General tab should be shown; if not, click it.

6. Type the name of the Connection agreement in the Name box.

7. Select the direction of "From Exchange to Windows" under the Replication Direction to make certain that the Exchange Server information is uploaded to Active Directory.

8. Select a server to run the service in the Active Directory Connector Service.

9. Click the Connections tab.

10. In the Windows Server Information area, type the name of the Windows 2000 Server in the Server box.

11. Select the Windows Challenge/Response mode for Authentication.

12. In the Authentication Connect As, click Modify and then select a user and click OK.

13. Under Password, type the user's password and click OK.

14. For the Schedule tab, click Always.

15. Click the From Exchange tab.

16. Under Exchange Recipients Containers, click Add.

17. Select the recipients' container that you want to have show up in Active Directory. To simplify this process, select the entire site rather than individual recipient containers.

18. Select all the objects to replicate.

19. If prompted, type an administrative user name and password.

ForestPrep and Site Configuration

When you run ForestPrep, you can run into several problems. First, if the ForestPrep application cannot access the Windows 2000 Active Directory or is not able to look up the site to which the domain controller belongs, it is probably an issue with the DNS configuration or an unavailable domain controller. Even if you are running ForestPrep directly on a domain controller that doubles as a DNS server, you can run into this issue if DNS is not configured or running properly.

To configure Windows 2000 to be a DNS client:

1. Right-click My Network Places.

2. Select Properties.

3. Right-click the network connection, usually named Local Area Connection.

4. Select Properties from the pop-up menu.

5. Select Internet Protocol and then click Properties.

6. Click Advanced.

7. Click the DNS tab.

8. Enter the IP address of each DNS server.

9. Check the Append primary and connection specific DNS suffixes checkbox.

10. Check the Append parent suffixes of the primary DNS suffix checkbox.

If DNS is configured correctly, this could also be a problem with the site configuration of the Active Directory. Usually to the problem is that a site is configured without IP subnets. To fix this issue:

1. Click Start | Programs | Administrative Tools | Active Directory Sites and Services.

2. Navigate to the Subnets node and right-click it.

3. Select New Subnet.

4. Enter the IP address and subnet mask for the new subnet.

5. Select a site to place this subnet in.

6. Click OK.

Removing an Exchange Server from the Active Directory

If all else has failed, you may just want to remove every iota of Exchange Server from the Active Directory and start from the beginning. This is not recommended for a production environment, but you should keep the process in your back pocket as an emergency backout plan should you have problems during implementation.

1. If there is an existing Exchange Server 5.5 Organization, open the Exchange 5.5 Administrator application and delete any Exchange 2000 server objects.

2. Click Start | Run and type **LDP** on a domain controller that is not the same as the Exchange 2000 Server.

3. Connect to the Active Directory.

4. Locate the Configuration\Services\Microsoft Exchange container and open it.

5. Right-click OrgName and select Delete.

6. Go up one level to Microsoft Exchange container, right-click it, and select Modify.

7. Type **heuristics** in the Attribute box and leave the Value box blank.

8. In Operations, click Delete | Enter | Run. You will see a note stating whether the operation succeeded.

9. Shut down the Exchange 2000 Server.

10. Reboot the domain controller.

11. You may now Run ForestPrep and DomainPrep and rebuild the Exchange 2000 Server as a Windows 2000 Server. Then you may install Exchange Server again.

More Information

Go to Microsoft's Web site to search for troubleshooting information. Also, there are several books available from www.syngress.com that document Windows 2000 Active Directory. These are:

- Managing Active Directory for Windows 2000 Server

- Mission Critical Windows 2000 Server

- Building Cisco Networks for Windows 2000

- Designing Directory Services

Take a look at our listing of other Exchange-related Web sites in our Appendices.

Summary

Exchange 2000 Server offers a fully integrated messaging system for Windows 2000 Active Directory. Unlike past versions of Exchange, Exchange 2000 uses the Active Directory as a native directory service instead of providing its own Directory Store. In the future, this system will make Exchange capable of integrating natively with any application that uses the Active Directory.

The Active Directory provides Exchange server with a storage location for information about mailbox users. Active Directory also provides Windows 2000 with the storage location for information about user accounts and network resources. This database is used similarly to a phonebook, since a user or another application can look up information about other user accounts and resources available through queries. The directory service also provides a centralized authentication service and a method to relate objects to one another within it. This means that you can apply policies to manage the way that user accounts and other network resource objects can act with each other, as well as manage the security access of one object to another.

The Active Directory provides a hierarchical storage area for objects. The largest unit of the Active Directory is a forest. It is comprised of one or more domains that trust each other using Kerberos trusts that are bidirectional and transitive in nature. The forest has a common schema, configuration, and global catalog. The Global Catalog is an index made up of partial copies of every object in the directory.

The domains within the Active Directory follow a Domain Name System (DNS) naming hierarchy. A forest can have multiple namespaces if needed. Trees of domains can be constructed through the DNS names, such as domain.com, parent.domain.com and child.parent.domain.com.

Within each domain, the administrator can construct a custom hierarchy to organize resources. This hierarchy is made up of containers called organizational units (OUs) that can be nested—that is, one OU can contain another OU, to create a tree structure of OUs. Each OU can contain user accounts, group accounts, computers, member servers, and other resource objects. The administrator can then apply policies to the OUs to manage the objects within them.

The forest's configuration is mainly the site topology. Sites are collections of IP subnets that are linked by reliable and available network connections. Sites can be changed to meet the growth and changes of an organization. Sites are used to localize Remote Procedure Calls (RPC) traffic. When client workstations query the Active Directory or log on to the Active Directory, they are aware of their own site through their IP subnet, and they direct their requests to domain controllers located in the same site. In addition, replication of the domain controllers' local database updates is made within a site on a frequent basis using RPC uncompressed traffic. Between sites, the replication traffic is compressed and can be either RPC or SMTP traffic depending on the configuration of the site and domain.

When you implement Active Directory with Exchange 2000 Server, you have the following process to follow:

1. Plan and design your Active Directory according to your business requirements.

2. Install Windows 2000 Servers (or upgrade Windows NT servers to Windows 2000, according to your plan) and apply the latest service pack.

3. Promote designated Windows 2000 Servers to domain controllers using DCPROMO following your design.

4. Change at least one domain in the forest to native mode.

5. Configure Active Directory sites with IP subnets, site links and site link bridges.

6. If you are upgrading an Exchange 5.5 Organization, then clean up your Exchange 5.5 Organization, install the latest service pack (at least SP3), and run the Exchange 2000 Server version of Active Directory Connector. Create connection agreements to synchronize data between Exchange 5.5 and Active Directory.

7. Run ForestPrep for the forest, using the Exchange Organization name that you selected in your design.

8. Run DomainPrep for each domain that will either host Exchange Servers or host Exchange Users.

9. Install the first Exchange 2000 server.

There may be some trouble spots during your implementation process. One of the primary problems that you may run into is in the DNS configuration. In addition, you may find that your site configuration needs to be adjusted.

FAQs
Visit **www.syngress.com/solutions** to have your questions about this chapter answered by the author.

Q: I want to use my Exchange 5.5 Servers as back-end servers with an Exchange 2000 front end so that I don't need to install the Active Directory. Is that possible?

A: No. You cannot use an Exchange 5.5 back-end server with Exchange 2000 front ends. Besides that, any Exchange 2000 server requires the Active Directory to provide the directory service.

Q: We have seven sites around the world. Each is connected via leased lines to our headquarters with varying bandwidth rates. There are two sites that have very low bandwidth available on their links that also suffer from unreliability. We want to place all our Exchange Servers at the headquarters along with all DNS and Global Catalog servers. Will this work?

A: When it comes down to it, it probably would function, as long as the network links were live and had sufficient bandwidth available. However, the first time that a user is not able to connect to a DNS server or a Global Catalog server (much less an Exchange Server), there will be a failure that you could have prevented through a different design. Your best bet is to make certain that you have a DNS server and a Global Catalog server in every site that is located across a WAN link and has a significant number of users. For Exchange Server, you should try to place an Exchange front end server in the same sites that you want to place a Global Catalog server.

Q: I went ahead and ran Exchange Server's Setup without running ForestPrep or DomainPrep first and it automatically started ForestPrep and DomainPrep by itself without a problem. Are you sure that these need to be run separately?

A: If you are running Exchange Setup on a Global Catalog server in the root domain of your forest, you won't need to run ForestPrep and DomainPrep separately. However, in all other cases, you will.

Q: If I set up replication between the Active Directory sites to occur once a week, will this interrupt my mail from replicating so that users won't receive new mail for a whole week if they are in that other site?

A: No. Routing groups that you create in the Exchange System Manager are responsible for message routing throughout your Exchange Server network. You will only see Active Directory objects and attributes, (such as a computer account that has joined a domain or a password that has just been changed) take a long time to replicate.

Chapter 3

Security Applications that Enhance Exchange 2000

Solutions in this chapter:

- **Understanding Your Security Needs**
- **Windows 2000 and Exchange 2000 Security Architecture**
- **Windows 2000 and Exchange 2000 Internal Security**
- **Firewalls**
- **Configuring Client Security**
- **Implementing a Smart-Card Environment**

Introduction

I remember seeing an IBM commercial a few years ago, that showed a couple sitting on a couch in front of a TV set. She was intently watching a program; he was working on a computer. Suddenly, he announced that that he had accessed the corporate payroll records for her company's executives, and she asked to have a look. "Too late," he announced. He had just sent the information to everyone in the company. What if someone with too much time on his or her hands and nothing better to do decided to poke around and read or even perhaps take some of the valuable intellectual property flying around in your corporate messaging system and post it on the Web? This picture strikes fear in the heart of any network administrator who does not want his or her company's name on the front page of a newspaper with this kind of exposure.

Sending messages is today's core business process. The emphasis on worldwide communication and collaboration is encouraged by management and supported by technology. Unfortunately, in their evolution to mission-critical status, messages have become a prime target for vandals and intruders. The popularity of Exchange server and the Outlook clients has made them the applications of choice when these individuals plan to mount their attack. The recent spate of worm viruses that took advantage of the Outlook clients' address book and Preview Pane feature are prime evidence that attacks are targeting current messaging systems' now robust and expanding feature sets.

Those of you coming from Windows NT 4.0 and Exchange 5.5 are used to managing the Exchange directory, connectors, the Windows NT Security Accounts Manager database, and a myriad of other products to secure your public-facing infrastructure. With the introduction of Windows 2000 and Active Directory (AD), security management of your Windows and Exchange environments is unified and consolidated into a single directory service. Furthermore, Windows 2000 has integrated many of the add-on applications that were once managed separately—such as IPSec, certificate authorities, Encrypting File System, and the Kerberos protocol.

The real advantage for administrators in the new Windows and Exchange 2000 world is that Windows 2000 security can be leveraged against Exchange 2000 and the overhead of additional security features is generally transparent to the user—PKI, Kerberos authentication, encrypted files and network communication, secure e-mail, and the list goes on. All of this works together for Windows 2000 and Exchange 2000 and all rely on Active Directory. Let us begin with a brief look at the need for Information Technology (IT) security and from *whom* and against *what* we are protecting.

Understanding Your Security Needs

If we take a step back from examining Windows 2000 and Exchange 2000 security specifically, several fundamental questions arise that need to be answered before we delve into specifics. What needs to be protected? Who is the enemy? What are we protecting against? How do we do it?

What Needs to Be Protected?

Before we get into enemies and attacks, let's discuss what we are protecting. Generally speaking, it is the reputation of the organization and the integrity of its valuable resources: people, productivity and property—both intellectual and physical. As IT professionals, we must focus on specifically protecting:

- The identities of your users and your network resources

- The organization's data (records, client information, intellectual property)

- The organization's infrastructure (data and voice network, computing resources, messaging and Web environments)

Who Is the Enemy?

The enemy can be categorized into two distinct groups: those who knowingly threaten your environment and those whose threat is involuntary. The latter group does not pose a significant threat to your Exchange enterprise. This group consists of the majority of employees—users, data-entry clerks, system operators, and programmers—who are ignorant of the impact that their errors have on security. While it may seem unbelievable that Carl in accounting or Jane in legal services may be the enemy, they directly and indirectly commit accidental errors that contribute to security problems. Sometimes their mistakes are the threat, such as a data entry error or a programming error that crashes a system. In other cases, their mistakes create vulnerabilities, which others can exploit. This group usually has no motives, methods, or goals for causing damage, and the damage is accidental.

The former group is the one you need to worry about. Notice that the division was between voluntary and involuntary users, not between those inside your organization and those outside. The most malicious threats consist of inside attacks by disgruntled or vindictive employees or by attacks committed by those from the outside just looking for a cheap thrill or to harm and disrupt your organization. Threats from without are significant in number and magnitude; however, they pale in comparison to what happens from the inside. A 1999 CSI/FBI Computer Crime and Security Survey estimated that unauthorized access and theft of proprietary information cost an average of $4,486,000 per year. The study also determined that 70 percent of unauthorized access is done from inside a company. The big difference is that the successful intrusion into a prominent organization from the outside will probably make the nightly news.

However, disgruntled or vindictive employees (present and past) are the most dangerous attackers. They usually have goals, objectives, and motives, and have legitimate access to corporate systems. They are familiar with existing security measures, resources, processes, and applications, and they most likely to know what actions might cause the most damage. Insiders can plant viruses, Trojan horses, or worms, and they can poke around in the file system, altering or deleting data.

The insider attack can affect all components of computer security. By browsing through a system, internal users can reveal confidential information. Trojan horses are a threat to both the integrity and confidentiality of information in the system. Insider attacks can affect availability by overloading the system's processing or storage capacity, or by causing the system to crash.

The angry folks are not the only ones who can harm an organization. Employees who are untrained in computers and are unaware of security threats and vulnerabilities are the likely cause of unintentional threats. Errors, omissions, and experimenting can cause valuable data to be lost, damaged, or altered.

A colleague of mine worked with a network administrator who was known to enjoy experimenting with different applications on any machine he could get his hands on. In one particular instance, he wanted to learn about a particular Web server and decided to install it on a local server. Unfortunately, the local server he chose was the sole server in his small organization that hosted the backup software and tape drives for backing up all file, database, and application servers. There was no apparent impact initially, but the next day my colleague, a senior network administrator who routinely checked the backups every day, discovered that the overnight backups did not run. In fact, the backup catalog was missing; when he attempted to run a manual backup he discovered that the backup application was corrupt. The organization, which produces massive amounts of database transactions daily, went without a reliable backups and the server was taken offline and essentially rebuilt from a base operating system up to a useful state. All tapes in the existing tape rotation needed to be recatalogued and the network administrator's network account was deleted as he was escorted out the door. The organization was put in a very dangerous place, and much time and effort (read money) was wasted to correct a mindless action of a careless employee.

An attacker could masquerade as an administrator and ask for passwords and user names. Employees who are not well trained and are not security-conscious can fall for this. Fortunately Windows 2000 and Exchange 2000 have a security infrastructure that supports strong authentication using external devices, such as smart cards, to positively identify that the user is who he or she says she is.

What Are We Protecting Against?

Attacks can be categorized into one or more of three types:

- Impersonation and forgery

- Unauthorized access to the corporate infrastructure

- Viruses

The "successful" execution of an attack in the first category normally leads to an attack in one or more of the other categories. There is a strong overlap between physical security and data privacy and integrity. Indeed, the goal of some attacks is not the physical destruction of the computer system but the penetration and removal or copying of sensitive information. As mentioned earlier, many of these attackers do it for the thrill of their "accomplishment" or for some type of physical reward—often financial.

Impersonation and Forgery

Impersonation is one of the most insidious forms of attacks because it steals the identity of another resource and performs the attack as if the innocent target is doing it. In many cases, the impersonator must commit forgery to cover any tracks. While the target can be a computing resource, such as a messaging or Web server, in most cases the target is a fellow human being. The launch of the Melissa virus in 1999 was accomplished by the virus author's breaking into the Internet account of an innocent person and e-mailing the virus to the world while masquerading as that innocent person.

Password Cracking

There are a variety of techniques a would-be attacker uses to assume the identity of something else, including password cracking, e-mail impersonation and eavesdropping, and network spoofing. Password cracking is a technique attackers employ to surreptitiously gain system access through another user's account. Weak passwords are often the cause because users often select passwords that are easy to remember. Phone numbers, home-town names, last names, names of children or the family pet, birth and anniversary dates, not to mention the infamous blank password or my personal favorite, "password", are not too difficult to guess. While these and similar passwords are the worst examples, any word in the dictionary is a poor choice because a password of this type is susceptible to dictionary attacks, a form of attack that uses "password auditing" software and a dictionary as the source of guesses.

Impersonation and Eavesdropping

With electronic mail being one of the most popular features of the Internet and within organizations, it has become a popular target for attackers. The major threats associated with e-mail are e-mail impersonation and eaves-dropping. The sender address on Internet e-mail cannot be trusted because the "impersonating" sender can create a false return address, and an individual could have modified the header in transit, or the sender could have connected directly to the Simple Mail Transfer Protocol (SMTP) port on the target computer to enter the e-mail. For eavesdropping, because e-mail headers and contents are transmitted in the clear text if no encryption is used, the contents of a message can be read or altered in transit, and the header can be modified to hide or change the sender, or to redirect the message. Network eavesdropping, or *sniffing*, allows an attacker to make a partial or complete copy of network activity, thereby capturing sensitive information such as passwords, data, and procedures for performing functions. The most prominent method is now to use a protocol analyzer or packet sniffer to monitor and examine the content of packets sent over the network. These tools can be used (no pun intended) right under our noses and we would be none the wiser, as it is very difficult to detect eavesdropping.

Network Spoofing

In network spoofing, the target is not a person and neither is the innocent victim. In this instance, a system presents itself to the network as though it were a different system by sending the target system's address instead of its own. The reason for doing this is that systems tend to operate within a group of other trusted systems. The Windows NT legacy domain trusts system is a prime example. Trust relationships are explicitly assigned from one domain to another. If a system can impersonate, or *spoof*, the address of a system in a trusted domain, then this new system can take advantage of all of the benefits—file system access, application permissions, access to the Internet, delegated security—that the "spoofed" system previously enjoyed. The actual situation here is that the individual who configured the "spoofing" system has virtually invisible access to the system in the trusting domain.

Unauthorized Access to the Corporate Infrastructure

Attackers need a platform to do their business. Most of what they would need can be found in corporate information technology infrastructure, such as SMTP mail relays, PBX telephone systems, and file storage. In addition, attackers may want to disrupt normal business operations, and usually in this case, the attacker has a specific goal to achieve.

Denial of Service

Denial-of-Service (DoS) attacks have become a common part of our vocabulary as prominent Web sites such as CNN and Yahoo! have been effectively shut down. A denial-of-service attack begins by exploiting weak security measures to make a service available. It is a growing trend on the Internet because Web sites are generally poorly secured and organizations and individuals with a system attached to an unsecured high-speed connection are a great place for the attacker to place a Trojan horse from which the attack can be launched. Once the attack is launched, it floods an unsuspecting Web site with a barrage of requests, and the Web site grinds to a halt because the Web servers eventually cannot respond. Organizations need to implement adequate security measures so that they are neither targets nor participants in DoS attacks. These attacks are also difficult to trace.

Packet Replay and Modification

Other methods of gaining unauthorized access to the corporate infrastructure are through packet replay and packet modification. *Packet replay* refers to the recording and retransmission of message packets in the network. Packet replay is a significant threat for programs that require authentication sequences, because an intruder could replay legitimate authentication sequence messages to gain access to a system. Packet replay is frequently undetectable, but can be prevented by using packet time stamping and packet sequence counting. *Packet modification* refers to one system's intercepting and modifying a packet destined for another system. Packet information may not only be modified, but could also be destroyed and the information lost.

Viruses

Attackers can develop harmful code known as viruses. With the rise in the use of e-mail, it has become more difficult to stop the spread of viruses than to launch them. Although there are hybrids, the most common viruses come in two distinct forms, Trojan horses and worms.

Spread of Viruses

Traditionally a virus developer would design a virus to implant somewhere, normally in some kind of storage media, and then perpetuate when a particular file was copied or when the infected media came into contact with other media. Now, using e-mail, a virus can be attached to a message and sent out to millions of unsuspecting recipients who may unknowingly send it on to millions more. Viruses open up a person's address book and send e-mail to everyone in the list. Regardless of their composition or behavior, viruses are a threat to any environment. They come in different forms and although not always malicious, they always take up time.

Trojan Horses

Trojan horses are malicious programs or software code hidden inside what looks like a normal program. When a user runs the normal program, the hidden code runs as well. It can then start deleting files and causing other damage to the computer. Trojan horses are normally spread by e-mail attachments. The Melissa virus and all of its variants caused denial-of-service attacks throughout the world using features of Microsoft Outlook to propagate. Later in this chapter, we will look at how this could have been prevented by securing the Outlook client.

Worms

Worm viruses are programs that run independently and travel from computer to computer across network connections. Worms may have portions of themselves running on many different computers. The I Love You virus and its variants are prime examples of worm viruses. Worms do not change other programs themselves, although they may carry other code that does. The greatest threat from a worm virus is that once all of the pieces are in place, it will launch and bring networks to a halt.

How Do We Protect Ourselves?

While it may seem to be an impossible task, protecting your environment against all of these nasty attacks is definitely possible. It really comes down to two tasks: protecting your messaging environment against known, readily identifiable threats, and protecting against the unknown. Naturally, protecting against the known threats and implementing safeguards to counter those threats is the easier task. To protect against the unknown you need to develop, implement, and enforce security policies and procedures, and the supporting technology, as a foundation to make sure that an attacker cannot slip through a crack. The security features that are integrated in and can be added to Windows 2000 for Exchange 2000 can accomplish these two tasks.

Your organization's security foundation must be configured to execute security measures for every user and server. Windows 2000's security architecture can be leveraged for Exchange 2000 with little additional configuration. It responds to security needs with the technology listed in Table 3.1.

Table 3.1 Exchange 2000 Security Needs Met by Windows 2000 Solutions

Security Measure	Windows 2000 Solution
Employ a method of verifying that the individual is who he or she says she is	Certificate-based Kerberos authentication
Protect the data where it is stored and only permit access to those who need it	Encrypting File System (EFS) Authentication (authentication, policies, anti-virus)
Protect the data as it is transmitted	Public key infrastructure (PKI) Encryption – IP Security (IPSec), Secure Sockets Layer (SSL), Transport Layer Security (TLS), Kerberos
Restrict the use of the network to those who are authorized	IPSec

Stay On Top of Security Updates

Security-conscious Exchange analysts will configure their individual environments as if the eyes of the world were on them. In a manner of speaking, this is not too far from the truth. There are those who lurk outside and within our gates, just waiting for an opportunity to gain access to what we have painstakingly built. Applying security updates as soon as they are available will deter many of those potential attacks.

One writer summarized the security breach formula as Goal + Method + Vulnerabilities = Attack (see www.microsoft.com/technet/security/secthret.asp). It sounds simplistic, but it is frighteningly accurate. On a positive note, by eliminating one variable on the operational

Continued

side of the equation, you can effectively prevent an attack before it happens, or at least hope to stop an attack in progress. The best factor to eliminate is vulnerability, and one way to accomplish this is to apply system and security updates as they are released. This must be done immediately because the attack method is already public information.

The process is really quite simple. A security hole or exploit technique will be posted on one or more of several security Web sites that follow Microsoft product security, notably www.ntbugtraq.com. Microsoft will acknowledge the problem, and will respond in short order with a hotfix. Potential hackers are monitoring these sites, and as soon as they find something to try out, they look for a victim. If you have properly applied Microsoft's hotfix to all affected machines, you will not be that victim. If you delay in carrying out the maintenance, you are vulnerable to those who are essentially armed with an instruction manual.

Walk through the following steps with every server:

- Use winver.exe to verify the latest Service Pack that has been applied.

- If you used hotfix.exe (highly recommended and available at ftp://ftp.microsoft.com/bussys/utilities/hotfix) to install hotfixes, run hotfix /l to list the interim fixes have been installed since the last Service Pack.

- Use Windows Update to download and install all critical and required updates.

- Keep your anti-virus software and signature files current.

- Monitor the Web sites for your operating system and any applications, especially for Exchange and IIS. Subscribe to a service that monitors changes to Web pages and notifies you of the change via e-mail.

Ensure that these activities are performed frequently (i.e., more than once per week) and that all changes are carefully documented for each server. This accomplishes two important tasks: first, your servers are updated to the same level and well-protected from attack; second, you track all changes on paper that you can hand off to your replacement when you are promoted for preserving the uptime of the infrastructure and the productivity level of your company.

Windows 2000 and Exchange 2000 Security Architecture

In the Windows NT Server 4.0 and Exchange Server 5.5 world, network administrators became accustomed to administering the network and the messaging system as two related, yet distinct, entities. This section will discuss the Windows 2000 security features that are leveraged for Exchange 2000 and explain the specific Exchange 2000 applications used to provide security to the messaging environment:

- Active Directory (AD)
- Public Key Infrastructure (PKI)
- Secure networking capability
- Client access

Active Directory

Active Directory is the directory service included with Windows 2000 Server. It replaces the Security Accounts Manager (SAM) in the Windows NT 4.0 domain controller as the security database. Active Directory is a secure, scalable, distributed, partitioned, and replicated database that stores network objects and their attributes in a hierarchical structure. In relation to Exchange 2000, Active Directory incorporates the Extensible Storage Engine (ESE), a separate directory in Exchange 5.5, to provide a single point of administration for network management. Its structure lends itself to centralized control that can be delegated on a component-by-component basis to individual administrators or computers.

Active Directory is a proprietary implementation of the x.500 directory service. Microsoft built it from the ground up to be closely, but not exactly, based on the x.500 standards (managed by ISO and ITU). A directory holds objects that represent various types of network resources, such as users, groups, computers, storage volumes and printers, which are described by attributes. Active Directory is fully integrated with and requires the Domain Name System (DNS).

Like every object in the Active Directory, access control lists (ACLs) govern how schema objects are protected so that only authorized users (members of the Schema Administrators group) may alter the schema.

In Active Directory delegation, a user is authorized by an administrator to perform a specified set of actions on a specified set of objects and object classes in some identified sub-tree of the directory. This delegated administration allows granular control over what can be done and who can do it without granting permissions that are beyond the needs of the role. Because Exchange 2000 is fully integrated within Active Directory, administrative roles and tasks can be delegated in exactly the same way.

The directory is part of the Windows 2000 Trusted Computing Base and is a full participant in the Windows 2000 security infrastructure. ACLs protect all objects in the Active Directory. The Windows 2000 access validation routines use the ACL to validate any attempt to access an object or attribute in the Active Directory. As a distributed database that contains everything that needs to connect to the network as well as the "rules" for who can do what, Active Directory is an ideal environment in which to use public key infrastructure to validate the identities of users and other resources.

Public Key Infrastructure

The purpose and basis of public key infrastructure is the provision of trust. Windows 2000 relies on public key cryptography to provide secure authentication and communication within a corporate network and beyond, and PKI needs Active Directory for authentication and certificate storage. PKI's role is to provide trusted security services—including confidentiality, authentication, digital signatures, and integrity. Public key cryptography uses two electronic keys—a public key and a private key, known as a key pair—that are generated by one of several public-key algorithms. A public key is available to anyone, while only its owner knows the private key. Public-key algorithms are designed so that if one key is used for encryption, the other is necessary for decryption. Furthermore, the private key is virtually impossible to derive from the public key. These keys are mathematically related, but the private key cannot be determined from the public key. The public key can be known by anyone, while the owner keeps the private key secret. The owner, as a result, can grant access to his or her information to those whom the owner trusts.

Public Key Infrastructure and Active Directory

A PKI needs a physical network infrastructure in a secure environment for a proper implementation. Like Windows 2000 and Exchange 2000, PKI relies on Active Directory for authentication, administration and management, and the storage of three objects (user object data, group object data, and security certificates). A PKI provides the means to bind public keys to their owners and helps in the distribution of reliable public keys in large, heterogeneous networks. Public keys are bound to their owners by public key certificates. These digital certificates contain information such as the owner's name and the associated public key and are issued by a reliable certification authority (CA).

Digital Certificates

Digital certificates, also called Digital IDs, are the electronic counterparts to driver licenses, passports, or membership cards. A digital certificate can be presented electronically to prove your identity, and thus, your permission to access information or services online. Digital certificates are used not only to identify people, but also to identify Web sites (crucial to secure e-business), servers, and software that is being sent over the Web. Digital certificates ensure the aforementioned trust element when you are communicating or doing business on the Internet—or any network, for that matter.

Digital signatures are used both to verify the identity of a user or server and to ensure that only the intended recipient can read a message. They verify identity and encrypt messages. Signing data does not alter it, but simply generates a string that is attached to the data. Web servers and browsers also use them to provide mutual authentication, confidentiality of the pages transferred, and integrity of the information. Digital signatures are created using one of several public-key encryption algorithms.

Certification Authority

A certification authority (CA) is a trusted body that issues, manages and revokes certificates. A PKI is often composed of many CAs that are organized hierarchically and linked by trust paths. The CAs may be linked in several ways. They may be arranged hierarchically under a "root CA" that issues certificates to subordinate CAs. The CAs can also be arranged independently in a network.

The number and arrangement of your CAs depends on many factors, based mainly on the size and complexity of your network. Even a small network can have multiple CAs if the organization is using an external body, such as VeriSign, Thawte, or Entrust, as the root CA. If your organization is geographically dispersed, you may want a subordinate CA in each location. In a Windows 2000 environment, Microsoft Certificate Server can be used on its own should you desire to design and manage your own certificates, or an external source may be used by itself, or it can be used in conjunction with MCS for the same purpose. For secure messaging, you can add an additional level of security by implementing Exchange 2000's Key Management Server (KMS).

Digital Envelopes

Digital signatures are not to be confused with digital envelopes. A digital signature positively identifies the sender and includes the sender's private key. A digital envelope is simply the wrapper around a message that encrypts the content. A public key and a private key are required to "unwrap" the message, once the identities of the sender and receiver have been established.

Secure Networking

Windows 2000 provides for secure networking using encryption at various layers of the Open System Interconnection (OSI) reference model. Microsoft has provided a suite of protocols and policies that can be implemented; these protocols lock down what connections can be accessed and how transactions will be made. IPSec, Secure Sockets Layer (SSL) and Transport Layer Security (TLS) encrypt data transmission at the transport layer, as illustrated in Figure 3.1.

Figure 3.1 Windows 2000 Security Protocols in the OSI Reference Model

Layer	Security Protocol
Application	
Presentation	
Session	
Transport	Secure Sockets Layer (SSL) Transport Layer Security (TLS) IPSec
Network	
Data-Link	
Physical	

Kerberos independently handles secure user authentication at the application layer for Active Directory and other application-layer protocols, such as DNS, File Transfer Protocol (FTP), and Hypertext Transfer Protocol (HTTP) (see Figure 3.2). IP security policies define what IP addresses to scan for, how packets will be encrypted, and how filters will be configured to take a look at all IP traffic passing through the object on which the IP security policy is applied.

Figure 3.2 Kerberos and Its Applications in the OSI Reference Model

Layer	Security Protocol	Applications
Application	Kerberos	Active Directory, HTTP, DNS, FTP
Presentation		
Session		
Transport		
Network		
Datalink		
Physical		

WARNING

When you implement encryption on the application layer, content filtering or virus checking across gateways is compromised. Encryption at the transport layer will give you greater control over what flows in and out of your network.

Client Access

There are many ways to access the Exchange 2000 information store: MAPI, POP3, IMAP and SMTP. In Exchange's previous life, Remote Procedure Calls (RPCs) were used for client-to-server and server-to-server communication; RPC communications have been replaced by pure SMTP. Each access protocol has its own distinct security method.

MAPI clients that access Exchange 2000 within a corporate network, such as Outlook 2000 or Outlook Express with a MS Exchange Profile, use Kerberos for authentication and IPSec encryption. POP3 and IMAP clients that access the Exchange Information Store across the Internet, such as Outlook Express using an Internet Mail Profile, can use a variety of authentication methods, including anonymous access, access using clear text transactions, SSL transactions, or NT Lan Manager (NTLM). For this type of client, the Web server is configured for a particular authentication method, decided by the hosting organization. While messages can be sent directly to an SMTP host for routing or delivery, SMTP is mainly used for server-to-server communication, replacing Remote Procedure Calls (RPCs).

MAPI is a proprietary Microsoft protocol that e-mail clients such as Outlook and Exchange use to communicate with Exchange Server when you add the Exchange Server Information Service to your messaging profile. An Exchange or Outlook e-mail client using MAPI can access a mailbox on the Exchange server only over a LAN/WAN or Remote Access Service (RAS) connection. When the client tries to establish a new mail session with the Exchange server, the server attempts to validate the user's logon credentials. For "down-level" clients the user authenticates using NT's challenge/response mechanism. Windows 2000 clients use Kerberos authentication.

NOTE

A "down-level" client is the classification Microsoft uses for any client that is running any version of a Microsoft operating system that preceded Windows 2000. Client machines running Windows 3.x, 9x, or NT Workstation are examples of "down-level" clients.

Windows 2000 and Exchange 2000 Internal Security

Windows 2000 security can be leveraged to provide Exchange 2000 with the secure environment it needs to protect the messaging service. This section will focus on configuring Windows 2000, Exchange 2000, and any additional applications for secure e-mail. Specifically, it will cover:

- Protocols
- Delegation
- IPSec
- Policies

Protocols

The main protocol components of the Windows 2000 secured networking suite are:

- NTLM
- Kerberos

- SSL
- Certificates

Note that Certificates are not a protocol *per se*; however, Kerberos and SSL are certificate-based protocols and any discussion of these protocols requires a definition of the role and function of the certificates they use. Key Management Services also functions with Microsoft's Certification Authority services.

NT LAN Manager

The NTLM authentication protocol is a challenge/response authentication protocol, and was the default for network authentication in Windows NT version 4.0 and earlier. Windows 2000 continues to support the NTLM protocol, but Kerberos is the new default. NTLM is the authentication protocol for users who have not yet moved to Windows 2000, or in Microsoft parlance, "down-level" clients. Kerberos authentication is available for Windows 95 and 98 clients through add-on products, but it's not available for Windows NT 4.0 or earlier.

In NTLM authentication, a challenge-response system is used to avoid revealing passwords directly over a physically insecure network. At its simplest, the server sends the user some sort of challenge, which would typically be a kind of random string. The user would then compute a response, usually some function based on both the challenge and the password. This way, even if an intruder captures a valid challenge-response pair, it will not help the intruder gain access to the system since future challenges are likely to be different and thus require different responses.

Prior to Windows NT 4.0 Service Pack 4 (SP4), Windows NT supported two kinds of challenge/response authentication: LAN Manager (LM) challenge/response and Windows NT challenge/response (also known as NTLM challenge/response). In addition, Microsoft has developed a new version of NTLM known as NTLMv2. This became available with Service Pack 4.

Before we launch into a description of each version of NTLM, see Table 3.2 for a comparison of features.

Table 3.2 Features in Different Versions of NTLM

Authentication Type	PW Length	Type	Security Application
LM	<7 characters	Uppercase, alphanumeric characters	Windows NT 3.51 and 4.0 authentication

Continued

Table 3.2 Continued

Authentication Type	PW Length	Type	Security Application
NTLM	14 characters	Lowercase plus LM	Windows NT 4.0 and 2000 authentication
NTLMv2			Negotiates message confidentiality

LM

LM authentication is the weakest of the three protocols because, although the passwords in LM can be longer than seven characters, the algorithm allows longer passwords to be attacked in seven-character chunks. Password characters can be drawn from the set of uppercase alphabetic, numeric, and punctuation characters, plus 32 special ALT characters.

NTLM

In contrast, NTLM uses all 14 characters in the password as a single contiguous unit and allows lowercase letters. Basically, increasing the length and character complexity in this manner means that although an eavesdropping hacker can attack in the same way as with the LM authentication protocol, it will take far longer for the hacker to be successful. Naturally, if your users are choosing shorter passwords, whole words, or blank passwords, NTLM won't help!

In Windows 2000, you have the capability to turn off NTLM support and go with a purely Kerberos model that provides a higher level of security for your network. Bear in mind that once you "flick the switch" and move your mixed-mode Windows 2000 environment into native-mode, you cannot go back. You may, however, find that you need to continue NTLM support on your Windows 2000 system for several reasons.

The first reason to continue NTLM support is if you have "down-level" clients and servers that use one of the LM/NTLM authentication methods listed above. Non-Windows 2000 machines can only use the NTLM protocol for network authentication in Windows 2000 domains. Second, your Windows 2000 machines use NTLM when authenticating to servers with Windows NT 4.0 and when accessing resources in Windows NT 4.0 domains. These reasons apply in a mixed-mode Windows 2000 environment.

The other reason to maintain a mixed-mode environment is for UNIX compatibility. While Kerberos was born in the UNIX world, you may also have to consider keeping NTLM support if you have UNIX clients using a Server Message Block (SMB) client to connect to your Windows 2000 domains, due to SMB client requirements. If the UNIX clients are using standard Transmission Control Protocol/Internet Protocol (TCP/IP) application protocols such as Telnet and FTP exclusively, you can then eliminate NTLM support. If your Windows 2000 clients are connecting to UNIX resources using an SMB daemon, you may want to consider disabling the SMB daemon and using a Network File System (NFS) client on the Windows 2000 machine.

NTLMv2

Microsoft refers to NTLMv2 as "NTLM on steroids." NTLMv2 improves both the authentication and session security mechanisms of NTLM. In addition, the NTLM Security Service Provider (SSP) now allows clients to control which version of NTLM to use and allows servers to decide which alternatives to accept. Finally, NTLMv2 allows clients and servers to require the negotiation of message confidentiality (encryption), message integrity, 128-bit encryption, and NTLMv2 session security. NTLMv2 is available on NT 4 systems with Service Pack 4 or higher.

Kerberos

Many of the protocols used in the Internet do not provide any security—notably TCP/IP. Tools to "sniff" passwords on the network are in common use by systems crackers; thus applications that send an unencrypted password over the network are extremely vulnerable. Worse yet, other client-server applications rely on the client program to be forthright about the identity of the user on the client-side. Kerberos provides the tools of authentication and strong cryptography to help you secure your information systems across the network in your entire enterprise.

Kerberos v5 is the native network authentication protocol for Windows 2000 and Active Directory. Kerberos uses strong cryptography so that a client can establish and prove its identity to a server (and vice versa) across a physically insecure network connection. After a client and server have used Kerberos to prove their identity, they can also encrypt all of their communications throughout the session to assure privacy and data integrity as they go about their business. Practically speaking, Kerberos is mostly used in application-level protocols, such as Telnet or FTP, to provide user-to-host security. It is also used, though less frequently, as the implicit authentication system of data stream or RPC mechanisms at the presentation layer. It could also be used at the network and transport layers for host-to-host security, in protocols like IP, User Datagram Protocol (UDP), or TCP—although such implementations are currently rare, if they exist at all. Because it is native to the operating system, there is no configuration for basic Kerberos authentication.

Mutual Authentication

Kerberos provides for mutual authentication and secure communication between Windows 2000 hosts in a native- or mixed-mode environment by manufacturing secret keys for any requestor and providing a mechanism for these secret keys to be safely propagated. It does not, *per se*, provide for authorization or accounting; however, applications can use their secret keys to perform those functions securely.

Kerberos allows entities communicating over the network to prove their identity to each other while preventing eavesdropping or replay attacks. It is designed to provide strong authentication for client/server applications by using secret-key cryptography and by having the secret keys distributed in a controlled fashion throughout the network based on the key distribution model presented by Needham and Schroeder (see "Using Encryption for Authentication in Large Networks of Computers," Communications of the ACM, 21, 1978). It also provides for data stream integrity (detection of modification) and secrecy (preventing unauthorized reading) using cryptography systems such as DES.

Kerberos works by providing principals (users or services) with tickets that they can use to identify themselves to other principals and secret cryptographic keys for secure communication with other principals. A ticket is a sequence of a few hundred bytes. These tickets can then be embedded into virtually any other network protocol, thereby allowing the processes implementing that protocol to be sure about the identity of the principals involved.

Kerberos authentication requires the existence of a trusted network entity that acts as an authentication server for clients and servers requesting authentication information. This authentication server is known the key distribution center (KDC). It has access to a database consisting of a list of users and client services, their default authentication parameters, their secret encryption keys, and other data. Authentication is typically a one-way process. This is the process by which a service authenticates the client. An advantage of Kerberos over NTLM is that it allows for mutual authentication, where the client authenticates the service.

Kerberos authentication occurs when special authentication model messages, *session tickets*, are passed among client applications, server applications, and one or more KDCs. Client processes acting on behalf of users authenticate themselves to servers by means of the session ticket. The KDC generates tickets, which are sent to the requesting client processes. Kerberos maintains a set of secret keys, one for every entity to be authenticated within a particular realm (a realm is the protocol's equivalent of a Windows 2000 domain) or domain. A client presents a ticket to the server as evidence that the principal is who it claims to be. The ticket presented to the server "proves" that a KDC authenticated the client.

The Kerberos protocol solves the eavesdropping problem with secret key cryptography. Rather than sharing a password, communication partners share a cryptographic key that is symmetric in nature. This means the single key can both encrypt and decrypt. To communicate, one side sends the other an encrypted message containing their name and local time, the other machine then decrypts the packet with the symmetric key and if the time is close to its time, then the match is OK. The fact that time is part of the encryption technology is why Windows 2000 machines need to be time-synchronized with a SMTP service. The idea is if two people know a secret they can communicate by encrypting a message with the secret and if they both know the secret they know the other person is who they say they are. The problem is the secret can't be sent as just text over the network because anyone with a network sniffer could find the "secret."

Exchange 2000 runs as a service in Windows 2000 Server and is treated as a network service with respect to Kerberos. By using Kerberos for Active Directory authentication, the user's identity is established at the beginning and used for the entire session. Exchange 2000 uses this verified identity to permit the user to sign into Exchange when the user is attached to the network—either locally or remotely through VPN or RAS. When the client needs to access Exchange, the client requests an Exchange service ticket from the Kerberos service. The service ticket is then used for authentication with Exchange 2000 Server. For subsequent access to the Exchange 2000 server, the client uses the service ticket, which increases authentication performance. Kerberos is not used to authenticate a user who is accessing mail through Outlook Web Access (OWA). OWA authentication methods are discussed later in the chapter as part of securing client access through a Web browser.

Secure Sockets Layer

Secure Sockets Layer (SSL) is a protocol that protects data sent between Web browsers and Web servers. SSL also ensures that the data came from the Web site it is supposed to have originated from and that no one tampered with the data while it was being sent (see Figure 3.3). Any URL that begins with "https" indicates that SSL has been enabled. The "s" added to http://... stands for *secure*. SSL provides privacy, integrity, and authentication in a private point-to-point communications channel. SSL also provides for selectable encryption and decryption of both request and response data being passed across network connections.

Figure 3.3 SSL Encryption Process

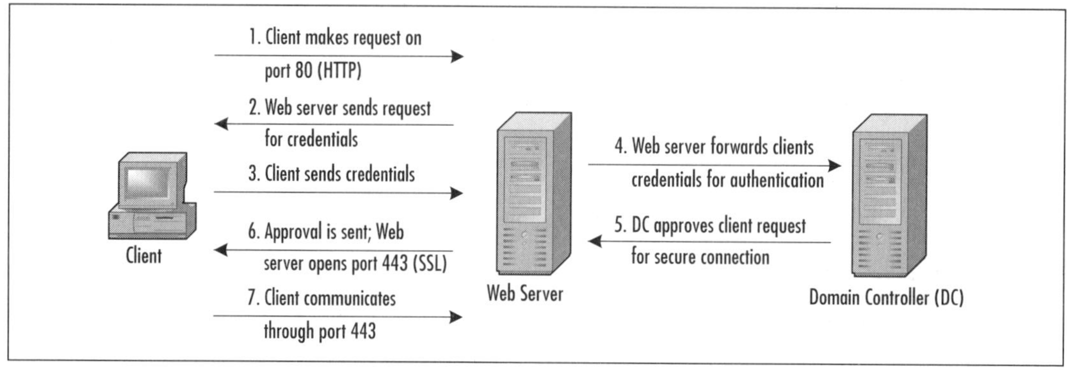

SSL provides a level of security and privacy for those wishing to conduct secure transactions over the Internet. SSL provides OWA users with the ability to communicate securely via an encrypted session. Because SSL protocol encrypts HTTP transmissions over the Internet, transactions cannot be "sniffed" by a would-be intruder. This is especially relevant to OWA users who are reading and sending e-mail, and accessing their schedule and address book across an Internet connection.

Companies that want to implement OWA over the Internet for their remote users through SSL need to contact a certification authority such as VeriSign to verify the identity of the user. Once the certificate has been obtained, the Internet Information Server (IIS) machine running OWA can be configured for SSL connections. Users don't have to do anything to trigger an SSL connection. The client portion of SSL is built into the Web browser, and IIS is configured for the appropriate client authentication method.

Certificates

Certificates provide a mechanism for gaining confidence in the relationship between a public key and the entity that owns the corresponding private key. Basically, you need a certificate to guarantee you are who you say you are; once you have proven that, you receive your key. The most common form of certificates in use today is based on the x.509 standard. The Internet Engineering Task Force (IETF) Request For Comments (RFC) 2459 profiles the x.509v3 certificate and the x.509v2 certificate revocation list (CRL), both of which are supported in Windows 2000. In fact, Microsoft started issuing a Certification Authority server capable of issuing x.509v3 certificates with Windows NT 4 Option Pack.

The Trust Relationship

A certificate can be thought of as similar to a driver's license. A driver's license is accepted by numerous businesses as a form of identification because the license issuer (a government institution) is accepted by the community as trustworthy. Because businesses understand the process by which someone can obtain a driver's license, they can trust that the issuer verified the identity of the individual to whom the licensed was issued. Therefore, the driver's license can be accepted as a valid form of identification.

Certification Authority

A certification authority (CA) issues certificates to requesters based on a set of established criteria. A CA acts as a guarantor of the binding between the subject public key and the subject identity information that is contained in the certificates it issues. In its simplest form a CA hierarchy consists of a single CA—though, in general, a hierarchy contains multiple CAs with clearly defined parent-child relationships. A child CA is also referred to as a *subordinate CA*. See Figure 3.4 for an illustration of a basic CA hierarchy.

Figure 3.4 Basic Certification Authority Hierarchy

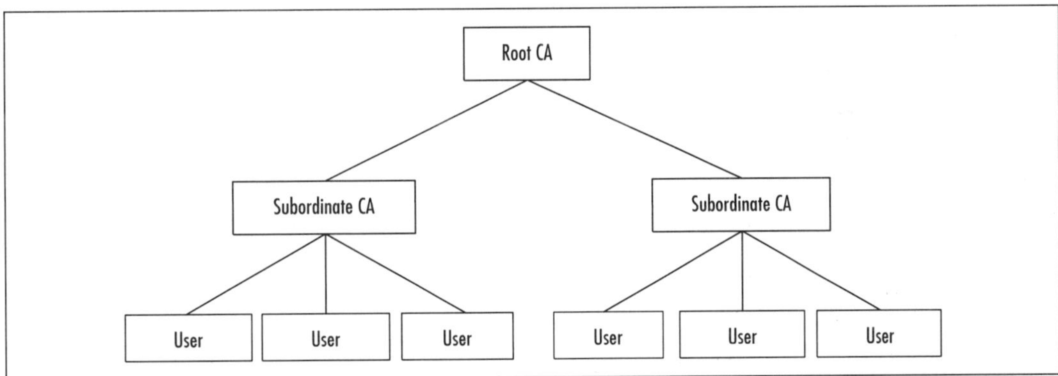

There is no requirement that all subordinate CAs within a company share a common top-level parent CA. The following list explains basic terminology:

- **Root CA** The CA at the top of a hierarchy is generally referred to as a *root CA* whose certificate is self-signed.

- **Self-signed certificate** A *self-signed certificate* is a certificate whose subject name and issuer name are the same and whose public key can be directly used to verify the signature attached to the certificate.

- **Issuing CA** A CA that issues end entity certificates is typically called an *issuing CA*.

- **Intermediate CA** An *intermediate CA* refers to a CA that is not a root CA, but one that only certifies other CAs in a hierarchy. A hierarchy with only a root CA does not contain an intermediate CA. A two-level hierarchy with a root CA and an issuing CA also does not contain an intermediate CA. By definition, hierarchies with more than two levels of CAs contain at least one intermediate CA.

- **Stand-alone and Enterprise CA** Windows 2000 supports two types of CA services: enterprise or stand-alone. The primary difference between the two CA services is in how certificates are issued. The *stand-alone CA* will issue certificates without authenticating the requestor and usually is configured to require a CA administrator to approve requests based on some out-of-band authentication. Third-party certificate authorities such as VeriSign can be the root CA for a Windows 2000 stand-alone CA (see Figure 3.5). *The*

Figure 3.5 Using an Internal CA as Subordinate to a Third-Party Root CA

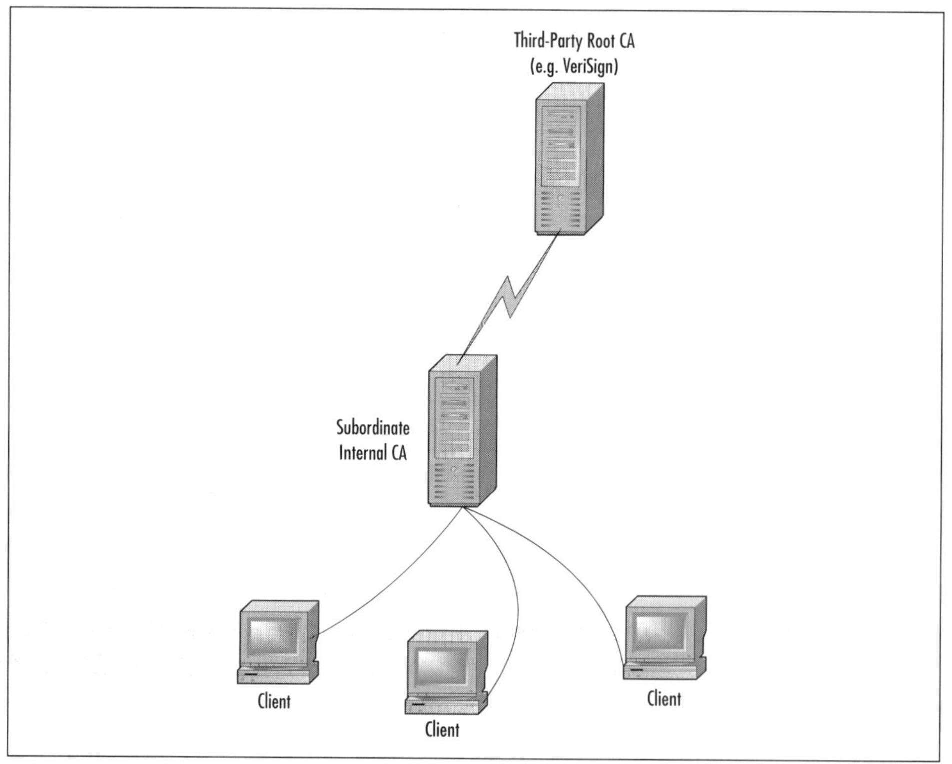

enterprise CA uses certificate templates to distinguish different types of certificates based on intended usage(s). Users may enroll for different types of certificates based on their access rights within a domain. An enterprise CA does require Active Directory.

Certificate Services and the Key Management Service

Key Management Service is an add-on component of Exchange 2000 Server that uses Windows 2000 Certificate Services to provide security on the application layer of the messaging system. It produces x.509v3 user certificates that Exchange 2000 and Outlook 2000 use for digital signature and encryption. The x.509v3 user certificates are recognized by Secure/Multipurpose Internet Mail Extension (S/MIME) clients and ensure interoperability among different clients when used across the Internet. Figure 3.6 shows the Windows 2000 Certification Authority with policy extensions added by KMS.

Figure 3.6 KMS Policy Extensions for Windows 2000 Certification Authority

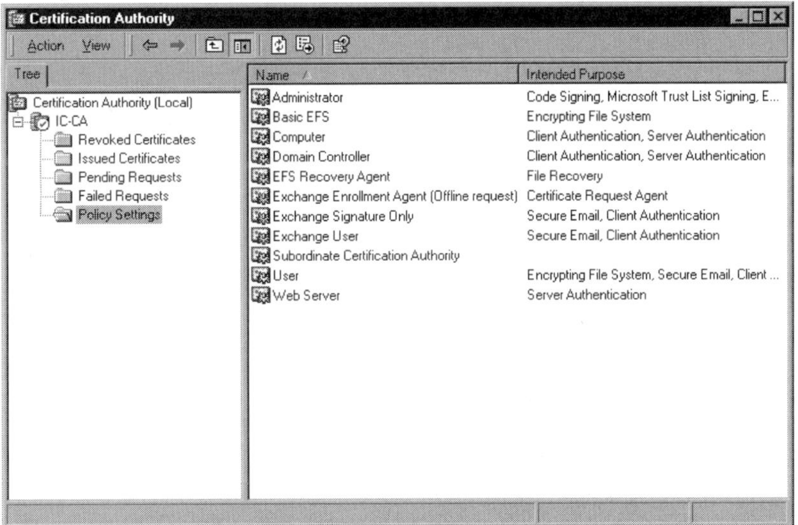

NOTE

The Enroll Agent (Computer), Exchange User, and Exchange User Signature templates of the CA must be enabled before KMS installs.

The strength of KMS is that it uses a variety of cryptographic technologies and methods as opposed to a single technique. The main KMS features are as follows:

- Encryption

- Hash functions

- Ciphers

- Algorithms

KMS can be configured to require more than one administrator to be present before performing each KMS task. Each task is initially configured to require only one password, and the first password is always "password" until it is changed. KMS implements a dual-key architecture—the "missile-silo" approach, which gives each enrolled user two key pairs and certificates: one used for encryption, and the other used for signing. Both keys are required to send and receive the message, much like the launch of a nuclear strike where two keys are required. KMS uses this architecture so the signing key does not need to be archived in KMS.

Earlier versions of KMS restricted KMS to just one server per site; however, Exchange 2000 KMS fits the site-based model. The KMS organizational unit becomes the Administrator Group and each new administrator group created allows KMS to install on or point to an existing KMS server. You can also enroll users in bulk by enrolling selected users, groups, or servers.

Delegation in Exchange

For Exchange 2000, delegation focuses on user administration. Parameters such as mailbox location and size limits are now just attributes of objects in Active Directory.

Integrating Roles

The same network administrator managing Windows 2000 accounts can manage these parameters in the same account properties pages. The advantage to administrative delegation in Exchange 2000 is that you can reduce the cost of administration by integrating roles. For example, a small organization may no longer need one person to manage network administration and another to manage the messaging system; the two roles can easily be combined.

Separating Roles

Alternatively, you can maintain separate roles by specifically assigning permissions to manage a set of objects. You are also able to delegate server administration using resource domains with Windows 2000 and Exchange 2000. Exchange 2000 servers can be organized into Active Directory organizational units and the administration of those organizational units can be delegated to the messaging administrators.

Permissions

Within an Exchange organization, permissions control access to resources. A permission provides specific authorization to perform an action. Permissions are a key component of Exchange administration; because they grant and deny access throughout an entire organization, they should be one of your first security considerations.

Administration Delegation Wizard

Exchange 2000 includes a tool called the Exchange Administration Delegation Wizard that simplifies permission management for delegating the appropriate permissions to Exchange administrators. Rather than assign permission to administrators individually, you can create groups of administrators and use Delegation Wizard to assign a set of administrative permissions to each group. Creating security groups with descriptive names and adding specific users to those groups simplify managing permissions across the organization.

NOTE

Administration Delegation Wizard is installed with Exchange, and cannot be run until the first instance of Exchange is installed in the organization.

If you need more control over permissions than Delegation Wizard provides, you can first use Delegation Wizard, then administer Active Directory permissions directly on Exchange objects by using System Manager. Extended permissions are specific to Exchange objects that are added to the standard Active Directory object schema.

A security descriptor manages all security information, including the permissions you associate with an object. Permissions are also inheritable; all objects in a hierarchy inherit the same permissions as the objects above them. Applying permissions at the highest possible level of the object hierarchy maximizes inheritance of permissions throughout the hierarchy. If you're planning a folder hierarchy of six tiers, it's easier to set the permissions at the top level and have each new folder inherit them than it is to build the hierarchy and then set each folder's permissions manually.

Roles

In Exchange 5.5, if you assign a role to a user or group, that user or group has the same permissions for all objects in that container. In Exchange 2000, you can specify user and group access by object class; for example, a user might have access to protocols and mailbox stores for a particular server, but not to security settings. If you have resources that require separate permissions, you can assign permissions to implement security policies that are as complex as you need them to be. You assign these tasks by assigning roles to users (see Figure 3.7). Table 3.3 describes these roles.

Figure 3.7 Assigning User Roles for Permissions

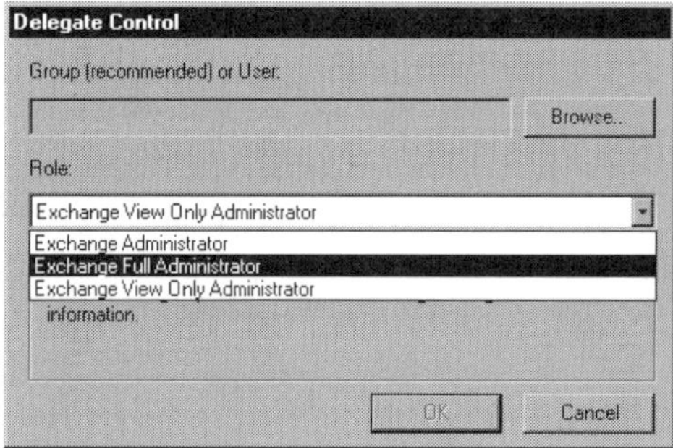

Table 3.3 Permissions Roles

Role	Description
Exchange Full Administrator	Grants the user permission to fully administer Exchange system information and modify permissions. Users assigned this role will have full control of the Exchange organization.
Exchange Administrator	Grants the user permission to fully administer Exchange system information, but not to modify permissions. This role may be useful where support staff need to administer the Exchange organization, but do not need to modify permissions.
Exchange View Only Administrator	Grants the user permission to view Exchange configuration information. This role may be useful where support staff need to view Exchange information, but do not need to change it.

Levels of Administration

One way to organize Administrator groups and easily grant the appropriate permissions is to create groups of administrators who have the same access privileges. The three levels of administration that should meet most organization's needs are enterprise administrators, administrative group administrators, and recipient administrators (see Table 3.4).

NOTE

Any user that you want to administer any level of Exchange 2000 must have at least Read permissions on the Exchange organization container.

Table 3.4 Administration Levels

Level	Title	Description
1	Enterprise Administrators	■ Windows 2000 Server installs default groups in the built-in container in Active Directory Users and Computers. The built-in local security group called Administrators has all permissions to manage the Windows 2000 Server domain. The Domain Admin and Enterprise Admin global security groups are members of the Administrators group and therefore also are granted all permissions in the Windows 2000 domain. ■ The Domain Admin and Exchange Admin global security groups are granted rights to administer the Exchange 2000 organization. These rights are inherited from the parent object—the server's Configuration container. ■ Note that Exchange System Manager hides the configuration container. You can view the configuration container by running Adsiedit.exe from Windows 2000 Server Support Tools.

Continued

Table 3.4 Continued

Level	Title	Description
		■ To assign users administrative privileges for the entire enterprise, add them to the Enterprise Admin group. By default, members of Enterprise Admin have nearly full control of both Active Directory and Exchange 2000.
2	Administrative Group Administrators	■ Many organizations might want to take advantage of the administrative group model. To do this, you create a global security group in Active Directory and grant this group one of the roles in the Exchange Administration Delegation Wizard for the specific administrative group. These permissions should be the same as those for Enterprise Admin, except that they are only valid within the selected administrative group.
3	Recipient Administrators	■ Recipient Administrators administer all aspects of user objects. You can use the built-in Windows 2000 Server Account Operators security group as a single location for recipient administrators. You should grant the Account Operators group the Exchange View Only permissions role using the Exchange Administration Delegation Wizard. Recipient administrators must be able to create accounts in Active Directory in addition to enabling a mailbox in Exchange 2000. ■ All user administration permissions must include rights to Active Directory in addition to Exchange. This reflects a change from earlier versions of Exchange where Exchange managed its own directory rather than relying on the operating system.

IPSec

IPSec is another new feature of Windows 2000 that is part of the integrated secure networking suite. IPSec is a framework of open standards for ensuring private, secure communications over IP networks. It uses cryptography-based security to provide access control, connectionless integrity, data origin authentication, and protection against replays, confidentiality, and limited traffic flow confidentiality. Because IPSec is provided at the network layer, its services are available to the upper-layer protocols in the stack, and are transparently available to existing applications.

IPSec enables a system to select security protocols, decide which algorithms to use for the services, and to establish and maintain cryptographic keys for each security relationship. IPSec can protect paths between hosts, between security gateways, or between hosts and security gateways. The services available and required for traffic are configured using IPSec policy. IPSec policy can be configured locally on a computer, or can be assigned through Windows 2000 Group Policy mechanisms using Active Directory (see Figure 3.8).

Figure 3.8 IP Security Policy Settings

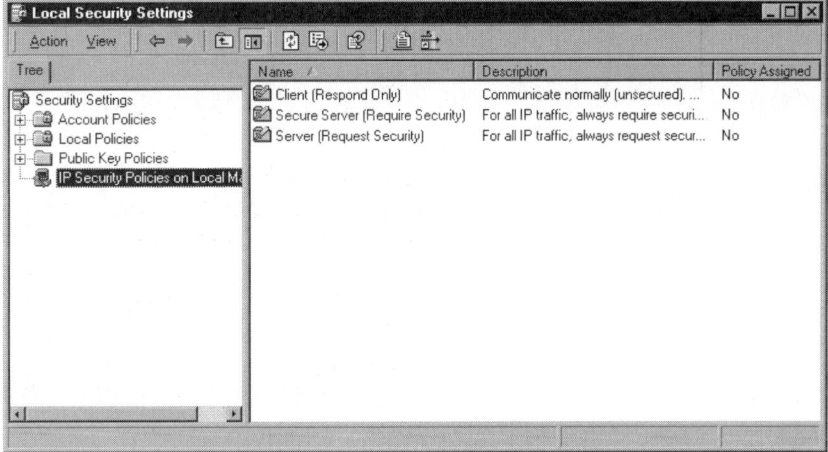

When using Active Directory, hosts detect policy assignment at startup, retrieve the policy, and periodically check for policy updates. The IPSec policy specifies how computers trust each other. The easiest trust to use is the Windows 2000 domain trust based on the Kerberos protocol. Predefined IPSec policies are configured to trust computers in the same or other trusted Windows 2000 domains.

Each IP datagram processed at the IP layer is compared against a set of filters that are provided by the security policy. IP can do one of three things with a datagram:

- Provide IPSec services to it

- Allow it to pass unmodified

- Discard it

Once the policy has been put in place, traffic matching the filters use the services provided by IPSec. When IP traffic (including something as simple as a ping in this case) is directed from one host to another, a Security Association (SA) is established via a short conversation over UDP port 500, (using the Internet Security Architecture Key Management Protocol, or ISAKMP), and then the traffic begins to flow. Because IPSec typically encrypts the entire IP payload, capturing an IPSec datagram sent after the SA is established reveals very little of what is actually in the datagram. The only parts of the packet that can be parsed by Network Monitor are the Ethernet and IP headers.

Although Certificate Services and KMS provide security on the application layer, IPSec provides security on the IP transportation layer (that is, Layer 3). IPSec also provides protection for the TCP/IP protocol stack, such as TCP, UDP, Internet Control Message Protocol (ICMP), and other protocols that send traffic at the IP layer. IPSec communication can transmit in blocks of data, with each block secured by a different key. This prevents an attacker from obtaining an entire communication with a single compromised key.

Security Policies

Security policies in Windows 2000 do more than simply establish the playing field for your users. They establish the ground rules and act as the referee as well. In a Windows 2000 environment they can be configured on any local machine (Windows 2000 Server or Professional) through the Local Security Policy tool, or for the enterprise through the Group Policy Tool. The key policies to configure are Account Policies (including Kerberos settings, Group Policies, and IP Security Policies).

The shortcuts for both tools are located in the Administrative Tools folder. The views that launch when the shortcut is clicked will look familiar as local and group policy settings are different snap-ins for the Microsoft Management Console (MMC). You could also add these snap-ins to a custom console or task pad.

Account Policies

Account policies are policies that are applied universally to every user account in your organization, or at least they should be. Normally, these settings begin as a corporate standard and are then implemented using the available technology. In Windows 2000, account policies are the first subcategory of Security Settings (see Figure 3.9). Notable account policies include password policy, account lockout policy, and Kerberos authentication policy.

Figure 3.9 Account Policies

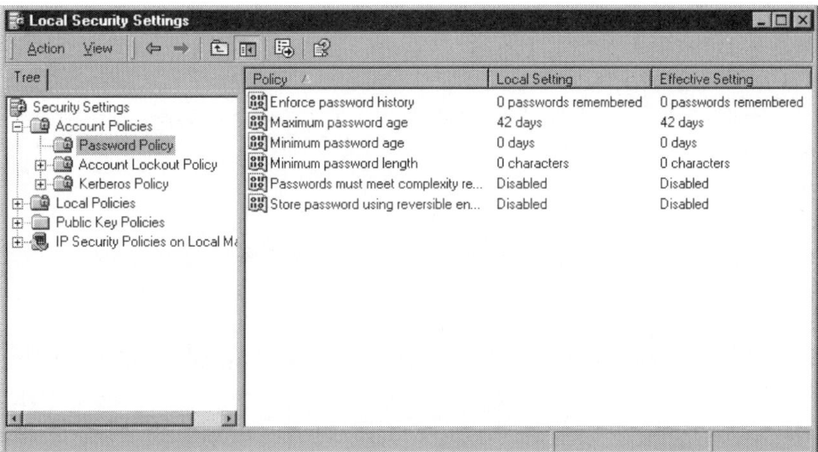

Password policies are set depending on the needs of the organization. If we think back to the weak or predictable password problem we discussed at the beginning of the chapter, it is possible to overcome this by specifying minimum password length, no blank passwords, and maximum and minimum password age. It is also possible to prevent users from reusing passwords and ensure that users use specific characters in their passwords, making passwords more difficult to crack.

Account lockout policies specify what happens when users fail to enter the correct password for an account. Users can be locked out after a specified number of failed logon attempts and the period of time that accounts are locked out for.

With the Kerberos authentication policy, you can modify the default Kerberos settings for each domain. While Kerberos works well in its default configuration, there may be a time where the settings need to be changed. A common setting to configure is the maximum lifetime of a user ticket, as seen in Figure 3.10.

Figure 3.10 Kerberos Policy Settings

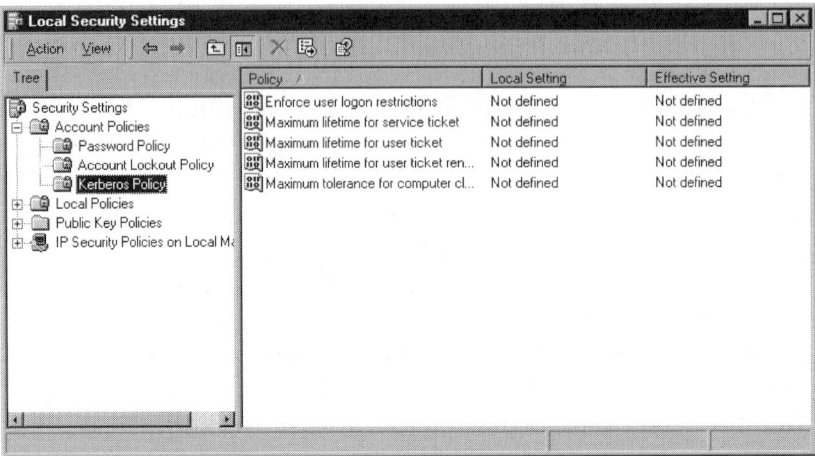

Group Policy

Group Policy is a way of forcing rules about computer configuration and user behavior. It is possible to have different policies throughout the company. As a user connects to a Windows 2000 domain controller that has Group Policy settings enabled, the policies are automatically downloaded to the user's computer and stored in the registry. Some of the settings include:

- Addition or removal of items from the desktop and control panel.

- Automatically installing software on users' computers without user interaction.

- Configuring Internet Explorer options for users, including security zones.

- Configuring network settings such as mapped network drives and permissions to view a computer browse list.

- Configuring system settings such as disabling computer shutdown options and the ability to run Task Manager.

Group policies in Windows 2000 are the best vehicle for controlling what your users see when they power up their machines, what they can do on their network, making network resources available to them, and securing what they do.

IP Security Policies

The Internet Protocol (IP) underlies the majority of corporate networks as well as the Internet. It is a stable, compatible, flexible protocol that is inherently unsecured. Due to its method of routing packets, IP-based networks are vulnerable to spoofing, sniffing, session hijacking, and man-in-the-middle attacks—threats that were unheard of when IP was first introduced.

The initial attempts to provide security over the Internet have been application-level protocols and software, such as SSL and TLS for securing Web traffic and Pretty Good Privacy (PGP) for securing e-mail. These applications, however, are limited to specific applications.

It is possible to make use of IP security policies in Windows 2000 to control how, when, and on whom IP security works. The IP security policy can define many rules, such as:

- What IP addresses to scan for

- How to encrypt packets

- Setting filters to take a look at all IP traffic passing through the object on which the IP security policy is applied

IP security policies in Windows 2000 are the logical representation of IPSec (refer back to Figure 3.8). As mentioned earlier, they can be configured on a local machine (Windows 2000 Server or Professional) through the Local Security Policy tool, or for the enterprise through the Group Policy Tool.

Firewalls

Firewall is a term that comes from the automotive industry. A firewall in a car is the barrier that creates a comfortable space for the passengers by protecting them from all of the heat and dangerous chemicals that fly around in the engine compartment. Most organizations have connected or want to connect their private networks to the Internet so that their users can have convenient access to Internet services, such as Web content and Internet e-mail. An Internet firewall creates that comfortable space for your users by restricting inbound and outbound access, and analyzing all traffic between your network and the Internet. The type of firewall can range from a simple packet filter to a variety of gateways that analyze traffic for each application type. It can be a single component, or it may be comprised of a combination of components such as routers, computers, networks, and software that protect any resource that can be reached from the Internet-reachable resources.

The main function of a firewall is to centralize access control. If outsiders or remote users can access the internal networks without going through the firewall, its effectiveness is diluted. For example, if a traveling manager has a modem connected to his office computer that he or she can dial into while traveling, and that computer is also on the protected internal network, an attacker who can dial into that computer has circumvented the firewall. If a user has a dial-up Internet account with a commercial ISP, and sometimes connects to the Internet from his or her office computer via modem, he or she is opening an unsecured connection to the Internet that circumvents the firewall. Firewalls provide several types of protection:

- They can block unwanted traffic.

- They can direct incoming traffic to more trustworthy internal systems.

- They hide vulnerable systems that cannot easily be secured from the Internet.

- They can log traffic to and from the private network.

- They can hide information such as system names, network topology, network device types, and internal user IDs from the Internet.

- They can provide more robust authentication than standard applications might be able to do.

Types of firewalls include packet filtering gateways, application gateways, and hybrid or complex gateways. *Packet filtering firewalls* use routers with packet filtering rules to grant or deny access based on source address, destination address, and port. They offer minimum security but at a very low cost, and can be an appropriate choice for a low-risk environment. They are fast, flexible, and transparent. Filtering rules are not often easily maintained on a router, but there are tools available to simplify the tasks of creating and maintaining the rules.

An *application gateway* uses server programs, or proxy servers, that run on the firewall. These servers take external requests, examine them, and forward legitimate requests to the internal host that provides the appropriate service, appropriately named *store-and-forward proxies*. Application gateways can support functions such as user authentication and logging.

Exchange Server and many other e-mail systems use a store-and-forward design, which inherently makes use of the proxy server. Clients connect to servers that reside on the local network. Servers in turn communicate with each other to transfer e-mail messages. Separate proxy services are unnecessary when Exchange Server is correctly configured. *Hybrid gateways* combine two or more of the above firewall types and implement them in series rather than in parallel. In medium to high-risk environments, a hybrid gateway may be the ideal firewall implementation.

Firewall Strategies and Exchange 2000

Because Windows 2000 and Exchange 2000 are designed to be connected to the Internet and to form foundational layers for your enterprise, you will be using them in conjunction with one or several firewalls. Just plunking down a firewall solution at the edge of your network is not the solution. The placement and use of your firewall is crucial and it depends as much on how users on the outside need to access your network as what your inside users need to do. Your firewall configuration must take into consideration the business needs of your organization as well as security. What you use your Exchange server for and how you choose to manage it will determine where you will place your firewall and what information you will allow to pass through it.

Firewall Placement

When connecting Exchange to the Internet, there are four firewall scenarios to consider. Bear in mind that the first three scenarios have been developed with the deployment of Outlook Web Access (OWA) as a prime consideration. The fourth scenario is for organizations that need to send mail to the Internet, but do not require external access to Exchange. We will be looking into client-side security in the next section. Each depends upon how protected your Exchange server will be and where you want to place the burden of administration.

As you can see in Figure 3.11, a firewall between the IIS/OWA server and the Microsoft Exchange Server may seem practical if several Web-enabled applications are already deployed on the IIS server and it is important to protect the Microsoft Exchange Server and domain controllers. In this configuration, all the client connections from IIS to the Microsoft Exchange Server are filtered by the firewall. Thus, users can access the IIS/OWA server without going through the firewall, but they must go through the firewall to access data on the Microsoft Exchange Server. This configuration is not recommended because the IIS/OWA server is not protected. Using this design, IIS (acting as a MAPI client to the Microsoft Exchange Server) requires similar access to the Microsoft Exchange Server and domain controller as a standard Outlook client.

Figure 3.11 Firewall between IIS/OWA Server and Exchange Server

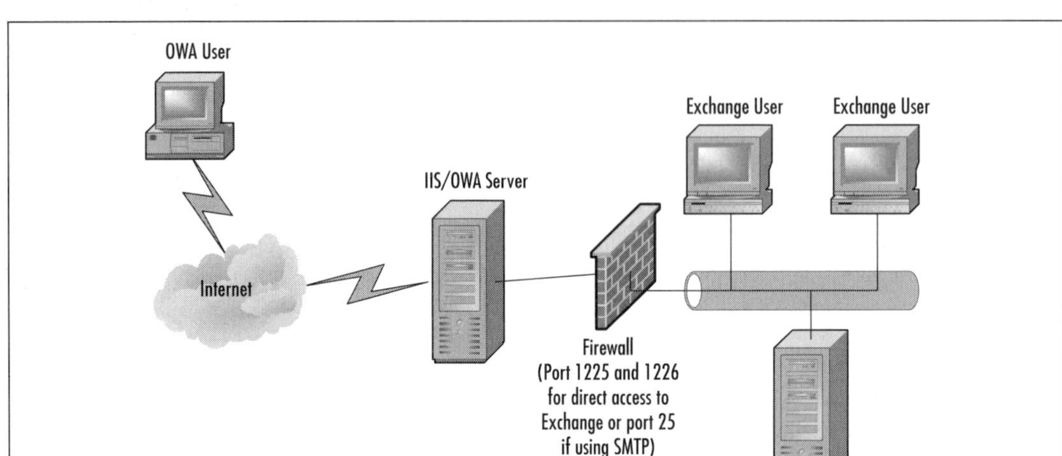

On the firewall, it is important to enable several TCP ports to allow the Outlook Web Access server to connect successfully to the Microsoft Exchange Server directory and information store. Because Microsoft Exchange Server randomly assigns ports for the directory and information store by default, you must statically map the ports that clients will use. Microsoft recommends mapping port 1225 to the directory and port 1226 to the information store.

WARNING

Do not assign ports immediately above the 1023 range to the directory and information store. This may cause other problems with Microsoft Exchange Server.

The most common and secure firewall configuration requires that users go through the firewall to access IIS/OWA and Microsoft Exchange Server computers. This configuration secures all information that flows into the IIS/OWA server (all incoming TCP packets must pass through the firewall or packet filter). This configuration is also useful for preventing Internet access to other applications and services running on your IIS/OWA server. The firewall is located outside of the organization to prevent any attacks or unwanted access to the servers. For this design, configure the firewall to pass HTTP on port 80.

In this scenario, as shown in Figure 3.12, the browser connects over TCP port 80 through the firewall to IIS. IIS then communicates with Microsoft Exchange Server to access Microsoft Exchange Server data. The IIS/OWA server then renders HTML for the client by sending the data through the firewall and over the Internet on TCP port 80. If SSL is being used to encrypt mail transactions to the client, port 80 is used for the initial contact and then 443 is used for the mail session.

Figure 3.12 Firewall between Internet and IIS/OWA Server

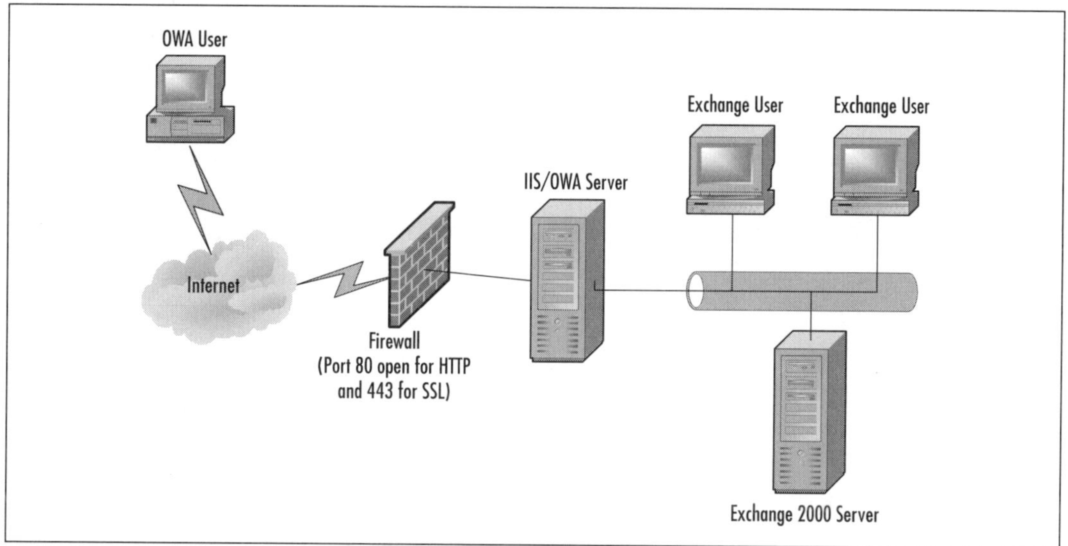

After enabling these ports on the firewall, test your configuration and verify that a browser can connect successfully with the Microsoft Exchange Server over the Internet. For test purposes, use Outlook (using TCP transport) to connect to the Microsoft Exchange Server. If you are able to connect with Outlook, the Outlook Web Access client will also connect. If Outlook does not connect to Microsoft Exchange Server, check the firewall settings and verify the Microsoft Exchange Server configuration.

The configuration shown in Figure 3.13 is emerging as a popular arrangement as organizations "Webify" their business processes. The IIS/OWA server sits between two firewalls in a Demilitarized Zone (DMZ). Internet users must go through the external firewall to access IIS/OWA; OWA connects through the internal firewall to connect with the Exchange server. This configuration is useful where Web applications that are used by both the public and employees reside either on the IIS/OWA server or on other Web servers in the DMZ. In the case where there are other Web application servers, they can use the IIS/OWA server's SMTP stack to conduct their transactions through the internal firewall to back-end database systems. Again, the external firewall has port 80 open for HTTP transactions (443 if using SSL) and the internal firewall has ports 25 and 80 open for SMTP and HTTP, respectively.

Figure 3.13 IIS/OSA in DMZ between Two Firewalls

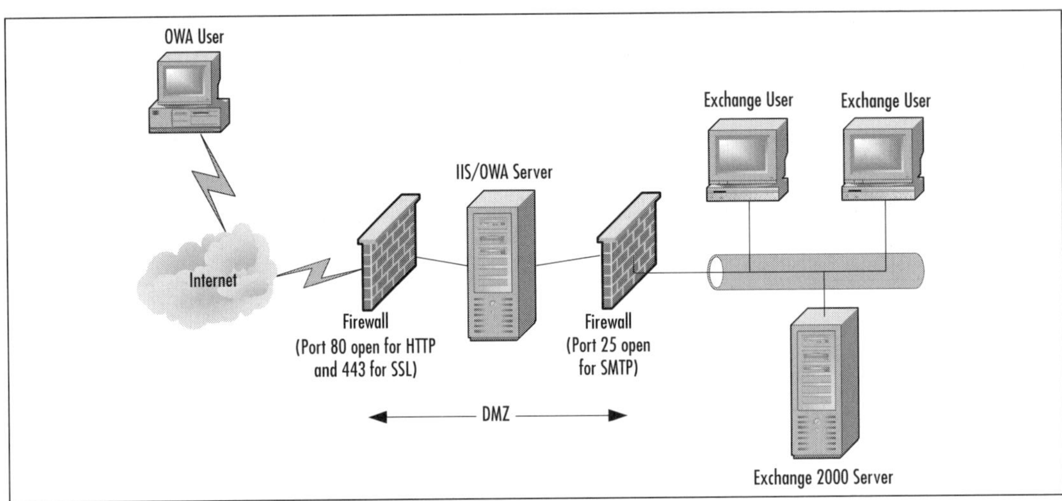

In the scenario shown in Figure 3.14, there is no external access to Exchange; OWA is not installed. Exchange connects to Internet through a firewall using Internet Mail Connecter on SMTP port 25.

Figure 3.14 Firewall Internet and Exchange Server, No OWA Access

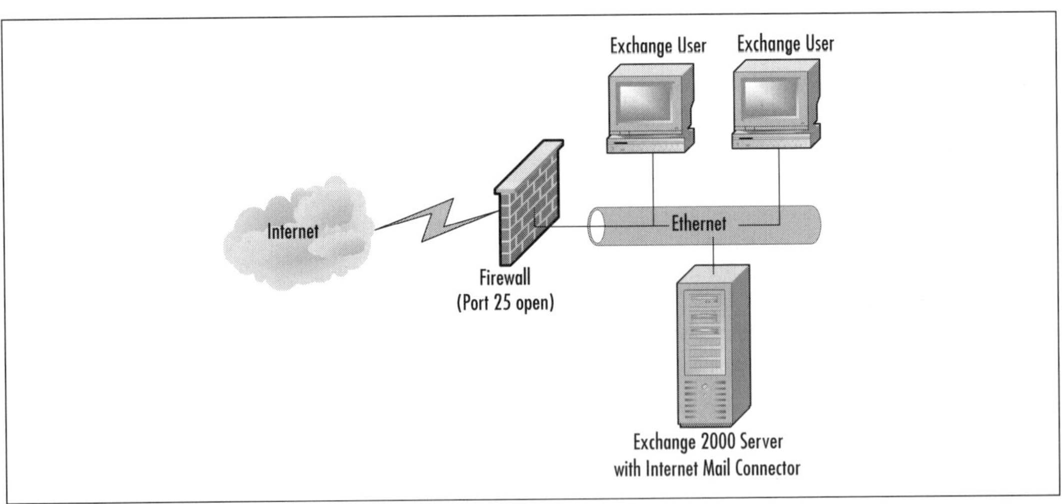

Firewall Administration

The most important consideration in administering your firewall is what services need to run through it *at a minimum*. The answer will tell you what ports need to be open and vigilantly monitored and audited. Attackers routinely use IP port-scanning software to find unsecured ports on firewalls. Any open or unsecured port can be an open door to your infrastructure. The table in Appendix A lists the ports that need to be left open for different Windows 2000 and Exchange 2000 protocol activities.

WARNING

Close all unnecessary ports. Run port-scanning software against your own firewall to find any ports you may have missed.

Configuring Client Security

An organization could have the most secure network and back-end systems that are locked down tighter than Fort Knox, but if the common points of access, the clients, are not secured, then all of that work invested in secure connectivity and servers has been wasted. Client-side security begins at back-end systems with authentication methods and encrypted communication.

Securing Outlook

To secure the Outlook client, be it the full-blown client, such as Outlook 2000, or its lighter-weight counterpart, Outlook Express, you must secure the place where it lives.

Encrypting File System

Windows 2000 users, especially those mobile types on notebook computers, can encrypt files and folders on their local hard disks using Encrypting File System (EFS). EFS is a new feature in Microsoft Windows 2000 that allows the protection and confidentiality of sensitive data by using symmetric key encryption in conjunction with public key technology. Only the owner of the protected file can open it and read just like a normal document. EFS is integrated into the NT file system (NTFS), and thus you set the encryption attribute for folders and files just as you would for other attributes. EFS provides users with privacy. Besides the user who encrypts the file, only a designated administrator (a *recovery agent*) can decrypt the file in cases of emergency recovery. EFS is a transparent operation in which file encryption does not require the user to encrypt and decrypt the file.

WARNING

Make sure that users do not use EFS on network drives, on their Program Files directory or on their local %systemroot% directory.

Digital Identification

A Windows 2000 user with the Outlook client who is directly connected to the corporate network proves his or her identity at the initial session logon through Kerberos authentication and will carry that digital identification throughout the session. "Down-level" clients will use NTLM and will not need to log in separately to Exchange 2000. If a user wants to use a different certificate, such as the case where a user is at a remote site and can access his or her mail using a POP3 connection, the user can do so by clicking on the Get a Digital ID button on the Security tab of the Account Properties page (Figure 3.15).

Figure 3.15 Selecting a Default Certificate (Digital ID) in Outlook Express

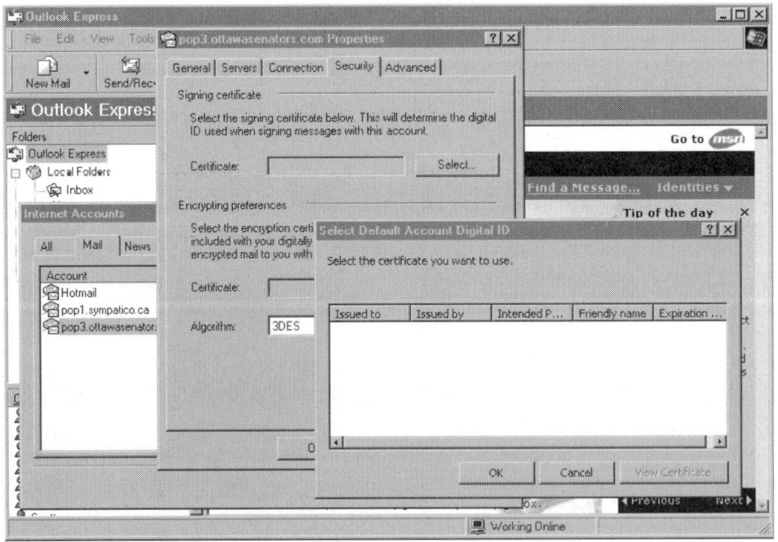

If you use Exchange 2000 Key Management Service, the MAPI client uses the CAST or Data Encryption Standard (DES) algorithms to encrypt the mail messages you compose on your computer, before they leave the client machine. A message remains encrypted until the recipient decrypts it on the fly by double-clicking the message to read it. The message also remains encrypted while stored in the mailbox. This process is an end-to-end (i.e., writer-to-reader) security measure.

Securing Web Browsers

Securing the Web browser is not much more than just loading it up with 128-bit encryption. Securing the browser begins on the back end where encryption levels and authentication methods are established. As browsers evolve, while they remain stateless with relatively little configuration required, they are becoming more feature-rich. These new generation browsers are bordering on rich-clients, and their lack of need for configuration is being replaced by a need for administration and maintenance. From a security perspective, many attackers are now exploiting security holes in Web browsers to infiltrate machines to execute malicious code or to read data in file systems. For organizations that have standardized on Internet Explorer, the Internet Explorer Administration Kit (IEAK) will help you manage your installation base for distributing maintenance releases and security updates, and for removing features that may produce headaches among the IT staff.

User Authentication

The Outlook Web Access server can authenticate users with one or more of the following types of security (see Figure 3.16).

Figure 3.16 OWA User Authentication Options

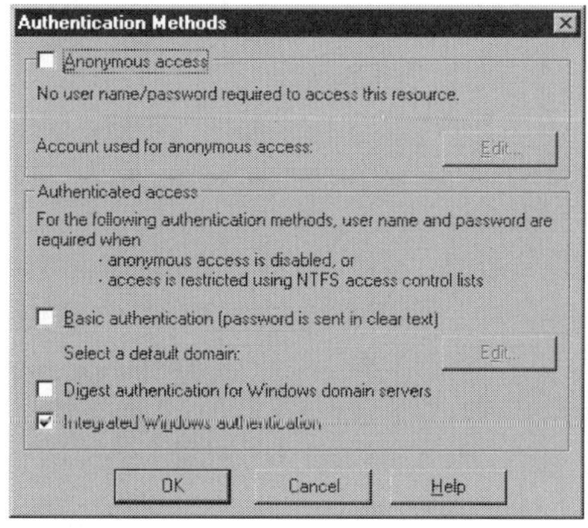

- Anonymous
- Basic (Clear Text)
- Basic (Clear Text) over Secure Sockets Layer
- Windows NT Challenge/Response (NTLM)

Anonymous

If Outlook Web Access is configured for Anonymous authentication, users can use Outlook Web Access without specifying a Windows NT user account name and password. Each time a user establishes an anonymous connection, IIS logs the user on with an anonymous or guest account, which is a valid Windows NT user account. By default, the anonymous account is IUSR_ComputerName. Anonymous authentication provides access only to resources that are published anonymously, such as public folders and directory content.

Advantages	Disadvantages
All browsers support Anonymous authentication.	Anonymous authentication is not secure.
Users are not prompted for credentials.	Users can only access the Global Address List and public folders that are configured for anonymous access.

Basic (Clear Text)

If Outlook Web Access is configured for Basic authentication, users must specify a valid Windows NT user account name and password in order to use Outlook Web Access. Both the user name and password are transmitted as clear text over the network to the IIS/OWA server. The advantage of Basic authentication is that users can access an unlimited number of resources, even if those resources are not on the user's Outlook Web Access server. For example, a user can access public folders on one Microsoft Exchange Server and e-mail on another Microsoft Exchange Server.

WARNING

Because Basic authentication transmits passwords across the network as unencrypted information, Microsoft recommends that you use SSL with Basic authentication, which encrypts all information passing through IIS.

Advantages	Disadvantages
All browsers support Basic authentication.	Basic authentication is not secure.
Users can access all Microsoft Exchange Server resources.	Users are prompted for a user name and password. Users must be granted the Log on Locally right on IIS.

Basic (Clear Text) over Secure Sockets Layer

If Outlook Web Access is configured for Basic authentication over SSL, users must specify a valid Windows NT user account name and password to use Outlook Web Access. Both the user name and password are transmitted as encrypted information over the network to the IIS/OWA server. As with Basic authentication, users can access an unlimited number of resources with Basic over SSL authentication, even if those resources are not on the user's Outlook Web Access server.

Advantages	Disadvantages
Most browsers support Basic over SSL authentication.	Performance can be slow as a result of the encryption.
Users can access all Microsoft Exchange Server resources.	Users are prompted for a user name and password.
Basic over SSL authentication is very secure.	Users must be granted the Log on Locally right on IIS.

Windows NT Challenge/Response (NTLM)

If Outlook Web Access is configured for Windows NT Challenge/Response, users must specify a valid Windows NT user account name and password in order to use Outlook Web Access. The user name and password are sent from the browser to the IIS server as encrypted information. A serious limitation of NTLM is that all resources the user wants to use must reside on the same server as IIS and Outlook Web Access. NTLM authentication is not supported if IIS/OWA and Microsoft Exchange Server are located on different computers.

Advantages	Disadvantages
NTLM authentication is relatively secure.	Users can access only resources on the IIS/OWA server.

Continued

Advantages	Disadvantages
Users are not prompted for a user name or password.	All browsers (for example, Netscape Navigator) do not support NTLM authentication.

Roaming Users

If several users share a computer to access e-mail using Outlook Web Access, Microsoft recommends disabling local caching on the browser. If caching is not disabled, messages accessed during the previous Outlook Web Access session may still remain on the local disk, making it possible for someone to see another user's messages.

For increased security, Microsoft recommends not using the Save Password feature in Internet Explorer. For other information about disabling local caching and the Save Password feature, see the user documentation for the Web browser.

Encryption

You can use SSL to implement transport-level encryption. To enable SSL, the POP3 server needs to have obtained and installed a digital certificate. You can obtain this certificate from a local Microsoft Certificate Server or from a third-party such as VeriSign (see Figure 3.17). To install the certificate, you must have installed Internet Information Server (IIS) on the Exchange server and used the IIS Key Manager to request and process the certificate.

NOTE

Don't confuse the IIS Key Manager with the Exchange Server Key Management Server.

After you install the certificate, a POP3 client can access the Exchange server over an SSL-encrypted transport session.

The e-mail client and the server go through a handshake to initiate the communication. If the e-mail client trusts the Exchange server's certificate, it uses the keys in the certificate to encrypt the transmission. This encryption process is independent of whether any applications running at higher levels have added encryption. If the client is a browser, install the highest encryption level that your country will allow. There are export restrictions on encryption algorithms.

Figure 3.17 Exchange 2000 Certificate for Installation to a Microsoft Certification Authority

You must configure both the e-mail client and the Exchange server to support SSL. To configure SSL support, go to the Advanced tab for the Internet Mail (POP3) Information Service (see Figure 3.18) and select the check box specifying that the server requires SSL. The client will then attempt to connect to the SSL (POP3) port (TCP port 995) of the server rather than the standard TCP port 110 used for POP3.

Figure 3.18 Configuring SSL Support via POP3 Advanced Settings

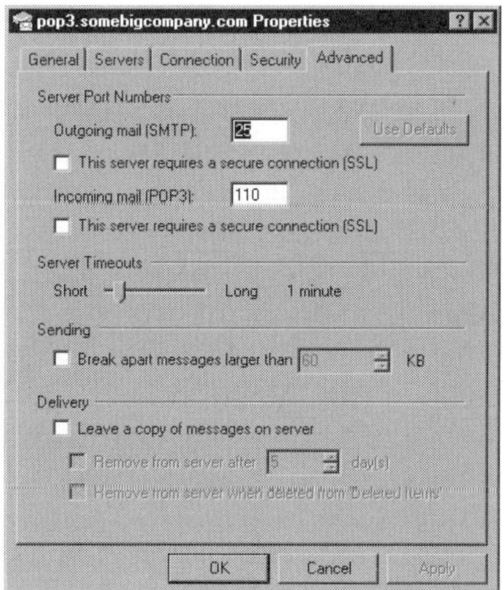

Implementing a Smart-Card Environment

Smart Cards are credit-card–type cards that contain a small amount of memory and sometimes a processor. They can store system logon information, such as the user's private key, along with passwords and other personal information. All the user needs is a reader and a personal identification number (PIN). Microsoft assisted in developing the standards for smart cards, and as a result, has implemented smart-card reader recognition (plug-and-play capability) and APIs for developers in Windows 2000.

Smart cards are a key component of the PKI that Microsoft has integrated with the Windows 2000. Smart cards enhance software-only solutions such as interactive logon, client authentication, and remote logon. Smart cards provide:

- Tamper-resistant storage for protecting private keys and other forms of personal information.

- Isolation of security-critical computations involving the private key from other parts of the system that do not have a "need to know."

- Portability of credentials and other private information between computers at work, home, or on the road.

Another security use of smart cards is file encryption utilities that use the smart card as the key to an electronic lock on files, or as a key for physical access in proximity security, such as building access.

The circuitry in a smart card derives power from a smart card reader after the card is inserted into the reader. Data communication between a smart card and an application running on a computer is performed over a half-duplex serial interface managed by the smart card reader and its associated device driver. Smart card readers are available in a variety of form factors and can be connected to a computer using an RS-232, PCMCIA or USB interface. As stated earlier, new versions of this hardware that have been developed to the smart card standard will be recognized plug-and-play devices in Windows 2000 and beyond.

In a typical smart-card logon environment, the user is required to insert his or her smart card into a reader device connected to the computer. Then, the software uses the information stored on the smart card for authentication. When paired with a password and/or a biometric identifier, the level of security is increased. Another security use of smart cards is file encryption utilities that use the smart card as the key to the electronic lock.

Authentication

According to Microsoft's Smart Card Logon White Paper, (see www.microsoft.com/technet/win2000/win2ksrv/technote/sclogon.asp) a smart card can be used to authenticate to a Windows 2000 domain in three ways. The first is interactive logon involving Active Directory, Kerberos and public key certificates. The second is client authentication where a user is authenticated using a public key certificate that matches an account stored in Active Directory. The third is remote logon that uses a public key certificate with the Extensible Authentication Protocol (EAP) and TLS to authenticate a remote user to an account stored in Active Directory.

Interactive Logon

Interactive Logon using a smart card begins when a user inserts a smart card into a smart-card reader that signals the Windows 2000 operating system to prompt for a PIN code instead of a username, domain name, and password. The card insertion event is equivalent to the familiar CTRL+ALT+ DEL secure attention sequence used to initiate a password-based logon; however, the PIN the user provides to the logon dialog is used to authenticate only to the smart card and not to the domain. A public key certificate stored on the smart card is used to authenticate to the domain using Kerberos.

Logon Request

After a user inputs a PIN to the logon dialog screen, the operating system begins a sequence of actions to determine whether the user can be identified and authenticated based on credential information the user has provided (PIN code and smart card). The logon request first goes to the Local Security Authority (LSA), which subsequently forwards it to the Kerberos authentication package running on the client. The Kerberos package sends an authentication service (AS) request to the KDC service running on a domain controller to request authentication and a Ticket Granting Ticket (TGT). As part of the AS request, the client-side Kerberos package includes the user's x.509v3 certificate, retrieved from the smart card, in the pre-authentication data fields of the AS request. An authenticator, included in the pre-authentication data fields, is digitally signed by the user's private key so that the KDC can verify the AS request originated from the owner of the accompanying certificate.

Once this is complete, the x509v3 certificate from the smart card is validated. This validation process consists of the verification of the smart-card certificate against the user's certificate credentials stored in Active

Directory and the authenticity of the certificate issuer. When complete, the user's private key is issued and a session token is granted. This essentially is the same authentication process as described in the Kerberos section. I do not want to oversimplify the use of these devices, but smart cards basically replace the first stages of the login process.

The real benefit of smart card technology is the portability of the user's credentials. The downside is that their use is subject to some basic human limitations. They can be forgotten at home, lost, or stolen. If the PIN code is written down in close proximity to the card, such as on a piece of paper in a wallet where the card is stored—or worse, written in pencil on the card itself (I have actually seen this)—then the finder of the card and PIN code can assume the smart-card owner's identity.

Offline Logon

When a user is disconnected from the network or the domain controller is unreachable due to failure somewhere along the network path, a user must still be able to log on to his or her computer. With passwords this capability is supported by comparing the hashed password stored by the LSA with a hash of the credential that the user supplied to the GINA during logon. If the hashes are the same, the user can be authenticated to the local machine.

In the smart-card case, offline logon requires the user's private key to decrypt supplemental credentials originally encrypted using the user's public key. If the user has multiple smart cards, then the supplemental credentials must be encrypted and referenced based on the hash of the certificate—to ensure that the user can perform an offline logon regardless of what card is used.

Smart Cards and Exchange 2000 Security

Secure e-mail is one of the best justifications for deploying smart cards to your organization because it allows users to share information confidentially and to trust that the integrity of the information was maintained during transit. Using either Outlook client, a user can select a public-key certificate issued by a trusted certification authority to use for digitally signing and decrypting secure messages. By publishing the user's certificate to a public directory in the enterprise or on the Internet, other users within a company or on the Internet can send encrypted e-mail to the user, and vice versa.

A smart card adds a level of integrity to secure e-mail applications because it stores the private key on the card, and protects it with a PIN. In order to compromise the private key and send signed e-mail as someone else, someone would have to obtain the user's smart card and the PIN. The

PIN could someday be replaced with a biometric template of the user's fingerprint, thus enhancing the non-repudiation aspect of digitally signed e-mail.

It is recommended that users who do not perform advanced tasks such as joining computers to domains or promoting servers to domain controllers be issued smart cards and not passwords. This category of user should represent a significant portion of a company's employee population. These users could be professional workers, suppliers, contractors, or anyone else who is not trusted to administer a computer or the network.

Windows 2000 supports a per-user account policy, with a smart card required for interactive logon, that requires a smart card to effect an interactive logon. What this means is that once the policy is set on an account, the user cannot use a password to log on to the account, interactively or from a command line. The policy applies to interactive and network logon only, but not to remote access logon which uses a different policy configured on the remote access server. While setting the smart card required for interactive logon policy on an account is not recommended for every user in an enterprise, it should be set for those users who are members of the Users group that are using smart cards to log on to a Windows 2000 domain.

Summary

Some may say that security measures are onerous or only for the paranoid. We think they are wrong. When it comes to protecting the worth or value of your organization, you cannot view the subject in any other way. Identify spoofing is *common*, as are attacks on actual data. With messaging, often it is not only what is stored that is the target of attack, it is the very identities of the users.

When you combine the security applications integrated with Windows 2000 and Exchange 2000 there are an overwhelming multitude of options for securing your messaging environment. The correct solution is multi-faceted, but it possesses five main characteristics:

- Positively identify the user, using strong authentication methods (Kerberos, smart cards, digital identification, and certificates).

- Secure your messaging clients and servers by applying all system and security updates.

- Secure and monitor your network traffic with IPSec and Windows 2000 IP Security Policies.

- Restrict who can do what with your network resources using Group Policy Objects and administrative delegation.

- Shore up, monitor, and audit your firewall (or firewalls); leave no open or unlocked doors.

The key to network security, and specifically to messaging security, is to apply the right degree of security at the right places and to balance it with productivity and usability. There is little sense in investing the majority of your time to secure features that are never used, nor is there any sense in locking down frequently used functions to the point that they are barely usable.

FAQs

Visit **www.syngress.com/solutions** to have your questions about this chapter answered by the author.

Q: I am going to be working with vendors and I need to verify that they sent their orders. How do I do that?

A: Use certificates from a stand-alone CA that is a child or subordinate to a third-party CA, such as VeriSign, to verify their identities.

Q: We have clients who are on the road quite a bit and tend to store their sensitive data, including e-mail, on their laptops. If they encrypt their files and directories containing this data, how can I as a network administrator get their files off if they are not around and the files are needed?

A: Once a user encrypts a file or folder on a local machine, only he or she can decrypt it, unless there is someone who is a recovery agent. If you need to access the files, make sure that you are a Encrypted File Recovery Agent for the domain to which these users' laptops connect.

Q: I will be deploying Outlook Web Access for our organization. How can I secure our Windows2000 IIS 5.0 server?

A: Use Microsoft's Windows2000 Internet Server Security Configuration Tool. It automates the security configuration process. It is available for download from www.microsoft.com/technet/security/tools.asp.

Q: I am implementing a firewall for my company. How do I know what ports to open and what to close? Once that is done, how can I test to see what state my ports are in?

A: You should close all ports by default, and then open only the ones that you know that are absolutely, positively necessary for your environment. For example, if you host your own Web server, use SSL for OWA, use SMTP for Internet messaging, and permit your users to use Instant Messaging, you should leave open ports 80, 443, 25, and 2980. You can check your port states by using ShieldsUp at www.grc.com.

Chapter 4

Basic Administration

Solutions in this chapter:

- Defining Tools Used to Administer Exchange 2000
- Adding and Configuring Users, Contacts, and Groups
- Maintaining Address Lists
- Administering Exchange Server Global Settings
- Managing Address Lists
- Creating and Administering System and Recipient Policies
- Managing Public Folders
- Managing Connectors

Introduction

As you learned in Chapter 1, this newest version of Microsoft's Exchange Server has evolved considerably from its predecessors. In Chapter 2, you learned how the Windows 2000 Active Directory (AD) replaces the duties formerly controlled by the Directory Services component of Exchange 5.5. Microsoft Exchange Server, more than ever before, is dependent on the underlying operating system. These changes are subsequently reflected in the tools that are used to administer Exchange 2000 Server.

In Exchange 2000, we say good-bye to User Manager for Domains and the Exchange Administrator program. Instead, Exchange 2000 distributes most administrative duties between two Microsoft Management Console (MMC) snap-ins—*User Management* through the Active Directory Users and Computers console, and *Server Management* through the Exchange System Manager console. This chapter describes how to use these tools to perform the many basic administrative tasks facing Exchange administrators on a day-to-day basis. Even though Exchange has become more complex, centralized management provided by the MMC helps ensure that basic Exchange administration does not become complex.

Leveraging the Active Directory is the biggest innovation in Exchange 2000. All Exchange-related objects are recipient objects held in the Windows 2000 AD hierarchy. As a direct result of this, the functionality of groups and e-mail converge, as security groupings from NT days now can be e-mail distribution lists as well.

Exchange 2000 also requires Internet Information Server 5.0 (IIS), which is installed by default in Windows 2000. IIS becomes the protocol gateway to the Internet for Exchange Server, providing Simple Mail Transfer Protocol (SMTP) and other protocol connectivity through the concept of virtual servers. Even with this requirement, an Exchange administrator doesn't have to be an IIS administrator as well.

The basic administrative functions covered in this chapter, complete with numerous screen captures, will prepare you for your journey into the very complex and powerful collaborative messaging product called Exchange 2000 Server.

Customizing the Microsoft Management Console (MMC)

Windows 2000 employs the Microsoft Management Console (MMC), Version 1.2, with a variety of specific "snap-ins" to administer server and workstation configuration, user and directory management, networking functions, application and storage management, and performance issues. MMC 1.0 was first introduced with the Option Pack for Windows NT 4.0. Microsoft is developing MMC 2.0 as a component of the Whistler project (the next version of Windows).

The MMC is a Windows-based application structured for Microsoft and third-party components to come together to provide management tools in a common interface, referred to as a Multiple Document Interface (MDI). One of the greatest features of the MMC is its customizability. Instead of separate executables, the application MMC.EXE uses various snap-ins, which in turn access their own DLL files in performing their tasks.

Most administrative duties for Exchange 2000 are achieved through two MMC snap-ins: User management is done through *Active Directory Users and Computers*, while Exchange Server management is generally performed through the *Exchange System Manager* snap-in. These snap-ins can be combined into one custom MMC interface and saved as an MMC file, which uses the .msc extension.

From a command line, or Start | Run, type **MMC** and press Enter. This will open an MMC template called Console1 by default (see Figure 4.1).

Figure 4.1 MMC Console Template

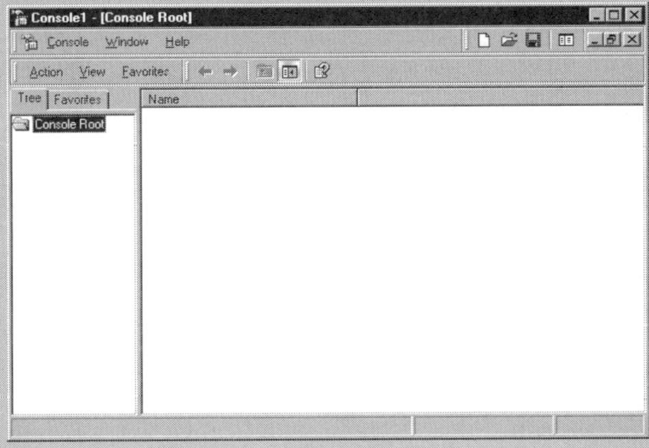

Continued

This interface provides no management functionality until snap-ins are added. Under the Console menu, choose Add/Remove Snap-In, then click the Add button for a list of Stand Alone Snap-Ins you can combine for your Exchange Management Console, as shown in Figure 4.2. You can add the snap-ins for Active Directory Users and Computers as well as the Exchange System snap-in. After you close the Add Snap-In dialog boxes, you see that the snap-ins now share the same interface (Figure 4.3). To save this simplest of console customizations, just choose Console | Save As and name the file as desired, using the .msc extension.

Figure 4.2 Adding Standalone Snap-In to Customized MMC Console

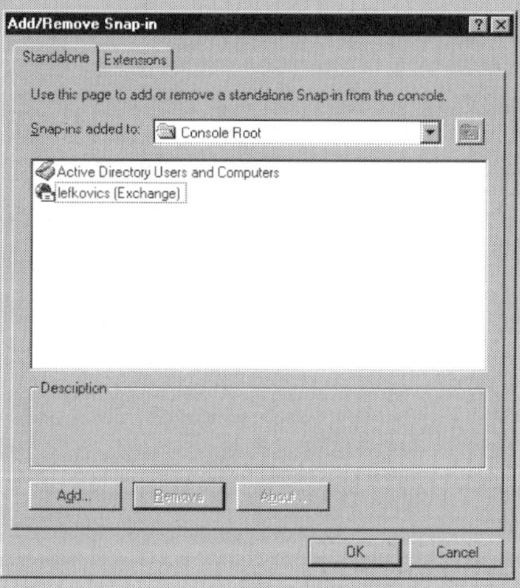

Figure 4.3 Customized MMC Console

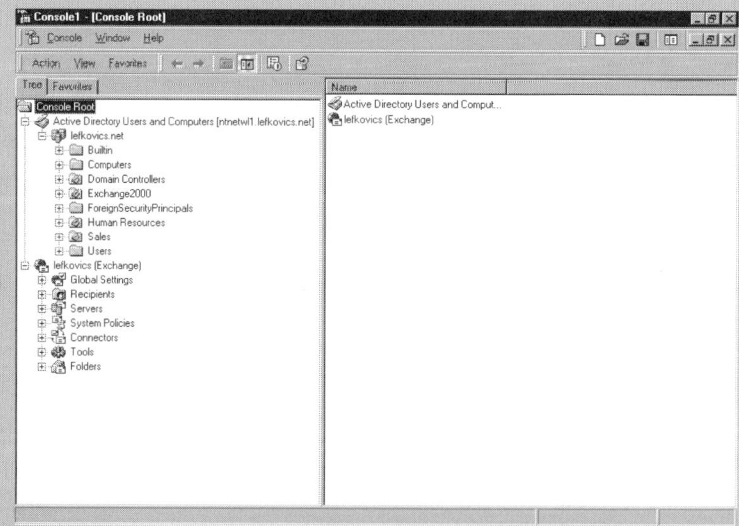

Continued

You can now make a desktop shortcut to your customized MMC file, and even share or distribute it to other administrators. When selecting certain snap-ins, you also have the opportunity to select individual extensions within that snap-in, perhaps for distribution to different levels of administrator. You can see the management potential for your organization!

Microsoft provides extensive documentation on managing your Windows 2000 organization, many of which can be found at the following Microsoft site entitled Exploring Management Services:

www.microsoft.com/windows2000/guide/server/features/managementsvcs.asp.

Exchange Administration Tools

Everything you need to administer Microsoft Exchange Server is accomplished through just a few MMC snap-ins. Most of the administration is done through the AD Users and Computers snap-in and the Exchange System Manager snap-in, as summarized in Table 4.1. These tools represent a clear separation of user and server administration from what you were used to in the legacy Exchange Administrator application. You could separate duties among administrators based on functions of the specific MMC snap-ins.

Even though the IIS hosts the protocols for Exchange 2000 communication, you only administer the default Hypertext Transfer Protocol (HTTP) Virtual Server, which is the default Web site, through the Internet Services Manager MMC snap-in. Any other HTTP Virtual Servers other than the default, as well as all the connecting protocols, are managed using the Exchange System Manager.

Table 4.1 Primary MMC Snap-Ins for Exchange 2000 Administration

MMC Snap-In	Administrative Tasks
AD Users and Computers	Creating and managing user accounts, contacts, and security groups Enabling and disabling messaging features Setting individual delivery restrictions and storage limits
Exchange System Manager	Managing global Exchange parameters, such as virtual servers, administrative and routing groups, address lists, and storage groups

Continued

Table 4.1 Continued

MMC Snap-In	Administrative Tasks
Internet Services Manager	Administering Internet Information Server, through which Exchange Server connects to the Internet
AD Sites and Services	Managing Windows 2000 site connectivity, including AD replication

In organizations where Exchange 2000 and Exchange 5.5 coexist through the Exchange 2000 Active Directory Connector, you still must use the Exchange 2000 tools to administer Exchange 2000 and the old Exchange Administrator (admin.exe) to manage mailboxes still residing in the legacy version.

Active Directory Users and Computers

The Active Directory schema determines the structure of the database holding the AD objects and their attributes. As you learned in Chapter 2, upon installation, Exchange 2000 extends the AD schema, actually adding new attributes, which can then be associated with the various recipient objects in the AD. Properties of users, groups, contacts, mailboxes, and public folders are all held in the Active Directory (see Figure 4.4). You can manipulate them as you would any other AD object.

Figure 4.4 Active Directory Users and Computers

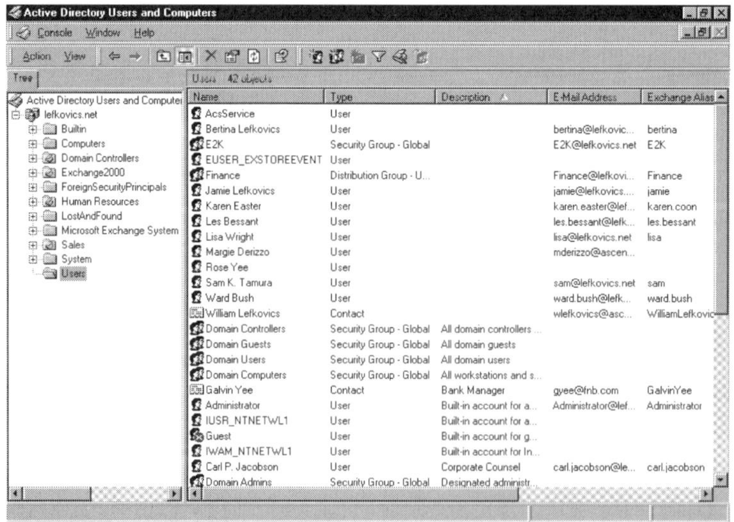

TIP

If you open Active Directory Users and Computers from the Microsoft Exchange folder in the Start menu, you'll see additional columns not available in the regular AD Users and Computers located in the Administrative Tools folder of a domain controller. These columns are E-Mail Address, Exchange Alias, and Exchange Mailbox Store.

Figure 4.5 is an example of the interface used to view and edit the properties of an AD object of type User. Exchange 2000 adds the Exchange-related tabs to edit attributes specific to the Exchange organization.

Figure 4.5 User Properties

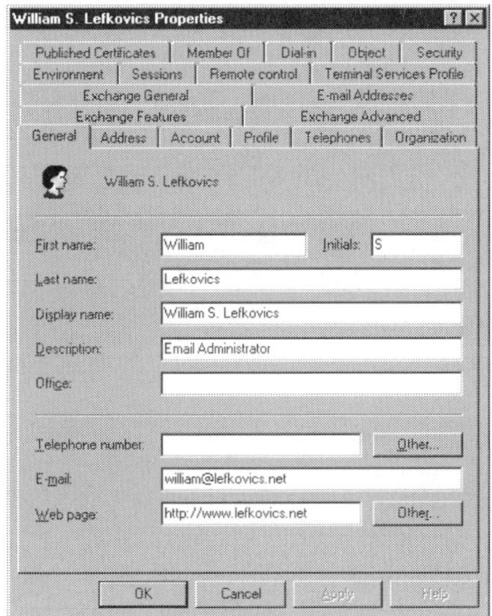

TIP

Some attributes in Active Directory Users and Computers are hidden by default. Open the View menu in the AD Users and Computers snap-in and choose Advanced Features. This will expose the Exchange Advanced tab in the User Accounts properties, for example.

Exchange System Manager

The foundation of an Exchange Server environment is an *organization*. In Exchange 2000, the boundary of an organization is the Active Directory Forest. An organization can not span multiple forests; therefore, a company with more than one Active Directory forest will have to deploy multiple Exchange organizations if messaging is needed for objects in all forests.

Within a forest, Windows 2000 forms sites, logical groupings of domain controllers optimized for replication and access by clients. Atop the Windows 2000 sites, Exchange 2000 uses routing and administrative groups to replace the concept of Exchange sites.

Upon installation of Exchange 2000, you no longer join a site as in legacy versions, but rather you have the option of joining an existing Exchange organization or creating a new organization. Once that decision is made and the organization name is selected, it cannot be changed! In Figure 4.6, the organization name is "lefkovics."

Figure 4.6 Exchange System Manager

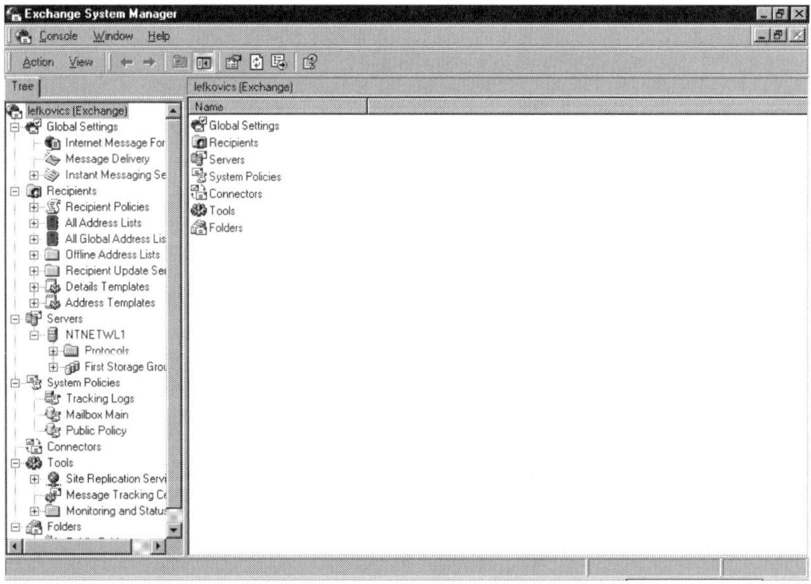

The Exchange System Manager snap-in contains several components required to administer your Exchange organization, as shown in Figure 4.6. We will review these components and how they are used for basic Exchange 2000 administration.

Global Settings represent system-wide configuration settings for your Exchange organization. Global settings are applied in messaging situations only when the equivalent settings on virtual servers or other AD objects are not configured.

The **Recipients** node in the AD Users and Computers console holds global settings for configuring recipient information and organization. You administer Recipient Policies and configure Address Lists and Templates using this section of the Exchange System Manager.

Under **Servers**, you have a list of Exchange servers and the ability to administer the various protocols and data storage on each of them. In Figure 4.6, you see there is only one Exchange Server (*ntnetwl1*) in the Organization *lefkovics*.

Within the **System Policies** node, you can configure any of the three types of system policies supported by Exchange 2000. System Policies can be applied to servers, mailbox stores, and public folder stores.

The **Connector** node allows you to add new SMTP or X400 connectors, as well as connectors to other messaging platforms, such as Lotus Notes or Novell Groupwise.

Message Tracking and Monitoring Tools, located in the **Tools** folder, are good troubleshooting assets should e-mail delivery come into question.

The **Folders** node allows you to administer Public Folders from the System Manager if required, including replication, addressing and folder restrictions.

Administering Users, Contacts, and Groups

As previously noted, administrative tasks in Exchange 2000 can be separated to user administration and server administration. We will start with managing the individual users and address the more global server and organization configurations later in this section.

Within Active Directory, you can categorize objects using logical containers called Organizational Units (OUs). In Figure 4.4, we created containers called Sales, Human Resources and Exchange 2000. In the real world, OUs might be based on department, geographic location or even object type, such as Contacts and Distribution Groups. You can use Organizational Units to control access to objects, assign group policy, or delegate administrative duties at a container level. However you choose to group AD objects with OUs, Exchange 2000 is not affected. In legacy versions of Exchange it was an arduous task to migrate mailboxes between containers, but with Exchange 2000, you can even drag and drop mail-enabled and mailbox-enabled objects between Organizational Units.

NOTE

The Organizational Unit (OU) hierarchy is not reflected in the Exchange 2000 Address Book.

As administrators at the recipient object level, we face many tasks on a regular basis. This chapter will cover these basic tasks:

1. Create a mailbox-enabled user.
2. Edit user account properties.
3. Mailbox-enable an existing user account.
4. Create mail-enabled contacts.
5. Create distribution groups.
6. Mail-enable an existing security group.

Probably the most common tasks required of the typical e-mail administrator would fall in the category of managing user information, from mailbox configuration to contacts and groups membership. Before initiating this discussion, let's review the terminology associated with recipient objects. Some terms used in previous versions of Microsoft Exchange Server have changed, as summarized in Table 4.2.

Table 4.2 Summary of Recipient Object Terminology from Legacy Exchange Versions

Term from Legacy Exchange Version	Equivalent Exchange 2000 Terminology
Mailbox	Mailbox-Enabled User
Distribution List	Mail-Enabled Group
Custom Recipient	Mail-Enabled User or Contact

Users, Contacts, and Groups are all recipient objects in the Active Directory. Recipient objects can be mail-enabled or mailbox-enabled.

Mailbox-enabled recipients are users with an associated mailbox and e-mail address; as such, they can send and receive e-mail messages.

Mail-enabled recipient objects, typically contacts or groups, have e-mail addresses, but no mailbox.

Consequently, mail-enabled objects can receive e-mail messages, but they are not able to store or send them. Messages sent to a mail-enabled recipient object are directed to the external e-mail address granted that recipient, much like custom recipients in Exchange 5.x. In the case of a mail-enabled group, an e-mail message is distributed to the members of the group.

Administering User Accounts

Like its predecessors, Exchange 2000 requires that mailboxes have a user account for authentication to resources. User accounts do not require mailboxes, of course, but mailboxes do require user accounts. A mailbox-enabled user account is probably the most common recipient in an Exchange organization. Most companies employ a naming standard for users, which you would need prior to creating a new user.

Creating Mailbox-Enabled User Accounts

We are going to use a real-world example to follow the step-by-step process for adding a new account. The legal department has just added a new corporate counsel, Carl P. Jacobson, to the company and has submitted a request for the systems administrator to create an account and mailbox for this new hire.

There are two ways to begin this process. In Active Directory Users and Computers, either right-click an existing user object or user template and choose Copy to start the *Copy Object User Wizard*, or select the container for the new user account, right-click and choose New | User to start the *New Object User Wizard*, as displayed in Figure 4.7. Remember, it is best to create OUs for your users. You can apply policies to them later.

Figure 4.7 New Object - User Wizard

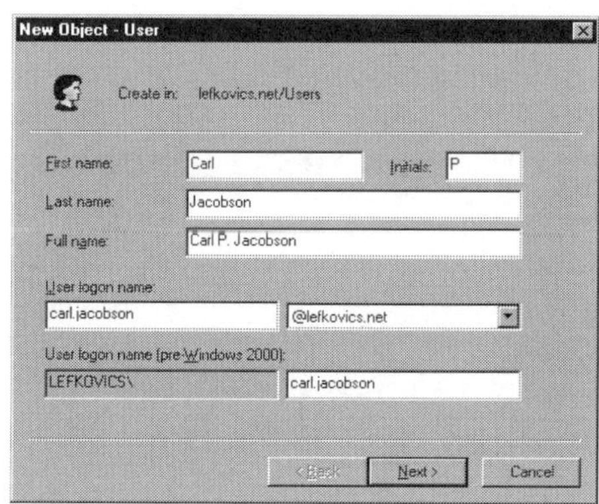

In our example, we have started the process to create a new user. The screen shown in Figure 4.7 is where you enter the name information, which should conform to the company's naming convention. The Full Name field is limited to 64 characters and, along with the login name, must be unique within the domain.

Next, you set the user's password for this new account, again based on company policy. For example, all new hires might be given a password initially with the requirement to change it upon first logon (see Figure 4.8).

Figure 4.8 Setting New User Password Information

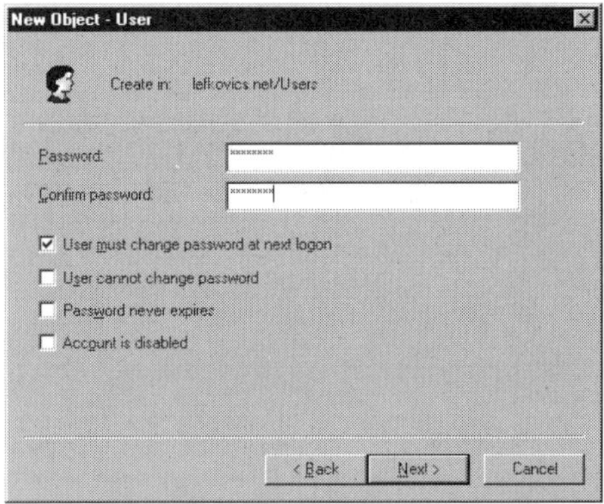

After you click Next, you come to the point where you can create an Exchange mailbox, as shown in Figure 4.9. By checking the box beside Create an Exchange Mailbox, you are creating a mailbox-enabled user account. If your Exchange organizations had multiple Exchange Servers, with multiple mailbox stores, the exact location for this mailbox could be selected at this point using the drop-down menus.

Figure 4.9 Create an Exchange Mailbox for a New User

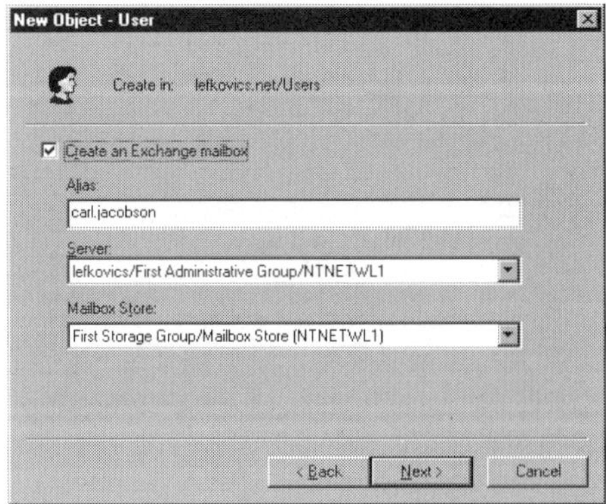

After choosing to create an Exchange mailbox for your new corporate counsel, you can click Next again to generate your new user account. A confirmation screen will summarize some properties for your new user, indeed showing that an Exchange mailbox will be created (see Figure 4.10). SMTP and X400 addresses for your new mailbox-enabled user account will be automatically created. E-mail addresses for any of the connectors to other messaging systems that have been configured will also be created at this time. The newly created account for Carl P. Jacobson will now appear in the AD Users and Accounts console, under the container *Users* in our example.

Figure 4.10 New User Account Creation Summary

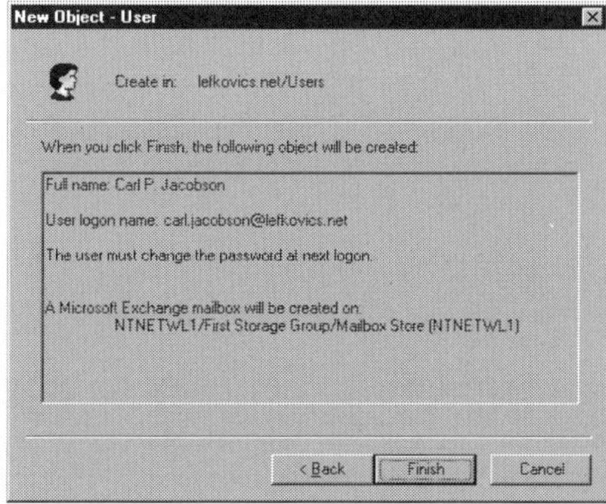

Configuring User Account Properties

After creating a new user account, you have other configuration information to update. We will go through a few of the Properties tabs on your new user account to enter Exchange-related attributes.

General User Account Properties

In this screen you can edit a user's name and display name as well as a few other fields. Most of the fields in these Properties tabs can be used as attributes to filter for Address List creation or other Lightweight Directory Access Protocol (LDAP) queries. The Description field in the General tab (seen in Figure 4.11) by default appears in the main windows of AD Users and Computers console. The e-mail and Web page fields are required to employ the Send Mail or Open Home Page action in a user or group in AD Users and Computers. The telephone number represents the user's primary work number, and the Telephones tab provides options for any other contact numbers.

Figure 4.11 General Tab of User Account Properties

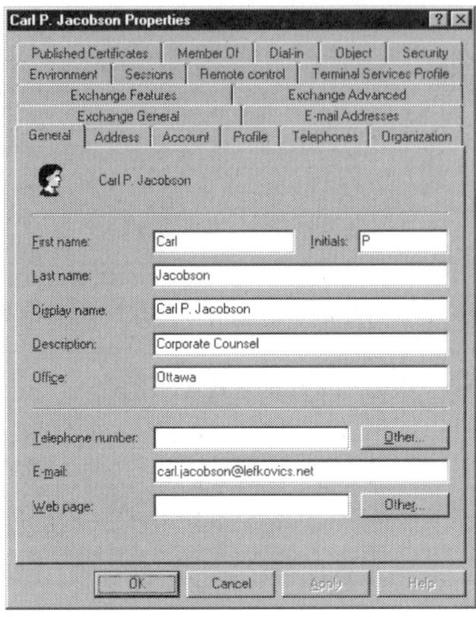

Entering Address Information in User Account Properties

Address information is entered in the self-explanatory fields in this window, shown in Figure 4.12. It should be noted that personal information entered into a user account is replicated across the AD and accessible by anyone with the appropriate permissions. Access to this information should probably be regulated by company policy.

Figure 4.12 Address Information in User Account Properties

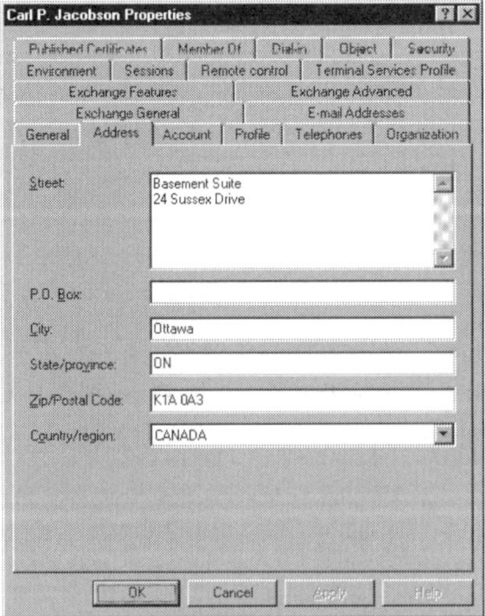

Other User Account Property Tabs

The Telephones tab contains fields that allow many different contact numbers for your user account. These include home numbers, mobile phone numbers, pager numbers, fax numbers, and voice-over-IP number. The Organization tab allows for other useful company attributes, such as Title, Department, and Company—each beneficial to the creation of address lists based in specific criteria, as you will see later in the section entitled "Creating Online Address Lists."

Configuring Exchange General Tab in User Account Properties

There are four main settings you can configure from the Exchange General tab of a user account's Properties settings, as shown in Figure 4.13: Exchange Alias, Delivery Restrictions, Delivery Options, and Storage Limits.

Figure 4.13 Exchange General Tab in User Account Properties

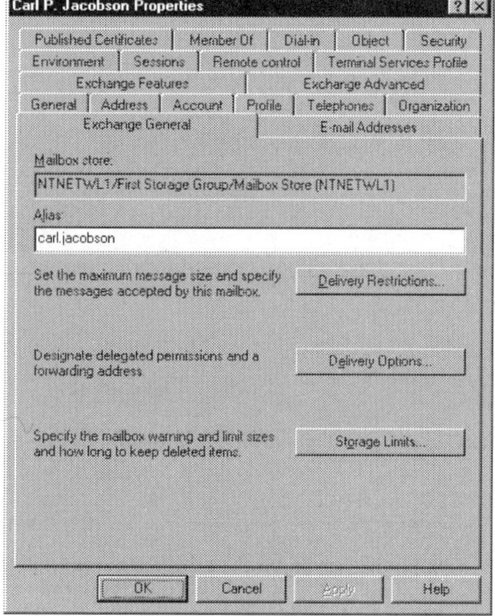

Every mailbox-enabled user account requires an Exchange Alias. The Exchange Alias is used in creation of the SMTP address, and if applicable, the MSMail address. If a user has a name change, you would update the user's name, their Display Name, which is used for X400 address creation, and their Exchange Alias.

NOTE

Even though you can set attributes for an individual user account, Organizational Units in most cases can be used to group users for whom settings will be the same, and applied using a group policy.

You also configure any user-specific delivery restrictions here, as shown in Figure 4.14. You can limit the incoming and outgoing message size. For our new user, we have set limits of 10,000 KB, or just under 10 MB. You should pay special attention to the units Microsoft has chosen for this attribute. I have seen people enter "5" intending "5,000." Individual delivery restrictions override global restrictions. E-mail messages exceeding the size restriction entered here will be returned as undeliverable and a Non-Delivery Report (NDR) will be generated and returned to the sender, with a copy sent to the postmaster. We will indicate an administrative account for NDRs when we configure our SMTP Virtual Server later in this chapter.

Figure 4.14 User Account Delivery Restrictions

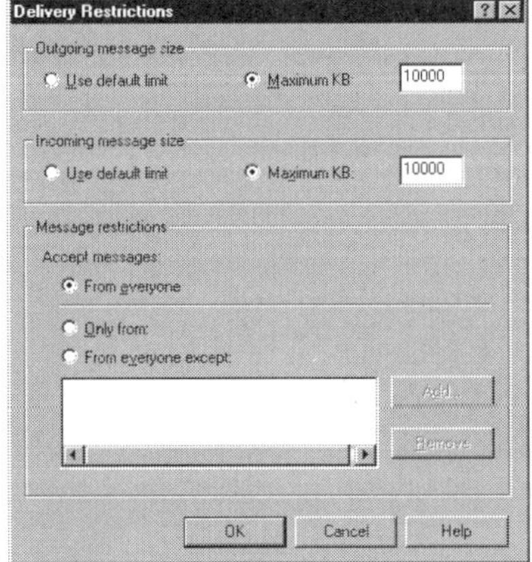

You can also limit message delivery to this recipient from other mail-enabled recipients in the AD, should that be required. By default, a mailbox-enabled user can receive e-mail from anyone.

The next button in the Exchange General dialog box presents other Delivery Options to configure for your new user. As shown in Figure 4.15, you can delegate access to this user's mailbox to another mailbox-enabled user in the organization. Adding users to this field grants them access to view the mailbox, as well as send e-mail on behalf of the user account associated with this mailbox.

Figure 4.15 User Account Delivery Options

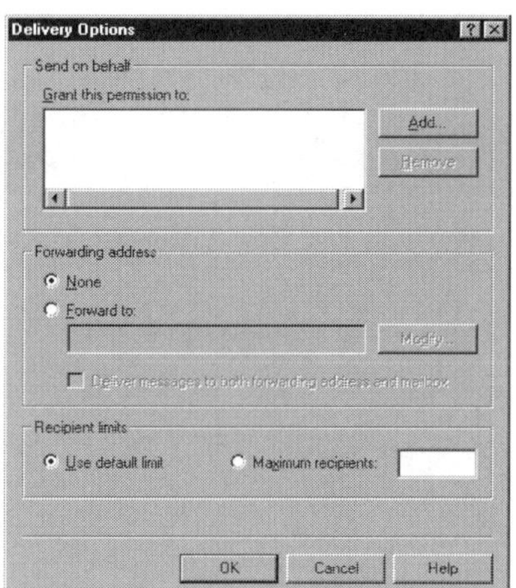

From the Delivery Options applet, you can also configure e-mail forwarding for this mailbox. E-mail can be forwarded to another mailbox-enabled or mail-enabled recipient in the organization. In legacy Exchange, you used a custom recipient for external mail forwarding; a mail-enabled contact with an external e-mail address in Exchange 2000 provides the same result. You have the option of keeping a copy of forwarded messages in this mailbox as well. Reselecting the None radio button will of course remove any forwarding settings you apply.

It may be beneficial in some organizations to limit the number of recipients a mailbox-enabled user can send to in any given e-mail. This restriction can prevent large mailstorms causing unnecessary server stress because a user decided to send a document to every user and group they could locate. *Recipients* in this case refers to the sum of users listed on the To:, Cc:, and Bcc: lines of an e-mail message. Setting a specific recipient limit here will override the global default of 5000.

You can also assess mailbox storage limits from the Exchange General tab. As displayed in Figure 4.16, applying mailbox size limits is very similar to previous versions of Exchange. Limits assigned an individual mailbox override global settings. For our new user, we have set Exchange to issue a warning e-mail daily if this user maintains a mailbox exceeding 50,000 KB. We have also assessed a restriction preventing this user from sending e-mail should his mailbox size exceed 100,000 KB. We have chosen to leave the Prohibit Send and Receive field blank, as we don't want NDRs returned to people e-mailing this user.

When an item is deleted from Outlook at the client, and then emptied from the deleted items folder at the client, the item still remains hidden in the mailbox store. The item remains hidden in the store for the period called the Deleted Item Retention Period. During this time period, a deleted item does not count against the mailbox storage limits and can still be recovered by the client if needed. We have chosen to override the deleted item retention period assigned to the mailbox store hosting this mailbox and apply a limit of 60 days to keep deleted items hidden.

Figure 4.16 Storage Limits

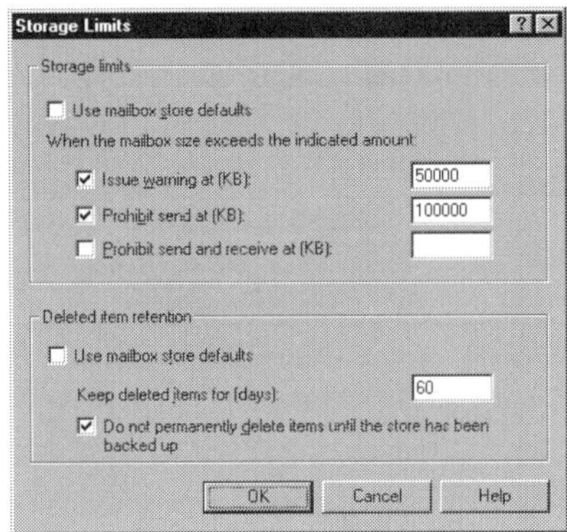

There is a final checkbox to ensure items are not permanently deleted until they are backed up, so that any item deleted finds its way to at least one backup set.

Enabling Other Exchange Features

Other Exchange 2000 features can be enabled from the Exchange Features tab of the mailbox-enabled user account properties, shown in Figure 4.17. The most likely option would be the Instant Messaging (IM) implementation within Exchange 2000. You can enable Instant Messaging from this tab, or by using the Exchange Task Wizard discussed in the next section. To enable Instant Messaging, you must know the Exchange Server that is running Instant Messaging and the Instant Messaging domain.

Configuring Alternate E-Mail Addresses for a Single User

In many organizations, there may be a need to assign an e-mail alias to an existing mailbox-enabled user account. Examples of this need might be a neutral inquiry address from a Website such as inquiry@domain.com, or a discrete address for the Human Resources Director to receive resumes, such as jobs@domain.com. In our example, we have added a generic SMTP address for legal questions as an alias. Inbound SMTP mail addressed to legal@lefkovics.net will now be routed to Carl P. Jacobson.

Figure 4.17 Exchange Features

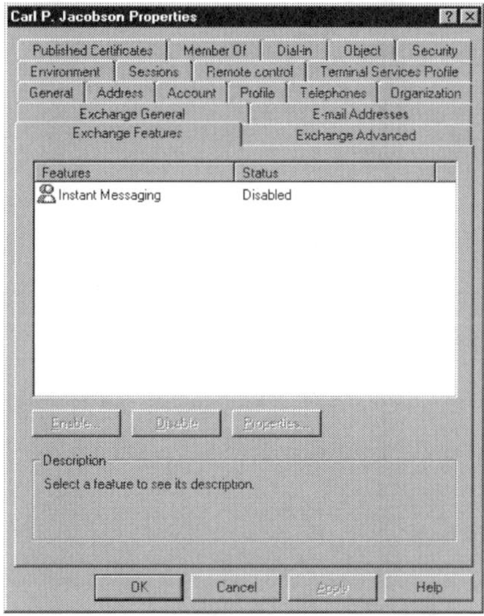

You add new addresses by selecting the New button at the bottom of the E-Mail Addresses tab in the mailbox-enabled user account properties (see Figure 4.18). You are then presented with a dialog box indicating the various address types you can add as aliases (see Figure 4.19).

Figure 4.18 E-Mail Addresses Tab

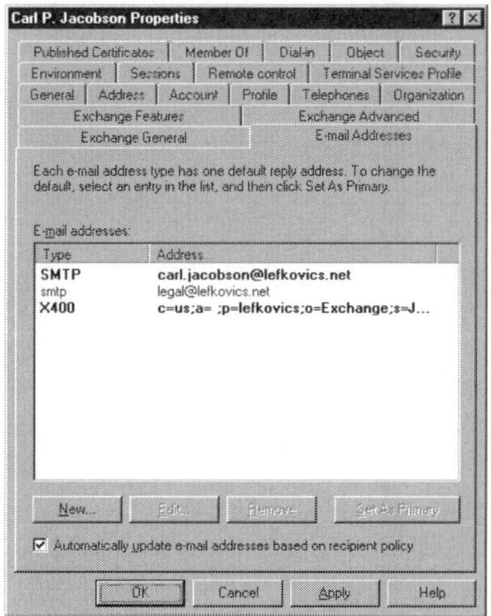

Recipient objects are not limited to a single e-mail address; however, they can only have one primary reply address per address type, which will display in bold font in the e-mail addresses tab. Here in Figure 4.19, the default SMTP reply address is set as carl.jacobson@lefkovics.net, which is what e-mail recipients will see in the To: field of their e-mail client when they reply to an e-mail from Mr. Jacobson. The default reply address can be changed by selecting an alternative address in the list, and clicking the Set as Primary button. This would be a typical step when a user has submitted a name change.

Figure 4.19 Selecting New E-Mail Address Type

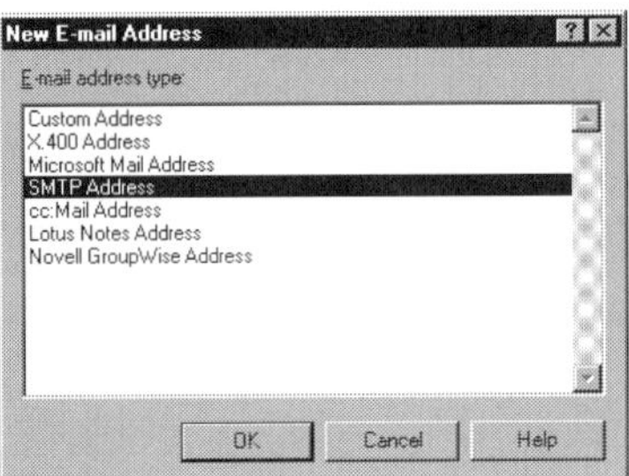

To add an additional SMTP address to this user account, you select SMTP address and click OK. Enter the full Internet address to be assigned to this user (see Figure 4.20). This address must be unique across the directory. Some all-purpose administrators can be overloaded with many different ones, from postmaster to hostmaster.

Figure 4.20 Entering New Internet E-Mail Alias

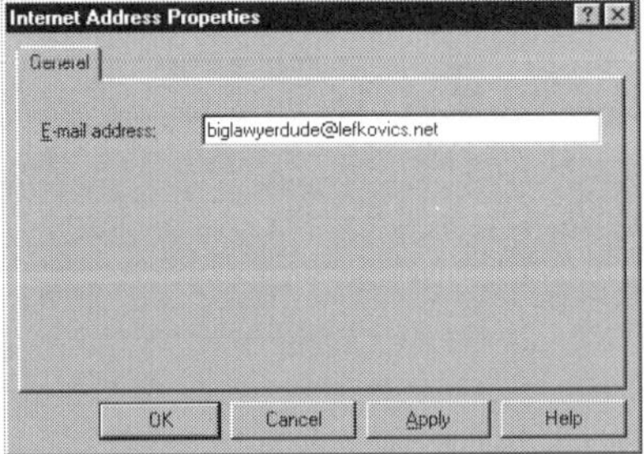

Configuring Settings in the Exchange Advanced Tab

The last user configuration tab we will review is the Exchange Advanced tab (Figure 4.21). The Simple Display Name here is meant for non-ANSI characters, specifically for systems that may be unable to read the regular display name for this user account.

Figure 4.21 Exchange Advanced Tab

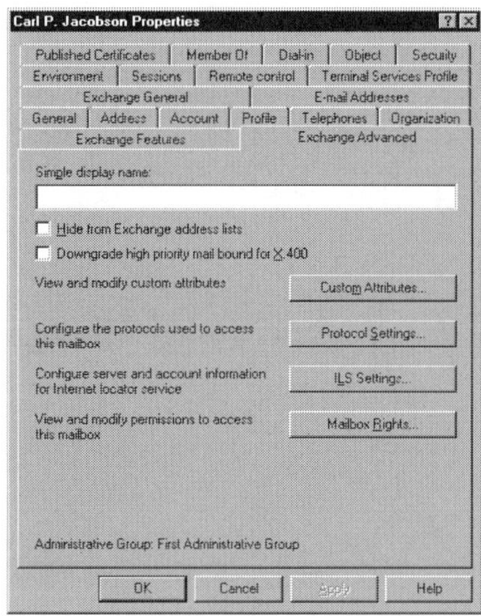

From this tab, you have the option of hiding this user from address lists, by checking the box accordingly. You cannot select which specific address list to hide the user from. This is a good feature for users who have just left the company, when you do not want to delete their mailbox immediately.

You can also configure certain protocol properties at the user level. If Post Office Protocol v3 (POP3) and Internet Message Access Protocol v4 (IMAP4) are enabled for all users, then they will be listed by default in the Protocol Settings dialog box, as shown in Figure 4.22. You can disable individual protocols at the user level, by selecting the specific protocol,

Figure 4.22 Protocol Settings

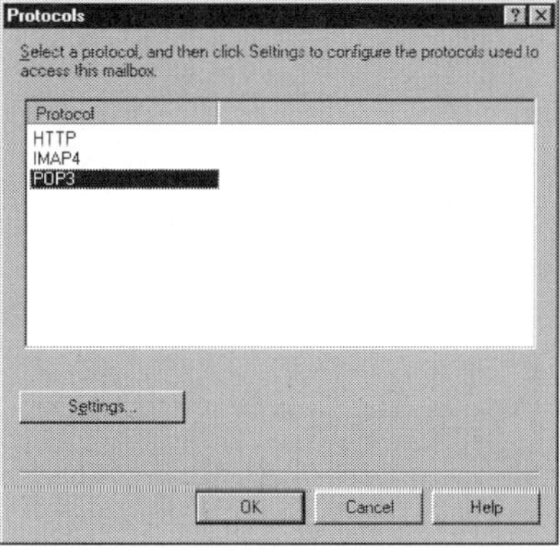

such as POP3, and clicking the Settings button. Then you deselect the appropriate checkbox in the Details dialog applet (see Figure 4.23). Here you can also override the message encoding defaults for the protocol.

Figure 4.23 Protocol Details

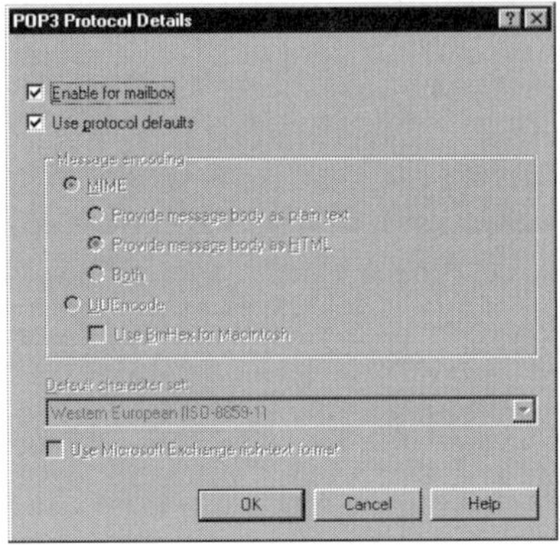

The last configuration setting we will cover in the Exchange Advanced Tab hides behind the Mailbox Rights button (see Figure 4.24). For our new user, we have opened the Permissions applet by selecting Mailbox Rights in the Exchange Advanced tab. From here you can add specific permissions to other users or groups to access this mailbox. Granting full mailbox access to another user here would allow that user to open that mailbox and perform all duties, including deleting information, by adding it to their profile in Outlook.

Figure 4.24 Mailbox Rights

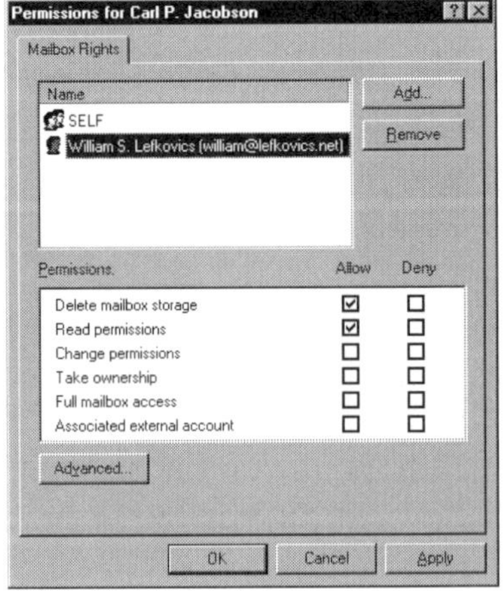

Our new Corporate Counsel, Carl P. Jacobson, is now configured and ready to use Exchange 2000. Changing attributes for new users like this should really be exceptions to the normal company defaults and should be limited for simplicity. Due to the high number of contracts amendments that a lawyer might send and receive, he may require a higher limit on individual e-mail size and mailbox storage than the normal defaults. Typically you need to maintain global settings that fit the majority of users and keep logical Organizational Units for applying group policies with these settings.

Mailbox-Enabling an Existing User Account

In some companies some users may not require a mailbox for their position. At any time, however, you can mailbox-enable an existing user or group of users. You do this by selecting the user(s) for whom you wish to create a mailbox in AD Users and Computers. You then choose Exchange Tasks in the right-click menu to start the Exchange Task Wizard, as shown in Figure 4.25.

Figure 4.25 Exchange Task Wizard

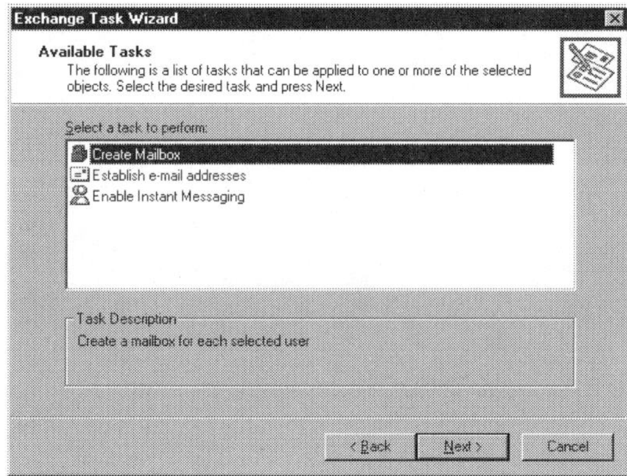

Selecting Create Mailbox and clicking Next will essentially take you back to the Create an Exchange Mailbox option you saw when you created a new user from scratch.

The Exchange Task Wizard also lets you just mail-enable the user. Mail-enabling a user is applicable for someone like a consultant, who needs to be authenticated to your domain for other work, but does not require a local mailbox. If you mail-enable the user, you can add an external e-mail address allowing him or her to be visible in address lists and work like a custom recipient in legacy Exchange with any e-mail directed to his or her external e-mail address.

Administering Contacts

In Exchange 2000, a contact created within the Active Directory is simply a person or entity that your organization needs to communicate with. A contact can have an external e-mail address and thus be mail-enabled and serve much like a custom recipient in legacy Exchange. A mail-enabled contact can then be included in Address Lists, as discussed later in this chapter in the section called Administering Address Lists.

Creating Mail-Enabled Contacts

When you need to include people who are not part of your domain in regular e-mail communications accessible by multiple users, it is beneficial to store them as mail-enabled contacts.

As our example for a new mail-enabled contact, we will add a fictitious bank manager contact, Galvin Yee of First National Bank, for our company. To create mail-enabled contacts:

1. Open AD Users and Computers.

2. Select the folder or organizational unit where you want this contact created.

3. Right-click and choose New | Contact to open the New Object window (see Figure 4.26).

Figure 4.26 New Object - Contact

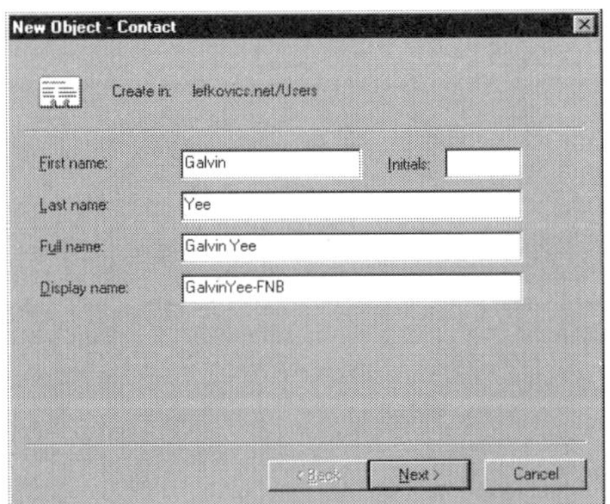

4. Enter the name and display name, which identifies the contact in the Global Address List (GAL).

5. Click Next to advance to the next window.

6. Enter the external e-mail address of this user. By clicking the Modify button, you can choose the type of address and then enter that address in full, as displayed in Figure 4.27.

Figure 4.27 Adding E-Mail Address to New Contact

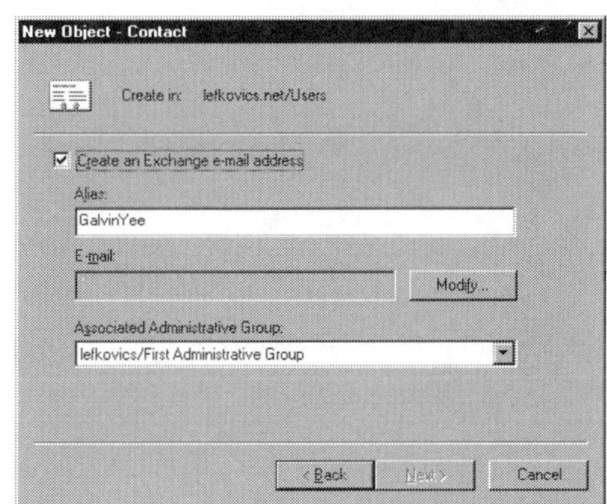

7. Click Next and Finish, which adds this new mail-enabled contact to the AD.

As you saw with a new user account, creation of the recipient object is not the last step. There are many properties for this contact that may need configuring as well (see Figure 4.28).

Figure 4.28 Properties for Mail-Enabled Contact

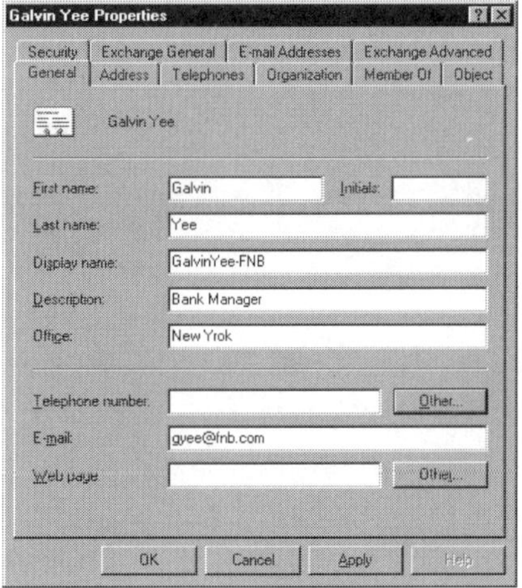

Again as in a user account, the attributes you complete for a mail-enabled contact can assist you in Address List generation and possibly other LDAP queries of the AD. The Address and Telephone tabs provide options for including specific contact information, much like a new user account. You can also hide this contact from the any address lists by checking the appropriate box in the Exchange Advanced tab.

Configuring the Exchange General Properties of a Mail-Enabled Contact

It is likely within an organization that a mail-enabled contact need not be accessible to all users. You can configure certain limitations for a mail-enabled contact, much as you did for a new user account.

You can apply a message size limit in the Exchange General tab. Figure 4.29 shows a case where a limit of 1,000 KB is selected. Messages exceeding this size will be returned to the sender with an NDR.

In our example, the bank manager only needs to receive e-mail from two people. You also configure this from the Exchange Tab of the Contact Properties (see Figure 4.29) by clicking Add and choosing the users or groups from whom this contact can receive e-mail messages.

Figure 4.29 Exchange General Tab

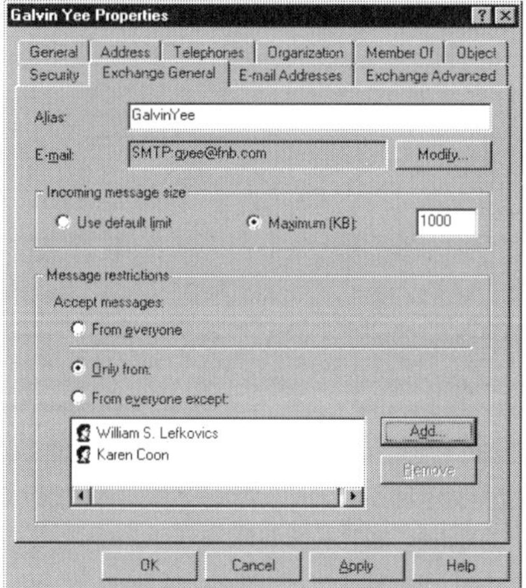

Configuring Alternate E-Mail Addresses for a Mail-Enabled Contact

A mail-enabled contact can have multiple e-mail addresses associated with it. You configure this using the E-Mail Addresses tab. For our example, we added another SMTP address, as shown in Figure 4.30.

Mail-enabled contacts are also automatically endowed with an X400 address and have the ability to activate addresses for any of the cross-platform mail connectors that have been installed and configured.

Figure 4.30 E-Mail Addresses Tab for New Contact

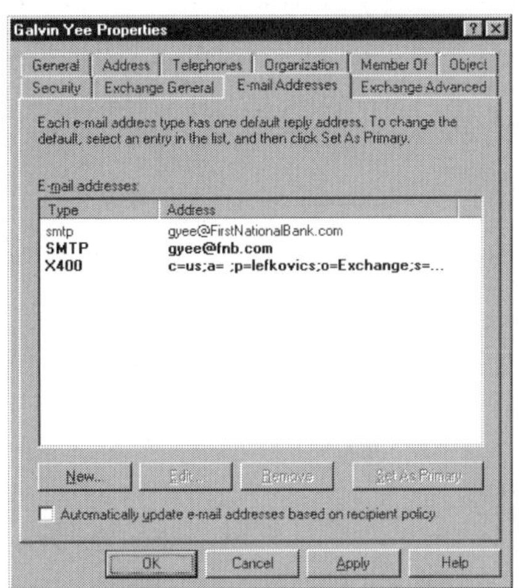

Administering Groups in Exchange 2000

As existed in NT, a *group* is a logical collection of users or objects with similar properties to simplify components of administration. The application of groups for the purposes of administering Exchange 2000 is slightly different and a very valuable tool.

Considering Administrative and Routing Groups

In legacy versions of Exchange Server, logical administrative entities were somewhat segregated using sites. Exchange 2000 leverages two special types of groups— *Administrative Groups* and *Routing Groups*—which, in concept, replace the use of sites.

Administrative Groups contain logical collections of Exchange objects that share the same levels of permissions, and can include any number of servers, server policies, routing groups, monitors, public folder trees, conferencing servers, and chat networks. The objects allocated to an Administrative Group may be considered for geographical, departmental, or perhaps political reasons, depending on your organization. As you add objects to a certain administrative group, those objects are granted the permissions of that group. In this manner, you can delegate specific server administration, routing management, and other Exchange-related administration to certain administrators. This same process allows you to limit those administrators to the permissions in that Administrative Group.

> **NOTE**
>
> Within the Administrative Groups container in Exchange System Manager, each legacy Exchange site connected to your Exchange 2000 organization would show its own administrative group and display a white folder icon.

Routing Groups are defined simply as collections of well-connected Exchange servers. Exchange servers contained within a routing group are assumed to be able to make quality point-to-point connectivity with each other at any time, much like what we expect in Exchange 5.x site topology. Connectivity between routing groups requires a bridgehead-to-bridgehead connector, such as a Routing Group Connector, analogous to the Exchange 5.x Site Connector. In Figure 4.31, two routing groups are connected—Bridgehead server to Bridgehead server—using a Routing Group Connector.

Figure 4.31 Basic Bridgehead-to-Bridgehead Topology

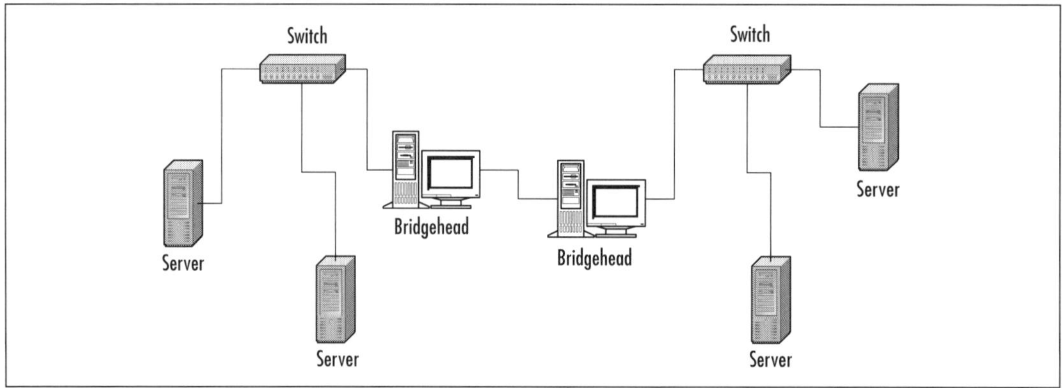

By default, the Administrative Group and subsequent Routing Group containers are not visible in the Exchange System Manager because they could be considered advanced tools for larger organizations. Companies with one or two Exchange servers would likely not require multiple administrative or routing groups. To display these containers, you must view the Properties screen for the Exchange organization atop the hierarchy in Exchange System Manager and select the checkboxes as shown in Figure 4.32. We will review and discuss further the use of Administrative and Routing groups for Exchange later in Chapter 6.

Figure 4.32 Displaying Administrative and Routing Groups in Exchange System Manager

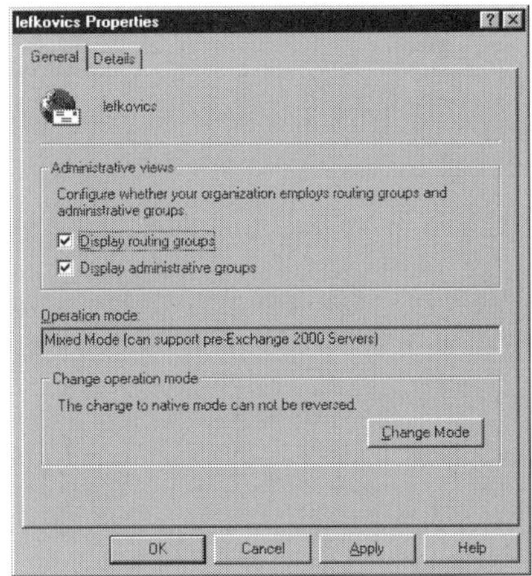

Both Windows 2000 and Exchange 2000 have two separate and independent modes. Native mode enables the product to take advantage of its full set of features while mixed mode allows for backwards compatibility to earlier versions.

When operating in mixed mode, Exchange 2000 follows the site concept you are familiar with in legacy Exchange versions, for both administration and routing issues. Each site represents a single routing group and moving objects between sites is not a simple step. Mixed mode limits your use of Active Directory to accommodate the read-only components of Exchange 5.5 that are replicated via the Active Directory Connector. Switching to native mode removes these limitations.

As you learned in Chapter 2, recipient objects can be connected to Active Directory and migrated to Exchange 2000. When you are finished with Exchange 5.5, you can convert to native mode in Exchange 2000 to leverage Active Directory's scalability and allow more routing and administrative options. The move from mixed to native modes is as simple as clicking a button (see Figure 4.32)—but be warned, it's not reversible.

Managing Security and Distribution Groups

In Windows NT we worked with Global groups and Local groups, which were configurable to restrict or grant access to resources. Legacy Exchange was equipped with Distribution Lists, which were mainly used to send messages to multiple people using a single address, and also to control access to public folders.

Now that the Exchange Directory Services is incorporated into Windows 2000 Active Directory, Windows 2000 Groups can be used as e-mail distribution lists and can control access to resources, eliminating potential duplication of tasks.

Rather than reproducing the membership of a Windows security group into a distribution list, you can selectively mail-enable Security Groups, including the built-in groups that you want to serve as e-mail distribution lists. Creating groups offers further administrative flexibility, yet poses another challenge by providing various scopes for group deployment, as outlined in Table 4.3. Universal Scope requires Windows 2000 to be in native mode, so the operating system and Exchange can take advantage of the scalability of Active Directory.

Table 4.3 Group Scopes

Scope	Native Mode	Mixed Mode	Group Membership
Domain Local Scope	Supports membership of accounts, global scope groups from any domain, and domain local groups from the same domain	Only supports accounts from global groups, but from any domain	Can be a member of another domain local group within the same domain Permissions can only be assigned to public folders of local domain.
Global Scope	Only supports accounts and global groups from the same domain	Only accounts from the same domain	Can be placed in any other group in any domain
Universal Scope	Supports accounts and groups from any domain	Cannot create Securily groups in this scope while in mixed mode	Can be placed in other groups

A very simplified example for Group Scope usage might be to use Universal Scope for groups of objects that need access to things from all areas of the forest. You would use Global Scope for objects that need permissions across domain boundaries. Alternatively, you would select Domain Local Scope to assign permissions to resources within a single domain.

To create a new Security or Distribution Group for Exchange 2000:

1. Open AD Users and Computers and navigate to the folder in which you want the group to reside.

2. Right-click the folder and choose New | Group; you will see the screen in Figure 4.33.

Figure 4.33 New Object - Group

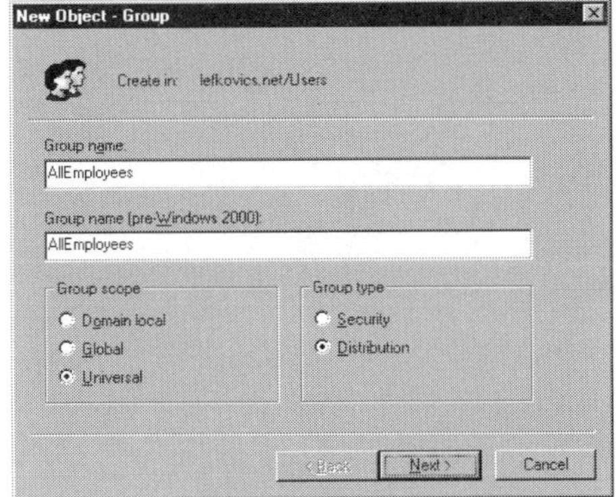

3. Enter the name of the group, then select the type of group and the scope to which this group applies. For our example, we have chosen a group type Distribution with a Universal Scope.

4. After clicking Next, you can assign the Exchange e-mail address, which is by default the group name. In our example, as shown in Figure 4.34, the e-mail address is AllEmployees@lefkovics.net.

5. Click Next and Finish to create your new group.

Figure 4.34 Assigning Exchange Address to the Group

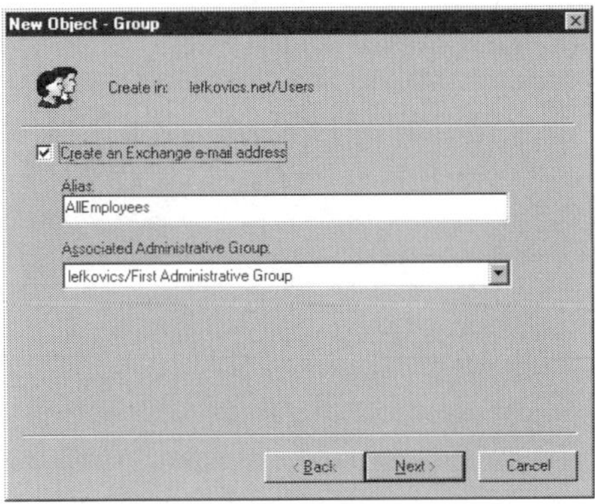

Your new group will now appear in the folder in which you created it; however, you still need to complete a few configurations in order to grant it some functionality. If you double-click the group (or right-click and choose

Properties) you can configure the properties of your group. Opening the properties of your distribution group, you see in the General tab the group name and e-mail address, as shown in Figure 4.35.

Figure 4.35 General Tab of Group Properties

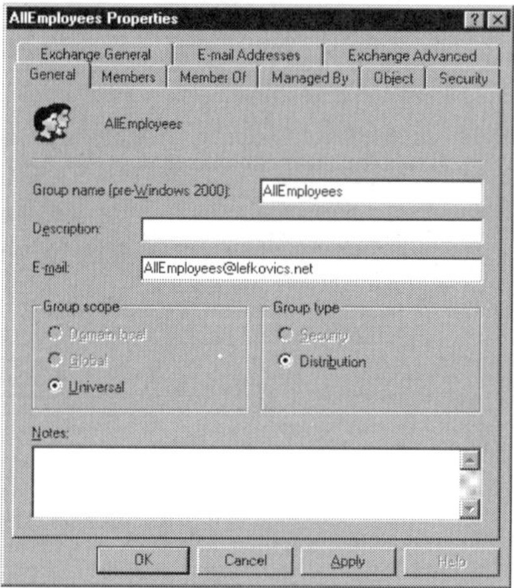

To add members to this group (which should be other mail-enabled groups because this example falls in the Universal Scope), you select the Members tab. Figure 4.36 shows a list of regional groups you have already added to this Distribution Group. You can click the Add button to display a list of objects that can be added, and select individual accounts or appropriate groups.

Figure 4.36 Adding Members to Group

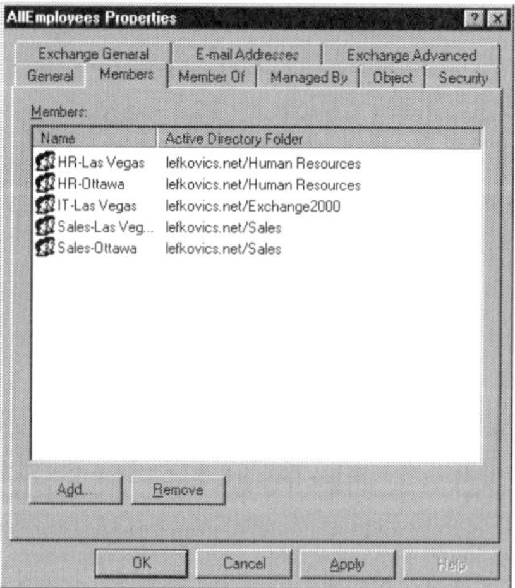

You can also set certain restrictions on both mail-enabled security and distribution groups starting with the Exchange General tab of the group properties. As shown in Figure 4.37, you can set the maximum message size for any e-mails going to a group in KB. In our example, we have limited e-mails to 5,000 KB and we have also prohibited Plant Workers from e-mailing to AllEmployees. Also from the Exchange General Tab, you can change the Exchange Alias for a group. This will generate additional e-mail addresses as outlined in recipient policy.

Figure 4.37 Exchange General Tab of Group Properties

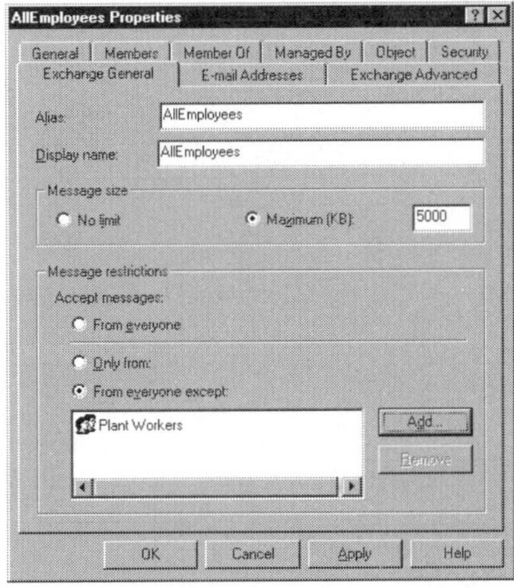

The generation of e-mail addresses for mail-enabled objects is driven by recipient policy. In the e-mail addresses tab, you can see the default addresses for objects as SMTP and X400 (Figure 4.38). This box would also include other addresses for installed and properly configured connectors if they were present.

There are other advanced settings you can add using the Exchange Advanced tab, as shown in Figure 4.39. Here, you can hide this group from Address Lists so it will not be displayed. Users with appropriate permissions will still be able to send e-mail to the group by addressing it by exact SMTP address. You can configure addresses to which reports should be sent in the event of delivery failures. You can also select servers that may be more suitable for expansion of groups for e-mail delivery.

Mail-Enabling an Existing Security Group

It is possible that in the past you may have deployed Windows 2000 security groups that did not have to serve as a distribution list and subsequently,

Figure 4.38 E-Mail Addresses Tab in Group Properties

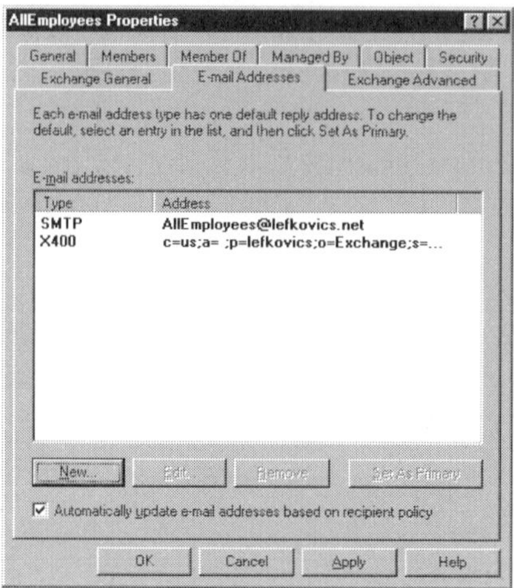

Figure 4.39 Exchange Advanced Tab in Group Properties

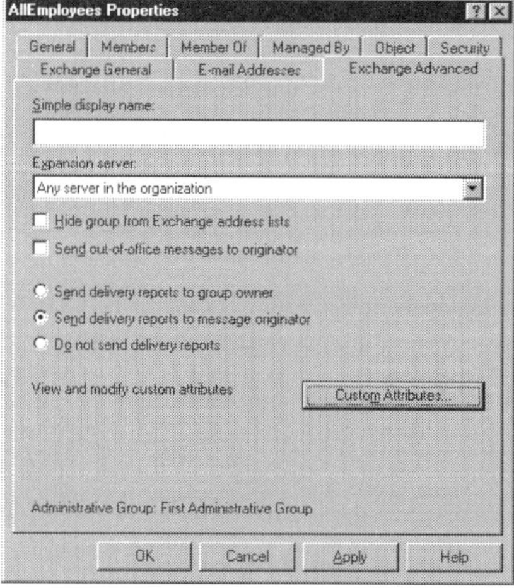

never had an Exchange alias assigned. You are able to mail-enable such existing groups to serve updated requirements. For example, perhaps workers in our call center in Las Vegas formerly required access to specific resources only, but we now need more timely communication with them.

To mail-enable a pre-existing group, activate the Exchange Task Wizard (Figure 4.40) by right-clicking the particular group for which you want to establish an e-mail address and select Exchange Tasks. From the wizard, you can request the addition of a new address, which will allow you to enter an alias for this group.

Figure 4.40 Exchange Task Wizard

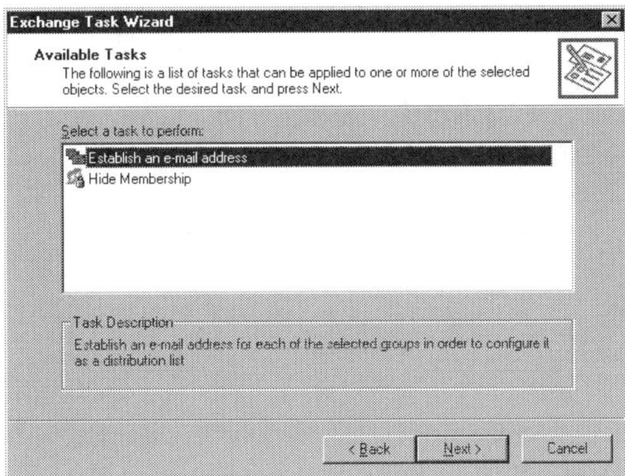

In this example, we are mail-enabling the security group entitled LasVegas and using that default as the Exchange alias (see Figure 4.41). This will grant the group the SMTP address of LasVegas@lefkovics.net.

Figure 4.41 Adding Exchange Alias

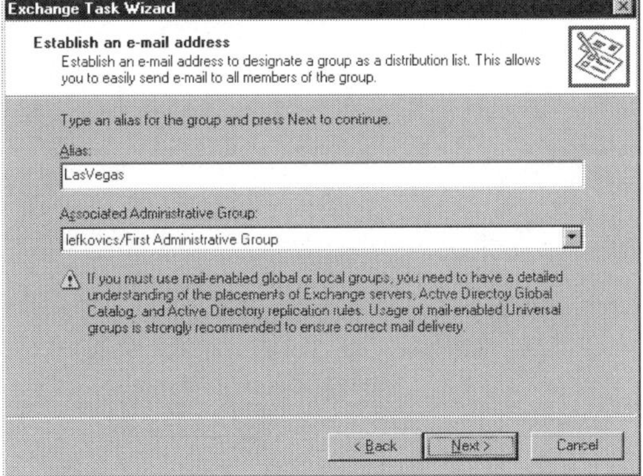

You then click Next and confirm the addition by clicking the Finish button. This Security Group now has an e-mail address that will receive any SMTP mail and distribute it to all of its mail-enabled membership.

Administering Exchange Server

So far, the chapter has focused on user management and the administration of recipient objects in general. As previously noted, the primary tool for administering global settings in Exchange 2000 is the Exchange System

Manager. As a rule, settings on individual objects override settings that apply to the organization as a whole. Ideally, those exceptions should be kept to a minimum to maintain a more organized administrative environment. It is easier to maintain groupings based on Organizational Units and policies than to maintain individual objects.

Configuring Exchange Global Settings

Within the Exchange System Manager, there are a few locations where you can configure how Exchange Server delivers e-mail. The Global Settings container grants you the ability to set blanket default settings across the organization. Objects that are configured to use default settings for e-mail conversion type and delivery restrictions will use the global settings.

In the Message Delivery Properties, under the Global Settings container within the Exchange System Manager, you can set the global settings for inbound and outbound message size. Any inbound or outbound e-mail exceeding these parameters will be returned to the sender as undeliverable. In Figure 4.42 we have set limits of 10,000 KB. In the same configuration screen you can control the global default value for the maximum number of recipients to whom an individual e-mail message can be addressed. In Figure 4.42 we have chosen to limit the number of recipient addresses to 100. These global settings can be configured through policies applied to groups, organizational units, or objects. If any mail-enabled object has not had a policy applied to it or an individual setting configured, then these default settings will be enforced.

Figure 4.42 Message Delivery Properties in Exchange System Manager

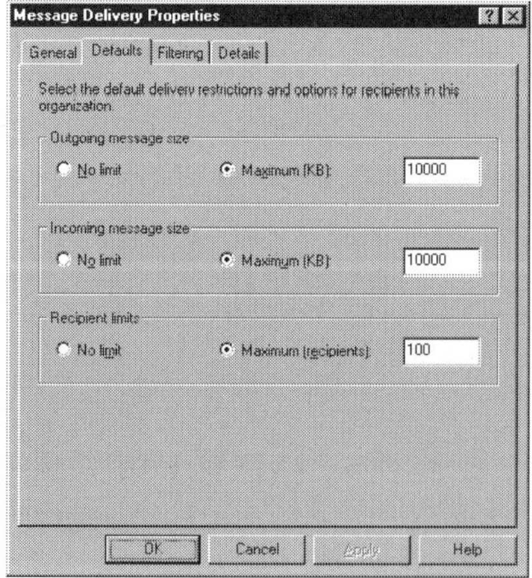

You are also able to configure message filtering, using the message delivery container properties. This setting, which is very similar to the message filtering option in Exchange 5.5 within the Internet Mail Services property pages, allows you to block inbound SMTP e-mail from specific domains or users. Figure 4.43 shows examples, including the format with which to add entries. You also have the option of sending an NDR back to the sender. If the Archive Filtered Messages is selected in the Filtering tab, then a folder will be created at the SMTP virtual server upon first receipt of an e-mail identified as one to be filtered. That folder will be located in the \\Exchsrvr\Mailroot\<vsi #>\Filter directory.

Figure 4.43 Message Filtering

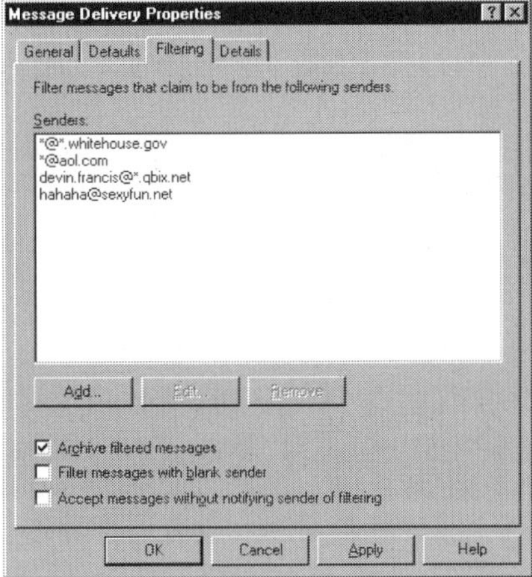

The last Global Setting we will look at is the configuration of Instant Messaging connectivity out of this server. As shown in Figure 4.44, you can indicate the presence of a Proxy Server and provide the appropriate Internet Protocol (IP) address and port. If you are passing through a firewall to connect your IM network to the Internet, then you can indicate the use of a firewall here as well.

Administering Address Lists

Exchange 2000 employs address lists to organize and present mail-enabled AD objects to clients. The address lists are kept up to date by a service called the Recipient Update Service (RUS), which runs pre-defined LDAP queries against the AD at regular, configurable intervals. Address lists are customizable and can be configured for both online and offline client access.

Figure 4.44 Instant Messaging Global Settings

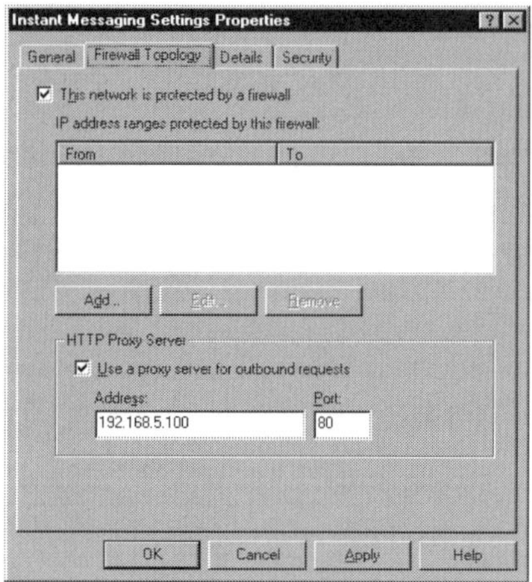

Managing Online Address Lists

In legacy versions of Exchange Server, you were able to take attributes common to a set of users and restrict clients' access to address book information based on these properties. These Address Book Views could be assigned in a client profile. Address lists in Exchange 2000 allow greater flexibility and ease of deployment. In this section we will discuss default address lists, how to create and configure address lists (including offline address lists), and how to control client access to address lists.

Default Address Lists

In legacy Exchange, the GAL is comprised of objects maintained within the Exchange Directory Services. When Exchange 2000 was installed, a set of default address lists was created, as displayed in Fig 4.45. For a small organization, the default lists probably provide sufficient functionality; however, larger deployments will find benefits for creating and customizing specific address lists. In Exchange 5.5, you were able to create Address Book Views (ABVs) by organizing directory entries into logical groupings and, in certain circumstances, limiting user access to unnecessary address list information. Address lists are more versatile in Exchange 2000, and easier to administer as well.

The basic contents of the default address lists are summarized in Table 4.4.

Figure 4.45 Exchange System Manager Showing Address Lists

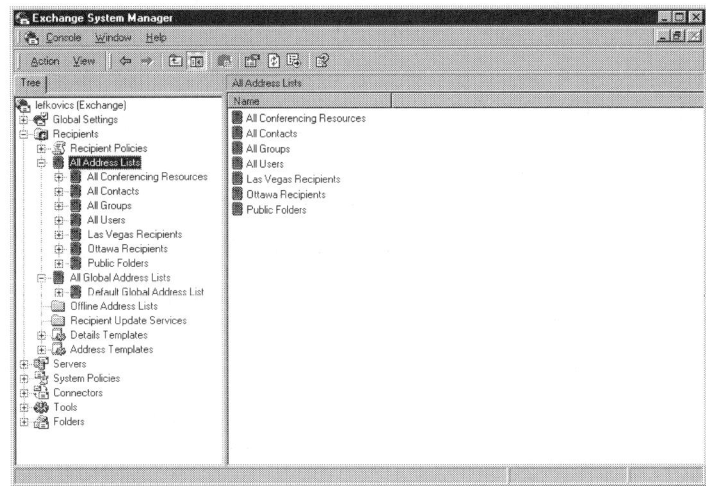

> **NOTE**
>
> Exchange 5.5 Address Book Views do not get migrated to Exchange 2000. Equivalent Custom Address Lists will have to be created to match the desired result.

Table 4.4 Default Address Lists

Default Address List	Address List Contents
All Conferencing Resources	Lists all conferencing resources within the organization
All Contacts	Lists all mail-enabled contacts within the organization
All Groups	Lists all mail-enabled groups within the organization
All Users	Lists all mail-enabled and mailbox-enabled users in the organization
Public Folders	Lists all the public folders in the organization
Default Global Address List	Lists all mail-enabled recipient objects, including Users, Contacts, and Groups. This list is synonymous with the legacy Exchange GAL
Default Offline Address List	Lists all mail-enabled recipient objects, allowing for client download for offline viewing

Creating Custom Address Lists

You can create custom address lists, based on a logical grouping of recipient objects by applying a filter on certain AD attributes. For example, you can create an address listing of recipients based on company department or perhaps office location.

To create a new address list specifically for the Ottawa office:

1. Start Exchange System Manager.
2. Navigate to the All Address Lists node, under Recipients.
3. Right-click and choose New | Address List.
4. It is best to select a logical name for this grouping, such as "Ottawa Recipients."
5. Click Filter Rules to set conditions for presentation in this list.
6. Select the Advanced tab and then click the Field button to reveal the numerous options.
7. In this case, select User and then City.
8. Set the Condition Field to "Is (exactly)" and the value to "Ottawa."
9. Click OK and Finish.

As you see in Figure 4.45, we selected a filter where the City attribute is exactly Ottawa. After completion, you will then see a new address list under the All Address Lists node in Exchange System Manager with the display title Ottawa Recipients. You have actually created a new preset LDAP query to the AD without entering any LDAP query code. If you look at the properties of the new address list you just created, it will show the actual LDAP entry to return the desired objects (see Figure 4.46). This new address list will be available to Outlook clients, in Corporate/Workgroup mode, the next time they open Outlook. This address list will continue to be updated as Ottawa users are added and deleted.

Editing and Removing Address Lists

Though you are unable to edit the properties of the default address lists installed with Exchange 2000, you can rename them or even delete them, though it might be useful to keep that master default Global Address List around if your users need to be able to search attributes of all other messaging recipients. You can amend the filter rules on the custom address lists that you created or rename the address list should another name be more suitable.

To modify the LDAP query statement for an address list:

Figure 4.46 Address List Properties showing LDAP Query

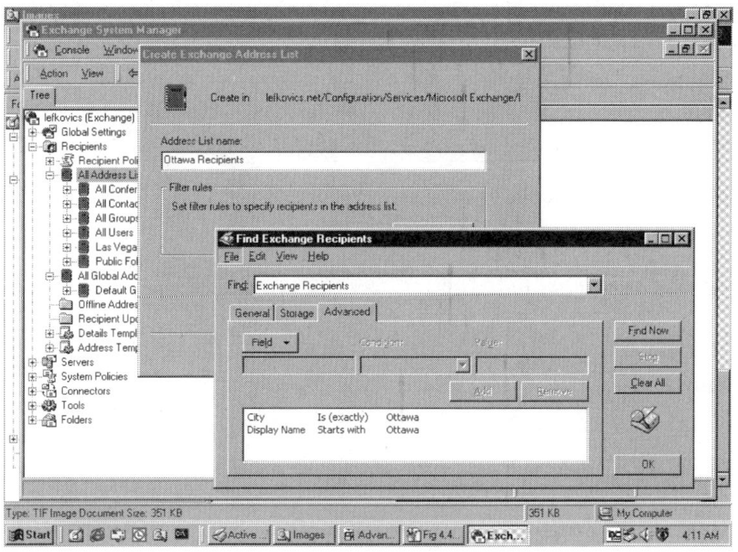

1. Open the Exchange System Manager.

2. Navigate to the specific address list that you need edited.

3. Right-click the address list and choose Properties.

4. Click the Modify button (see Figure 4.46) to get the screen to change the Filter Rules.

To rename an address list, open the Exchange System Manager and navigate to the specific address list under the Recipients node. Right-click and choose Rename, type the appropriate name change, and press Enter. In the same menu you see the option to delete as well.

NOTE

You must have a Recipient Update Service running for each domain that has recipients in the forest, or changes to attributes will not populate the Active Directory.

Address list changes across an enterprise are dependent on AD replication and the RUS. The RUS is integrated with the Exchange System Attendant and by default will verify list membership every ten minutes when set to Always Run. If your company was very stable and you had reason to minimize network traffic, you could adjust the frequency that the RUS queries for changes following a custom schedule.

You may need to access changes for your clients immediately. In this case, you can force RUS updates to expedite the replication process. To manually update custom address list changes:

1. Start the Exchange System Manager.

2. Navigate to Recipients | Recipient Update Service folder in the console tree.

3. When selecting the RUS folder, the update services are listed.

4. You can update the address list changes for the entire enterprise by selecting Recipient Update Services (Enterprise Configuration) or just a specific domain.

5. Right-click the update service and then select Update Now, as shown in Figure 4.47.

Figure 4.47 Manually Updating Address List Information

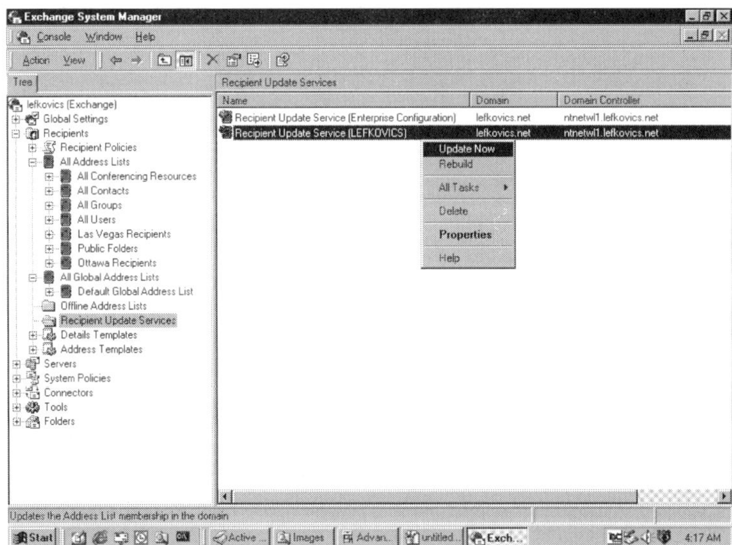

Setting Client Permissions for Online Address Lists

By default, our Exchange users have access to all of our address lists; however, depending on organizational requirements, this may not be preferred. To explicitly allow access to a group or user to an address list:

1. Start the Exchange System Manager.

2. Navigate to the specific address list for which you wish to adjust permissions under the Recipients node. This address list may be a default one or a custom list you created.

3. Right-click the address list and choose Properties.

4. Click the Security tab to view the permissions for this address list.

5. Ensure that Allow is checked beside Read Permissions for those groups or users that you wish to have access.

6. Remove read permissions by deselecting Allow for those users or groups that should not have access to this address list.

WARNING

When restricting recipient read permissions to an address list, do not select the Deny box, but only clear the Allow box. By selecting Deny, you may be trying to deny a permission granted to the recipient by its parent; thereby causing unintended effects.

Managing Offline Address Lists

Much like online address lists, Exchange 2000 creates a default offline address list as well. The offline address lists are downloadable to clients so that they may still browse the GAL or the offline address lists to which they have been granted access. Offline addresses are stored on an offline address list server, which, in larger organizations, should be a server that is not overburdened with other tasks. The process of transmitting offline address lists to clients and of rebuilding offline address lists can be resource-intensive.

Creating Offline Address Lists

The default offline address book contains the GAL, but you may require that certain users receive a more customized set of address information. When you create an offline address list, it gets stored in a system public folder as a single data file, even though it may contain multiple offline lists. Creating a new custom offline address list is very simple. Let's make a new one for our Washington office:

1. First, open Exchange System Manager.
2. Right-click the Offline Address Lists folder in the console menu.
3. Choose New | Offline Address List.
4. Give the list a name and select your Offline Address List server (see Figure 4.48).

Figure 4.48 New Offline Address List

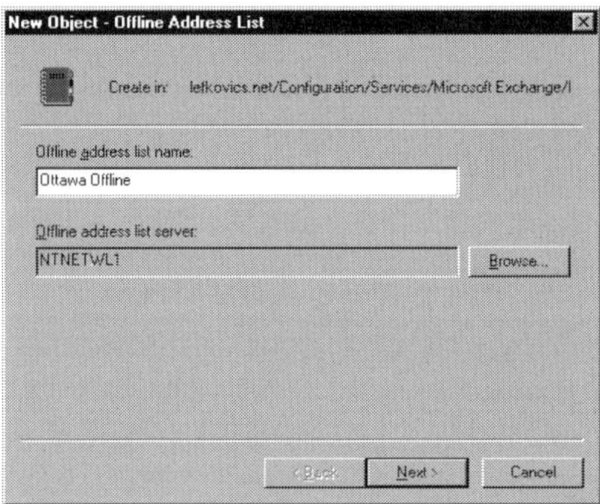

5. After clicking Next, select other specific lists to be included in this Offline List (see Figure 4.49) This will only show lists you have permission to read.

Figure 4.49 Selecting Address Lists to Add to Custom Offline Address List

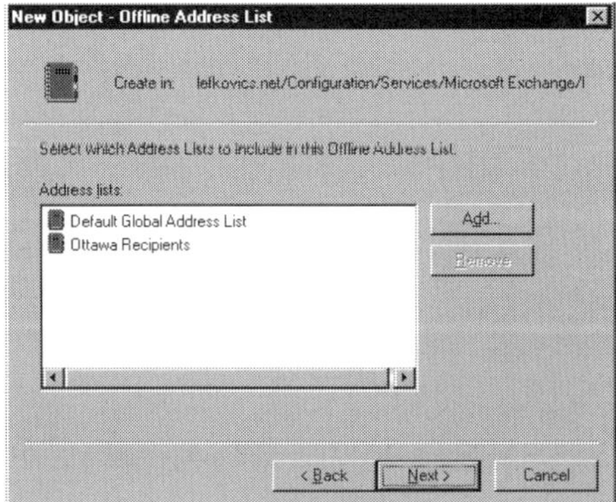

6. Add the individual lists you need and click Next, and then Finish.
7. Once built, these lists will be available to Outlook clients.

Editing and Removing Offline Address Lists

Just like online address lists, the offline address lists can be renamed or deleted. Within the Exchange System Manager, navigate to the offline address list you need to change, then right-click and select the menu option for renaming or deleting.

Rebuilding Offline Address Lists

Changes made to address lists are not automatically updated to the offline lists. The offline address lists go through a process of rebuilding as part of a daily maintenance. The offline address list rebuilding schedule is customizable. In larger organizations especially, rebuilding offline address lists should be scheduled for a period of low Exchange Server activity.

To change the scheduled rebuild of an offline address list:

1. Open the Exchange System Manager.

2. Navigate to the Offline Address Lists folder.

3. Right-click the offline address list you want to configure and choose Properties to see a property page similar to Figure 4.50.

4. You can change the Update Interval using the drop-down menu, or set your own custom schedule.

Figure 4.50 Offline Address List Property Page

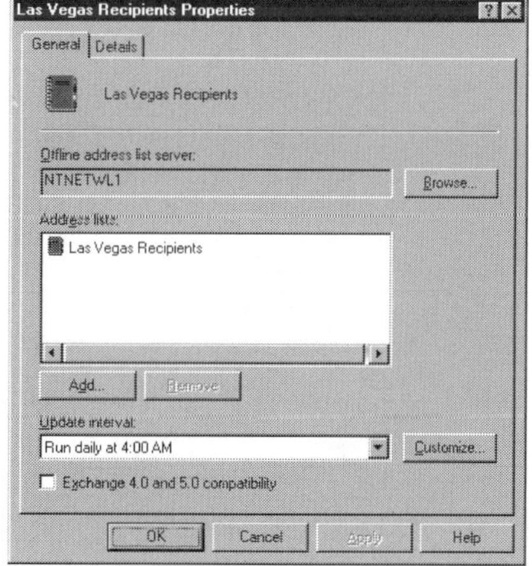

You can also force the rebuilding process by manually requesting an immediate rebuild. To manually rebuild an offline address list, right-click the offline address list in Exchange System Manager and choose Rebuild. Again, especially in larger organizations, the rebuild process can take a fair amount of time, as indicated by the alert generated when requesting a manual rebuild, such as our Las Vegas Recipients Offline Address List, shown in Figure 4.51.

Figure 4.51 Rebuild Offline Address List Alert

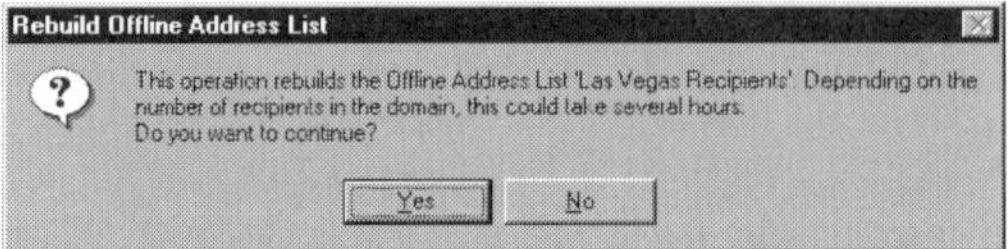

Customizing Address Book Templates

Exchange 2000 provides you with another powerful opportunity to make the product work even harder for your organization, and that is the ability to customize the graphical interface for address book recipients.

Details Templates are equipped with a set of controls that are used to interpret its graphical presentation of Address List views to the user. You can modify the contents of Details Templates to change how the user views properties of objects in Address Lists. This is just a customization process.

Table 4.5 Template Controls for Customizing Address Book Templates

Template Control	Control Function
Label	Adds a text label within the template
Edit	Adds single-line text fields, or multiline text boxes
Page Break	Determines the beginning of a tab, and defines where to set the text
Group Box	Creates a panel for a group of controls
Check Box	Adds a check box with a text label
List Box	Creates a list box with optional scroll bars
Multi-Valued List Box	Creates a list box that can display multiple values
Multi-Valued Drop-Down	Adds a selection list with multiple values

Exchange 2000 provides seven customizable templates: User, Group, Public Folder, Search Dialog, Mailbox Agent, Contact, and Exchange Send Options. These templates can be viewed in the Exchange System Manager. You need to navigate to the Recipients node and choose Details Templates. Selecting the desired language will reveal the list shown in Table 4.5. Figure 4.52 shows the controls used to present the user information in an address list view. Figure 4.53 shows the default address list view.

Figure 4.52 Details Template

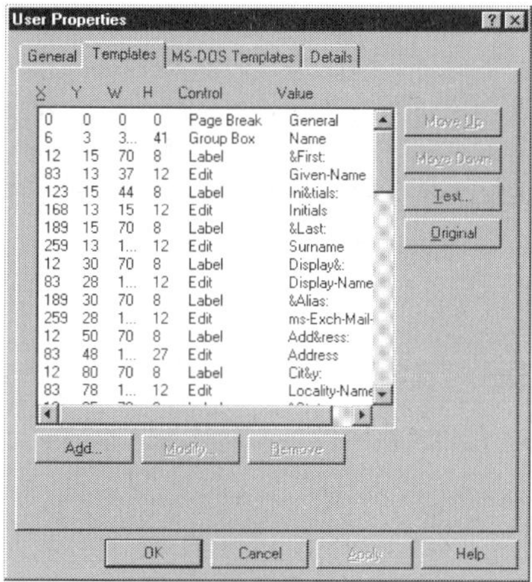

Figure 4.53 Default View of Address Book Item (User Template)

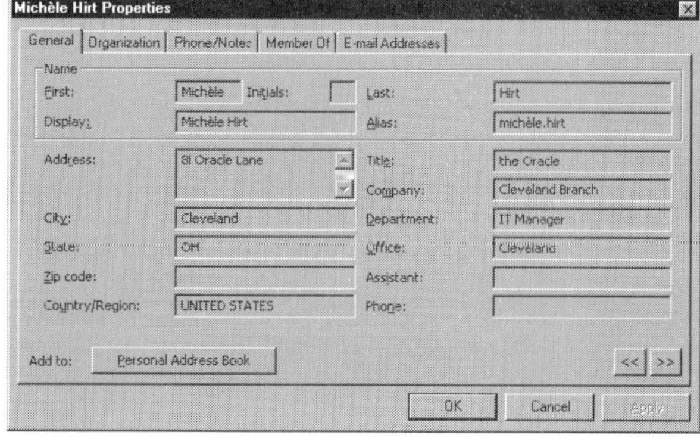

Managing Policies on Exchange 2000

Policies are a collection of configuration settings that apply to a specified group of objects. Exchange 2000 includes two types of policies to assist in administration. *System Policies* are configuration templates applied to Exchange servers, mailbox stores, or public stores. *Recipient Policies* take the place of the Site Addressing container from the legacy Exchange Administrator program, allowing you to apply sweeping changes to e-mail addressing on mail-enabled objects throughout your organization.

Administering System Policies

You have three different classes of System Policies to help shape your Exchange 2000 organization. Configuration settings entered through these policies are held in the configuration container within the AD and as such get replicated to all domain controllers. These policies are administered using the Exchange System Manager snap-in. The System Policy container is under the Administrative Groups folder in Exchange System Manager, as shown in Figure 4.54.

Figure 4.54 System Policies in Exchange System Manager

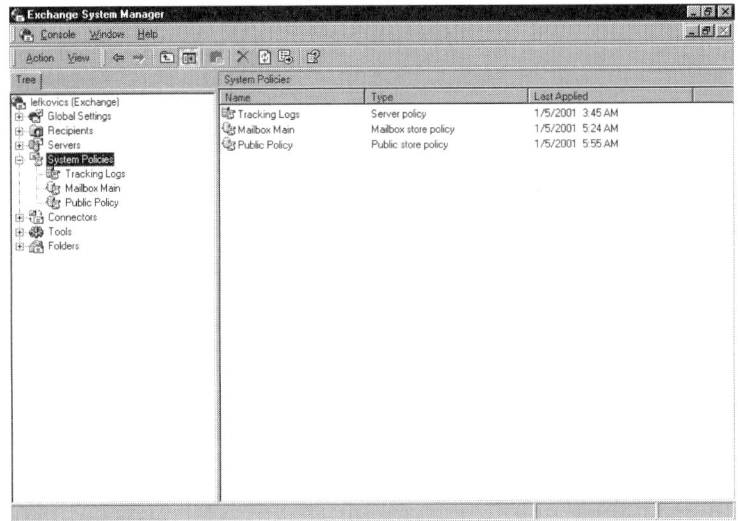

NOTE

By default, there is no Systems Policy container within Microsoft Exchange System Manager. To create one, right-click the administrative group to which you want to apply a system policy and choose New | System Policy Container.

Configuring Server Policy

A Server Policy in Exchange 2000 is used to enable message tracking, enable subject logging, and remove log files based on their age (measured in days). Without discussing the ethical issues, message tracking is a useful tool for monitoring inappropriate e-mails through the company, tracing the path a message takes from sender to recipient, searching for messages based on message attributes, and confirming receipt of messages. If you enable message tracking, you must also be aware that tracking logs can grow fairly quickly. Setting log file maintenance to allow for older logs to be deleted is important, especially where lack of unlimited hard drive space is an issue.

To create a new Server Policy you must jump through a few hoops:

1. Open Exchange Systems Manager.

2. Navigate to the System Policy container under Administrative Groups.

3. Right-click System Policy to reveal the menu.

4. Choose New | Server Policy.

5. When the New Policy window appears, check the box beside General and click OK.

6. You now should see the Server Policy Properties page where you must first assign a descriptive name for this policy on the General tab.

7. Your policy options are listed on the General (Policy) tab, as shown in Figure 4.55. In our example, we have checked off both Subject Logging and Message Tracking and have chosen old log files to be removed after seven days.

8. Click OK to create the policy.

   You are not quite done at this point. You have created a new Server Policy; however, it has not been applied to a server.

Figure 4.55 General (Policy) Tab

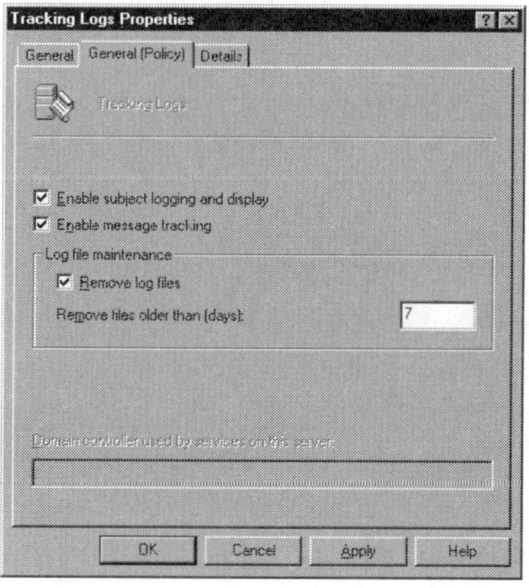

9. Right-click the new policy you created and choose Add Server (see Figure 4.56).

10. Select the server to which you want this policy applied and Add it to your list. Then click OK.

    When you choose your new Server Policy in the left side of the console, the server you added will appear in the right frame.

Figure 4.56 Adding Server to Server Policy

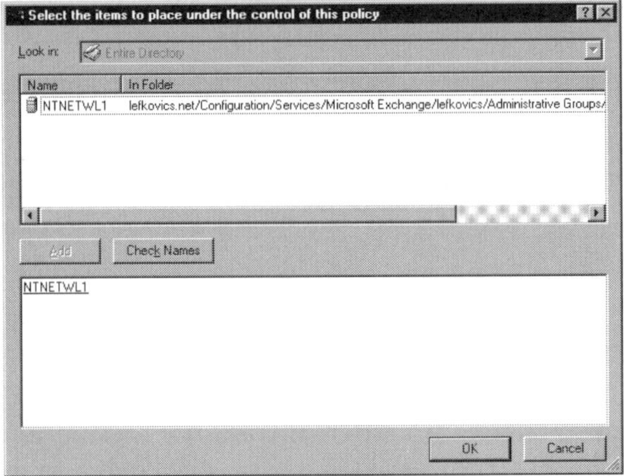

Configuring Mailbox Store Policy

Mailbox Store Policies allow you to set deleted item retention parameters, mailbox storage limits, and maintenance rules on a store-by-store basis. It is important to note that implementation of a Mailbox Store Policy will prevent you from modifying these settings in the individual Mailbox Store properties, as they will appear dimmed. To create a new Mailbox Store Policy:

1. Right-click the System Policies container in the Exchange System Manager.

2. From the drop-down menu, choose New | Mailbox Store Policy.

3. From the New Policy window, select the components you want to configure, as shown in Figure 4.57. The boxes you check off in this list determine the properties tabs available to configure.

4. After clicking OK, you again must enter a descriptive name for your new policy.

5. As you see in Figure 4.58, the General (Policy) tab allows you to determine which Public Store and Offline Address List is the default for this Mailbox Store.

Figure 4.57 New Policy Options

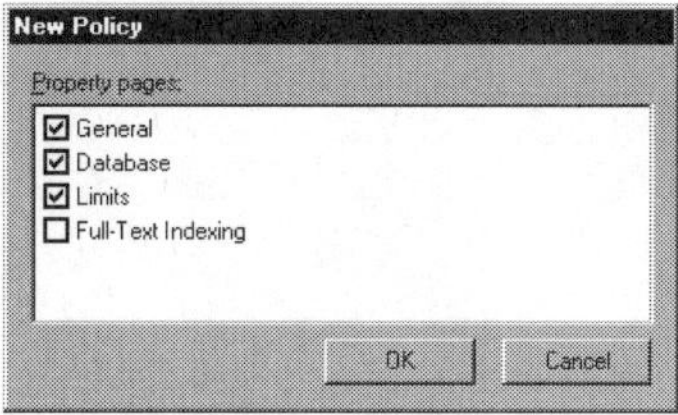

Figure 4.58 General (Policy) Tab

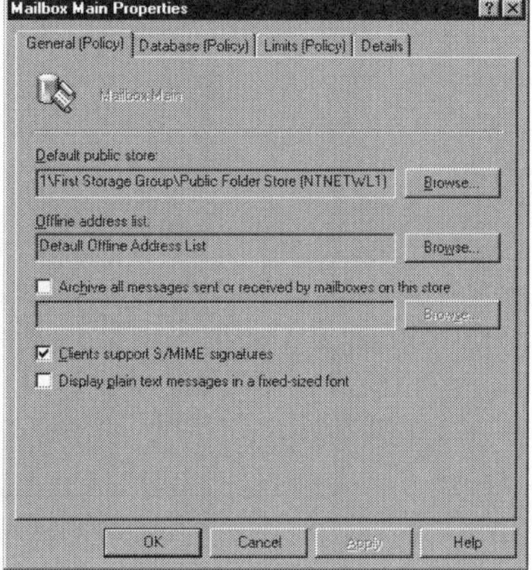

6. From this tab you also control whether you archive all messages sent or received through this store. If you choose archiving, you must then select a destination folder or mailbox.

7. By default, it is assumed that mail clients can use Secure Multipurpose Internet Mail Extension (S/MIME) signatures, such as Outlook 98/2000.

8. You can also choose to have the text of inbound e-mail converted to a fixed font.

9. From the Database (Policy) Tab, you can adjust the online maintenance schedule of the mailbox store from the default of 11:00P.M. to 3A.M. if necessary. You should schedule this maintenance when the database activity is at its lowest for the day.

10. The Limits (Policy) tab, as shown in Figure 4.59, allows you to control mailbox storage limits as well as how long items that are deleted by the client get saved in the store.

Figure 4.59 Limits (Policy) Tab

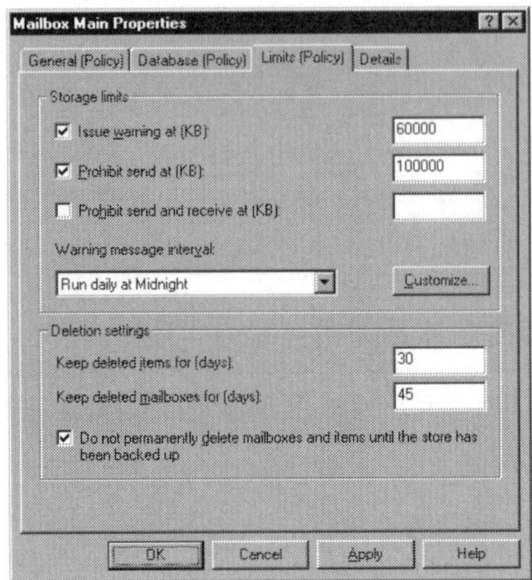

11. Configure the three steps of storage limits in increasing size. In our example, Figure 4.59, we have chosen to issue a storage warning to the client if their mailbox exceeds total storage on the Exchange Server of 60,000 KB. At 100,000 KB, we have selected to prohibit the client's ability to send messages.

12. Be careful applying a value to the Prohibit Send and Receive option because e-mail inbound to a user with a mailbox this size will force NDRs sent back to the original sender. For our example, we have left this blank.

13. By default, Exchange checks the mailbox sizes at midnight each day, then applies the restriction or sends the e-mail notification to those boxes that match the criteria you set above.

14. You also need to configure Deleted Item Retention from the Limits (Policy) tab, for both messages and mailboxes. Settings of 15 to 30 days are common for many organizations.

15. You can also check the box requiring a backup of the mailbox store prior to any permanent purge of deleted items. This ensures that the deleted items contents find their way to at least one backup tape before disappearing.

16. When you click OK for the Mailbox Store Properties window, you commit your settings to the newly created policy.

17. Just as in the Server Policy, you must still select the object of these configurations. In Exchange System Manager, right-click the new mailbox store policy and choose Add Mailbox Store.

18. Select the desired store(s) to which you want this policy applied and click OK.

Configuring Public Store Policy

The setup and configuration for Public Store Policies mirror the Mailbox Store procedure. Just as you witnessed with Mailbox Store Policy, options in the Properties screen of the Public Store are dimmed if a Public Store Policy has been applied to it.

To create a new Public Store Policy:

1. First locate the System Policies container in the desired Administrative Groups node and right-click.

2. Choose New | Public Store Policy from the drop-down menu.

3. As earlier, you must grant this policy a name before configuring the settings.

4. In the General (Policy) tab, you again have the default setting of allowing for S/MIME enabled clients, with plain fixed font left unchecked.

5. From the Database (Policy) tab, edit the scheduled maintenance for this public store. Online maintenance is best performed at periods of lowest database activity. The default is set from 11:00P.M. until 3:00A.M.

6. As shown in Figure 4.60, the Limits (Policy) tab has a few differences for public stores. The Issue Warning box indicates the size that that public store can get as a whole before a warning is issued. The Prohibit Post setting determines the size the public store can become before not allowing further posts. And the Maximum Item Size, of course, indicates that largest message that the public store can receive.

7. You can set Deleted Item Retention on a public folder through a policy as well. This is set numerically in days, as shown in our example.

8. The Age Limit setting determines the length of time an item can remain in the public store before facing deletion.

9. You have a policy setting that is specific to public folders, and that is replication. In the tab Replication (Policy) you can set the interval for replication. The interval is defaulted to Always Run, allowing you to enter the setting in minutes.

Figure 4.60 Public Folder Policy Limit (Policy) Tab

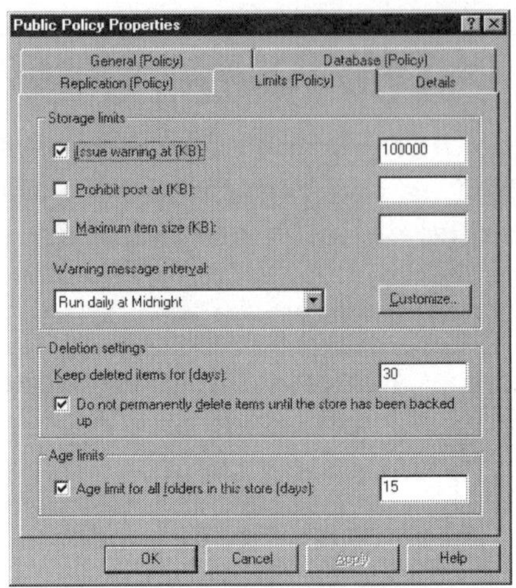

10. You can also restrict message size for replication. Typically, you would set this the same as the message size limitation for posting to the public folder.

11. Click OK to create the public folder policy.

12. Last, add the public folder stores to which you want this public store policy to apply.

All the server policies above can be edited and reapplied within your organization anytime. Within a system policy, individual stores and servers can be removed or added by selecting the Add Server or Add Store options in the right-click menu. It should also be noted that should you need the system policy changes to take effect immediately, you can apply the policy immediately by right-clicking the specific System Policy and choosing Apply Now. System policies are easily deleted though the right-click menu as well.

Administering Recipient Policies

As suggested earlier, Recipient Policies are used to govern e-mail addressing in the organization, and can be applied to any mail-enabled recipient object. At installation, Exchange 2000 creates a Default Recipient Policy that will apply to all mail-enabled objects in the AD. The default recipient policy can be modified to reflect company-wide changes in your organization, but if needed, multiple recipient policies specific to groups of recipients can be implemented. The e-mail addresses for a recipient policy could include those required for connecting to foreign systems through connectors such as Lotus Notes, Groupwise, MSMail or Lotus cc:mail, as well as the default or additional SMTP and X400 addresses.

Even though you can create multiple recipient policies within an organization, only one recipient policy can be applied to any given recipient object. Multiple recipient policies are beneficial for filtering objects for multiple domain addressing. For example, the management team of a holding company might need to receive e-mail for several domains under its control, whereas individuals within one of those companies may only require e-mail addressed to that specific domain. If no other recipient policy is applied to an object, then the default recipient policy is assumed.

Creating a New Recipient Policy

Creating a new Recipient policy is quite simple.

1. First open Exchange System Manager and expand the Recipients node.

2. Right-click Recipient Policies and choose New | Recipient Policy.

3. In the General tab of the resulting Properties window, enter a descriptive name for this new policy.

4. By clicking the Modify button, you can determine the parameters that recipients must meet to be assigned this policy (see Figure 4.61). The Find Exchange Recipients dialog box is your interface to the LDAP-driven filter of the AD recipients by server, store and even individual attributes.

Figure 4.61 Find Exchange Recipients

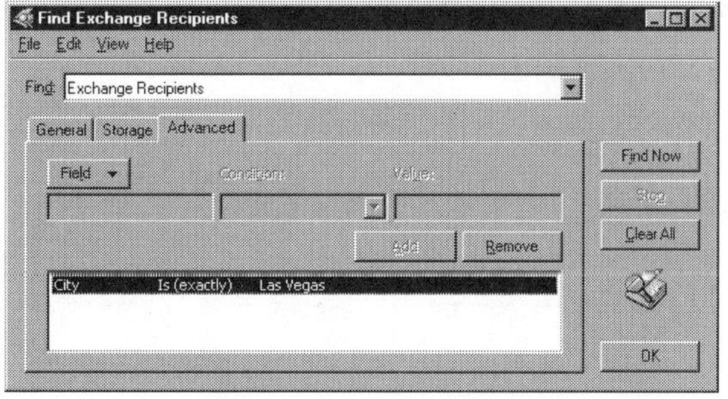

5. You can then assign your address generation scheme in the E-Mail Addresses tab. By default, the SMTP and X400 addresses are enabled in a new recipient policy. You have to activate any other address in the E-Mail Addresses tab of the Recipient Policies properties, as shown in Figure 4.62. If your company received e-mail

for multiple domains you could add the second SMTP domain here as well, starting with the "@" sign.

6. After confirming the chosen addresses, click OK to create the policy.

Figure 4.62 E-Mail Addresses for Recipient Policy

A recipient policy can be changed at any time and reapplied or deleted if no longer needed. You can change its membership by amending the filter information; you can add, remove, or disable e-mail addresses; and you can alter the relative priority of the policy. Individual recipient objects in the AD have an e-mail address tab in their properties, as we saw earlier in this chapter. Changes made to an individual recipient will override any recipient policy that has previously been applied.

NOTE

Although you can edit the Default Recipient Policy, you cannot remove the policy. This policy is required by Exchange 2000.

Changing Recipient Policy Priority

Recipient policies represent a valuable resource, especially for larger organizations that may have multiple companies in multiple cities all with recipients in the same AD structure and the same Exchange organization. Multiple recipient policies can be assigned a priority, in the event that membership overlaps. An object can only have one recipient policy applied to it, even if it qualifies as a member of multiple policies. A user moving from one department or location to another may require a change in recipient policy. That change can be reflected in a change in policy priority when the user was moved from one group or organizational unit to another.

The default recipient policy retains the lowest priority, but others can be moved up and down the list. You change recipient policy priority by right-clicking the specific recipient policy whose priority you wish to change, then choosing All Tasks | Move Up (or Move Down).

Forcing Recipient Policy Updates

It should be noted that changes to recipient policies do not get updated in the same manner as system policies. Recipient policies depend on the update interval of RUS, which you configure using the Exchange System Manager. By default, the RUS is set to Always Run for updates, but can be scheduled at times of less traffic for busier deployments. By instructing the RUS to update , you can also force an AD update of recipient policies that have been added or amended:

1. Navigate to the Recipient Update Service under the Recipients node of the Exchange System Manager console.

2. Expand the Recipient Update Services to show the RUS in the right pane. There will be a separate RUS for each domain in the AD forest, as well as an enterprise-level RUS.

3. Right-click the RUS and choose Update Now, as you did back in Figure 4.47.

Administering Exchange Server Protocols

In Exchange 2000, the actual function of connecting Exchange to the Internet has been passed to the IIS component of Windows 2000, as it is responsible for the various Internet protocols. You still administer the use of these protocols by Exchange primarily through the Exchange System Manager, with the exception of some aspects of the HTTP Virtual Server. Exchange uses the concept of Virtual Servers to communicate with the IIS.

The IIS maintains a special database of metadata called Metabase. Specific changes in the AD get periodically updated in the metabase by the Metabase Update Service. The changes made in AD through the Exchange System Manager overwrite settings made in IIS, so the best practice would be to administer as much as possible through the Exchange System Manager.

A virtual server in Exchange 2000 represents a combination of an IP Address and a Transmission Control Protocol (TCP) Port. Each virtual server must be unique in this combination. For example, you can have multiple virtual servers share the same IP address, as long as they have differing TCP Ports. Table 4.6 shows the default TCP ports for specific Internet protocols. See Appendix A for a more comprehensive listing of ports.

Table 4.6 Default TCP Ports for Protocols

Protocol	Default TCP Port	TCP Port with Secure Sockets Layer (SSL)
SMTP	25	—-
IMAP4	143	993
POP3	110	995
HTTP	80	443
NNTP	119	563

In Exchange 2000, the default SMTP Virtual Server assumes and extends what was formerly the Internet Messaging Service (IMS) in Exchange 5.5. Figure 4.63 shows the various virtual servers for the protocols.

Figure 4.63 Virtual Servers in Exchange System Manager

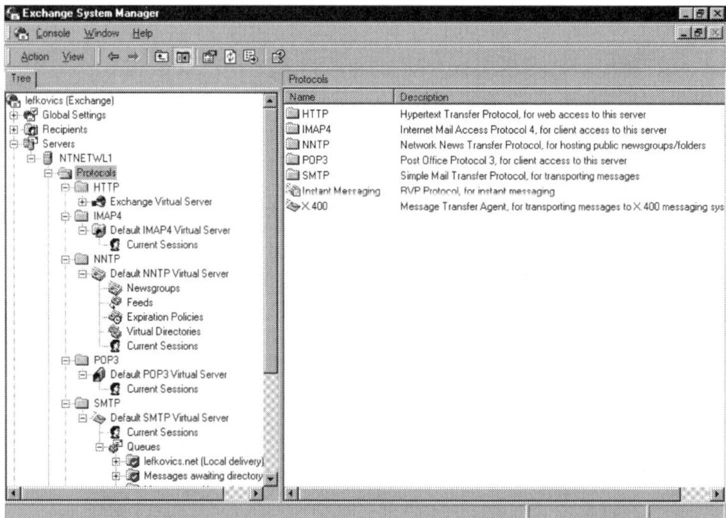

Configuring SMTP Virtual Servers

Exchange 2000 installs a Default SMTP Virtual Server to connect Exchange to the outside world. Though it is named as default, you can change the name at any time by right-clicking and choosing Rename.

There are several property pages to configure in an SMTP virtual server. If you navigate within Exchange System Manager to the Servers container, then through the Protocols to the SMTP folder, you can see all the SMTP virtual servers available to you. You can create a new virtual server by right-clicking the SMTP folder under Protocols and choosing New | SMTP Virtual Server, as long as you have a unique IP Address/TCP Port combination. It is possible to have multiple SMTP Virtual Servers on an Exchange Server, but typically it would not be necessary. All inbound SMTP mail will arrive at port 25 and you can only have one virtual server per port. The SMTP Virtual Servers rely on multithreaded processes, so there is no performance gain to multiple outbound ones. If you need to host multiple default domains, then multiple virtual servers are possible as long as the IP address/TCP port combination is still unique.

Figure 4.64 shows the General Tab of the SMTP Virtual Server properties. From here you can set the IP address for this virtual server. Since SMTP binds to port 25 as a standard, it is recommended to maintain that setting, so any additional SMTP Virtual Servers would require another IP address to maintain a unique IP Address/TCP Port combination. You could limit connections in terms of their number and their timeout from this page.

Figure 4.64 General Tab of SMTP Virtual Server Properties

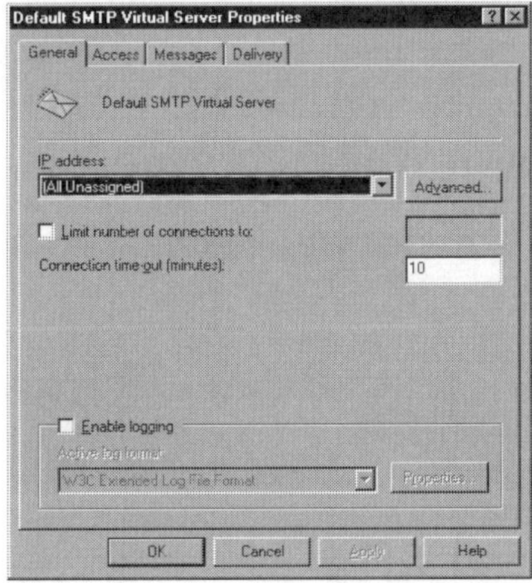

The SMTP Virtual Server also lists queues for e-mail movement within Exchange System Manager. SMTP messages that are awaiting some action

before being able to progress will be visible here. The System Manager also maintains the connection state of the virtual server, and will indicate the status as Active, Ready, Remote, Frozen, Retry, or Scheduled.

With your SMTP Virtual Server providing connectivity to the Internet, you must configure who out there can connect to your server and send mail. The settings to control virtual server access are shown in Figure 4.65.

Figure 4.65 Controlling Access to SMTP Virtual Server

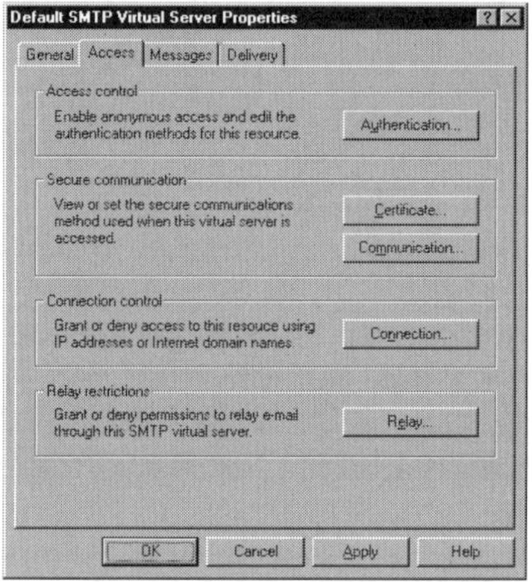

First, you can control access to a virtual server through authentication requirements. Within the authentication window, you select Anonymous for unknown external addresses to connect with your server and transfer SMTP messages inbound to your organization, as you can see in Figure 4.66. Basic authentication requires usernames and passwords; however, they are sent in plain text format. You could encrypt this information using Secure

Figure 4.66 Authentication to the SMTP Virtual Server

Sockets Layer (SSL) and a security certificate. Integrated Windows Authentication provides a little more security for authentication. One or more of these authentication methods can be selected.

You can also restrict virtual server access using the Connection Control button. From here you are able to restrict or to explicitly allow access to a virtual server from another resource by IP Address, subnet, or domain name.

Another very important step is configuring the relay restrictions. You must ensure that only the clients you allow can send mail using your server. Preventing SMTP relay in Exchange 5.x has long been a hot topic in Exchange newsgroups, especially when IMAP4 or POP3 clients are required valid access as well. Chapter 7 will cover SMTP relay in more detail. Figure 4.67 shows the relay configuration screen. In our example, we have allowed relaying by one specific domain, plus all that successfully authenticate.

Figure 4.67 Relay Restrictions for SMTP Virtual Server

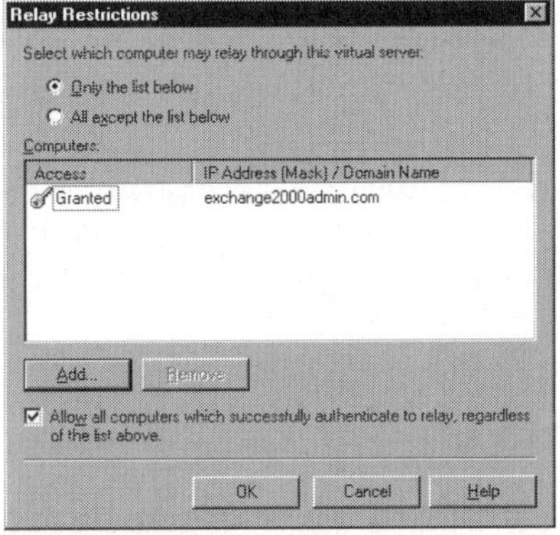

The configuration process of an SMTP virtual server allows you to set some limitations to message size and also to set certain connection parameters. In the example in Figure 4.68, we have applied a message size restriction of roughly 12MB. We also have accepted the default of 20 messages per connection for SMTP. When two SMTP servers negotiate a connection for message transfer, a limitation of about 20 messages is beneficial because the servers can and will make concurrent handshakes. If there are 40 messages to send, two sessions of 20 messages running concurrently will tend to be faster than consecutive transfer.

In the SMTP Virtual Server configuration, we set the destination mailbox for copies of Non-Delivery Reports (NDRs); typically you would use postmaster@<domain.com>, which may be an alias on a single account or perhaps a distribution group containing a few e-mail administrators.

The last field in the Messages tab of SMTP Virtual Server properties allows you to forward e-mail to another host serving the same SMTP

Figure 4.68 Messages Tab in SMTP Virtual Server Properties

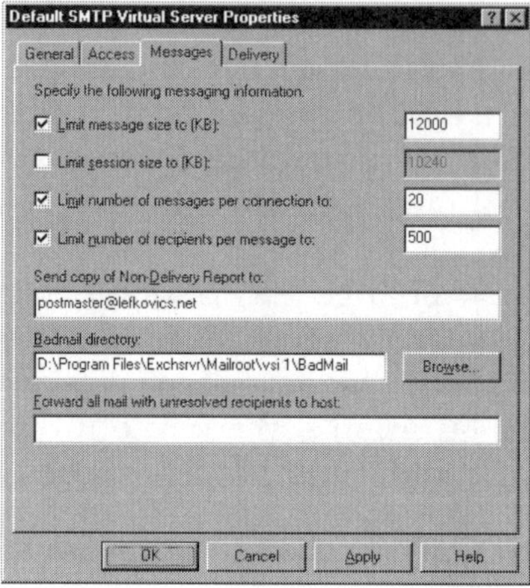

domain. If the recipient does not resolve as a mail-enabled or mailbox-enabled recipient object in the AD, then the e-mail could be forwarded to a Unix host operating SendMail for the same mail domain.

When SMTP mail can resolve its destination host, but the host is not available to receive e-mail, the SMTP Virtual Server will retry at configurable intervals. Figure 4.69 outlines the default settings for undeliverable e-mail.

Figure 4.69 Retry Intervals on SMTP Virtual Server

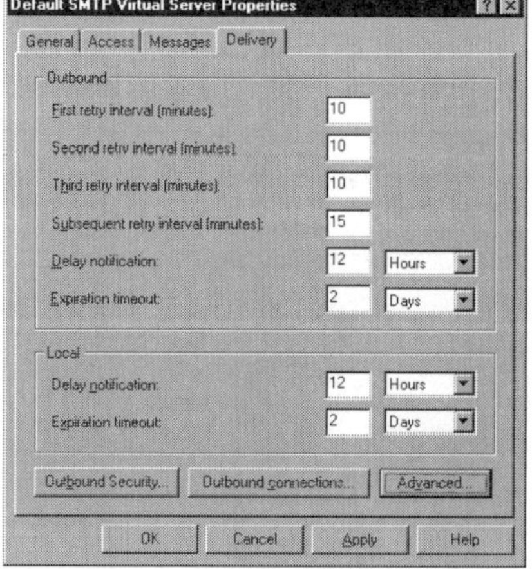

Configuring IMAP4 and POP3 Virtual Servers

IMAP4 and POP3 Virtual Servers are even easier to configure than SMTP. The authentication steps are much the same. Both these protocols have a different setting within Message Format for MIME settings, as shown in Figure 4.70.

Figure 4.70 Message Format Settings for POP3 Virtual Server

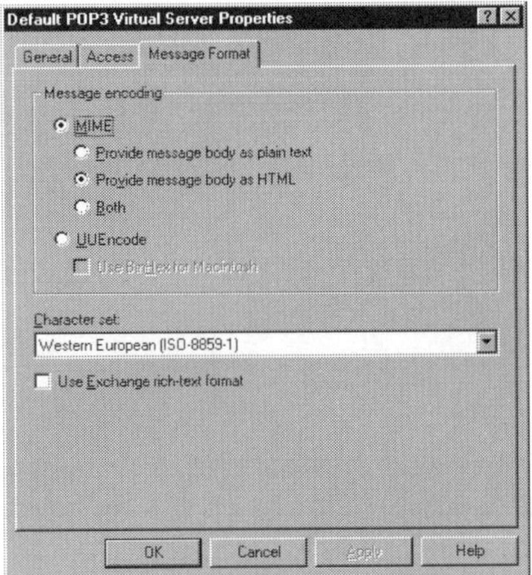

When changing configurations on an existing virtual server, regardless of the protocol, it is generally a good idea to pause the service to prevent subsequent connections. Connections that have already been established will remain through completion, as long as the service is paused and not stopped; that way, any changes to settings that you might make will get applied more cleanly.

Managing Exchange Data Storage

Exchange 2000, like its predecessor, employs an information store (formerly private information store) and a public folder store. The information store can support multiple storage groups. Each storage group can support multiple mailbox stores. By default, Exchange installs one of each on each of the servers. An example of the containers is shown in Figure 4.71.

Administering Mailbox Stores

Legacy Exchange servers provided you with one database for your mailboxes. Exchange 2000 allows you to partition the database into multiple Mailbox Stores within a parent container called a *storage group*. A benefit of having the store separated into smaller segments is that in the event of

Figure 4.71 Data Stores in Exchange System Manager

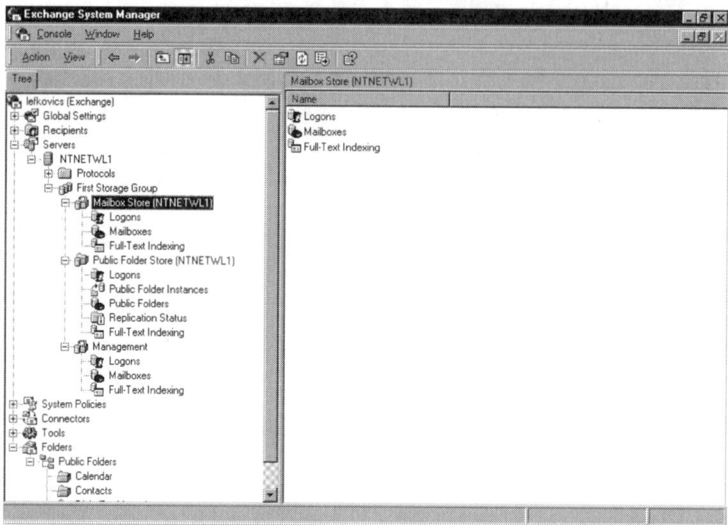

failure, the unit of recovery is smaller, thereby impacting fewer users. Each storage group has its own single set of transaction log files, even with multiple mailbox stores.

Under the Server container in the Exchange System Manager, you can select the individual server you wish to administer and select the appropriate storage group. Figure 4.72 shows the General tab of the default storage group. Because transaction logs are associated by storage group, here you have the ability to apply circular logging, which is disabled by default. If you intend to maintain an organization that supports up to the incident restores, then circular logging should remain disabled. The properties in Figure 4.72 also show the path to the databases that reside in this storage group.

NOTE

Single Instance Storage is maintained over the multiple mailbox stores within a single Storage Group.

As indicated, a storage group can hold multiple mailbox stores. The first mailbox store, created by default, is always made up of co-components priv1.edb and priv1.stm (see Figure 4.73).

Figure 4.72 Configuring Storage Group

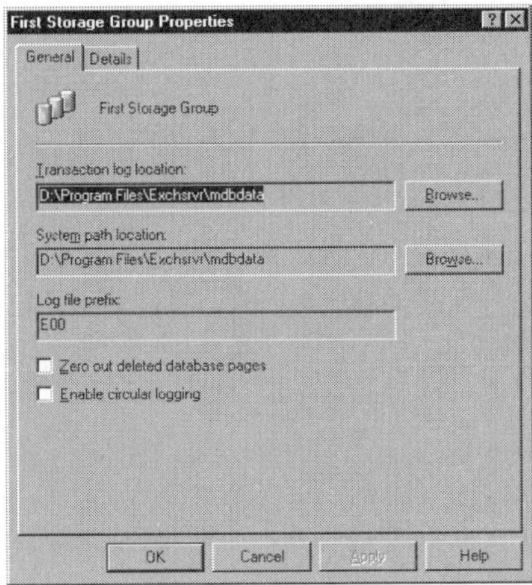

Figure 4.73 Database Tab in Mailbox Store Properties

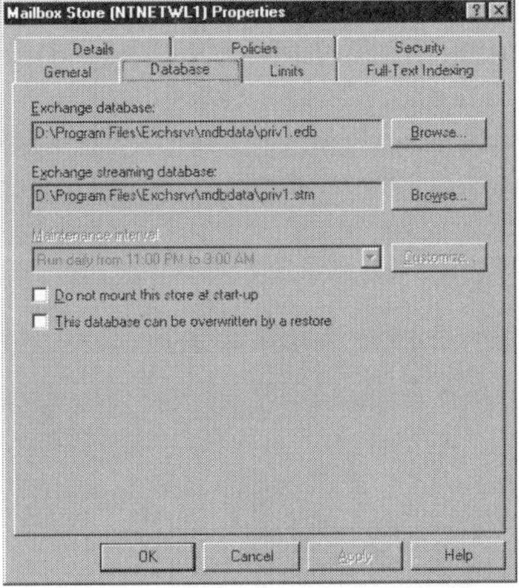

Within the default first storage group, there is a default mailbox store, but you can still add separate mailbox stores. In our example in Figure 4.74 we are adding a mailbox store called Management to our server NTNETWL1. Because of the presumed relative importance of management's e-mail, this mailbox store will have assigned to it more lenient deleted item retention and larger mailbox size allocation.

When creating a new mailbox store, you can select the offline address book available for that store. Also, each mailbox store must be associated with what becomes its default public folder store. In our example, we selected the only public store available.

Figure 4.74 Creating a New Mailbox Store

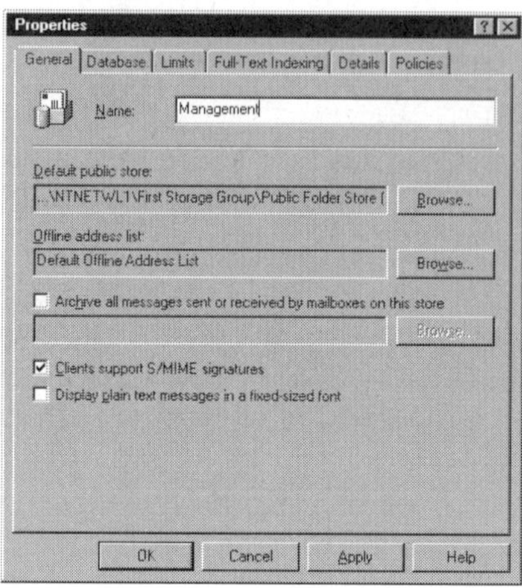

Storage limits are configurable by mailbox store and not across the entire storage group—although that would be very simple with a mailbox policy, as described earlier in this chapter. Because we are creating a group for Management, we have chosen storage limits of 100,000 KB to issue a warning, and 150,000 KB to prohibit send (see Figure 4.75). Again we have chosen not to prohibit receive. We have also allocated a longer deleted item retention period than we did elsewhere in this chapter.

Figure 4.75 Limits on Mailbox Store

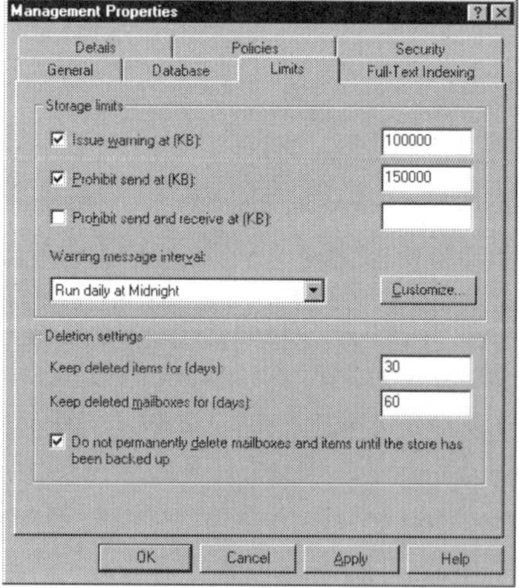

By not setting a limit for Prohibit Send and Receive, you help to ensure e-mails don't get bounced back to the original sender, either injuring your reputation or causing the sender grief, perhaps even costing you a client. Disallowing Send should be enough to force most users to provide some mailbox housecleaning. You might even keep an in-house whitepaper on e-mail archiving in the IT public folder for user reference.

Many of the settings we just looked at were configured earlier in this chapter when we were covering the step-by-step creation of a mailbox policy. The implementation of a mailbox policy will eliminate the need to set these configurations for all mailbox stores. When a mailbox store has been added to a mailbox policy, the settings are applied as in the policy and the specific configuration pages applicable to those settings become dimmed. The specific policies that have been applied to a mailbox store are visible in the Policies tab of the mailbox store properties pages, as shown in Figure 4.76.

Figure 4.76 Policies Tab of Mailbox Store

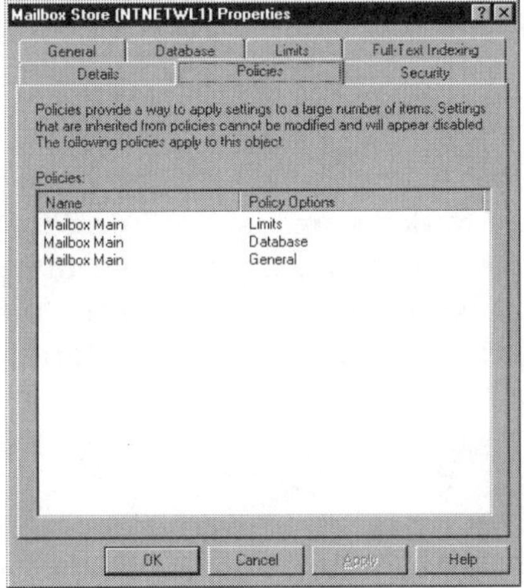

Mailbox stores can be easily renamed, should that be needed. We recommend short names, as this helps when troubleshooting from the command line. Navigating to the specific mailbox store in Exchange System Manager and right-clicking the mailbox store container will present the menu. Choose Rename and assign a descriptive logical name for the store.

Mailbox stores can also be deleted, after all objects have been removed, by either deleting or migrating to other containers. After deleting the store, it may be necessary to go into Windows Explorer and delete the actual files manually.

Administering Public Folders

In my experience in Exchange, starting with Exchange 5.0, many companies underutilize the potential and power of public folders. Exchange 2000 makes public folders even more attractive as a means of sharing documents, messages, and other collaborative data across the enterprise or perhaps to specific groups.

At installation, Exchange 2000 installed a single default hierarchy set of public folders in a single default public folder store. Current Messaging Application Programming Interface (MAPI) and IMAP clients can only support viewing a single public folder hierarchy, but Exchange 2000 supports multiple public folder stores, each with their own hierarchy. Browsers, using WebDAV and applications utilizing the Installable File System (IFS) can access multiple public folder hierarchies. The IFS allows access to public folders and mailboxes as shared network drives.

Administration of public folders can be separated into two components; administering the public folders themselves, and maintaining the public folder store.

Maintaining Public Folder Store

Administering the public folder store is very similar to managing the mailbox store. The Properties pages are very similar. The biggest difference is the presence of a Replication tab in the public folder store. Public folders are replicated to create multiple instances that allow a greater number of users to access them simultaneously.

In our example in Figure 4.77, we have assigned a message limit for 10,000 KB for replication. Objects greater than that will not replicate.

Figure 4.77 Replication Tab in Public Folders Properties

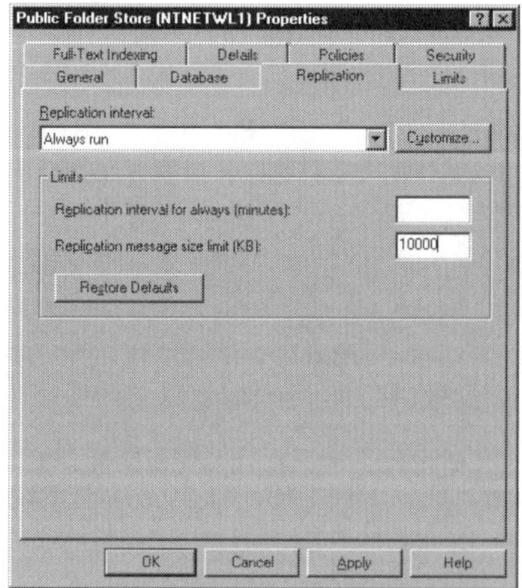

The other element that differs slightly from mailbox stores to public stores resides in the Limits page of the store properties. The public folder store can have enforced deletion for objects over a certain age. In Figure 4.78, that age is set to 15 days, after which they will be permanently deleted. You can see in this example that we have also requested a warning when the store reaches the 100,000 KB level.

Figure 4.78 Limits in Public Folder Store Properties

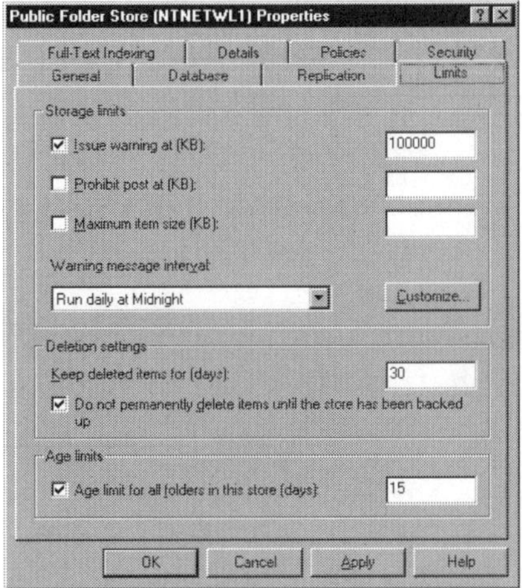

Managing Connectors

It is likely your Exchange organization is connected to the Internet. It is also probable that at some point in time you will connect your Exchange Server to another legacy messaging server, or connect your routing group to another routing group, either within an Administrative Group or across to other groups.

Table 4.7 summarizes the main Exchange 2000 connectors and briefly describes their functionality.

Table 4.7 Exchange 2000 Connectors

Connector	Functionality
Routing Group Connector	Connects two Exchange 2000 Routing Groups Easiest connector to configure SMTP-based
SMTP Connector	Connects a Routing Group to other routing groups (in the same Admin Group) or a foreign SMTP RFC821-compliant messaging system

Continued

Table 4.7 Continued

Connector	Functionality
X400 Connector	Connects a Routing Group to other routing groups (in the same Admin Group) or a foreign X400-based messaging system that conforms to X400 standard

Configuring Routing Group Connectors

A Routing Group Connector, it should go without saying, requires two routing groups. It is the easiest of the connectors to configure. Routing groups are designed or chosen to optimize message flow and are SMTP-based. Routing Group Connectors provide some logical connectivity between groups.

Setting up a Routing Group Connector is not difficult, but it does require the Exchange System Manager to be displaying Routing Groups. To set up a Routing Group Connector:

1. Within Exchange System Manager, navigate to the routing group to which you want to add the Routing Group Connector (RGC).

2. Expand the routing group and right-click the Connectors folder and choose New | Routing Group Connector.

3. On the General tab, assign the RGC a descriptive name. In our example in Figure 4.79, we have called it *Atlantic*.

Figure 4.79 General Tab of Routing Group Connector Properties

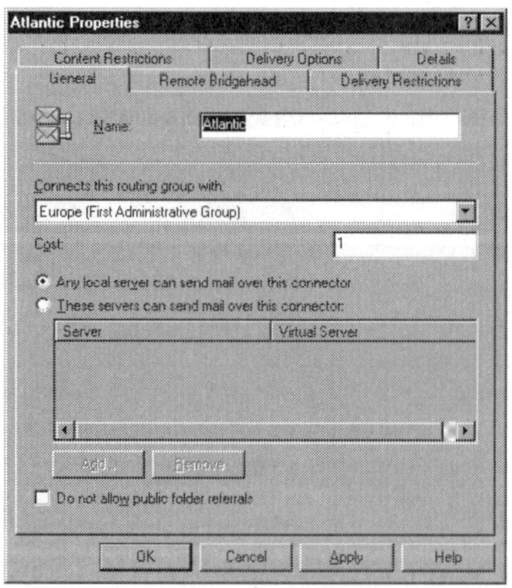

The Routing Group Connector must be able to connect with a remote bridgehead virtual server in order to form the connection. This remote server is added in the Remote Bridgehead tab of the RGC Properties. As shown in Figure 4.80, we have allowed all the different types of messages in our sample, but we have chosen to reject all messages over 500 KB. This is a good feature if your bandwidth across the connector is limited.

Figure 4.80 Content Restrictions on Routing Group Connector

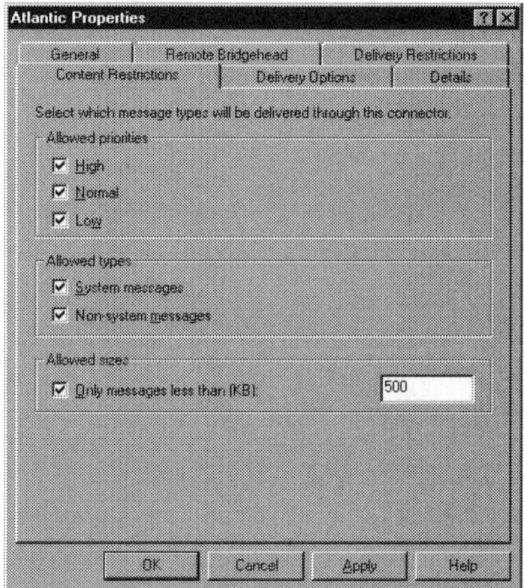

You can also set some specific restrictions across your connector. You can select who does or who doesn't have permissions to send e-mail across the connector using the Delivery Restrictions tab, as shown in Figure 4.81. We have chosen to reject messages from the Plant Workers who do not need access to recipient objects in the other routing group.

Figure 4.81 Restriction on Routing Group Connector Properties

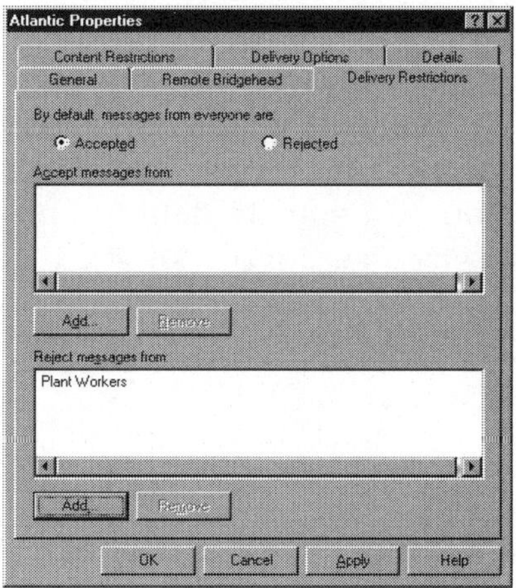

Finally, you do have a little control of the amount of bandwidth that gets used and when. In Figure 4.82 we have configured to not allow e-mails exceeding 500 KB to pass, except on a custom schedule, which was set to early morning hours. Otherwise, we have set the connector to accept and deliver traffic as it is received.

Figure 4.82 Delivery Option for Routing Group Connector

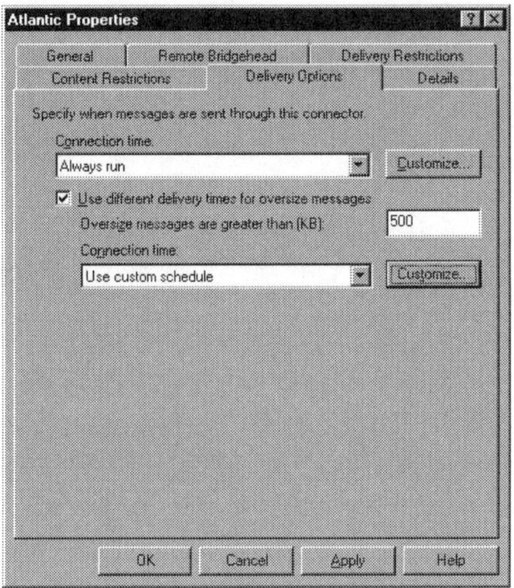

Configuring SMTP Connectors

Routing Group Connectors are the easiest to configure; however, they are not capable of all the functionality of an SMTP Connector. SMTP Connectors can connect to foreign messaging systems, utilize authentication and encryption for outbound security, and specify remotely initiated message delivery.

Installing an SMTP Connector has a few more configuration steps than an RGC. First, as in Figure 4.83, you must grant the new connector a name and select local bridgehead servers. In our example, we have called it *Asia*. The SMTP Connector will use a Domain Name System (DNS) Mail Exchanger (MX) Record to send messages to a foreign system.

Much like the RGC, you can specify delivery times through the connector based on message size (see Figure 4.84). Unlike the RGC, however, in an SMTP Connector, the connector can queue mail for remotely triggered delivery. Permissions to allow this of a client must be expressed here.

Figure 4.83 General Tab for SMTP Connector

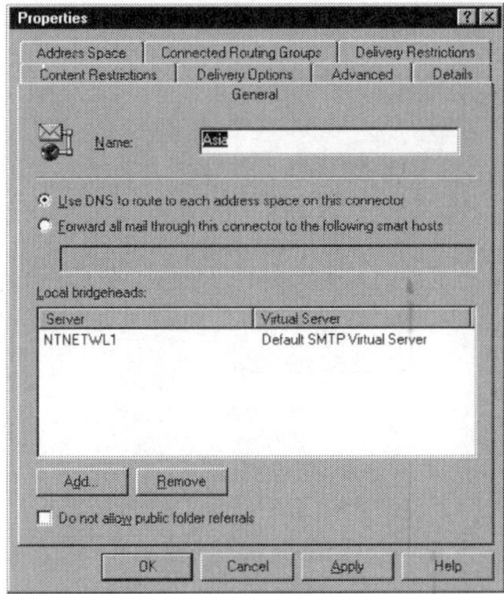

Figure 4.84 Delivery Options for SMTP Connector

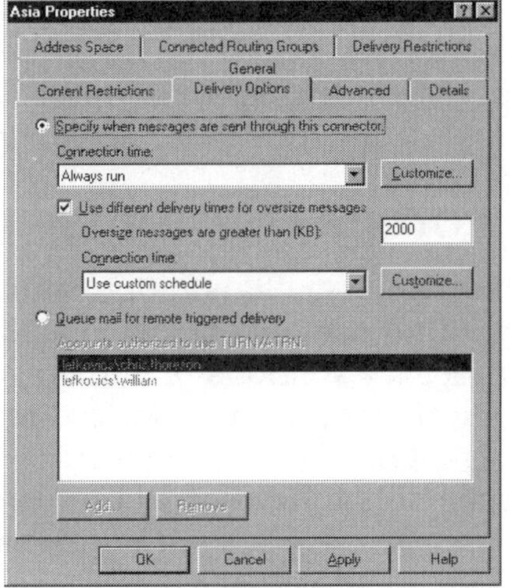

In the Advanced tab, you can configure how the SMTP Connector handles EHLO/HELO when communicating to external SMTP servers (Figure 4.85). This also determines how the connector will deal with queues held on the server at the other end.

Figure 4.85 Advanced Tab of SMTP Connector

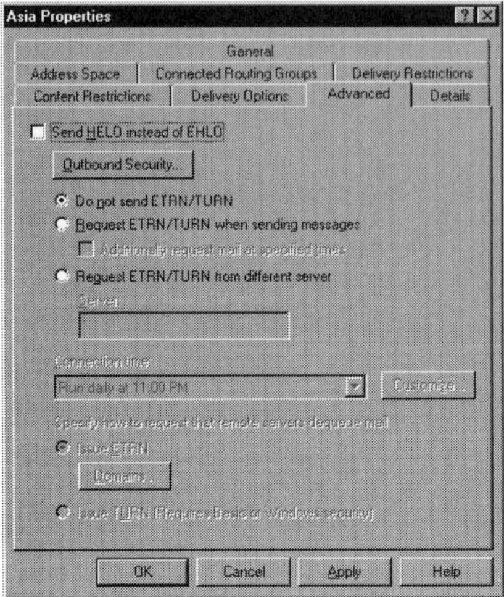

X400 Connectors

An X400 connector would be deployed to provide a messaging route between routing groups, or between an Exchange routing group and a foreign X400 System. Between routing groups, the X400 is only recommended for times of very low bandwidth.

Connectors to Foreign Systems

Connectors that allow messaging collaboration with foreign systems are very specific components that are part of the installation steps for Exchange 2000. As with legacy versions of Exchange, several connectors to other mail servers are supported, as summarized in Table 4.8.

Table 4.8 Exchange Connectors to Foreign Messaging Systems

Connector	Description
Microsoft Mail Connector	Connects to Microsoft Mail Servers for message delivery Synchronizes directory information and calendar items using MSMail Dirsync protocols and the Schedule+ Free/Busy Connector
Lotus cc:Mail Connector	Connects to cc:Mail networks with directory synchronization to Active Directory

Continued

Table 4.8 Continued

Connector	Description
Lotus Notes Connector	Connects and synchronizes directory information with Lotus Notes servers, enabling meeting notifications from Notes
Novell Groupwise Connector	Connects and synchronizes directory information between Groupwise and Active Directory with some supported calendaring functionality

Summary

As you have witnessed in this chapter, the administration of Exchange 2000 has evolved along with the product. The tools we use to perform day-to-day administrative tasks have changed, leveraging the Microsoft Management Console. Many of us have spent several years developing our skills on the Exchange 4.0 and 5.x products, but a lot of that thinking must be set aside to make way for Active Directory and management of objects from non-Exchange programs.

Exchange 2000 is heavily integrated with Windows 2000, especially the Active Directory. All the Exchange objects that used to reside in the Directory Services component of Exchange Server now make their home in the Exchange-updated AD schema, replicated to domain controllers through Active Directory replication.

Exchange 2000 is a powerful product, but you have equally powerful tools to administer it. You can configure similar components within Exchange through the use of policies: server policy to manage servers, mailbox policy to administer mailbox stores, and public folder policy to set up public folder stores. You can also distribute e-mail addressing very simply throughout the organization with recipient policies. It is efficient wherever possible to manage *groups* (as opposed to users). Now that groups can be mail-enabled as distribution lists were in previous Exchange products, this is more relevant than ever before.

Exchange also now allows partitioning of the information stores to make your recovery unit potentially smaller—and therefore less time-consuming and less intrusive to other users.

The protocols you know and love are all supported in Exchange 2000; in some aspects their use has improved as virtual servers now replace part of the IMS functionality from Exchange 5.x.

FAQs Visit **www.syngress.com/solutions** to have your questions about this chapter answered by the author.

Q: What primary tools do we use to administer Exchange 2000?

A: There are two main complementary administration tools for Exchange 2000:

Active Directory Users and Computer – for administering users, contacts, and distribution groups

Exchange System Manager—to manage Exchange Server, virtual servers, and group policies

Q: One of the executive secretaries in our company, Karen Coon, got married over the weekend to her beau, Earl Easter. First thing Monday morning, she proudly requests that her username and e-mail information be immediately changed to reflect her new married name. How do we do that?

A: This process is fairly simple. You must open Active Directory Users and Computers and locate the recipient object Karen Coon. If necessary, you can perform a search of the AD to locate this user's account. Right-click the user and choose Rename. Change the name to her married name and press Enter. This will bring up a window to change her display name and login name as well. After that, open the Users Properties window and select the E-Mail Addresses tab. Click New E-Mail Address, enter her new e-mail address and click OK. After it is added to the list of e-mail addresses, you need to select it again and click Set as Primary for her new address to be her reply address. Leave her e-mail address reflecting her maiden name on the system to receive any e-mail addressed to that address.

Q: Our company, ReallyBigGuys.com, just purchased another firm, exchange2000admin.com. We are retaining their staff under our original business name. We are merging all messaging functions of both companies to our existing Exchange 2000 server organization. MX records have been pointed to our server for both domains and we've been asked for inbound e-mail to be received for both domains and with SMTP addressing for the new people to be received with either domain. What do we do to allow both domains?

A: The answer lies in Recipient Policies. Open the default recipient policy and select the E-Mail Addresses tab. Click Add and input the new domain as shown in Figure 4.86.

Figure 4.86 Adding Additional SMTP Addressing to Recipient Policy

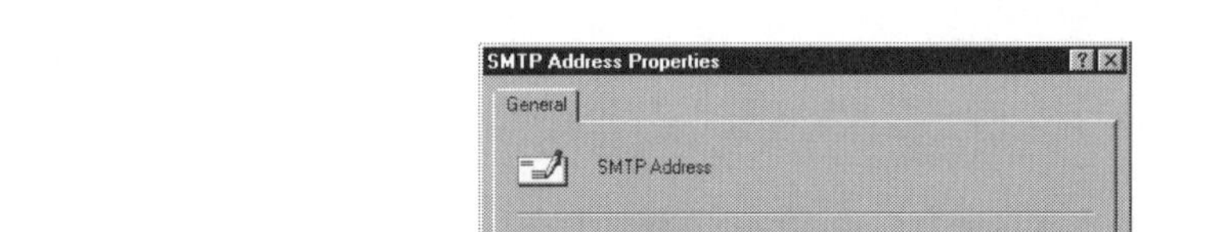

Q: We have a user for whom we wish to remain mailbox-enabled for internal issues, but we do not want him to send or receive external e-mail. How do we configure that?

A: The trick here is that users need an SMTP address to send and receive e-mail. But that SMTP address does not need to conform to the default recipient policy. You can create a recipient policy with a bogus SMTP address specifically to apply to users that should have no external e-mail. The address may be something like <username>@com.domain. To restrict a user from sending e-mail, you must create an SMTP connector and restrict the user (or an appropriate group they belong to) by adding them to the Reject Messages From window.

Chapter 5

Client Access to Exchange 2000 for E-Mail

Solutions in this chapter:

- **Physical Access between a Client and an Exchange Server**

- **Exchange Clients using MAPI**

- **Exchange Internet Clients: POP3 and Outlook Web Access**

- **LDAP Clients**

- **Troubleshooting Exchange Clients**

Introduction

Although Exchange Server is a powerful groupware system, it is also primarily an electronic messaging system—that is, it allows users to send and receive e-mail. Once you've installed a server, configured it, and created user accounts, your next challenge is getting people online and using the system.

For many people, e-mail is the central hub of their professional lives. Given how crucial e-mail can be to workflow, the ability to quickly connect an end user to Exchange Server from any physical access point to the network and from any one of many client types is an invaluable skill.

Exchange 2000 Server provides e-mail to many types of clients. It supports standard protocols that are used on a wide variety of messaging systems, such as:

- Post Office Protocol, version 3 (POP3)

- Simple Mail Transfer Protocol (SMTP)

- Internet Message Access Protocol, version 4 (IMAP4)

- HyperText Transfer Protocol (HTTP)

- Lightweight Directory Access Protocol (LDAP)

- Remote procedure calls (RPCs)

Exchange 2000 Server uses Outlook 2000 as its native client and Outlook Web Access (OWA) as its Web client. When you want to exploit the full functionality of Exchange 2000 Server, you are best served by using Outlook 2000. If you want to provide a client that is universally accessible via the Internet, you should select Outlook Web Access. Other client applications can access Exchange Server using the standard protocols, as we explore further in this chapter.

Microsoft uses two terms to distinguish between the two types of Outlook clients. If you are looking for a *rich* environment, select Outlook 2000 because it provides the most features. If you are looking to *reach* from your environment to different types of clients, select Outlook Web Access because it provides the fastest access from a distance and works with most Web browsers, regardless of the operating system.

Physical Access

The concept of physical access is simply based on connecting a client physically on a route that leads to the server. The first step toward setting up client connectivity to the Exchange Server is providing a physical path between the client and the server.

Messaging protocols are primarily Application and Presentation layer protocols, as designated by the Open Systems Interconnection (OSI) Reference Model. The layers below the Application and Presentation layers provide network connectivity and the physical infrastructure. These layered protocols make the messaging system independent of the underlying infrastructure, as illustrated in Figure 5.1.

Figure 5.1 Messaging Protocols Are Independent of Underlying Infrastructure

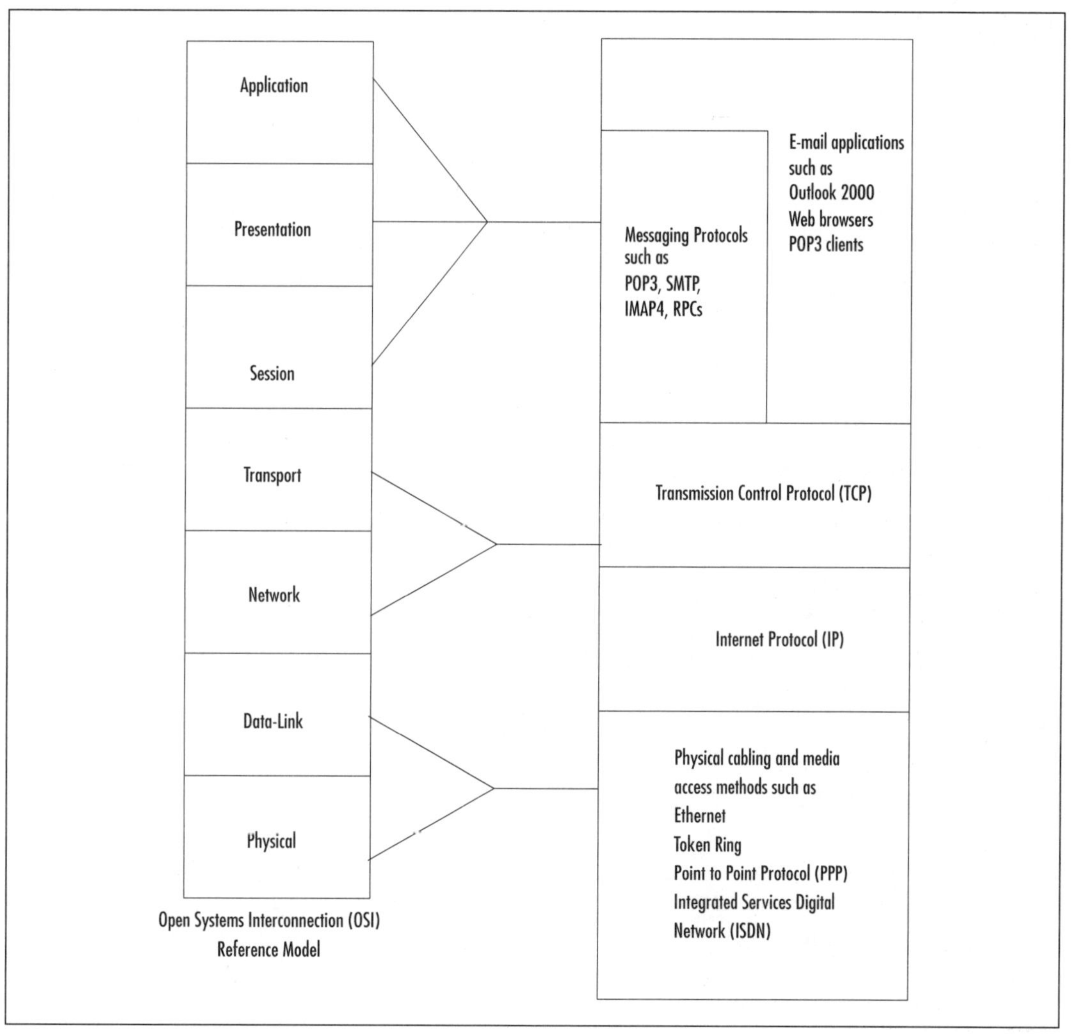

WARNING

Only two requirements must be met by any network over which you want to run Exchange 2000: It must support Transmission Control Protocol/Internet Protocol (TCP/IP) and provide Domain Name System (DNS) services. These requirements are needed by Active Directory, which provides directory information to Exchange Server. If any link in the chain does not support TCP/IP, you could encounter a failure to connect physically to Exchange 2000.

Messaging services can be supplied via the Internet from an Exchange Server. When users need to access their e-mail from remote locations, and when the Exchange Servers are connected to the Internet, you can configure the clients to retrieve e-mail over the Internet with Exchange 2000's and Windows 2000's Internet connectivity services.

Some of the most common ways for a client to gain physical access to the messaging system are:

- Local area networks (LANs)

- Wide area networks (WANs)

- Remote access via dial-up modems

- Remote access via virtual private networks (VPNs) over the Internet

Local Area Networks

Connecting a client computer to the same LAN that links to the Exchange Server is a configuration with the least likely interruption to service due to a physical problem. LANs are typically constructed of reliable wiring and few points of failure.

The Network and Transport layers provide the addressing and routing of data throughout the network. TCP/IP is required as the Layer 3 and Layer 4 protocol due to Exchange 2000's reliance on Windows 2000 Active Directory and, in turn, the Active Directory's reliance on TCP/IP. When you connect a mail client on a LAN, you simply connect it to the same network on which the Exchange Server is located, as shown in Figure 5.2.

Figure 5.2 Connecting a Mail Client on a LAN

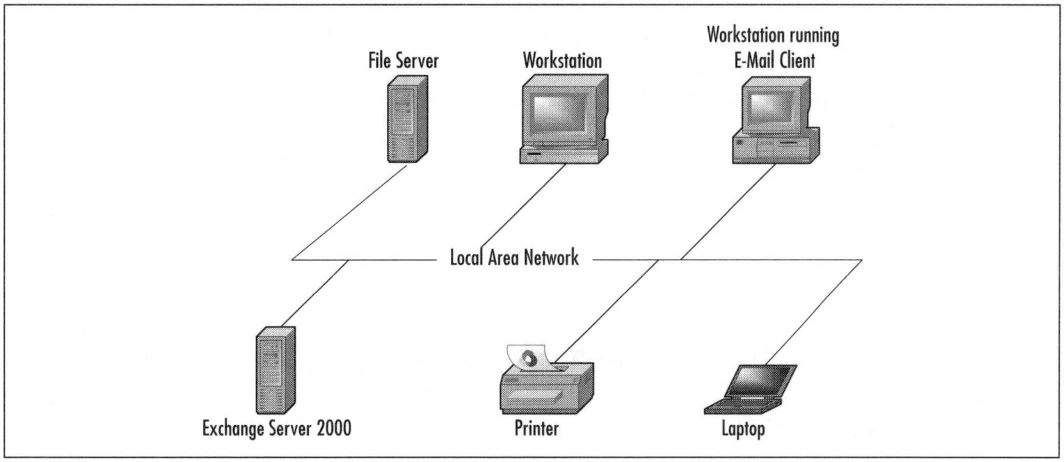

Wide Area Networks

Connectivity to an Exchange Server over a WAN is only slightly different from the connectivity you establish over a LAN. The WAN brings about a routing component as well as multiple types of physical and Data-Link layer topologies. WAN links tend to be less reliable and slower than LAN links. There is a tremendous number of types of WANs that you could have.

NOTE

You will rarely, if ever, connect a client or an Exchange Server directly to the WAN link. In fact, if you do connect directly to a WAN link, it probably will be with the Exchange Server and will be for its use as a router as well as a messaging server. The problem with this setup is that you will have a tremendous amount of overhead on the server, reducing its performance as both a messaging server *and* a router.

When you connect your network client to the LAN, it routes traffic through one or more network segments to eventually reach the network segment that connects to the messaging server, as shown in Figure 5.3. The Network and Transport layer protocols, in this case TCP/IP, run over each of the segments, providing the routing functions between the segments.

Figure 5.3 Connecting a Mail Client to Access an Exchange Server over a WAN

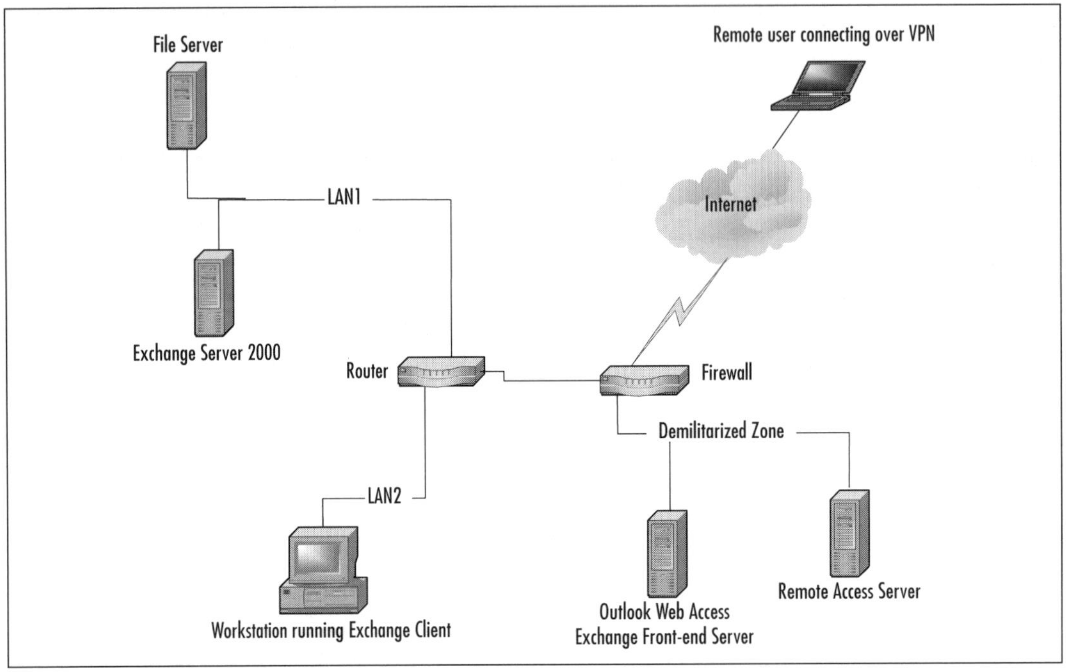

Dial-Up Connections

Remote access servers (RAS) provide dial-up connections to the enterprise network, or intranet. Dial-up connections can use the following types of connections (for more detail on these types of connections via RAS, read the Physical Networking section in Appendix B.

- Analog

- Digital subscriber line (DSL)

- Integrated Services Digital Network (ISDN)

Each of these RAS dial-up connections uses a special adapter on the machine, which is then connected to a telephone line. Analog connections can use a modem with a standard telephone line. DSL links require a filter on a telephone line as well as a DSL adapter. ISDN connections use an "ISDN modem," which is actually a codec to code and decode digital signals. Depending on the type of ISDN connection, it can connect to a standard telephone line, or it might require a leased line. Your telephone company might not offer DSL or ISDN, so make certain to check with the company • before planning to using them for RAS connectivity.

Speeding Up Exchange over a Dial-Up Link

When you use a remote connection, you are stuck with a very slow link to your messaging server. It can be several minutes before you connect to the Exchange Server and are able to work on your e-mail. But you can do at least one thing to optimize remote access for Outlook 2000. This involves editing the registry on a Windows 9x or 2000 computer, which is deeply frowned upon by Microsoft, since mistakes can ruin the entire operating system. Before you start the registry edits, you should fully back up the system, including making a copy of the registry … just in case. Once you are ready to start:

1. Click Start | Run.

2. Type **regedit** and press Enter.

3. Navigate to HKLM\SOFTWARE\Microsoft\Exchange\Exchange Provider.

4. Open the Rpc_Binding_Order Key. The value should be similar to ncalrpc,ncacn_ip_tcp,ncacn_spx,ncacn_np,netbios,ncacn _vns_spp. Each of these items separated by a comma represents a different type of protocol. RPCs will try binding to each protocol in the order listed until it reaches one that can connect Outlook 2000 to the Exchange Server.

   - Ncalrpc binds to local RPCs, which means that the Outlook client checks to see if the Exchange Server is running locally before checking the network. This is fine if you are running Outlook on your server, but it's probably not your first choice otherwise.

   - Ncacn_ip_tcp binds to TCP/IP. If connecting to Exchange 2000, you will want to use this as your first item.

   - Ncacn_spx binds to Novell's Sequence Packet Exchange (SPX) protocol. With Exchange 2000, you will probably not use this item.

   - Ncacn_np binds to the Named=Pipe protocol.

   - Netbios binds to NT's NetBIOS version protocol. With Exchange 2000, you will probably not use this option, but you could possibly use it for older versions of Exchange.

Continued

> ■ Ncacn_vns_spp binds to a Vines network protocol. This is
>   the least likely protocol that you would use.
>
> 5. For Exchange 2000 Server, change the order of the protocols
>   to ncacn_ip_tcp, ncalrpc,netbios,ncacn_np,ncacn_spx,ncacn
>   _vns_spp in the key and then click OK.

Virtual Private Networks

VPNs leverage the Internet to provide access to private networks for remote
users. A VPN is a "tunnel" from a remote client through a public network
to a private network, creating a connection that emulates a direct connection to the private network. Data that travels across the VPN connection is
encrypted. You may create a VPN connection from any Internet-connected
location, although some manufacturers have implemented only their proprietary VPN solutions to work over a dial-up connection. A VPN tunnel is
depicted in Figure 5.4.

Figure 5.4 VPN Tunnel

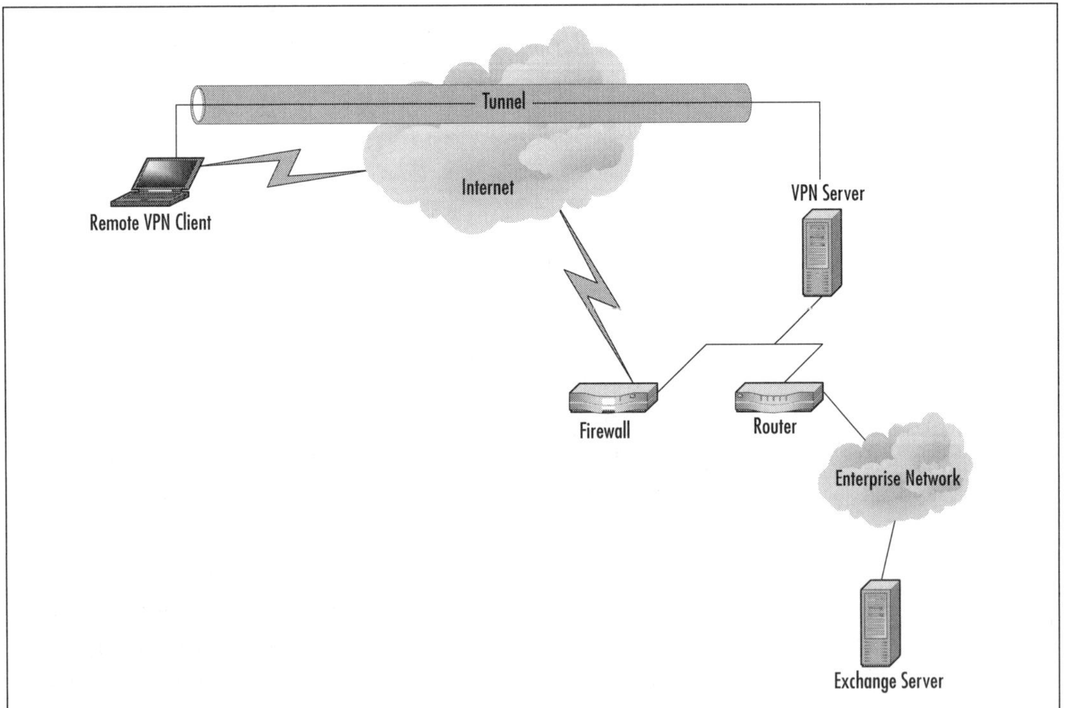

A VPN requires the following components:

- **VPN server** Provides VPN connections to remote access clients or routers.

- **VPN clients** Hosts that initiate VPN connections to the VPN server.

- **Encapsulation** Private data is encapsulated with a header, allowing data to traverse the public internetwork.

- **Tunnel** The path that the data travels.

- **Encryption** Private data is encrypted at the sending VPN host (either client or server) and decrypted at the receiving end.

- **Authentication** The VPN server verifies that the VPN client has appropriate permissions for access to the private network.

For more information on encryption and authentication, please see Chapter 3.

In Exchange 2000, a client that accesses the server using a Messaging Application Program Interface (MAPI), such as Outlook 2000, must use a VPN connection in order to use mail services over the Internet. However, POP3, IMAP4, and Outlook Web Access clients can connect directly over the Internet if the Exchange Server is connected directly to the Internet. Non-MAPI clients can connect as shown in Figure 5.5.

Figure 5.5 Non-MAPI Clients Connect to Exchange Directly

VPN Authentication and Encryption Protocol Considerations

Many businesses are implementing VPNs to reduce their costs for maintaining dial-up servers. Using a VPN server means that you need only a single server (or very few redundant servers) and a single Internet connection (or few redundant Internet connections) to provide multiple people with access to the internal network or intranet. If you are looking for more information about VPN protocols, read the VPN Protocol Details section in Appendix B.

IPSec

Internet Protocol Security (IPSec) is a standard for security that is implemented at the Network layer of the OSI Reference Model. This is in contrast to earlier security models that implemented security at the Application layer. IPSec enables data to travel through the network in a completely secure manner. IPSec itself is used with both VPN connections and dial-up connections for remote users.

To implement IPSec in Windows 2000:

1. Right-click My Network Places and select Properties.

2. Double-click any connection. IPSec will be applied to all connections that use TCP/IP, even though you configure it for only one connection.

3. Click on Internet Protocol (TCP/IP). It should already be checked. Click the Properties button.

4. Click the Advanced button.

5. Click the Options tab.

6. Click IP Security, and then click the Properties button.

7. Click the radio button for "Use this IP security policy" and select the policy from the drop-down box. If you are using a client machine, select "Client (Respond Only)." If you are using a server machine, select either "Secure Server (Require Security)" or "Server (Request Security)." This dialog box is shown in Figure 5.6.

8. Click OK and close all dialog boxes.

Figure 5.6 IP Security Configuration

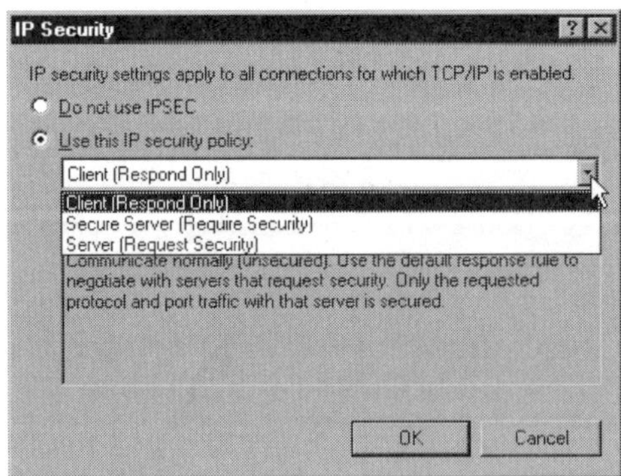

PPTP

Point-to-Point Tunneling Protocol (PPTP) is an extension to Point-to-Point Protocol (PPP) that creates a private tunnel that secures information sent across the Internet to a private network. This works best with a dial-up connection. PPTP is a Microsoft specification for VPN. In order to create a PPTP connection on a Windows 2000 client:

1. Right-click My Network Places, and select Properties.

2. Double-click Make New Connection. The New Connection Wizard will start.

3. Click the Next button.

4. Select "Connect to a private network through the Internet," as shown in Figure 5.7. Then click Next.

Figure 5.7 Connect to a Private Network Through the Internet

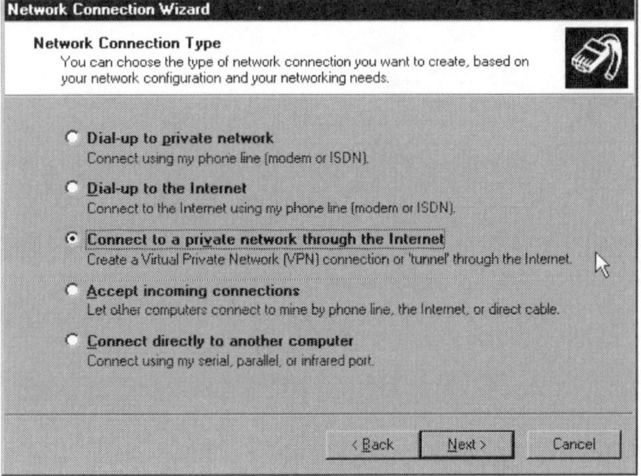

5. Select a connection, or the option to not dial up the Internet. If you select the option to not dial up the Internet, you may use the PPTP connection over a nondial-up line, such as when you are connected to a LAN that is connected to the Internet. Click Next when finished.

6. Type in the IP address of the VPN server to which you will connect with PPTP, and then click Next.

7. Select whether all users or just yourself will have access to this VPN connection. Then click Next.

8. Type in a name for the connection, and click Finish.

9. The new connection will show up in the My Network Places Properties dialog box as a new connection icon. Right-click the icon, and select Properties.

10. Click the Networking tab.

11. Drop down the box that states "Type of VPN Server I am calling," and select Point to Point Tunneling Protocol (PPTP), as displayed in Figure 5.8. Click OK and close the dialog boxes.

Figure 5.8 Configuring the VPN Connection for PPTP

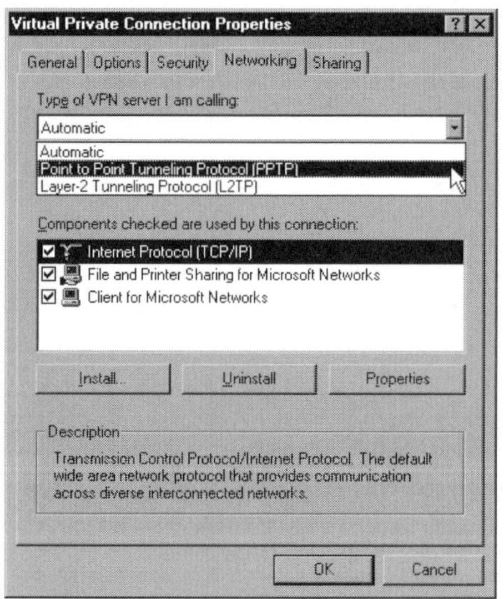

L2TP

Layer 2 Tunneling Protocol (L2TP) is a VPN tunneling protocol standard that is based on the concepts presented by Microsoft's PPTP and Cisco's Layer 2 Forwarding (L2F) protocols. L2TP is more secure than PPTP and should be your preferred method of connection, if you have the option of either PPTP or L2TP. L2TP is supported natively by Windows 2000. You can create a L2TP VPN connection in the identical way that you use to create a PPTP connection, except that you select L2TP instead of PPTP, which is shown in Figure 5.8.

VPN Security Considerations

When you use a VPN for remote users, your e-mail travels through a "tunnel" built across the Internet and then into your internal, private network. It is imperative to secure remote users' connections in order to prevent mail interception and attacks on the network.

There is no required additional configuration for the Exchange Server to simply provide e-mail access to clients that connect over a VPN. However, you can make changes to your network to protect it from potential attacks. (This process is reviewed in detail in Chapters 2 and 7.) The types of attacks that you may encounter are:

- Denial of service (DoS)
- E-mail forgery
- E-mail relaying
- Theft of data
- Viruses

Firewalls

Adding a firewall between the internal network and the Internet can protect against DoS attacks. The firewall is used to reduce the number and types of packets that can be sent from the Internet into the private network. DoS attacks are denoted by multiple, repeated transmissions of network packets that utilize so much of the network's bandwidth that users are unable to log on and servers cannot respond to requests. Exchange 2000 operates in a network with a firewall, but you must be aware of the types of traffic that use certain ports and be very specific about how to filter or disable that traffic. For example, SMTP uses TCP port 25, and if you disable that traffic altogether, you will not be able to send or receive e-mail via SMTP on the Internet.

Denial-of-Service Attacks

DoS can be aimed specifically at e-mail servers by overwhelming the servers with SMTP, IMAP4, POP3, or NNTP connections. This type of attack will keep the server's central processing unit (CPU) so busy that it cannot respond to other requests or perform scheduled operations. To prevent these types of attacks, you can configure Exchange 2000 to deny connections to virtual servers from a list of IP addresses or a specific domain name. Using Windows 2000 Performance Monitor, you can monitor the CPU utilization for each server and the number and location of connections that each Exchange Server receives. If messages from a particular domain name or IP address dominate the server's usage, you can deny that domain name or IP address the right to connect.

E-Mail Forgery

E-mail forgery can be prevented by validating the "from" address by the SMTP mail server. Exchange 2000 Server supports this SMTP function.

Using Exchange 2000 Server's SMTP Relay Control, you can ensure that the incoming SMTP IP address is included in a list of approved addresses and, if it is not, prevent that e-mail from being transmitted. E-mail forgery occurs when a person sends an e-mail using someone else's domain name as the "from" address. This is a practice used by persons who send *spam* e-mail—that is, unsolicited e-mail. E-mail forgery is another form of e-mail relaying, where a person bounces his e-mail through another domain's e-mail server. This is a practice for people who want their e-mail messages to remain anonymous, perhaps for nefarious reasons. Such relayed e-mail can be traced to the bounced domain, causing problems for that domain's owners.

Encryption

Encryption is the optimal way to prevent data theft. Encryption scrambles the data that is sent from one network node to another so that the only way to read it is to have the unscrambling key. Exchange 2000 Server supports encryption based on Transport Layer Security (TLS), Secure Sockets Layer (SSL), and IPSec. Data theft occurs when traffic is monitored, or *sniffed*, by a network node. A person who has set up this type of network node easily reads unencrypted traffic. Data theft can also occur when an unauthorized person gains access to a network server and can download files. This second type of data theft can be prevented by a firewall.

Viruses

A virus detection software package is the best defense against viruses. Most third-party virus detection software programs provide hot fixes to immediately eradicate an invading virus. Regardless of whether you connect to the Internet, viruses abound in e-mail systems. They are particularly prevalent in high-end e-mail systems. For example, Exchange 2000 and Outlook 2000 both support a tremendous scripting capability. However, that same scripting capability makes them primary targets for scripted viruses. Most of these scripts are sent as attachments to e-mail rather than the content of the e-mail itself. When a user receives such an e-mail virus, the user can delete the e-mail without causing damage. But if the user opens the attachment, the virus wreaks havoc on the local computer or the e-mail system, depending on what the virus is scripted to do. Usually, the virus copies itself to the computer and then forwards itself to people listed in the recipient's e-mail address book.

TIP

If you use a firewall on your network, you can design bridgehead servers to manage Internet e-mail while remaining servers handle internal e-mail requests. This system reduces the number of servers that can be affected by a malicious attack from an Internet user. A bridgehead server in this scenario can be designed with two separate SMTP virtual servers and two separate network adapters. One adapter is connected to the internal network and the other connected to the Internet or a demilitarized zone (DMZ). The external virtual server can be configured to allow relaying of e-mail for the internal virtual server, thus preventing e-mail relaying at the same time it diminishes the number of servers that could be affected by a DoS attack.

Using Windows 2000 Routing and Remote Access Servers

You can configure Windows 2000 servers with the native Routing and Remote Access Service (RRAS) to provide either dial-up or VPN connections to remote users. These servers are able to authenticate directly to the Active Directory, so users can take advantage of a single logon. Your network can have several RRAS servers at various locations. Some can provide dial-up connections; others provide VPN connections, or a single server can provide both dial-up and VPN connections. Distributing the RRAS across the network can help reduce costs of telephone access for dial-up users. However, the RRAS that provides VPN connections should be located at the point at which the network connects to the Internet, as shown in Figure 5.9.

Windows 2000 RRAS can provide either L2TP or PPTP connections. The server will authenticate a remote client before opening a VPN connection. The session then creates the tunnel for packets to flow. Packets are encrypted at the sending device and then decrypted at the receiving device.

Clients

Migrations are not easy, mainly because you are removing something established and replacing it with something that behaves in an entirely different way. The following factors could affect a migration:

- The network might not be prepared; it might not support the bandwidth, the hardware, or the protocols needed.

Figure 5.9 VPN Servers Sit Next to the Internet Link

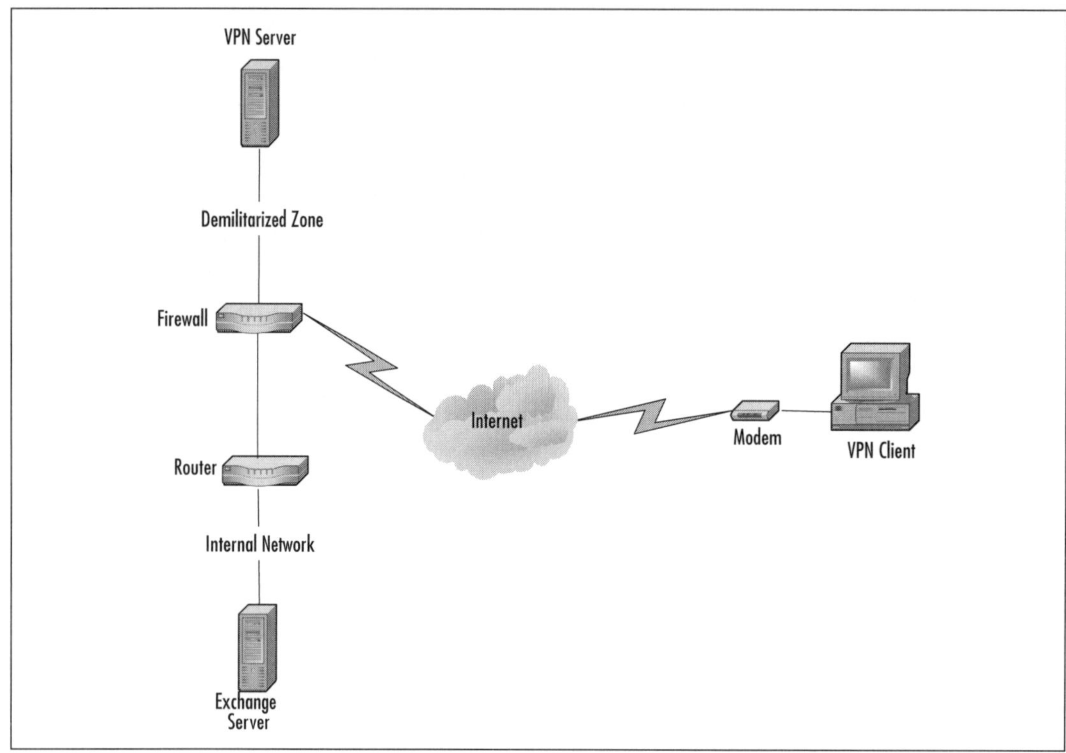

- The administrators might not be prepared; they might not be able to quickly optimize or adjust settings due to lack of familiarity.

- Usually the users are the most unprepared, having never used the new system before.

The remainder of this chapter covers some of the top client application installation issues that you will encounter as an administrator. In the MAPI Clients section, we discuss how to install Outlook 2000 on an individual workstation. In addition, we review how to roll out Outlook 2000 using Group Policies so that you can install multiple workstations simultaneously using Active Directory. We also cover non-MAPI clients such as Outlook Web Access that you can use to connect to Exchange Server.

MAPI Clients

The Messaging Application Program Interface (MAPI) is a standard method for messaging clients to use to access a messaging server. Several MAPI clients have been created for the current and past versions of Exchange Server. These clients are:

- Outlook 2000

- Outlook 98

- Outlook 97

- Exchange client 5.0

- Exchange client 4.0

Outlook 2000 is both a component of Office 2000 and the client shipped with Exchange 2000 Server. Outlook 2000 is optimized for use with Exchange 2000, but that does not prevent people from using older MAPI clients. The fact that older clients can be configured to work with Exchange 2000 Server can help bridge the gap between an older version of Exchange and migrating to the new Exchange 2000 Server.

New in Exchange 2000 Server, MAPI clients use the Windows 2000 Active Directory to resolve address names. Outlook 2000 clients (and Outlook 98 clients that have been upgraded with the Outlook 98 Archive Patch) access a Windows 2000 Active Directory Global Catalog server directly using a referral service under Exchange 2000. Older MAPI clients use the Exchange 2000 Server DSProxy service to intercede on behalf of Active Directory. As a result, older MAPI clients generate more traffic on the network. DSProxy acts as a stand-in for the client because the older clients were programmed to communicate directly with Exchange to obtain address book information, as displayed in Figure 5.10.

Figure 5.10 DSProxy

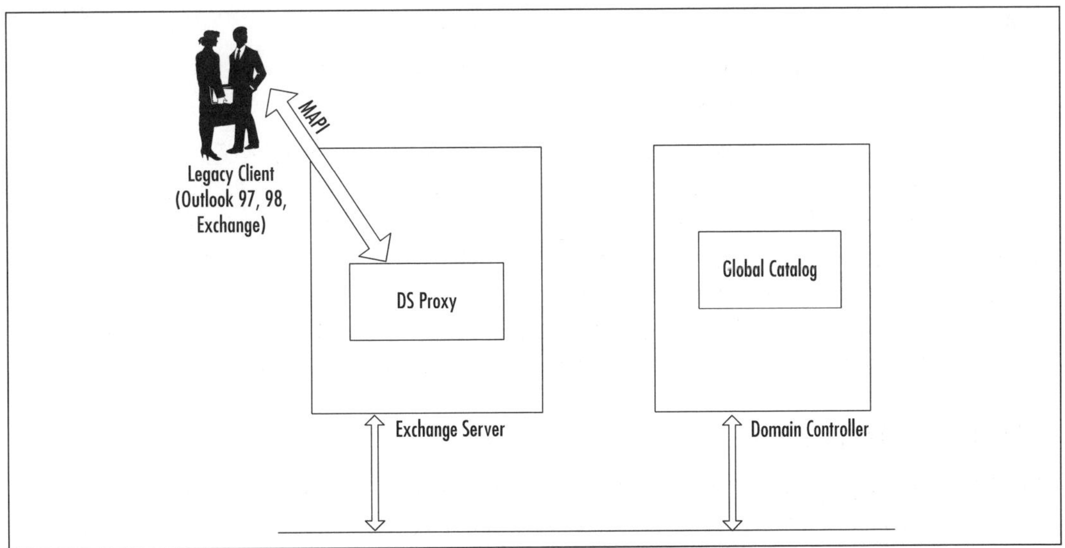

Outlook 2000

Microsoft Outlook 2000 is not only an e-mail client application; it also is a personal information manager with calendaring, tasks, and contact management. Outlook 2000 extends into collaborative groupware through its meeting management and task assignments. Using Outlook 2000's object model, administrators can customize Outlook 2000 to meet their organizations' needs through the creation of custom forms and scripts using Visual Basic Scripting Edition (VBScript). The object model is the same method that is used by Visual Basic to create applications. Objects, such as a button or a text window, are added to an Exchange mail form, and a programmer applies programming information to each of those objects.

The Outlook 2000 application, shown in Figure 5.11, provides Notes, a Journal for application usage, Sticky Notes, and the ability to manage folders.

Outlook Storage Options

Outlook can store information centrally on the Exchange Server or the POP3 server, or it can store information locally in personal storage (.PST) files, or it can synchronize online information to be accessible offline in offline storage (.OST) files:

- .PST files store mail items, contact items, tasks, notes, and a calendar on a local hard drive. These files are not part of your mailbox in the Exchange information store, but you can copy or move items from the Exchange information store to them. If you want to create a .PST file, you can click the File menu in Outlook 2000 and select New | Personal Folders. Type a name for the file in the Save In box, and make certain you place the .PST file in a location in which you want it to be stored. Click Create. You will be prompted with a Name box, and you can type a name here that will display in Outlook. The default for this name is Personal Folders. You can install Personal Folders even if you don't connect to an Exchange Server information store.

- .OST files are copies of the mailbox located on an Exchange Server. An . file with the .OST extension enables you to work with mail when you are not connected to the Exchange Server. To create an offline storage file, you must first be online and connected to Exchange. Then within Outlook 2000, click the Tools menu and select Services. Select the Microsoft Exchange Server option, and click the Properties button. Click Advanced, and then click Offline Folder File Settings. Type the path and the name of the new .OST file. When prompted, click OK to create the new file. Click OK, and then click OK again to close. You can use offline folders only if you have already set up Outlook to use Exchange Server. The main contents of your mailbox will be synchronized in the .OST file. Any folders that you may have created will need to be manually flagged for synchronization. If you want to synchronize a public folder, you can do so by copying a shortcut to the public folder to your Favorites; then, after viewing the Properties of that favorite shortcut, click the Synchronization tab and select "When offline or online." When you want to synchronize your .OST file with the Exchange Server, click the Tools menu and select Synchronize, and then select All folders.

Figure 5.11 Outlook 2000

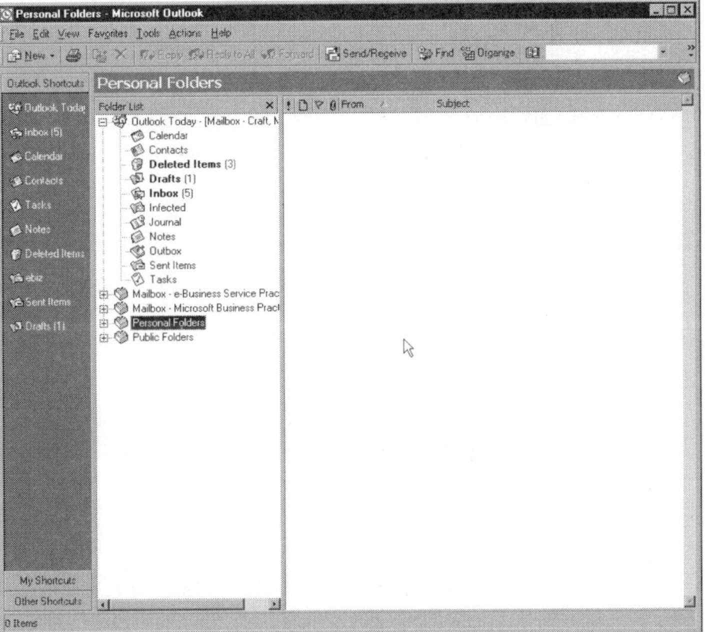

Folder Home Page

Of all Outlook 2000's innovations, the one that makes Outlook 2000 a candidate for an e-business application is that Outlook 2000 can associate a folder with a HyperText Markup Language (HTML) page. This becomes the folder home page and replaces the default folder view. Furthermore, an administrator can place a script in that folder home page that uses Outlook's object model to access information in the folder. If it is desired, an administrator can integrate that folder home page into an intranet or extranet site. This makes it easy for an organization to use Web information and Exchange information in the same document. Another benefit of the folder home page is that it enables users to access the contents of Exchange public folders through a Web page without actually running Outlook 2000. However, since the folder home page uses Outlook's object model to provide this information, Outlook 2000 must be installed on the user's workstation.

You can make any Internet Web page a home page for an Outlook folder. As you can see, the Web page will not allow you to work with mail items, since it effectively obscures them from view. This means that you must edit a Web page to include Outlook commands in order to access and utilize the Outlook information. However, if you do create a Public Folder home page, you will have a much richer environment for your public folder. You must be a folder owner in order to apply a home page to an Outlook public folder. To do so:

1. Right-click the folder.
2. Select Properties.
3. Click the Home Page tab.
4. Check the box to "Show home page by default for this folder."
5. Type the URL for the home page in the Address box, as shown in Figure 5.12, or click the Browse button and browse for a Web page.

Figure 5.12 Applying a Home Page to a Public Folder

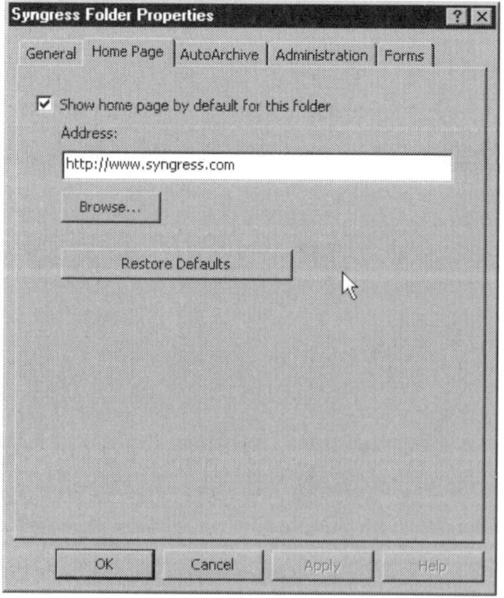

6. When you are finished, the home page will display as shown in Figure 5.13.

Figure 5.13 A Home Page Displayed When a Public Folder Is Selected

> **TIP**
>
> Microsoft has an easy-to-use tool to help administrators design folder Web pages. It's called the Team Folders Wizard. Microsoft provides the Team Folders Wizard for download at www.microsoft.com/exchange/downloads/tfwizard.htm.

Installing Outlook

Installing Outlook 2000 is simply a matter of running Setup from the Outlook 2000 CD or a share point that you've configured, then following the options as prompted by the setup application. The following section covers how to set up an Exchange profile. The "Advanced" section shows you how to create an Outlook installation package that you can customize and make part of your group policies for installing software.

The Basics

Many organizations deploy Outlook 2000 as part of Office 2000. If you have Outlook 2000 already installed, you can configure it to access an Exchange Server by following these steps:

1. Right-click the Microsoft Outlook icon on the desktop, and select Properties.

2. If you would like to create a new profile rather than change the current one, click the Show Profiles button.

3. Click Add and you will see the dialog box illustrated in Figure 5.14.

Figure 5.14 Adding a New Profile

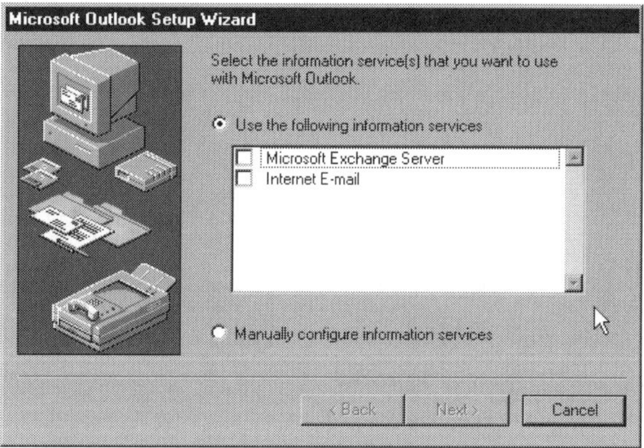

4. Check the box for Microsoft Exchange Server, and click Next.

5. Type in the name for this profile, and click Next.

6. Type in the name of the Exchange Server and then the name of the Mailbox, and click Next.

7. In the next dialog box, select whether or not you will need to have offline storage. If you need offline storage, click the Yes radio button. Otherwise, click No. After either choice, click Next.

8. Click Finish.

You can add many other information services to profiles. Briefly, they are:

- **Internet e-mail** This is a service to connect to a POP3 and SMTP mail server. If you use this service, you cannot connect to an Exchange Server in the same profile because both this service and the Exchange Server service use MAPI.

- **Microsoft LDAP directory** The LDAP service enables you to connect to a directory service in order to search for addresses. You can connect to multiple LDAP directories by adding multiple instances of this service.

- **Microsoft Mail** The Microsoft Mail service will connect Outlook 2000 to legacy Microsoft Mail servers.

- **MS Outlook Support for Lotus cc:Mail** This service will connect Outlook 2000 to a Lotus cc:Mail mailbox.

- **Outlook address book** The Outlook address book allows you to create an address book that is accessible when you use a MAPI service.

- **Personal address book** The personal address book lets you create an address book that is accessible without using any type of Exchange Server connection or MAPI service.

- **Personal folders** Personal folders are separate storage for mailbox items. You do not require a connection to an Exchange Server to use personal folders.

TIP

To absolutely ensure that your Outlook 2000 deployment performs at its best, you should download and apply the Service Pack. Service Packs for Outlook 2000 can be downloaded from http://officeupdate.Microsoft.com.

Advanced: Outlook Installer Package for Group Policies

Let's face it: Installing Outlook 2000 is a fairly straightforward task, if your only goal is to get the application loaded onto a workstation. However, if you have a goal of loading multiple workstations or of customizing the installation and reducing errors, well, that's more of a challenge. Outlook 2000 uses the new Windows Installer. This tool, in conjunction with Active Directory, allows you to roll out Outlook 2000 using a Group Policy and assign the software to groups of workstations or users, as you see fit. Effectively, the process is as follows:

1. Download the Office 2000 Resource Kit from www.microsoft.com/office/ork/2000/download/ORKTools.exe and install it on your workstation.

2. Create a share point on a file server. For Windows 2000, this means adding a file folder and then right-clicking on the file folder and selecting Sharing from the pop-up menu and then adding the user(s) or group(s) who should be allowed to access the files and install Outlook. Read-only permissions should be sufficient for installers, but make certain that you can modify and add extra files if you need them. Your share point will take the Universal Naming Convention (UNC) name of \\Server\share.

3. Run SETUP /A from the Outlook CD, placing the Outlook 2000 files on the file server share point created in Step 2, which creates an administrative installation point.

4. Run the Custom Installation Wizard from the Office Resource Kit tools. If you selected the defaults during installation, you should be able to click Start | Programs | Microsoft Office Tools | Microsoft Office 2000 Resource Kit Tools | Custom Installation Wizard.

5. Click Next at the Welcome screen.

6. When you are prompted, select the data1.msi file from the Outlook files by clicking the Browse button and locating it across the network, and then clicking Open.

7. Click Next to open the data1.msi file. You are then prompted to either select an existing .MST (a Windows Installer Template file) or not to use an existing one. Select not to use an existing one; you will automatically create a new .MST file. Click Next.

NOTE

An .MSI file is an installation file that requires the Windows Installer. The Windows Installer Service ships as a service in Windows 2000 and in Windows Millennium Edition (ME). (Older versions of Windows can apply a service pack to be able to use the Windows Installer Service.) The Windows Installer provides a standardized method for installing applications. It is integrated with the software distribution features of group policies in Active Directory. An .MST file is a customized template for the Windows Installer Service that directs how an application will be installed. You can check http://officeupdate.Microsoft.com for downloadable service pack .MSI files. Then you can deploy a service pack without having to visit your end users' desks!

8. You are then shown a path and filename for the new .MST file; either accept that path and filename or type in a new one and click Next.

9. You are now making selections that will be used in your template file. The path and organization name are first, as shown in Figure 5.15. Type in the path to which Outlook should be installed, and then type in the name of your organization. Click Next.

Figure 5.15 Path and Organization Name in Custom Installation Wizard

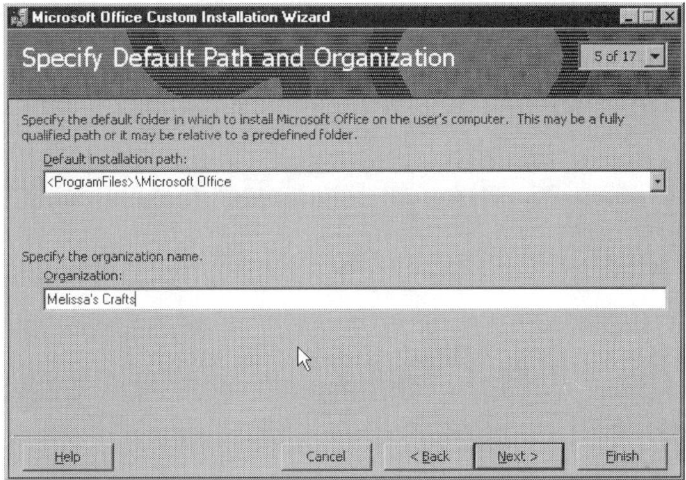

10. Now you will be prompted to define how previous versions of Outlook will be treated. To reduce the confusion that users face and to increase the available disk space, you should probably select the options to remove all previous versions. This is illustrated in Figure 5.16. Click Next.

11. Next, you need to select which features to install on the local workstations, which to run from the network, and which to not install at all. You do this by clicking the down arrow in the box to the left of each component and selecting the option, as shown in Figure 5.17. Once you have selected all the items and configured the installation of the files as you want them to occur, click Next.

12. You are next prompted for profile configuration. You can use the default settings (doing so is not recommended), or you can migrate the settings that the clients already are using, or you can specify an existing .OPS file. Click Next.

Figure 5.16 Remove Previous Versions of Outlook Automatically

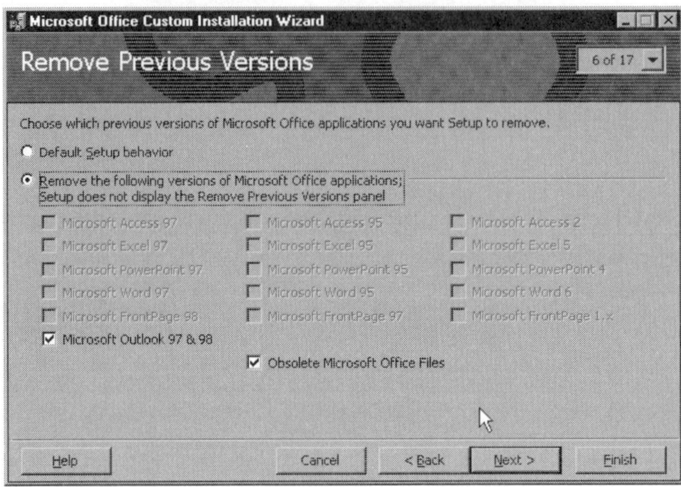

Figure 5.17 Selecting Files and Run Location

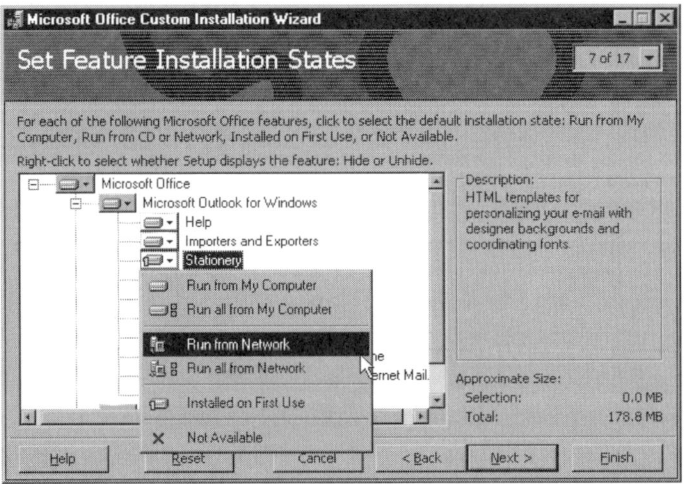

NOTE

An .OPS file describes the options for configuration of Outlook 2000. These options are found in the Tools menu under the Options item. You can create an .OPS file by running the Office Profile Wizard, which is downloadable from www.microsoft.com/office/ork/2000/download.

13. The following screen lets you specify any additional files to be copied to the workstation during installation. Normally this is not necessary. If you need to install more files, click the Add button, select the files, click the Add button, then click Next.

14. The next dialog box lets you set registry settings. If you have an .REG file, you can add the entire file by clicking the Import button and selecting it. Otherwise, you can add individual registry settings as you deem appropriate. Again, this is normally not necessary. Click Next when finished.

NOTE

An .REG file is a text file that lists the registry entries that can be applied to a Windows machine. When you apply an .REG file, the registry is updated with its contained registry entries.

15. Shortcuts can be modified for the Start menu and desktop on the following screen, shown in Figure 5.18. You can add any new shortcuts, remove the defaults, or change them as you would like your users' desktops to appear by using the Add, Modify, and Remove buttons. Click Next when you have finished this step.

Figure 5.18 Change Shortcuts to Modify Users' Desktops

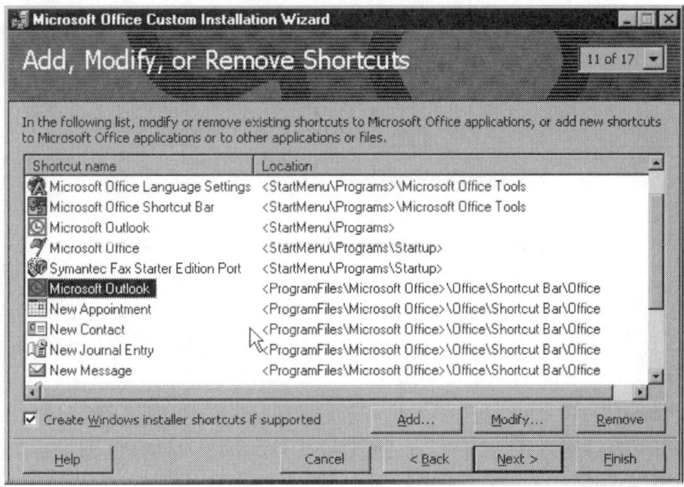

16. The following dialog box lets you specify any additional network share points that have an administrative installation of the Outlook 2000 files. If you have additional network shares, click the Add button and type them in. When you're done, click Next.

17. Next, you are prompted to type in additional programs to install after the Outlook 2000 installation has finished. If you add another setup program here and the application cannot be installed in an unattended manner, it will not be as easy to roll out multiple workstations, so select your setup files carefully and make certain to include all the switches that might be needed to ensure an unattended installation. Click Next when done.

18. The dialog box shown in Figure 5.19 allows you to configure Outlook's profile. Click each item in the left windowpane and customize that item in the right pane. Then click Next.

Figure 5.19 Configure the Outlook 2000 Profile

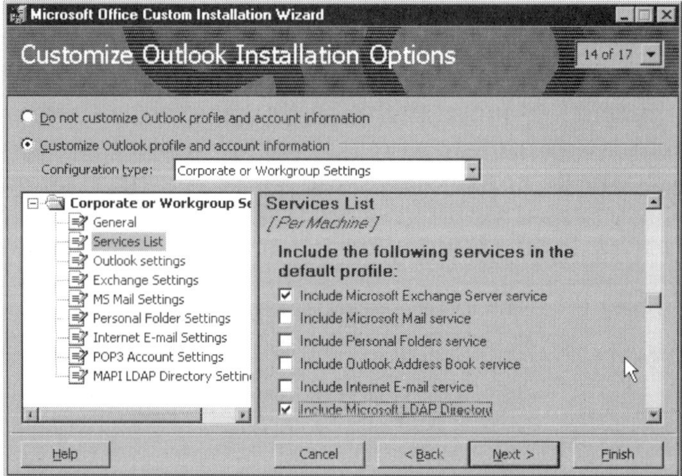

19. The next dialog box gives you the option to install Internet Explorer, version 5 (IE5), as part of the Outlook 2000 installation. For this exercise, don't choose IE5, but you might want to do so when you work with Outlook 2000 on your network. If you choose to install IE5, you should consider downloading and using the Internet Explorer Administration Kit (IEAK) and customizing the IE5 installation prior to the Outlook 2000 installation. Make your selections, and click Next.

20. The next dialog box lets you select items that appear during setup and make changes to them so that users will see something different. If you are performing an unattended installation, there is not much reason to make any changes. Click Next when you're finished.

21. The final dialog box allows you to save your changes. Click Finish.

22. To test the unattended installation, at a workstation, type:

```
\\Server\share\setup /t \\server\share\file.mst /q:n /wait
```

23. For further automation, open the setup.ini file in the \\server\ share\ location and change the line under the [MST] section to read MST1=file.mst, where file.mst is the file you created.

24. To set up the group policy, open the Active Directory Users and Computers console on a domain controller.

25. Navigate to the Organizational Unit that represents the users or computers who you want to have using Outlook 2000, and right-click it.

26. Select Properties, and then click the Group Policy tab.

27. Click New.

28. If you are installing software on computers regardless of who logs on, navigate below the Computers node. Otherwise, if you want users to have Outlook 2000 regardless of where they log on, navigate below the Users node. Expand the Software Settings.

29. Right-click Software Installation, and click New | Package.

30. Under File name, type the share point and data1.msi file. Click Open, and then select whether to Publish or Assign. If you publish the file, users can find it in the Control Panel under Add/Remove Programs. If you assign the file, it will automatically install.

31. Close all Windows and test the group policy by logging on as a user or on a computer to which Outlook was assigned or published.

TIP

To really impress your users, you can download the Outlook Bar Shortcuts Configuration Wizard from www.microsoft.com\ork\office\2000\download. Then customize the shortcuts in the Outlook bar for users, giving them shortcuts to public folders. You should also look at the Custom Maintenance Wizard for ongoing administrative maintenance.

Outlook 98

When you configure Outlook 98 to access an Exchange Server, you will find that it is the exact same process as configuring an Outlook 2000 profile. Not only that, but Outlook 98 follows a nearly identical method for installation; however, it *does not* support the Windows Installer, as Outlook 2000 does. To roll out these versions, you can use a Network Installation Wizard (in place of the Custom Installation Wizard), which you can download from www.microsoft.com/office/ork/download/setupniw.exe. The resulting template file is a .STF file, rather than an .MST file, and is not native to being used in Group Policy software installations. The easiest way to deploy multiple machines using Outlook 98 is to run the setup installation referencing the .STF template file from a script. We'll show you how to do this in the next paragraph.

Unattended Installations

Unattended installations reduce the time it takes to deploy multiple workstations, which lets you modify the registry and leaves no room for human error (once the installation file has been tested to work correctly). If you intend to run an unattended installation of Outlook 98, you should make the following changes:

1. Create an administrative share point by running SETUP /A from the Outlook CD and placing the files on a network server.

2. Run the Network Installation Wizard v2.0, which you can download from www.microsoft.com/office/ork/download/setupniw.exe.

3. Make changes to the Outlook.stf file using Network Installation Wizard. When you have finished, save your changes.

4. Open Outlook.stf, make any custom changes to the file, and save it.

5. On the client workstations, run \\server\share\SETUP /t d:\path\outlook.stf /q:n.

Outlook Web Access Clients

Outlook Web Access is an HTML client for Exchange Server. When a client connects to an Exchange Server running Outlook Web Access, its Web browser appears to have an Outlook e-mail client interface. Under Exchange 2000, Outlook Web Access is automatically installed and ready to use as long as Internet Information Services (IIS) is running.

One of the major benefits of using Outlook Web Access is that it is a nearly universally accessible e-mail client. Even if no client that can access

Exchange Server is available for a workstation, it can use Outlook Web Access if it has a browser. For example, if an organization wants to provide access to e-mail access to employees from home using Internet access but does not want to pay for or support e-mail client applications on users' personal computers, it can do so through Outlook Web Access. This not only allows users to be able to have a wide variety of operating systems and hardware types, but it does not require any installation beyond a browser. In another example, an organization can implement OWA for a business unit that uses UNIX machines; although they have compatible Web browsers, no Outlook application is available for them.

Another benefit of Outlook Web Access is its low-bandwidth utilization. If your network connects to other sites that have a high latency due to a slow or unreliable link, Outlook Web Access is a viable solution. Figure 5.20 depicts a network in which Outlook Web Access is deployed in a remote site due to a satellite link to that site. All clients in the remote site connect using Outlook Web Access; those in the other sites use Outlook 2000.

Figure 5.20 Using Outlook Web Access in High-Latency Networks

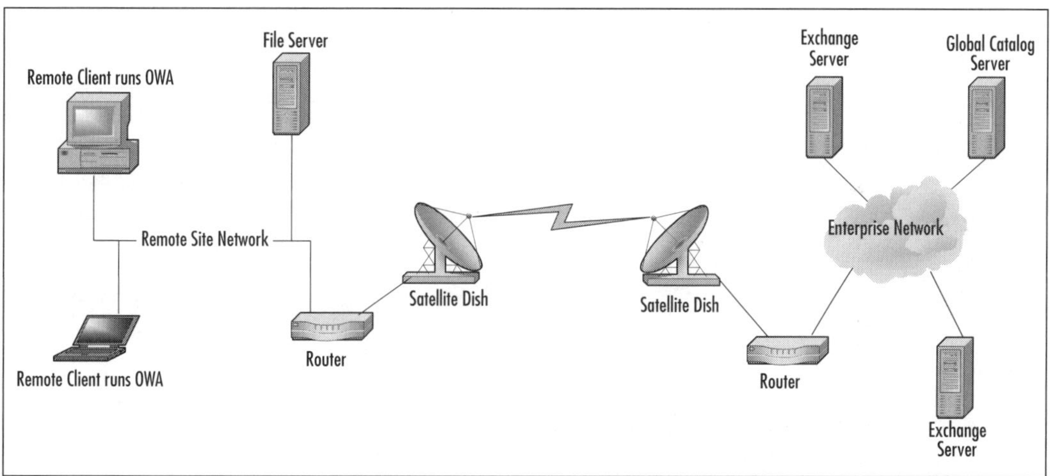

Finally, when you have a user that roams around the network, Outlook Web Access is a good solution because all e-mail resides on the Exchange Server. User-specific profiles and storage files do not reside on the local PC, so there is less administrative overhead. For example, Joan works in a laboratory that has seven workstations. Depending on the project Joan works on, she could be sitting at any one of those workstations or even a combination of two or more workstations during a single day. Since Joan shares the laboratory with 20 other technicians, it would be laborious to create 21 profiles on each of the seven workstations; however, it is not a hardship to allow Joan and the other technicians to use their own URLs on any particular workstation at any time in the lab.

OWA in Exchange 2000 is different from OWA in Exchange 5.5. OWA in Exchange 5.x was based on Active Server Pages (ASP) technology for access to the Exchange information stores. OWA in Exchange 2000 is based on Exchange 2000's Web Storage System. Administrators can define addresses for Exchange Server resources such as user mailboxes or specific folders. For example, http://owa.domain.com/exchange automatically directs a user to his own mailbox if he is previously authenticated. When a client types in the Exchange Server OWA address, IIS5 receives the OWA requests and passes the client to the OWA scripts related to the URL address that the user typed into the browser.

You can use URLs in conjunction with various commands rather than use the graphical interface. This capability makes it easy to integrate Exchange Server into your intranet or Internet Web site. To use a URL and a command together, use a syntax similar to http://owa.dom.com/exchange/folder?command=option. Table 5.1 lists some of the URLs and commands that you can use.

Table 5.1 OWA Commands

URL	Command	Purpose
Owa.dom.com/exchange/user	N/A	Opens a specific user's mailbox
Owa.dom.com/exchange/user/calendar	N/A	Opens a specific user's calendar
Owa.dom.com/exchange/user/tasks	N/A	Opens a specific user's tasks folder
Owa.dom.com/exchange/user/contacts	N/A	Opens a specific user's contacts folder
Owa.dom.com/exchange/user//item	N/A	Opens a specific item in the user's inbox
Any Exchange URL	View=myview	Displays the Outlook View named myview
Any Exchange URL	Sort=column	Sorts by the column named column

Continued

Table 5.1 Continued

URL	Command	Purpose
Owa.dom.com/exchange/user/calendar	Date=yyyymmdd	Displays that date in the calendar
Any Exchange URL	Cmd=navbar	Displays the navigation bar
Any Exchange URL	Cmd=new	Creates a new default item in the folder
Any Exchange URL	Cmd=options	Sets options
Owa.dom.com/exchange/user/item	Cmd=reply	Replies to an e-mail

Migrating from Exchange 5.5 OWA

The differences between Exchange 5.5 OWA and Exchange 2000 require you to perform a migration from the older version of OWA if you have customized the OWA ASP files in Exchange 5.5. To do so:

1. Install one or more Windows 2000 Servers with IIS5.

2. Install and configure Exchange 2000 Server on designated servers across the enterprise network.

3. Configure the Exchange 5.5 server that provides OWA to be a front-end OWA server to the Exchange 2000 back end. Users will use this Exchange 5.5 server for OWA, which then looks to the directory for the data location on Exchange 2000.

4. Customize the Exchange 2000 Server with OWA to meet your needs.

5. Pilot the Exchange 2000 OWA interface, and if it functions correctly, redirect all OWA traffic to the Exchange 2000 OWA server by using the URL that you have specified for the Exchange 2000 OWA server *or* by changing the URL to point only to the Exchange 2000 OWA server..

6. Take the Exchange 5.5 OWA server offline and set it aside until you are assured that there are no problems. (Depending on the size of your organization and OWA usage, this waiting period should be between a week and a month.)

7. Upgrade the Exchange 5.5 server to Exchange 2000 and place it on the network or decommission it.

Outlook Web Access Authentication

When you use OWA over the Internet, you should pay close attention to the way in which you secure the servers. In a single Exchange Server environment, configuration is straightforward. However, a multiple-server environment requires a little more thought because there is a chance of an authentication conflict. Optimally, you should configure all servers with the same authentication. A front-end server will use the authentication you configured for IIS, whereas a back-end server uses the authentication method set for Exchange Server. When you use different types of authentication on the front-end and back-end servers, such as Basic authentication on one and Windows Integrated on the other, users will probably require the right to log on locally to the front-end server. Since you will be using OWA, you should definitely use SSL with whatever authentication method you've selected. (For more security information, please review Chapter 3.)

You can apply the type of authentication you want to use for OWA through the Internet Services Manager utility. The steps to follow are:

1. Click Start | Programs | Administrative Tools | Internet Services Manager.

2. If you are running the utility on a different computer, you can connect to the OWA computer by clicking the Action menu, selecting Connect, and then typing in the name of the OWA server.

3. Once you are connected, locate the Web site that contains the Exchange directories. By default, Exchange directories are placed in the default Web site.

4. Right-click the Web site name and select Properties.

5. Click the Directory Security tab. You will see a dialog box similar to the one in Figure 5.21.

6. Click the Edit button under the Anonymous Access and Authentication Control box. The Authentication Methods dialog box appears, as shown in Figure 5.22. Select the authentication method that you prefer, and click OK until the dialog boxes are closed. Read the following sections to learn what each of these methods will mean for your OWA implementation.

Basic Authentication

Basic authentication is a clear text challenge response method. This method requires a user to enter a username, a domain, and a password in order to use OWA. Basic authentication can be used with a front-end server, and it can be used with any type of browser. The biggest drawback

Figure 5.21 Directory Security

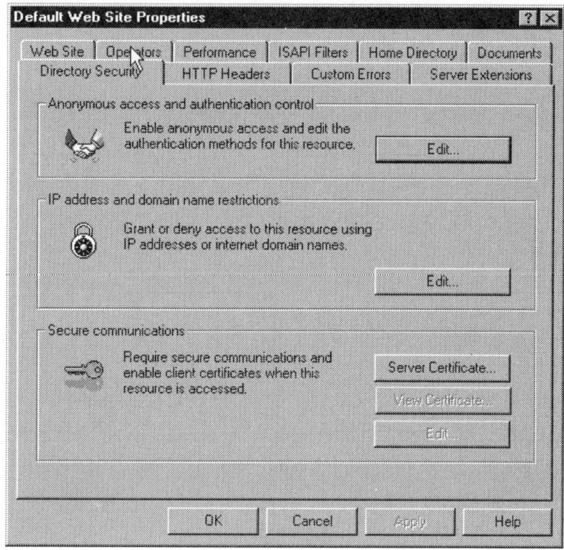

Figure 5.22 Authentication Methods

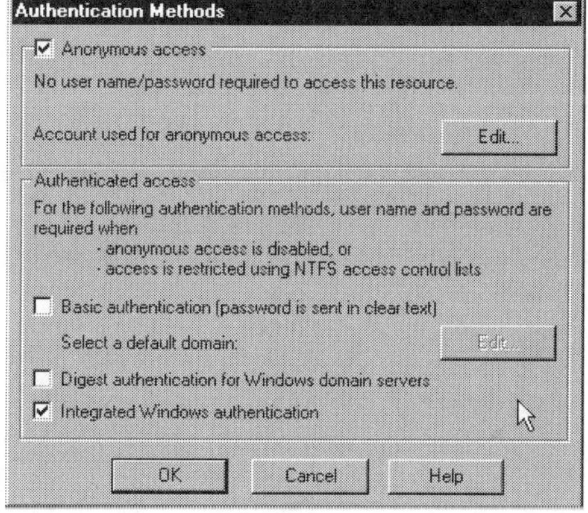

to basic authentication is that the user's name, domain, and password are transmitted across the network in clear text; anyone monitoring the transmission can pick it up, so it is not secure.

Integrated Windows Authentication

Integrated Windows Authentication operates best when the workstation uses Windows 2000 and Internet Explorer 5 because then it will use

Kerberos (an Internet standard authentication protocol also used by Active Directory). Any other Windows version (Windows 95, 98, or NT) can also authenticate using the Integrated Windows method, but they all use the legacy NTLM (NT LanMan) authentication. The nice thing about Integrated Windows authentication is that, unlike Basic authentication, the user's name, password, and domain are encrypted, and users who have already authenticated to the network are not prompted for their passwords when they access OWA. The biggest challenge with this method is that all the client workstations need to run 32-bit Windows and Internet Explorer, version 4 or 5.

Digest Authentication

A client uses digest authentication when it is challenged by the server to hash a value sent by the server. The client hashes the value along with the username, password, and domain name using Message Digest 5 (MD5) authentication and sends the hash and the original message to the server, which then knows that the client is valid (or not). Digest authentication works on any browser that is HTTP version 1.1 compliant. One of the problems with digest authentication is that you must be running the Exchange server (either a front-end or a back-end server) on a Windows 2000 domain controller.

Anonymous Access

Anonymous access is completely nonsecure. It is useful for providing access to general public folders on an intranet. Public folders that are provided via this method must be published, and then anonymous access must be specified explicitly. To use anonymous access, you configure each public folder that you want to provide to general users separately.

Secure Sockets Layer

SSL, although not an authentication method, offers high security through encryption for the entire transmission of data. What this means is that you can use Basic authentication on your Exchange Server and then secure the communication with OWA clients over SSL. Most Web browsers support SSL.

Disable OWA Access

OWA is automatically enabled for any user with a mailbox. If you want to deny a user access to Outlook Web Access, you complete the following steps:

1. Click Start | Programs | Administrative Tools | Active Directory Users and Computers.

2. Click the View menu.

3. Select the Advanced Features option so that it is enabled.

4. Navigate to a user that you intend to disable and right-click on the user object.

5. Select Properties from the pop-up menu.

6. Click the Exchange Advanced tab. This dialog box is shown in Figure 5.23.

Figure 5.23 Exchange Advanced Options

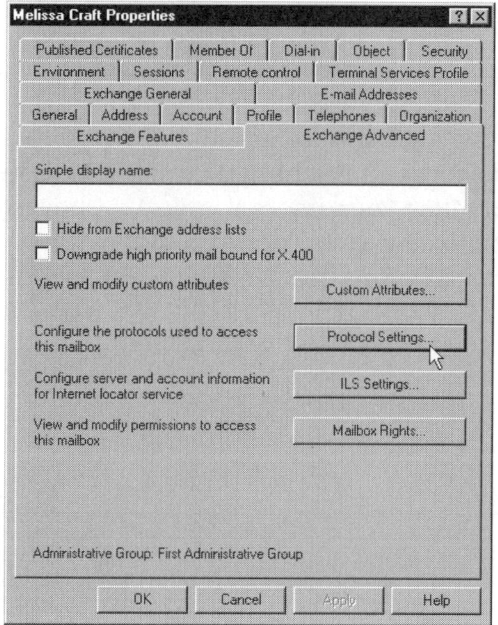

7. Click the Protocols Settings button.

8. Select HTTP and click the Settings button. Note that you can disable IMAP4 and POP3 using this same method for any user.

9. Disable HTTP by unchecking the box, as shown in Figure 5.24.

Exchange Server Placement

When you place the OWA servers, you need to consider where the Internet connection is located. Keep the following general rules in mind for your design:

Figure 5.24 Disabling OWA for a User

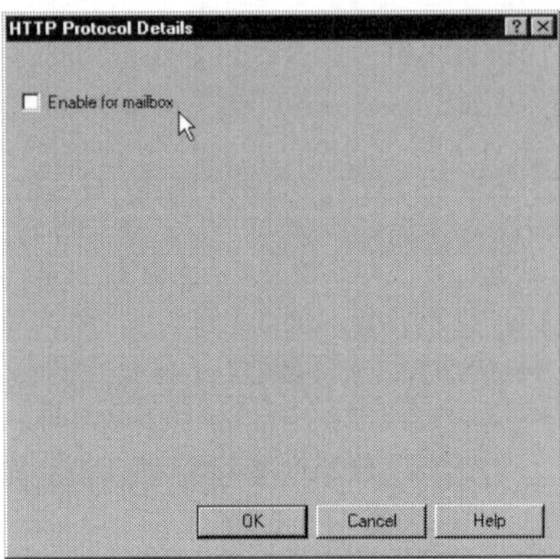

- Place front-end servers within your private network if you do use VPN, or access to Exchange over the Internet will not be allowed. A VPN will allow your users to use MAPI clients and give you a greater amount of security by not exposing your entire set of e-mail services directly to the Internet. This concept is illustrated in Figure 5.25.

Figure 5.25 VPN Used with Exchange

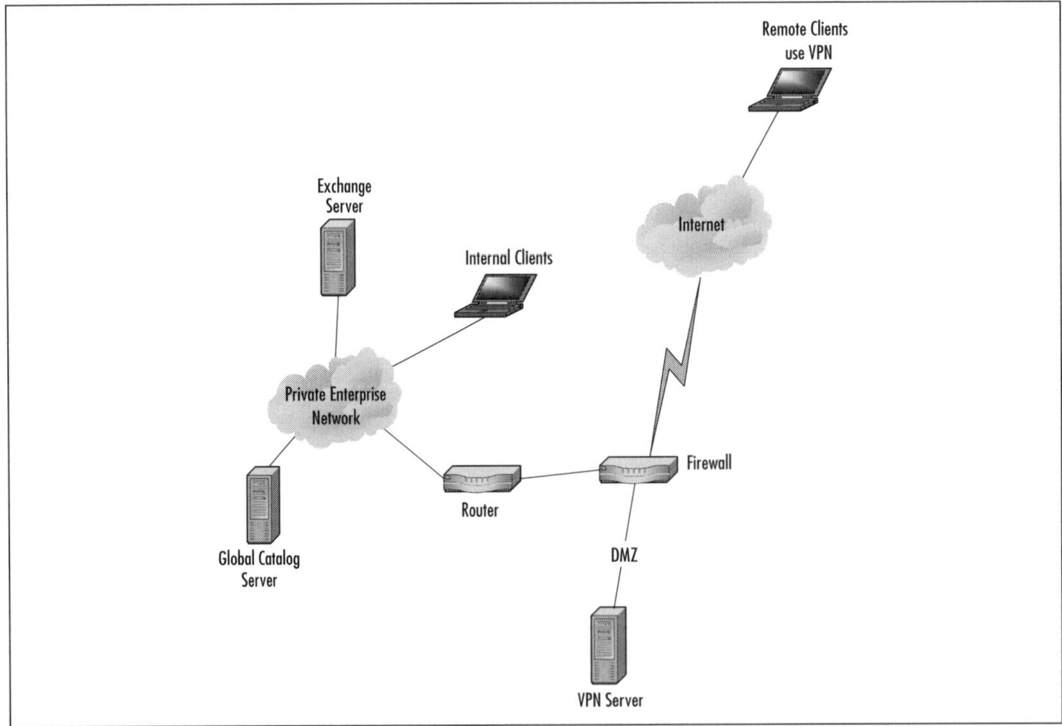

- Place back-end servers within your private network, whether you use a VPN or not.

- Place front-end servers on the DMZ if you do not use VPN.

- Maximize the use of front-end servers by letting both internal and Internet-based clients access them.

- Use dual-homed front-end servers if you place them directly on the Internet. An example of an Exchange system that is exposed to the Internet is shown in Figure 5.26.

Figure 5.26 Exchange on the Internet

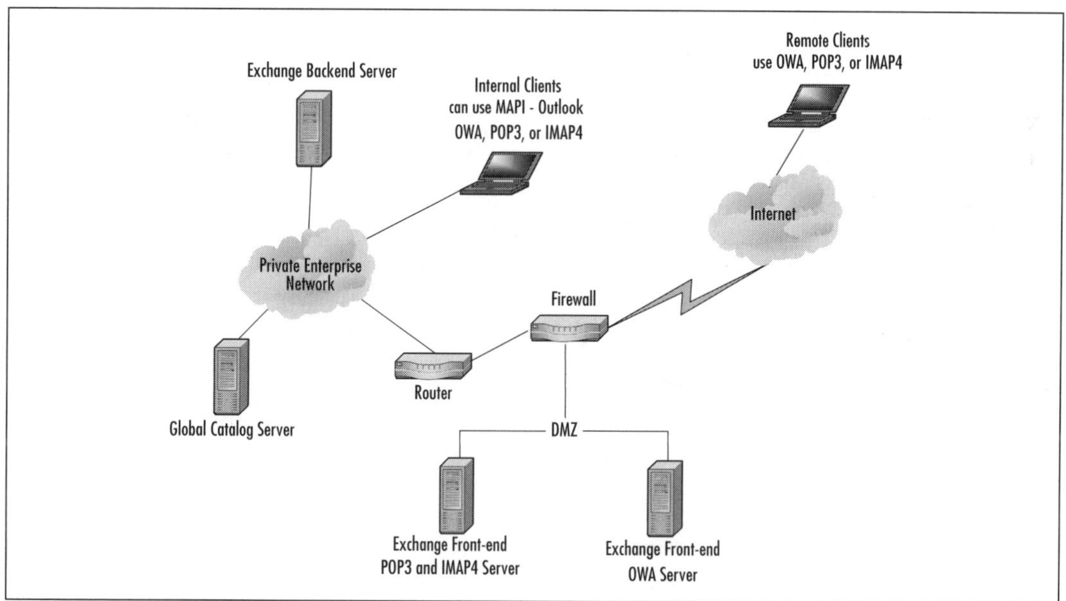

OWA is configured by default for access to mailboxes and public folders. In fact, after OWA is installed, IIS will have four new virtual IIS directories:

- **/exadmin** Used by the OWA Exchange Administration tool for public folder administration.

- **/exchange** Provides the root for mailboxes.

- **/exchweb** Keeps graphics and other files used by OWA.

- **/public** Provides the tree for public folders.

In order to define a front-end server, open the Exchange System Manager program and right-click the server. Then check the box for "This is a front-end server." Next, reboot. You can also disable the Exchange information store to optimize performance.

Internet Explorer, Version 5

OWA works best when it is used with Microsoft Internet Explorer 5. One of the main advantages of this combination is that IE5 does not need to communicate with the OWA server each time a user clicks the graphical interface. This reduces network traffic and optimizes performance from the user's perspective. Another advantage is that IE5 fully implements the Outlook interface, so users have the best experience when using IE5 with OWA. This interface is shown in Figure 5.27.

Figure 5.27 IE5 with OWA

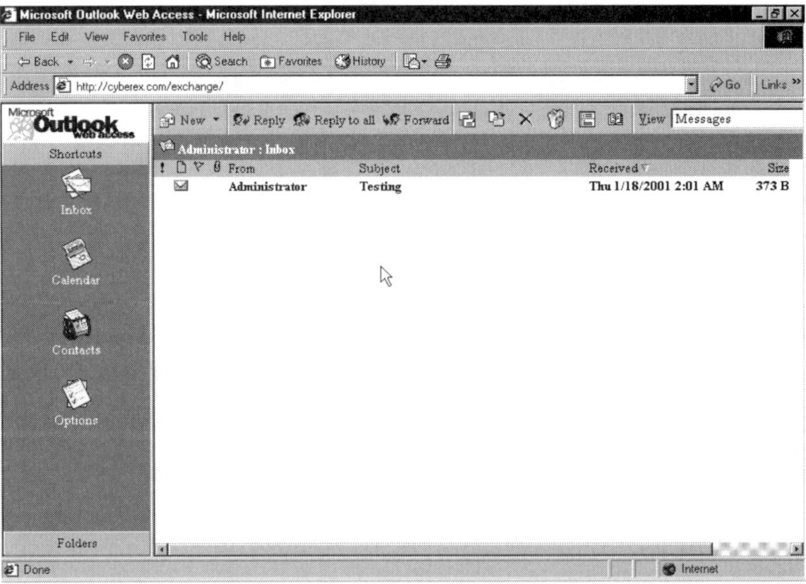

IE5 supports Dynamic HTML (DHTML) and Extensible Markup Language (XML) and it supports WebDAV, an HTTP extension that lets a browser manipulate data on a server using HTTP. A great deal of the OWA interface functionality is related to DHTML and XML. WebDAV is the means by which IE5 can manipulate content of e-mail messages, render the client at the client side (thus optimizing server performance), and access the metadata for documents. (Metadata is the information *about* the document, such as the date that the document was last saved.) To find out more about WebDAV, visit www.webdav.org.

Netscape Navigator

IE5 provides the best browser for OWA, but other browsers are supported, too. OWA requires that any other Web browser supports:

- HTML, version 3.2
- JavaScript

One of the most popular Web browsers other than Internet Explorer is Netscape Navigator. The OWA interface for Navigator does not have the same capabilities as for IE5. For example, using Netscape Navigator, you are prompted for a name and password in cases in which IE5 would have supplied the credentials on your behalf. Figure 5.28 displays the OWA interface on Netscape Navigator, version 6.

Figure 5.28 OWA Using Netscape Navigator

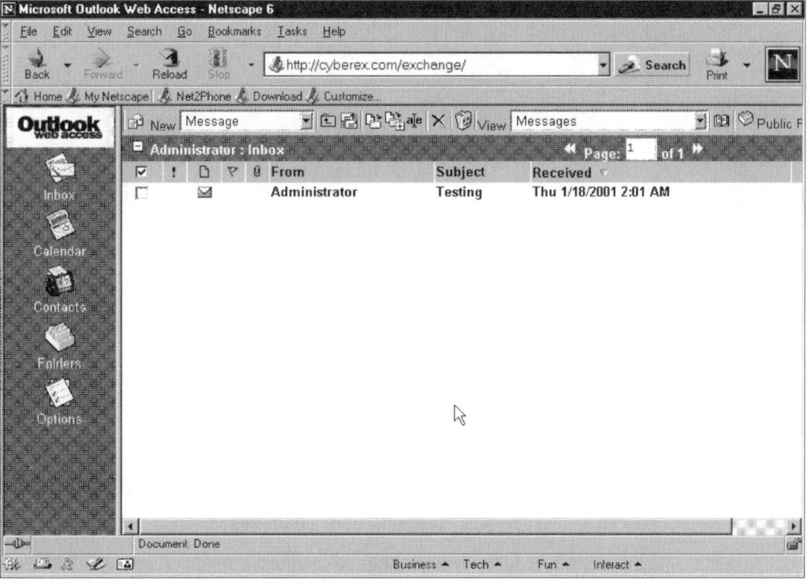

POP3 and IMAP4 Clients

Both POP3 and IMAP4 are Internet standards for messaging but not for sending mail, only for retrieving mail. POP3 is used more pervasively than IMAP4 and is a popular e-mail client provided by Internet service providers (ISPs), largely due to the reduced administrative overhead POP3 requires. POP3 clients typically are configured to download all e-mail to the local client's store, and only after it is stored will the user take action on the e-mail. IMAP4 has more functionality than POP3, since a client can use IMAP4 to read e-mail that is stored on the e-mail server and to access public folders. IMAP4 and POP3 cannot send e-mail nor access a directory service; hence they rely on SMTP to handle the sending of messages and LDAP to gain access to a directory service.

When you migrate from Exchange 5.5 to Exchange 2000, your POP3 and IMAP4 clients will be affected. If you simply upgrade the existing Exchange Servers, you can use the same server names and addresses for the Exchange Servers. If you migrate to different Exchange Servers with new names, you need to edit these names. In addition, you need to change the name for the LDAP server to the name of a global catalog server because Exchange 2000 will not provide directory services natively.

Migrating a POP3 Client to Use Exchange 2000 Server

If you are using a third-party POP3 server and are migrating to Microsoft Exchange 2000 Server, you will find that your migration will be very straightforward. Since most POP3 servers require users to download their e-mail to their local client application, the server is little more than a pass-through point to the Exchange Server system. If you use SMTP servers that are separate from the POP3 servers, you should migrate the SMTP servers first and, if possible, use the same DNS name for the Exchange SMTP servers that you used for the older ones. This results in no configuration being required at the client side.

Then you should migrate the POP3 servers to Exchange. First, make certain that all users have logged on and downloaded their e-mail. Then take the POP3 servers offline. Finally, configure POP3 on the Exchange Servers. If possible, use the same DNS names as were used on the old POP3 servers. If you cannot use the same DNS names on the POP3 or SMTP servers that were migrated, you need to make changes to every client application and to the Mail Exchange (MX) records on the DNS servers in your organization. Later on, you can roll out the Outlook 2000 client or have users try out OWA, but it is not required in order for users to receive their e-mail.

Outlook Express

Outlook Express is the e-mail client bundled with Microsoft Internet Explorer. Outlook Express supports both IMAP4 and POP3, so you can use this client regardless of which type of protocol you configure on your Exchange Server.

To configure Outlook Express to access either POP3 or IMAP4:

1. Launch Outlook Express.
2. Click the Tools menu.
3. Select the Accounts option.
4. Click the Add button.
5. Select Mail. You will see the dialog box shown in Figure 5.29.

Figure 5.29 Display Name Dialog Box in Outlook Express

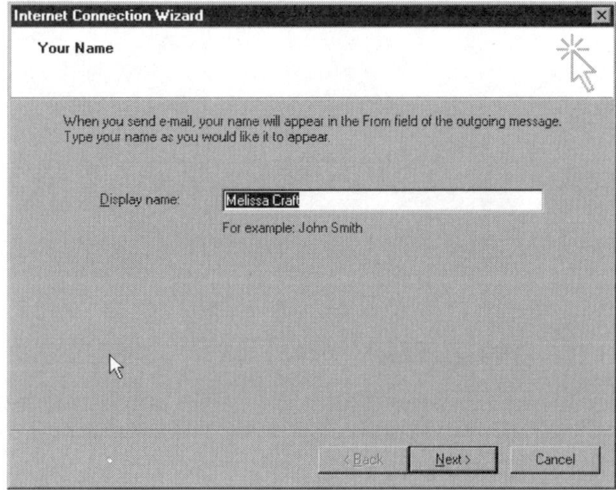

6. Type a name to become your display name. When people receive an e-mail from you, this name will show up in the "From" field. Click Next.

7. You are next prompted to type in an e-mail address or to sign up for a new account. Since you are configuring Outlook Express to access an Exchange Server, you want to use the SMTP address you have configured for the user in the form of user@domain.com. Click Next.

8. The next screen, shown in Figure 5.30, allows you to select the type of protocol that will be used to access the e-mail account.

Click the drop-down box and select from POP3, IMAP, or HTTP. Type in the name of the server providing that protocol in the top box, and then type in the SMTP server in the lower box. Click Next.

9. Next you are prompted to type in the account name and the password for it. Type in the information, and click Next. At the final dialog box, click the Finish button.

Figure 5.30 Select POP3 or IMAP

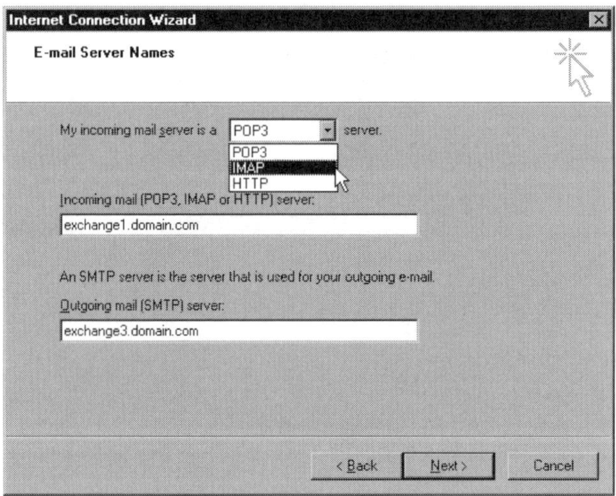

Netscape Navigator Mail

Netscape has bundled an e-mail client in Navigator, version 6. You can download the Netscape browser and e-mail client from www.netscape.com. This e-mail client supports POP3 and IMAP4. To configure Netscape:

1. Launch Netscape.

2. Click the Tasks menu.

3. Select Mail.

4. Select ISP or e-mail provider, and click Next.

5. Type in the name that you want to appear in the "From" box, and then type in your e-mail address, which is in the format *yourname@yourdomain.com*. Click Next. You will see the dialog box shown in Figure 5.31.

6. Select POP3 for the server type, and type the name of the Exchange POP3 server. Under Outgoing SMTP Server, type the name of the SMTP server. Click Next.

Figure 5.31 Netscape Mail Server Configuration

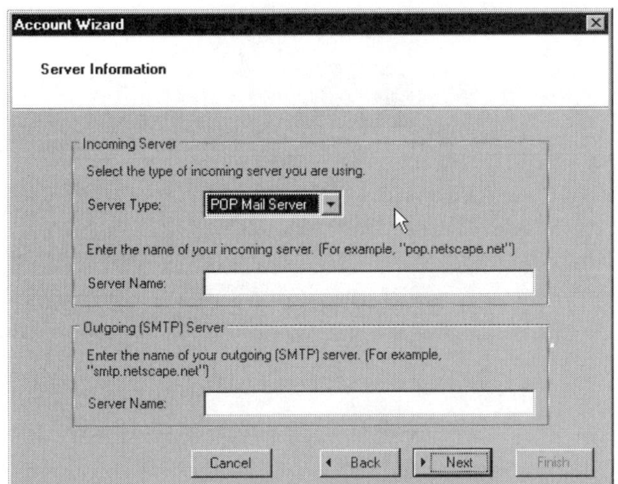

7. The next dialog box asks for your username, type in the name of the mailbox user and click Next.

8. You are then prompted for the Account name, which is simply an easy way to organize multiple e-mail accounts, so you can name it anything. Click Next.

9. When presented with the summary, verify that it is correct, and click Finish.

Eudora

Eudora is a popular free e-mail program available on the Internet that supports POP3 and SMTP. You can download Eudora Light from www.eudora.com/eudoralight/. To configure Eudora to access your Exchange Server for POP3 e-mail:

1. Launch Eudora Light. These instructions work with Eudora Light, version 5.0.2.

2. The first time that you launch Eudora Light, you will be prompted for configuration. Otherwise, click the Tools menu and select Options.

3. In the left-hand navigation bar of the Options window, click the Getting Started icon. Type in the mailbox username in the Mail Server (Incoming) account box. You will see the dialog box shown in Figure 5.32.

Figure 5.32 Getting Started with Eudora Light

4. Type in the user's full name in the "Real name" box; this name will appear in the "From" box when e-mail is sent from this account.

5. Under "Return address," type in the SMTP address for the mailbox user. Type in the SMTP Server (Outgoing) name in the box.

6. Click OK.

LDAP Clients

LDAP is a protocol that is used to access a directory service. It is a used to look up names and addresses that are stored in a directory service. In the case of Exchange Server, this is Active Directory. Because Exchange Server no longer contains its own directory service, when you query with an LDAP client, you are querying an Active Directory Global Catalog server. Even though Exchange Server offloads this function to the Active Directory—which, by the way, increases its messaging performance—you still can access Exchange Server contact information, distribution lists, and addresses using LDAP.

LDAP Background

LDAP was originally created to access X.500 directories, since the original X.500 client had a significant overhead (considered *heavy*, hence the reason LDAP is considered *lightweight*). LDAP has been transformed and has become a standard directory access protocol. X.500 is a standard that defines how a directory service can be organized through a hierarchical namespace. This namespace defines object attributes, which are further denoted by short abbreviations shown in parentheses, as follows:

- Organization (O)
- Organizational Unit (OU)
- Country(C)
- Common Name (CN)

There are many other defined object attributes, and the X.500 directory is extensible to include custom objects that an organization deems necessary. The organization of these directory attributes is shown in Figure 5.33.

Figure 5.33 X.500 Hierarchy

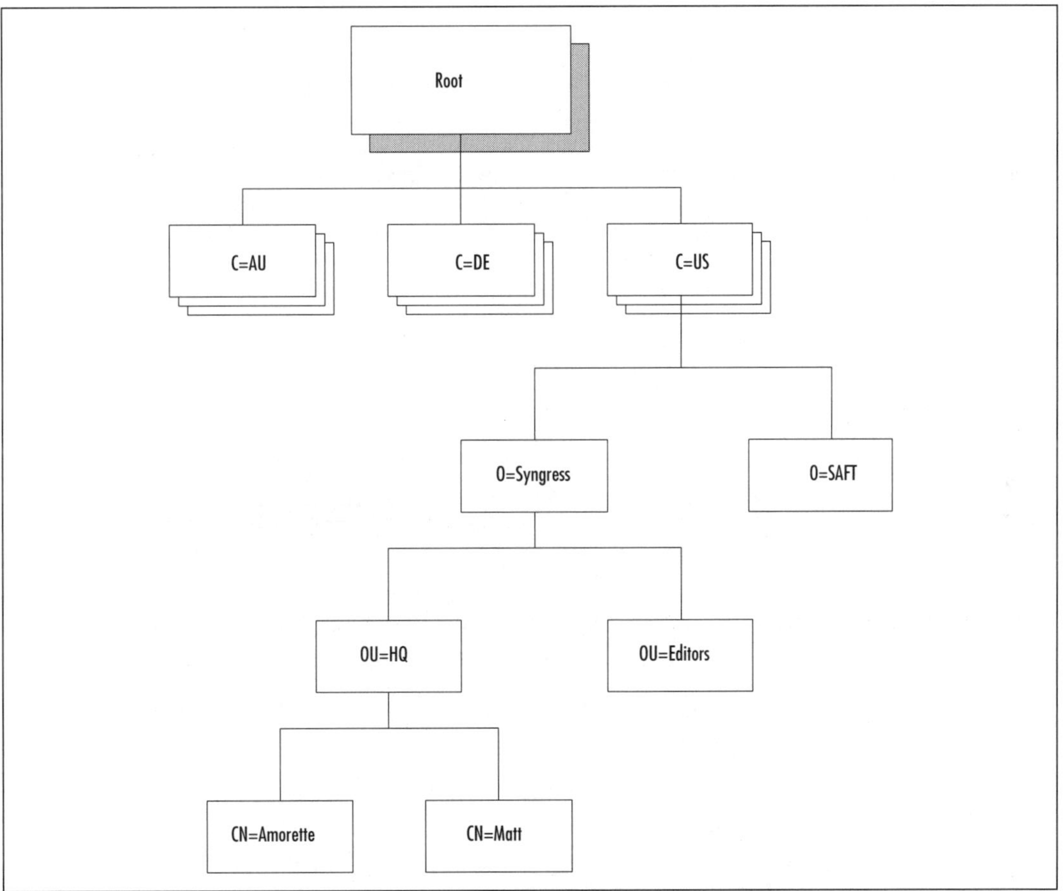

As you can see by Figure 5.34, Active Directory that provides the directory service to Exchange Server implements an X.500-*like* hierarchy. Active Directory is not an X.500 directory service in the strictest sense, but it does use LDAP for directory access.

Outlook Express LDAP

You can configure Microsoft's Outlook Express, version 5 (which comes with IE5), to access an LDAP server. The method of doing this is similar to configuring Outlook Express to access a POP3 e-mail server:

1. Launch Outlook Express.

2. Click the Tools menu.

3. Select the Accounts option.

4. Click the Add button, and select Directory Service from the pop-up menu. You will see the dialog box shown in Figure 5.34.

Figure 5.34 Adding an LDAP Account

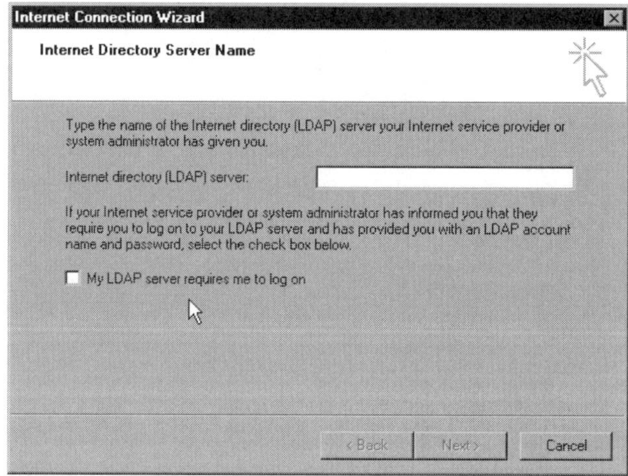

5. In the box for "Internet directory (LDAP) server," type the DNS name of a global catalog server and check the box that states "My LDAP server requires me to log on." Click Next.

6. You will be prompted for the account name and password. Check the box for secure password authentication. Click Next.

7. Figure 5.35 shows the next screen, which prompts you to select whether the LDAP server should be checked for e-mail addresses. The answer to this question, as far as Exchange 2000 Server is concerned, is Yes. Select that radio button, and click Next.

8. The last screen congratulates you for completing the information in the wizard correctly. Click the Finish button.

Figure 5.35 Checking the LDAP Server for E-Mail Addresses

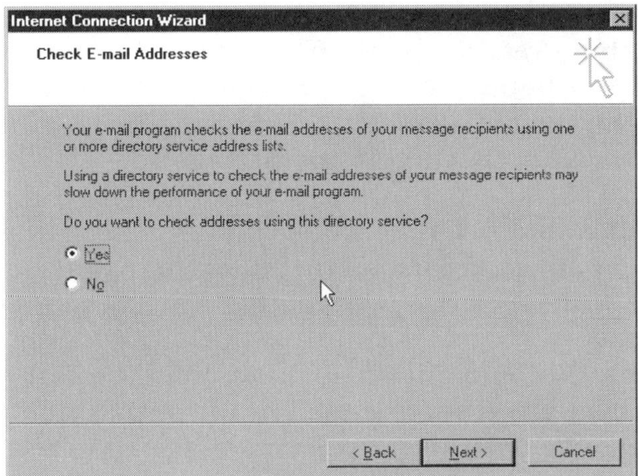

Troubleshooting

E-mail is usually one of the most critical applications running on the network. Most users keep their e-mail client application open all day long and even check it after hours for news and updates, responses to their inquiries, calendaring information, tasks and reminders, and of course, for incoming e-mail. You should select an e-mail client that allows users to have full functionality but requires the least amount of troubleshooting—in effect, something that's *easy* to run, maintain, and troubleshoot.

Outlook 2000 and Outlook Web Access are your best bets. Outlook 2000 provides the most functionality, and OWA provides the easiest access to e-mail. If your users are up to it, you might even be able to show users how to use both of these e-mail clients at appropriate times—using Outlook 2000 when they are in the office and connected directly into the LAN and using OWA when they are dialing up the network from their homes or connecting over the Internet to read e-mail.

WARNING

When users turn on the Mark My Comments feature in Outlook 2000, they need to ensure that they do not hit the Insert key accidentally. If they do, the comment mark (the user's name in parentheses) is placed between each and every letter that is typed rather than just at the beginning of the sentence. Of course, to fix this problem, you just need to press CTRL and Z until all the overly marked text is removed and then hit the Insert key again before typing further.

Stuck in the Middle of the Outbox

One of the most common problems occurs when a user moves from online to offline without realizing the differences in how e-mail is handled. An e-mail can appear to be "stuck" in the outbox, or the user could be confused by the fact that no e-mail is being received. The resolution, of course, is to guide the user to connecting to the network.

Another problem occurs when a user has sent a message, thus placing it in the outbox, but before it has a chance to be transmitted, the user goes into the outbox and opens the message to make changes. Most users will think that the message is still being sent, because it is sitting in the outbox, so they just close it and save the changes. However, the user needs to click the Send button again in order for that e-mail to be transmitted. If a user has a stuck e-mail in the outbox and is connected to the network, have the user open up the message and click the Send button, then watch it disappear.

The Missing Files

When you have Outlook 2000 deployed across your network, you might find that some of the features you thought were unnecessary are actually things a few users need. These users will phone to tell you that they are missing part of Outlook or that they can't do something that they want to do, even though the online help says they should be able to. Here are some tips for handling these issues:

- If the Outlook 2000 files were installed, but the service is not installed, you can easily add an Outlook feature. Click the Tools menu, select Services, click the Add button, and then select the service.

- If an optional component needs to be installed, you need to shut down Outlook 2000 and reboot. Open the Control Panel, and then open Add/Remove Programs. Select Outlook 2000, and click the Add/Remove button, or under Windows 2000, click the Change button. If you do not see Microsoft Outlook, click Microsoft Office 2000, as shown in Figure 5.36. The Setup program will start (make certain that you have the Office 2000 or Outlook 2000 CD-ROM or installation files available), and you can add or remove components as necessary.

- If a user wants to use offline storage files but during installation selected "I do not travel with this computer," you can add the offline feature only while connected to the Exchange Server. Click the Tools menu, select Services, select Microsoft Exchange Server, click Properties, click the Advanced tab, check the box for "Enable offline use," and click the Offline Folder File Settings buttons to configure the offline storage file settings.

Figure 5.36 Changing Microsoft Office 2000 Options to Add Functionality to Outlook 2000

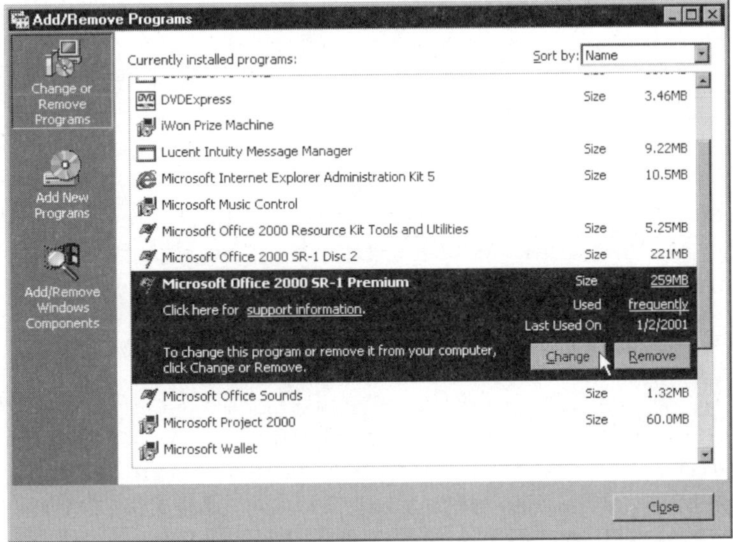

POP3 Oddities

Even though POP3 is one of the most common protocols used for e-mail connectivity, it can still be the root of the problem for an end user.

User Misunderstanding

One problem that occurs is a simple misunderstanding. Some users do not know that Outlook Express and Outlook 2000 are two separate applications and do not have the same capabilities. They could try to set up their Outlook Express application to connect to the server; when they can't get it to work, they will call and say that Outlook doesn't work. Of course it doesn't—because you didn't expect anyone to use POP3, so it wasn't enabled on the server. There are two ways you can fix this mistake:

- Stick by your corporate standards and make the user install Outlook 2000 (or use OWA if that's available).

- Enable POP3 on the Exchange Server.

Given that adding more e-mail client applications only increases the amount of administration that you have to do, you will be best served by having users access the server only via approved e-mail client applications.

Attachments

Another POP3 problem can occur with attachments. Some attachments come through as a whole mess of gobbledygook at the end of the message, renamed to other file formats such as binary (.BIN) files, or they are translated into an illegible text message before the client receives them. Not all attachments are created equal, and since POP3 clients don't understand native Exchange message format, a translation occurs on the server before the user receives the e-mail and attachment. If the POP3 client doesn't understand the type of attachment that Exchange Server sends it, you have problems. You can experiment with the conversion format that Exchange uses to make certain that the majority, if not all, of the attachments are handled properly for your users' POP3 clients. This is done in the Exchange System Manager by adjusting the Message Format options in the POP3 Properties.

Protocol Logging

If you can't figure out a problem that is happening with a POP3 client, you can turn on POP3 protocol logging. Protocol logging will work only as a troubleshooting system for each individual POP3 server; it won't solve problems that occur on an organization- or sitewide basis. To turn on protocol logging:

1. Before starting, make a verified backup of your server and registry so that you can restore the registry if necessary.

2. On your Exchange Server that provides POP3, open the registry with REGEDIT by clicking Start | Run, typing **regedit,** and pressing Enter.

3. Navigate to HKLM\SYSTEM\CurrentControlSet\Services\ MSExchangeIS\ParametersSystem, as shown in Figure 5.37.

4. Double-click the value named POP3 Protocol Logging Level or create one by right-clicking and selecting New | DWORD Value.

5. Change the value from the default 0, which equals no logging, to either a 1, which equals minimum logging, or a 4, which is the maximum logging.

6. Close the Registry Editor when you are finished.

7. Either stop and restart Exchange Services or reboot the server.

Figure 5.37 Changing POP3 Logging in the Registry

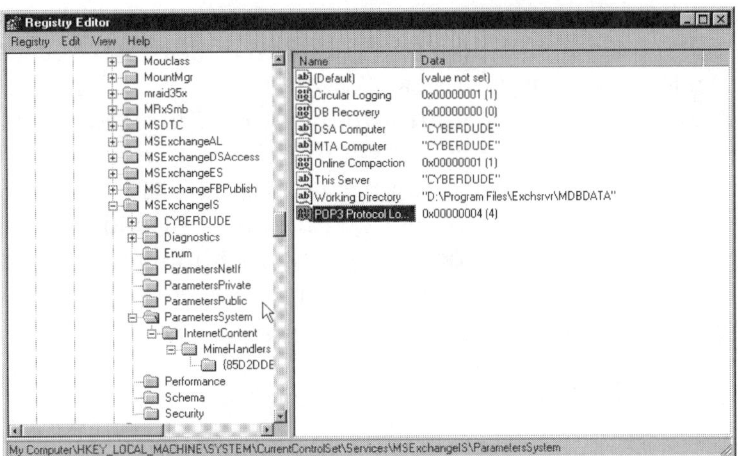

Summary

Exchange Server is very flexible from the standpoint of a client application. Not only can you deploy an Outlook 2000 client to connect to Exchange, but you can also connect:

- A variety of Message Application Programming Interface (MAPI) clients

- Outlook Web Access (OWA), the native HyperText Transfer Protocol (HTTP) client, using Internet Explorer, version 5 (IE5), or other Web browsers such as Netscape Navigator

- Any type of client that can access an IMAP4 server

- Any type of client that can access a POP3 server

- Any Lightweight Directory Access Protocol (LDAP) clients

Each type of client drives different requirements of your Exchange Servers and of the migration path that you take from your current messaging system toward the Exchange 2000 Server system. For example, a migration from an existing POP3 server to an Exchange Server will not require an entirely new client application. Likewise, if you had an existing Exchange 5.5 network using Outlook 98 as the client application, you could upgrade the Exchange 5.5 network to Exchange 2000 without needing to make changes at the client side. In summary, the richer your client product feature, the more you will have to upgrade and configure. The reach clients (browsers, OWA) will have fewer configurations.

The best rich client to use with Exchange 2000 is Outlook 2000. You can roll this client out as a part of Microsoft Office 2000 or as a separate application. Outlook 2000 offers the most functionality of a client application, with custom forms and designer capabilities as well as support for Visual Basic Scripting. Outlook 2000 supports folder home pages, making it an integral component of an organization's intranet or extranet. As for rich clients, any browser will work, but if you use IE 5.0, you have less traffic over the network due to integration with AD.

The biggest challenge that any administrator will find in managing an e-mail system is troubleshooting the client applications. An administrator needs to be prepared for requests for new messaging features as well as handling messaging errors that occur on the client side.

FAQs

Visit **www.syngress.com/solutions** to have your questions about this chapter answered by the author.

Q: Our network uses Novell NetWare v4.12. We also use GroupWise. This is a native IPX/SPX environment, and we use a proxy service through Border Manager to allow Internet access. If we migrate to Exchange 2000 Server, what should be the first thing we tackle?

A: Your first item of business is to deploy TCP/IP across your network, so that each client workstation can access it natively. You should make certain to deploy DNS servers in strategic locations to ensure that all workstations can locate a DNS server at all times. TCP/IP is an absolute requirement before deploying Exchange 2000 and connecting clients physically to it.

Q: We are using a Windows NT v4.0 network with a PPTP VPN running on a RAS server for Internet users. Can we still use this RAS server after upgrading to Windows 2000, Exchange 2000, and Outlook 2000?

A: Yes, you can use the same RAS server. You might want to upgrade the RAS server to Windows 2000 for a couple of reasons, however. First, the RAS server under Windows 2000 supports the Active Directory natively, so security is stricter. Second, with Windows 2000 RAS servers, you can migrate your users to L2TP, which offers a more secure connection over an Internet VPN. Outlook 2000 should function over any of these configurations.

Q: We have an engineering group that uses Sun UNIX boxes for their workstations. They've been using a POP3 server and an SMTP server for e-mail to connect to our Exchange 5.0 system. The rest of the users on the network use Outlook 97 to connect to e-mail. Our CIO is challenging us to provide a single client that will work on any of these systems. What should we do?

A: You should deploy Outlook Web Access for all users and install Internet Explorer for all users to give them the most functionality.

Q: Can Outlook Express resolve e-mail addresses in Exchange 2000 Server?

A: Yes. You must configure Outlook Express to be an LDAP client to the Active Directory and then, during configuration, select the item that enables the directory service to be used when resolving e-mail address names.

Chapter 6

Deploying Exchange 2000 Server

Solutions in this chapter:

- **Green Field Deployment**
- **Upgrading from Previous Versions of Exchange**
- **Testing Your Scenario**

Introduction

Deploying Exchange 2000 can be a very simple or very complex process. The complexity of your deployment will depend on several factors—but mostly it will depend on the complexity of your existing messaging environment. If you currently have no messaging system (there are a few of you out there) or if your existing messaging system consists of one or two servers running Exchange Server 5.5, then deployment is a fairly simple process. However, if your existing messaging system supports 225,000 users across four continents and 500 physical locations with varying levels of network connectivity and reliability, your Exchange 2000 deployment may be a tad more complex.

Most deployments will fall somewhere between these two extremes. If your current messaging environment is an earlier version of Microsoft Exchange, or if you are going to deploy Exchange 2000 and not migrate your existing messaging environment, this chapter will outline for you several methods for deploying and upgrading to Exchange 2000. Is the process still complex? Sure, but if it were easy, your boss could access the data center between the front nine and the back nine, run the Exchange 2000 Deployment Wizard, and be done before it was his turn to tee off. As you will see, this is not the case.

One of the unique aspects of upgrading from Windows NT 4.0 and Exchange Server 5.5 to Windows 2000 and Exchange 2000 is that two "directories" are being upgraded or consolidated into a single Active Directory. Windows NT 4.0 was only the security subsystem for Exchange Server 5.5. Exchange Server 5.5 has its own directory. Windows NT 4.0 accounts are associated with Exchange Server 5.5 mailboxes, but they are two different directories (if you can call the NT 4.0 Security Account Manager—or SAM—a directory). Exchange 2000 lost its directory to Windows 2000 Active Directory. The Windows 2000 security subsystem is Active Directory, not an NT 4.0 SAM. This means that when you upgrade your Windows NT 4.0 SAM to Active Directory you also will be upgrading your Exchange Server 5.5 directory to Active Directory, consolidating the two into a single directory.

This poses several challenges that must be carefully planned for and tested. Microsoft has provided the tools to manage this process effectively, but it's up to you to make sure the tools are used correctly and in the proper order. This chapter will give you the information you need to upgrade your directories to Active Directory.

Upgrading the directory is only half the story. Everything else needs to be upgraded from Exchange Server 5.5 to Exchange 2000. This includes mailbox servers, connectors, public folder servers, and bridgehead servers.

Fortunately this process is fairly straightforward. The main challenge here is getting from point A to point B. If you have ten Exchange Server 5.5 sites you want to consolidate into three Exchange 2000 routing groups spanning two Administrative Groups, the process becomes more complex and requires more planning. As you can see, the key word here is *planning*.

Green Field Deployment

Before we delve into the complexities of upgrading from Exchange Server 5.5 to Exchange 2000, there are some basic deployment strategies that can and should be used during deployment. Also, if you are not upgrading from a previous version of Exchange but are migrating from a different messaging system such as cc:Mail or Lotus Notes, you will likely deploy Exchange 2000 and migrate messaging data from your existing messaging environment to the new Exchange 2000 organization. This type of Exchange deployment, a so-called green field deployment, simply takes an Exchange 2000 design and deploys it across the organization. The term *green field* is used to symbolize rolling out the product onto a green field of grass that has never been touched. It is something we Exchange administrators dream of.

Preparing Active Directory

Exchange 2000 makes a considerable number of changes to the Active Directory schema and configuration partition. These changes are made when the first Exchange 2000 server is installed in the Active Directory forest. They are necessary to support the objects and attributes required by Exchange 2000.

Remember, as explained in Chapter 2, a single schema and configuration partition exists for every Active Directory forest. The Active Directory schema and configuration partitions are hosted on each and every domain controller in the forest; they can only be modified by members of the Active Directory Schema Administrators Group. This means that when Exchange 2000 Server setup makes changes to the Active Directory schema and configuration partition, these changes must be replicated throughout the Active Directory forest to each domain controller. It also means that an administrator who is a member of the Schema Administrators Group must install the first Exchange 2000 server.

This poses a couple of issues:

- The Schema Administrators Group should contain a very limited number of administrators, most of whom will likely be centralized at one or two locations within the company. Typically, these administrators are not your Exchange implementers. It is impractical in a large organization to think these members of the Schema Administrators Group are the only administrators in the company who could run Exchange 2000 setup.

- It would be best if many schema modifications could be made early in the deployment of Active Directory, well before Exchange 2000 is deployed, so that the Exchange 2000 schema modifications could be included in the schema during the Active Directory deployment. This would avoid an excessive replication overhead when Exchange 2000 is finally deployed.

- Let me repeat this. Don't wait until your Exchange deployment plan to perform modifications to your Active Directory Schema. You want to make these changes in the early stages of your Active Directory/Windows 2000 deployment of domain controllers.

These potential difficulties with Exchange deployment were discovered during the Exchange 2000 beta process. Exchange 2000 setup always installed the product, but also performed special modifications to Active Directory when first run. The answer was to create a setup switch that ran a special Exchange 2000 setup process.

Using ForestPrep

This setup switch is named /forestprep. Forestprep is run once by a Schema Administrator to prepare your Active Directory for Exchange 2000 by making changes to the Active Directory schema without actually installing Exchange 2000.

As seen in Figure 6.1, forestprep makes the necessary changes to the Active Directory schema and establishes the Exchange 2000 organization by making modifications to the Active Directory configuration partition.

If your organization will deploy Exchange 2000, but is currently in the planning or deployment phase of your Windows 2000 project, then consider incorporating the Exchange 2000 schema and configuration partition changes into your Active Directory deployment by using forestprep at the early stages of your Active Directory deployment.

TIP

By running Exchange 2000 setup with the forestprep switch on the Active Directory Schema Master, the forestprep schema modifications will take considerably less time.

Figure 6.1 Exchange 2000 Setup Schema Modifications

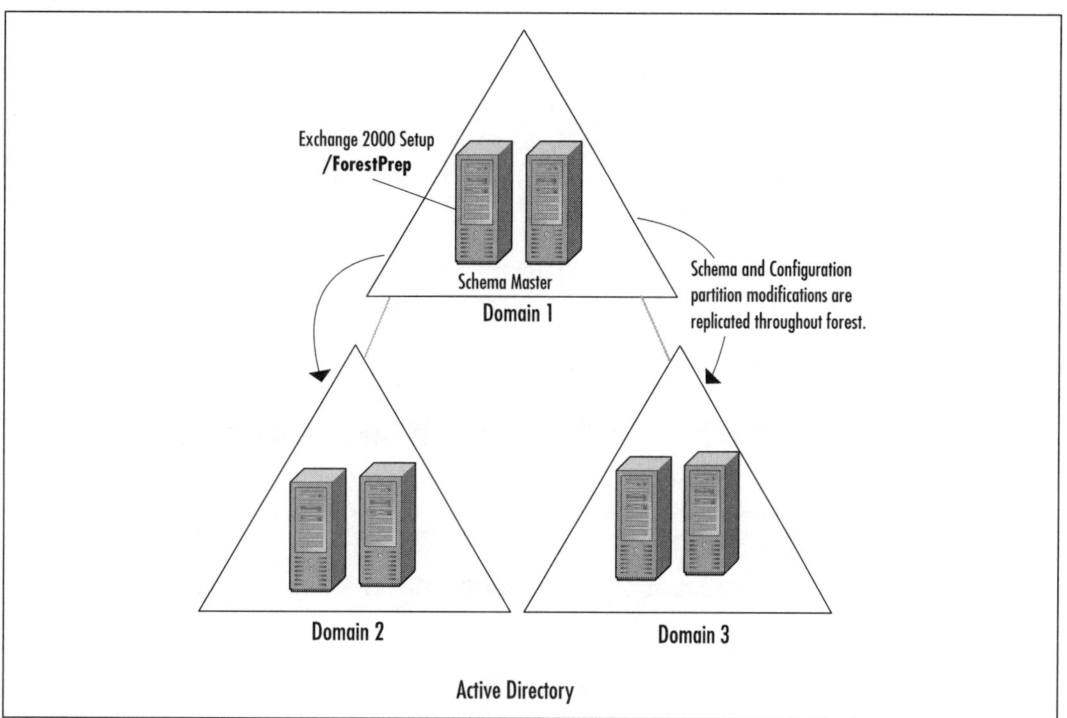

This can be done by having a Schema Administrator run forestprep in the root domain on the Active Directory domain controller designated as the Schema Master over a weekend—or whenever the schema and configuration partition changes can be replicated across the organization efficiently and without impacting system performance.

When running Exchange 2000 setup with the forestprep switch, Exchange 2000 setup will prompt you for the following information:

- Your 25-digit product identification code. This code is located on the Exchange 2000 compact disc jewel case.

- An indication that tells whether you are creating a new Exchange 2000 organization or joining an existing Exchange Server 5.5 organization. You must have the service account name and password if joining an existing Exchange Server 5.5 site. You must also have the Exchange version of the Active Directory Connector (ADC) installed in the forest. The reasons for this will become clear later in this chapter.

- The organization name. This should be defined in your Exchange 2000 design or functional specification. Choose this name wisely, because it cannot be changed.

- The Active Directory user you want to specify as the initial Exchange 2000 Administrator. This account will be granted permission on the Exchange 2000 objects and object containers created in the Exchange 2000 portion of the Active Directory configuration partition.

When you use the forestprep setup switch, ForestPrep is the only choice—as shown in Figure 6.2—when selecting components.

Figure 6.2 ForestPrep Component Selection

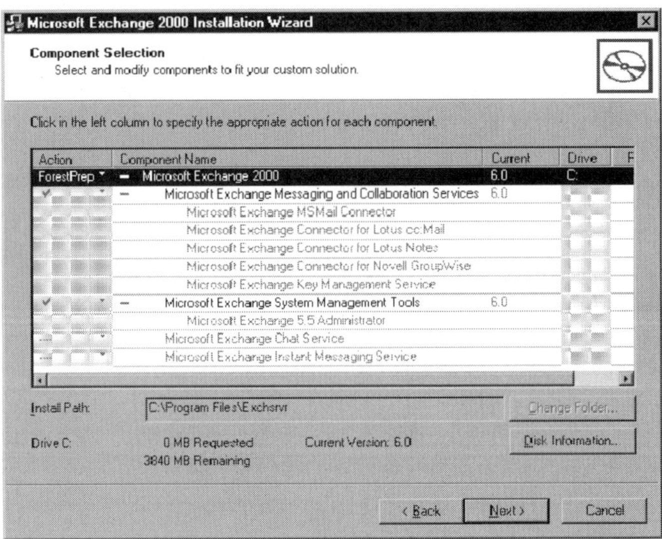

Setup will fail if you are not logged in as an Active Directory user who is a member of the Schema Administrator Group, or if Exchange 2000 setup is unable to successfully write changes to the Active Directory schema.

WARNING

Be careful when starting Exchange 2000 setup with the forestprep switch on the command line. If you misspell /forestprep, the standard Exchange 2000 setup will start and allow you to install Exchange 2000.

If you run Exchange 2000 setup without first running Exchange 2000 setup with the /forestprep switch, the schema and configuration partition modifications will first be made, then Exchange 2000 will be installed. You do not have to run /forestprep before an Exchange 2000 server can be installed, but it is a best practice and recommended by Microsoft.

Preparing Your Domains

Several of the same principles that apply to forestprep also apply to the Active Directory domains. An administrator who has Domain Administrator permissions for that domain needs to have Exchange 2000 setup do several things to each Active Directory domain.

Exchange 2000 administrators do not need any special permissions in Active Directory other than those granted them by the Exchange Delegation Wizard from within the Exchange System Manager. This means that you can have a group of Exchange 2000 administrators who can only manage the Exchange 2000 objects and object containers in Active Directory. They don't have to be domain administrators or have any other special permission in the domain. This type of division is preferred by many organizations, but can become an issue during setup when Exchange is first being installed into the Active Directory domain. This is because Exchange 2000 setup performs the following tasks:

- A user account named EUSER_EXSTOREEVENTS is created for use with the script event host.

- An Exchange Domain Servers domain global group is created; this group contains all computers running Exchange 2000 in the domain.

- An Exchange Enterprise Servers domain local group is created; this group contains all computers running Exchange 2000 in the enterprise.

- Each of these groups is granted permission on objects in the Active Directory domain.

An administrator who has permissions in the domain can only perform these tasks by running Exchange 2000 setup with the domainprep switch.

Using DomainPrep

Like forestprep, domainprep is a command-line switch used during deployment to prepare each Active Directory domain. If there are no Exchange implementers in the domain who are members of the Domain Administrators Group, then an administrator who is a member of the

Domain Administrators Group can run domainprep to prepare the domain for Exchange 2000.

When running Exchange 2000 setup with the domainprep switch, DomainPrep will be the only component you can select, as shown in Figure 6.3.

Figure 6.3 DomainPrep Component Selection

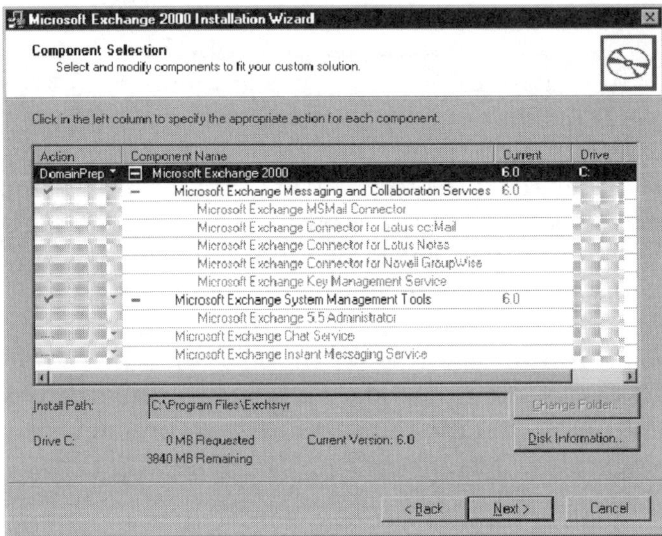

Setup will fail if you are not logged in as an Active Directory user who is a member of the Domain Administrators Group when domainprep is being run or when the first Exchange 2000 server is installed into the domain.

If you run Exchange 2000 setup without first running Exchange 2000 setup with the /domainprep switch, the domain modifications will be made; then Exchange 2000 will be installed. It is not necessary to run /domainprep before installing an Exchange 2000 server into the domain, but it is the best practice and recommended by Microsoft.

WARNING

As with forestprep, if you misspell /domainprep when starting Exchange 2000 setup with the domainprep switch on the command line, the standard Exchange 2000 setup will start and allow you to install Exchange 2000.

Deploying Servers Running Exchange 2000

Once the forest and domains have been prepared for Exchange 2000, it's time to get down to deploying Exchange 2000 servers. Exchange 2000 servers should be rolled out in a manner that provides the most efficient use of implementation resources and the most complete user experience. You would not want to deploy Exchange 2000 servers populated with user mailboxes across several routing groups, and only then connect those routing groups with connectors using bridgehead servers. A general guideline for deploying Exchange 2000 servers (not relevant when upgrading) includes:

- Establish the Administrative Groups and apply permissions using the Exchange Delegation Wizard, per your Exchange 2000 design using Exchange System Manager.

- Establish the Routing Groups per your Exchange 2000 design using Exchange System Manager.

- Deploy Exchange 2000 bridgehead servers in each routing group per your Exchange 2000 design.

- Connect routing groups with the connectors specified in your Exchange 2000 design.

- Test connectivity.

- Deploy mailbox and public folder servers per your Exchange 2000 design; populate with user mailboxes and public folder data.

This straightforward approach to deployment can be modified to include migration and coexistence. It will become apparent that planning and testing are the key ingredients to a successful Exchange 2000 deployment.

Establishing the First Administrative Group

When you install Exchange 2000, setup looks for a list of Administrative Groups that the new server can be installed into. If no Administrative Groups exist, such as when the first server is installed, an Administrative Group is created named *First Administrative Group*. It's not a very useful name and will likely not be included in your Exchange 2000 Administrative Group design.

To better control which Administrative Groups exist and which Administrative Groups the Exchange implementers install their servers into, you can establish all your Administrative Groups *after* forestprep has been run and *before* you install your first Exchange 2000 server. This is done using these steps:

1. Run Exchange 2000 setup with the /forestprep switch to prepare your Active Directory forest.

2. Run Exchange 2000 setup with the /domainprep switch to prepare your Active Directory domain.

3. Run Exchange 2000 setup and only select the Exchange 2000 Management Components.

4. Start the Exchange System Manager and create all the Administrative Groups defined in your Exchange 2000 design.

5. Install your first Exchange 2000 server and select the Administrative Group the server will be installed into as defined by your Exchange 2000 design or functional specification.

Incorporating these steps into your Exchange 2000 deployment plan will ensure that you establish the Administrative Groups before Exchange servers are installed. When your assisting Exchange implementers proceed to install their Exchange 2000 servers, they will have a complete drop-down list of Administrative Groups to choose from. There will be no question, when following the instructions provided by your deployment plan, which Administrative Group to install their server into.

WARNING

You cannot move Exchange 2000 servers between Administrative Groups. This means that the Administrative Group selected during setup is the Administrative Group where that server will reside unless reinstalled.

Creating Administrative Groups in this way only pertains to new Exchange 2000 organizations. If you install an Exchange 2000 server into an Exchange Server 5.5 site, the Administrative Groups will be created in Active Directory in the same topology as the Exchange Server 5.5 sites. This is because Exchange 2000 treats Administrative Groups like Exchange Server 5.5 sites during coexistence.

Deploying Exchange Using Terminal Services

Windows 2000 Terminal Services is included with Windows 2000. This handy feature allows you to connect to a remote server and establish a session on that server that emulates the remote servers console. It's like actually being there.

In remote locations that will host an Exchange 2000 server, it may be desirable for *you* to install Exchange 2000, not the local system administrator. Finally we administrators can ensure a remote exchange installation is installed according to our requirements. This is possible using Windows 2000 Terminal Services. The local system administrator prepares the Windows 2000 server, joining the domain and installing Windows 2000 Terminal Services. You, or another Exchange 2000 implementer, then establish a Windows 2000 terminal services session with the remote server and install Exchange 2000.

NOTE

It is not necessary to use terminal services to manage the Exchange 2000 server. All configuration of the server is contained in the configuration partition of Active Directory and can be accomplished using Exchange System Manager.

Deploying Support for Multiple Languages

Exchange 2000 includes all supported languages, once they are installed. The languages supported by Exchange 2000 are shown in Figure 6.4.

Figure 6.4 Exchange 2000 Language Support

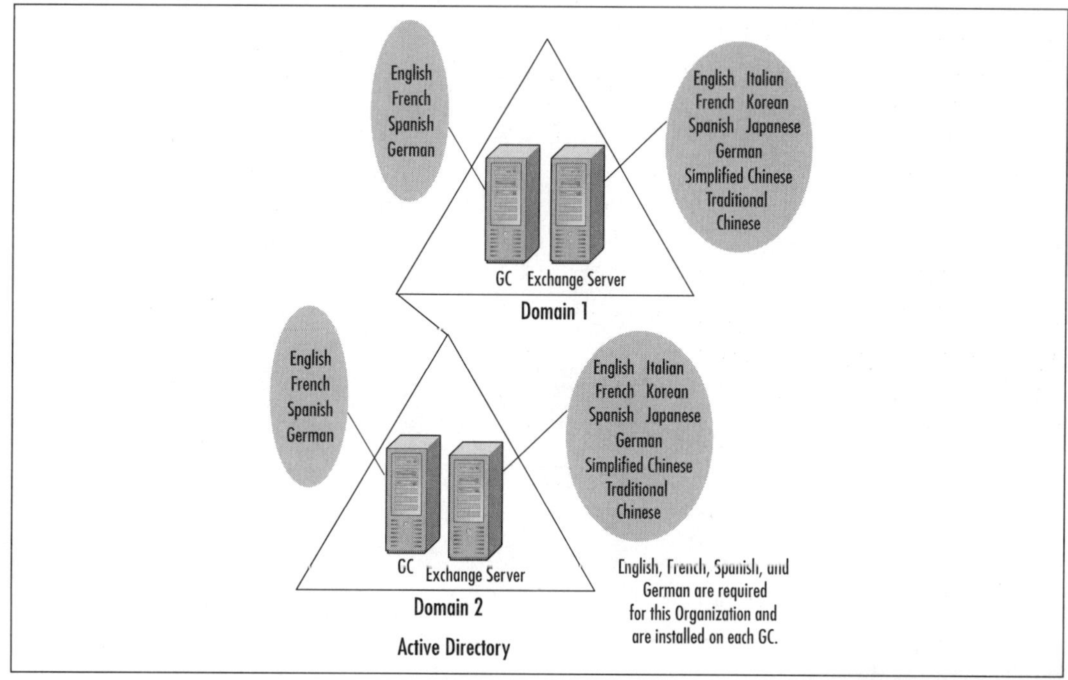

There is no reason to install additional language support for Exchange 2000. However, Windows 2000 Active Directory does *not* include all languages with the default installation. Since Exchange 2000 relies on Active Directory for its directory services, if you require additional language support for your Outlook 2000 users, it will be necessary to implement that additional language support on all Active Directory domain controllers configured as global catalog servers.

To install additional language support on your Active Directory global catalog servers:

1. From Control Panel open Regional Options.

2. Select the languages you need to support in the Languages setting for the system.

3. Restart the domain controller configured as a global catalog server.

Deploying Exchange on a Windows 2000 Cluster

With the advances in Windows 2000 clustering and the ability to support multiple Exchange 2000 information stores on a single Active/Active Windows 2000 cluster, the consolidation of several Exchange 5.5 servers into one or more large Windows 2000 clusters running Exchange 2000 is becoming more popular. As seen in Figure 6.5, many economies—including greater availability —can be realized by having fewer large servers.

Figure 6.5 An Exchange 2000 Cluster

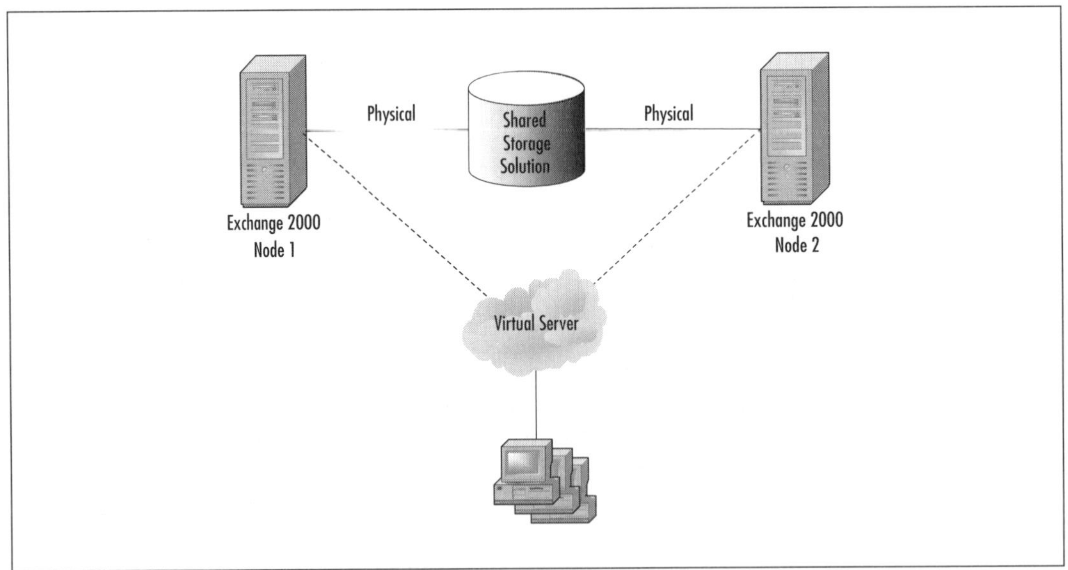

If your Exchange 2000 design calls for Exchange 2000 to be installed on a Windows 2000 cluster, there are some guidelines to follow.

- The same Exchange 2000 components must be installed on both nodes of the cluster.

- Exchange 2000 must be installed into the same drive letter and directory for both nodes of the cluster.

- After Exchange 2000 has been installed on the cluster, a virtual server must be created. To do this you create a resource group and define computer resources such as a TCP/IP address, network name, and shared disk, for the cluster nodes. Once complete, you will have a functioning Exchange 2000 server that is made up of multiple nodes. Take this time to test the cluster and its fail-over functionality before creating or moving mailboxes to the server. Take a look at Chapter 11 "Why or Why Not to Cluster Exchange 2000" to learn more about clustering Microsoft Exchange 2000.

Unattended Installation

Exchange 2000 is using a new setup engine for Microsoft BackOffice products. The Software Installation Toolkit (SIT) provides the ability to perform an unattended setup. An unattended setup is done in two phases.

- First, an unattended setup file is created by running Exchange 2000 setup with the **/createunattend** command-line switch. This switch causes Exchange 2000 setup to walk through the setup process and prompt the installer to define the type of installation that will be done—including the components to install, and the Administrative Group and routing group that the server will be installed into. Then, rather than installing the server, an unattended setup file is created with an .ini extension.

- Next, Exchange 2000 setup is run with the **/unattendfile** command-line setup switch that uses the information in the unattended setup file (created in the first phase) to install the Exchange 2000 server.

It is also possible to encrypt the unattended setup file that is created by using the **/encryptedmode** command-line setup switch. This way neither the implementer at the remote site nor anyone else along the way can view the content of the unattended setup file, which may contain a service account password if the Exchange 2000 server will coexist with Exchange Server 5.5.

Depending on the type of deployment your organization calls for, you may want to use unattended setup files during your deployment of Exchange 2000. If you choose to do so, make sure you test the creation of the unattended setup file and its use during installation.

Deploying Exchange System Manager

Exchange 2000 is configured and managed using two tools. The configuration of Exchange 2000 is done using the Exchange System Manager and recipients are managed using Active Directory Users and Computers. From the Exchange System Manager you can define and configure global settings, Administrative Groups, routing groups and their connectors, along with servers and their objects such as information stores. Exchange recipients, such as users, mail-enabled contacts, mail-enabled groups, and public folders are created and managed using Active Directory Users and Computers, not Exchange System Manager. This is fundamentally different from previous versions of Exchange where the Exchange Administrator was used to configure Exchange and to manage Exchange recipients.

Now with Exchange 2000, your Exchange administrators will manage Exchange using Exchange System Manager, and the administrators that manage Active Directory users, contacts, and groups will manage Exchange recipients using Active Directory Users and Computers. When a user is created using Active Directory Users and Computers, the administrator can choose to create a mailbox for that user and choose which Exchange server the mailbox will be created on.

The ability to manage Exchange recipients is not built into the standard Active Directory Users and Computers. Rather, this functionality is added when the Exchange System Manager is installed. For deployment, this means that you must install the Exchange System Management components on all computers where recipients are managed using Active Directory Users and Computers, as well as those workstations where Exchange will be managed using Exchange System Manager.

Upgrading from Previous Versions of Exchange

Now that you have a textbook understanding of how to deploy Exchange 2000, the real work begins. How do you get from your existing Exchange Server 5.5 organization running on Windows NT 4.0 to Exchange 2000 running Windows 2000 with Active Directory? That is the task at hand. In this section we will try to arm you with the information and tools necessary to answer that question with a reasonable degree of certainty.

There are two components that need to be addressed in upgrading an Exchange Server 5.5 to Exchange 2000: upgrading the directory and upgrading the messaging infrastructure. The directory upgrade is more difficult to manage, because two directories with duplicate accounts need to be melded into a single Active Directory. The messaging system upgrade is heavy lifting because of the sheer volumes of data that need to be migrated or upgraded. With enough information, planning, and testing, your upgrade will be a challenging and successful project.

Upgrading the Directories to Active Directory

Understanding how your Windows NT 4.0 directory and Exchange Server 5.5 directory will come together to make up your Windows 2000 Active Directory is very important to the success of your migration project. The goal is to consolidate two different directories with similar object types into a third directory, maintaining dependencies along the way (Figure 6.6).

Figure 6.6 Merging Two Directories into Active Directory

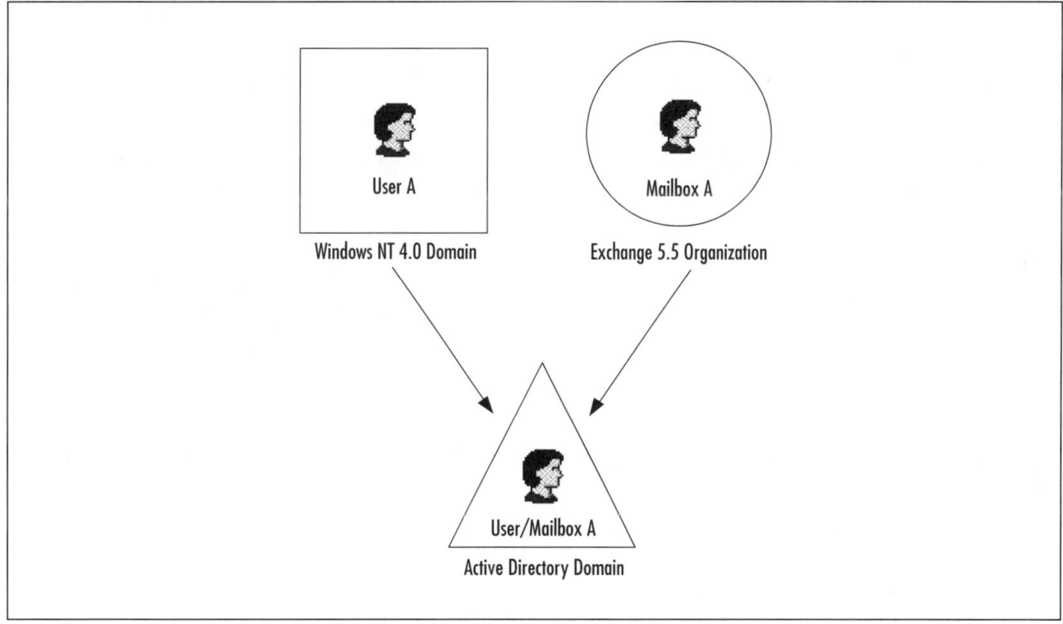

For most companies that have multiple Exchange sites and/or NT 4.0 domains there will be a period of coexistence between Windows NT 4.0, Exchange Server 5.5, and Active Directory. To make coexistence between these messaging systems possible, certain restrictions had to be placed on how you can configure Exchange 2000 during coexistence. Like Windows

2000, which has a mixed mode to support coexistence with Windows NT, Exchange 2000 has a mixed mode to support coexistence with Exchange Server 5.5. When the first Exchange 2000 server is installed, the organization is in mixed mode. Once there is no longer any need to support Exchange Server 5.5 servers or services, the Exchange 2000 organization can be configured for native mode. Make certain you no longer need to coexist however, because once you flip this switch there's no going back.

For Exchange Server 5.5 to coexist with Exchange 2000, the Exchange 2000 servers must look and feel like another Exchange Server 5.5 server. To accomplish this, certain restrictions are placed on the flexibility of Exchange 2000 Administrative Groups and routing groups (see the sidebar titled *Making Exchange 2000 look like Exchange Server 5.5)*. In mixed mode, the Exchange 2000 Administrative Group and the routing group are directly associated, so that they look to Exchange Server 5.5 like another Exchange Server 5.5 site. The restrictions on how Administrative Groups and routing groups can be configured while in mixed mode are as follows.

- Routing groups cannot span Administrative Groups.

- A server in a routing group cannot belong to a different Administrative Group.

- Mailboxes cannot be moved between Administrative Groups.

- Administrative Groups can contain multiple routing groups, but Exchange 5.5 servers will not recognize more than one routing group and will treat all Exchange servers in the Administrative Group as if it were a single site.

When you install your first Exchange 2000 server, after running forestprep and domainprep, coexistence between the Exchange Server 5.5 directory and Active Directory will be established. From the Exchange Server 5.5 directory, Exchange configuration information will replicate to Active Directory, and you will see Administrative Groups starting to appear that will mirror the sites defined in Exchange Server 5.5. During coexistence, therefore, your Administrative Groups will mirror your Exchange Server 5.5 sites, locking your administrative model into something similar to what you had with Exchange Server 5.5.

Making Exchange 2000 Look Like Exchange Server 5.5

When planning your Exchange 2000 deployment, it's important to understand the basic components of an Exchange 2000 organization. This is important because, as the person responsible for planning the deployment, you need to be familiar with how Exchange Server 5.5 and Exchange 2000 fit together. In previous versions of Exchange, the Exchange organization was made up of sites. Exchange sites defined the administrative model, how messages flowed through the organization, and the X.500 namespace. Each of these aspects of an Exchange site would likely have a unique set of design considerations. The ideal Exchange 5.5 administrative model was different from the ideal routing model. However, since these two design points are folded into a single object—the site—this often leads to compromises during the site design process. Usually, Exchange Server 5.5 sites were designed on the basis of available network bandwidth, with the administrative model taking a back seat. The consequence is that most Exchange organizations have a loose administrative model where users who are defined as Exchange Administrators within a site have full control over all objects in that site.

In Exchange 2000 sites no longer exist. They have been dismantled into three independently configurable components: Administrative Groups, Routing Groups, and the Active Directory namespace (Figure 6.7).

Each of these Exchange 2000 components can be designed independently of the others to meet specific design considerations. This is only true when Exchange 2000 is in native mode. When in mixed mode, to support coexistence, Administrative Groups and Routing Groups are dependent.

An administrative model that meets your organization's requirements can be implemented without affecting the routing topology, and vice versa.

Administrative groups

Objects in Exchange 2000 are contained in manageable groups named Administrative Groups. The objects in an Administrative Group inherit the permissions assigned the Administrative Groups. Administrative Groups can, but don't have to, contain any Exchange 2000 object. This means that all your routing groups and public folder hierarchies can be contained in one centralized Administrative Group, while your Exchange 2000 server objects are contained in regional Administrative Groups. This type of flexibility allows for new administrative models not previously available with Exchange.

Continued

Figure 6.7 Exchange 2000

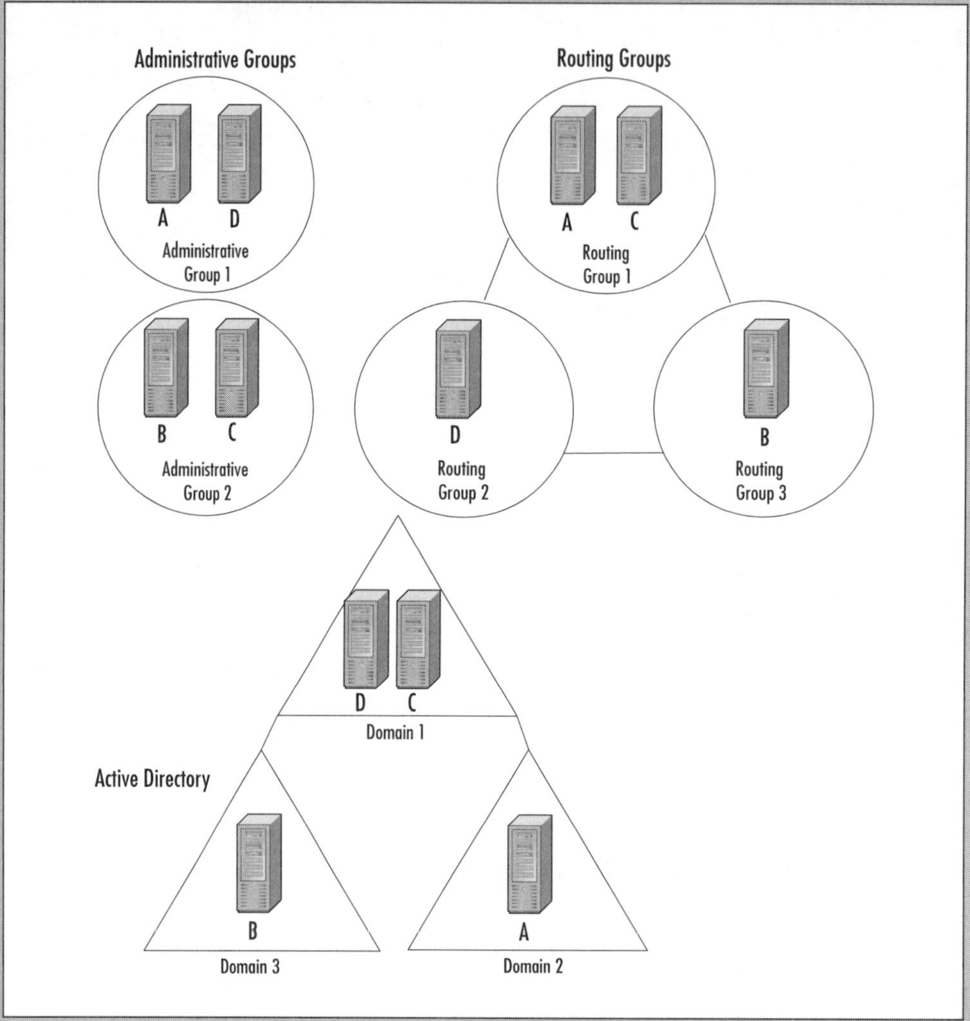

Routing groups

Message flow within and between routing groups is similar to previous versions of Exchange. Messages are delivered between servers within a routing group in a single hop, or point-to-point. Between routing groups, messages are routed through bridgehead servers and across connectors. Despite similarities in how messages flow, there are vast differences between the inner workings of Exchange Server 5.5 and Exchange 2000 message transfer. Some of the major changes to message transfer in Exchange 2000 include SMTP being the primary protocol

Continued

> used to deliver messages within a routing group and the preferred protocol between routing groups. Also, Exchange 2000 is much smarter about how to route a message between routing groups. The state of all connectors that connect routing groups is contained in a database on all servers. Once a connector fails, all servers are notified, and that connector will not be used again until it becomes available.
>
> Those who are responsible for your Exchange 2000 deployment should have a working knowledge of Exchange 2000. Too often those who design the Exchange 2000 topology get all the training while those who do the deployment, it is assumed, will be able to get by on their Exchange Server 5.5 skill set. This may not be the case. After reading this chapter, I think you'll agree.

When to Consolidate before Deploying

When you coexist with Exchange Server 5.5, you inherit the Exchange Server 5.5 site topology into your Exchange 2000 organization. What's more, you can't move servers between Exchange 2000 Administrative Groups to reorganize once the coexistence phase of your deployment is complete. This means that if your Exchange 2000 design or functional specification has a different Administrative Group structure than your Exchange Server 5.5 site topology, you're in a bind (but not alone). There are two approaches to overcoming this problem.

- After your upgrade to Exchange 2000 is complete, you can go to native mode and move mailboxes between Administrative Groups (not servers, mind you, just mailboxes). You could then create additional Administrative Groups that contain Exchange 2000 servers, and move users out of unwanted Exchange Server 5.5 sites, then retire those sites.

- With Exchange Server 5.5 service pack 1 you can move servers between Exchange Server 5.5 sites using the Move Server Wizard. This presents the other option. You could reorganize your Exchange Server 5.5 site structure to look like your Exchange 2000 Administrative Group structure using the Move Server Wizard, then upgrade from Exchange Server 5.5 to Exchange 2000, resulting in the Administrative Group structure defined in your Exchange 2000 design.

Neither of these options are inviting. Each would require a great deal of effort and resources in addition to extending the deployment process and causing more end-user downtime. However, until Microsoft releases an

Exchange 2000 version of the Move Server Wizard, there are not many other choices.

Tools Used to Upgrade the Windows NT 4.0 SAM

Despite the lack of a Move Server Wizard for Exchange 2000, Microsoft has provided us with several useful tools for upgrading our Windows NT 4.0 directory to Active Directory. The simplest method of upgrading, of course, is the in-place upgrade method. This takes your existing Windows NT 4.0 domain structure and upgrades it to Active Directory. However, as with Exchange 2000, where you may not want the same directory structure as Exchange Server 5.5, many organizations will want to migrate from an existing Windows NT 4.0 directory structure to a new Active Directory directory structure, preserving as much user data as possible. Fortunately, there's a tool to do just that: the Active Directory Migration Tool (ADMT).

Using the Active Directory Migration Tool

The Active Directory Migration Tool (ADMT) provides an efficient way to migrate accounts and trusts from Windows NT 4.0 domains to Active Directory domains. It is a feature-rich tool (Figure 6.8) that works with Windows 2000 to retain SID data as objects are moved from one domain to another.

Figure 6.8 Active Directory Migration Tool

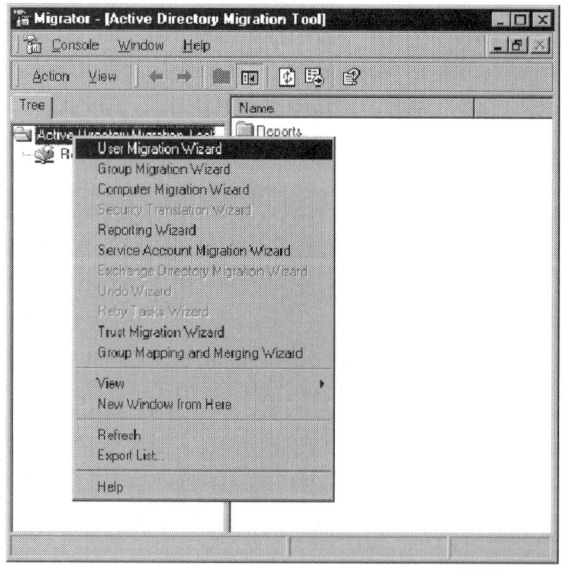

When a user is moved from a Windows NT 4.0 domain to an Active Directory domain the user's SID, which is the identification key that allows that user access to resources in the NT domain, is copied to an attribute of the Active Directory user. This attribute, named SIDHistory, is used to grant the new Active Directory user access to the resources still contained in an NT 4.0 domain. It is this attribute that allows for a controlled and phased migration from Windows NT 4.0 to Active Directory using ADMT.

NOTE

ADMT has a look-before-you-leap feature, which lets you run ADMT without affecting either domain.

Tools Used to Upgrade the Exchange Server 5.5 Directory

Active Directory is made up of three types of partitions: domain partitions (one for each domain), a configuration partition, and a schema partition. The Exchange Server 5.5 directory contains data we want to upgrade into the domain and configuration partitions (the schema is upgraded during setup). To accomplish this we use the Active Directory Connector (ADC).

Using the Active Directory Connector

The ADC plays a crucial role in Exchange Server 5.5 and Active Directory coexistence. The ADC synchronizes directory objects between Exchange Server 5.5 and Active Directory, both recipient directory objects and configuration directory objects. This allows organizations that have maintained an attribute-rich Exchange Server 5.5 directory to bring that data across to their Active Directory and keep it synchronized. The configuration objects of Exchange Server 5.5 sites are synchronized to Active Directory so that Exchange 2000 servers have knowledge of the sites, servers, and other configuration objects necessary to coexist. For coexistence, it is required to use the Exchange 2000 version of the ADC.

During synchronization, Exchange Server 5.5 objects are matched with equivalent Active Directory objects.

- Exchange Server 5.5 mailboxes are equivalent to Active Directory mail-enabled users.

- Exchange Server 5.5 distribution lists are equivalent to Active Directory mail-enabled groups.

- Exchange Server 5.5 custom recipients are equivalent to Active Directory mail-enabled contacts.

There are two versions of the ADC, one that comes with Windows 2000 and a version that is included with Exchange 2000. The Windows 2000 version can only synchronize mail recipient objects with Active Directory users and can be used to populate Active Directory and to centralize administration of the two directories. The Exchange 2000 version of the ADC also synchronizes mail recipient objects between directories. However, the Exchange 2000 version of the ADC also synchronizes configuration objects between Exchange Server 5.5 and Active Directory, allowing for coexistence between the directories.

NOTE

Exchange 2000 setup will not allow an Exchange 2000 server to join an Exchange Server 5.5 site if the Exchange 2000 version of the ADC is not installed in the enterprise.

The ADC performs synchronization by associating portions of one directory with a portion of the other directory. These associations are defined in what are called *connection agreements*. Connection agreements are established between Exchange Server 5.5 sites and Active Directory domains to define what objects from each directory should be synchronized and where. A container in the Exchange Server 5.5 directory, such as a recipient container, is associated with a container in the Active Directory domain, such as an Organizational Unit (OU). The objects in these containers are synchronized based on the schedule defined in the connection agreement.

Synchronization occurs using Lightweight Directory Access Protocol (LDAP) between an Exchange Server 5.5 server with Service Pack 3, a Windows 2000 server running ADC, and a Windows 2000 domain controller configured as a global catalog server (Figure 6.9).

WARNING

If you are going to run Exchange Server 5.5 on a Windows 2000 server, you must change the Exchange LDAP port to something other than port 389, which will be used by Windows 2000.

Figure 6.9 The Active Directory Connector

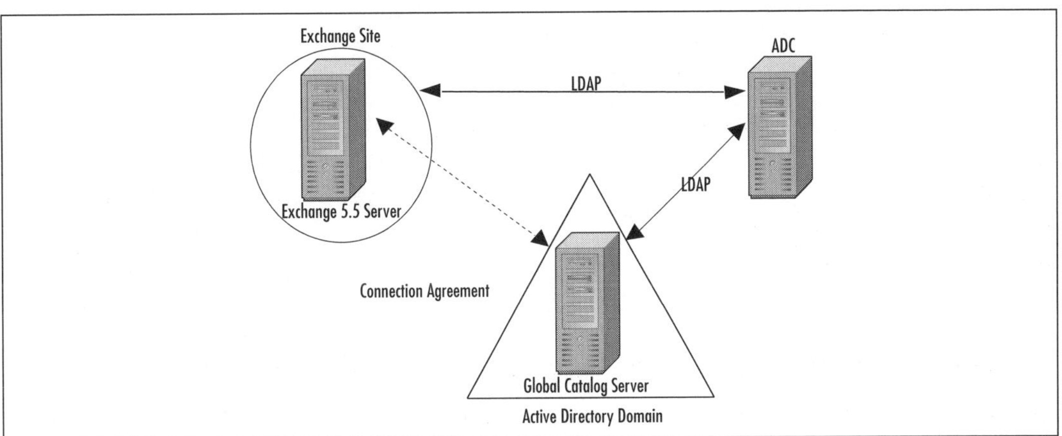

User Connection Agreements

User Connection Agreements define which object containers in each directory will have their objects synchronized. Therefore you must plan carefully
which containers in each directory you want objects to synchronize
between. You must define and configure User Connection Agreements to
assure objects are synchronized between your two directories properly. It is
important to define where ADC connection agreements are needed in your
environment before implementing the ADC.

In Figure 6.10 there are two Exchange Server 5.5 sites and a single
Active Directory domain. If you want the recipients from each site to be synchronized with different domains or with different OUs within a domain, as
in Figure 6.10, then you must define multiple connection agreements. In this
case, two connection agreements are defined to synchronize objects from
each site to the domain. This is a simple example of how connection agreements are used, but you can see the importance of making sure you correctly defined where you want your objects in each directory synchronized.

Connection Agreement configuration is very flexible, and therefore can be
complex. The connection agreement can be configured for one-way synchronization, in either direction, or two-way synchronization, based on your
requirements. One-way connection agreements only write changes to the
directory in one direction. This can be useful in lab or pilot projects where
you don't want Active Directory to affect your production Exchange Server
5.5 directory. It is also possible to configure the types of objects a connection
agreement will synchronize. To define the connection agreements necessary
for your organization, you must analyze the objects in your Exchange Server
5.5 directory and your Active Directory design to determine where the
Exchange objects will reside after you upgrade to Exchange 2000.

Figure 6.10 User Connection Agreements

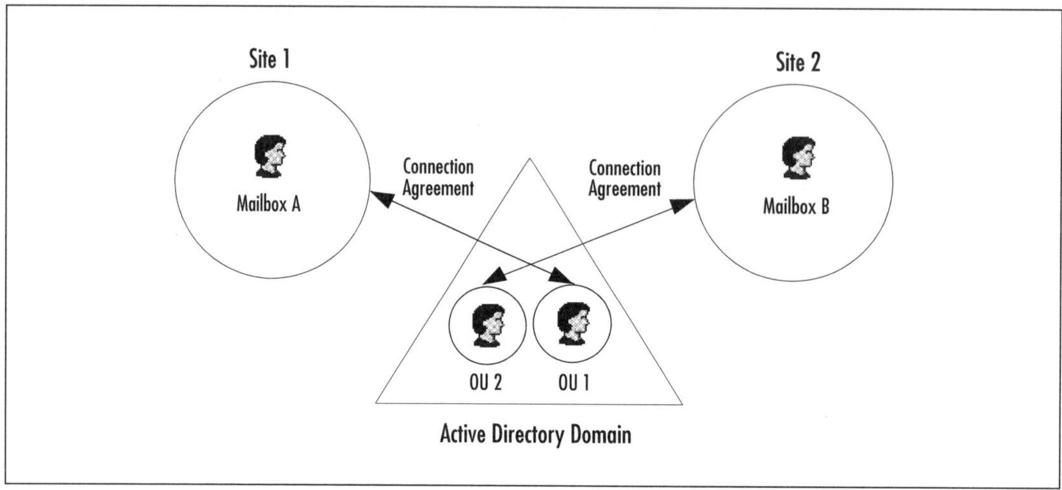

Figure 6.11 Object Synchronization

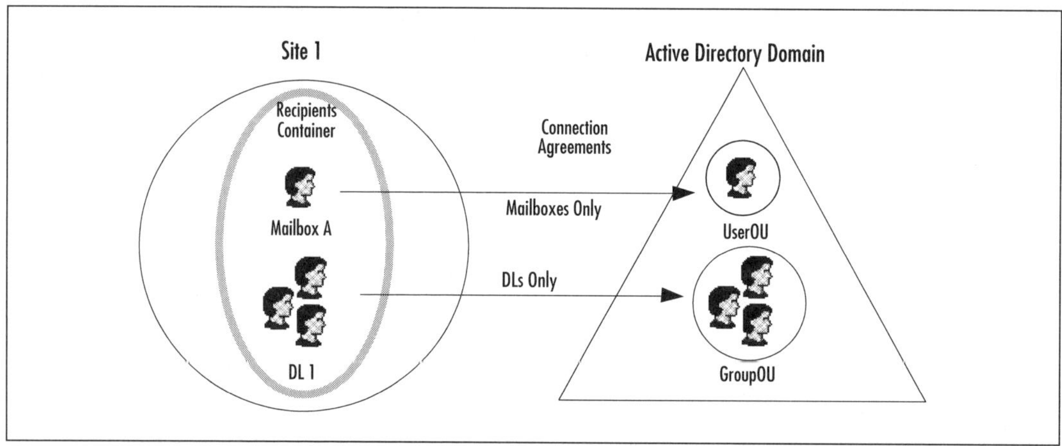

Another example of the flexibility of connection agreements can be seen in Figure 6.11, where there are two connection agreements between Site 1 and Domain A. One connection agreement is configured between the Exchange Server 5.5 site recipient's container and an Active Directory OU named UserOU. This connection agreement is configured to only synchronize *mailbox* objects from Exchange Server 5.5 to Active Directory. The other connection agreement, between the recipient's container and an OU named GroupOU, is configured to only synchronize *distribution lists* from Exchange Server 5.5 to Active Directory. So, even if you have multiple types of objects in a recipient container or OU, you can synchronize the objects in those containers by object type.

It is also possible to have multiple connection agreements configured to synchronize the same type of objects to two different destinations. This may be necessary when users from multiple NT 4.0 domains have mailboxes in a single site. When those domains are upgraded to Active Directory domains, connection agreements are put in place to synchronize the objects in the two domains with the single site. The ADC is capable of determining which connection agreement will synchronize each object because of an attribute that is written to the object. This allows for two connection agreements from the same site to two different Active Directory domains. However, what happens when you create a new object in the Exchange Server 5.5 site? Which domain will it synchronize with? That is determined by which connection agreement is configured as the *primary connection agreement.* At least one connection agreement per site and domain should be defined as the primary connection agreement. The primary connection agreement will create new objects in the destination directory, if one does not exist. Though not required, it is recommended that only one primary connection agreement be defined for each site and domain to avoid creating duplicate objects in the forest.

In Figure 6.12 both Site 1 and Site 2 has two user connection agreements, one with Domain A and another with Domain B. The user connection agreement between Site 1 and Domain A is defined as a primary connection agreement. The user connection agreement between Site 2 and Domain B is defined as a primary connection agreement. When a new object, such as a custom recipient, is created in Site 1, a contact object will be created in Domain A. When a new object—such as a distribution list—is created in Site 2, a mail-enabled group will be created in Domain B. If both connection agreements from Site 1 were defined as primary connection agreements, it would be possible for duplicate objects to be created in domain A and domain B.

In multisite and multidomain environments, plan carefully to assure objects are going to be synchronized as needed. Where you defined your user connection agreements and which ones you designate as primary connection agreements will depend partly on the ultimate location of your user accounts. It is important to fully understand the ADC and how it is used in different environments. You will quickly realize the ADC and its configuration can be quite complex and should be planned and deployed carefully.

Figure 6.12 Primary Connection Agreements

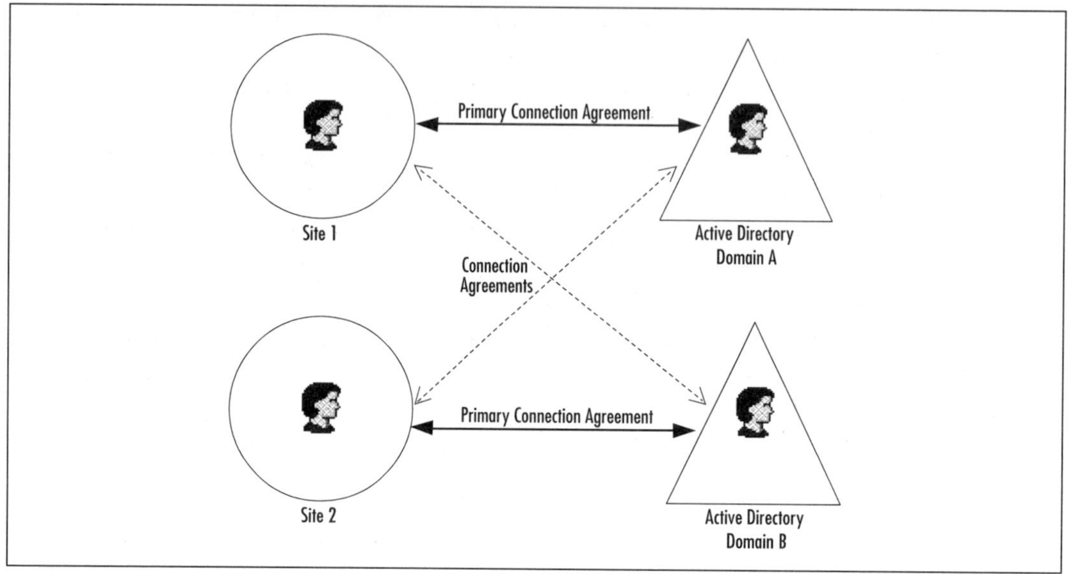

Public Folder Connection Agreements

Exchange Server 5.5 public folders are both containers that store public folder items in the public information store, and recipients that have an address in the Exchange 5.5 global address list. The public folder recipients are contained in the Exchange 5.5 directory like any other recipient. Every public folder must have an address in the Exchange 5.5 directory, though it may be hidden. These addresses are used for various things and make up part of the Exchange 5.5 public folder system.

When coexisting with Exchange 2000 it is necessary to have these public folder addresses represented in Active Directory so that the Exchange 2000 public folder system continues to work as usual. Synchronization of public folder addresses between Exchange Server 5.5 and Active Directory is achieved using public *folder connection agreements*.

One public folder connection agreement should be set up between each Exchange 5.5 site and Active Directory. There is very little to configure in the public folder connection agreement; however, they are important to include in your deployment plan—along with definitions of user connection agreements.

Configuration Connection Agreements

User connection agreements and public folder connection agreements are at the heart of a directory upgrade solution and planning for them is critical.

However, the Exchange 2000 version of the ADC can also synchronize the configuration portion of the Exchange directory to the configuration portion of Active Directory. This is just as important to the deployment process because it enables Exchange 5.5 servers and Exchange 2000 servers to coexist. When Exchange 2000 servers coexist with Exchange Server 5.5 servers in an Exchange Server 5.5 site, they must know the configuration of the Exchange Server 5.5 organization. When a change is made to an Exchange Server 5.5 directory—for instance, when a server is removed from the site—that change is synchronized though the configuration connection agreement to Active Directory. The Exchange 2000 server that's a member of the Exchange Server 5.5 site then knows the server no longer exists in the site. Directory configuration synchronization is supplied through one or more configuration connection agreements. Fortunately, Exchange 2000 setup automatically defines the configuration connection agreements necessary to support coexistence. When you are installing the first Exchange 2000 server into an Exchange Server 5.5 site, setup checks Active Directory to confirm you have installed the Exchange 2000 version of the ADC. Setup will not continue unless the ADC is installed because setup requires that you have defined the configuration connection agreements necessary to support coexistence.

Site Replication Service

The ADC and its configuration connection agreements are but one component required for coexistence. Another is the Site Replication Service (SRS). Within an Exchange site, the Exchange Server 5.5 directory services communicate directly with one another using remote procedure calls (RPCs). When an Exchange 2000 server is put into the Exchange 5.5 site, it also must participate in directory replication. However, as we know now, the Exchange 2000 server doesn't have a copy of the directory that has been moved to Active Directory. Since Exchange 2000 has no local directory, the SRS provides an Exchange Server 5.5 directory service during coexistence.

NOTE

The SRS is only used for coexistence. The client and administrator interface have been disabled.

The SRS is a pseudo-directory that runs on the Exchange 2000 server only for replication to and from Exchange 5.5 servers. The SRS directory becomes part of the Exchange site, communicating with the other Exchange

Server 5.5 servers using RPC. When a directory change from an Exchange 5.5 server is replicated to the SRS on Exchange 2000, the SRS accepts the directory change. From there, the directory change is synchronized with Active Directory through the configuration connection agreement.

As shown in Figure 6.13, as changes are replicated around the Exchange site, they are replicated to the Exchange 2000 SRS. The ADC configuration connection agreement in Domain A synchronizes these changes and replicates them to the configuration partition of Active Directory.

Figure 6.13 Site Replication Service

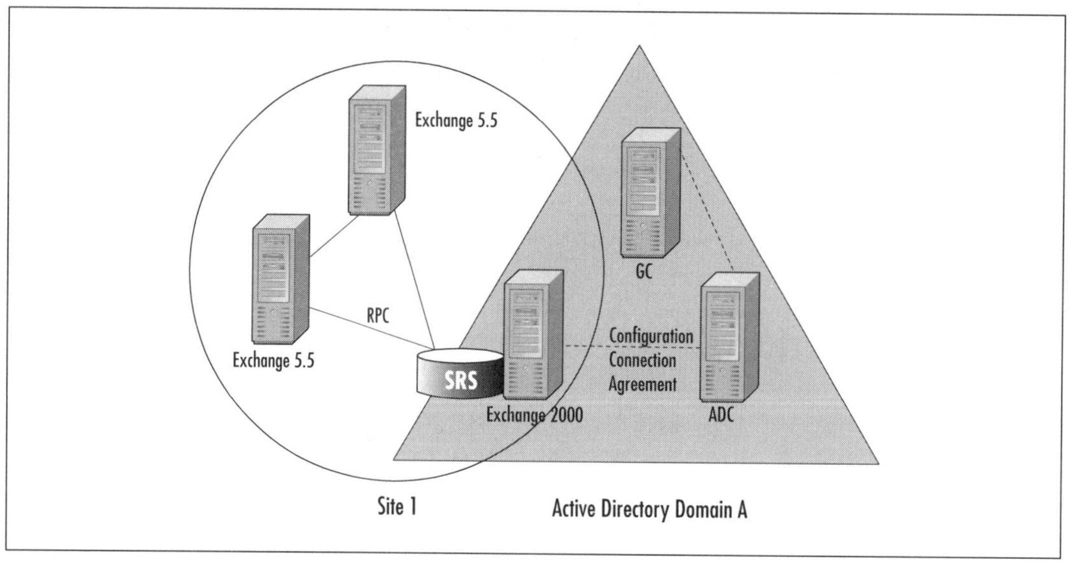

Using the Active Directory Account Cleanup Wizard

During the upgrade and during synchronization, objects such as user accounts can be created by an in-place upgrade, the ADMT, or the ADC. In some cases it is possible that one or more of these tools may create duplicate Active Directory objects. When this happens it will be necessary to use the Active Directory Account Cleanup Wizard, or ADClean. Duplicate accounts can be created during migration when two or more directories, such as Windows NT and Exchange Server 5.5, are consolidated into a single Active Directory. ADClean (Figure 6.14) merges these accounts, preserving the important attributes of both and creating a single account.

Figure 6.14 Active Directory Account Cleanup Wizard

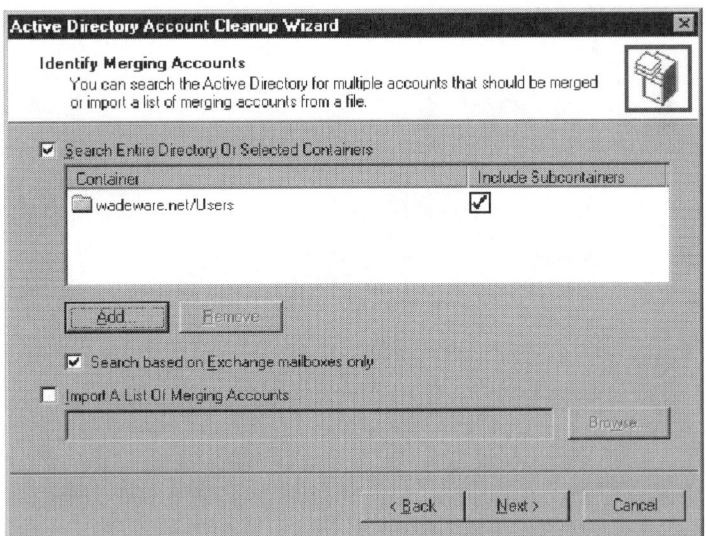

For example, if you use the ADC to create accounts in Active Directory, then upgrade a Windows NT 4.0 domain to Active Directory, you will be left with two accounts for each user: one created by ADC and the other created by upgrading the domain. ADClean will consolidate these duplicate accounts. During the consolidation, group and distribution list membership is preserved (as well as the SIDs of each account) so resource access is not affected.

Directory Upgrade Scenarios

Now that you are familiar with the tools that will be used during the upgrade and deployment of Exchange 2000, it is important to understand the impact they will have on the directory when they are used. In your deployment it may be necessary to use the tools in a particular order, especially if you are doing a phased deployment of Exchange 2000 or Windows 2000. This section outlines some of the possible directory upgrade scenarios, showing which tools are used and the impact they will have.

Using the In-Place Upgrade Method

The simplest and most straightforward approach to upgrading your directory is an in-place upgrade. Upgrading the Windows NT 4.0 primary domain controller (PDC) in-place to Windows 2000 creates Active Directory accounts. The ADC is then configured to synchronize Active Directory and the Exchange Server 5.5 directory (Figure 6.15).

Figure 6.15 In-Place Upgrade then ADC

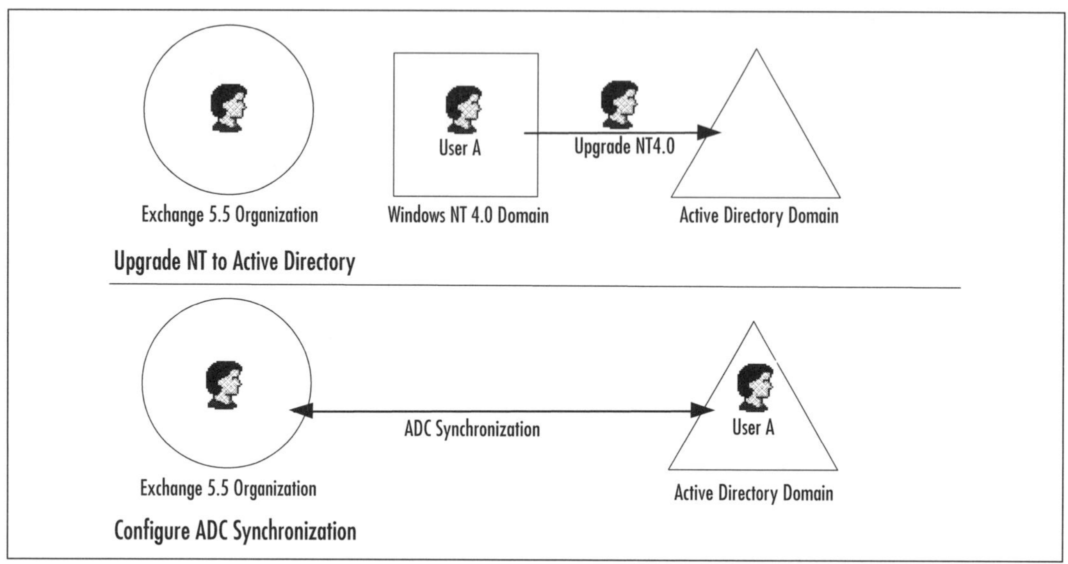

This is a common upgrade approach for smaller- to medium-size organizations and organizations that plan on keeping a similar Active Directory domain topology as they had with Windows NT 4.0. One advantage to this method is each user's original security identifier (SID) is preserved during the upgrade and stored in the upgraded users Active Directory account. This allows the upgraded user to access resources inside and outside their domain.

Upgrade Using ADMT then ADC

Active Directory is quite different from Windows NT 4.0. The reasons for and capabilities of Active Directory domains are different from those of Windows NT 4.0 domains. Because of this, many organizations are moving to a new Active Directory domain topology. This migration from an NT 4.0 domain topology to a new Active Directory domain topology will include moving users and computers between domains using ADMT. The ADMT, like an in-place upgrade, preserves the SID from the source objects as they are moved to the destination domain. Once the objects have been moved to the destination domain, the ADC is configured to synchronize between Active Directory and Exchange Server 5.5 (Figure 6.16).

In this scenario, the Windows 2000 deployment project is in full swing before the Exchange 2000 deployment begins. Once Active Directory users have been moved from their NT 4.0 domain to their Active Directory domain and the ADC is configured, the Exchange directory upgrade is essentially complete. Upgrading the Exchange Server 5.5 servers to Exchange 2000 will keep the association between mailbox and directory object in place.

Figure 6.16 Migrating Using ADMT then ADC

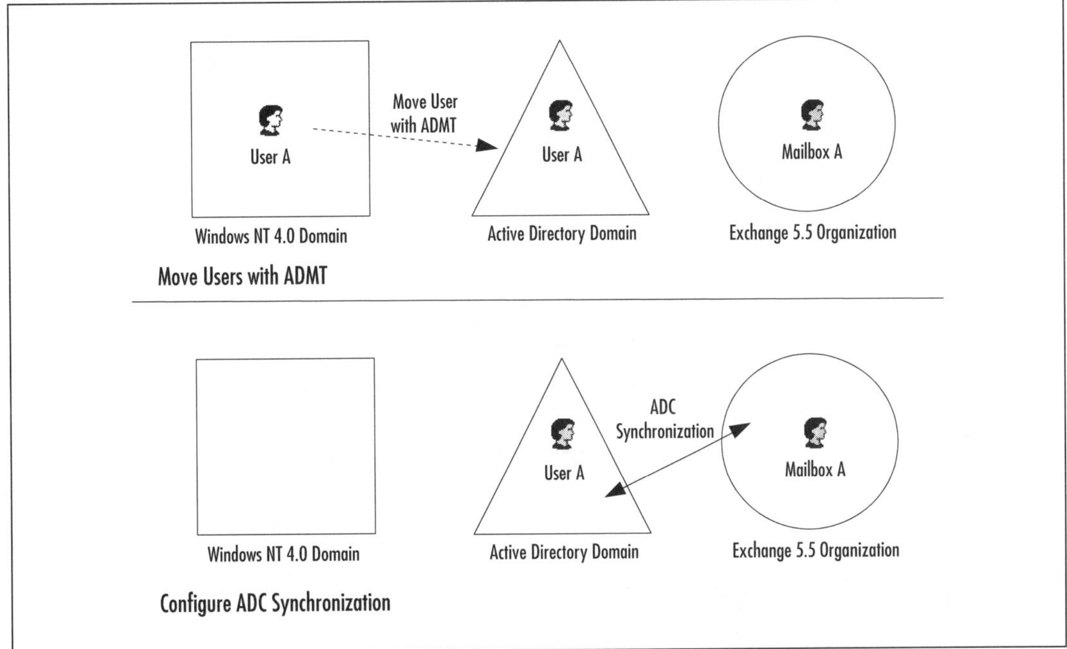

ADC then In-Place Upgrade then ADClean

Up to this point, the scenarios in this chapter have assumed Windows 2000 and Active Directory are deployed before Exchange 2000. However, many organizations don't want to wait for Windows 2000 and Active Directory to be fully deployed before they can enjoy the benefits of Exchange 2000. It is possible to begin the deployment of Exchange 2000 before Active Directory has been deployed throughout the organization. To accomplish this, at least one Active Directory domain must be created that will host Exchange 2000 servers and recipient objects. The recipient objects in Active Directory will only be used by Exchange 2000 clients for address book lookups. The users will continue to log on to their NT 4.0 accounts to access their NT 4.0 resources.

The Active Directory domain created to support Exchange 2000 is called a *transition domain*. The ADC is used to create and synchronize all Windows NT user accounts to the transition domain. The ADC creates disabled Active Directory users that in turn make up the global address list for Exchange 2000 users (Figure 6.17). You can then upgrade your Exchange Server 5.5 servers to Exchange 2000 (Figure 6.18).

Figure 6.17 Using the ADC to Create Disabled Accounts

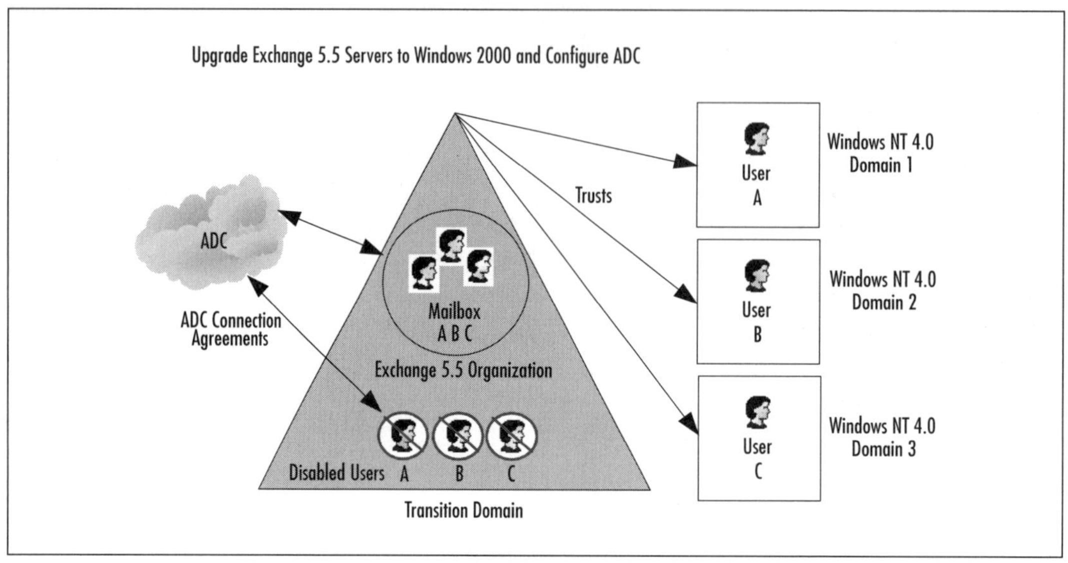

Figure 6.18 Upgrading Exchange 5.5 Servers to Exchange 2000

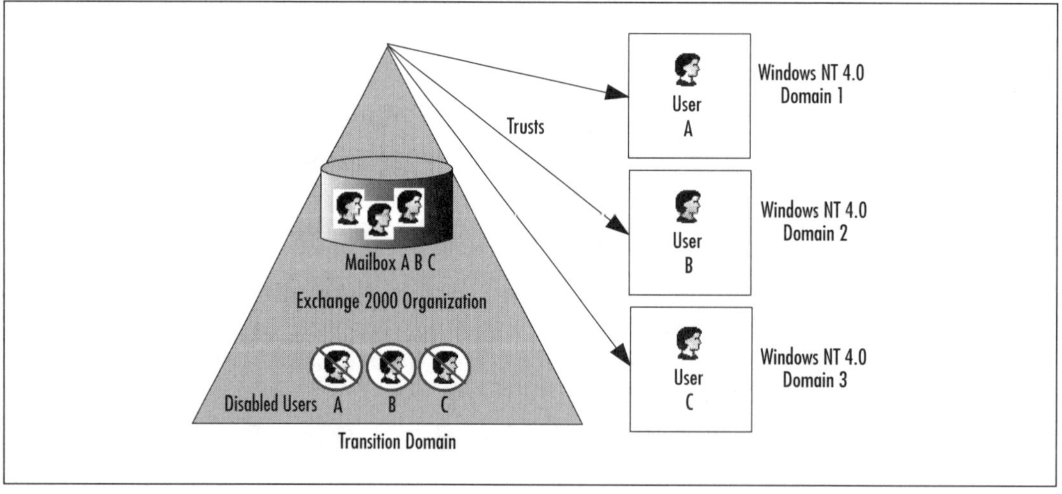

Once complete, you continue to have your NT 4.0 account domains in place; however, once your users access their Exchange mailbox, the mailbox will reside in an Active Directory domain and be hosted on Exchange 2000. With this configuration, you can benefit from Exchange 2000 in a Windows NT 4.0 environment indefinitely, and upgrade your Windows NT 4.0 domains to Windows 2000 at your leisure.

Once you are ready to upgrade your NT 4.0 accounts domains to Active Directory domains, duplicate accounts will be created in Active Directory: one that was created by the ADC and another that was created by the NT domain upgrade. Therefore, as you upgrade your NT 4.0 domains to Windows 2000, you must run ADClean to consolidate the duplicate accounts (Figure 6.19). The disabled Active Directory account created by the ADC in the transition domain will be merged into the account residing in the upgraded Active Directory domain (Figure 6.20).

Figure 6.19 Upgrading NT 4.0 Domains to Active Directory

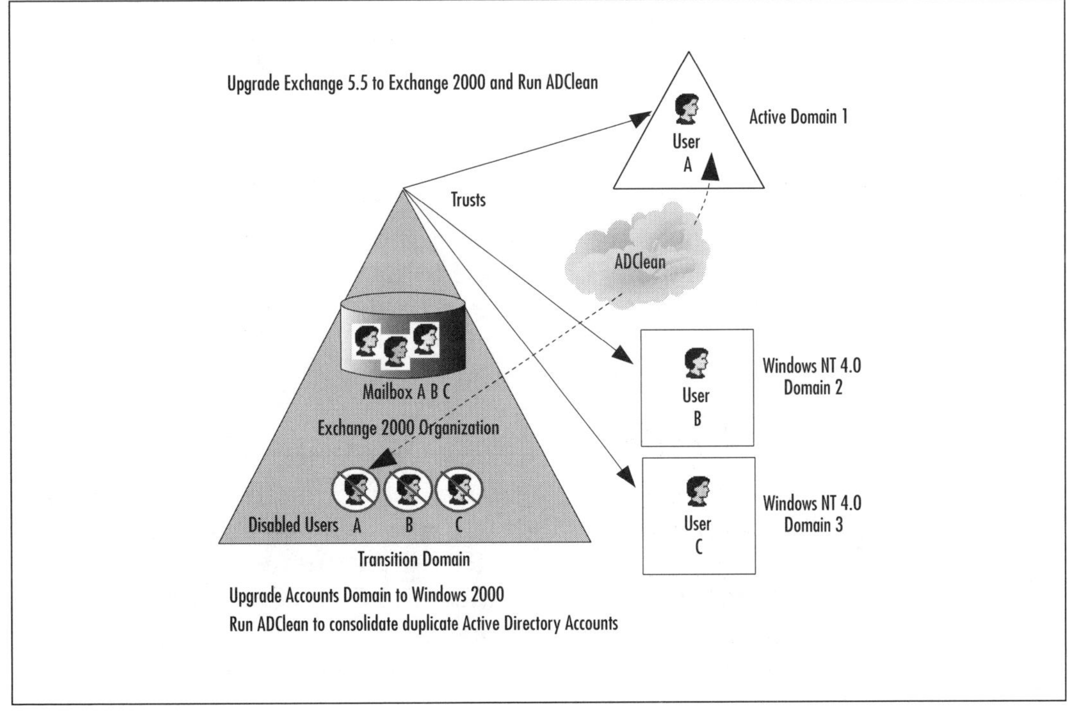

Figure 6.20 Confirming ADClean Merged Duplicate Accounts

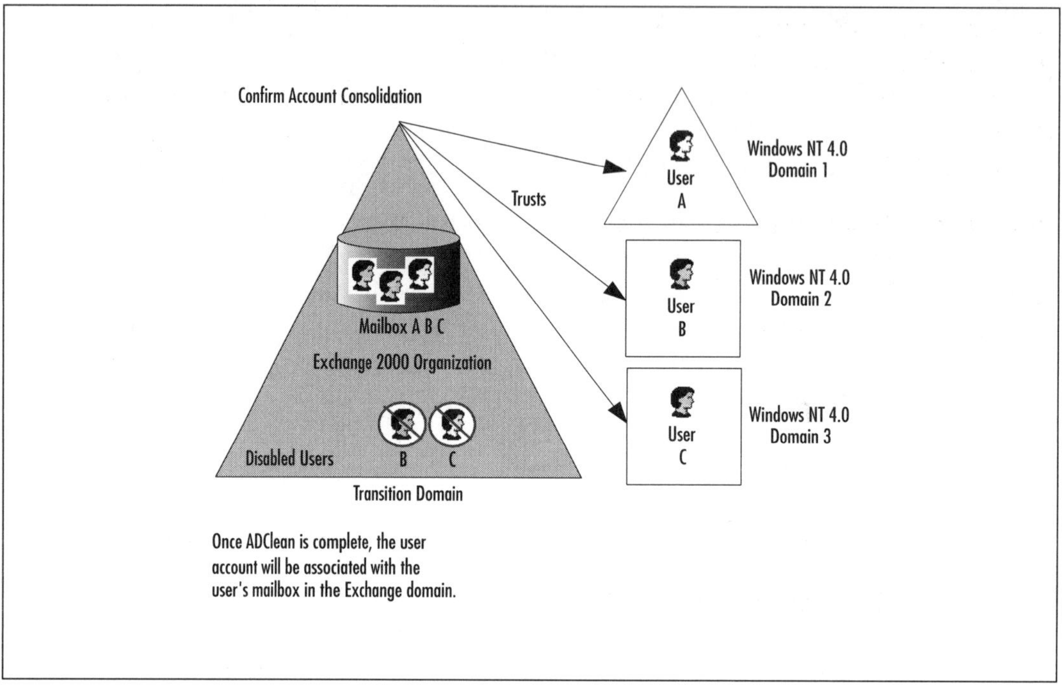

The remaining NT 4.0 account domains can be upgraded following the same process. Once the domains have gone to native mode, the Exchange 2000 servers can be moved to the domains where their users reside and the transition domain can be retired.

NOTE

The first domain in a forest plays a special role in the forest and cannot be removed. It is for this reason that you may want to establish your Active Directory forest with a domain that will continue to be at the root of your domain structure. In this instance, the Exchange 2000 domain would be the second domain in the forest.

Upgrade Using ADC then ADMT then ADClean

Another scenario where duplicate accounts are created is one that uses ADMT to migrate accounts from NT 4.0 to Active Directory after the ADC has been configured and has created disabled Active Directory accounts for each Exchange 5.5 mailbox. This scenario is similar to the previous one; however, rather than upgrading the NT 4.0 accounts domains in place, the NT 4.0 accounts are being migrated to new Active Directory domains using ADMT.

As before, the ADC creates disabled user accounts in a transition domain (Figure 6.21). This time, however, the NT 4.0 accounts are moved using ADMT to a new Active Directory domain (Figure 6.22).

Figure 6.21 Active Directory Users Created by ADC

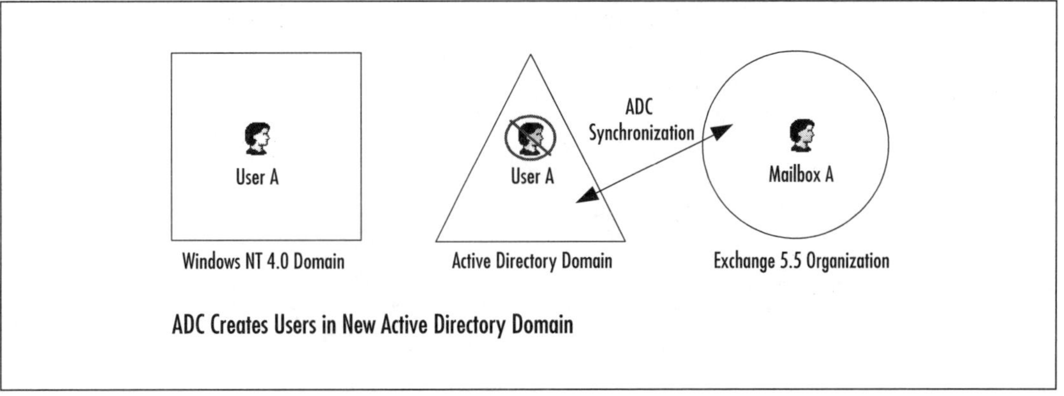

Figure 6.22 ADMT Creates Duplicate Accounts

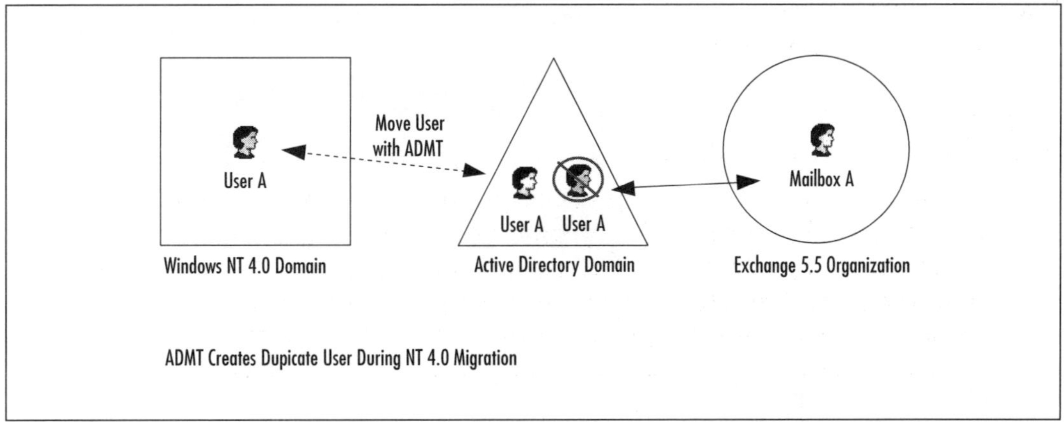

This creates duplicate accounts: one created by the ADC, the other created by the ADMT. ADClean is then run to consolidate duplicate accounts (Figure 6.23). The disabled Active Directory account created by the ADC in the transition domain is merged into the account residing in the new Active Directory domain (Figure 6.24).

Figure 6.23 ADClean is Used to Merge Twin Accounts

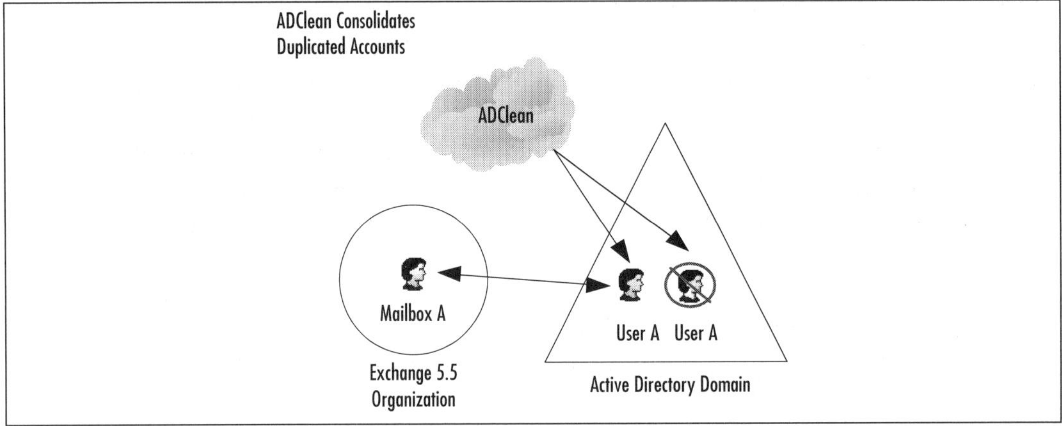

Figure 6.24 Twins are Merged and One Account Remains

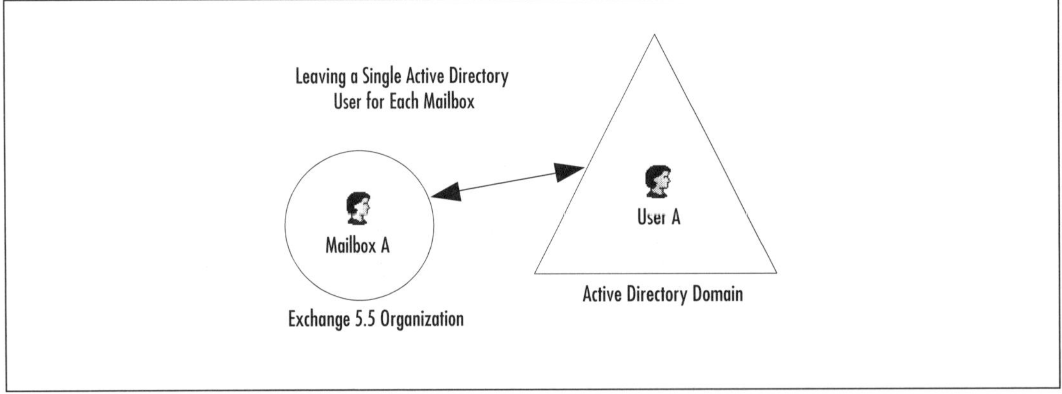

Directory Upgrade Considerations

Trying to meld two different directories into one can be challenging. It can also raise some complexities that require a creative solution. One of these challenges is due to the fundamental difference in how permissions are applied to public folders in Exchange 2000 and Exchange Server 5.5. In Exchange 2000, Active Directory objects such as users and groups are used to apply permissions to public folders. In Exchange Server 5.5, Exchange objects such as mailboxes and distribution lists are used to assign permissions to public folders. This means, for the purpose of applying permission to public folders, there must be an Exchange distribution list equivalent in Active Directory. Unfortunately, the equivalent is the Active Directory Universal Security Group, which only exists in Windows 2000 native mode.

When to Require a Native Mode Domain

To support public folder security coexistence between Exchange Server 5.5 and Exchange 2000 public folder permissions, it is necessary to have at least one native mode domain in your forest. A user connection agreement is configured between Exchange Server 5.5 and the native mode domain to synchronize groups between the two directories. When synchronization between the Exchange site and Active Directory domain occurs, the Exchange 5.5 distribution lists will become Active Directory universal security groups in the native mode domain. Universal security groups have their group membership published in the global catalog (Figure 6.25). When the public folder hierarchy is replicated between Exchange Server 5.5 and Exchange 2000 servers, Active Directory universal security groups will be used wherever Exchange Server 5.5 distribution lists have been assigned permissions to public folders.

Figure 6.25 Native Mode Domain for Public Folder Coexistence

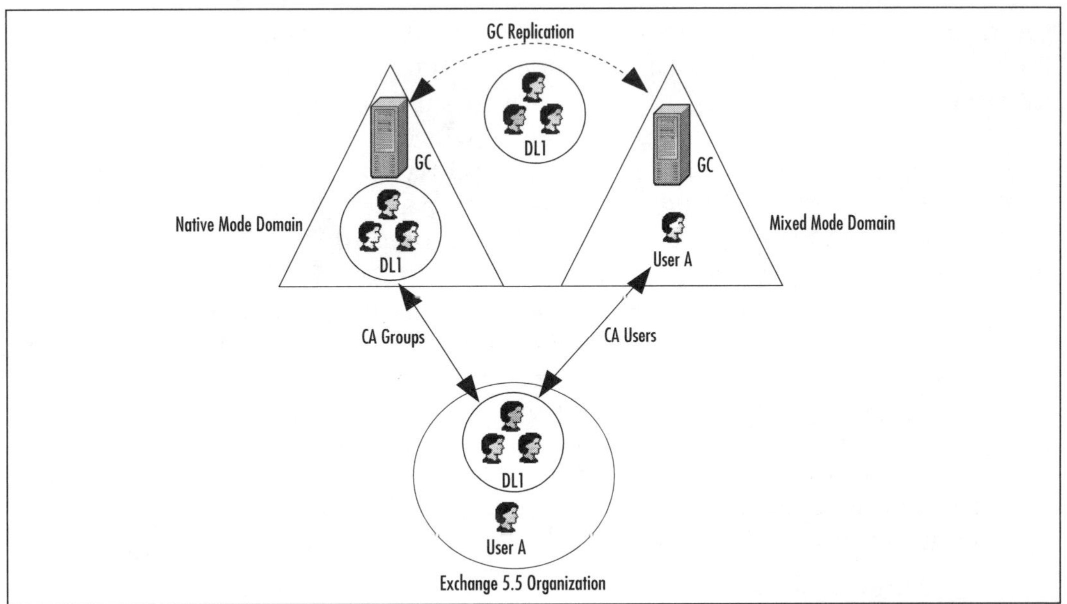

This works because universal security groups are included, along with their membership, in the global catalog. Since Exchange Server 5.5 distribution lists are being translated into universal security groups in the native mode domain, a representation of the distribution list is included in Active Directory. This representation of distribution lists, in the form of universal security groups in Active Directory, allows for public folder permission to be consistent between Exchange Server 5.5 and Exchange 2000. The Exchange 2000 servers in the mixed mode domains are able to access these security principles from the global catalog and then use them to apply permissions to public folders. If you choose not to set up a native mode domain, and distribution lists are being used to apply permissions to public folders, you will lose those permissions. Permissions will have to be manually applied using Domain Global Groups or user objects.

The other option, which may make sense in smaller organizations with limited numbers of public folders, is to forego this problem and its complex solution by manually reassigning permissions to public folders once they have appeared in Active Directory. This way, you don't have to create a native mode domain or the special connection agreements to support it.

How to Successfully Use Universal Groups

Another important consideration with Exchange 2000 is the use of Active Directory global and universal groups. Windows 2000 Active Directory experts will tell you that you should avoid using universal groups and try to use global groups whenever possible. This is because there is a certain amount of overhead associated with universal groups. This overhead is incurred when a user logs in and because universal group membership is included in the global catalog and must be replicated throughout the organization.

On the other hand, Exchange experts will tell you that you should avoid using global mail-enabled groups and try to use universal mail-enabled groups. This is because global group membership is *not* available outside of the global group's domain. So if a user in one domain sends a message to the global group in another domain, the Exchange 2000 server in the sending user's domain will expand the global group from the other domain and find no members. The Exchange 2000 server wrongly deduces that there are no recipients and the message goes nowhere. The Exchange experts will tell you that if you use universal groups, whose membership is replicated to all global catalog servers, you'll never have this problem.

Another more practical solution would be to define the *expansion server* attribute for each global group to be an Exchange 2000 server in the domain that hosts the global group. This way, when a user from one domain sends a message to a global group in another domain, the

Exchange 2000 server that expands the global group is from the global group's domain. It queries a domain controller in the local domain for the global group membership, the global group is successfully expanded, and the mail is delivered. Unfortunately, there is no group policy to force an expansion server to be specified on all global groups. The policy required here is a procedural one. In order to successfully use mail-enabled global groups in a multidomain environment, an operational policy has to be put in place that requires the creator of a global group to specify an expansion server that exists in the domain where the global group is being defined. This way you can use mail-enabled global groups without incurring the overhead of universal groups, and still be assured that messages will be delivered to their destination.

Upgrading the Messaging Environment

Once you have chosen an upgrade path for your Exchange 2000 deployment from Windows NT 4.0 and Exchange 5.5 to Active Directory, you must consider how to upgrade your messaging environment from Exchange Server 5.5 to Exchange 2000. Upgrading from Exchange Server 5.5 to Exchange 2000 is a considerably different upgrade from that of previous versions of Exchange to Exchange Server 5.5. This is because the structure of the Exchange 2000 organization has changed. Based on this, it may be reasonable to consider the move to Exchange 2000 as more of a migration than an upgrade, especially if your Exchange 2000 design is much different that your current Exchange Server 5.5 design. With that said, there are two approaches to moving to Exchange 2000 from Exchange Server 5.5:

- If your Exchange 2000 design is similar to your Exchange Server 5.5 design, upgrade your messaging environment in place, taking care to maintain connectivity to any foreign messaging system, such as the Internet, during the upgrade.

- If your Exchange 2000 design is considerably different from your Exchange Server 5.5 design, migrate your existing Exchange Server 5.5 environment to Exchange 2000. This way, your focus is on deploying the Exchange 2000 design and migrating data from the legacy Exchange system to Exchange 2000.

It is also important to move familiar functionality from your Exchange Server 5.5 environment to your Exchange 2000 environment. The look and feel of the client should not change without proper training and change management of the end users. This includes features like:

- Creating Exchange 2000 Address Lists that are similar to your Exchange Server 5.5 Address Book Views

- Defining an Exchange 2000 offline address book server

- Creating Exchange 2000 recipient policies that provide users with the same e-mail addresses they had in Exchange Server 5.5

By comparing your Exchange 2000 design (which may define things like Address Lists) and your existing Exchange Server 5.5 environment, you can list those things that need to be configured in Exchange 2000 as they were configured in Exchange Server 5.5—as well as those things that will be new to users and require training or some other form of communication.

Performing an In-Place Upgrade

The first approach to getting to Exchange 2000 is the in-place upgrade. The in-place upgrade offers the path of least resistance, but it may only be practical in a few servers in your organization. After upgrading your Exchange Server 5.5 servers to Windows 2000, you simply run the Exchange 2000 setup to install the new software and upgrade the information stores. Exchange servers that do not have any data on them, such as connector servers, need not be upgraded. Simply reinstall Exchange 2000 and implement the connectors defined in your Exchange 2000 design. The in-place upgrade is the preferred method of upgrade in smaller environments with a limited number of servers, when the same hardware is to be used. There are several reasons why an in-place upgrade may not be the best choice for some of your servers:

- The server to be upgraded must be taken offline to do the upgrade. Other methods do not require this.

- If you are using Exchange 4.0 or 5.0, you'll first have to upgrade to Exchange Server 5.5 before going to Exchange 2000. How long the upgrade will take depends on the size and number of folders in the information store and the version of Exchange you are upgrading from. Again, other upgrade methods do not require you to upgrade to Exchange Server 5.5 first.

Performing a Move-Mailbox Upgrade

The move-mailbox method curtails many of the disadvantages of the in-place upgrade. The move-mailbox method entails moving mailboxes from existing Exchange servers to new Exchange 2000 servers. Unlike the in-place upgrade method, the move-mailbox method does not require that the Exchange server be taken offline, nor does it require that the Exchange servers be version 5.5. The new Exchange 2000 server joins the existing Exchange Server 5.5 site, coexisting with Exchange Server 5.5 through the ADC and SRS. Once the Exchange 2000 server belongs to the Exchange 5.5 site, mailboxes are simply moved from the old Exchange servers to the new Exchange 2000 servers (Figure 6.26). This method will be popular with organizations that plan to support Exchange 2000 on new hardware.

Figure 6.26 Move Mailbox Upgrade Method

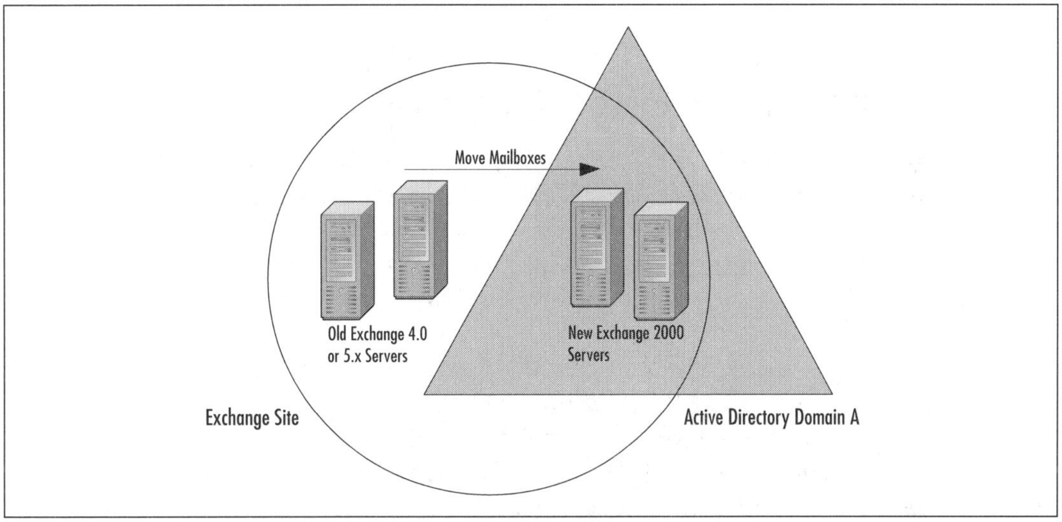

If you have dedicated connector servers, which do not host mailboxes or public folders but are bridgeheads to other sites or the Internet, the move-mailbox method doesn't apply. This is where your approach becomes more like a migration than an upgrade. The connector servers, and the bridgeheads that connect your Exchange 5.5 sites, will be replaced with Exchange 2000 servers that have their own connectors. There really is no upgrade for this process. It's more in line with a standard deployment. How you schedule the deployment tasks that will support your new Exchange 2000 architecture with the upgrade tasks that will bring your user data over to Exchange 2000 is what can separate a quality deployment plan from a mediocre deployment plan.

Using the Leapfrog Method

The move-mailbox method of upgrading to Exchange 2000, with all its advantages, does require new hardware. To move your existing Exchange mailboxes to Exchange 2000 requires new Exchange 2000 servers. For organizations whose current server hardware will support Exchange 2000, an added twist to the move-mailbox method can be used. The *leapfrog migration method* entails adding only a few new servers to the migration, moving users from existing Exchange servers to the new server, then installing Windows 2000 and Exchange 2000 on the old servers and moving the mailboxes from the next Exchange server to the newly installed Exchange 2000 server (Figure 6.27). If you're not familiar with the term *leapfrog,* it's the name of a children's game in which the last person in a line leaps one by one over the others to move to the front of the line.

Figure 6.27 Leapfrog Upgrade Method

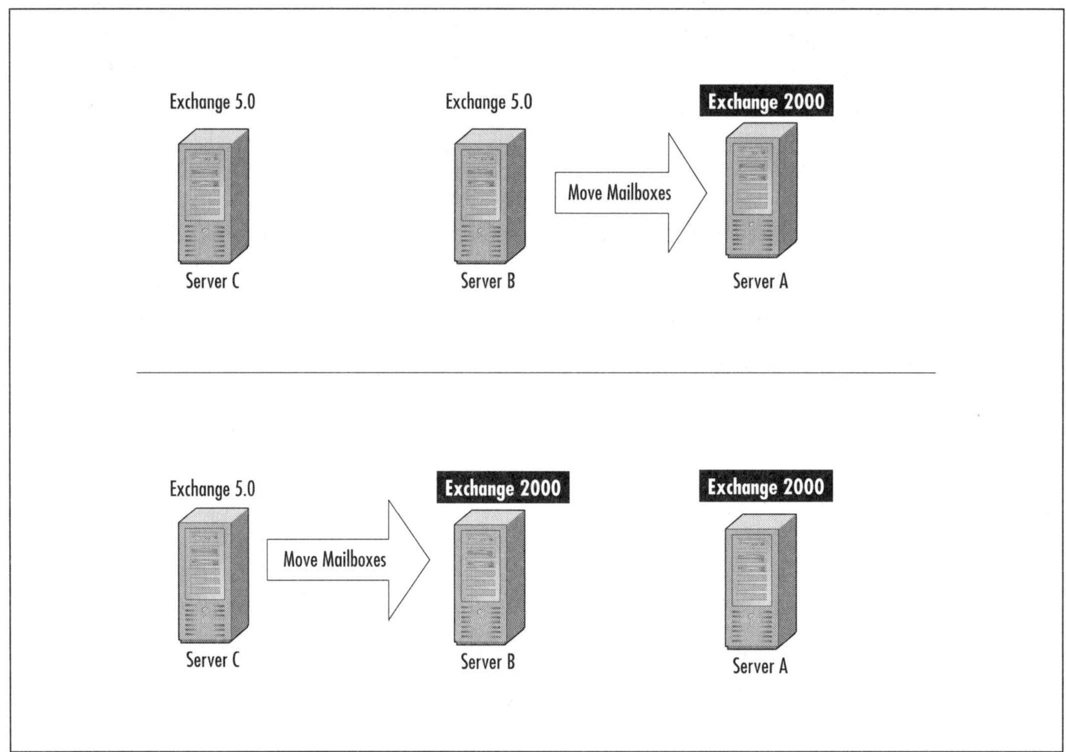

This leapfrog process is repeated until all servers have been upgraded to Exchange 2000. All the advantages of the move-mailbox method apply here, with a couple of additional advantages:

- Only a few new servers are required to get the leapfrog started.
- Once all mailboxes have been moved off a server, the computer can be wiped clean and a fresh Windows 2000 and Exchange 2000 installation can occur without upgrading anything.

As you can see, the deployment plan that defines your leapfrog process would have to be very specific. Scheduling mailboxes to be moved and servers to have Windows 2000 and Exchange 2000 installed, all the while ensuring that your mixed Exchange 5.5 and Exchange 2000 environment continues to support your users.

> **NOTE**
>
> Other methods for upgrading do exist. Some, such as the swing-server method, are just variations on the leapfrog method, with no real added value. Others, like the forklift method, are not supported by Microsoft at this time. For further information, refer to the Microsoft Web site at www.microsoft.com.

Moving to a New Organization

There are also tools available to move mailboxes to entirely new Exchange 2000 organizations. This method of migrating may be attractive to organizations that do not want to coexist. However, the tools available are somewhat cumbersome; they should be carefully tested to assure the results meet your requirements and are within your threshold for pain.

Using the Exchange Mailbox Migration Program

The Exchange Mailbox Migration program, or *exmerge*, is a tool that moves mailboxes between organizations through the use of personal store files (.pst). This process can be done in one or two phases. The one-phase process assumes the mailbox names are identical between the organizations. The two-phase process allows you to map the destination of the .pst files to new mailbox names in the new organization.

There are many drawbacks to this type of migration. For one, the single instance relationship within the information store is lost, resulting in an increase in information store size. Another is that migrated messages may have to be readdressed if replied to. Remember, the reply address will be for the old organization, not the new organization, so this can be a mess. Make sure you understand the ramifications of using *exmerge* and try it out in the lab before writing it into your deployment plan.

Upgrading Supporting Servers

Much of the focus on upgrading to Exchange 2000 has to do with upgrading mailbox servers and directories. As you know, however, there are other services and components that make up an Exchange organization. These components are just as necessary to the delivery of messages as the directory and mailbox servers, and their upgrade and deployment must be planned just as carefully.

When upgrading an Exchange Server 5.5 organization to Exchange 2000, the goal of most upgrades is to move messaging and directory data from one system to another without disrupting user availability or performance. Supporting servers, such as connector servers or bridgehead servers, do not have any data to upgrade—so in some cases it may not make sense (or even be necessary) to upgrade a particular server to Exchange 2000. Rather, it's the functionality that needs to be upgraded to Exchange 2000.

For example, if an Exchange Server 5.5 organization has two Exchange 5.5 servers configured with the Internet Mail Service (IMS) to send and receive messages from the Internet, it's not necessary to do an in-place upgrade of those servers—mainly because the Exchange 2000 SMTP connector is very different from the Exchange Server 5.5 IMS. To replace the two IMS servers there would only be one SMTP connector with two bridgehead servers configured. Here you can see that it's the functionality of the IMS that's being upgraded, not the service itself.

Upgrading Connector Servers

As with the example above, other types of connector servers should also be considered for the service they provide and the role they play in the architecture. This is key. If your Exchange 2000 organization has three routing groups connected by routing group connectors, and your Exchange Server 5.5 organization has three sites connected with X.400 connectors using bridgehead servers, the focus should be on how to implement the routing group connectors to connect the routing groups, not how to upgrade the X.400 servers.

NOTE

When a connector server is upgraded in place, the connectors on that server will also be upgraded. However, there is not a one-to-one correlation between Exchange Server 5.5 connectors and Exchange 2000 connectors. Make sure you understand what an in-place upgrade of a connector server will mean for your organization.

Upgrading Client Access Using Front-end Servers

Another service provided by Exchange Server 5.5 that is very different in Exchange 2000 is Internet client access. Internet clients are those clients that use Internet standard protocols to access mailboxes. These protocols include Post Office Protocol 3 (POP3), Internet Message Access Protocol 4 (IMAP4), Hypertext Transfer Protocol (HTTP), and Network News Transfer Protocol (NNTP). Exchange 2000 has the ability to separate the components that make up a messaging system into different physical servers: front-end servers that manage Internet client requests and back-end servers that store data. In Exchange Server 5.5 Internet clients have to connect directly to the server that hosts the user's mailbox. In Exchange 2000, with front-end servers, the Internet client only needs to connect to the front-end server and the front-end server will pass the requests to the appropriate back-end server. This way, the front-end server can be placed in a demilitarized zone (DMZ) or outside a firewall to provide added security and the Internet client does not need to know the specific mailbox server where their mailbox resides.

> **NOTE**
>
> MAPI clients, such as Outlook, must connect directly to the mailbox server and cannot use front-end servers. However, Outlook will automatically redirect user profiles if a user mailbox changes from one server to another.

The deployment of front-end servers in an Exchange 2000 organization does not replace any existing servers in an Exchange 5.5 organization. However, users must be made aware of the existence of the front-end servers and how to configure their Internet clients to connect to them. This should be defined in the deployment plan.

Testing Your Scenario

By now you should have a better understanding of what goes into a deployment plan that will take your existing Exchange organization and upgrade it to Exchange 2000. Several choices will have to be made about which method you will use to upgrade your directories and messaging system to Exchange 2000. Whichever method or combination of methods you choose must be tested and proven to be viable in your environment.

When your Active Directory and Exchange 2000 design was being developed, it is very likely that one or more candidate designs considered for your organization were tested in a lab. You should use this same lab to test your chosen deployment methods. This can be done in two phases:

- **Tools and Configuration Phase** This phase uses the lab to test the tools used during the migration. Several tools have particular requirements, such as trusts between domains, registry modification requirements, and the like. This phase allows you to become familiar with each tool and what it takes to make the tool work in your environment.

- **Upgrade Walkthrough Phase** Here the lab is configured to emulate your production Exchange Server 5.5 environment and to test how each of your chosen methods work in upgrading to your Exchange 2000 design.

Much can be learned from the lab. You may discover that your choice for upgrading to Exchange 2000 does not work within the parameters you define. It may require too much user downtime for your Active Directory deployment to be completed. Once you've completed your lab testing, you should have a complete understanding of how you will deploy Exchange 2000. You should be confident in the steps required to accomplish the upgrade or migration. Nothing should be learned during the actual production upgrade; all learning should be done in the lab.

Once you've nailed down your deployment plan from what you've learned in the lab, you may want to consider performing a pilot deployment of Exchange 2000 to a select group of users across your organization. This pilot is another way for you to confirm that the deployment path you've chosen is the right one for your organization. You may find that outside the lab you discover steps that need to be added to your deployment plan. Typically, lessons learned during a pilot are that more end-user or administrator training is needed, and also that end-user expectations need to be well defined before their mailbox server is upgraded, so that they know what to expect from the upgrade. This will go a long way in keeping your customers satisfied and making your deployment a success.

Summary

Deploying Exchange 2000 should not be taken lightly—especially in an organization that currently uses Exchange or another messaging system. What your deployment looks like will depend a lot on where your organization is in its Active Directory deployment. Each point along your Active

Directory deployment may have a different impact on your deployment plan. Your Active Directory deployment may be in one of the following phases:

- **No Active Directory** If your company is currently running Windows NT 4.0, and has no current plans to deploy Active Directory company-wide, then your deployment plan will include a segment on establishing an Active Directory domain, setting up coexistence, then upgrading your Exchange 5.5 servers to Exchange 2000.

- **Deploying Active Directory at same time as Exchange 2000** If your company plans on deploying Active Directory at the same time Exchange 2000 is being deployed, you will want to make sure your deployment plan outlines how the two deployments will affect each other, along with any dependencies that are created by Active Directory or Exchange 2000. Coexistence will be established between directories and care will be taken to manage the creation of twin accounts.

- **Mid-Active Directory deployment** If your company has already begun deploying Active Directory and will not finish before your Exchange 2000 deployment begins, you'll have to anticipate the possibility of duplicate accounts created by your deployment. Familiarizing yourself with the Active Directory deployment plan and coordinating deployment schedules will help to assure both deployments are successful.

- **Active Directory fully deployed** If your company has fully deployed Active Directory, your task will be to move the Exchange 5.5 directory data into Active Directory and upgrade your Exchange 5.5 messaging system to Exchange 2000.

Once you've nailed down your directory upgrade strategy, you can begin to review your options for upgrading your existing messaging system. Your goal is to upgrade your existing messaging environment to an Exchange 2000 organization that matches the Exchange 2000 design. Your choices here include:

- **Upgrading your servers in place** This is the most straightforward approach and best suited for smaller organizations or organizations that have a limited number of servers in a limited number of physical locations. The in-place upgrade may also be well suited for the remote offices of large organizations that will continue to host an Exchange server in the Exchange 2000 organization.

- **Moving your existing Exchange mailboxes to new Exchange 2000 servers** This approach will likely be the most common method of upgrading to Exchange 2000. This method does not require you to upgrade from Exchange 5.5, nor does it require the server to be offline during the upgrade.

- **Moving your existing Exchange mailboxes to existing servers reconfigured as Exchange 2000 servers** Another common upgrade solution, the leapfrog method, is a variation of the previous method, where mailboxes are moved off existing Exchange servers that are then wiped clean. Windows 2000 and then Exchange 2000 are installed. Mailboxes from the next existing Exchange server are moved to this Exchange 2000 server and the cycle continues until all Exchange servers have been upgraded to Exchange 2000.

- **Combining different upgrade methods** Large organizations may find it makes most sense to employ a combination of the above methods, depending on the location within the organization that is being upgraded. The servers in the server farm at headquarters may be upgraded using the leapfrog method, while servers at remote offices are upgraded in place.

- **Migrating your mailboxes to a new Exchange organization** As one of the most radical methods of upgrading to Exchange 2000, this migration may be used in organizations where the Exchange 2000 design is drastically different from the existing Exchange organizations. It may also be used when companies that have multiple Exchange organizations want to consolidate into a single Exchange organization and Active Directory forest.

Microsoft has provided us with the tools necessary to deploy Exchange 2000. It is up to us to put these tools to good use. In doing so, we will take a set of complex tasks and perform them in a controlled manner that will result in a successful upgrade to Exchange 2000. By choosing your directory upgrade strategy and messaging system upgrade strategy, then developing a deployment plan that articulates how they will be applied to your organization, you will be able to realize your goal of upgrading to an Exchange 2000 design.

FAQs

Visit **www.syngress.com/solutions** *to have your questions about this chapter answered by the author.*

Q: Can I move servers between Administrative Groups once I switch my Exchange 2000 organization to native mode?

A: No. At this time there is no supported way to move servers between Administrative Groups. For this reason, you will want to pay close attention to how you will move from your existing Exchange organization to your new Exchange 2000 organization.

Q: If I use ADClean, is it a sign that I've not planned my deployment well?

A: No. There are certain deployment scenarios where it makes the most business sense to deploy and configure the ADC before NT 4.0 accounts are upgraded. When this is the case, ADClean is necessary.

Q: Should I be aggressive in moving my organization to native mode?

A: It depends on your requirements. If you *ever* want to coexist with Exchange 5.5 again, do not switch to native mode.

Q: We currently use the version of the ADC that comes with Windows 2000 to synchronize our directories. Can I use this version to configure coexistence with Exchange 2000?

A: No. Exchange 2000 requires the version of the ADC that comes with Exchange 2000 for coexistence. This is because this version provides configuration and public folder connection agreements.

Q: Does the ADMT allow you to perform a dry run to check for any errors?

A: Yes, the ADMT has a look-before-you-leap feature that you should take advantage of.

Q: Don't I have to be a domain administrator to run Exchange 2000 setup?

A: If the forest has been prepared using forestprep and the domain has been prepared using domainprep, then you don't need any special Active Directory permissions to install Exchange 2000. You do, however, need permissions on the local computer.

Chapter 7

Defending Exchange 2000 from Attack

Solutions in this chapter:

- **What Are the Potential Threats to Exchange 2000?**
- **Considering Defense Strategies**
- **Protecting Mailbox Stores and Clients**
- **Firewall and Gateway Strategies**
- **Managing Exchange 2000 Security**

Introduction

Exchange 2000 is a powerful messaging and collaborative application running on Windows 2000. It truly is the first application to leverage Active Directory (AD) and Windows 2000 security to the fullest. By itself, however, Exchange 2000 is not complete in that other utilities, applications, and/or hardware are required to make sure that our chosen messaging solution remains the killer application it is.

Most Exchange Server deployments do not run Exchange by itself. We depend on numerous third-party applications to complement Exchange as a complete, secure messaging system. These products include firewall applications or appliances, antivirus software, and server management products.

Even with our best efforts, our messaging system—due to the very nature of the product—is most likely the weakest link in network security. The increasing volume of data that comes and goes through our Simple Mail Transfer Protocol (SMTP) portals is phenomenal as companies and individuals increasingly depend on e-mail as a source of information and document exchange. Through public folders or specific connectors to other messaging products, Exchange 2000 is also a share point for documents of all types.

As administrators, we must realize that using a product that is central to our information-sharing world carries its share of vulnerabilities. We cannot stop all possible attacks, but we can certainly be prepared and prevent almost all of them.

What Are the Potential Threats to Exchange 2000?

Microsoft produced Exchange 2000 to be a powerful messaging application as well as a versatile development platform. In many ways, Exchange was built with the developer in mind, with the new Web Storage System, a new version of Collaborative Data Objects (CDO), and Active Directory integration. This versatility actually opens Exchange to abuse or attack. The vulnerability of these potential attacks depends on our specific deployment of Exchange Server and the measures we take to limit our exposure. As administrators, we might witness certain security attacks, against which we should ensure that we are protected. These security risks are outlined in Table 7.1.

Table 7.1 Security Risks for Exchange 2000

Security Risk	Description
Physical location	We must ensure that our mail servers are in a secure location, accessible only to authorized individuals.
Denial of service (DoS)	This involves any task that overwhelms our Exchange server so that it is no longer able to multitask. This event can be internal or external, intentional or accidental.
Data interception	An individual captures packets in order to obtain privileged access to our Exchange server. This packet capture could obtain a password or capture a session for later impersonation by replaying.
Viruses, including macro virus	A virus is malicious code that interferes with operation of Exchange or clients. This is often code that attempts to propagate through e-mail submission or macro code.
Trojan horse	This is a program or code that appears harmless but typically breaks security and can further damage installations.
Personnel issues	Individuals attempting to obtain access to our Exchange server by some means of misrepresentation.

When we prepare to deploy Exchange 2000 in our organization, it is necessary for us to consider all the third-party products that complement the application. We must ensure that we have the proper backup software if we use a third-party product, any management software that we might need, and, of course, antivirus software. Our Exchange server represents the greatest likelihood of introducing infected files into our network.

Unsolicited Commercial E-Mail

SMTP on the Internet, as outlined in Request for Comments (RFC) 821, does not by design require authentication. Due to the ease of forging SMTP header information and the resulting anonymity, a large amount of e-mail traffic over the Internet occurs in the form of *unsolicited commercial e-mail (UCE)*, also called *spam*. Regretfully, UCE is part of the reality of maintaining an Internet e-mail presence today.

There are two separate but related concerns regarding UCE and its occurrence in the enterprise. The first issue we face as e-mail administrators is simply the copious unwanted inbound spam that we receive on a daily basis. Try as we might, we can't stop it completely, but it is possible to sensibly use a couple of native tools to lessen the impact of spam. The second issue involves the more serious matter of allowing SMTP relay on the Internet.

The Internet Mail Consortium (www.imc.org/ube-relay.html) has performed several surveys over the years to determine the percentage of mail servers that are vulnerable as open SMTP relays. The consortium's research indicates that more than 6 percent of SMTP mail servers on the Internet are still vulnerable to abuse by spammers. Although this figure represents a significant decline over the last few years, it is still about 6 percent too much.

You can report open SMTP relays and research the problem a little more deeply at several online resources:

> www.mail-abuse.org
>
> www.orbs.com
>
> www.abuse.net

Considering Defense Strategies

Our Exchange servers cannot sit by themselves, unprotected from potential danger. They need the help of third-party applications, informed administrators, and educated users.

Setting Policy

Every working day, employees access company information using company equipment to perform their company-assigned tasks. Do not underestimate the importance and value of a corporate policy statement (CPS) as it applies to computer equipment.

Your company could have a policy manual that every employee who is to receive network access must read and sign, agreeing that he or she will adhere to the relatively strict guidelines outlined. New hires would not get network access until this document was returned to the IT director. This manual would serve as your initial position on the importance of your network and messaging systems and your leverage for enforcement of security issues internally.

Since our Exchange server is probably the primary gateway for information traveling to and from the company, there must be specific instruction pertaining to its use. Some items to include in an IT policy regarding employee e-mail are:

- Guidelines for e-mail usage

- Disclosure of e-mail monitoring practices

- Allowances for attachments

- Notifications of virus issues

- Explanation of e-mail restrictions (mailbox size, logon hours)

> **NOTE**
>
> Here's a brief list of some online sources to assist you in creating an IT policy:
>
> - System Administration, Networking and Security (SANS): www.sans.org/newlook/resources/policies/policies.htm
> - International Information Security Foundation: http://web.mit.edu/security/www/gassp1.html

Educating Users

Employees and guests who access your network and Exchange server are resources your company needs to operate as a business. Too often you can spend time and money on hardware or software solutions to try to prevent users from misbehaving, without communicating sufficiently with the end users. Some products, such as antivirus software, are essential in today's corporate networks, but great value is returned in maintaining user education.

Users must be educated on basic e-mail practices, many of which the MIS department could take for granted, such as recognizing a virus attachment. Checking with the sender of a "FW: Joke" attachment before opening that attachment might seem paranoid behavior to users at first, but with some training, they could feel and act like heroes. Try not to overestimate or underestimate the people who use the network from day to day.

Outlook, as the primary e-mail client for Exchange 2000, is a complex and powerful application. Our company offers employees Outlook training classes in our resource room to any department requesting it, and we have recently started an internal Outlook Tip of the Day e-mail, customized to meet our company's (and users') specific needs.

Protecting the Message Store

By the very nature of the product, our Exchange Server is likely the weakest link in the security chain of our network. It must be accessible via a variety of methods and has a large volume of documents, files, and information flowing bi-directionally through it. It also is a significant storage facility for e-mail and a repository for document sharing. We must grant it great attention in protecting it from the various security risks outlined at the beginning of this chapter.

Physical Security

It might sound almost silly to mention, but your physical Exchange server should be kept in locked, secure chambers with restricted or monitored access. There are two trains of thought on this rule. The first concern is administrators—or perhaps individuals with more malicious intent—toying with Exchange 2000 without supervision. Access to the server console should be available only to specific administrators. The second line of reasoning is more circumstantial in nature. Most companies deploying Exchange 2000 want their messaging systems available 24 hours a day, seven days a week. Having their mail servers physically located near active people invites trouble. One small client spent weeks trying to determine why their server rebooted suddenly at around 11:00 nightly. After installing a video camera, they learned that the cleaners, in need of a power outlet for the vacuum, would unplug the server and plug it in again when they were done.

Antivirus Protection for Exchange

Any point of entry for data in a network is a potential portal for viruses, Trojan horses, or worms. Such an introduction could occur via an e-mailed document through the Exchange server, an inbound file sent FTP, or even a floppy with a project that a staff member took home to his infected computer and subsequently brought back to the office. A basic network showing points of protection is displayed in Figure 7.1.

There are several basic methodologies to protecting our network from viruses, and all of them depend on keeping the software up to date in a timely manner. The optimum virus protection scenario is a multitiered, multivendor approach, as outlined in Table 7.2.

Figure 7.1 Antivirus Installation Points

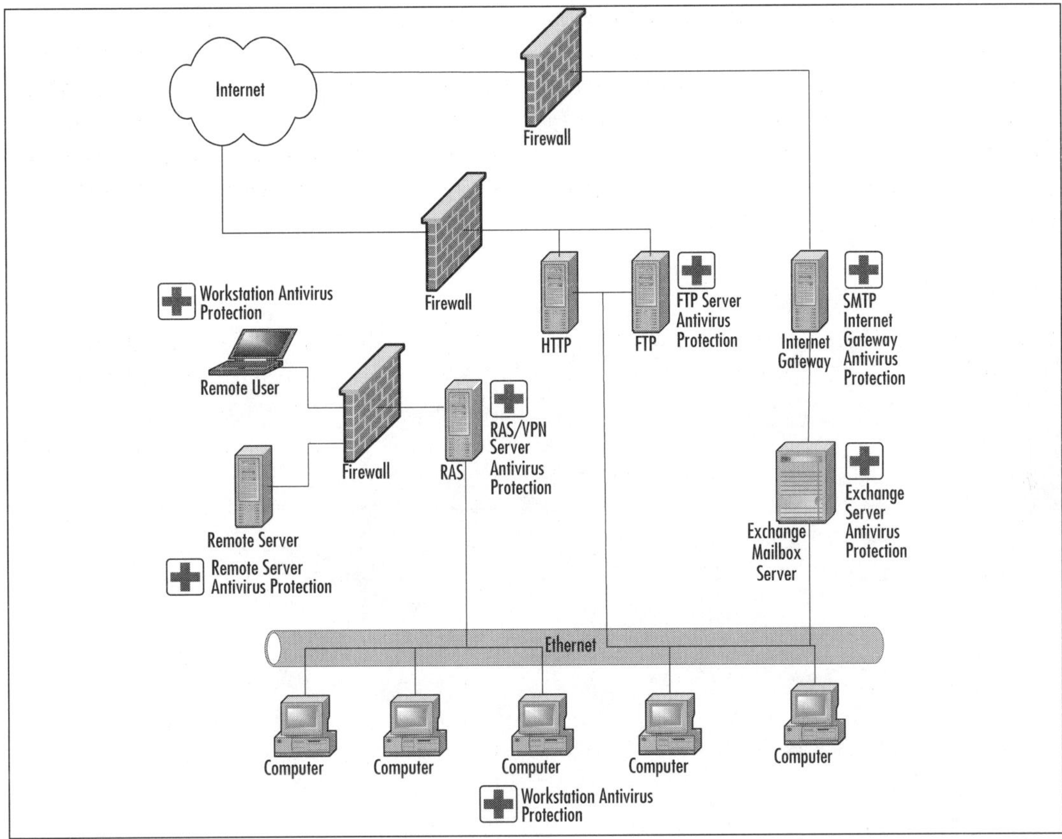

Table 7.2 Antivirus Approaches for an Exchange Server Network

Location of Antivirus Strategy	Description of Approach
Perimeter or gateway	Most perimeter-based products scan SMTP messages for viruses and content but could also protect HTTP and FTP portals.
Exchange server and information stores	Exchange-aware antivirus software is needed to protect at the Exchange mailbox store level and perform scans of the Exchange databases.
Workstation	Each workstation should have an antivirus solution running as well, hopefully in the form of a real-time scanning engine to catch infected documents before they enter an Exchange container.

We can deploy an antivirus product at the gateway into our Exchange organization. Third-party virus checkers can scan incoming SMTP messages for malicious code, checked against a self-contained signature database file. Some products also can provide content filtering at the SMTP gateway as well, quarantining e-mails containing specific words or perhaps deleting attachments based on file extension.

For the SMTP service running on the Internet Information Service (IIS), antivirus solution developers can leverage the use of protocol and transport event sinks to capture and process inbound and outbound SMTP messages.

Introduction to Protocol and Transport Event Sinks

We know that Microsoft Exchange 2000 Server features many radical changes from its predecessors. One of the more significant developments is the move to SMTP as the primary transport protocol for messaging. The actual SMTP service for Exchange resides in the IIS component that is installed by default for Windows 2000 Server. Within the SMTP transport event architecture, we are able to customize message flow and even add certain actions based on a set of specific rules. The SMTP protocol is extensible using Protocol Events to add ESMTP commands or modify the existing commands.

What does this mean? Well, using tools such as Visual Basic, C++, or even Collaborative Data Objects (CDO), we are able to "capture" SMTP e-mail as it passes through the SMTP Service within IIS and customize what it does, where it goes, and what it looks like. We will see increased use of these events as Exchange 2000 grows in the number of deployments.

There are numerous applications for these customized *event sinks*:

- **For protocol events** You can collect information based on SMTP connections such as originating IP address and length of connection. You can also customize ESMTP commands to capture other properties of SMTP mail for monitoring purposes.

- **For transport events** You can isolate e-mail, both inbound and outbound, and scan it for specific text or virus patterns. You can assign custom routing based on header information. You can also append text to the body of e-mail in either direction, such as adding a legal disclaimer to e-mail.

Continued

The Event architecture allows you to code custom behavior based on specific events that you can watch for using sinks in the SMTP service. This is a powerful tool for compiling server-side applications in conjunction with Exchange 2000.

For more information on SMTP transport and protocol event sinks, search the online Microsoft Developers Network (MSDN) library at http://msdn.microsoft.com/library/default.asp. Information on SMTP server events for Windows 2000 can be found in the Platform Software Development Kit (SDK) documentation.

Some antivirus vendors have products that "understand" the data structure within the information stores in Exchange Server in order to scan e-mails and attachments at the store level. It is not recommended to run a file-based virus scanner against the Exchange Server information stores. If you intend to scan the mailboxes within Exchange, you must deploy an antivirus software solution specific to this task.

WARNING

Use only antivirus software specific to Exchange 2000. The API used to scan the store might be very similar, but the differences from the legacy versions of Exchange, including the new feature allowing multiple mailbox stores, can cause undesirable results and possibly damage.

Antivirus products that run on Exchange Server operate in one of two modes. Either they must take the form of a Messaging Application Program Interface (MAPI) client with rights to all mailboxes so that they can simultaneously log into each mailbox and scan messages on arrival, or they must leverage the Antivirus Application Programmers Interface (AVAPI). The AVAPI, added in Exchange 5.5's Service Pack 3 and still available to independent software vendors (ISVs) in Exchange 2000, allows more direct access to tables within the information store database. Essentially, attachments get scanned even before a client has access to the file. The overall performance of this process is much more efficient than the MAPI avenue, resulting in a lighter load on the server. With any antvirus software running on our Exchange server, we are looking at a 10 to 15 percent CPU performance hit, depending on messaging patterns. This should be taken into consideration when doing capacity planning for your deployment.

MAPI-based protection also seems to fail under duress simply because it cannot keep up. There also exists a small chance that a client will open an inbound attachment before the MAPI scanner has cleared it to be virus-free. The first antivirus software vendor to stop using MAPI to scan the store was Sybari's Antigen product.

NOTE

For more information on the antivirus API, consult Microsoft Knowledge Base Article Q263949 and MSDN at http://msdn.microsoft.com/workshop/security/antivirus/overview/overview.asp.

Vendor Solutions

Any third-party software that goes near our Exchange server must be a well-known, quality product from a reputable vendor. This is especially important for Exchange Server-based antivirus software, for which the intrusive nature of the product makes it necessary that it be trustworthy.

Of the server-based antivirus solutions, the current favorites in the Exchange 2000 newsgroups certainly are Sybari's Antigen and Trend Micro's ScanMail products. The two products offer similar features and results, and both boast ease of installation and administration.

We must consider what we look for and expect in an antivirus solution for our enterprise. There are several important characteristics of the software and the vendor to review:

Product performance Does the solution work as advertised and catch all viruses, Trojans, and worms that it should? At the server level, does it provide quality protection while not significantly influencing message flow?

Administration Does the antivirus software allow effective, central administration while not growing too complicated to use on a day-to-day basis?

Update deployment Does the mechanism for installing virus data file updates work effectively, whether to clients at workstations or on the server itself? Does it allow you to easily update remote users as well?

Product integration How does the product work in conjunction with other related solutions? In some cases, the antivirus product and SMTP content filtering product could be the same, as in the case of Trend Micro's ScanMail. The Baltimore Technologies (formerly Content Technologies) line of Sweeper products work well together.

Vendor updates For antivirus software, it is important for suppliers to respond quickly and communicate efficiently in releasing new virus signature files for their customers. When the Loveletter virus hit, the newsgroups were full of administrators asking about patches. The fastest vendor responses got the best marks.

Technical support Responsiveness of vendors' help desks is not important unless you have a problem and you need assistance *now*. It's very hard to inoculate something when the vendor takes days to return your call.

Total cost of ownership Any company that has an Exchange server really must operate an antivirus software solution. The amount of money companies are willing to spend on that solution varies greatly. A low retail desktop solution costs a lot if an administrator must go out to every workstation to apply updates, whereas a more costly product could run an update service to almost allow the clients to update the workstations themselves, saving money later.

System performance Any antivirus solution will cost in terms of CPU cycles and memory usage. What that cost is, or how much your system is negatively impacted by operating the software, adds to your judgment of an appropriate antivirus solution.

Remote administration Can you check the status of the system from another computer, perhaps even from home over a virtual private network (VPN)?

Ease of installation Is a large learning curve associated with administering this product?

Sybari's Antigen is extremely simple to install and operate in a test lab. Trend Micro's ScanMail was also effective on Exchange 2000. Recommended antivirus solutions for Exchange 2000 include:

- Sybari Antigen 6.0 for Exchange 2000 (www.sybari.com/products/antigen_exchange.asp)

- Trend Micro ScanMail 5.0 for Exchange 2000 (www.antivirus.com/products/smex/)

- Mail essentials for Exchange 2000 (www.gfi.com/me/mailessentials.htm)

- GroupShield for Exchange 2000
  (www.mcafeeb2b.com/products/groupshield-exchange/default.asp)

- MAILSweeper for Exchange
  (www.mimesweeper.com/products/exchange/default.asp)

- Panda Antivirus for Exchange Server
  (www.pandasoftware.com/com/pgvi/exchange/exchange.asp)

NOTE

Several buyer's guides on the market compare and contrast products. *Network Computing* magazine hosts an archive of them, including an antivirus software comparison from January 8, 2001: www .networkcomputing.com/ibg/home.

There are also industry certifications for security products, including antivirus software. The two primary certifications come out of the ICSA and West Coast Labs. Most of the major antivirus vendors are tested specifically against Exchange Server as well:

- ICSA Labs (ICSA Certification): www.icsalabs.com/html/ communities/antivirus/certification.shtml

- West Coast Labs (Checkmark Certification): www.check-mark.com/ cgi-bin/redirect.pl

The ICSA (now called TruSecure) also produces an annual *Computer Virus Prevalence Survey.* ICSA has produced this survey for six years, showing a significant increase in virus incidents over that time. The numbers suggest that a typical company in 2000 received between 14 and 91 virus incidents per month, per 1,000 PCs. The survey can be downloaded for free at www.icsalabs.com/html/communities/antivirus/index.shtml.

Cluster Server Considerations

Not every antivirus application that runs on Exchange 2000 will work on Exchange 2000 in a clustered environment. This is due to differences in how antivirus applications interact with external storage (Exchange databases).

For example, both Sybari Antigen and Trend Micro's ScanMail advertise fail-over support for clustered Exchange 2000 servers. The product must be installed on both nodes of the cluster to facilitate successful fail-over. For more information, contact your antivirus vendor

Client-Side Protection

Workstations might not be the primary point of entry for viruses, Trojans, and worms, but they are the primary point of deployment. We should consider using a different antivirus software product for the desktops than the one we deploy at the server or gateway level. It is unlikely that all vendors will come up with the next signature patch at the same time. Having multiple vendors prevents you from putting all your eggs in one basket.

Protecting the Workstation

We can deploy file-based antivirus software at the workstation level to provide real-time scanning of documents that pass through each station. If an infected document, perhaps existing as an e-mail attachment in a mailbox within the Exchange mailbox store, is opened at the client, a real-time monitor at the client should then catch a known virus. A file-based virus scanner at the client workstation is not very effective against an Outlook personal folders file (.pst) or an offline folders file (.ost); however, it should catch infected documents before they become part of the Outlook folders or Exchange mailbox.

The effectiveness of any antivirus product depends on both the vendor producing updates to the signature files in a timely manner and the administrator ensuring that the updates are applied where they are needed as quickly as possible. Certainly a combination of at least two of the outlined protection methods would be more secure and complete than any one alone. You would also do well to use a different vendor product for each level of protection to improve your chances of maintaining a virus-free network.

Even with the best antivirus software and with the latest patches applied, however, your protection is not guaranteed. The creation and distribution of antivirus software updates are reactive, not proactive. The coding of a new virus always precedes the coding of the fix to prevent it from spreading. You must rely on common sense and user education to recognize and tackle viruses in general.

Protecting the Outlook Client

Toward the end of March 1999, the corporate Outlook world was thrust into a reality it had only passively acknowledged earlier. The Microsoft Word macro virus named Melissa had struck. Outlook's versatility and scriptability did not allow it to discern the ethical intent of the programmer. We can hardly blame Microsoft for that, though, can we?

The Melissa virus was a wake-up call for the messaging sector of information technology. It was the first major virus outbreak to exploit features of MAPI and propagate itself using e-mail and the Outlook address book. Companies and administrators, this author included, were scrambling to beef up their antivirus products on their Exchange servers and within their organizations as a whole.

NOTE

For more complete coverage of the Melissa virus outbreak, consult www.cert.org/advisories/CA-1999-04.html and http://support.microsoft .com/support/exchange/content/whitepapers/melissa.doc.

With Melissa exposing our industry nonchalance, we should be grateful that its payload was little more than its annoying ability to reproduce. A couple of months later, a more serious virus emerged from the Middle East: Worm.ExploreZip. If we didn't learn with Melissa, the message certainly hit home with Worm.ExploreZip: *Do not open unexpected attachments!* The payload with this virus was far more severe. It damaged data on computers' local drives as well as some networked drives by replacing any Word, PowerPoint, and Excel files with useless files that were 0 bytes in size. Some companies lost a large amount of relevant data as the executable file zipped_files.exe was opened by unsuspecting recipients of the virus e-mail.

Part of the destruction left behind by these viruses comes in the form of corporate embarrassment at propagation of these incidents. Almost a year after Worm.ExploreZip, our very human need to be loved superceded our common sense as we opened a Visual Basic Script e-mail attachment called Loveletter.vbs—another attachment that, when executed, propagated itself using e-mail. Some organizations witnessed their Exchange servers almost grind to a halt as copies of the virus were spread through global address lists of thousands of users. Information stores grew rather quickly. The incidents were so overwhelming, Microsoft assembled an ILOVEYOU virus eradication kit that included the utilities ISSCAN.exe and Exmerge.exe to scour the information store and rid the databases of the script attachment. The ILOVEYOU virus saw countless permutations with varying degrees of effectiveness over the next several months.

More recently, in November 2000, some of us decided to see what a Spanish Christmas is like. The Navidad.exe worm does make changes in the Windows registry and takes a little more effort to repair. It still needs a MAPI-compliant e-mail application, such as Outlook, to distribute itself to others.

All these virus epidemics have one thing in common. In each case, the attachment had to be executed by user action. The most important tool we have as administrators is user education. Your users need to get the message: It will not stick if you do not click!

Microsoft received a great deal of criticism for the ease of and extent to which viruses are able to execute on its products. This is the same ease that allows developers to extend the functionality of Outlook as a customizable application and versatile corporate e-mail client solution. Microsoft's reply came in the form of the Outlook security patch.

Microsoft Outlook Security Patch

Although not revolutionary, the Outlook E-mail Security Update provides a little more security by disallowing a lot of what was previously automatic to scripts like loveletter.vbs. First, the update prevents selected users from executing selected attachment types directly from the e-mail. They are first required to save the attachment to disk (see Figure 7.2).

Figure 7.2 Attachment Security Warning

Microsoft also implemented modifications to prevent other applications from programmatically accessing address information and sending capabilities without approval from the user. After the update is installed, executing the ILOVEYOU virus would generate a dialog box asking the user if he or she wants to grant the application access to the components needed to e-mail itself. The Outlook Object Model Guard will pop up for every programmed send. The update also heightens the security settings for HTML in Outlook, which goes from Internet Zone to Restricted Zone, and for Macro Security in Office.

Assuming that e-mail for users is being delivered to an Exchange Server mailbox, the Outlook Security update also empowers administrators to enforce security measures across the domain or create an exempt

Figure 7.3 Outlook Security Patch Administration

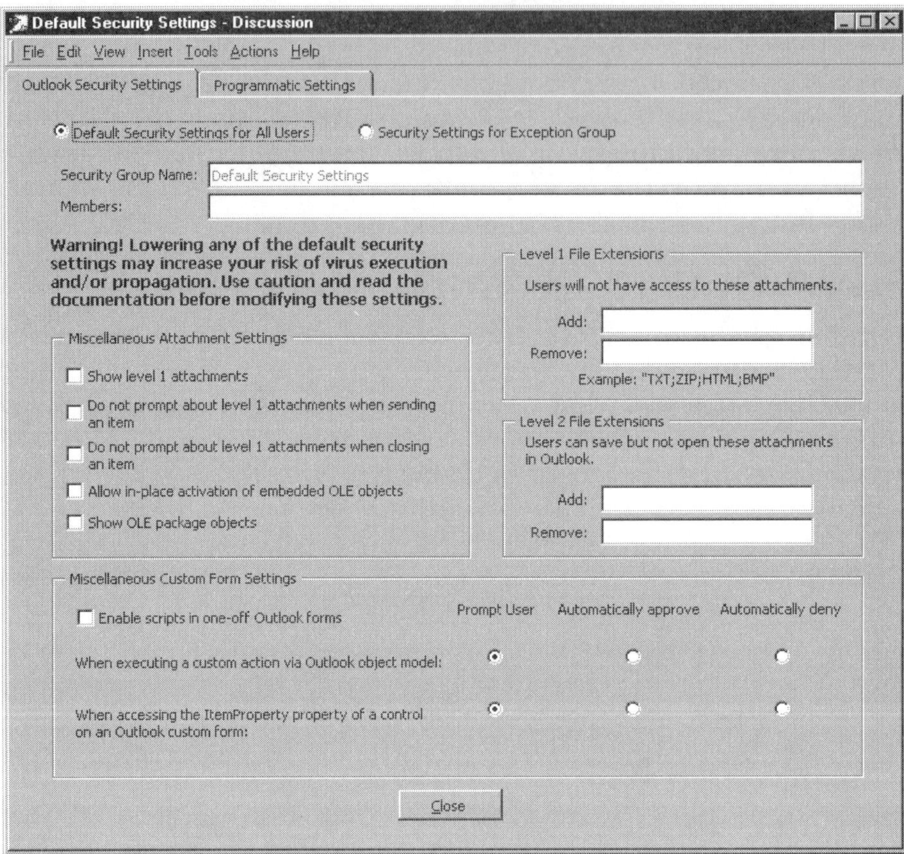

group. Figures 7.3 and 7.4 show the basic form used to assign the extent of e-mail security granted with the latest updates.

The Programmatic Settings, shown in Figure 7.4, show the many instances in which you can cause the user to be prompted when an application tries to send e-mail.

You should note that there is no easy uninstall for the Outlook security patch. If your end users feel too restricted in their everyday use of Outlook after this implementation, the only fix is an uninstall of Office 2000 or Outlook 2000 if Outlook is installed without the Office suite.

Figure 7.4 Outlook Security Patch Administration: Programmatic Settings

Default Security Settings - Discussion

File Edit View Insert Tools Actions Help

Outlook Security Settings | Programmatic Settings

	Prompt User	Automatically approve	Automatically deny
When sending items via Outlook object model:	●	○	○
When sending items via CDO:	●	○	○
When sending items via Simple MAPI:	●	○	○
When accessing the address book via Outlook object model:	●	○	○
When accessing the address book via CDO:	●	○	○
When resolving names via Simple MAPI:	●	○	○
When accessing address information via Outlook object model:	●	○	○
When accessing address information via CDO:	●	○	○
When opening messages via Simple MAPI:	●	○	○
When responding to meeting and task requests via Outlook object model:	●	○	○
When executing Save As via Outlook object model:	●	○	○
When accessing the Formula property of a UserProperty object in the Outlook object model:	●	○	○
When accessing address information via UserProperties.Find in the Outlook object model:	●	○	○

Close

Vendor Solutions

Recommended antivirus software vendors offering desktop solutions include the following:

- Trend Micro Office Scan (www.antivirus.com/products/osce)

- Norton Antivirus 2001 (www.symantec.com/nav/nav_9xnt)

- Computer Associates Inoculate*IT* (www.cai.com/products/inoculateit/inoculateit_prodinfo.htm)

- McAfee VirusScan (www.mcafeeb2b.com/products/virusscan/default-desktop-protection.asp)

- Sophos Antivirus for Windows (www.sophos.com/products/antivirus/savnt.html)

- Command Central AntiVirus Expert 2000 Desktop (www.avx.com)

Firewall and Gateway Strategies

Without a doubt, you should place some form of firewall between your Exchange servers and the Internet. There are two primary types of firewall. The first is a *passive packet filter router*, in which packets are passed through the firewall and on toward their destinations based on compliance with a rule set. You can envision this system as resembling a pegboard you might see at a hardware store, with some of the holes filled in. The other primary type of firewall is more active and often called a *proxy firewall* because it relies on daemons for authentication and packet forwarding.

The presence of a firewall should not mislead you into taking lightly the security measures you learned in Chapter 3. Consider your network as your home. If you go out for the evening, you still lock the front door of your house, even though anyone with the right talent and tools *could* still find a way inside. As long as your Exchange server is connected to the Internet, there is a way into your network, and as long as there is a way into your network, you must not neglect your internal security.

Typically, a firewall allows you the ability to block ports that aren't in use. For Exchange 2000, IIS5 hosts the protocol services that connect Exchange Server to the Internet. Each protocol has a default TCP port through which packets are passed (see Table 7.3).

Table 7.3 TCP Ports Used by Exchange 2000 Server Protocols

Protocol	Default TCP Port
SMTP	25
POP3	110
POP3/SSL	995
IMAP4	143
IMAP4/SSL	993
NNTP	119
NNTP/SSL	563
LDAP	389
LDAP/SSL	636
HTTP	80
HTTP/SSL	443

Firewall products on the market vary greatly in cost and functionality. Like any product involving network security, it is important to get a quality brand-name product that you trust and are most comfortable with administering. Some firewall vendors include:

- Cisco PIX Firewall (www.cisco.com/warp/public/cc/pd/fw/sqfw500)

- Checkpoint Firewall-1 (www.checkpoint.com/products/firewall-1/index.html)

- Raptor Firewall (http://enterprisesecurity.symantec.com/content/productlink.cfm)

And a personal favorite, at the best price:

- IPF on OpenBSD (www.openbsd.org)

Point of Entry Protection

Antivirus applications can operate at all entrance points on the network. Viruses enter through SMTP, HTTP, and even FTP. Gateway products are available to catch unwanted code before it even enters your network. With the trend toward wireless devices, some gateways use Wireless Access Protocol (WAP). There are also antivirus products to scan WAP gateways.

Antivirus applications for Internet Gateways include:

- Trend Micro InterScan VirusWall (www.antivirus.com/products/isvw)

- Norton Antivirus 2.0 for Gateways (http://enterprisesecurity.symantec.com/content/productlink.cfm)

- Aladdin eSafe Gateway (www.aks.com/esafe/gateway/index.asp)

Handling Inbound UCE

We've all seen the e-mail messages offering "easy money" or X-rated products. The full Outlook MAPI client has built-in rules using the Rules Wizard to assist in filtering UCE. Using these rules, much of the inbound UCE can be redirected to another folder for later review or sent directly to the Deleted Items folder and beyond to the Recycling Bin. This process is not perfect, however, so retaining the filtered messages for later confirmation of condemned status is recommended.

You are also able to filter e-mail from specific domains, e-mail addresses, or IP addresses using Exchange 2000. In Exchange 5.5, message filtering was available in the Properties of the Internet Mail Service (IMS). As explained in Chapter 4, you can implement message filtering of a specific domain or e-mail address using the Message Delivery Properties under Global Settings in the Exchange System Manager (see Figure 7.5).

Figure 7.5 Message Filtering: Global Settings

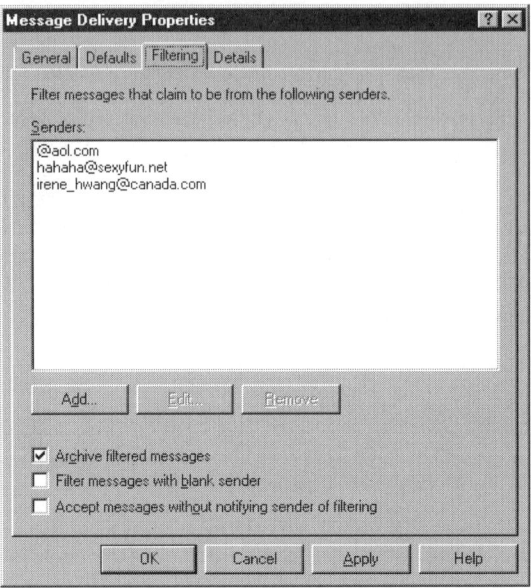

It is clear that you could spend a great deal of time accumulating a database of filtered domains and e-mail addresses using this functionality at the server level. Minimizing the amount of spam that finds its way to the end user, however, will, in a small way, add to the overall efficiency of your company.

You can also filter junk mail at the client level in most cases. Outlook has a built-in rule that can be selected to send suspected spam to a specific folder, including the Deleted Items folder if desired.

Vendor Solutions

Numerous third-party applications on the market can add to the native filtering functionality of Exchange Server. These applications aim to block junk-mail traffic or mass e-mailing DoS attacks by filtering these message prior to their arrival in the message store:

- Trend Micro's ScanMail Version 5.0 for Exchange 2000 (www.antivirus.com/products/smex)

- Sybari Antigen 6.0 (www.sybari.com/products/antigen_exchange.asp)

- Content Technologies WEBSweeper (www.us.mimesweeper.com/products/msw4smtp/default.asp)

- MailMarshall 4.0
  (www.marshallsoftware.com/MailMarshal/default.asp)

Preventing Unwanted SMTP Mail Relay

Much of the spam we see is actually relayed off unsuspecting SMTP servers. The consequence at the company level for not preventing this abuse takes many forms.

To have your server be the launching pad for a mass e-mailing of spam is in itself a DoS attack. Depending on the degree of the relay, your server will be very busy dealing with junk e-mail and won't be able to tend to your legitimate internal or external requests in a timely manner. Besides that, when others receive UCE bounced off your server, you will face two issues. The first is the embarrassment of falling victim to the abuse. The second is facing either the multitude of angry replies requesting removal from a list you know nothing about or dealing with the nondelivery reports (NDRs) for all the incorrect e-mail addresses in the mass mailing. When the recipient receives the UCE and replies to it, it is your address, not the address of the original sender, that will appear in the To: field.

An SMTP relay in itself is not bad; indeed, you could require it for external clients to send e-mail from your server. If you do not maintain proper control of which clients or addresses can access your resources, however, you could inadvertently expose your server as an SMTP relay.

A simple Telnet session to port 25 will disclose whether your virtual server can be abused as an SMTP relay. From a DOS prompt, execute the following:

```
Telnet <IP Address> 25

HELO

MAIL FROM: nobody@nowhere.com

RCPT TO: somebody@externaladdress.com

DATA

This is a relay test

<Enter>

.

<Enter>
```

If you can get through this conversation, you are able to relay from the address with which you connected in starting the Telnet session. In Exchange 2000, you can restrict the ability of others to relay using settings at the Access tab in the SMTP Virtual Server Properties applet, as shown in Figure 7.6.

Figure 7.6 Access Tab of SMTP Virtual Server Properties

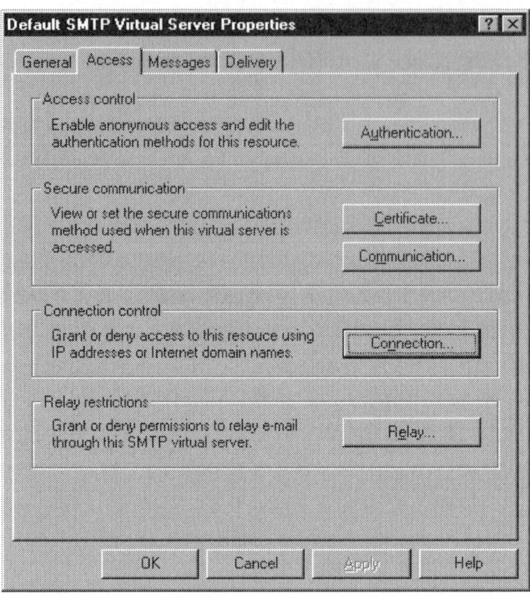

Within the Relay Restrictions setting, you can explicitly grant or restrict relay access by IP address, by subnet, or by domain. Restricting by domain results in a reverse DNS process for each SMTP connection and uses a great deal of server resources. In this tab, you can also require a client to authenticate before allowing any relay (see Figure 7.7).

Figure 7.7 Relay Restrictions for SMTP Virtual Server

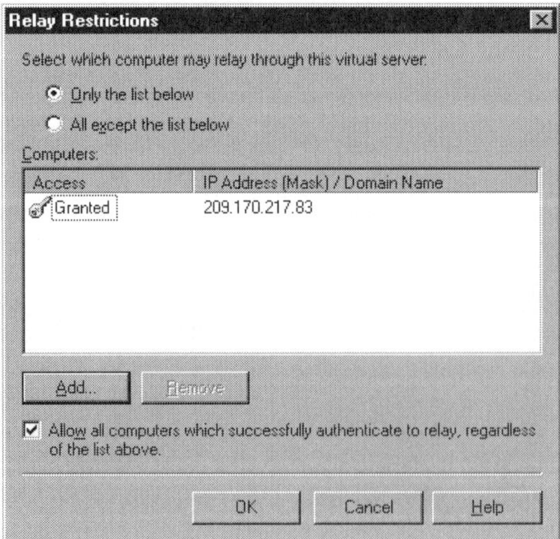

Configuring SMTP Protocol Logging

Every time a computer makes a connection with your SMTP virtual server, a "conversation" takes place that is very similar to the step-by-step Telnet session listed earlier in this section. The standard for this communication is outlined in RFC 821.

> **NOTE**
>
> A number of places online host a database of RFCs, many of them universities, such as the University of California at Berkeley and Ohio State University (www.cis.ohio-state.edu/hypertext/information/rfc.html).

IIS on Windows 2000, which hosts the SMTP service for Exchange, affords you the ability to log connections made to your Exchange server specifically by protocol. This log file is useful for diagnosing connectivity issues as well as investigating suspicious activity. You can show possible patterns of UCE mail within the log file and take action to block that specific IP address if necessary.

To enable SMTP logging, navigate to the SMTP Virtual Server within Exchange System Manager. You can then open up the Properties page and, at the bottom of the General tab, select Enable Logging, as shown in Figure 7.8.

Figure 7.8 Enable SMTP Logging

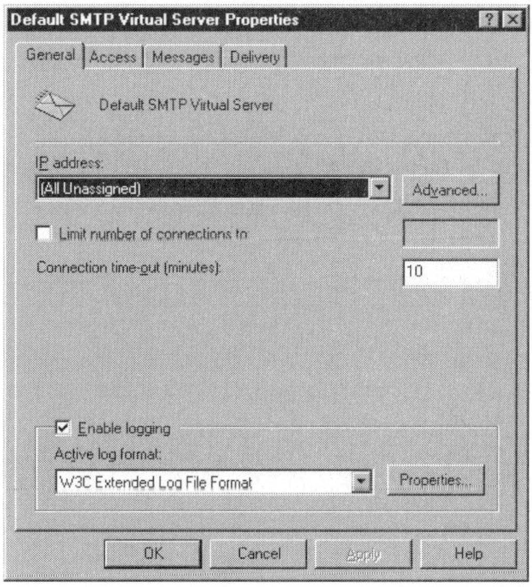

The SMTP log can be recorded in one of several formats. We use the W3C Extended Log Format due to the flexibility it provides in determining the components of the SMTP traffic that are logged. An example of SMTP log file output using the W3C Extended Log Format is shown in Figure 7.9.

Figure 7.9 Sample SMTP Log File in W3C Extended Log Format

```
ex010118.log - Notepad
File  Edit  Format  Help
#Software: Microsoft Internet Information Services 5.0
#Version: 1.0
#Date: 2001-01-14 10:18:47
#Fields: time c-ip cs-username s-sitename s-computername s-ip s-port cs-method sc-status sc-bytes cs-bytes time
10:18:47 - OutboundConnectionResponse SMTPSVC1 NTNETWL1 - 25 - 0 99 0 1472 -
10:18:47 mgate.sybari.com OutboundConnectionCommand SMTPSVC1 NTNETWL1 - 25 EHLO 0 4 0 1983 -
10:18:47 mgate.sybari.com OutboundConnectionResponse SMTPSVC1 NTNETWL1 - 25 - 0 64 0 2093 -
10:18:50 mgate.sybari.com OutboundConnectionCommand SMTPSVC1 NTNETWL1 - 25 MAIL 0 4 0 3776 -
10:18:50 mgate.sybari.com OutboundConnectionResponse SMTPSVC1 NTNETWL1 - 25 - 0 32 0 4246 -
10:18:50 mgate.sybari.com OutboundConnectionCommand SMTPSVC1 NTNETWL1 - 25 RCPT 0 4 0 4246 -
10:18:50 mgate.sybari.com OutboundConnectionResponse SMTPSVC1 NTNETWL1 - 25 - 0 36 0 4346 -
10:18:50 mgate.sybari.com OutboundConnectionCommand SMTPSVC1 NTNETWL1 - 25 DATA 0 4 0 4356 -
10:18:50 mgate.sybari.com OutboundConnectionResponse SMTPSVC1 NTNETWL1 - 25 - 0 48 0 4447 -
10:18:50 mgate.sybari.com OutboundConnectionResponse SMTPSVC1 NTNETWL1 - 25 - 0 42 0 4577 -
10:18:50 mgate.sybari.com OutboundConnectionCommand SMTPSVC1 NTNETWL1 - 25 QUIT 0 4 0 4587 -
10:18:50 mgate.sybari.com OutboundConnectionResponse SMTPSVC1 NTNETWL1 - 25 - 0 39 0 4677 -
10:19:19 - OutboundConnectionResponse SMTPSVC1 NTNETWL1 - 25 - 0 99 0 7200 -
10:19:19 email.ascentrausa.com OutboundConnectionCommand SMTPSVC1 NTNETWL1 - 25 EHLO 0 4 0 7200 -
10:19:19 email.ascentrausa.com OutboundConnectionResponse SMTPSVC1 NTNETWL1 - 25 - 0 55 0 7200 -
10:19:19 email.ascentrausa.com OutboundConnectionCommand SMTPSVC1 NTNETWL1 - 25 MAIL 0 4 0 7200 -
10:19:19 email.ascentrausa.com OutboundConnectionResponse SMTPSVC1 NTNETWL1 - 25 - 0 68 0 7210 -
10:19:19 email.ascentrausa.com OutboundConnectionCommand SMTPSVC1 NTNETWL1 - 25 RCPT 0 4 0 7220 -
10:19:19 email.ascentrausa.com OutboundConnectionResponse SMTPSVC1 NTNETWL1 - 25 - 0 47 0 7220 -
10:19:19 email.ascentrausa.com OutboundConnectionCommand SMTPSVC1 NTNETWL1 - 25 XEXCH50 0 7 0 7220 -
10:19:19 email.ascentrausa.com OutboundConnectionResponse SMTPSVC1 NTNETWL1 - 25 - 0 20 0 7220 -
10:19:19 email.ascentrausa.com OutboundConnectionResponse SMTPSVC1 NTNETWL1 - 25 - 0 6 0 7220 -
```

Hosting

For smaller companies, investing in protective technologies can prove very burdensome in terms of cost and administration. To alleviate this stress, these companies might leave the burden of virus scanning and content filtering to their Internet service provider (ISPs) or their *e-mail hosts*. Some of those hosting services could themselves use Exchange 2000 as their messaging and collaboration platform.

You can find a listing of more than three dozen hosting and collaboration-services partners at the following Microsoft Exchange site link: www.microsoft.com/exchange/techinfo/hosted.htm.

Managing Exchange 2000 Security

Most of the effort we expend in installing and maintaining Exchange 2000-specific applications on the best server hardware helps make our jobs more manageable in the long run. So, our Exchange Server installation is protected by a firewall. It has antivirus software that keeps messaging traffic clean. Our users have been given the skills to operate their client to the fullest. What could go wrong?

As administrators, we must remain proactive in monitoring the products we have in place to protect the integrity of our information and our Exchange Server installation. Review the logs on a regular basis; the firewall logs prove quite adventurous at times if all activity is monitored.

A best practice is to check your Exchange Server's application event log every morning to ensure that the previous night's online backup was successful and that the database had no integrity issues itself, which would likely get reported here from the online maintenance processes or the nightly online backup, which does some checks on its own. In addition, check antivirus logs just to see what was captured, blocked, or otherwise cleaned.

Antivirus companies are reactionary by nature. On the discovery of a new virus, they must work to create a patch that eradicates this new virus and then send the patch to everyone in their databases of registered customers. Administrators should ensure that they are on the e-mail alert list, especially if their antivirus software is not configured for autodownloading of vendor patches. To keep your network in the best position to defend against malicious code, do your best to keep all clients and portals on the most recent antivirus update patch.

Along with ensuring that your company policy is adhered to and monitoring your information sources, you should also stay on top of vulnerability issues for Exchange 2000, the Windows 2000 operating system, and any third-party application.

Even with all that attention, it is likely we'll see another Melissa. The format will be different, but it could be as devastating.

NOTE

We strongly recommend that any Windows administrator be subscribed to the Microsoft Security Bulletin Notification Service to receive e-mails of vulnerabilities as they are published: www.microsoft.com/technet/security/notify.asp.

Summary

Exchange 2000 was designed to work as a central repository for sharing documents, storing communications and schedules, and distributing information. Our dependency on Exchange Server as a mission-critical information application for the enterprise is ever increasing. As more ISVs leverage the powerful developmental platform Exchange 2000 provides and as more companies migrate to the product, more network engineers and administrators will have to work and learn to secure and ensure that it performs as the mission-critical application it is.

Protecting your Exchange 2000 deployment involves the inevitable use of third-party software, probably on multiple levels to help ensure that the information continues to flow and that the integrity of that information remains intact.

Your stable Exchange environment will require a firewall product between itself and the Internet. You will also need some antivirus software, preferably deployed at multiple levels through the organization, from the gateway to the server to the desktop and back. You could require some solid enterprise-level backup and management solutions to help make the administration duties more efficient.

You also must ensure that your client software isn't a weak link to maintaining the uptime of your messaging product. Securing Outlook from accidental distribution of a virus saves embarrassment before your peers and anger from your clients and potentially saves hours of late-night IT time.

FAQs

Visit **www.syngress.com/solutions** to have your questions about this chapter answered by the author.

Q: How do I allow only specific external users to send e-mail through my Exchange server?

A: Security against unwanted SMTP relay is configured through the SMTP Virtual Server Properties. From the Relay button in the Access tab, you can explicitly allow or deny relay privileges while also requiring that any client qualified to relay also be authenticated.

Q: What kind of resources does a server-based antivirus software solution consume?

A: You must be aware that any other application you deploy on your production Exchange servers will cost you in overall performance for the messaging application. Antivirus software is one of the bigger resource consumers, though it is much better now with the use of the antivirus API. There are many issues to consider, such as type of user, presence of connectors, and hardware, but you should anticipate a 10 percent decrease in maximum users with a coexisting store-based antivirus solution.

Real-Time Communication in Exchange 2000

Solutions in this chapter:

- **The Value of Instant Messaging to Your Business**

- **Implementing Chat Services**

- **Can Conferencing Server Keep Your Travel Budget Down?**

Introduction

Real-time means live communication. E-mail is *nearly* real-time. (When I am walking down the street and my RIM BlackBerry receives my e-mail from our Exchange server, I'm pretty excited about it, but I guess that's Southern-style real time). Real-time communication means live communication from one-to-one and many-to-many users. Microsoft has products that meet all the different expectations of real-time communication. In this chapter, we'll review Instant Messaging, the feature in Exchange 2000 that tells you when other people are online at their computer. We'll also go over the Chat service, which allows users to communicate in text mode in a virtual conference room. Finally, we'll go over Microsoft's feature-rich conferencing product, Exchange 2000 Conferencing Server. Each of these three products offers a level of real-time communication that is differentiated by the number of features it can utilize, the level of complexity to configure on the server and the client side, and the number of client applications that can use the technology. This chapter will review the concepts, planning tips, and methods of installation and configuration for each of these real-time products.

The Value of Instant Messaging to Your Business

Instant messaging, very simply, allows you to monitor a contact list to see who is online and active on their computer, and to communicate back and forth in real time. The tough question for an administrator is: does your business require immediate access between individuals that other methods are not providing? Instant Messaging (IM) provides your clients, vendors, and staff instant access to you while you are actively working on a computer and your presence is noted. This can either be extremely useful or extremely nonproductive. Conversely, you can send your clients, vendors, and staff members instant messages when your situation is urgent and you need to reach them. Or is that what pagers and cell phone are for? At least when using pagers and cell phones the user has a record of the message being sent. Remember, real-time also means that nothing is stored. One of the mottos of IM is, "We don't store anything." So, once communication ends, data disappears.

The good news is that Instant Messaging can be integrated into your organization's technical infrastructure. This section discusses the benefits of Instant Messaging, how it works to help you effectively utilize real-time communication, then reviews how to install, configure, and use Instant Messaging from both the server and the client side.

Architecture

Currently there is no definitive industry standard for Instant Messaging. The Instant Messaging client and server functionality offered by Microsoft do not automatically allow for interoperability to other Instant Messaging products such as that provided by America Online—at least not yet. The Instant Messaging Presence Protocol (IMPP) standard is under review as an industry standard, but in the meantime, Microsoft utilizes a protocol known as Rendezvous Protocol (RVP) in the products discussed in this section. The Microsoft offering for Instant Messaging consists of two client products, Microsoft Network (MSN) Messenger Service and Exchange Instant Messaging Client, and one server product, Microsoft Exchange 2000 Instant Messaging Server.

MSN Messenger Service

Currently, the MSN Messenger Service is a client that is available for download from the MSN Web site (www.msn.com). It is available to the public and works with the Microsoft MSN messaging back-end. It does not work with Exchange 2000 Instant Messaging back-end.

NOTE

Authentication to use the MSN Messenger Service is based on the account that you established in the Microsoft/MSN Passport program. You have to register your personal information to get a Passport account. All of this is done on the public Internet. You create a "buddy" list of people and are alerted by the MSN Messenger Service when they are online.

Exchange 2000 Instant Messaging Client

This client is available as a download from Microsoft's Web site, as well as on the Exchange 2000 install media under the I386\instmsg folder. This client will work with both the Microsoft MSN messaging back-end and the Exchange 2000 Instant Messaging back-end. Currently it looks and functions as the MSN Messenger Service, but it allows you to use more features. You will still be required to have a Passport account in order to connect to the MSN messaging back-end. You are required to use Microsoft Internet Explorer version 5.0 (make sure to read the latest release notes to ensure you have the correct software installed on your system). Figure 8.1 shows to which two messaging services the two clients can connect.

Figure 8.1 Instant Messaging Client Connections

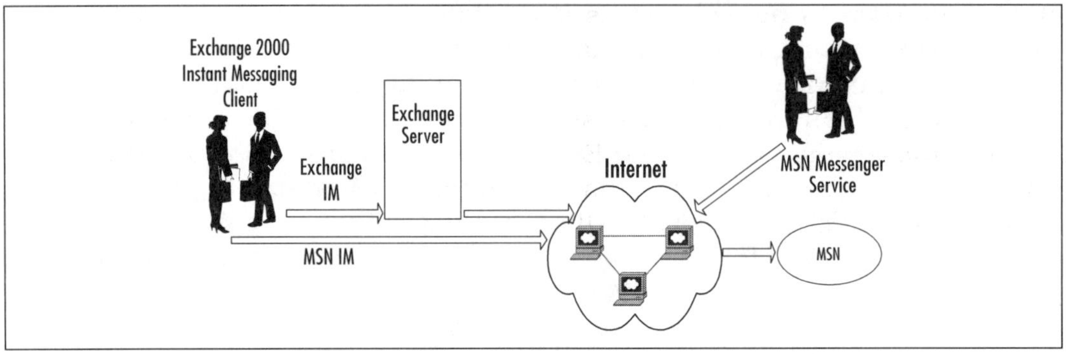

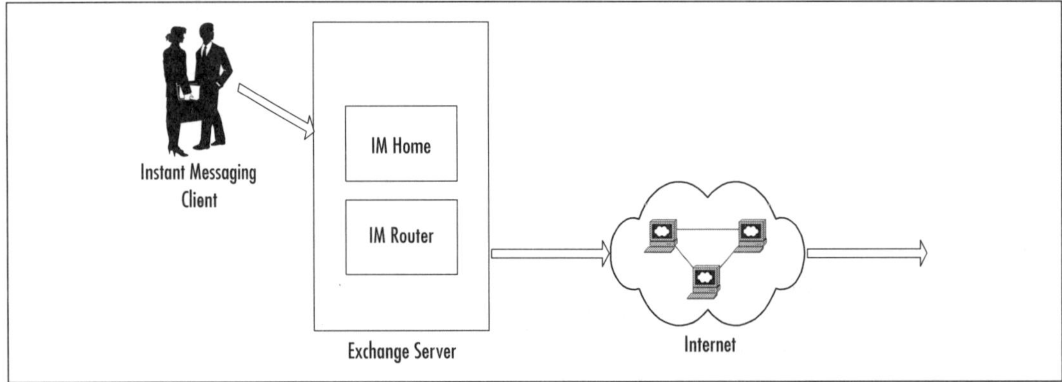

Exchange 2000 Instant Messaging Server

The Instant Messaging Server is an Exchange 2000 server with the Instant Messaging (IM) component installed. There are two main components to the Exchange 2000 Instant Messaging Server, the IM home server component and the IM routing server component. Figure 8.2 shows a typical single-server IM environment. With just one server, you will place both the IM Home and the IM routing components on the same Exchange Server.

Figure 8.2 Instant Messaging Single Server Configuration

Both IM components interoperate closely with the Internet Information Server (IIS) and the Hypertext Transfer Protocol (HTTP) services. The Microsoft client and server products both communicate using the Rendezvous Protocol (RVP), which is a subset of HTTP.

IM Home Server

The Instant Messaging home server component provides a home for your clients who wish to use IM. It does not have to be the same Exchange server that hosts their private e-mail. The home server component monitors if you are online and provides that presence information to subscribers (those individuals who wish to know when you are online). *Presence information* is when the Exchange server is sensing you are working at your computer (it actually monitors for keyboard activity). Presence information can be classified in a few ways:

- Online
- Busy
- Be Right Back
- Away from Computer
- On the Phone
- Out to Lunch
- Appear Offline

A client can modify their presence information with the IM client if they wish to give more information, such as "Be Right Back" and "On the Phone." The IM home server component will monitor for changes in this presence information and will send all state changes to those people subscribing to you. Microsoft recommends having no more than 10,000 IM concurrent user connections on an IM home server.

IM Routing Server

The Instant Messaging routing server component can be combined with or can be separate from the IM home server component. The IM routing server connects requests in and out of the IM server and works closely with IIS. The IM routing server can process connection requests from a client at IMHomeServer1 to IMHomeServer2 using HTTP or proxy redirection. It also processes connection requests from the Internet to a client's IM home server. Microsoft recommends having no more than 20,000 IM concurrent user connections on an IM routing server. If you have more than one home server, you will need a separate routing server. With one home server, you do not need a separate routing server.

By placing the IM home server and IM routing server on different Exchange servers, as in Figure 8.3, you are distributing the routing load to the IM routing server (the front end).

Figure 8.3 Instant Messaging MultiServer Configuration

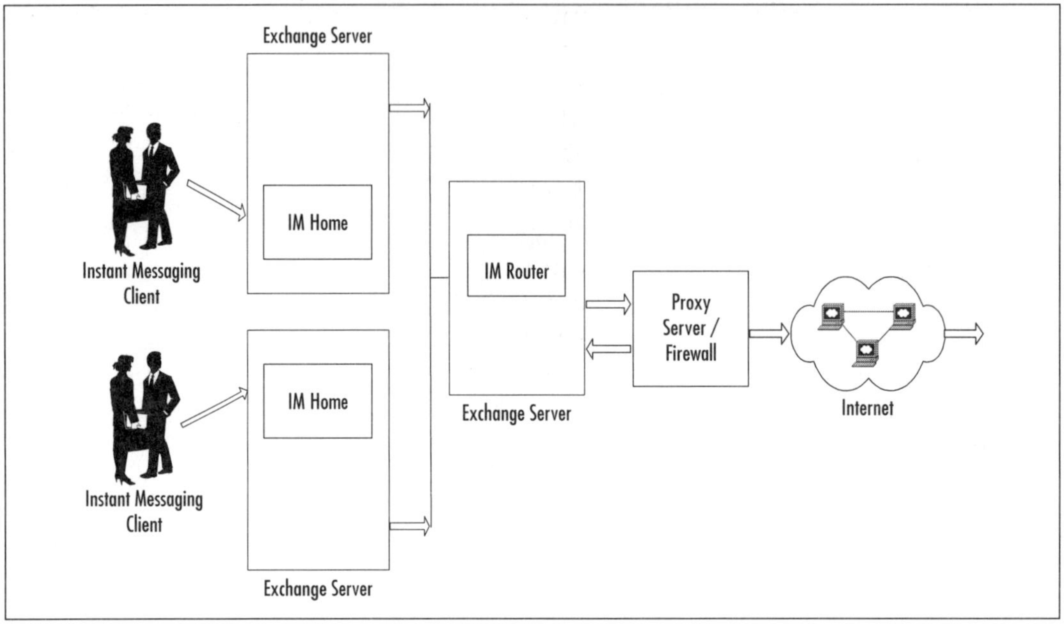

Furthermore, this multiserver configuration can prevent the name of your home servers from being exposed to the Internet. The routing server is registered in the external Domain Name System (DNS), and is responsible for authentication into the Instant Messaging environment. Communication takes place over port 80, using HTTP, so you would only have to expose port 80 through your firewall. The HTTP/RVP verbs that should be passing over your connection should be SUBSCRIBE, NOTIFY, PROPPATCH, and PROPFIND.

Before You Install Your Instant Messaging Servers

Let's take a look at a few troublesome areas to make sure your Instant Messaging installation is worry-free.

- **Security** When possible, do not expose your IM home server to the Internet. Install the home server and routing server on two physically separate servers. You should allow limited access to the IM routing server and place one (if not two) firewalls (in a DMZ implementation as reviewed in Chapter 3) between the sets of IM servers.

- **Performance and Fault Tolerance** Depending on the size of your organization, you may want to have more than one IM routing server. This would reduce the load on the servers, and give you fault tolerance in case one of the servers was offline. As mentioned above, Microsoft's rule of thumb is 20,000 concurrent connections on a routing server and 10,000 concurrent connections on a home server. If you require fault tolerance, then you would want multiple routing servers in case one of the routing servers was offline.

- **Naming convention** You may want to use **im** as the Instant Messaging server name so subscribers can search for you more easily. You may also want to consider having the **im** address be exactly the same as the e-mail address. This would require configuring your DNS with SRV records. A subscriber's Microsoft Instant Messaging client would then contact the target DNS server at your company, query DNS for the RVP service, and then connect to the target IM router that was identified by DNS.

NOTE

It is recommended that you name your Instant Messaging Routing Server **im**, for Instant Messaging. This would in turn have a Fully Qualified Domain Name (FQDN) of **im.company.com.** DNS would have **im.company.com** registered with A records and exposed to the Internet. One would assume that your company e-mail addresses would be similar, and therefore make it easier for your friends and business associates to contact you either way.

For example, an e-mail address of john.doe@company.com would assume an Instant Messaging address of john.doe@im.company.com. (This is also assuming that your company is going to connect your IM to the Internet. Many businesses may not want their users IM-ing to the Internet, and will successfully implement IM for intranet use only.)

Implementing Instant Messaging

To install Instant Messaging you can go to Add/Remove Programs in Control Panel, select the drop-down Action to Change by Microsoft Exchange 2000, as seen in Figure 8.4, and then you can select Install for Instant Messaging and the Chat Services. You can also just run the install setup from the Exchange CD again.

Figure 8.4 Installing Exchange 2000 Instant Messaging

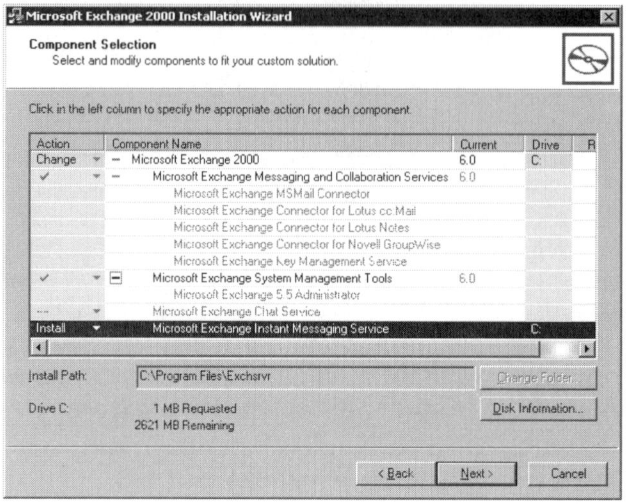

Once you have installed Instant Messaging, you must configure the server. Go into Exchange System Manager, select the server where you installed Instant Messaging, and choose Protocols | Instant Messaging (RVP). Right-click Instant Messaging (RVP) and select New | Instant Messaging Virtual Server. Create a user-friendly name for your virtual server and select the IIS Web site that will enable Instant Messaging. IM then prompts you for the server's valid DNS domain name. You can put in the Fully Qualified Domain Name (FQDN) for both a home server or a router server. Or, if you want to avoid the proxy server, for home servers you can just put in the server name—something generic, such as server1. A router server requires the full name to assist in routing.

You are next prompted to choose whether you want your IM server to be a home server, meaning that it will host user accounts. If you do, then select "Allow this virtual server to host Instant Messaging user accounts." If you want your IM server to be a routing server, just click Next. All IM servers are capable of being routing servers, but they do not all have to host accounts.

After configuring the Internet virtual server, verify that the DNS has the appropriate A and PTR records for the server you identified. In our example you would see an A record for the virtual server im.company.com. Also, if the FQDN of your virtual server does not exist, you may have to create the following SRV record, as seen in Figure 8.5. For more information on DNS records, see Chapter 2.

Figure 8.5 DNS SRV Record for rvp

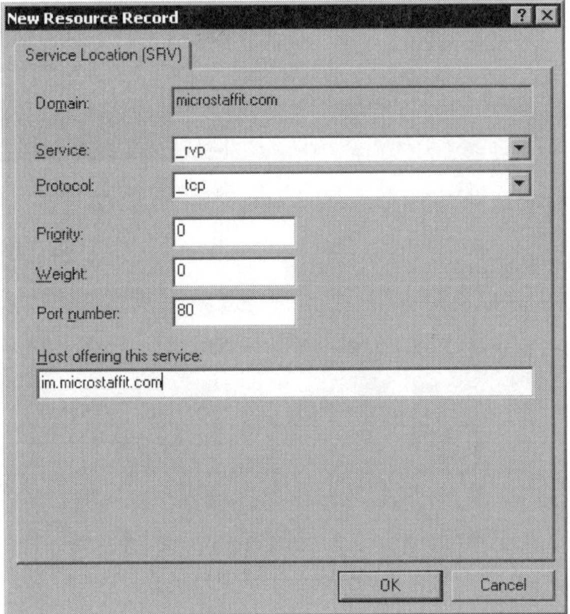

User Administration

Once Instant Messaging is configured, you need to enable your users. Instant Messaging is disabled by default. To enable users:

1. In the Microsoft Management Console (MMC), run Active Directory Users and Computers.

2. Find the user(s) you wish to enable, select them, right-click, select Exchange Tasks, and you should see Figure 8.6.

3. Choose Enable Instant Messaging and select Next.

You can then browse and select an IM home server and an IM domain name for your users, as Figure 8.7 indicates.

Take the time to look at the Task summary when the wizard is complete. You should see something like this:

```
CN=user2 jones,OU=CorpOU,DC=microstaffit,DC=com:

Instant Messaging User Address: user2@im.microstaffit.com

Public URL: http://im.microstaffit.com/instmsg/aliases/user2

Home Server URL: http://im.microstaffit.com/instmsg/aliases/user2
```

Figure 8.6 Enabling Instant Messaging for Users

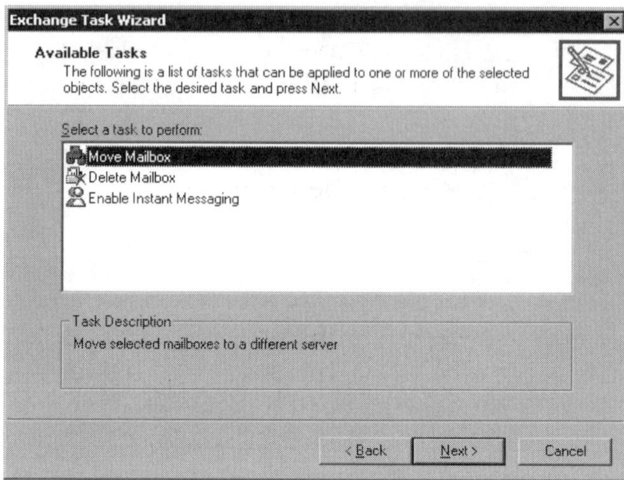

Figure 8.7 Configuring a User's Instant Messaging Home Server and Domain

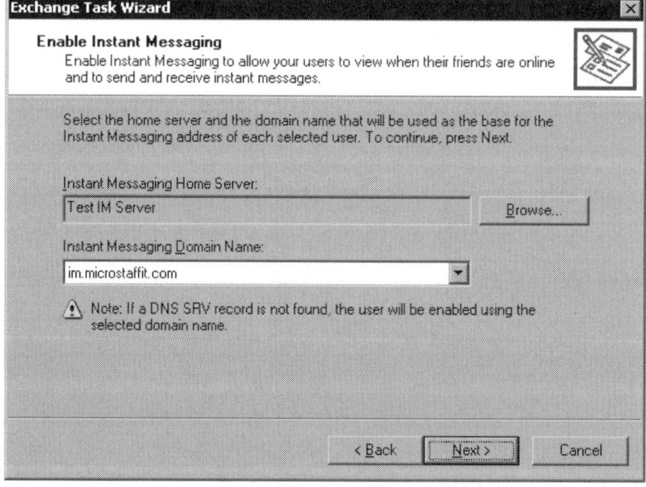

Notice you now have an Instant Messaging user address, plus two URLs. The public URL and the home server URL are how HTTP finds you with Instant Messaging. When an IM user types into their client application the specific user they are looking for, such as user2@im.microstaffit.com, the client application actually translates that SMTP address to a URL such as: http://im.microstaffit.com/instmsg/alias/user2. The IM client will then use HTTP (just as a Web browser does) to locate the destination. However, the destination is not a Web page, but *user2.*

Public and home server URLs can be the same, as the example above shows. In a multiserver configuration, you would have home servers and routing servers. The public URL would be based on your routing server's server name, and your home server URL would be based on the IM home server that hosts your account. When external clients attempt to subscribe to your account, they would use the public URL. The public URL would be translated at the routing server, and it would re-route the HTTP traffic through to your home server. The external users would never know your home server name.

Client Configuration

To install Instant Messaging on the clients, you can distribute to your clients the mmssetup.exe file found on the Exchange install CD. The only installation configuration they require is to enter their e-mail address to identify themselves. They will need to create their own buddy lists. Figure 8.8 shows what the Exchange Instant Messenger client looks like.

Figure 8.8 Exchange Instant Messaging Client

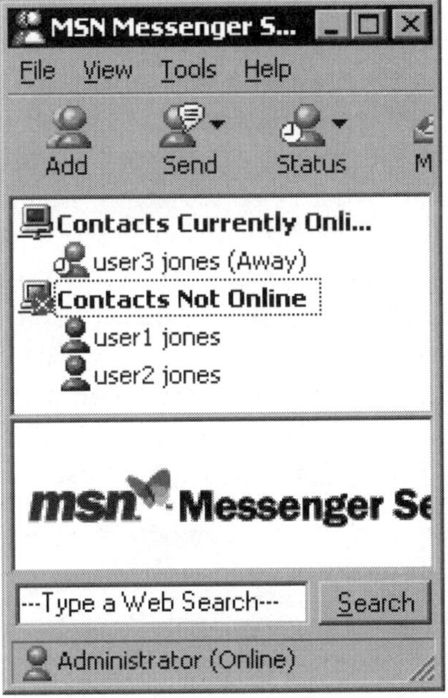

Troubleshooting

The first problem you may encounter will be in the DNS setup of the IM servers.

- Make sure you have valid DNS names and have configured DNS correctly with A and PTR records.

- Perform nslookup and tracert to determine if you have configured the settings correctly.

- You might require an _rvp record with the FQDN for the IM Virtual Server in DNS.

- Look to www.microsoft.com/exchange for more information.

Using Chat Services

When people get together to talk casually, they *chat*. At the office, a discussion is like a formal chat. When you want to have a discussion with your team about a last-minute requirement a customer has asked to put into your product, you may not require a conference room, video cameras, speakers, microphones, etc. Also, you know that Instant Messaging won't do to discuss this requirement, as you need to have everyone present. One solution is to use a chat room that your company would reserve just for these occasions.

Exchange 2000 provides for a chat service on the server. You, the system administrator, can create chat communities, administer the communities, ban users, and create channels, classes, and more. You can configure security on your users and chat rooms. If you don't have a chat service in your organization, you may want to think about how your team may benefit from such a discussion service. The biggest problem with chat sessions is that they may require some form of monitoring or facilitating—like any meeting—to keep participants communicating within established parameters. If your company can manage that, chat will be a very useful tool for geographically dispersed teams and individuals.

Implementing Chat Services

The installation of chat is easy. However, the administrative effort is complex, because you are responsible for monitoring and facilitating the chat rooms. Chat is based on RFC 1459, Internet Relay Chat protocol, known as IRC or as IRCX for the IRC Extension version that Microsoft created. Chat sessions typically use TCP Port default ports 6667 and 7000, but you can configure chat to use ranges 6665 through 6668. Make sure you coordinate this with your network administrator so the firewall can be configured to allow chat traffic through.

TIP

If you are migrating your Exchange 5.5 chat service to Exchange 2000 chat, make sure you change your Exchange 5.5 chat ports to alternate ports, such as 6663 or 6669 first. You can install Exchange 2000 on the same server, and it will claim ports 6667 and 7000. You will then essentially be running two chat services on one physical server, which will allow you to test your new Exchange 2000 chat service before removing the old.

Server-Side Installation

To install chat services, go to Add/Remove Programs in the Control Panel, select the drop-down Action to Change by Microsoft Exchange 2000, and then select Install for Chat Services (see Figure 8.9). You could also run the Exchange setup from the CD.

Figure 8.9 Installing Chat Service

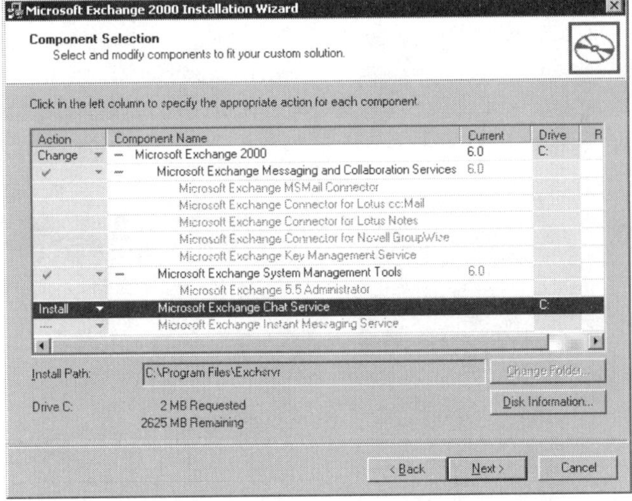

Once the product is installed, you find a new container called Chat Communities in Exchange System Manager, as shown in Figure 8.10.

By right-clicking on the Chat Communities container, you can create new communities (also known as *rooms*). Here we have created a community called OlympicHopefuls. The Properties screen of the chat communities has four tabs for you to complete, as you can see in Figure 8.11.

Figure 8.10 Chat Communities for Chat Services

Figure 8.11 Chat Community Property Pages

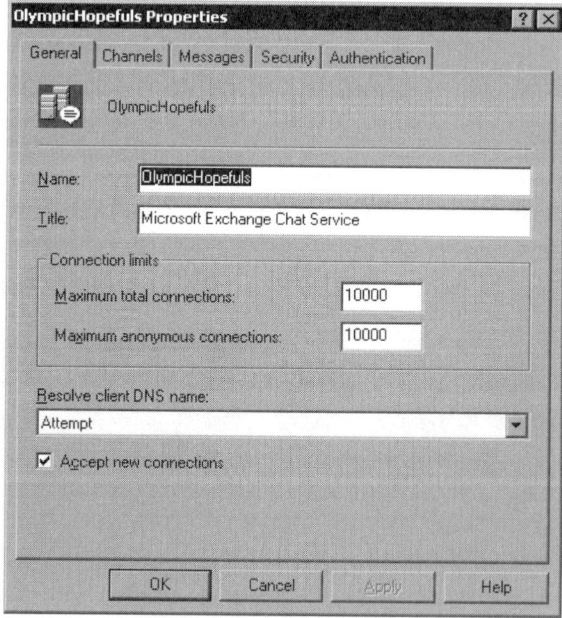

You should go through each tab and familiarize yourself with the configuration possibilities. Options that you should consider for security purposes would be:

- Limiting the number of connections (users) to your chat community sessions.

- Attempting DNS name resolution of the users.

- Requiring authentication to your chat server.

In Olympic Hopefuls, you can see the default containers created: Channels, Bans, and Classes. You can structure your chat communities by creating *channels*. Channels can start when the chat service starts. You can specify subject matter, topics, content rating and language. With a *Ban* you can ban certain people from chatting in your community. This can be based on their user name, their nickname, and even their IP address (using DNS name resolution). With *Classes*, you can create a *class* called *Syngress*, where you will only allow users with the suffix of *syngress.com* to participate in the discussions.

Next you will want to configure the IRCX container settings. Select the IRCX container under the Protocols tab, as seen in Figure 8.12. Add those communities that you want to host on your Exchange server.

As you can see in Figure 8.13, we have added two communities to our chat server.

Figure 8.12 IRCX Protocol in Exchange 2000 Server

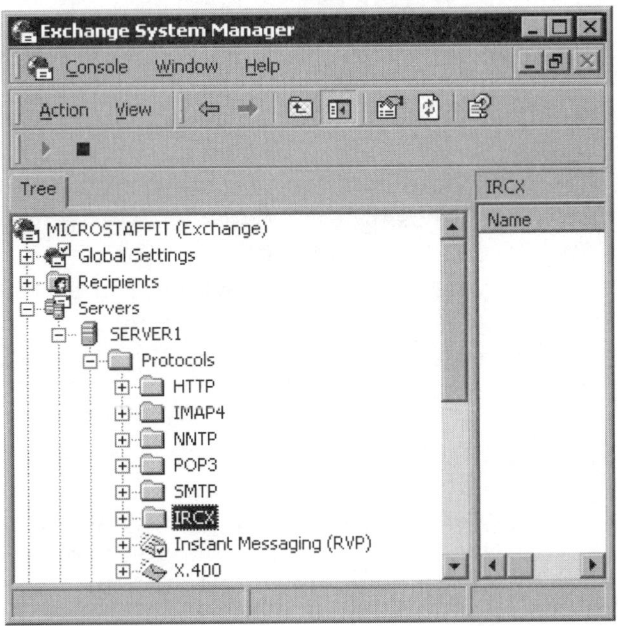

Figure 8.13 Hosted Chat Communities

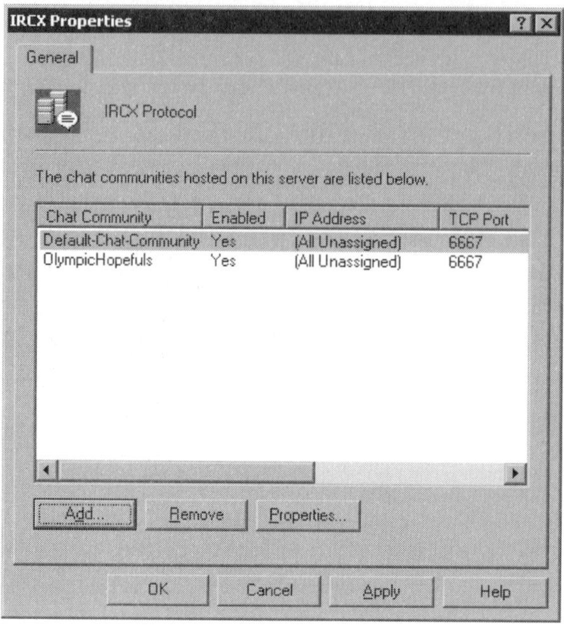

Client-Side Configuration

Now that you have configured the server, it is time to verify that it works.
Find Exchange 5.5 Service Pack 3 (SP3) and get the Chat 2.1 client (the
Chat 2.0 client will not work with Exchange 2000). Once you install it on
your desktop, you have a small amount of configuration to complete. If you
do not get Figure 8.14 immediately when you start chat, then go to View |
Options and complete the necessary Properties screens (most of them are
optional—you can choose a cartoon character to represent you, you can
have sounds played when you talk, you can whisper, and so on).

For connections, we have selected to go to server1, and to join the session in Room1. We enter the room and begin talking about the new
requirements in Figure 8.15.

Troubleshooting Chat

Besides the headache of being a babysitter for chat rooms, what types of
problems may you have? Clients may have problems connecting, or once
connected they may have problems getting authenticated, or you may have
too many people on your system.

If your clients are having problems connecting to your chat service,
you should attempt to connect from different locations. One way to test

Figure 8.14 Initial Chat Connection Configuration

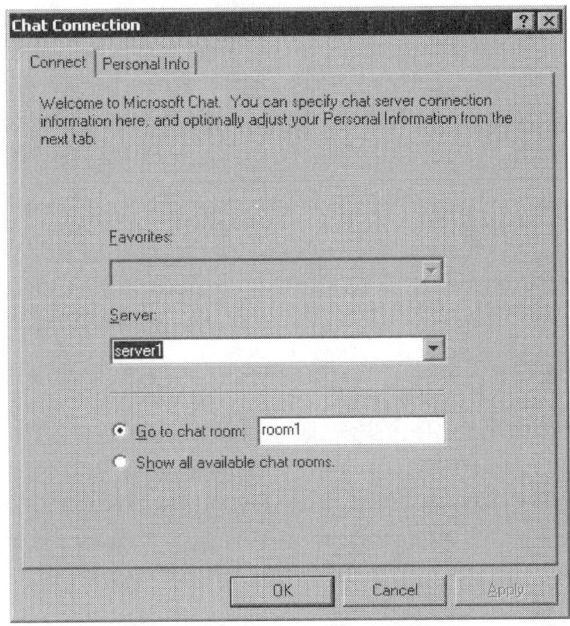

Figure 8.15 Chat Session with Two Users, Little and Biggy

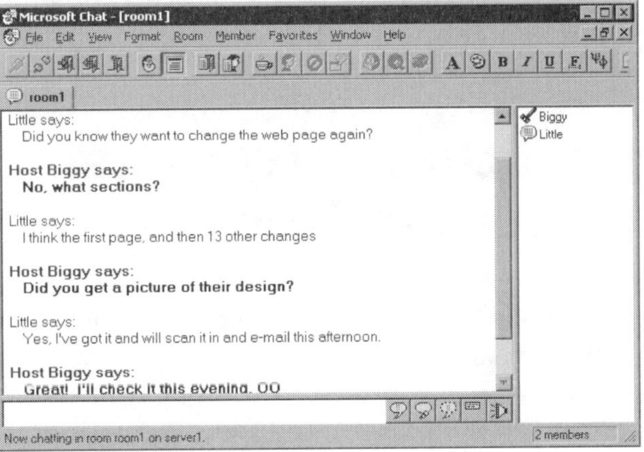

connectivity to your chat server and eliminating potential problems with the client is to open a TCP port 6667 session from a client computer to the chat server using the Telnet application. To do this, run Telnet by clicking Start ? Run and typing **telnet servername 6667** where *servername* is your chat server name. If you do connect, then type your username or nickname appropriately by entering:

```
USER    username
NICK    nickname
```

Your connection is working if you are getting feedback from the chat service. This would indicate that your problem is likely with your chat client or how it's configured. If you do not get feedback from the chat client, then start with basic TCP/IP troubleshooting techniques:

1. Ping the server name; if it comes back, then you know you can reach their server.
2. Ping the gateway name to verify you can leave the network.
3. Ping your IP address to verify your TCP/IP is working.
4. Telnet to other ports, such as 7000, 6665, 6667, or possibly 6668.

If users are having problems getting authenticated, then review your security settings on the individual communities. Check the Security tab on the Community Properties screen. You can also drill down into the community, and check to see who is banned, how the classes are set up, as well as the security settings on the channels. There are a lot of ways to confuse authentication.

You should consider running the performance monitoring tool Performance Logs and Alerts on your chat server if you are experiencing performance problems and you believe there may be too many users on the chat server. One way to alleviate performance problems is to limit the number of users that can connect to the chat server, or to distribute some communities to other chat servers.

Can Conferencing Server Keep Your Travel Budget Down?

Exchange Conferencing Server should be viewed as a software conferencing solution for small to medium organizations or for groups within large organizations. It not only can keep your travel budget down, but it enables you to have meetings more often because the total cost of implementation is low. Having a fully multimedia-resourced meeting with your entire national or international team on a more frequent basis should improve communications and subsequently efficiency within your organization. Microsoft has created a full-feature real-time communication product in Exchange 2000 Conferencing Server (ECS). Whether end-users have Outlook, NetMeeting, or other T.121 clients, they can invite users to a conference, schedule a conference room, join the conference, and manage the conference, all from their desktop. This can be implemented by utilizing a lower-cost technology already in place—your intranet, the Internet, and WAN connections.

ECS is more complex than chat and Instant Messaging—but don't let it scare you off. This section provides enough information for you to install and configure your own Exchange Conferencing server to begin testing the possibilities for your organization. Try it! Exchange 2000 Conferencing Server allows the sharing of video, audio, data, shared whiteboards, and chat facilities. With desktop cameras, speakers, and microphones, end users can participate fully in online meetings. If the end-users don't have the multimedia peripherals, they can attend and participate via T.120 services, such as chat, whiteboard sharing, and application sharing. If the conference attendees all require a white paper to review before the next sessions, ECS will distribute files to everyone. The same transport is used, and it can be delivered in the background.

Background

Chat and NetMeeting were predecessors of ECS, and their best features are integrated into ECS. One feature from chat that looks similar in ECS is the windowpane that opens up and allows (chat) communication. Each user's statements are annotated with their full name—not nickname—and you can see which users are participating in the chat. NetMeeting features (known as T.120 services) available in ECS are application sharing, the whiteboard, and file transfer. However, what is different from NetMeeting is that a conference is hosted by the Exchange Conferencing Server, not by an individual NetMeeting user. In NetMeeting, if the originating user left the conference, the entire conference would drop; this is not the case in ECS. Also, NetMeeting would only allow for one video session between two clients, whereas Exchange Conferencing Server allows for multiple video sessions in a single conference.

ECS does this by using multicast technology in Windows 2000 to transmit a conference to many individuals efficiently. ECS can transmit to these groups directly without incurring the traffic that a unicast transmission would require to each computer.

Components

Exchange 2000 Server is a different product from Exchange 2000 Conferencing Server. You do not have to install Exchange Server and Conferencing Server on the same system. You must have an Exchange server installed and running in *the same domain* as the conferencing server, but ECS does not have to be on the same physical computer as Exchange.

Unicast, Multicast, and MADCAP

What is the difference between unicast, multicast, and MADCAP? (This is where your studying for Exam 70-216 pays off.) Briefly, *unicast* directs a packet to a single destination. For example, when you connect to a file server over IP from your desktop to save a file to the server, you are sending packets of data to that server only. You are not sending packets of data to other computers on the network. If you were to send a file to multiple computers using unicast, there would actually be multiple copies of the file sent over the network. This would affect network bandwidth. Most server-to-server and client-to-server communication uses a unicast session.

In a *multicast* session, a packet is directed to a single IP address, but a group of computers are "assigned" that specific IP address. Multicast IP addresses fall in the Class D class range from address 224.0.0.0 to 239.255.255.255. For more information on multicasting and address assignment (specifically Intranet versus Internet IP addressing), see any book on Windows 2000 Networking, RFC 1112, RFC 2236, or consult www.isi.edu/in-notes/iana/assignments/multicast-addresses. Multicasting is efficient in conferencing solutions, as the central conference host can simultaneously send the packets of data to a group of computers using one IP address. This means applications such as video conferencing servers can send out video conferencing packets to one IP address, but multiple video conferencing clients receive the packet—producing no more network traffic than a unicast packet, but providing all clients with the same video stream. If you were to send a file to multiple computers using multicast, there would be just one copy of the file sent over the network.

MADCAP (Multicast Address Dynamic Client Allocation Protocol) is the protocol that enables you to configure multicasting in Windows 2000.MADCAP was previously known as Multicasting Dynamic Host Configuration Protocol (MDHCP). This allows you to set up a multicast scope in DHCP, with the multicast scope containing a range of multicast IP addresses. A multicast scope behaves like a unicast scope, except that one IP address is given to multiple hosts.

Reserving a Conference Room

Let's look at some of the components of ECS to help understand how the product works. First, this section will explain how one would reserve a conference room manually to help you understand the simplicity of the product; then it will explain how it is implemented in Exchange 2000 Conferencing Server. Figure 8.16 illustrates how people would do this manually.

Figure 8.16 The Conference Management Service and Components

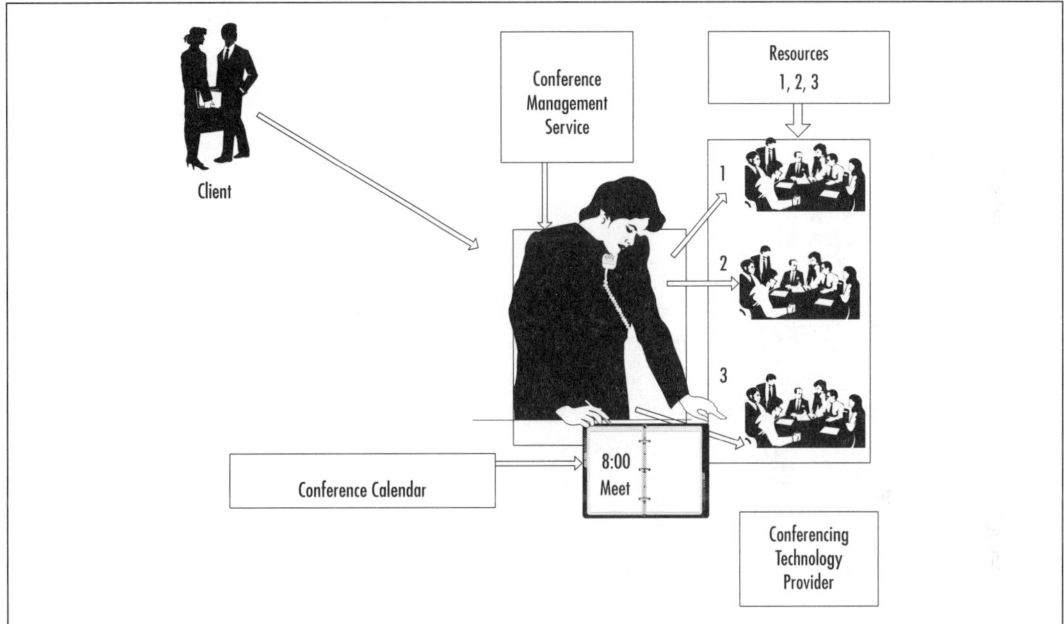

Conference Management Service (CMS) You should view this as a reservation system. You have to have at least one CMS to manage your Exchange Conferencing Server. You may want to install a second CMS on a different computer for fault tolerance. In Figure 8.16, the woman on the phone is representing CMS, the reservation system. She is receiving requests for conference rooms from clients, and she reserves them on her calendar organizer that she keeps on her desk.

Conference Calendar Mailbox In Exchange Conferencing Manager, you, the administrator, must create what is called a Conference Calendar Mailbox. This is the calendar for the conferences. It is an Exchange mailbox that holds all the information about the meetings being scheduled (you will create this mailbox in the implementation section later in this chapter). In Figure 8.16, the Conference Calendar Mailbox would be the equivalent of the woman's calendar organizer.

Clients (Reserving a conference room) To reserve a conference room in real life, you have some options: you can call over the phone or visit the reservationist and she can guarantee you a room immediately, or if you want to send her an e-mail requesting a conference time, she'll send you back a confirmation of which conference room she got and for what time. You will then have to send your participants a second e-mail notifying them of the conference room and time. With regards to client software, the client that you will use to schedule a conference will either be Outlook or a browser interface (Outlook Web Access, or OWA).

Conference Resources A Conference Resource is the room or resource that you would need when holding a conference. These resources are mailbox-enabled. CMS uses these accounts when scheduling conferences. When you create these conference resources, (as you will do later in this chapter) you must define what multimedia resources are available. So in real life, you would say that a conference room has a projector, a speakerphone, a whiteboard, or a computer that you display to the wide screen. Similarly, when creating a conference resource in ECS, you define if it is video and/or data enabled. So in Figure 8.16 above, you can see that we have three rooms available for conferences.

Confirmation The confirmation of the location of the conference room is a URL. Following the URL path at the correct time will take you to the virtual conference room.

In summary, the Conference Management Service (the woman in Figure 8.16) reserves a resource (a room) and writes it in her conference calendar mailbox (organizer). If she was called over the phone or in person (Outlook 2000) she can tell the originator immediately (a URL). If she was sent an e-mail or left a note (browser, or pre-Outlook 2000 product) she will have to send the originator back an e-mail with the confirmation information (a URL).

Joining and Managing Conferences

Now that we have the basic reservation system in place, let's proceed to joining and managing a conference.

To join a conference, clients have a few options:

1. Copy the received URL in a browser, and it will connect you to the conference room.

2. In Outlook, right-click on your meeting and join the conference.

3. In Outlook, open up your meeting, and double-click on the URL.

4. Go to the web site http://conferencingserver/conferencing/list.asp and view a list of scheduled conferences, then click on the one you wish to attend.

Once you are in the virtual conference room, you will see a window with the features appropriate for your conference (video, data, etc.). You will also have *Conference Access Web pages*. These are the Web pages that clients can use for information when attending the conference (found at the site just previously mentioned in the fourth option above, and as shown in Figure 8.17).

Figure 8.17 List of Available Conferences

Conference Technology Providers (CTP)

Microsoft provides two conference technology providers: Data Conferencing and Video Conferencing Providers. With ECS, your conference is being transmitted using both data and video/audio. You can have the Conference Technology Provider(s) that comes with Exchange Conferencing Server or you can utilize a Third Party CTP. (If you are familiar with the Open Systems Communication, or OSI, stack, think of CTP as working at the transport layer.)

- **ECS Data Conferencing Provider** The Data Conferencing Provider service brings ECS the true power of data conferencing. The Data Conferencing Provider is the service that allows the chats, the whiteboard sharing, the application sharing, and the file transfer. The Data Conferencing Provider must be installed on the same server as the CMS; you can also install it on other servers for more multipoint control units (MCUs). The install component T.120 MCU/H.3.23 Conference Bridge is the MCU for T1.20 data conferencing clients and a bridge for H.323 clients.

- **ECS Video Conferencing Provider** The Video Conferencing Provider service that ECS utilizes is what managers really get excited about. The video transmission is provided via the multicast IP broadcast to directed groups of users/computers. Remember you must have a MADCAP server on your network for the Video Conferencing Provider to work on the *server*. Conversely, if your *client* does not support multicast and you are to join a conference that has video, the T.120 MCU/H.3.23 Conference Bridge can "bridge the gap." Through H.323 (unicast), the T.120 MCU/H.3.23 Conference Bridge connects to your NetMeeting client and allows you to participate.

When you participate in an ECS conference, you'll notice the user interface is divided up into two sections. One shows the audio/video of all those participating (assuming audio/video is available), and the other allows for data conferencing services such as chat, whiteboard, file-sharing, etc. The video portion of the conference is provided by the EDC video conference provider through a multicast or H.323 session. The data portion of the conference is provided by the ECS Data Conferencing provider which uses T.120 services that come from Netmeeting (Netmeeting is included on all Windows 2000 clients).

So to put all these components together, take a look at Figure 8.18.

Figure 8.18 Key Components of the Exchange Conferencing Server

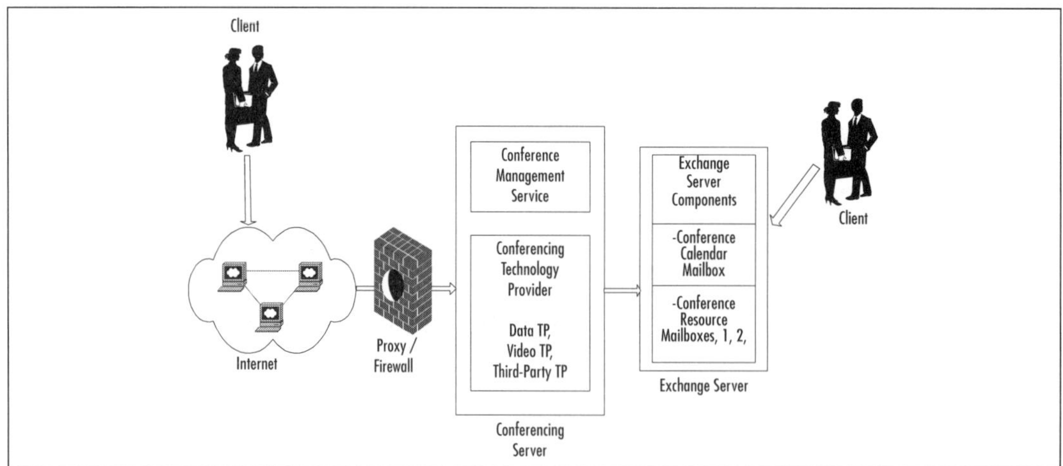

T1.20 and H.323

When you think of T.120, think data and think point-to-point (unicast). Netmeeting is a T.120 client and ECS takes advantage of Netmeeting on the client during a conferencing session. Data sharing can be sharing files, sharing text words via chat, sharing applications, and sharing diagrams via a whiteboard. T.120 is an International Telecommunications Union (ITU) standard to enable multipoint data conferencing. An ECS server with the *T.120 MCU/H.3.23 Conference Bridge* installed allows desktops to participate in real-time data conferencing. The component that enables this is the Data Conferencing Provider.

When you think of H.323, think video and think point-to-point (unicast). ECS provides audio and video streaming capabilities through IP Multicasting and also through H.323 compatibility. Clients that support Multicasting (such as Windows 2000) are the preferred EDS clients because multicast is much more efficient than point-to-point (unicast). However, many organizations do not have Windows 2000 on every desktop. H.323 can be configured on the ECS Video Conferencing Provider to allow non-Windows 2000 clients, such as Windows 98, to participate in the video/audio portion of a conference. Remember though, H.323 services are point-to-point so that a unicast session is established with each H.323 conferencing participant and the economies of multicast are not realized.

As mentioned earlier, clients that do not support multicasting can connect to ECS if they are H.323 compatible and the ECS Video Conferencing Provider has been configured to support H.323. H.323 is also an ITU standard, and it enables point-to-point audio and video stream conferencing. An ECS server with the T.120 MCU/H.3.23 Conference Bridge installed allows desktops to participate in real-time audio and video conferencing.

Installing Exchange Conferencing Server

The first server in a domain that has CMS installed is known as the *top-level server*. To install Exchange Conferencing Server you need to have the following:

- Windows 2000, Active Directory

- An Exchange 2000 server in the same Active Directory domain

- IIS in the same Active Directory site

- Certificate Services (if security on your conference rooms is required)

- MADCAP (MDCHP)

When you install from the Exchange Conferencing Server CD, you will get the choices shown in Figure 8.19. We described these earlier, with the exception of the Conferencing Manager, which is the MMC add-in. Think of how the Exchange Administrator program could be installed on some systems and not installed on some—the same is true for the Conferencing Manager. You don't have to install the Conferencing Manager on every system; just on those systems from which you plan to administer the conference.

Figure 8.19 Installing ECS

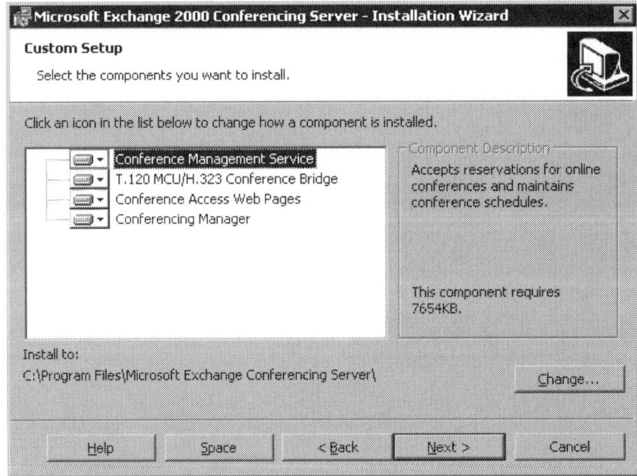

So, for a single server, you can select all of these components and install them on one server, as in Figure 8.20.

Also, you can separate the components and install them on different servers, as in Figure 8.21.

Configuration

Now let's review how to configure the Conferencing Server, and then the client components. This section will get your Conferencing Server up and running, but be sure to then read the online documentation that comes on the Conferencing Server CD (as well as the online help) for detail on security, administrative groups, policies, and so on.

Figure 8.20 Exchange 2000 Server and Exchange 2000 Conferencing Server

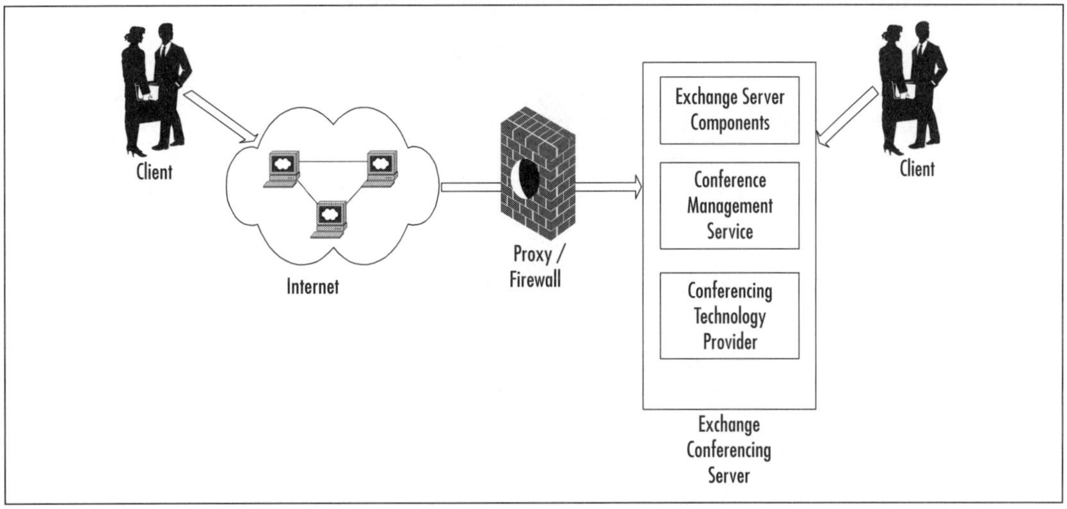

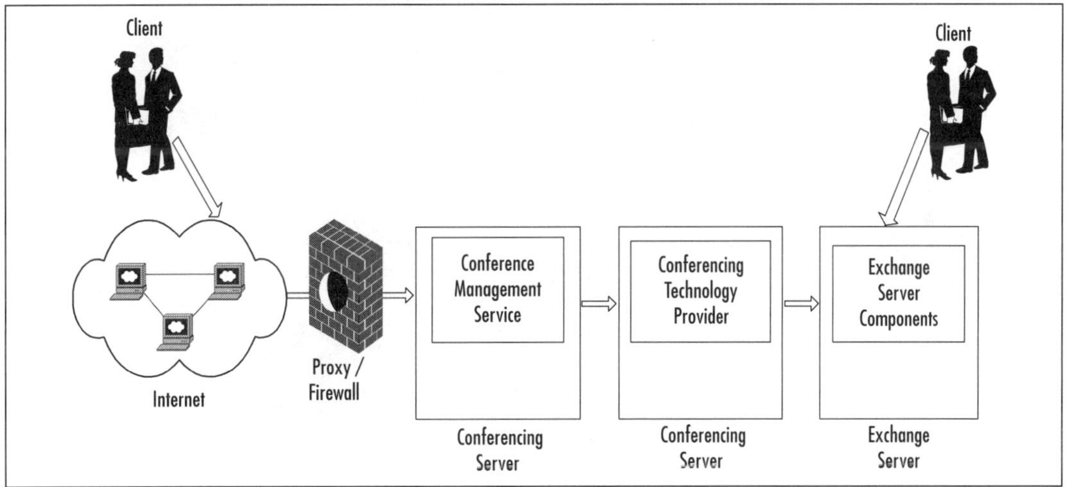

Figure 8.21 Exchange Server and Conferencing Server on Separate Servers

Server Side Configuration

First you'll create the Conference Calendar mailbox. This is the resource that keeps track of all the meetings and registrations. Next, you'll create conference resources (similar to rooms). Third, you'll create a profile that can access the Conference Calendar mailbox to make sure it is working.

Create a Conference Calendar Mailbox

The following steps describe how to create a Conference Calendar Mailbox.

1. In Conferencing Manager, right-click Properties for the Default-First-Site-Name Conferencing Site under Exchange Conferencing, as shown in Figure 8.22.

   If you are not prompted to create a Conference Calendar Mailbox, select the General tab and click the Modify button, as shown in Figure 8.23.

Figure 8.22 Creating a Mailbox under Default-First-Site-Name Conferencing Site

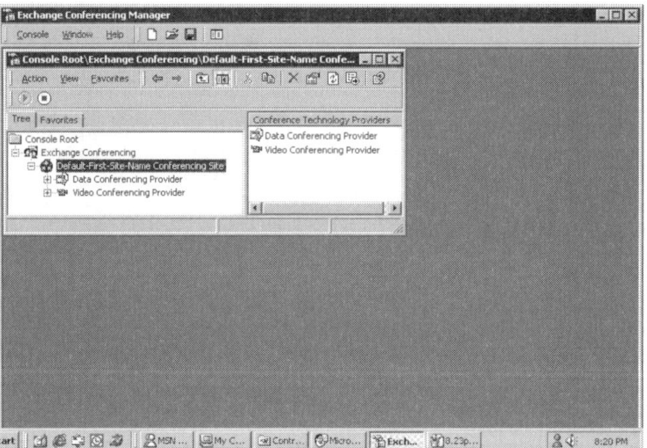

Figure 8.23 Properties Page of Default-First-Site-Name Conferencing Site

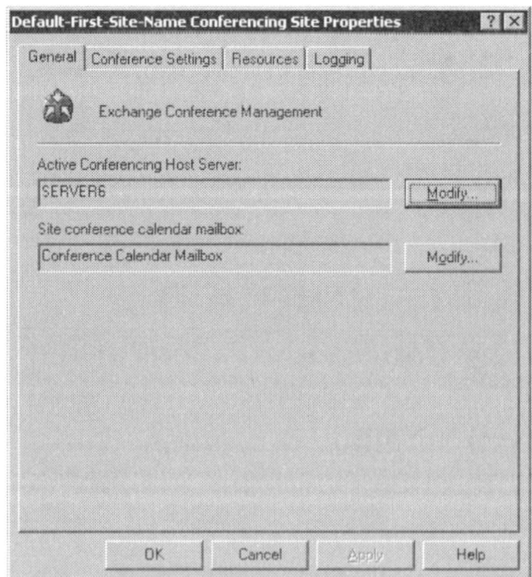

2. In the next screen, as shown in Figure 8.24, you will select *Create* to create a mailbox. You will create this mailbox just like any other account mailbox, except that you will be asked to provide a password for the mailbox.

Figure 8.24 Creating a Conference Calendar Mailbox

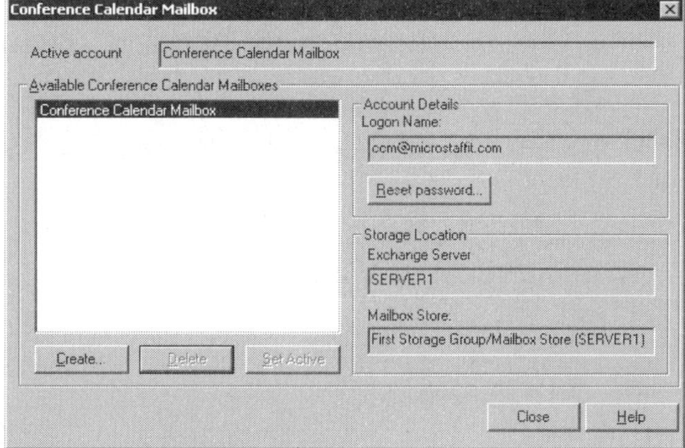

3. Once you create the mailbox, you can modify the Conference settings:

- The name of the URL for the conferences (default HTTP://SERVER/conferencing)

- How early participants can join (default 20 minutes)

- How much participants can extend a room reservation (default 0 minutes)

- Whether you will allow the conference organizer to extend the room reservation

- Whether you will allow the conference organizer to change room resources

NOTE

You might want to change room resources if there are too many participants for the room size.

Create Conference Resources

Now you need to create conference rooms, or *Conference Resources*.

1. Select the Resources tab and you should get a window similar to Figure 8.25.

Figure 8.25 Creating Conference Room Resources

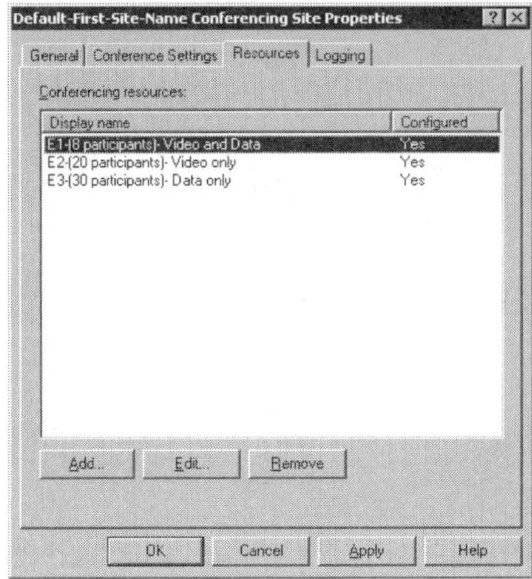

2. Select Add, and create a Resource, as in Figure 8.26.

Figure 8.26 Conference Room Resource Properties

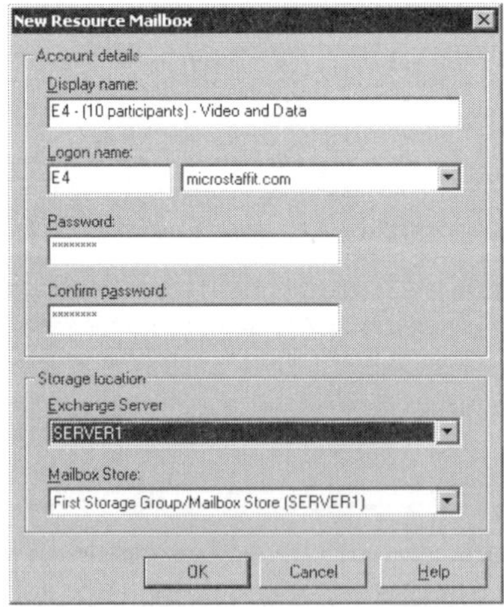

3. After you put in your resource information, you should identify the type of Conferencing Provider it will host, such as Data Conferencing Provider or Video Conferencing Provider, as in Figure 8.27.

Figure 8.27 Assigning Conference Technology Providers to a Conference Resource

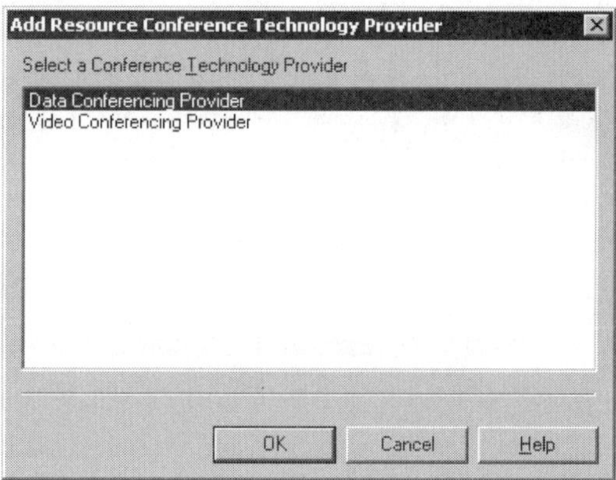

If you choose Video Conferencing Provider, you will be prompted to configure basic parameters. In our example, we used the defaults and everything worked fine (we used a Philips 646 Digital Camera; USB Device, Model Number PCA646VC.) Notice at the top of the Properties screen in Figure 8.28 you can enable H.323 Data Providers. This is where you enable H.323 for non-Windows 2000 clients. Notice at the bottom of the Properties screen you are to choose the multicast scope that is applicable for this conference resource. We have a multicast scope called TestMulticast-ECS.

Figure 8.28 Defining the Video Conference Provider Parameters

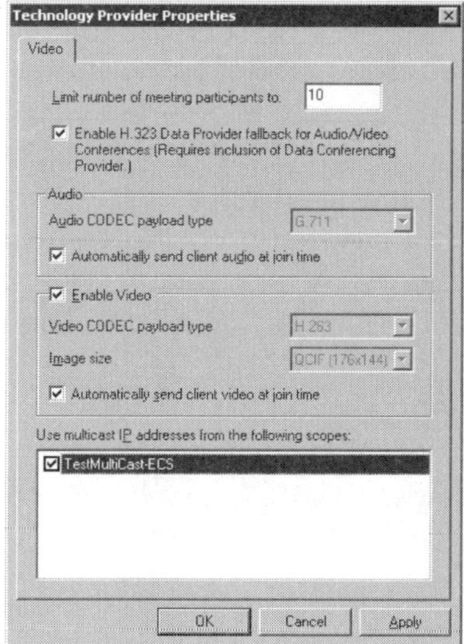

4. Next, if you choose the Data Conferencing Provider, you will only be prompted for the number of meeting participants.

    To verify the mailboxes you created, you can go into Active Directory Users and Computers and look at the objects under the Microsoft Exchange System Objects. You will have to be using the Advanced View, which you get by selecting View | Advanced Features. This is shown in Figure 8.29.

Figure 8.29 Viewing ECS Mailboxes from Active Directory Users and Computers

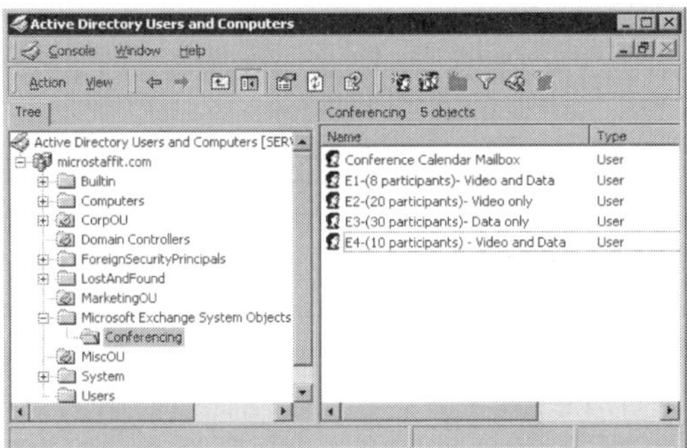

5. Your next step to verify that your Conference Calendar Mailbox exists is to create a profile and log on to the mailbox. Make sure you have the right security permissions or you won't be able to open up the mailbox and review the calendar.

TIP

The key to good Conference Resource usage is logical naming conventions. Users will only be able to see the Display name of the resource in the Global Address List, so it is important that it is representative of the resources and participant number. It is recommended that you put in the type of resource you have, such as voice or data, and the number of participants it can manage. Also, if you have a large organization, you also might want to add a geographic name. The resources we used are similar to

E1- (8 participants) – Voice and Data

Because our Conference Server resource is in Columbia, South Carolina (noted CAE) we could also have called it:

E1-(8)-CAE-Voice and Data

Client-Side Configuration

Now let's start scheduling and joining conferences. Our test lab used Windows 2000 systems, so multicast was not a problem.

Scheduling a Conference with Outlook 2000

Once Outlook 2000 is installed, go to Calendar to create a meeting. In our test lab, Outlook did not show the Microsoft Exchange Conference Drop Down. We looked this up in Microsoft TechNet, and it said to create the following file in Notepad. (We tried this in WordPad, but it did not work.)

```
File outlookreg.reg

REGEDIT4

[HKEY_CURRENT_USER\Software\Microsoft\Office\9.0\Outlook\
ExchangeConferencing]
```

Name this file outlookreg.reg, then double-click it. You will receive the query, "Are you sure you want to add the information in (XYZ) to the registry." (There is yet another confirmation pop-up after that.)

You will have to deploy this fix to your clients running Outlook if you want them to use this. We don't know how long Microsoft intends for this to be the normal way, so keep checking their Web site! You can manually add the Exchange Conferencing key to the registry. The file above may be useful for organizations that want to push out the registry entry using SMS or a logon script or a group policy.

Now that you are back in Outlook, you can schedule a resource and invite attendees, as in Figure 8.30, which shows a typical Outlook calendar appointment. Notice that the online meeting field is checked and Microsoft Exchange Conference is selected.

You can see the names of those invited by looking at the To... field. In this example, we invited user1, user2, user3 and user4. Notice that the Resource was listed as a conference resource mailbox from a previous step, and it automatically accepted, as the meeting has a URL already. You can see in Figure 8.31 that you select a resource for a meeting by going to the Select Attendees and Resources tab and then, in the Resources Field, choosing a resource from the pull-down menu of All Conferencing Resources.

Figure 8.30 Scheduling a Resource and Inviting Attendees

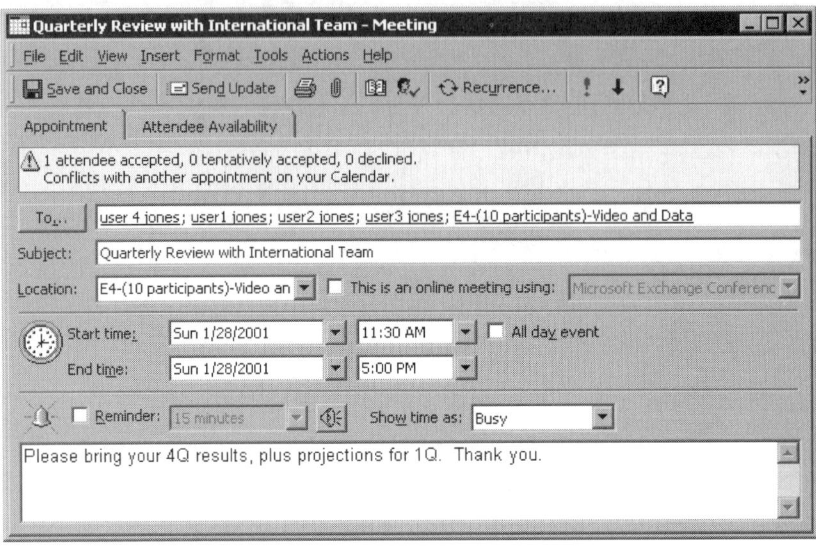

Figure 8.31 Attendee Availability of a Meeting

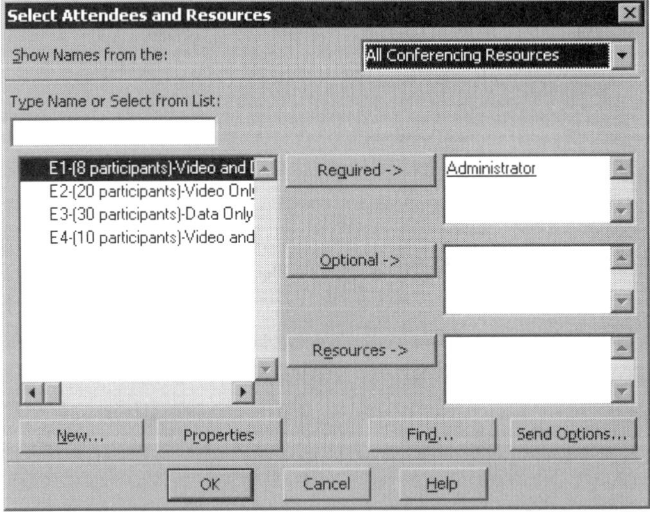

Joining a Conference from Outlook 2000

When user3 received the e-mail invitation, for example, they opened their calendar in Outlook, which looked similar to Figure 8.32.

Figure 8.32 User3 Daily Calendar Showing Conferences

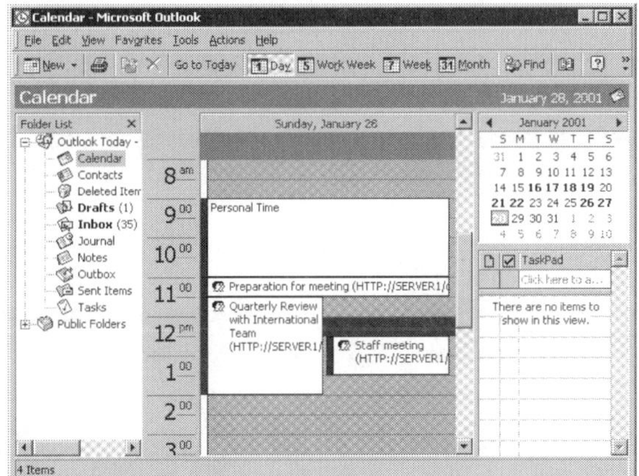

When it came time for user3 to join the meeting, they had the option of using Outlook, NetMeeting, or the conference schedule Web page. Since this was a videoconference, the user chose Outlook 2000. When they right-clicked the appointment time, it prompted them to join the conference, and they accepted. The first time they started the client they were prompted to install Exchange Conferencing Client Access and Exchange IP Multicast Conferencing Client. (In this case, the browser pops up on the desktop, and the user gets a selection of conferencing tools in the browser window, as in Figure 8.33.)

Figure 8.33 Conferencing Window

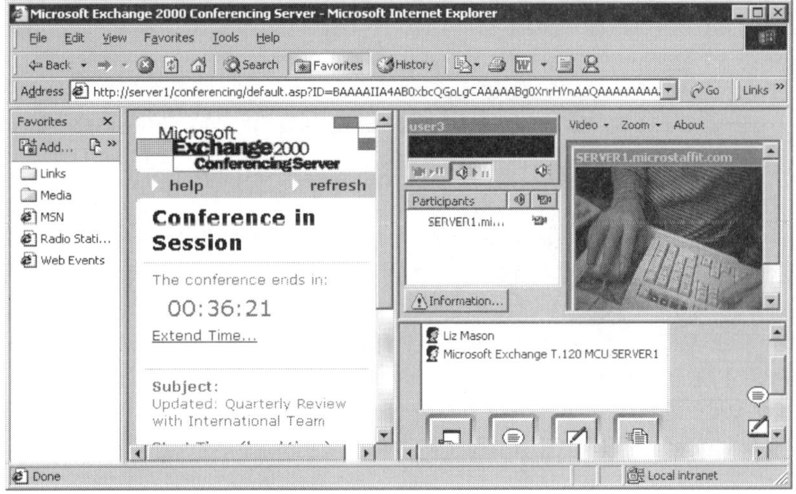

You can see in the left-hand pane that the conference is in session. The conference will end in 58 minutes, and the start date and time are noted. The organizer of the meeting is noted, and the user can send them an e-mail. If you are the organizer, it is possible here for you to extend the meeting or to change the resource.

You may decide to join another meeting going on at the same time, as shown in Figure 8.34.

Figure 8.34 Multimedia Conference in ECS

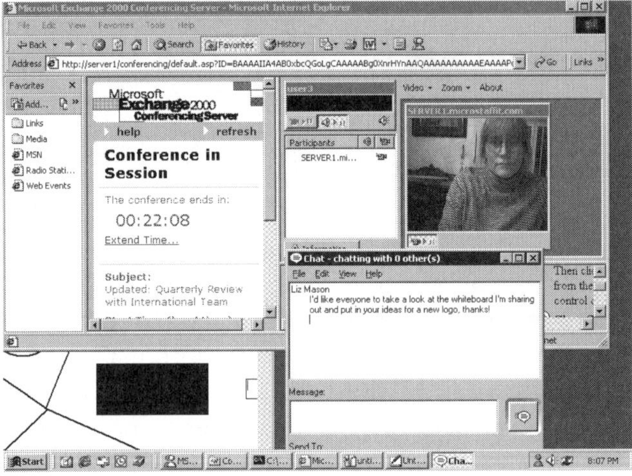

Here the participants, as well as the resources,, are noted in the middle of the pane. The icons at the bottom of the pane indicate you can share applications, transfer files, chat, and share a whiteboard. You can see on the right side of the pane that we have started a chat session, and that our video window is showing one individual.

Joining a Conference from Outlook Web Access

Let's say you decide to join the meeting with Outlook Web Access. You know you have a meeting scheduled that requires whiteboards, chatting, and sharing applications, so you need a T.120-compliant client. You'll also need a computer with NetMeeting 3.01 installed and IE 5.0. (A Frames Capable browser is a requirement, so you will need at least IE 4.01 or Netscape 4.5.). When you connect to the Exchange server at http://server1/exchange, you are directed to your home mailbox, for user3. Next, you return to your calendar and see a very similar calendar interface, as Figure 8.35 indicates.

Figure 8.35 Outlook Web Access View of Calendar

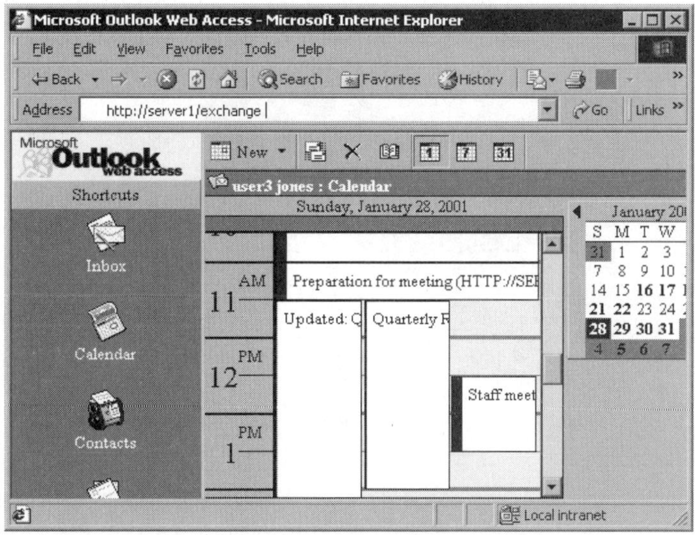

When you double-click the calendar appointment, the browser completes itself with:

```
HTTP://SERVER1/conferencing?id=BAAAAIIA4AB0xbcQGoLgCAAAAAgbIoO/X/
AAQAAAAAAAAAEAAAAAK/gsy48ZJtwaMiXarJgY=
```

You'll then be taken into the browser to join the conference in progress.

Scheduling a Conference with Outlook Web Access

Next you want to reserve a conference room via your browser interface. In Calendar, you create an appointment just as you did in Outlook 2000. Remember, when creating a meeting in pre-Outlook 2000 products or in a browser interface, you don't get the instant reservation confirmation and URL—you have to wait to get a message from the CMS, as in Figure 8.36.

Also, remember you can join a conference from the conference schedule Web page: http://*conferenceserver*/conferencing/list.asp.

Troubleshooting

There are many areas in which you can experience problems in ECS (we'll assume you can troubleshoot Exchange for any mailbox problems you may have). A simple way to determine what is going on is to look at error and auditing logs. First, check out the Event Viewer to see what it reports, and next, look at ECS-specific log files. Under C:\program files\Microsoft Exchange Conferencing Server\server1.ecs, you will find logfiles that contain

Figure 8.36 Response from CMS when Waiting for a Reservation Confirmation

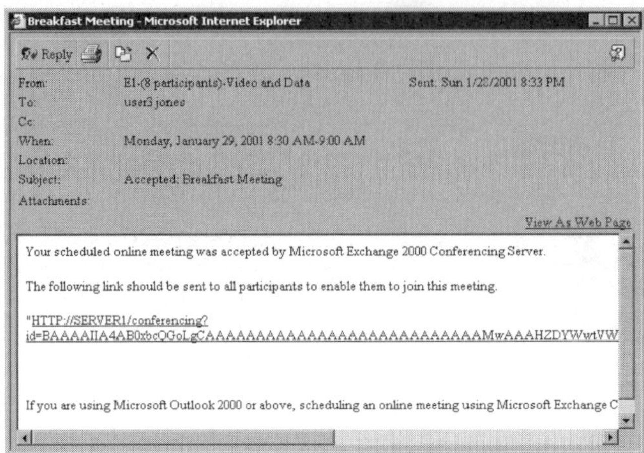

data on the Exchange Conferencing Server. The data collected can actually be configured in Exchange Conferencing Manager (ECM). In ECM, right-click the site name for the CMS log file, and right-click the Data Conference Provider for the ECS log file. Select which values you want logged, as in Figure 8.37.

Figure 8.37 Setting Logging Parameters for ECS

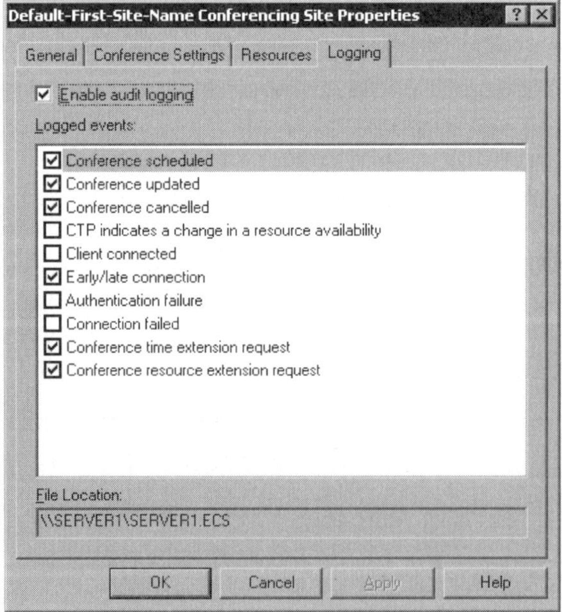

You should then find in C:\program files\Microsoft Exchange Conferencing Server\server1.ecs, (shared out as \\server\server1.ecs) the log files, as in Figure 8.38. These two log files should help you start troubleshooting client reservation and conference joining problems.

Figure 8.38 Files CMS20010117, DCS20010117 Containing ECS Logging Information

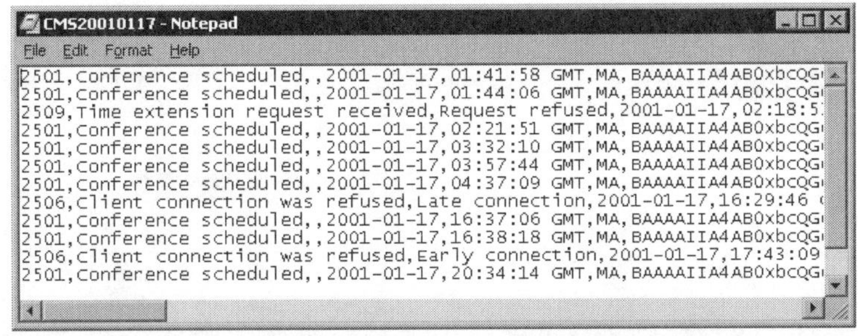

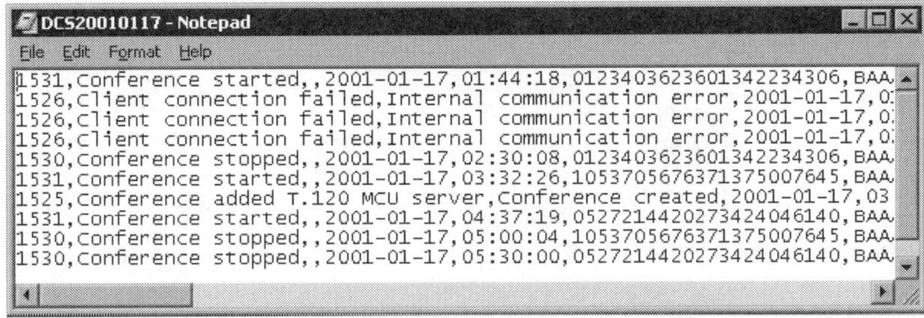

If you are unclear about what resources are reserved, you can open up your conference calendar mailbox, as in Figure 8.39, and review who has what resources reserved.

If you have problems with peripherals, try taking the peripherals out/off and then back on. If you have problems connecting to ECS, sometimes just waiting a few minutes helps (usually after a reboot you may mistakenly think the system is ready).

Finally, the On-Line Help can be *very* useful. Look for sections on troubleshooting the following:

- Exchange Conferencing Server

- Conference Management Service

- Data Conferencing Provider

- T.120 MCU Servers

- H.323 Bridge Servers

- Video Conferencing Providers

Figure 8.39 Conference Calendar Mailbox

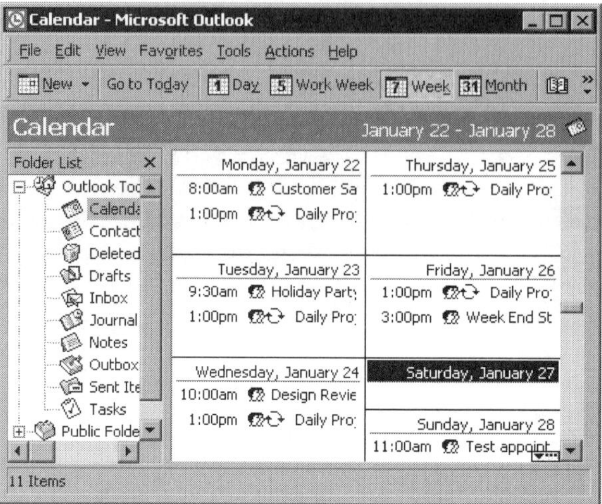

More Information

www.microsoft.com/exchange/productinfo/ECS_Support.htm

www.microsoft.com/exchange/techinfo/E2Kuptodate.htm

Exchange Conferencing Server Online Documentation

Exchange Conferencing Server Online Help

Exchange Online Documentation

Exchange Online Help

Summary

Microsoft provides three excellent real-time communication solutions in Exchange 2000. To implement these solutions successfully, it is important that you thoroughly understand your company's business communication needs. Instant Messaging can be useful when trying to get a quick answer to a problem or trying to find out if a peer is available. End-users understand e-mail addresses, so this could be an easy transition for them. Chat, although dwarfed by Exchange Conferencing Server, does have a place in the business world. You can reach out to customers who may not have video or audio conferencing facilities. You can initiate chat sessions on product lines, solicit feedback, and monitor a customer hotline. At a fairly low cost, you can be an ASP and create chat communities for your customers. In using

Exchange Conferencing Server, you can use technology that is probably already available in your company, purchase a few multimedia peripherals, and then begin communicating more frequently to geographically dispersed team members.

The key to implementing these products is testing and prototyping. Make sure you have spent some time understanding the products before implementing them live. Make sure your users understand the benefits of these products by promoting mini-workshops on scheduling and facilitating virtual conferences. Finally, monitor chat sessions and Exchange Conferences on a periodic basis to understand how participants use and view their new tools. This will help make your real-time program more successful.

FAQs

Visit **www.syngress.com/solutions** to have your questions about this chapter answered by the author.

Q: How do I use Instant Messaging to communicate with external users?

A: With Microsoft's products, you would install MSN Messenger Service and configure it to monitor internal to your organization using Exchange, and then external to your organization using the MSN Internet program. Other programs such as AOL cannot be currently monitored.

Q: How can chat help my company?

A: The public is Internet-savvy. They understand e-mail, Instant Messaging, and chat rooms. If you want to create a forum for customer feedback and input, chat (appropriately monitored) can do that. Also, a chat session with employees in different parts of the world may help reduce conference call costs.

Q: What client products work best with Microsoft Exchange 2000 Conferencing Server?

A: Outlook 2000 is the client product of choice. It integrates well with ECS, and offers you more functionality. You can use Outlook Web Access, and connect to your Exchange Server, and subsequently your Conference Resource as well. Currently IE 4.0 and Netscape 4.5 are the versions that are supported. Also, to meet your T.120 compliance requirement for data sharing, NetMeeting 3.01 works well.

Chapter 9

Application Service Providers

Solutions in this chapter:

- **Defining Application Service Providers**

- **Hosting Services Using Exchange 2000 and Active Directory**

- **Architecture for Shared Hosting**

- **Scaling Exchange 2000 and Active Directory**

- **Planning and Configuring the Active Directory and Exchange 2000 Hosting Infrastructure**

Introduction

Application Service Providers (ASPs) are having an increasing impact on how small- and medium-sized companies handle their messaging infrastructure. In today's Information Technology (IT) climate, it is very difficult and expensive to find administrators who can not only administer messaging services, but who can also configure, implement, and enhance those services.

An ASP can help companies by outsourcing the implementation, configuration, and maintenance of a variety of services, including messaging. Although companies will likely derive financial benefits from reduced cost of ownership, they will also reap the benefits of allowing their overutilized staff to concentrate on more important projects than commodity messaging.

This chapter covers the basic architecture of hosting Exchange 2000; it then covers configuring Active Directory and Exchange 2000. It is written assuming that "you," the reader, are an administrator or a manager in an ASP company. The configurations are specific to using Active Directory and Exchange 2000 in a hosting scenario. In many cases, the same configurations apply to a corporate environment as the hosting environment and, as such, are covered elsewhere in this book.

Defining Application Service Providers

An ASP provides access to applications (including the entire infrastructure for supporting that application) to customers who pay for access to the application in the form of a subscription. Customers access the application over the Internet or via a private leased line to the ASP's data center. Essentially, an ASP is an outsourced IT department or function for a company that "rents" an application. This would be similar to timeshare access to mainframe computers.

ASPs provide services in the form of delivering access to an application. These applications can include messaging, portals, Customer Relationship Management (CRM) applications, and financial applications.

ASP Definitions

ASPs define the level and quality of service that will be offered to a customer by developing a *Service Level Agreement* (SLA) with the customer. The SLA defines such parameters as response time for clients, storage quotas, availability of services, network bandwidth, concurrent users, and data recoverability. For example, a typical SLA may provide the following:

- Access 24 hours per day, seven days a week
- 1000 users full connectivity at all times
- Previous night restore of all data within four hours
- Guaranteed bandwidth of 512 Kbps
- Sub-second response time

An ASP needs to have sufficient monitoring and reporting capabilities in order to quantify the parameters of the SLA and determine if the SLA has been met. The SLA will also have provisions for enforcement of the SLA, which might include refunds or discounted service if the requirements of the SLA have not been met.

Provisioning is another important concept to define. In general, *provisioning* is the process by which services are made available to subscribers within an automated system. (Companies that utilize the services of an ASP are called *subscribers*.) Microsoft currently has sample code called Web Admin available that shows how Active Directory users and Exchange Mailboxes can be provisioned using a simple Web interface that could be accessed by subscribing companies' administrators. Microsoft also has a sophisticated, transactional provisioning system called Microsoft Administration and Provisioning System (MAPS) that takes eXtensible Markup Language (XML) definition files as input.

ISP vs. ASP

There is some overlap between what would be considered an ISP and an ASP. An ISP provides a network connection. Most ISPs also provide application services such as e-mail. Therefore, most ISPs are also ASPs. The primary differences are concurrency, services, and SLAs.

- ISPs provide bulk e-mail services using simple protocols such as Post Office Protocol v3 (POP3) and Internet Message Access Protocol v4 (IMAP4). ISPs typically have less stringent SLAs, with very little data recoverability built in. ISPs also have very different usage trends, where most subscribers are

Continued

> individual users who would use the services predominately in the evenings. The users of an ISP also have much less *concurrency*, that is, the number of users in the ISP that use the system at the same time.
>
> ■ ASPs may also provide simple messaging services, but can also provide high-end, or premium, messaging services such as calendaring. ASPs also have SLAs that may be much more specific, with tight provisions for performance and availability. Lastly, ASPs are essentially outsourcing the messaging services for a company, and can expect much greater concurrency.

NOTE

More information on Web Admin and MAPS is available on Microsoft's application hosting Web site at www.microsoft.com/apphosting.

ASP Messaging Service Models

ASPs can provide messaging services in a *dedicated service* or *shared service* model.

Dedicated Service Model

An ASP can offer a higher level of service that dedicates the hardware, Active Directory, and Exchange 2000 to a subscribing company. You would set up the infrastructure in the same way that you would in the shared service model described in the next section; however, only one subscriber company would be hosted on the server or servers, the Active Directory forest, and the Exchange 2000 organization. Other differences lie in how the infrastructure is managed and how the customer will connect to the ASP to access the services. Typically, a private network connection would be utilized. Management of the infrastructure would be the responsibility of the ASP; however, in a dedicated service model there is flexibility in allowing the customer some degree of management.

Shared Service Model

In a shared service model, multiple subscriber companies share a single Active Directory forest and domain. Subscribers are isolated from other subscribers by partitioning their users and groups into dedicated Organization Units (OUs). Further isolation is configured for Exchange 2000 Address Lists, so that different subscribers do not have access to each other's address information.

The shared service model is the recommended configuration for hosting Exchange 2000, because it allows you to host many users and subscriber companies on a single infrastructure. This allows hosting to be cost-effective for the subscriber—and more profitable for the ASP.

Hosting Services Using Exchange 2000 and Active Directory

All of the Exchange 2000 configuration data is stored in Active Directory, and Exchange 2000 will also use it for looking up recipient information. Active Directory will also host the directory data needed by your subscribers. Active Directory provides the database to store users and groups, as well as the Exchange 2000 configuration. It also authenticates users.

Exchange 2000 provides the ideal platform for hosting messaging services. In addition, Exchange 2000 offers collaborative services and extensive development opportunities that can be utilized, as well as support for many third-party applications that can enhance an ASP's service offerings. Depending on the SLA and service model that a customer subscribes to, Exchange 2000 can be very flexible in service offerings, as well as providing excellent scalability and reliability.

At the foundation of the ASP offering will be the core messaging services that allow the customer to send and receive messages, store messages, and access Exchange 2000 data using a Web client. These services include accessing and storing messages using the Messaging Application Program Interface (MAPI) and a MAPI client such as Outlook 2000, POP3, IMAP4, and the Web interface that is built into Exchange 2000: Outlook Web Access (OWA).

Using Exchange 2000 to Host Basic Messaging

You can provide access to basic messaging by utilizing the POP3/IMAP4 protocols to give subscribers the capability to receive messages, and Simple Mail Transfer Protocol (SMTP) to relay outgoing messages. This access is typically temporary, and subscribers will only connect to the servers to download or send messages. Therefore, the SLA for this type of service might not stipulate any provision for backup and restore of lost messages.

Using Exchange 2000 to Host Premium Messaging

MAPI provides a premium set of features for accessing data in Exchange 2000. Using MAPI, you can provide not only messaging, but also calendar, contact, and several other useful management features. MAPI clients also provide folder capabilities, which allow clients to create folders, move and copy messages between folders, as well as use the local Personal Folders for storing messages locally. MAPI clients also have access to Public Folders. In addition, MAPI clients can access Exchange 2000 Address Lists, which are not available when using the other protocols to access the core messaging services. (LDAP clients can access the Exchange 2000 Address Lists, but LDAP clients cannot access the core messaging services.) This directory capability is a great differentiator for a premium messaging service; it gives subscribers functionality they are potentially already using and will make the transition to hosted messaging smoother. You can also use MAPI and Outlook 2000 to provide customers with custom development features integrated with Outlook 2000, and to utilize the integration capabilities of Office 2000.

When providing MAPI services, you will most likely allow subscribers to store message data on the Exchange 2000 servers. This will impact how you architect the servers, and would be considered a premium service, including backup and restore elements dictated by the SLA.

Using Exchange 2000 to Host Basic Web Messaging

Many ASPs will want to make basic messaging available to subscribers via the Web, but they will not include the full feature set that is part of the default OWA client included in Exchange 2000. It is possible to create a custom Web page that reuses OWA components, such as the interface into the *inbox*, which allows users to send and receive messages. See Chapter 5 for more information on Exchange 2000 clients.

Using Exchange 2000 to Host Premium Web Messaging

The default OWA client that ships with Exchange 2000 is a full-featured messaging client that includes messaging, folder capabilities, calendar, contacts, and access to public folders. You can also use OWA to search the Exchange 2000 Address Lists for messaging recipients. As with premium messaging, subscriber data is stored on the Exchange 2000 server.

Hosting Other Services Integrated with Exchange 2000 and Active Directory

Although this chapter focuses on providing messaging capabilities with Exchange 2000 and Active Directory as the basis for your hosting platform, there are many possibilities beyond messaging to provide services to subscribers. These include real-time conferencing, instant messaging, custom applications, and third-party add-ons.

Exchange 2000 Conferencing Server

You can use Exchange 2000 to provide real-time conferencing services based on H.323- and T.120-compliant video and audio capabilities. Features include audio, video, chat, whiteboard, application sharing, and file transfer. See Chapter 8 for more information on Exchange 2000 Conferencing Server.

Exchange 2000 Instant Messaging

Exchange 2000 also includes Instant Messaging capabilities that allow for the immediate transmission of messages to other Instant Messaging contacts. Instant Messaging also includes presence information that allows other Instant Messaging users to monitor your status—such as busy, out of office, or on the phone. Again, see Chapter 8 for more information on Instant Messaging.

Custom Applications

Exchange 2000 provides an excellent platform for application development, whether via a Web browser, or with Outlook 2000 and Office 2000. The development environment is based on the Web Storage System, and includes a Software Development Kit (SDK) and tools for the developer.

NOTE

For more information on the Web Storage System SDK, visit the Microsoft Developers Network Web site at http://msdn.microsoft.com.

Third-Party Add-ons

There are many third-party add-on products for Exchange 2000. Some of the more effective hosting capabilities for third-party add-ons are virus protection, unified messaging, personal devices, fax products, and feature enhancements (such as adding a spelling checker to OWA).

Architecture for Shared Hosting

The Exchange 2000 and Active Directory hosting infrastructure can be complex, depending on the type of service you will be offering; the numbers of users and companies you will be hosting; the security requirements; and the SLA provisions for performance, reliability, and disaster recovery. Much will depend on the degree to which your architecture will need to scale to meet your SLA requirements.

This architectural overview below is based on a shared Active Directory forest and Exchange 2000 organization for the subscribers to the ASP's services. The other model would be a dedicated model; as mentioned in the previous section, the architecture would be the same.

Architectural Overview

Figure 9.1 shows an overview of a typical architecture for hosting Exchange 2000. It consists of a Demilitarized Zone (DMZ) and back-end servers.

DMZ

The DMZ contains several servers and optional services. The function of the DMZ is to protect the back-end servers from unauthorized or malicious connections from the Internet, similar to an enterprise DMZ. Any connections that originate from the Internet will pass through the DMZ and the Exchange front-end servers, which then make proxy client requests to the back-end servers. With this architecture, clients originating from the Internet never make direct connections to the back-end servers.

The DMZ contains the following servers and services: the outer firewall, the external Domain Name System (DNS), the Exchange 2000 front-end servers, Internet Protocol (IP) load-balancing services, security services, virtual private network (VPN) services, provisioning services, Operations Support Systems/Business Support Systems (OSS/BSS) services, and the inner firewall.

Outer Firewall

The outer firewall is the initial port-filtering mechanism that allows access from the Internet based on Transmission Control Protocol/User Datagram Protocol (TCP/UDP) ports.

Figure 9.1 Architectural Overview

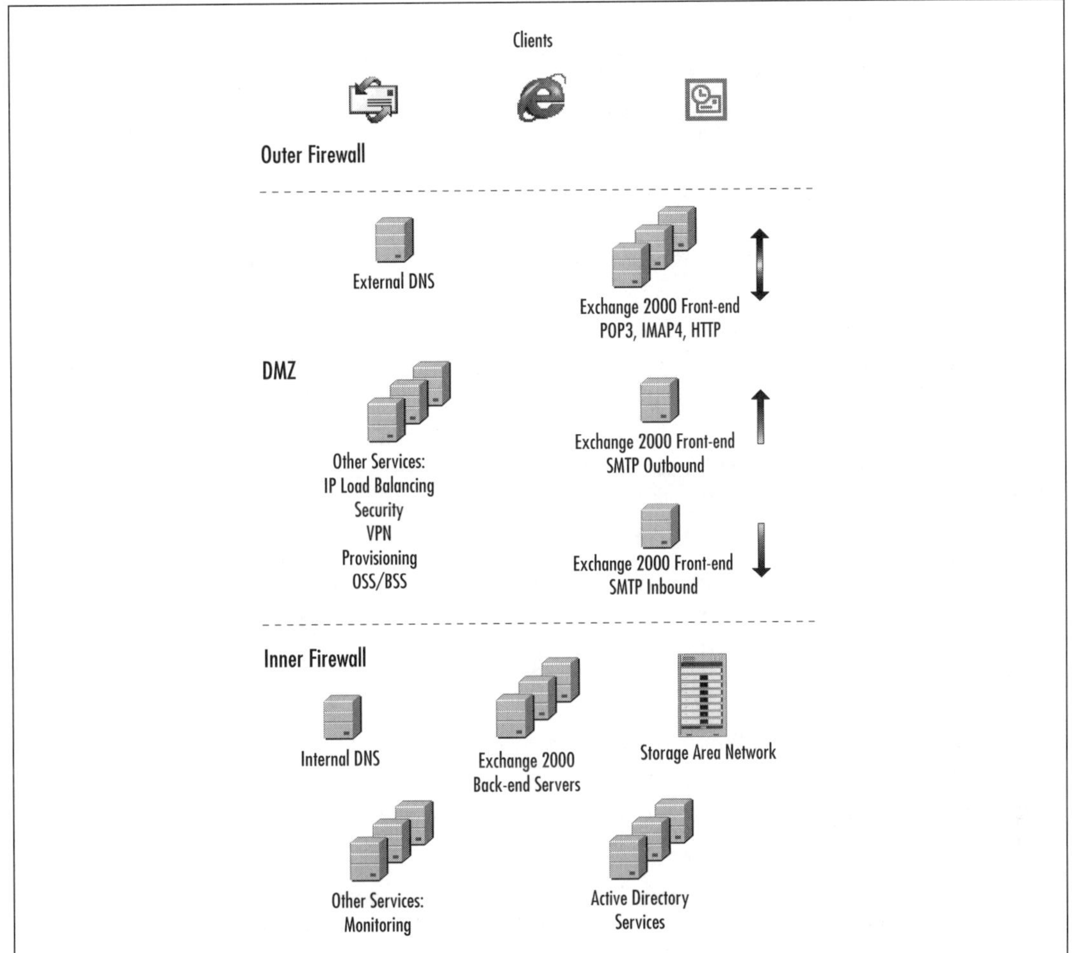

External DNS

The external DNS contains the necessary records to allow clients from the Internet to connect to the Exchange 2000 front-end servers. It contains only a subset of the DNS records for the ASP's systems. It also may contain some of your subscriber's DNS records if you are managing the namespace for your subscriber.

Exchange 2000 Front-end Servers

The front-end servers are the connection point for POP3, IMAP4, and Hypertext Transfer Protocol (HTTP) clients. The front-end servers then make proxy requests to the back-end server where the messages are located. Front-end servers provide several advantages in the Exchange 2000 architecture:

Unified Namespace You can configure one DNS name and point it to multiple front-end servers. A client does not have to be configured to connect to the specific back-end server that holds their mailbox, as the front-end server will proxy the request on behalf of the client making the connection. For example, you could create a DNS record for Company1 as mail.company1.com. This record would point to multiple IP addresses, one for each front-end server. This capability allows you to scale Exchange 2000 and spread the client connection load across multiple servers. You could also utilize an IP load-balancing solution to have one namespace that points to multiple front-end servers.

Offload Secure Sockets Layer (SSL) Processing The front-end servers can handle SSL-encrypted sessions for clients so that the back-end servers don't have to maintain these sessions.

Secure Server Placement Front-end servers can be placed in a DMZ that secures the back-end mailbox servers from outside connections. With this configuration, clients never need to connect to the back-end server—only the front ends make the connection.

NOTE

Front-end servers cannot communicate with back-end servers using SSL (only clear text connections are allowed); however, clients can connect to front-end servers using SSL. MAPI clients, such as Outlook 2000, cannot utilize a front end, and must connect directly to the back-end Exchange 2000 servers.

IP Load-Balancing Services

In order to obtain fault-tolerance and load balancing among the front-end servers, an IP load-balancing solution should be deployed.

Security Services

Various security services will need to be deployed, depending on requirements. These include Remote Authentication Dial-In User Service

(RADIUS), Proxy Services, anti-spam, and anti-virus services. These services may also include encryption, if you are not enabling encryption on the front-end servers.

VPN Services

These services will provide a connection point for clients that will be utilizing tunneling protocols to gain secure access to back-end services. These services will most likely be utilized in a premium messaging service that utilizes MAPI and Outlook clients.

Provisioning Services

Automated provisioning services allow subscribers to create, or *provision*, their accounts and mailboxes. For example, you can implement a provision service that may let you enter user identification information on a Web site. The provisioning system would than automatically create an Active Directory user and Exchange 2000 mailbox and, additionally, set up the necessary billing information to charge the subscriber company.

OSS/BSS Services

Any billing or other subscriber services could be located in the DMZ to facilitate subscriber access.

Inner Firewall

The inner firewall provides very limited access for the servers in the DMZ to access back-end servers. This prevents any other unauthorized access from outside the DMZ.

Back-end Servers

The back-end servers contain the directory and messaging servers, as well as the following optional services: the Exchange 2000 back-end servers, storage area network servers (SANS), the internal DNS, Active Directory servers, and monitoring services.

Exchange 2000 Back-end Servers

These servers store the subscriber message data. Front-end servers connect to the back-end server to retrieve messages for clients using the POP3, IMAP4, or HTTP protocols (see Figure 9.2). MAPI clients connect to the back-end servers directly to retrieve their messages.

Figure 9.2 Client Connections to Front-end and Back-end Servers

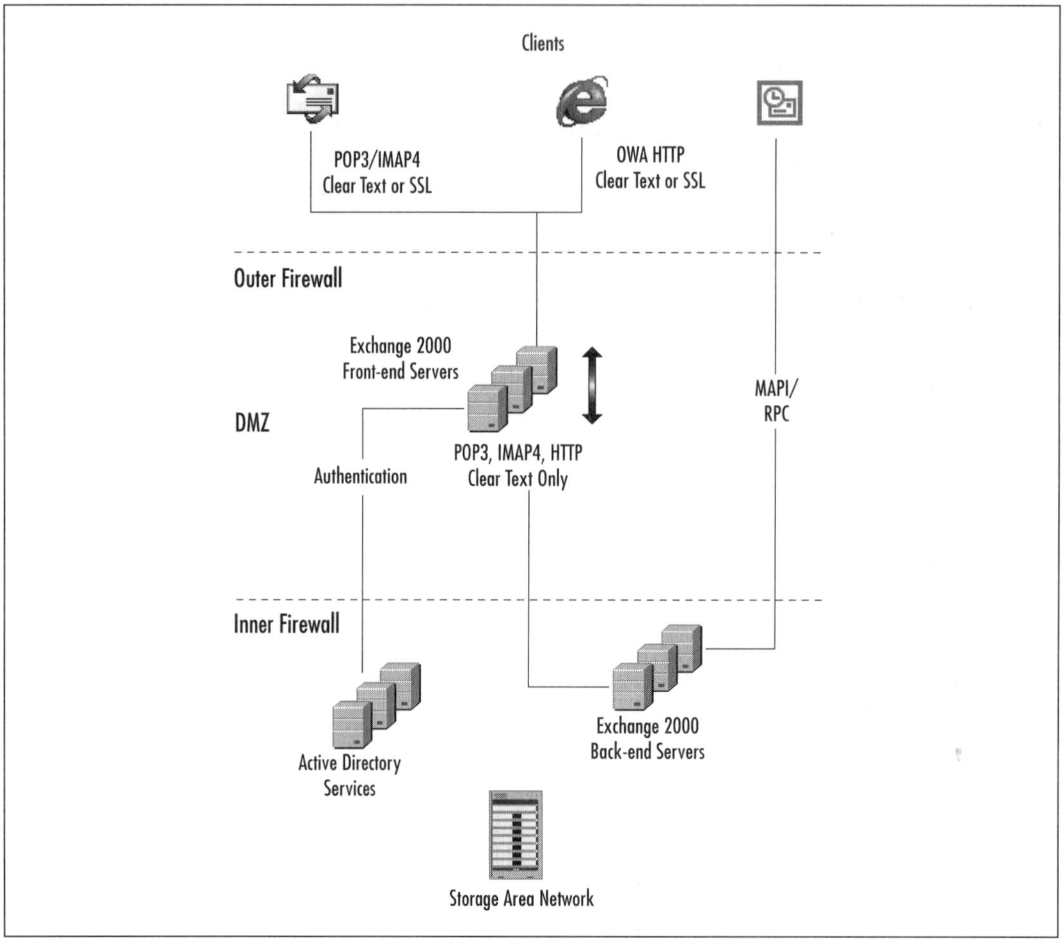

Storage Area Network Servers

The Exchange 2000 databases can be stored on a storage area network (SAN). Using a SAN and striping with mirroring or parity is one of the primary conditions for determining scalability of the back-end Exchange 2000 servers.

Internal DNS

The internal DNS contains records for the back-end servers, as well as servers in the DMZ. In addition, the internal DNS contains all necessary records for Active Directory. The internal DNS will only be used by these servers, and would not be accessed by clients outside of the back-end server or DMZ.

Active Directory Servers

These include the domain controllers and Global Catalogs for the Active Directory forest. In most environments, starting with two domain controllers that are also Global Catalogs will be sufficient. As the number of directory objects grows, more domain controllers and Global Catalogs will need to be added. Table 9.1 gives you some guidelines on how many domain controllers and Global Catalogs are necessary for a given number of subscriber users.

Table 9.1 Domain Controller Sizing

Server Configuration	250,000 Users	500,000 Users	1,000,000 Users
Number of Processors	4	4	4
RAM (GB)	3	3	4
Number of DC Servers	2	3	4

Monitoring Services

In order to quantify how well you are meeting the requirements of your SLA, you will need detailed monitoring to collect the metrics defined in the SLA. For example, if you have a requirement in your SLA for sub-second response time, then you would need a tool that measures and reports server latency based on the ports being used by the subscribing company. There are several commercially available monitoring tools that have this capability.

Scaling Exchange 2000 and Active Directory

Scaling Exchange 2000 and Active Directory for use in an ASP environment is important in achieving an economy of scale with a set investment in an infrastructure. You want to be able to start with ample capacity and scalability in order to add subscribers quickly without having to modify your hardware to do so. In a shared model, subscribers will share the same infrastructure, so in order to capitalize on your hardware investment, you want to be able to scale the platform to as many subscribers as possible.

Scaling Exchange 2000 for an ASP is similar to the corporate environment, except that an ASP environment could potentially host hundreds of thousands or millions of users on a single Exchange 2000 and Active Directory infrastructure. Scaling for an ASP is primarily a factor of meeting the requirements of the SLA with a minimum investment in hardware, and then making configuration changes to the hardware as subscribers are added. The SLA may have provisions for a certain response time or specifications for a certain amount of storage quota. So scaling is necessary to be able to meet current and future performance and storage requirements.

Performance is a matter of reducing bottlenecks to achieve the desired result. The primary bottlenecks for Exchange 2000 and Active Directory are memory, processor, and disk access speed. Scaling to reduce these bottlenecks can be achieved by *scaling up*, which involves expanding the capacity of the server by augmenting memory, process, and disk access speeds. Scaling can also be achieved by *scaling out*, which is simply adding more back-end or front-end servers. In the case of disk access speed, you can add spindles to a stripe set until you reach the performance objective.

Storage requirements can be met simply by scaling up your servers—that is, by adding more disk capacity to the SAN. However, part of the planning for your Exchange configuration will be how many stores and storage groups to configure, and how many users to put on each store. Although it is possible to continue adding users to a store—and the corresponding disk space to accommodate those users and their quotas—until you reach maximum performance limits, you still might have elements of your SLA that require minimum restore times. This can limit the number of users you will put on a store, hence the number of users on a server, based on how long it will take to restore a particular store. In this case, you might need to scale out (by adding more servers) to meet storage capacity requirements.

Planning and Configuring the Active Directory and Exchange 2000 Hosting Infrastructure

Planning your hosting infrastructure involves determining the configuration that will meet the SLAs you have in place with subscribers. In a shared model, you will plan your infrastructure so that subscriber companies are isolated from each other.

There are also several specific configuration changes that need to be implemented as part of deploying Exchange 2000 and Active Directory in a hosted environment. This section will outline some of the planning details and configuration changes that will need to be made, or specific configurations for hosting that go beyond what has previously been discussed in this book. Two fictitious companies, *company1* and *company2* will be used as an example in the sample configurations in this section.

> **WARNING**
>
> This section contains steps that will instruct you to make changes to Active Directory and the registry. Make sure you have a backup of your data and understand how the utilities work before making any changes to Active Directory or the registry.

Windows 2000 and Active Directory

We'll begin with configuring Windows 2000 and Active Directory for hosting, after which we will configure Exchange 2000.

Forest and Domains

In the shared model documented in this chapter there would be one Active Directory forest and one domain. This architecture supports the shared model, and allows you to minimize complexity in your shared architecture.

It is possible to give a particular subscriber a dedicated domain that is part of your shared forest so that they would have more control over their administration, security, and configuration; however, this would complicate your shared architecture. If possible, you would want to dedicate a forest and domain to subscribers that have more extensive requirements.

Domain Controllers and Global Catalogs

Domain controllers should be made Global Catalogs to facilitate better performance for Exchange lookups.

When installing Active Directory on the first domain controller, ensure that you set the Permissions option to be compatible only with Windows 2000 Server. This option is presented during the DCPromo process when you establish the forest, and will configure the environment to be more secure. Specifically, it omits the Pre-Windows 2000-Compatible Access built-in group from having read access to many of the directory objects.

User Identification

Users that are part of subscriber organizations will need to be uniquely identified within the forest and domain. There are three account attributes that need to be unique:

- E-mail Addresses (e.g., SMTP)

- User Principal Name (UPN)

- Pre-Windows 2000 User Logon Name

E-mail addresses must be unique and are automatically generated by Exchange 2000 Recipient Polices. The user portion of the SMTP address is derived from the alias defined for the user when creating their Exchange 2000 mailbox. Although the alias itself does not have to be unique, the full SMTP address must be unique. Typically the user portion of the SMTP address will match the user portion of the UPN.

The UPN is a user identification that takes the format of an SMTP address. It is comprised of a user portion (the prefix) and a domain portion (the suffix) in the following format:

```
user@<upn_suffix>
```

For example, if we have a user called *user1* at *company1*, their UPN would be *user1@company1.com*. Using a UPN suffix that matches the subscriber company domain allows us to have multiple users in the Active Directory that may have the same user name, but still maintain uniqueness between companies because the UPN will be different. However, you will still have to have unique user names for the users that share a common UPN suffix. Depending on the messaging service being hosted, you may use the UPN for all subscriber logon authentication.

Adding a UPN Suffix

You can use the Active Directory Domains and Trusts Microsoft Management Console (MMC) to add the UPN suffixes for the subscriber companies you will host. Go to the properties of Active Directory Domains and Trusts and add UPN suffixes as shown in Figure 9.3.

Clients that do not authenticate using Kerberos or that do not support UPN logon subsequently utilize the Pre-Windows 2000 User Logon Name. The Pre-Windows 2000 user name must be unique across the domain. It takes the following format:

```
<AD_Domain_Netbios_Name>\user
```

The user portion is identical to the same value as the user portion defined for the UPN. However, since it must be unique itself across the domain, you must change it. A useful format is to use the company name as part of the user name for the user portion of the Pre-Windows 2000 account. In our example of *user1* from *company1*, you could use the format *user1@company1*. So, the full Pre-Windows 2000 account would be in the following format:

```
<AD_Domain_Netbios_Name>\user1@company1
```

Figure 9.3 Adding a UPN Suffix

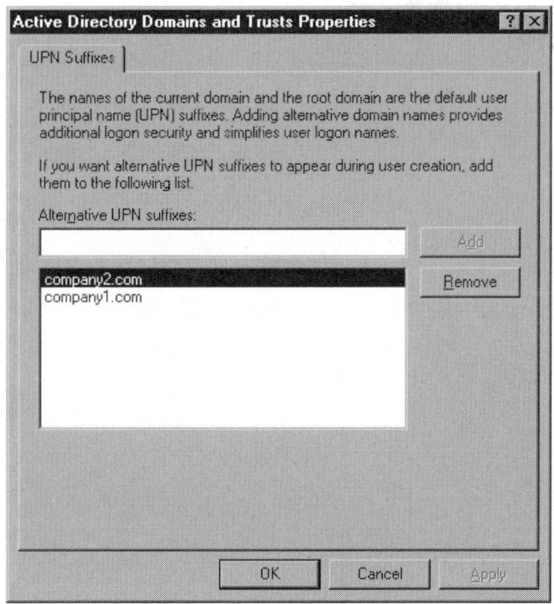

You will also use this format for the Pre-Windows 2000 account name value for distribution and security groups.

Creating Organizational Units

In order to isolate subscriber companies you can use Organizational Units (OUs) to partition a particular company's users and groups from each other. It is best to first create a parent OU, and then specific company OUs. Figure 9.4 shows the OU structure for *company1* and *company2*.

The parent OU hosting in Figure 9.4 is necessary so that you have the flexibility to modify the configuration of your subscriber OUs without affecting the system level containers, such as the Users container, under the domain.

Configuring Security Groups

Once you have configured the UPN, decided on the format of the Pre-Windows 2000 account, and created your OUs, you can create the subscriber's security groups for the users and administrators of each subscriber company in order to secure objects in Active Directory and Exchange 2000. The following are examples of the security group accounts you will need:

Figure 9.4 Organization Units

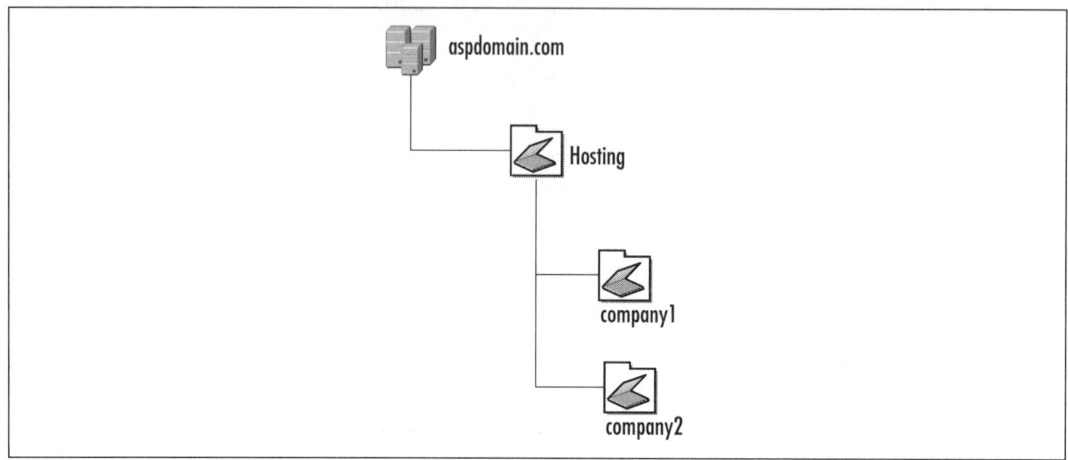


```
Name: Allusers@customer1

Pre-Windows 2000 account name: allusers@customer1

Name: Admins@customer1

Pre-Windows 2000 account name: admins@customer1
```

Do not establish an e-mail address for these security groups. If your subscriber needs groups for distributing mail, use Distribution Groups.

Securing Organization Units

You need to secure the OUs you have created for your subscribers in order to isolate them from a security standpoint. With OUs properly secured, users from other subscriber companies will not have access to another subscriber's directory data; therefore, they will not be able to access directory information, such as phone numbers, in another subscriber's OU.

There are two basic steps for securing your subscriber OUs. First, you need to secure them so that only users from the subscriber can view the contents of the OUs, and second, the list of OUs under the parent hosting OU needs to be secured so that a user can only list the OU they are a member of. In order to use list permissions, Active Directory must first be enabled to use List Object Permissions.

NOTE

Enabling List Object Permissions will also be needed for securing address lists, which will be discussed later in the chapter.

Use the following steps to enable List Object Permissions:

1. Use ADSIEdit.exe to edit the properties of the following object:

   ```
   cn=directoryservice,cn=windowsnt,cn=services,cn=configuration,dc=
   <AD Domain Components>
   ```

2. Set the dsHeuristics attribute to 001, and then close the Properties windows.

NOTE

ADSIEdit.exe is part of the Windows 2000 Support Tools on the Windows 2000 Server CD.

Now that you have enabled List Object Permissions for Active Directory, you will add the subscriber Allusers security groups to the Hosting OU for List Object Access. Use the following steps to allow List Object Permissions on the Hosting OU:

1. Right-click the Hosting OU and then click Properties.
2. Click the Security tab.
3. Clear the Allow inheritable permissions from parent to propagate to this object check box.
4. Click Copy to copy the parent permissions to the Hosting OU.
5. Highlight Authenticated Users, and then click Remove.
6. Click Add, and then double-click the Allusers@company1 security group.
7. Click OK.
8. Click Advanced.
9. Highlight the Allusers@company1 group, and then click View/Edit.
10. Uncheck all checkboxes except for the allow checkbox next to List Object, and Read All Properties.
11. Click OK, OK, and then OK to close the Hosting OU properties dialog box.
12. Repeat for each subscriber company Allusers security group.

TIP

To streamline some of the permissions processes you can create a security group that has all of the subscriber Allusers groups as members, and then use this group to apply the List Object Permissions on the Hosting OU.

Now you can secure your subscriber OUs so that only members of the subscribers Allusers group can see the contents of their corresponding OU. Use the following steps to secure your subscriber OUs:

1. Right-click the Customer1 OU, and then click Properties.

2. Click the Security tab.

3. Highlight the Authenticated Users, and then click Remove.

4. Click Add.

5. Double-click the Allusers@customer1 security group, and then click OK.

6. Verify that the Allow check box next to the Read permission is checked.

NOTE

You should also remove the Authenticated Users built-in group from the default system containers in Active Directory, such as the Builtin, Computers, Domain Controllers, and Users containers.

Now your OUs are secured from reading and listing the contents.

External DNS

If you will be handling namespace management for your subscribers, you will need to create a primary zone in the external DNS for the subscribers DNS domain. Additionally, you will need to create Mail Exchange (MX) and Host (A) records for your subscriber domain that point to your Exchange 2000 front-end servers. Typically you would have an A record such as mail.company1.com that would point to one or more front-end servers, or to an IP Load Balancing service. The MX record would point to your inbound SMTP server or servers or your IP Load Balancing service.

Additionally, your external DNS will need to be able to accomplish name resolution for all of the back-end Exchange 2000 servers, as well as the Active Directory Servers.

Internal DNS

The internal DNS should be located on your Active Directory domain controllers and configured as "Active Directory integrated." Depending on how you have configured your front-end servers, you may also need to add records for your front-end servers so that the back-end servers can resolve their host names. Typically, your front-end servers will be using the internal Active-Directory-integrated DNS as their primary DNS, and will automatically add host records via dynamic update. If this is the case, you will not need to manually add any records for the front-end servers to the internal DNS.

Configuring Exchange 2000

Now that you have configured Active Directory and Windows 2000, you can begin configuring Exchange 2000 for hosting.

Configuring Front-end Exchange 2000 Servers

Use the following steps to enable an Exchange 2000 server as a front-end server:

1. Bring up the properties of the Server object in Exchange System Manager.

2. Check the This is a Front-end server check box, and then click OK.

3. Restart the IISAdmin service.

Configuring Recipient Policies

The Recipient Policy applies e-mail addresses to users and groups. In our example, we have *company1* and *company2*. Users in *company1* need an SMTP address applied that matches the format user@*company1.com*, and users in *company2* need an SMTP address that matches the format user@*company2.com*.

You will need to ensure that only users in *company1* get the *company1* SMTP address. You will accomplish this by creating the Recipient Policy and configuring an LDAP filter to find the correct users. You have great flexibility in creating your LDAP filter, and the following example will work, but you may find other filters that better fit your requirements. You will create LDAP filters that will search for users based on their Pre-Windows 2000 account names. The guidelines established in this chapter dictate that users and distribution groups have the format that uniquely identifies the object within the domain. For example, *user1* in *company1* would have a Pre-Windows 2000 account name of *user@company1*. A distribution group in *company1* would have the format groupname@*company1* for its Pre-Windows 2000 account name. The following example shows the LDAP filter that will be configured for *Company1*:

```
(&(|(&(objectCategory=person)(objectClass=user))(objectCategory=group))(
samAccountName=*company1))
```

In this LDAP filter you are searching for users or groups that have a Pre-Windows 2000 Account Name that ends in *company1*. The attribute 'samAccountName' is the Pre-Windows 2000 account name.

The Recipient Policy will apply the *@company1.com* SMTP address to all users that match this LDAP filter. In this Recipient Policy, we will also remove the default SMTP address for the domain, as this will not be needed in our configuration.

WARNING

The default domain SMTP address is required for Outlook Web Access to function correctly if you will be using the default Exchange virtual directory. In our configuration we will be creating custom virtual directories for each subscriber company, so the default SMTP address is not necessary.

To create the Recipient Policy for subscribers, use the following steps:

1. Open Exchange System Manager and expand the Recipients container.

2. Right-click Recipient Polices, and then click New, Recipient Policy..

3. Enter Company1 as the name of the Recipient Policy, and then click Modify.

4. In the Find drop-down box, select Custom Search, and then click the Advanced tab.

5. Figure 9.5 shows the LDAP filter we will be in adding in this step. In the LDAP Query box enter the following LDAP filter:

```
(&(|(&(objectCategory=person)(objectClass=user))(objectCategory=
group))(samAccountName=*company1))
```

6. Click Find Now to verify the query is functioning correctly, and then click OK.

Figure 9.5 Recipient Policy LDAP Filter for Company1

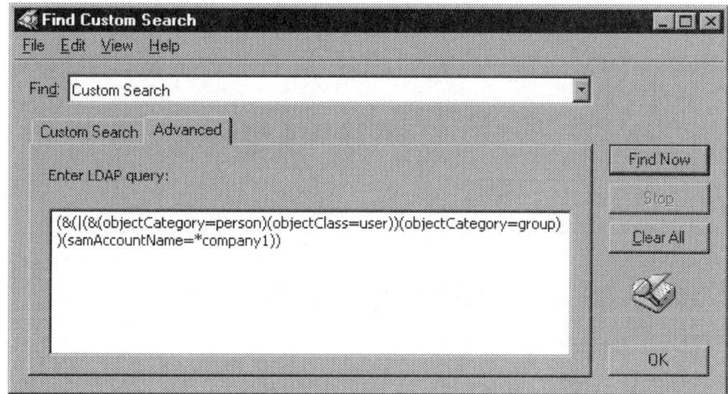

7. Click OK on the message.

8. Click the E-Mail Addresses tab.

9. Click New…, highlight SMTP, and then click OK.

10. In the Address field enter @company1.com, and then click OK.

11. Check the box next to the new SMTP address to enable it, and then click Set as Primary.

12. Remove the check in the box next to the default SMTP address that matches the domain, to disable it. The E-Mail Addresses configuration should be as shown in Figure 9.6.

Figure 9.6 Recipient Policy E-Mail Addressees for Company1

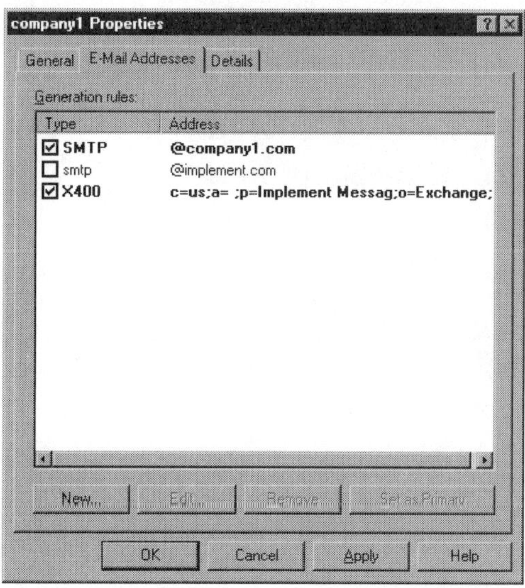

13. Click OK, and then Yes to complete the creation of the Recipient policy for *company1*.

14. Repeat for each subscriber company.

Configuring SMTP Connectors

Although all of the Exchange 2000 servers use SMTP natively, you will be using dedicated SMTP bridgeheads to be able to handle message traffic.

Configuring Mail Directories

By default, SMTP servers will spool messages awaiting delivery in the Exchange 2000 install directory structure. For better throughput on your SMTP servers, you can configure the SMTP mail directories in a different location than the default. For best performance you can move them to a disk subsystem or SAN that supports striping with parity or striping a mirror set.

Use the following steps to move the SMTP mail directories:

1. Stop all Exchange and Internet Information Services.

2. Move the 'vsi 1' directory under the Mailroot directory located in your Exchange server directory structure to the desired location.

3. Open ADSIEdit and bring up the properties for the following object:

```
CN=1,CN=SMTP,CN=Protocols,CN=<server name>,CN=Servers,CN=First
Administrative Group,CN=Administrative Groups,CN=<organization
name>,CN=Microsoft
Exchange,CN=Services,CN=Configuration,DC=<Domain Components>
```

4. Set the path to the new location for the following attributes:

   - msExchSmtpBadMailDirectory

   - msExchSmtpPickupDirectory

   - msExchSmtpQueueDirectory

5. Restart the Microsoft Exchange System Attendant and verify that that three 1005 events in the Windows 2000 Event Log, Application View, have been generated—indicating that the paths in the metabase were updated.

6. Restart the Exchange server.

Outbound SMTP Server

For the outbound SMTP server, you will configure an SMTP connector with the default address space (*). This bridgehead will then be used by all of the back-end servers to transfer messages destined for outbound connections.

You will also want to configure the outbound SMTP server to use the external DNS for name resolution when transferring messages. By default the SMTP bridgehead will use the internal DNS, but for message transfer, you can configure it to use the external DNS by using the following steps:

1. Right-click the SMTP virtual server on your outbound SMTP bridgehead.
2. Click the Delivery tab, and then click the Advanced button.
3. Click the Configure button, and then enter the IP address for the external DNS.

Inbound SMTP Server

The inbound SMTP server does not require any specific configuration; however, the MX records configured in the external DNS should be configured to point to the inbound SMTP server or servers.

Configuring Address Lists

Address lists are only available to MAPI clients. However, address lists and the address book are compelling reasons for utilizing a premium messaging service. Remember, they do need to be secured, so if a MAPI client subscriber looks at the address book, they only see the address lists and entries from their own subscriber company. Users have access to the default Global Address Lists and you can create optional address lists for a subscriber.

Configuring the Default Global Address List

Before creating a default Global Address List for your subscriber companies, you should first delete the default Global Address List in the system. Use the following steps to delete the default Global Address List:

1. Open Exchange System Manager.
2. Expand the Recipients, All Global Address Lists.
3. Right-click the Default Global Address Lists, and then click Delete.
4. Click Yes on the confirmation message.

Now you can create a default Global Address List for your subscriber company. You will define membership of the list by defining an LDAP filter similar to the one used for the Recipient Policy created earlier. In this LDAP filter, membership will be defined using the SMTP e-mail address for a specific customer. You will create one Global Address List per subscriber company. Users will only see one Global Address List, and in this case it will be the one they are a member of. Exchange will not show them a Global Address List of which they are not a member.

Use the following steps to create a default Global Address List for *company1*:

1. Open Exchange System Manager.

2. Expand the Recipients, All Global Address Lists.

3. Right-click All Global Address Lists, and then click New, Global Address List.

4. Enter Company1 in the Address List name box, and then click Filter Rules…

5. Click Field, User, E-mail Address.

6. In the Condition drop-down box, select Ends with, and then enter company1.com in the Value box.

7. Click Add, and then Find Now to verify the list contents.

8. Click OK, and then Finish to create the Global Address List.

9. Repeat for each subscriber company.

Configuring Address Lists

Custom address lists can also be created and should be based on hierarchy that uses the subscriber company name that has an address lists container that does not have entries, except for other address lists. Although this is not required, it allows you to add multiple address lists under that parent and have the correct permission automatically propagate from the parent. Otherwise you would have to manipulate the permissions on every address list you add. Figure 9.7 shows the address lists in System Manager created for *company1* and *company2*.

TIP

To create empty parent address list containers that will hold your subscriber address lists, create the address list, go to the Filter Rules, and then uncheck all of the recipient types that the list could show. The address list will then be empty of recipients, and you can add more address lists.

Figure 9.7 Address List Hierarchy

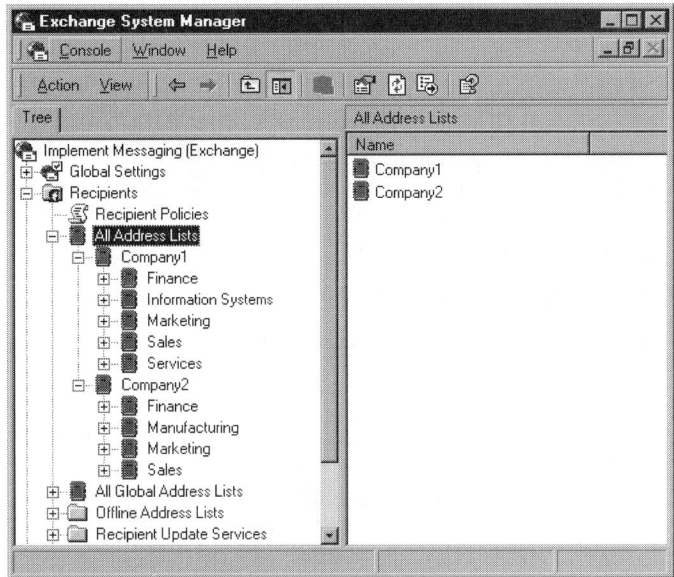

Securing Address Lists

Global Address Lists and address lists must be secured to isolate a particular company's address book information.

Use the following steps to secure the default Global Address List:

1. Open Exchange System Manager.

2. Expand Recipients, All Global Address Lists.

3. Right-click the Company1, and then click Properties.

4. Click the Security tab.

5. Clear the Allow inheritable permissions from parent to propagate to this object check box, and then click Copy.

6. Highlight Authenticated Users, and then click Remove.

7. Click Add, double-click the Allusers@company1 group, and then click OK.

8. Highlight the Allusers@company1 group, and then clear all permissions except for the following: Read, Execute, Read Permissions, List contents, Read properties, List object, Open address list.

9. Click OK, and then click Yes to acknowledge the message regarding Deny permissions.

10. Repeat for all subscriber global address lists.

When securing address lists you will establish security on the parent address list container using the same steps used to secure the Global Address List. If you do not want to use the parent container, you can create multiple address lists for subscriber companies based on the root All Address Lists container, but you will have to apply permissions on each address list to secure them. In addition, you will also have to secure the All Address Lists container so users can only view it and the parent containers they have access to. This is similar to how we secured Organizational Units earlier in the chapter, and as such, it requires that Active Directory have List Object Permissions enabled.

Use the following steps to secure the All Address Lists container:

1. Open Exchange System Manager.
2. Expand Recipients, All Address Lists.
3. Right-click All Address Lists, and then click Properties.
4. Click the Security tab.
5. Clear the Allow inheritable permissions from parent to propagate to this object check box, and then click Copy.
6. Highlight Authenticated Users, and then click Remove.
7. Click Add, double click the Allusers@company1 group, and then click OK.
8. Highlight the Allusers@company1 group, and then clear all permissions except for the following: Read properties, List object, and Open address list.
9. Click OK.
10. Repeat for all subscriber groups.

TIP

To streamline some of the permissions processes, you can create a security group that has all of the subscriber *Allusers* groups as members, and then use this group to apply the List Object Permissions on the All Address Lists container.

Now you can secure the parent address list containers for your subscriber companies:

1. Open Exchange System Manager.

2. Expand Recipients, All Address Lists.

3. Right-click the Company1, and then click Properties.

4. Click the Security tab.

5. Clear the Allow inheritable permissions from parent to propagate to this object check box, and then click Copy.

6. Highlight Authenticated Users, and then click Remove.

7. Also remove any Alluser groups inherited from the All Address Lists container.

8. Click Add, double-click the Allusers@company1 group, and then click OK.

9. Highlight the Allusers@company1 group, and then clear all permissions except for the following: Read, Execute, Read Permissions, List contents, Read properties, List object, Open address list.

10. Click OK, and then click Yes to acknowledge the message regarding Deny permissions.

11. Repeat for all subscriber parent address list containers.

Now you can add custom address lists for subscriber companies, and they will inherit their correct permissions from the parent address list container. Once the address list has been secured, only members of the specific subscribers *Allusers* group will be able to see them.

In Figure 9.8, we see what user1 in company1 can view in the Address Book on Outlook 2000.

Figure 9.8 User1 Address Book

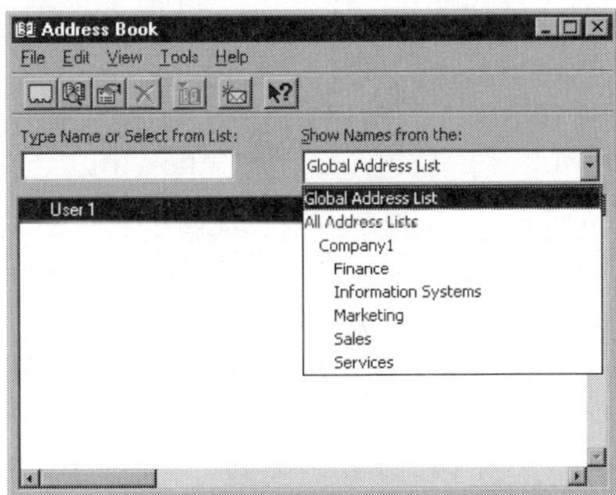

In Figure 9.9, we see what user2 in company2 can view in the Address Book on Outlook 2000.

Figure 9.9 User2 Address Book

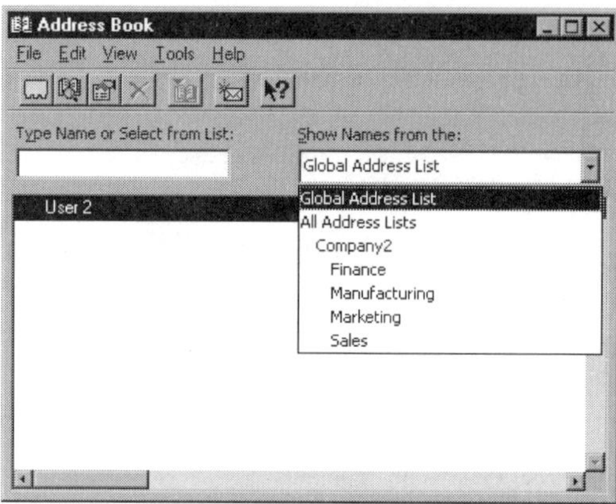

Configuring POP3/IMAP4

There is very little that is different between ASP hosting and regular corporate configurations when configuring POP3 and IMAP4. You can, however, turn off unneeded services. The Microsoft Exchange Information Store (MSExchangeIS), Microsoft Exchange Message Transfer Agent (MTA) stacks, and Microsoft Exchange System Attendant (MSExchangeSA) services are not needed, and they can be changed to a manual startup. In addition, the default Mailbox Store and Public Folder Store are not needed, and they can be deleted. You will need to modify the startup of the POP3 and IMAP4 service to remove the dependency on the MSExchangeIS service.

Use the following steps to remove the MSExchangeIS dependency:

1. Open Regedt32.exe.

2. Remove 'MSExchangeIS' from the following keys:

```
HKEY_LOCAL_MACHINE\System\CurrentControlSet\Services\IMAP4SVC
and POP3SVC\DepenedOnService
```

You can now change System Attendant and Information Store to manual, remove the Public and Mailbox stores, and restart POP3 and IMAP4.

Configuring HTTP

There are several steps for configuring HTTP for use in a hosting environment.

Configuring Virtual Directories

You will create a virtual directory for each company on both the front-end and back-end Exchange servers. The virtual directories must be configured to use the domain that matches the subscriber company SMTP domains you configured when creating your Recipient Policies, because OWA will look for a user based on their SMTP addresses when specifying the alias in the URL. For example, if you are accessing OWA by specifying the default Exchange virtual directory using the following syntax:

```
http://server/exchange/alias
```

With the above syntax, Exchange will try and find the user in Active Directory by combining the alias portion of the URL with the SMTP domain the virtual directory is configured for. In this case, it would be alias@defaultdomain.com.

However, our example user's SMTP address is user1@company1.com, as a result of the Recipient Policy we created earlier. In Figure 9.10, you can see the dialog box brought up when creating a virtual directory that will allow you to specify the SMTP domain the virtual directory will be created for.

Figure 9.10 Virtual Directory Domains

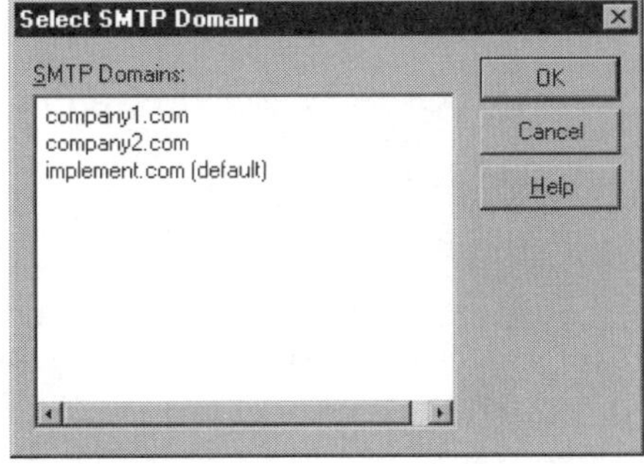

So, we need to create virtual directories that are configured for the subscriber SMTP domains so that when user1 logs onto OWA with the following URL, then the Exchange server will be able to find the user object in Active Directory:

```
http://server/company1/user1
```

With this syntax, Exchange will look for *user1@company1.com*, and be able to find the user object in Active Directory.

To configure subscriber virtual directories:

1. Open Exchange System Manager.

2. Expand Administrative Groups, First Administrative Group, Servers, <Front-end server>, Protocols, HTTP.

3. Right-click Exchange Virtual Server, and then click New, Virtual Directory.

4. Enter company1 in the Name text box, and then click Modify.

5. Click company1.com, and then click OK.

6. Click OK to create the virtual directory.

7. Repeat for each subscriber company.

8. Repeat for back-end Exchange servers.

NOTE

Because the default Exchange alias will not work for users who do not have the default SMTP domain as an address, you should restrict access to this virtual directory.

Configuring UPN Logon

By default, users will log on to OWA using the following syntax:

```
<AD_netbios_domain_name>\pre-windows 2000 account
```

For example, *user1* logging into OWA would use the following syntax:

```
Aspdomain\user1@company1
```

It is also possible to use the UPN to logon, and has the advantage that the user will not need to remember a different account for logging on to OWA. To configure OWA to use UPN, you need to configure "\" (backslash) as the value for the Domain field on the Basic Authentication configuration for each virtual directory (front-end and back-end) that will use UPN.

Configuring the Base DN Search Scope

OWA has the capability to search the directory for user information. You will need to restrict this capability in order to limit it to a particular OU by modifying the msExchQueryBaseDN attribute in Active Directory for each subscriber user that will use OWA.

Use the following steps to configure the msExchQueryBaseDN for *user1* in *company1*:

1. Run ADSIEdit.exe.

2. Expand OU=Company1,OU=Hosting,DC=<Domain Component> in the Domain partition.

3. Right-click CN=User1, and then click Properties.

4. Set the msExchQueryBaseDN attribute to the following:

```
OU=Company1,OU=Hosting,DC=<Domain Component>
```

5. Repeat for each user.

Configure Service Startup for HTTP

Exchange Services and the stores can be stopped as described earlier in the Configuring POP3/IMAP4 section.

> **NOTE**
>
> MSExchangeSA must be started to make configuration changes.

Configuring Storage Groups

Stores and Storage Groups will be shared amongst subscriber companies. Although it is possible to offer enhanced storage services and dedicate a part or the entire storage infrastructure to a particular subscriber, this will limit the number of subscribers that can coexist on a single mailbox server. The SLA should dictate the level of service and parameters that define the storage requirements and services offered.

As with the general performance and scalability issues discussed earlier, your storage configuration should allow for maximum concurrent users and should be able to scale up to handle more users. How far you scale up an individual server will be impacted by the SLA requirements for recoverability and availability. If there are stringent limits on the time it takes to restore, then that might limit the number of users you co-locate on the same store. High availability requirements will also impact storage decisions, and you will most likely implement Windows Cluster Service to address availability requirements.

The following guidelines can be used to help in determining storage configuration:

- Use Redundant Array of Independent Disks (RAID) in a striping with mirroring configuration (RAID 0+1).

- Locate each storage group and accompanying databases on their own disk volumes (RAID 0+1), with each mailbox database in its own directory.

- Locate the transaction logs for each storage group on their own dedicated volume with mirroring enabled (RAID 1).

- Use Storage Area Networks, and maximize the number of disks in the stripe sets

- Ensure disk controllers are write-enabled (disable write-back), or ensure adequate battery backup for the controller.

Security Considerations

Security considerations for an ASP hosting Exchange 2000 will be similar to a corporate implementation that offers messaging capabilities to users from the Internet. In the previous section on Configuring Exchange 2000 we covered aspects such as securing Address Lists, which would make this implementation different than the typical corporate environment. See Chapter 3 for more information about security in general, and then use this chapter to extend security to the ASP environment.

Additional Resources

The following Web sites provide additional information for ASPs hosting Exchange 2000: www.microsoft.com/apphosting and www.allaboutasp.org.

Summary

Active Directory and Exchange make a superb platform for hosting messaging in an ASP environment. Once you have a network infrastructure in place (firewalls, security, and other networking services such as VPN), you can then configure your Active Directory for hosting. Keep in mind the following configuration tasks:

- Plan your user identification and then configure UPN suffixes.

- Configure and secure Organization Units.

- Configure external and internal DNS servers.

Once Active Directory is configured, you can then configure Exchange 2000 by completing the following tasks:

- Configure front-end servers.

- Design and configure Recipient Policies.

- Configure SMTP connectors.
- Configure and secure address lists.
- Configure your protocols; POP3, IMAP4, and HTTP.
- Configure storage groups.

FAQs

Visit **www.syngress.com/solutions** to have your questions about this chapter answered by the author.

Q: Will Web users be able to search the address lists?

A: They can search Active Directory, but not address lists themselves.

Q: How can I secure what Web users can search in Active Directory?

A: By configuring the msExchQueryBaseDN attribute to the domain name of the OU where you want their search capability to start from.

Q: How can an address list be secured from other subscriber companies?

A: By using Active Directory permissions, you can secure it to be viewable only by members of a security group configured for the subscriber company.

Q: How can an ASP have two users from different subscriber companies with the same name retain uniqueness?

A: Use User Principal Names to give users a unique identity within the Active Directory forest.

Chapter 10

Is Your Backup and Restore Really Working?

Solutions in this chapter:

- Exchange 2000 Architecture Overview
- Tools and Products to Back Up Exchange 2000 Data
- Types of Backup Procedures
- Preventing Data Loss: What to Back Up and Why
- Planning Data Loss Prevention and Recovery
- Implementing Backup
- Implementing Restore Scenarios
- Troubleshooting

Introduction

In this chapter, we discuss the various types of failures that can occur with an Exchange server and ways to recover from them. Many users have started using their mailboxes as their primary file stores. However, this way, if the server crashed, they wouldn't be able to get at any of their documents. If you use your Exchange server as a part of your company's business processes, such as workflow applications or e-commerce, your entire business can be made idle by a failure.

There are many ways for your Exchange server to stop working properly—from running out of disk space to a complete server crash and quite a few possible scenarios in between. Databases can become corrupted, and users can accidentally delete a message. This chapter attempts to prepare you for these events.

The best way to recover from a disaster is to prepare for a disaster before it happens. In this chapter, we focus primarily on using NTBackup to back up your Exchange server to tape, but some other tools and utilities, including third-party backup software that might have more options than NTBackup, can be used. In addition, you are no longer required to back up to tape; Windows 2000 introduces the option to back up to a file. Other options include backing up individual mailboxes for fast recovery.

We also explore how to perform the various functions necessary to restore Exchange data. We discuss best practices for backing up and restoring an Exchange database and other services and how to recover individual mailboxes.

Exchange 2000 Architecture Overview

To be able to properly back up and restore your Exchange information, you must first understand how Exchange stores information. This section reviews some of the key components in Exchange that should be backed up and explains how they interrelate.

Database Components

Exchange uses the Extensible Storage Engine (ESE) for its databases. This technology is made up of several different components. They are:

- **The database file has an extension of .edb** This file contains folders, mail messages, attachments, calendar items, and the like and is used by Messaging Application Program Interface (MAPI) clients (such as Outlook) to store RTF messages and attachments. This file is organized into 4 KB pages, and each page has a checksum to ensure that the data is valid.

- **The streaming database file has an extension of .stm** This component is new in Exchange 2000 and is used to store native Internet content, Multipurpose Internet Mail Extension (MIME), such as that used by Web clients. This file is also made up of 4 KB pages.

- **Log files** These files have an extension of .log. Exchange uses log files to keep a record of all the transactions that have occurred. To make Exchange faster, log files can contain information that has not yet been committed to the database file. Two reserve log files, Res1.log and Res2.log, are used to reserve storage space in case the Exchange server runs out of disk space.

- **Checkpoint file** This file is named Edb.chk. A checkpoint file keeps track of the transactions that have been committed to the database and those that still need to be committed.

Exchange uses all these components to store information. An Exchange database is actually composed of the Exchange database (.edb) file, the streaming database (.stm) file, and the log files.

Transaction Logging

The use of both a database file and transaction logs provides fault tolerance and improves performance. When Exchange needs to write information to the database, it first writes the information to a transaction log and the cached database in memory and then later writes the information to the database file. This allows Exchange to write to the database in a more optimal manner. If the Exchange server gets too busy to write all the information to the database, it can delay writing that information until it is less busy. In this case, the data is written only to the transaction log. Then, when the server is less busy, it can write information in bulk to the database file.

WARNING

Transaction logs should not be thought of as regular log files. They are critical to the proper function of the Exchange databases. Do not delete any log files from the Exchange Server directory or you might not be able to start the database.

If a failure such as a power failure causes the server to stop, Exchange can replay the transaction logs when it is restarted. In addition, if you place the log files and the database files on different drives and you have a failure of the database drive, you can recover using the backup, and Exchange will automatically replay all the log files. This way, the server will be recovered to the state it was in just before the drive failed, without losing any data.

Every log file is exactly 5 MB (listed as 5,242,880 bytes in Windows Explorer). If you find a log file that is not exactly this size, it usually damaged.

In order to save hard drive space, Exchange offers the option of using circular logging. When circular logging is enabled, log files that have been committed to the database are deleted from the disk. Although this option does save disk space, it also has a number of side effects. First, differential and incremental backups are disabled, but more important, if we have the failure of the database drive we spoke of earlier, you can restore data only up to the last backup. Since the log files are not available, Exchange is not able to replay the transaction logs up to the time of the failure. Exchange 5.5 had circular logging enabled by default; Exchange 2000 has it disabled by default.

To increase the functionality of Exchange, Exchange 2000 now supports up to four storage groups on a server. Each storage group can have up to five databases, so you can now have up to 20 databases on a single Exchange 2000 server. Each storage group uses a common set of log files. Therefore, multiple public and private databases can use a common set of log files, as shown in Figure 10.1.

Figure 10.1 A Simple Storage Group with Log Files

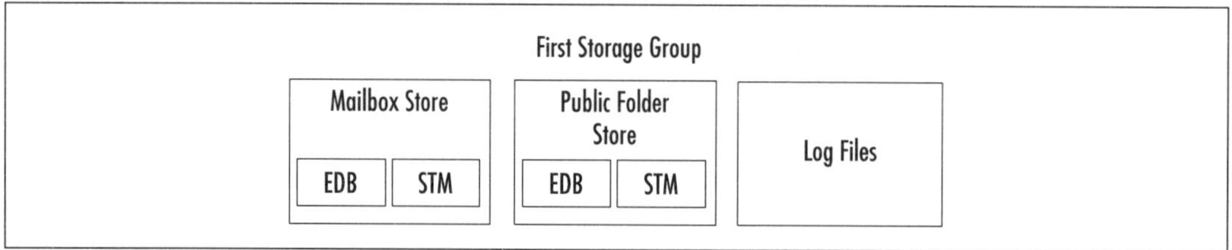

Internet Information Server

Exchange 2000's tight integration into Internet Information Server (IIS) allows you to dedicate servers for specific tasks. Exchange 2000 allows you to configure front-end servers, which are used to communicate with Web; Post Office Protocol, version 3 (POP3); and Internet Message Access Protocol, version 4 (IMAP4) clients. Moving these protocols to a front-end server reduces the load on servers dedicated to Exchange database operations.

Exchange 2000 uses the following IIS protocols:

- **Simple Mail Transfer Protocol (SMTP)** Since SMTP is the default protocol used by Exchange 2000, it is used to communicate with other Exchange 2000 servers as well as to communicate with other mail servers on the Internet. Exchange 2000 adds features to the default SMTP loaded with IIS.

- **HyperText Transfer Protocol (HTTP)** Used so that clients can access their Exchange mailbox from a Web browser. Outlook Web Access provides an interface that is very similar to a standard Outlook client.

- **Network News Transfer Protocol (NNTP)** Used to link Exchange to Internet newsgroups. Exchange can import messages from a newsgroup or post messages to a newsgroup.

Certificate Authority and the Key Management Server

Since SMTP sends messages in clear text, anyone who happens to be between the sender and the receiver of a message can potentially read that message. To keep this from happening, you need to encrypt your messages before they are sent over a network. The receiver of the message then needs to decrypt the message to be able to read it.

To encrypt and decrypt messages, Exchange 2000 uses both the Certificate Authority (CA) and the Key Management Server (KMS). CA allows the use of private and public keys. Using two keys allows a user to encrypt a message with the recipient's public key, and since only the recipient has access to the private key, only that user can decrypt it. The CA is used to publish public keys so that anyone can get a users' public key to send an encrypted message.

KMS is used to store users' private keys. This way, if a user loses his or her private key, it can be recovered from KMS. KMS is also used to allow administrators to open encrypted messages—for example, in case a user has left the company and one of his messages needs to be retrieved.

Site Replication Service

To maintain coexistence with Exchange 5.5, Exchange 2000 uses the Site Replication Service (SRS). This service allows an Exchange 2000 server to look like an Exchange 5.5 server. Other Exchange 5.5 servers are then able to share Directory information with the Exchange 2000 server.

Exchange 2000 Back Up Basics

Now that we have an understanding of how Exchange operates, we can discuss how to back it up. As we have just discussed, there is a lot more to Exchange 2000 than just the e-mail stored on it. All of the services we just talked about need to be restored in case of a failure.

Online Backups

Online backups are still the preferred method of backing up Exchange databases. Online backups allow you to back up your databases and still allow clients to access Exchange. Online backups also clear the committed log files if circular logging is disabled. Only a Normal online backup verifies the checksum on every page in the database, so that if any part of the Exchange database is corrupt, Exchange will log an error to the Event Log.

Since the database is still in use during an online backup, there could be changes to the database during the backup. If Exchange allowed the database to change during the backup, there would be inconsistencies in the data. To prevent this problem, Exchange uses a *patch file*. This file has an extension of .pat. A patch file records all the transactions to the database during the backup, similar to the way a log file works. Once the backup is complete, the patch file is then backed up, and all the events written to the patch file are committed to the database.

You need to ensure that the backups do not overlap with system maintenance, or online defragmentation might never run. If backups for a storage group begin while a database in the storage group is being defragmented, the defragment process ceases.

Offline Backups

Offline backups are still possible in Exchange 2000, but they require dismounting the database you are backing up. While the database is dismounted, users will be unable to access their mailboxes.

As we said before, Exchange now uses two files for each database. For offline backups, both the Exchange database (.edb) file and the stream (.stm) file need to be backed up and restored together to keep the database in a consistent state. Log files do not need to be backed up.

Exchange 2000 Restore Basics

Backups in Exchange 2000 are very similar to those in Exchange 5.5, but there are several key differences between the restore processes.

In Exchange 5.5, the Information Store is recovered with the Information Store service stopped. The backup software communicates with the Exchange System Attendant. In Exchange 2000, the backup software communicates directly with the Information Store service to restore databases. In order to restore a database in Exchange 2000, the Information Store must be started, with the database to be restored dismounted. This way, you can restore one database without affecting users homed on other databases.

To restore a database, Exchange copies the database, log files, and patch files from the backup to the appropriate directories. Then the recovery process starts. The recovery process involves replaying the log files and patch file.

This is called a *hard recovery*. Exchange not only replays the log files that were restored from backup but any log files that are available. This way, if you are recovering from a failure of the database drive, the undamaged log files will be replayed, and the Exchange server will have lost no data.

In Exchange 5.5, this registry key is used to replay the log files and apply the patch file. This process is also referred to as a hard recovery. The function of the Restore in Progress key is now handled by a file named restore.env. During a restore, Exchange places this file in a temporary directory specified before the restore starts (see Figure 10.2).

Figure 10.2 Specifying a Temporary Directory for a Restore with NTBackup

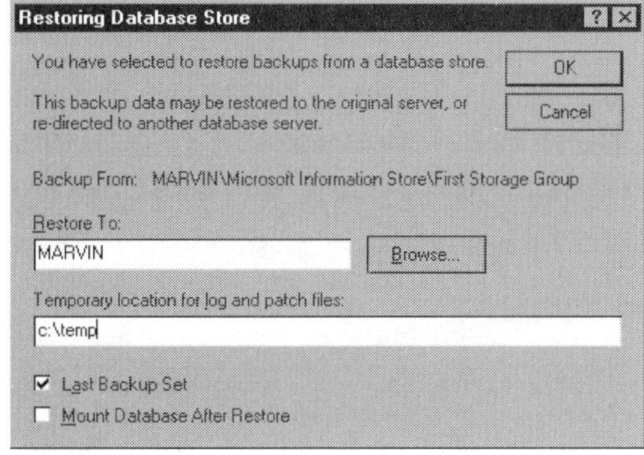

A subdirectory is created under the temporary directory for each Storage group but not for individual databases. Be careful if you are restoring multiple databases in a single storage group so you don't use the same temporary folder. If you do, the restore.env file will be overwritten and the hard recovery process will not be able to run properly; consequently, you'll have to restore the database again.

A new feature in Exchange 2000 is that it will not perform a soft recovery on a database if it needs a hard recovery.

The hard recovery process starts when you check the Last Restore Set option for the backup. After the backup completes, Exchange runs the hard restore automatically. If you forget to check this option, you can start the hard recovery process manually by running eseutil /cc.

To restore all the databases in a storage group, it is recommended that you restore them all at the same time. Since all the databases on a storage group share log files, restoring all the databases together allows Exchange to replay all the log files at the same time.

Restoring Individual Mailboxes

The moment to decide how you will restore a single mailbox or email message is not when the CEO calls to say he accidentally deleted a message and needs it for his client meeting in 15 minutes. You should plan for this situation before it happens, and it is almost guaranteed that it will happen sooner or later. As discussed earlier, you have some different ways to get the CEO his email back, but the only way you'll get it restored before his meeting is if you have planned for it.

Microsoft Tools

Remember, Microsoft does *not* provide the functionality to restore an individual mailbox with NTBackup. The ability to restore an individual mailbox is called a *brick-level backup*, and it simply isn't in Microsoft's code today. (Brick-level backups allow you to restore individual mailboxes or mail items easily). However, you can use the tool called ExMerge. ExMerge is able to export data from mailboxes to .pst files. You can create a batch script that copies all the information from a user's mailbox with ExMerge and save this data to a shared backup server. It isn't a complete solution, but it does work.

Third-Party Products

Some third-party software vendors frequently allow backing up of individual mailboxes, and some applications support backing up individual public folders. ARCserve 2000 by Computer Associates and Backup Exec from Veritas both have very good brick-level backup features. Both allow you to select individual mailboxes that are to be backed up individually. Using these tools, you can select the executives' mailboxes to be backed up individually.

Tools and Products to Back Up Your Exchange 2000 Data

There are several methods to prevent loss of Exchange data. NTBackup is a free utility on Windows 2000 that is used for making backups and doing restores, but you can use other utilities, such as third-party backup products and the Microsoft ExMerge utility to back up individual mailboxes. For system administrators, backups are our primary method for saving data, but they're not the whole solution. Several functions—namely, the mailbox recovery and deleted item recovery features—are built into Exchange 2000 to prevent data loss.

NTBackup

NTBackup is a free utility for performing backups and restores. It can perform online and offline backups of Exchange databases to tape drives or to files.

NTBackup performs online backups of Exchange by communicating directly with the Exchange services. This communication allows NTBackup to perform backups of the Exchange databases while they are running. During a backup, Exchange copies the contents of the database and logs to backup. Since the database files and log files cannot change during the backup, Exchange commits all database changes to patch files. After the database and log files are backed up, the patch file is backed up. Then the patch file is committed to the database, just like a log file.

NTBackup can back up and restore the Windows 2000 System State data, including the information required to restore Active Directory (AD), the CA, or the IIS. Backups can be started manually or scheduled to run automatically. However, NTBackup does have its limits. Since it cannot back up individual mailboxes, you might decide that another utility or software application is better. In addition, if you have a tape library or need to set up more intricate backup schedules, NTBackup is not for you.

WARNING

The version of NTBackup.exe 5.0.2172.1 should not be used to back up Exchange 2000 data. You can check your version by right-clicking NTBackup.exe and selecting Properties or by looking at the Help About feature. If your system is running version 5.0.2172.1, download the latest version of NTBackup from the Microsoft Exchange 2000 Web site. The version should be at least 5.0.2195.1117.

Third-Party Backup Products

Several third parties make backup software that integrates with Exchange 2000. These products offer additional features over NTBackup, such as the important brick-level backup. Check with the software vendor to see if your software supports brick-level backups. Keep in mind that if you do a full database backup and a full brick-level backup, you are essentially performing two full backups of the Exchange server. As mentioned earlier, you might want to create two databases in a storage group and place your brick-level users in the second database. If two databases are not for you, plan for additional time to perform both backups.

Many backup products also have support for more backup hardware options than NTBackup. These options include tape libraries that can automatically change tapes when necessary and the ability to stream data to multiple tape drives at the same time.

A complete list of supported third-party software vendors is available on Microsoft's Exchange Web site (www.microsoft.com/exchange). The site lists backup applications that are certified by Microsoft to work with Exchange 2000. Other software might also work with Exchange 2000 but is not certified by Microsoft. Check with your software vendor to see if its product works with Exchange 2000.

Two of the most well-known backup products are Backup Exec from Veritas Software and ARCserve*IT* from Computer Associates. The latest version of Backup Exec is certified to work with Exchange 2000 and adds some interesting features, including:

- The ability to back up and restore individual mailboxes with brick-level backups

- The ability to relocate a database to a different Exchange server or storage group

- Built-in drivers for many of the most current backup devices, including autoloaders

- The ability to stream backups to use multiple tape drives simultaneously, which allows for data mirroring, striping, and striping with parity

For more information on Backup Exec, check out Veritas' Web site at www.veritas.com. The latest version of ARCserve 2000 also has some improvements over NTBackup:

- Backs up individual mailboxes with To:, cc:, and bcc: information

- Allows databases to be restored from local or remote machines

- Allows scheduled jobs to be repeated by day, date, time, and interval

For more information on ARCserve 2000, go to the Computer Associates Web site at www.cai.com/arcserve.

ExMerge Utility

Microsoft has updated the ExMerge utility to work with Exchange 2000. This utility is used to import or export Exchange mailbox data to Personal Store (.pst) files. The ExMerge utility can be used in batch mode by supplying an .ini file and can be scheduled with the Task Scheduler utility. You can use ExMerge to back up all the mailboxes on your server or only the ones you determine are more important, such as company executives' mailboxes, your boss' mailbox, or most important, your own.

Using the ExMerge utility together with NTBackup could give you the flexibility to back up the Exchange databases as well as individual mailboxes, or you could find it easier to use a third-party utility.

Mailbox Recovery and Deleted Item Recovery

Exchange 2000 has two features that can help you recover data without restoring from backup. The first is the Deleted Item Retention feature. When a user deletes an item, it goes into that user's Deleted Items folder. If the Deleted Items folder is emptied (the folder can be set to empty automatically when Outlook exits), items in that folder might not be deleted immediately. Deleted items are retained until the Deleted Item Retention period expires. Before that period expires, the user can recover mail items. This setting defaults to 0 days, so make sure that you change this setting *before* you need it.

The second feature is the Deleted Mailbox Retention feature. By default, if a mail-enabled user's Active Directory account is deleted, the mailbox is not deleted for 30 days. Before the Deleted Mailbox Retention period expires, you can reconnect that mailbox to another Active Directory user account.

Types of Backup Procedures

Just as in other backups in Windows 2000, Exchange 2000 has different types of backups: normal, incremental, differential, and copy. Normal backups are simply full backups of the Exchange database. Incremental backups work by backing up only the data that has changed since the last incremental backup. Differential backups work by backing up all the data that has changed since the last Normal backup. Copy backups are just that—a copy of the data written to a backup, without modifying how incremental or differential backups are run. Although Exchange 2000 performs essentially the same function with these terms, they way they work is quite different.

Each backup type requires a different procedure to restore. These are listed in the author's order of preference for Exchange restores; the easier and faster the restore, the better!

- Normal backups simply require restoring the last normal backup.

- Differential backups require not only the last normal backup but the last differential backup as well.

- Incremental backups require restoring the last normal backup and every incremental backup since.

- Backups are restored the same way as normal backups. Simply restore a copy backup to restore the state of your database.

Normal Backups

Normal backups are full backups of the Exchange databases. Normal backups work by copying the Exchange database files and the log files to the backup device, then clearing the log files. Therefore, the best way to reduce the amount of space used by the Exchange log files is to simply perform a full normal backup.

During a normal backup, Exchange checks the checksums on each page of the database. If an error is found, an event is logged.

Normal backups are the easiest to restore from, since only one backup session needs to be restored. The disadvantage of normal backups is that they take the most time, because all the Exchange database files and log files need to be backed up. If you have the time, do a full backup every night.

NOTE

Since the databases in a storage group share log files, you need to back up all the databases in a storage group to purge all the log files.

Differential Backups

Differential backups are similar to incremental backups in that only the log files are backed up. The difference is that differential backups do not clear the log files after they complete. This way, to recover a database, you need only the last full backup and the last differential backup. For instance, let's say you do a normal backup on Sunday and then do a differential at 11:00 PM every Monday, Tuesday, and Wednesday. If you want to restore Exchange data that was deleted on Wednesday at noon, you would only have to restore the normal from Sunday and the differential from Wednesday.

Differential backups might be a good compromise between normal and incremental backups, but if you have a lot of database activity, so much data will have changed since your last normal backup that a differential backup could take almost as long as simply running a normal backup. Time the various types of backup and see what is best for your organization.

Remember, differential backups require that circular logging be turned off. Fortunately, circular logging is now turned off by default in Exchange 2000.

Incremental Backups

Incremental backups work by backing up only the log files of the Exchange database. The database itself is not backed up. After the log files are backed up, they are cleared. Incremental backups are the fastest to perform but require the most work to restore. To perform the restore, you need to first restore the latest normal backup and then every incremental backup since the normal backup.

If you are thinking about using incremental backups as part of your backup strategy, remember that when your server is down, the last thing you want to be doing is frantically searching through tapes looking for the right backups. For instance, let's say that you do a normal backup on Sunday and then do an incremental at 11:00 PM every Monday, Tuesday, and Wednesday. If you must restore Exchange data that was deleted on Wednesday at noon, you would have to restore the normal from Sunday and the incremental from Monday, Tuesday, and Wednesday.

Since incremental backups work by backing up the committed log files, circular logging must be disabled to run incremental backups.

Copy Backups

Copy backups are just what their name implies. They only copy the database information to tape. They do not modify the log files in any way.

Copy backups are generally used to archive historical data, since they don't interfere with incremental or differential backup rotations.

Remember, normal backups are preferred over differential or incremental backups. It is much easier to restore a single normal backup than a normal backup and one or more differential backups. A normal backup checks the Exchange database for corruption, and it also clears the log files. If normal backups are not feasible, you can perform weekly normal backups and daily incremental or differential backups.

When to Back Up

Once you have determined the kinds of backup you will be performing, it is necessary to determine when the backups will occur. It is best to perform backups when the Exchange server is not being heavily utilized, so 8:00 AM Monday is probably not the best time for most organizations. Generally, late evening backups work out well, but only if you don't have a significant network utilization at night or global operations that have employees around the globe.

In most situations, daily backups are sufficient, but some situations call for more frequent backups—for example, if you were using your Exchange infrastructure as a foundation for a workflow application. In such cases, it might be necessary to back up twice or more every day.

You also have to choose your rotation schedule. A *rotation schedule* is simply a list of the backup types that will be done on particular days. For example, a daily backup rotation involves full backups performed every day. A weekly rotation is a full backup once per week and incremental or differential backups every other day. Table 10.1 presents examples of various backup rotations.

Table 10.1 Comparison of Rotation Methods

Backup Type	Sunday	Monday to Saturday	Advantage	Disadvantage
Daily	Full	Full	Easiest to restore. Only one backup set is required to restore all data.	Takes the longest to backup, since all data must be copied to tape or disk.
Incremental	Full	Incremental	Fastest backups, since only data since the last incremental backup needs to be copied to tape or disk.	Hardest to restore (need to restore the last normal and all incremental backups).

Continued

Table 10.1 Continued

Backup Type	Sunday	Monday to Saturday	Advantage	Disadvantage
Differential	Full	Differential	Faster backups, since only data since the last normal backup needs to be copied to tape or disk.	Harder to restore (need to restore both the last normal and the last differential backups).

Preventing Data Loss: What to Back Up and Why

In this section, we drill down into the various types of data that need to be backed up: static and dynamic data. *Static data* is data that changes infrequently, such as the executable files used for an application or Windows 2000. *Dynamic data* is data that changes frequently, such as Exchange databases or other data files. To effectively design your backup strategy, you need to understand what needs to be backed up frequently and what can be backed up less frequently.

We also discuss things that can happen to cause you to lose data. A crashed hard drive is just one of the possibilities. Other events that can cause data loss are users accidentally deleting mail or other items, administrators accidentally deleting mailboxes, viruses deleting mail items, or a corrupted Exchange or Active Directory database.

Finally, we discuss the various services on which Exchange depends. A loss of any of these services could mean that Exchange data is lost, too. These services include Exchange-related services such as the Key Management Service or Site Replication Service as well as other services such as the AD and CA. Current backups of these services are as critical as backups of your Exchange services.

Types of Data to Back Up

Static data refers to data that changes infrequently. Examples of static data are:

- Windows 2000 operating system files
- Exchange 2000 Server application files

- Other application files, such as backup software and antivirus software

- Management scripts, such a batch files for backup, archive, and the like

Static data needs to be available if a restore is necessary, but it does not need to be backed up frequently. One way to make sure that you have static data backed up is to make backing up this information part of your change management procedures.

Dynamic data is data that changes frequently. Examples of dynamic data are:

- Exchange database files

- Exchange log files

- The Active Directory database

- The KMS database

- System state information

Dynamic data needs to be backed up frequently to prevent data loss. Backups of dynamic data should be automated, and the logs of those backups should be checked for any errors.

Types of Losses

There are many ways to lose Exchange data. If you look at the "Implementing Restore Scenarios" section toward the end of this chapter, you will see that we address scenarios on how to back up and/or restore the following problems that can occur:

Scenario 1: A mail-enabled user is accidentally deleted by an Exchange administrator. This situation can come about when an administrator accidentally deletes the wrong user or if the user left the company and another person needed access to the mailbox.

Scenario 2: A mail item is accidentally deleted by a user. This can happen when a user deletes an item, then later finds out he or she shouldn't have done so, or if a user accidentally deletes the wrong item. The mail item can also be deleted by a virus or some other malicious program.

Scenario 3: An information store database becomes corrupted. Although corruption of Exchange databases is fairly rare, it does happen; usually it is caused by storage systems that fail, such as hard drive failures.

Scenario 4: A server drive fails. Unfortunately, hard drive failures happen all too frequently. If the drive is part of a redundant array, data loss is unlikely. However, if a drive is not in a redundant array and it crashes, data loss is the result. Drives can also fail if invalid data is written to the file table or boot sector.

Scenario 5: Complete server failure. This might happen in the case of a natural disaster, such as a fire or earthquake.

Scenario 6: Corruption or loss of the Active Directory database. The AD database can be lost when a server fails or corrupted when an administrator makes a change that causes the corruption. If the AD is not available, Exchange has no way to associate a user object with a mailbox, so the user might not be able to access his or her mail. Redundant AD servers will help in this situation, but is possible to replicate corrupt information between AD servers. The only way to recover from this situation is to perform an authoritative restoration of the Active Directory.

Scenario 7: The Key Management Server and/or Certificate Authority databases are corrupted or lost. As we discussed earlier, the KMS and CA handle encrypting and decrypting of data. If the KMS gets lost or corrupt, users might not be able to decrypt encrypted messages, which is essentially the same as lost data. Loss of the CA causes problems with the Certificate Revocation list, which won't result in lost data but will definitely be troublesome for Exchange administrators.

Scenario 8: An Exchange Connector is lost. Obviously, loss of the connector information will result in lost connectivity with other systems.

Scenario 9: The SRS database is lost. As discussed in Chapter 6, the Site Replication Service is used to replicate directory information between Exchange 2000 and Exchange 5.5 servers. Loss of the SRS database will result in directory information not being replicated between the two systems.

Scenario 10: The IIS Metadata is lost. Since Exchange 2000 uses IIS to manage its SMTP and NNTP connections, loss of the IIS configuration will result in lost connectivity to other Exchange 2000 servers, Internet Mail connectivity, and Usenet news.

Planning Data Loss Prevention and Recovery

Just as with Exchange 5.5, backups of the Exchange databases are critical for restoring from a failure. If the database becomes corrupted or if the server suffers from a drive failure, restoring the databases could be the only way to retrieve data. Because Exchange 2000 can now have up to 20 databases per server, you need to plan your database backups more carefully than in Exchange 5.5. You can select any combination of databases to back up. You can back up each one separately or all of them together.

Since Exchange 2000 now stores data in a stream (.stm) file as well as the old Exchange database (.edb) formats, it will be necessary to consider both file types if you are performing offline backups.

This section discusses your choices of backup devices and suggests some best practices related to backups and restores.

Backup Devices

You have several options when choosing where you store your data. You need to determine your risk level, the budget you have available, and the amount of control you need over your backups before you can determine which of these options is best for your organization.

Tape Library

To centralize administration of Exchange backups across the enterprise, many companies have installed tape libraries. These libraries are devices that have one or more tape drives and hold many more tape drives. The software that controls the device is able to change the tape that is in the tape drive, with no manual intervention. This allows the software to use different tapes for different tasks, and the software can simply exchange a full tape for an empty one.

The advantage of using a few tape libraries over a tape drive in each server in your organization is that it provides easier administration. The log files are in a central location, so you don't have to connect to different servers to review the log files. In addition, because the tape drive is located centrally, you have more control over how and when tapes are changed and when tape drives are cleaned.

The disadvantage in using tape libraries is that you have to purchase additional hardware and software in order to implement this system.

Compaq, Hewlett-Packard, IBM, Exabyte, and other companies all make tape libraries that are rack mountable, hold around 10 DLT tapes, and can have one or two tape drives. These devices are great for backing up a few servers, because they can back up to 700 GB of data without changing tapes. If you plan your backups right, you might have to change tapes only once a week. These devices usually have tapes in a cartridge so that you can easily remove all 10 tapes at once and replace the cartridge with another cartridge of 10 tapes. You could probably change all 10 tapes in 30 seconds or less. If 10 70 GB tapes aren't enough, some devices are capable of holding up to 30 Terabytes (TB) of data.

Local Tape Drives

It is also possible to install a tape drive in each Exchange server. The advantage of this method is primarily speed. Data will travel over SCSI channels rather than over the network. The disadvantage is administration. You might have servers in remote locations that lack support staff. Imagine your frustration if you tried to restore from a backup only to discover that no one has been changing the tapes on your server.

Backup to a File

In Windows 2000, there is now an option to back up to a file. By backing up to a file, you can back up the Exchange databases quickly when utilization is low and then move the file to some other media later. This method can be useful for 24 x 7 or global organizations. By connecting the Exchange server to a storage area network (SAN), the Exchange server can be backed up quickly, then the slower operation of moving the data to tape can occur without impacting users.

Best Practices for Backups and Restores

Consider the title of this chapter: *Is Your Backup and Restore Really Working?* The authors of this book cannot begin to count the number of times they've been at customer sites only to find that the backups did not work or did not back up what they were supposed to, or that the customer was trying to do a full Windows 2000 and Exchange 2000 restore on a server that holds the tape device—and they can't find the device drivers. The following sections are best practices we've created based on these experiences.

Test Your Backups Monthly

Include as part of your backup and restore plan a monthly test of your Exchange server. That's right, test it monthly! You need to verify all the scenarios at least once in the beginning, and then when you are sure you are backing up the right components, you can scale back and just do a test restore on the databases in each storage group each month.

Consider Services Related to Exchange

As discussed earlier, Exchange 2000 integrates with AD, CA, and IIS, and loss of any of these services could result in data loss (or the inability to get data). In large organizations, another group could be responsible for backing up these services. If this is the case, it is necessary for the Exchange administrator(s) to coordinate with these groups to ensure that backups are being performed properly. If you are responsible for these services, it is necessary that you are able to back up and restore these services properly. Restores of these services should also be tested regularly.

Keep Half Your Database Drive Space Free

By making sure your drives are never more than half full, you gain two significant advantages. First, you can defragment the database using the same drive. When Exchange defragments a database, it works by copying the data from the original database file to a temporary one, then replacing the original file with the defragmented one. If you can keep both the original database and the defragmented database on the same drive, the defragmented database does not have to be moved between drives. Second, when you are restoring a database from backup, it is recommended that you make a copy of the database. That way, if you can't restore from backup, you might still be able to fix the corrupted database. If you have half your drive space available, you can quickly make a backup copy of corrupt databases before you attempt to restore. To make sure you maintain 50 percent free space, you can set up alerts in Performance Monitor, or you can use third-party utilities that alert you when free space exceeds a threshold.

Keep an Eye on the Backup Logs

The best way to find out if your backups are running successfully is to look at the backup logs. Most problems with backups are reported in the backup logs. Ideally, you should review the backup logs every time a backup runs. Several third parties make utilities that proactively monitor event logs. These utilities can monitor the event logs of several servers and notify you if certain errors are logged to any of the servers.

Keep an Eye on the Event Logs

When backups are run, Exchange runs a data verification process on the Exchange databases. This is done to make sure that backups are done of valid data. If the Exchange server detects damage to the database, it logs an event error numbered 1018. This event should be taken as a strong indication that data is corrupted. Frequently, data corruption is caused by failing hardware, such as a disk drive or disk drive controller. In any case, you should take immediate steps to determine the cause of the problem and rectify it.

1018 Errors

When Exchange 2000 writes a data page, it writes a data header. In this data header is a page number and checksum. Exchange submits this request to the file system, and the file system returns the result to Exchange. Faulty hardware can return a successful write before the data has been successfully written to disk. When Exchange accesses the page later, it checks that the page number is the correct one and recalculates the checksum. A 1018 error occurs when Exchange 2000 returns a page that has a bad checksum or an incorrect page number. Exchange retries on the page multiple times before it actually returns the 1018. A 1018 can be caused by many things, including the following:

- **Failing hard drive** Run Chkdsk to verify that all the drives are healthy. If they are not, check to make sure that all SCSI drives are terminated properly. If you're still having problems, try swapping out disks.

- **Running antivirus software or disk utility software that is not compatible with Exchange** Try disabling any of these types of software you are running and see if the problem persists.

- **Using NTFS compression** If you are using NTFS, make sure that you have the drive uncompressed.

- **Using write-back caching on your disk controller card** Some cards have a nonvolatile cache that is protected by battery or nonvolatile memory. If your card does not have this feature, turn write-back caching off.

If you have 1018 errors, you have two choices to fix them. The first option is to restore from backup. Second, you can try to repair the errors. The Eseutil is able to check the database for bad pages and try to repair them. If it is unsuccessful at repairing the bad pages, it will remove them, and any data in those pages will be lost. After running Eseutil, make sure that you run Isinteg to clean up any inconsistencies created by removing pages.

Document Your Exchange Network

As we will see a little later in the chapter, it is often much easier to recover from a failure when you have adequate documentation. Certain information is critical to restoring your Exchange server and is much easier to get before the failure. Some things that you should be sure are in your document are:

- The Administrative Group(s) to which your servers belong
- The organization name to which your servers belong
- The names of the storage groups on each server
- The names of the databases on each server
- The components installed on each server

Have Components in a Central Location

In order to perform any kind of data recovery, you need certain things before you start. You will be able to recover data much faster if you have all the following supplies in an easy-to-find place:

- **Hardware** A server that has sufficient hard drive space to which to recover. Ideally, this server would be identical to your other servers. The server can have Windows 2000 and Exchange 2000 installed.
- **Install media** You need to have the same version of the operating system that was originally installed (Windows 2000 Server, Advanced Server, or Datacenter Server) and Exchange Server.
- **System backups** Full drive backups of system drives and other drives with applications or data and a system state backup.
- **Exchange database backup(s)** These should have the information store databases and any other databases, such as the SRS database or KMS database.

Have Backup Hardware Standing By

It is crucial that you have backup hardware at the ready! You should have at least one backup server, preferably identical to your other Exchange servers. This backup hardware can be used for your test restores, for recovering single mailboxes, or to replace a server that's suffered a failure. This machine could have Windows 2000 and Exchange 2000 already installed so you can more quickly recover individual mailboxes.

Store Backup Tapes at a Safe Offsite Location

It is important to note that having backup tapes sitting next to the server won't help you recover your server if there is a fire in the server room. The tapes will simply be destroyed along with the server. This is also true of other natural disasters, such as earthquakes, tornadoes, and hurricanes, or even the work of vandals—maybe your competitor wants to put your company out of business, or maybe your staff is using your backup tapes to transfer MP3 files for personal use.

The way to avoid all these situations is to store your backups at a secure, offsite location. Many companies will perform this service for you. They come in once a week, pick up your tapes, and store them at a secure location, safe from vandals and fire. Alternatively, you could take a set of tapes home once a month for safekeeping.

Implementing Backup

Now that we have a backup plan, we need to know how to implement it. This section discusses how to perform various operations to back up Exchange data.

First, we examine how to use NTBackup to perform backups of the Exchange databases as well as other services, such as Active Directory or Certificate Services. Next, we look at how to use the ExMerge utility to back up individual mailboxes. We see how to back up all mailboxes on a server or only selected mailboxes. Next, we test the backups to make sure that they are functioning properly. It is much better to learn that your backups aren't working *before* you have a failure than after.

Finally, we see how to restore the various services we have backed up, including Exchange databases, Exchange services, and other related services.

Using NTBackup to Back Up Exchange Databases

Exchange databases can easily be backed up using NTBackup. Remember to check for version 5.0.2195.1117 or later. As you can see in Figure 10.3, to select which items to back up, first open the Backup tab. Databases are backed up by opening the Microsoft Exchange Server, opening the server you want to back up, and selecting the databases to back up.

It is recommended that you can back up all the databases in a storage group at one time. This method groups all the log files into one backup. If you back up the databases separately, the log files get backed up each

Figure 10.3 Selecting the Exchange Databases to Back Up

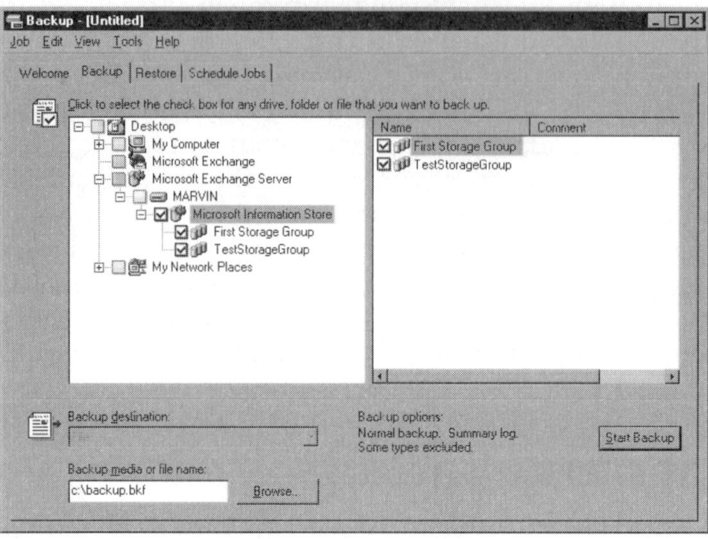

time. Furthermore, if you restore the databases separately, the log files get played out incompletely each time.

The version of NTBackup packaged with Windows 2000 now has a graphical user interface (GUI) for scheduling jobs. Now you don't have to try to figure out the correct command line to schedule the job with the "at" utility. See Figure 10.4.

Figure 10.4 Scheduling a Backup Job in Windows 2000

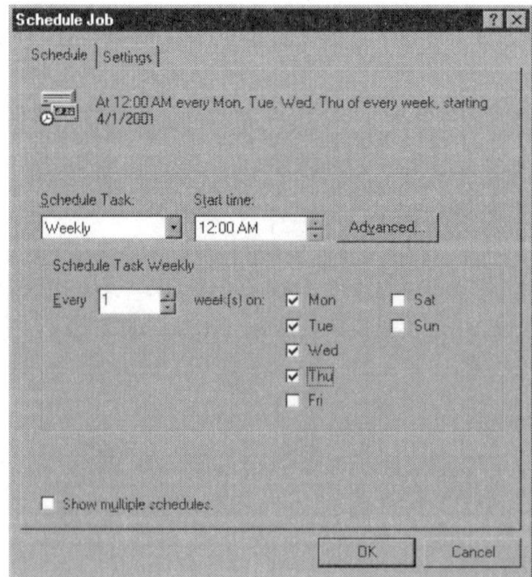

Using NTBackup for Other Exchange Databases

Exchange databases other than the Information Store databases can also be backed up using NTBackup. These databases are listed in NTBackup under the server name, just like the Information Store databases.

The other Exchange databases—the Site Replication Server database and the Key Management Server database—are backed up the same way as Information Store databases. When you open your backup utility, you will see those databases listed along with the Information Stores. Figure 10.5 shows the Key Management Server database being selected for backup. Simply select the database you want to back up and run the backup.

Figure 10.5 Selecting Other Services to Back Up

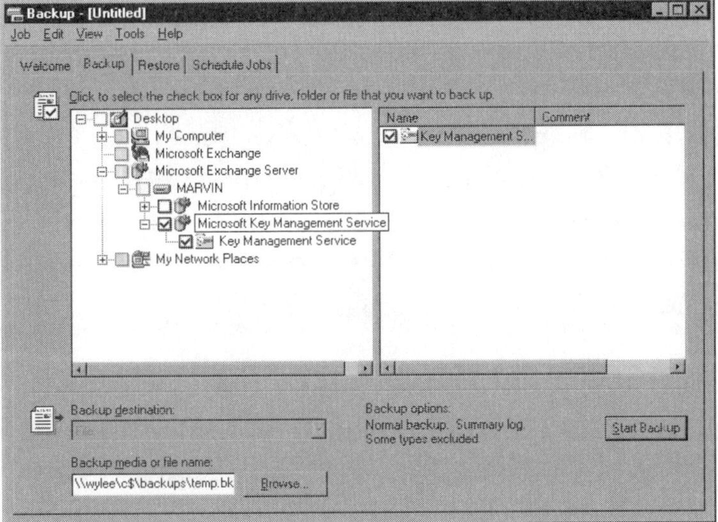

Backing Up Other Services

The other services that Exchange requires (Active Directory, Certificate Authority, and Internet Information Server) can all be backed up by including the System State data in your backups. Some services also allow backups from within their respective management utilities.

Internet Information Services

In the Internet Services Manager, you can right-click on a server and click Backup/Restore Configuration to back up IIS. You can use this function to back up or recover your IIS configuration. To back up the IIS configuration:

1. Right-click the server, and select Backup/Restore Configuration.

2. A menu of the existing (if any) backups of the IIS configuration is displayed. You can select Create backup... to start a backup.

3. You are prompted to enter a name for the backup. Enter one, and select OK.

The backup configuration is stored in the c:\winnt\system32\inetsrv\ MetaBack directory.

Certificate Authority

The Certificate Authority has a functionality similar to that of the IIS. To back up a CA:

1. Right-click a server, select All Tasks, and select Backup CA. The CA Backup Wizard will run. Here, you can back up the Certificate Authority private key and certificate and the issued certificates and pending requests.

2. Select both the private key and CA certificate and the issued certificate log and pending certificate request queue.

3. To make sure your backups aren't used by unauthorized parties, you must enter a password at this time.

4. Click Finish to perform the backup.

Using ExMerge to Back Up Mailboxes

Before you begin trying to back up mailboxes, make sure that the account you've selected to run ExMerge has "Receive as" and "Send as" permissions on all the mailboxes being backed up. When you schedule your backups, you can select the account that will run the process, as shown in Figure 10.6. Make sure that this user has rights to access the mailboxes you want to export.

Figure 10.6 Setting the User Account That Will Perform the Backup

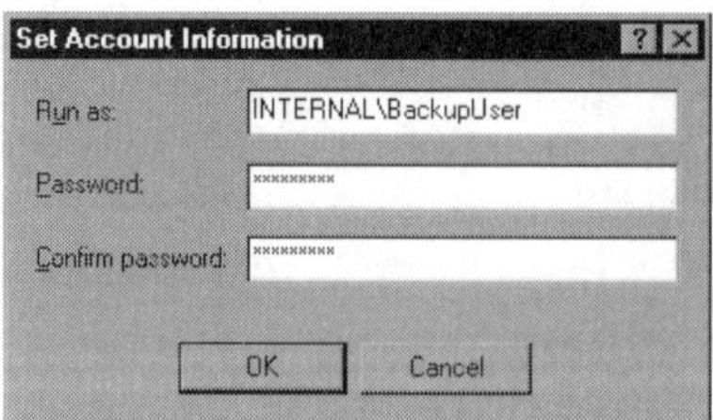

The ExMerge utility can be found on the Exchange 2000 CD, in the \support\utils\i386\exmerge directory. This directory has a document that shows all the options available with ExMerge and an .ini file that briefly describes each section. Let's look at how to automate mailbox backups using ExMerge.

In the ExMerge.ini file, you can specify the action you want to perform with ExMerge. This is done using the MergeAction setting. MergeAction has the following options:

- **0** Export to .pst file (the default)
- **1** Import from .pst file
- **2** Both export and import (move from one server to another)

If MergeAction is set to 0, you must specify SourceServerName. If the value is set to 1, you must specify DestServerName. If the value is 2, you most specify both options.

If you don't want to run ExMerge on all the mailboxes on a server, you can use a file to specify which mailboxes to run ExMerge on. The file should be a list of mailbox distinguished names (DNs), each on a separate line. In the ExMerge.ini file, set FileContainingListOfMailboxes to the name of this file, including the path, if necessary. You can also specify mailboxes on other servers in your organization by specifying the DN of the mailbox. ExMerge will automatically connect to the other server and export the mailbox.

Test Your Backups

In order to be absolutely sure that your backups are working properly, you should periodically perform a test restore. Test restores are the best way to find out if your backups are really working and that you're really backing up everything you need. They are also a good way to train administrators on how to restore an Exchange server.

Your test restore will depend on what you have responsibility for backing up in your department. If you work in an organization that does not give you the ability to backup or restore Active Directory, you might only be able to test your ability to restore your Exchange databases. However, if you can coordinate with the Active Directory admins or if you have the administrative rights, this might be a good time to see if you can restore your Active Directory at the same time.

Implementing Restore Scenarios

Now that we know how to back up your Exchange server, let's examine how to restore from those backups. Frequently, the restore method is as simple as opening your backup software and selecting the information to restore, but there are a few occasions when it is more difficult.

Restoring an Exchange 2000 Server

Earlier in this chapter, the section "Types of Losses" presented various scenarios in which you might lose data. Here we address how to recover that lost data.

Performing a Full Restore

Use the full restore procedure in the event of Scenario 5: Complete server failure. This procedure could also be necessary in Scenario 4: Server drive failure, if the drive lost was the boot partition.

To restore an Exchange server from a total failure, the recovery process is fairly straightforward, as long as your backups are working properly and the server object still exists in Active Directory.

First, configure the hardware with the same drive setup as the old machine. Then reinstall Windows 2000 using the same computer name as the old machine, but do not join the domain. Make sure that you use the same drive letters and paths for your installation. If the server had any service packs installed, install those next. Next, restore the system drive and system state from backups. You will need to restart the server after restoring the system state data.

When the server reboots, install Exchange 2000 with the /disaster-recovery switch. This option reads the configuration of the Exchange server from Active Directory. Make sure that you select the same Exchange components that were installed on the server originally. When setup finishes, you can then restore your databases from backup. If all went well, you should be able to mount your databases and be up and running.

Restoring a Corrupted Database

Use this procedure in the event of Scenario 3: Corrupted Information Store database. If a database on the server should become corrupted, it is a fairly simple process to restore from backup. You can restore any combination of databases at a time, but every database being restored needs to be dismounted before you begin the restore. Databases in the same storage group can still be mounted while other databases are being restored. The Information Store must be started to restore data.

When the restore of a database begins, Exchange copies the database files to the disk and then copies the log files and patch file to the temporary directory. Before Exchange can start the database, the log and patch files need to be replayed. To do this, Exchange starts another copy of the Extensible Storage Engine. This is done so that other databases in the same storage group are not affected by the restore process. Up to 16 instances of the ESE can run on an Exchange server at one time. If you are performing multiple restores concurrently, you need to keep in mind the number of instances of the ESE.

TIP

Before you restore a database, it is best to make a copy of the database file, just in case you can't restore from backup and need to try to fix the corrupted database.

If you are using NTBackup, open the Restore tab and find the backup session set you want to recover. This process is shown in Figure 10.7.

Figure 10.7 Selecting Exchange Databases to Restore

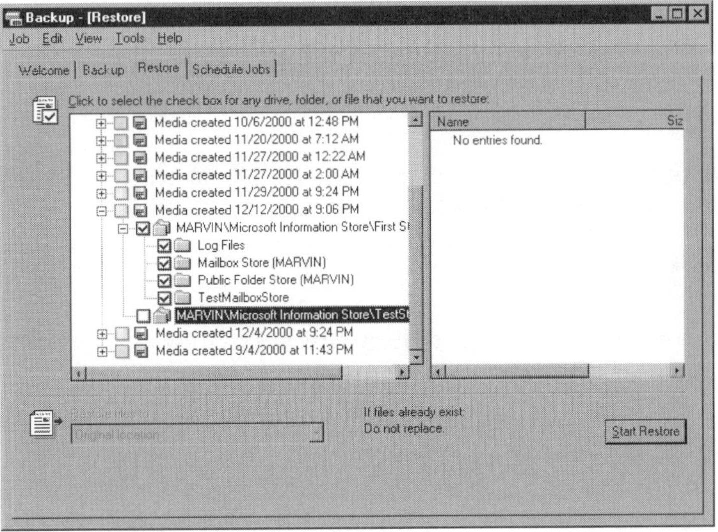

If you are restoring only a normal backup, you can select Last Restore Set to start the recovery process. Otherwise, if you are also restoring incremental or differential backups, leave the Last Restore Set unchecked until you get to the last incremental or differential backup. When all the restores have run, Exchange starts the hard recovery process on the database. When this process finishes, you can mount the database.

Restoring the KMS and CA Databases

Use this procedure in the event of Scenario 7: Corrupted or missing KMS or CA database. As we said earlier, Certificate Authority information is stored in the system state. Restoring the system state restores the Certificate Authority.

Another way to restore the Certificate Authority is to use the backup and restore utility in the CA MMC snap-in. To use this method, you need to start with a server with the same name as the original server. To restore the CA:

1. Add the Certificate Services in Add/Remove Windows Components. Make sure you select the same CA type. In addition, select the Advanced Options check box.

2. Click Import to import your .p12 file backup. When you backed up the CA, you were prompted for a password to protect the backup. Enter that password now. Confirm that the information displayed about the CA is correct. Then the Installation Wizard completes the install of CA.

3. Start the CA MMC, and change the policy settings to add the additional certificates required by Exchange.

4. Restore the issued certificates in the CA MMC using the CA Restore Wizard.

The KMS database can be recovered the same way as Information Store databases. To restore the KMS database:

1. With the KMS service stopped, make sure that the KMSDATA directory is empty.

2. Start the KMS service, which will start in a semi-running state.

3. Restore the database using NTBackup.

Restoring the Site Replication Service

Use this procedure in the event of Scenario 9: Corrupted or missing SRS database. The SRS is also restored like the Information Store databases but with a few additional steps:

1. Make sure that there are no *.edb, *.log, or *.chk files in the SRS directory.

2. Start the SRS service.

3. Open Exchange System Manager, right-click the Administrative group to which the server belongs, and click Properties. On the General tab, click the Modify button to change the password on the Exchange service account. Enter the same password used by the Exchange 5.5 service account.

4. Recover the SRS database in NTBackup as you would any other database.

Restoring the Active Directory

Use this procedure in the event of Scenario 6: Corrupted or missing Active Directory database. If you lose the Active Directory database (either from corruption or accidentally removing all servers from the forest), you have to restore AD from backup.

AD is restored from system state data. This requires rebooting the server into the Directory Services Restore mode and performing the restore, using the following steps:

1. Restart the server.

2. When the boot menu appears, press the F8 key to see the boot options.

3. Select the Directory Services Restore Mode option.

4. Select the operating system installation you want to recover.

5. Log on using the username and password you supplied Active Directory when it was installed.

6. Click OK (to acknowledge that you are in Safe Mode).

7. Run NTBackup, which you can run from the Start Menu | Programs | System Tools | Backup option.

8. Click the Restore tab.

9. Select the media to restore from.

10. Leave the option of Restore Files to box at Original Location.

11. Click Start Restore.

12. Restart the computer after the restore completes.

When the server restarts, the server will connect to any other Active Directory servers in the domain and start the replication process. Any changes made to the directory that have replicated to the other servers will replicate to the server you just restored. This might not be what you want if you are trying to recover from a corrupted Active Directory. In that case, you need to perform an *authoritative restore* (the previous restore process is referred to as a *nonauthoritative restore*). You can perform an authoritative restore by doing the following:

1. Perform a nonauthoritative restore as described previously.

2. After the server reboots, perform Steps 2 through 6 to again run Windows 2000 in Directory Services Restore Mode.

3. At a command prompt, run Ntdsutil.

4. Type **authoritative restore**, and press Enter.

5. Type **restore database**, press Enter, click OK, and click Yes.

For more information on authoritative and nonauthoritative restores, check out the Microsoft TechNet Web site at www.microsoft.com/technet.

Deleted Mailbox Recovery

Use this procedure in the event of Scenario 1: Mail-enabled user accidentally deleted. In Exchange 2000, when a mail-enabled user account is deleted, the Exchange server flags the associated mailbox for deletion but does not actually delete the mailbox. After the Mailbox Retention period expires—by default, 30 days—Exchange purges the mailbox from the system. If you accidentally deleted a user, as long as you haven't exceeded the Mailbox Retention period, you can reconnect the mailbox to another user object. This can be an existing mailbox that is not Exchange enabled, or you can create a new user account and connect the mailbox to it.

Deleted Item Recovery

Use the following procedures in the event of Scenario 2: Mail item accidentally deleted.

Using Deleted Item Retention

As in Exchange 5.5, Exchange 2000 supports deleted item recovery. If a user wants to recover a deleted item, he or she can run the Deleted Item Recovery option from Outlook, see which items can be recovered, and recover the desired items. The delete item retention time can be set for each database and is set to 0 days by default.

To recover a deleted item, open Outlook, and select the Deleted Items folder. Then click Tools | Recover Deleted Items. That brings up a screen that looks like Figure 10.8. Now just select the item to be restored, and click the icon at the top of the screen.

Figure 10.8 Deleted Item Recovery

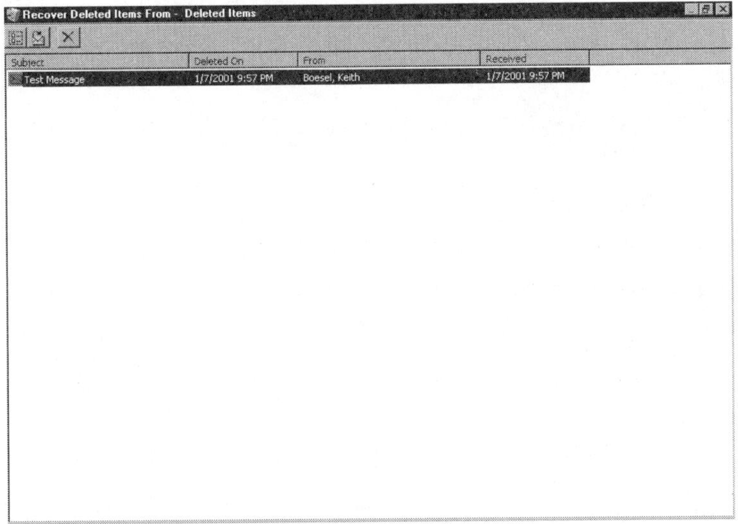

From Brick-Level Backup

To restore an item from a brick-level backup, the method is very similar to restoring an Exchange database. Simply open the backup set, select the items to restore, and select the destination. For more information on restoring brick-level backups, check out Veritas' Web site at www.veritas.com, Computer Associates' Web site at www.cai.com, or your preferred backup vendor's Web site.

From ExMerge

A previous section reviewed how to use ExMerge. To restore, you can use ExMerge to import from a .pst to a mailbox, but it is usually easier just to open the .pst file in Outlook, especially when it is only a single message that you need to recover. To do this, simply open Outlook, click Tools | Services, click the Add button, and select Personal Folders (see Figure 10.9). Then enter the path to the .pst file you exported. Now you can browse the backup file to retrieve the lost message(s).

Figure 10.9 Opening a .pst File to Export Data

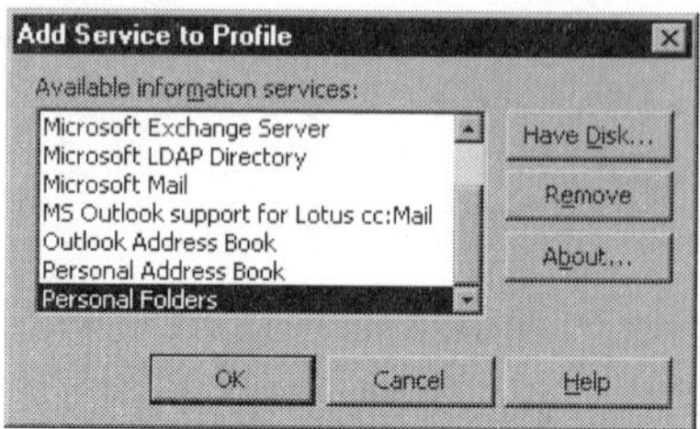

From a Complete Database Restore

If all the other methods fail, you might have to restore the entire Exchange server in order to restore one or more lost mail items. In order to restore mailboxes from an Exchange 2000 database backup, you need a separate server in a separate forest. This is because each mailbox in the Active Directory is given a globally unique identifier (GUID), and each GUID must be unique in the Active Directory. Therefore, if you want to restore a mailbox from a database, you must restore it into a separate Active Directory forest.

Once you have created your separate forest, do the following:

1. Install Exchange. If you are restoring from a server in the First Administrative Group, simply install Exchange into the default administrative group. If you need to restore from a server that wasn't in the First Administrative Group, things get more complicated. In order to install a server to a different administrative group, the group needs to be added to Active Directory before setup starts. To do this, you can run Exchange 2000 Setup with the /forestprep switch. Then run Setup again and install only the Exchange System Manager. Once this process is complete, run the Exchange System Manager, and create a new administrative group with the correct name. Then run Setup one more time and install Exchange 2000. When you are asked which administrative group to use, select the one you just created.

2. Once you have Exchange server installed in the correct administrative group, you might need to create a new storage group. If the database you are restoring was not in the First Storage Group, create that group. Then create a new database with the same name as the one you are restoring.

3. Dismount the database, and restore the database from backup.

4. Once you have restored the database, you must get access to the mailbox you want to recover. To do this, open the mailboxes under the database you restored, right-click Mailboxes, and select Run Cleanup Agent. The Exchange System Manager then marks with a red X the mailboxes that are not linked to Active Directory user accounts, as shown in Figure 10.10.

Figure 10.10 The Mailbox Cleanup Agent

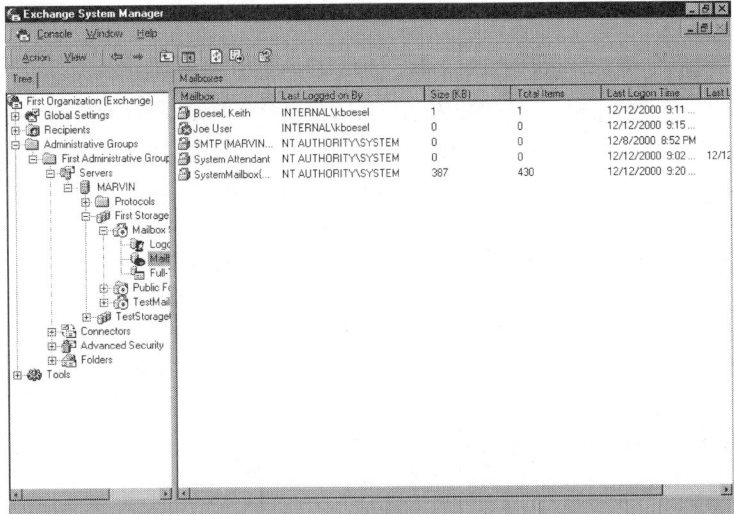

At this time, you can right-click a mailbox and click Reconnect. This action brings up a list of user accounts in Active Directory. You might notice that only user accounts that do not have mailboxes are listed. When you select an account, the mailbox is reconnected to that user account. Then log in as that user to access the mailbox.

As you can see, several pieces of information are required to perform this procedure, including the administrative group, storage group, and database names. If you are trying to recover this information from a server that has failed, it could be difficult to find. In such situations, it is helpful to have thorough documentation.

Restoring an Exchange Connector

Use this procedure in the event of Scenario 8: Loss of an Exchange connector. Most connector information is stored in the registry. Therefore, the first step to restoring a connector is to restore the system state. In addition, certain connectors have additional requirements to restore functionality:

- **MSMail** The shadow post office needs to be restored. This is a set of files stored in \connect\msmcon\maildata and its subdirectories. Restore these files from a backup.

- **Cc:Mail** Only the import.exe and export.exe files need to be restored to their original locations. The connector recreates all other files automatically.

- **Lotus Notes** You will need to restore the Notes client software directory and subdirectories, including the Notes.ini file and the \conndata directory in Exchange.

- **Novell GroupWise** Restore the GroupWise Gateway Network Service and the \conndata directory in Exchange.

Troubleshooting

Even when you have your backup and restore strategy all planned out, you still might run into problems. This section presents some troubleshooting scenarios that could occur in the course of upgrading from Exchange 5.5, experiencing a corrupted database, or locating errors in the backup log.

Understanding the LegacyExchangeDN Identifier

If you upgraded an Exchange 5.5 server to Exchange 2000 and you want to recover a mailbox from a database restore, you have to perform an extra step. In order to communicate with Exchange 5.5, Exchange 2000 uses a unique identifier, called a legacyExchangeDN, for each object. The legacyExchangeDN is used to map Active Directory names with Exchange 5.5 directory names. When you upgrade an Exchange 5.5 server to Exchange 2000, the Setup program sets the organization name of the new server to match the old organization name and matches the administrative group to the old Exchange 5.5 site name. You can change the name of an administrative group, but the legacyExchangeDN never changes. Therefore, when you restore a database that was upgraded from Exchange 5.5, you must set the name of the administrative group to match the legacyExchangeDN.

In order to determine your legacyExchangeDN, you can use a utility called ldifde that comes with Windows 2000. The ldifde utility allows you to view the raw attributes of Active Directory objects.

To determine the legacyExchangeDN, run ldifde with the following arguments:

```
Ldifde -f OUTPUTFILE.TXT -d "CN=ADMINISTRATIVEGROUP, CN=Administrative
Groups, CN=ORGANIZATIONNAME, CN=Microsoft Exchange, CN=Services,
CN=Configuration, DC=SUBDOMAIN, DC=DOMAIN,
DC=COM -l legagacyexchangedn -p base
```

(Note that the code has been line wrapped and spaces added after commas to improve readability.)

For example, to get the legacyExchangeDN from an Exchange server that was not upgraded from 5.5, you would use the following command:

```
C:\>ldifde -f temp.txt -d "CN=First Administrative Group,
CN=Administrative Groups, CN=First Organization, CN=Microsoft Exchange,
CN=Services, CN=Configuration, DC=internal, DC=domain, DC=com" -l
legacyexchangedn -p base
```

In these examples, *outputfile.txt* is the name of the file created by ldifde; *administrativegroup* is the administrative group to which the server belongs; *organization* is the name of the organization to which the server belongs; and *subdomain, domain,* and *com* refer to the Active Directory domain name to which the server belongs.

If you search the output file for the text *legacyExchangeDN*, you will find a line that looks something like this:

```
legacyExchangeDN: /o=Microsoft/ou=North America
```

Now that you know this information, you can install Exchange. The server must be a member of the administrative group that matches its legacyExchangeDN. In the previous example, you'd need to put the server in the North America administrative group. To do this, follow the instructions we discussed earlier to install Exchange to a different administrative group.

More Information on Legacy Exchange Distinguished Names

Exchange 5.5 used a DN to uniquely identify all objects in its directory. The DN contains not only the name of the object but also where it resides in the directory. An example of a DN in Exchange 5.5 is:

```
/o=Microsoft/ou=North America/cn=Recipients/cn=Joe
```

Continued

> The reason that you couldn't move an object between sites in Exchange 5.5 is that the DN contained the path to the object. If you moved the object, Exchange would not be able to find the object in its hierarchy.
>
> In Exchange 2000, a GUID is used to uniquely identify each object in the directory. With a GUID, you can move objects around in Exchange 2000. So that Exchange 2000 can communicate with Exchange 5.5, Exchange 2000 assigns each object a legacyExchangeDN. Even if you change the name of the administrative group to which a server belongs, the legacyExchangeDN never changes.

Backup Problems

If you have problems with your backup, you could be forced to try to fix a damaged database rather than restoring from backup. Another problem might be errors popping up in backup log (hopefully, you're looking at these logs!). The next sections help you through these issues.

Corrupted Database

To recover from a corrupted database, the best method is to restore from a recent backup. If such a backup is not available, you might be able to recover most of the information in the database. There are a couple of steps you need to undertake in recovery:

1. Make sure that you look in the event log at all the errors related to Exchange, the operating system, and networking to see what is going on in the background.

2. Look up any errors in Microsoft TechNet to see what Microsoft says about recovery procedures.

3. Review Chapter 12 on the use of Eseutil and Isinteg to make sure that you understand if and how you should use these repair tools.

4. Contemplate using the command:

   ```
   Eseutil /ppriv1.edb /spriv1.stm
   ```

   where priv1.edb is the filename and path of the EDB file, and priv1.stm is the name and path of the associated stream file.

Again, review Chapter 12 and Microsoft TechNet before using these tools.

Errors in the Backup Log

For various reasons, you will get errors in the backup log. You should first check the following items:

- Is there enough space on the tape, or if you are backing up to a file, is there enough space on the drive?

- Is the tape bad? Try another tape.

- Is the tape drive working properly? First, try cleaning the drive. If that doesn't work, try replacing the drive. If you have your backup hardware standing by, you can borrow the tape drive to see if that is the cause of the problem.

- Does the account that is running the backup have the appropriate permissions?

- If you are using NTBackup, check out the Microsoft TechNet Web site. Microsoft frequently posts fixes for common problems on this Web site. The address is www.microsoft.com/technet.

- If you are using another company's backup utility, check its Web site for resources.

Summary

As you can see from this chapter, a lot of knowledge, planning, and testing are required to be sure you can recover from a failure. In order to put together a good disaster recovery plan, you need to know what data needs to be backed up, how you are going to back it up, and how to restore it in case of failure. Ideally, you will have, in one convenient place, everything you need to recover from a failure. Your disaster recovery toolkit should include backups, installation media, and documentation showing exactly how to recover from each type of failure.

If you have a good disaster recovery plan, you are well on your way to being able to recover from any type of failure. However, just having a plan is not enough. The plan must be implemented if it is to do any good. Any deviation from the plan could cause disaster.

In order to implement the plan, you need a good working knowledge of how to use the tools available to you. Know how to use NTBackup or the third-party product you have selected to perform backups of various services and how to restore them. To use the tools effectively, you need to understand how Exchange uses log files to increase performance and fault tolerance.

You should check the various log files frequently and perform test restores monthly. There is no sense doing daily backups if the tape drive fails and no one notices for two months. Exchange will also notify you when Exchange databases are corrupted. If you monitor the event logs personally or with automated software, you have a good chance of knowing about a failing system before it turns into a disaster.

FAQs

Visit **www.syngress.com/solutions** to have your questions about this chapter answered by the author.

Q: Why doesn't NTBackup allow you to perform backups of individual mailboxes?

A: To store information most effectively, Exchange stores all information from a database in one large file. If each mailbox had an individual file, storage would be more difficult and less efficient. For example, if you send a message to three people whose mailboxes are all on the same database, Exchange stores that information only once. If each mailbox had its own file, this action would be impossible.

Q: I get an error message when I try to back up my Exchange server. It says, "Error attaching to device SERVER\Microsoft Information Store\First Storage Group." What's the problem?

A: You are trying to perform an incremental or differential backup without having first done a normal backup.

Q: You talked about a hard recovery, but is there such thing as a soft recovery?

A: Yes. A soft recovery is automatically run if the Information Store detects that it was not shut down properly. You could also get an error message that says, "MSExchangeIS could not start in a timely fashion." This is because a soft recovery is being run on a number of databases, and the Information Store could not start in the 120 seconds Windows 2000 uses to determine if a service has started properly.

Q: I restored my server from a offline backup, but I can't run isinteg-patch. What's wrong?

A: The isinteg -patch command was required in Exchange 5.5 when a database was restored from backup. In Exchange 2000, the Information Store automatically runs this process.

Chapter 11

Clustering Your Exchange 2000 Server

Solutions in this chapter:

- **How Cluster Service Works**

- **How Network Load Balancing Works**

- **How Exchange 2000 Can Utilize Cluster Service and Network Load Balancing**

- **The Benefits of Clustering Your Exchange 2000 Server**

- **How to Install Cluster Service and Network Load Balancing**

- **How to Install Exchange 2000 on a Cluster**

Introduction

So you've got your server outfitted with redundant disks, CPUs, and power supplies. You've got error-correcting code memory, and you've configured your disk array for fault tolerance, but there are still a few points of failure—the server's motherboard and the servers operating system, to name a few. You've noticed that client network response time to your key production file server is getting worse. To top it all off, a failure of the motherboard and a dreaded Blue Screen of Death (BSOD) has caused your Exchange server to stop . . . and your phone is starting to ring.

Microsoft provides two services in Windows 2000 Advanced Server and Datacenter Server to help prevent poor response time and to keep your clients connected to your Exchange server: Microsoft Cluster Service and Network Load Balancing Service.

The first, *Microsoft Cluster Service,* was initially released with Microsoft Windows NT 4.0 Enterprise Edition. If a server is not functioning or if an application is not working, Microsoft Cluster Service will transfer the failing resources on the first server to a predesignated working server. This transfer process is called *failover.* Originally failover worked only with two servers in NT 4.0. Microsoft has since expanded the Cluster Service in Windows 2000 Datacenter so that it allows four-way clusters. A *four-way cluster* is a configuration of four servers connected to a shared storage area that can fail services between any two of the servers in the cluster. Microsoft claims that Datacenter server can be used to provide solutions that are available 99.999 percent (a term that is also referred to as *five nines*) of the time. This works out to services being offline for about 5 minutes per year.

The second of these technologies is the *Network Load Balancing Service,* or *NLBS.* This service does not use the shared storage technology; instead, it requires all servers in the cluster to be on the same network segment. It uses an IP-based load-balancing method to increase availability and scalability. NLBS uses multiple servers configured identically. You can have up to 32 members in a NLBS cluster. When a request is received, only one of the servers responds. For example, you can build an NLBS cluster to provide your company's home page. You would configure multiple IIS servers with NLBS and copy the same Web pages to each server. When a request for the home page was received, only one of the servers would reply with the page. Since all the servers have the same pages, it doesn't matter which server returns the home page. Users receive their pages from different servers to distribute the load across the cluster.

If you find that the servers in the cluster are unable to keep up with the number of requests they are receiving, you can add servers to the cluster. This action redistributes some of the load to the newly added servers. If one of the servers in the cluster should fail, the other servers detect the failure and redistribute those requests to other servers in the cluster.

Exchange 2000 Server is written to utilize both these technologies. Both were originally released with Windows NT Server 4.0 Enterprise Edition, and both have been improved in Windows 2000. This chapter first explores these technologies; then we find out how Exchange 2000 is able to use them to increase availability and performance.

Throughout this discussion, we use the term *high availability* as opposed to *fault tolerance* because fault tolerance generally refers to an instantaneous or near-instantaneous recovery. High-availability services might experience a short outage during a failure. We'll talk about the reasons that this is true later in the chapter.

Understanding Cluster Service and NLBS

In Microsoft Windows NT Server 4.0 Enterprise Edition, Microsoft released *Cluster Service* and the *Windows Load Balancing Service (WLBS)*. Prior to the release of Cluster Service, its code name was Wolfpack. You will also see it referred to as Microsoft Cluster Service, or MSCS. Cluster Service is used to provide highly available services to the network. It cannot be used to load-balance applications.

Microsoft's updated Network Load Balancing Service (NLBS), released with Windows 2000, is used to provide highly available and load-balanced applications to the network. You can use both Cluster Service and NLBS to support applications that are mission critical to your organization. Since each service uses a different technology, each is better suited to certain types of applications than the other. Table 11.1 shows which technology can be used for each type of application.

Table 11.1 Benefits of Cluster Service and NLBS

Application	Cluster Service	NLBS	Benefit
Sharing Web pages		X	High availability Load balanced
File/print services	X		Provide highly available file and print services
Database	X		Make a SQL database highly available

Continued

Table 11.1 Continued

Application	Cluster Service	NLBS	Benefit
Messaging/mail	X		Make your Exchange server highly available
Terminal services		X	High availability Load balanced
E-commerce Web site	X	X	The best solution for this application is to use both technologies: ■ Use NLBS for the front-end servers that provide Web pages ■ Use Cluster Service to provide highly available data on the back end using a clustered SQL server
Virtual private networking		X	High availability Load balanced

What Is Microsoft Cluster Service?

Microsoft Cluster Service is used to make services highly available. Cluster Service uses two or more servers attached to a shared storage. Since any of the servers in the cluster can access this storage area, any of those servers can run services based on that storage. The downside to Cluster Service is that only one server can access a logical drive on this shared storage area. The storage area can be split into multiple logical drives to allow multiple servers to access the shared storage, but only one server can access a given logical drive.

In Figure 11.1, we have two servers that are connected to the shared storage area. The shared storage is split into three logical drives, and each logical drive can be accessed by one of the servers to provide services to the network. This shared storage can be connected with SCSI or Fibre Channel connections, but both nodes must be able to access the same storage area. This is referred to as *common bus architecture.*

What Is Network Load Balancing?

Microsoft has updated the *Network Load Balancing Service (NLBS)* in Windows 2000. NLBS lets multiple servers respond to requests from the network. To use Terminal Server as an example, an NLBS cluster of

Figure 11.1 A Basic NLBS Cluster

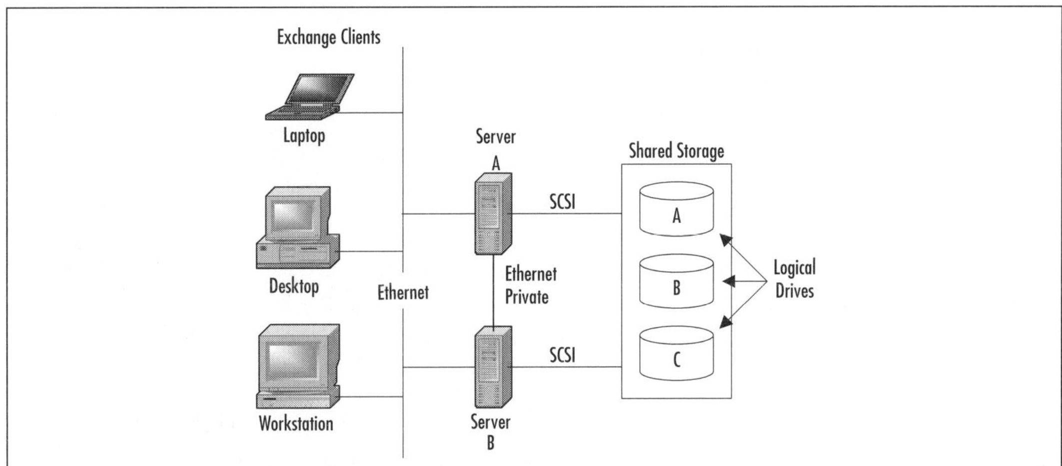

Terminal Servers will allow multiple servers to provide terminal services to clients. When a client attempts to use terminal services, it sends out a request to initiate the connection. Only one of the Terminal Servers will reply to the request. The client continues to communicate with this one Terminal Server. Other clients may connect to other servers in the cluster.

The WLBS requires all the servers in a cluster to be on the same network segment. An algorithm decides which server should respond to a given client request. All servers in a cluster periodically send out *heartbeat messages.* These messages are intended to let the other nodes in a cluster know that the server is still working properly. Whenever a heartbeat message is received from a new machine in a cluster, or if a heartbeat message is overdue from a server, the cluster starts a convergence process. During this process, the servers in the cluster determine which servers will handle which requests. Once the cluster has converged, each server knows to which requests it should respond without communicating with the other servers in the cluster. For example, when a cluster converges, it decides that Server A will handle all requests from 192.168.X.X. When a request for a Web page comes in from 192.168.5.10, all servers in the cluster know that Server A will handle that request. All the other servers simply drop the request, but Server A responds with the Web page requested.

If all the servers are configured the same way, all the clients will get the same information. If a server fails, the other servers are able to detect the failure and automatically take that server out of the cluster. This feature makes the WLBS highly available as well as load balanced.

As far as Exchange goes, NLBS can be used only to cluster front-end servers. Using front-end servers, you can move the Outlook Web Access services to dedicated servers, letting your back-end servers concentrate on other services. We'll talk about this topic in more detail in a moment.

Architecture

In this section, we go into more detail about how Microsoft Cluster Service uses shared storage and common bus architecture to provide highly available services. We look at some of the ways nodes in a cluster communicate with each other and how resources are moved between the nodes in case of failure. Once we've reviewed how Cluster Service works, we discuss how Exchange 2000 can use the Cluster Service to provide highly available services to the network. Finally, we explore NLBS and how it works.

Cluster Service Basics

To understand how to cluster Exchange properly, you must first have a basic understanding of how Windows 2000 performs clustering. To do that, you need to know the definitions of several terms:

- **Cluster** The collection of servers used to provide high-availability services to a network.

- **Node** A single server that is a member of the cluster. In Windows NT 4 Enterprise Edition and Windows 2000 Advanced Server, there are two nodes in a cluster. Windows 2000 Datacenter Edition supports up to four nodes in a cluster. We concentrate most of our discussion in this chapter on two-way clusters.

- **Resource** Something provided to the network by the cluster. This can be a physical resource, such as disk space, or a logical resource, such as an IP address or a service (like Exchange). Resources can be "owned" or reside on only one node at a time.

- **Resource group** A logical grouping of resources. Also referred to as a *virtual server* or, in the case of Exchange, an Exchange Virtual Server (EVS).

- **Virtual server** A collection of resources, listed in Exchange Manager as a resource group.

- **Shared storage** External storage that is accessible by two or more nodes of a cluster.

- **Heartbeat** Heartbeat messages are sent out from each server periodically in order to notify the other members of the cluster that it is still working properly. Heartbeat messages are sent every 1.2 seconds.

Now that we have some of the terminology out of the way, let's look at how Cluster Service works. If we look at Figure 11.2, we see that both servers are connected to shared storage. This allows any server in the cluster to use that storage to provide services to the network.

Figure 11.2 A Simple Cluster

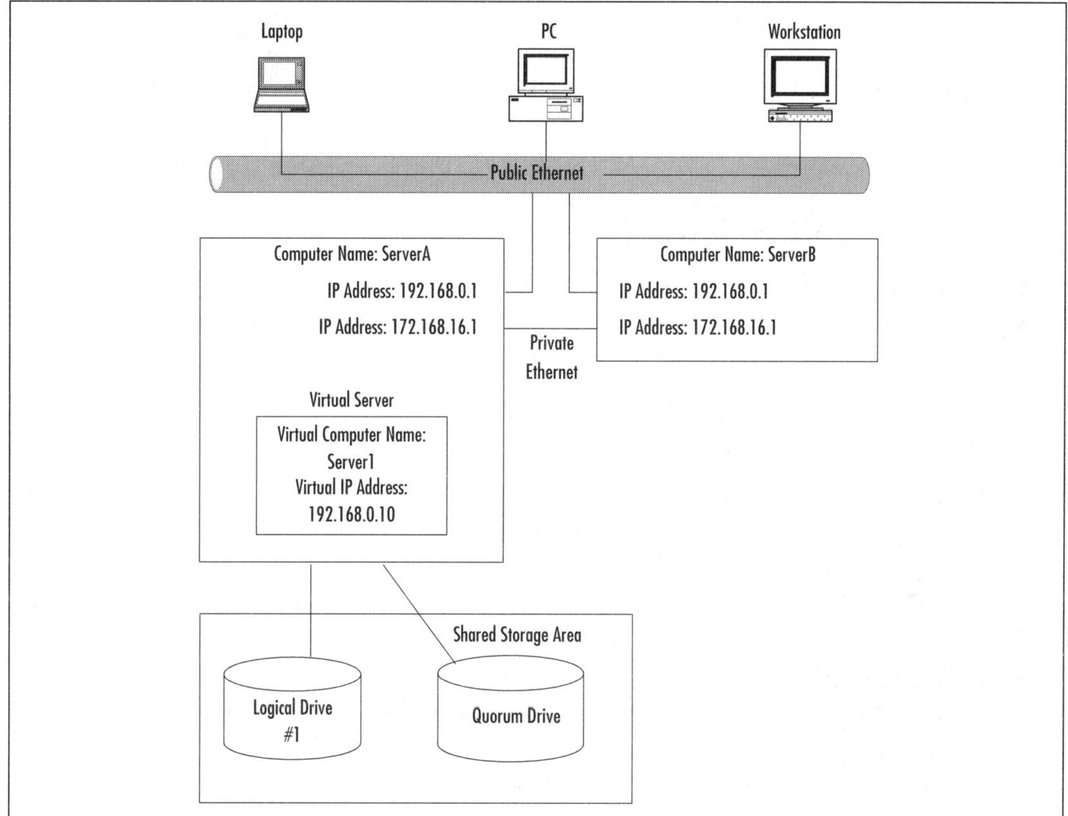

Quorum Drives

To manage the cluster, Cluster Service maintains a *quorum drive.* Figure 11.2 shows that the virtual server connects to such a drive. This drive holds a copy of the configuration database, which is a file called quolog.log. The database is used to recover failed resources in case of a network failure. Since nodes usually communicate with each other through the network, loss of connectivity would leave the nodes unable to determine which server should start which resource groups. In this case, the quorum drive is used to determine the servers that should start particular services. When installing Cluster Service, you need to specify a quorum drive that is on shared storage.

Networking Details

Because all nodes of a cluster send out heartbeat messages every 1.2 seconds, cluster nodes are typically configured with two network cards—one for connection to clients (we call this the *public network*) and one for communications between the nodes (which we call the *private network*). This structure ensures that no traffic on the network interferes with the heartbeat messages, since two lost heartbeat messages start the failover process. If you are using a two-node cluster, an Ethernet crossover cable will work fine for this application. Figure 11.2 shows both networks connected to each server. The public network is used to communicate with clients, and the private network is used for communications within the cluster.

It is possible to use a single network for both public and cluster communications, but since heartbeat messages are UDP packets, it is quite easy for a packet to be dropped. If two heartbeat messages in a row are not received, the failover process starts. Using a single network card for both public and cluster communications should be done only in a lab environment where a failover will not impact production applications.

TIP

Set the private network to be used only for cluster communications and the public network to be used for both cluster communications and client access. This way, if the private network fails, the public network that hosts both cluster communications and client access will allow your cluster to keep running normally. Remember, you are sending more traffic out on the public network, and the heartbeat can get lost.

You can make this setting when you first install Cluster Service or later by opening Cluster Manager, right-clicking the cluster name, opening Properties, and moving the private LAN to the top of the priority list.

Resource Groups

To make administration of the Cluster Service easier, Microsoft uses *resource groups*. Resource groups are just what they sound like: logical groupings of resources that are combined for administrative purposes. Each usually has its own IP address, computer network name, and some service that it provides to the network. When a user wants to use services that are on a particular resource group, they connect directly to the computer network name resource in that group. They don't know on what node the resource is being hosted. Because the network name fails over between nodes of the cluster, the user does not have to know on which physical server the resource group resides. Therefore, resource groups are often referred to as *virtual servers.* Using the example in Figure 11.3, a user can open a file from the FilePrint1 virtual server without knowing the name FilePrint1 does not represent a physical server. It doesn't matter whether FilePrint1 exists on the Cluster1 or Cluster2 physical server; the user connects the same way.

Figure 11.3 Virtual Servers

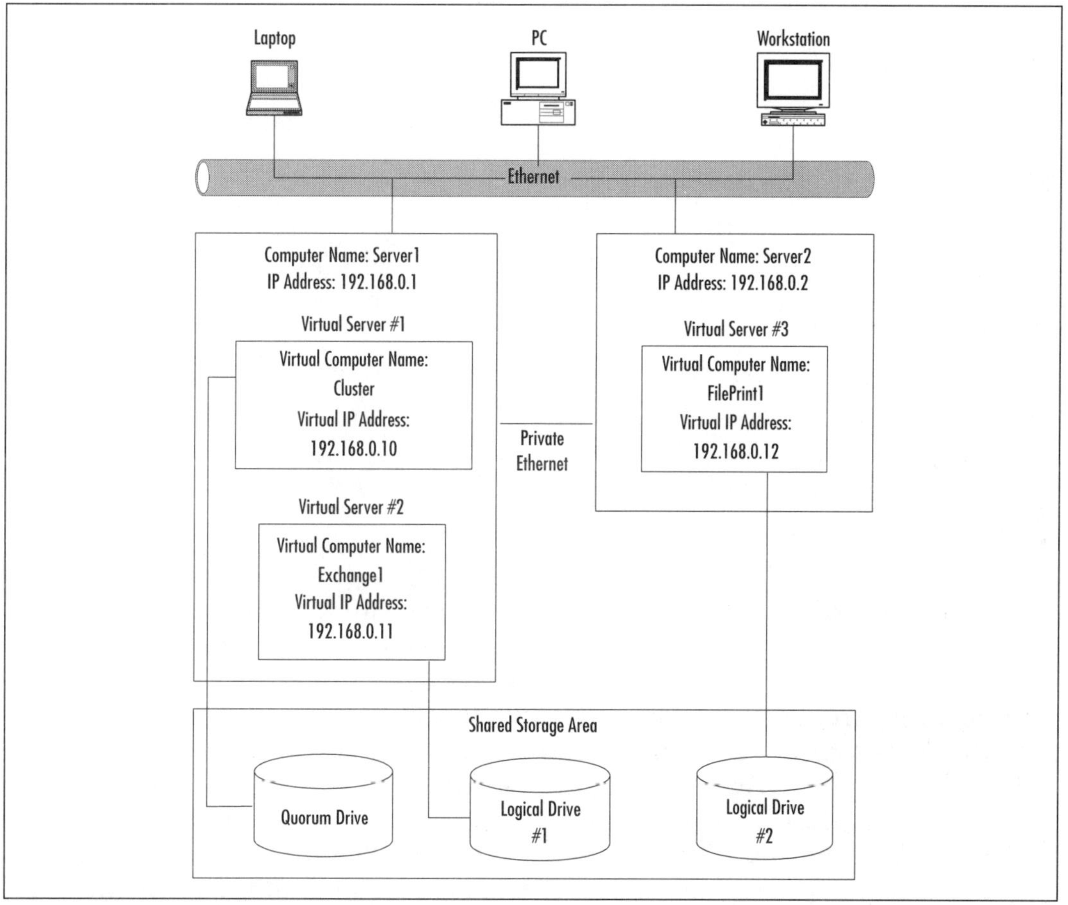

When Cluster Service is first installed, a default resource group called *Cluster* is created by default. This resource group is used to manage the cluster. It is recommended that you do not add services to this group. For example, if you added Exchange services to the Cluster resource group and needed to move the group to a different server, the Cluster Service would first have to stop all the Exchange services before the group could be moved. It is best to create additional resource groups for other services.

The Failover Process

When a problem occurs, the Cluster Service moves the resource group from the failed server to the server that is still online (see Figure 11.4). Since the IP address and the computer name move with the services, the user might have no idea that the resource group has moved to the other node of the cluster.

Figure 11.4 Virtual Server Moves to Node 2

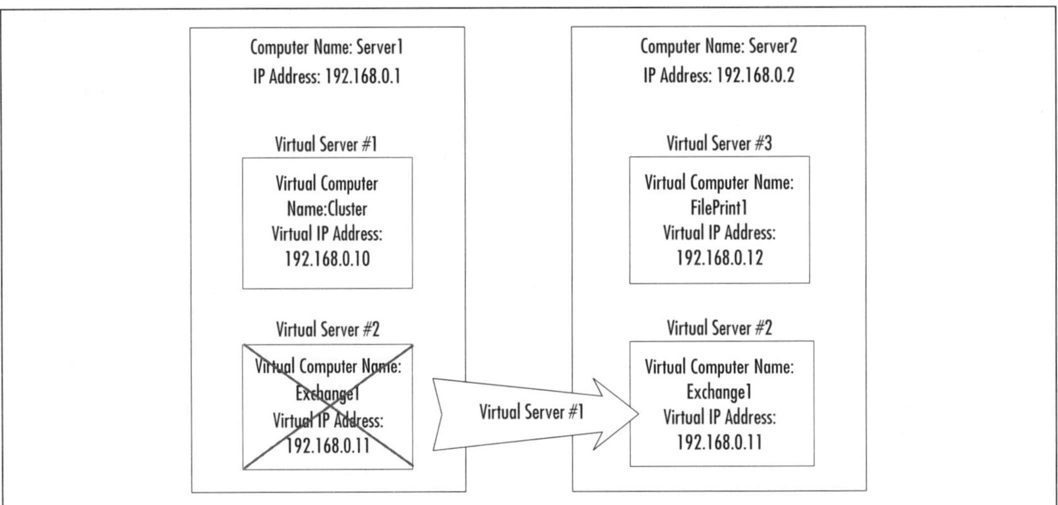

If one node of a cluster server has failing resources, the other node in the cluster is able to gain access to the shared storage through a common bus and restart the necessary resource services. Let's use DHCP as an example resource service. We made sure that we installed the DHCP configuration files on the shared storage area. Let's say that Server A is currently running the DHCP service. So, Server A reads and writes files on the shared storage. Now let's say that a component on the motherboard of Server A fails, and the server freezes. Server B, the other node in the cluster, which has been monitoring Server A all along, stops receiving these monitoring heartbeat messages from Server A. Because of the lost heartbeat message, Server B determines that Server A is for some reason no longer available and looks to see what resources Server A was running. Since Server A was running DHCP, Server B accesses the shared storage area used by DHCP and restarts the DHCP service on Server B. This process could take a few moments, but in the case of DHCP, it will probably restart before anyone even notices. More complicated services that have a longer startup period, such as Exchange, could therefore appear to be down for a short period of time while in fact the services are being restarted.

During the time between the failure of the first server and the second server bringing all the services online, the virtual server would appear to be down. If an application on the client side has the ability to reconnect to a lost connection on a server, the application simply reconnects to the virtual server and continues functioning. Some applications could require the user to retry the connection manually.

Each node in the cluster can have multiple resource groups running on it at any time, and each resource group can have multiple resources associated with it.

The Cluster Service uses several methods to determine that a failure has occurred. We briefly discussed the heartbeat messages. If a heartbeat message is not received when it is expected, the Cluster Service begins to initiate a failover. Another method is the use of *resource monitors*. Resource monitors communicate with resource DLLs, which are programs written specifically for an individual application. A resource DLL may monitor the status of a particular service or perform some other function to make sure that the virtual server is performing properly. If a resource DLL detects a failure, it notifies the resource monitor, and the virtual server is shut down and restarted on another node in the cluster. For example, say that for some reason, a virtual file server could no longer share its HumanResources directory because the administrator inadvertently deleted the share name using Windows Explorer. Although the cluster node would still be sending out heartbeat messages, the resource DLL would see that the share was no longer working and move the virtual server to another node in the cluster.

With Windows 2000 Advanced Server and Datacenter Server, resource DLLs are included for the following services:

- File and print shares
- Physical disks
- Microsoft Distributed Transaction Coordinator (MSDTC)
- Internet Information Services (IIS)
- Message Queuing server
- Network addresses (IP addresses)
- Network names

- Distributed File System (DFS)
- Dynamic Host Configuration Protocol (DHCP)
- Network News Transfer Protocol (NNTP)
- Simple Message Transfer Protocol (SMTP)
- Windows Internet Naming Service (WINS)

In addition to these services, Microsoft includes resource DLLs with the following applications:

- Exchange Server
- SQL Server

Exchange 2000 Cluster Basics

Since Exchange 2000 was written to be cluster-aware, you can implement Exchange 2000 on a Windows 2000 Advanced Server or Datacenter Server cluster.

Exchange 2000 clusters function the same way as any other clustered application. When Exchange Setup is run, it places its databases on the shared storage area of the cluster. Unlike Exchange 5.5, Exchange 2000 places the application files on the local drive. Exchange 5.5 places both the database files and application files on the shared storage. Figure 11.5 shows the placement of files in Exchange 2000.

Figure 11.5 Exchange File Placement

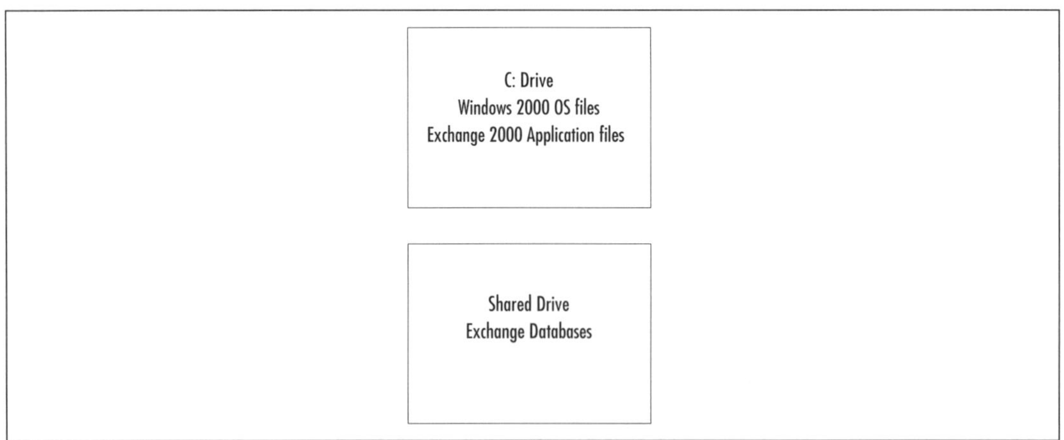

If one server should fail, the second server will attach to that area of shared storage and start the information store.

To determine if a failure has occurred, the Cluster Service uses the heartbeat messages, but it also uses a resource DLL. The resource DLL for Exchange 2000 is named ExRes.dll. ExRes monitors the various Exchange services and communicates with the Cluster Service resource monitor. If a service fails, the ExRes communicates with the resource monitor, which initiates a failover. The ExRes could also try to restart a failed service before trying to fail over. For example, if the Internet Mail Service fails on Server A, ExRes first tries to restart the service. If that is not possible, ExRes then moves the virtual server over to Server B. If an Exchange database were corrupted, the database would be dismounted. The ExRes would determine that the database is dismounted and try to remount the database. Since you can't mount a corrupted database, the remount process would fail. Then the ExRes would attempt to move the virtual server to another node. Of course, no other node in the cluster would be able to mount the database. The virtual server would bounce between nodes in the cluster, unable to start on any of them. Eventually, the cluster would determine that none of the nodes of the cluster could mount the database, and it would give up. Figure 11.6 shows a corrupted database being moved between two nodes of a cluster.

Figure 11.6 A Corrupted Exchange Database

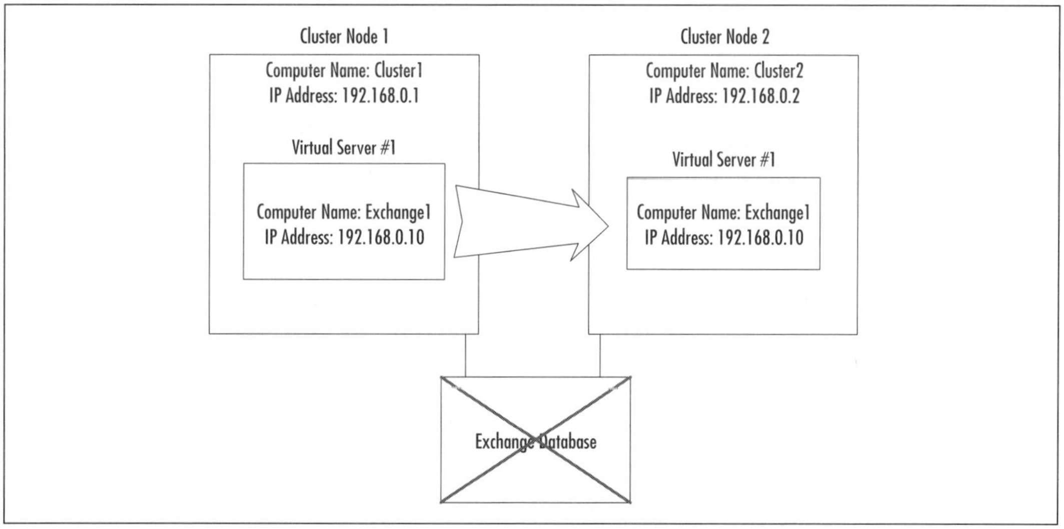

Network Load Balancing Basics

NLBS works by distributing incoming traffic from client requests between multiple servers. For NLBS to work, all the servers need to be on the same network segment.

NLBS can be used to cluster:

- **Web servers** Make your company's Web site highly available.

- **Streaming media servers** Deliver your company's training from load-balanced servers.

- **Virtual private network (VPN)** Make your remote access highly available.

- **Terminal Servers** Create a Terminal Server farm for high availability and load balancing.

As you can see from Figure 11.7, the cluster appears as a single server to the client. If DNS is configured to point to 192.168.0.1, any one of the three servers may respond to the client's request for a Web page.

Figure 11.7 An NLBS Cluster

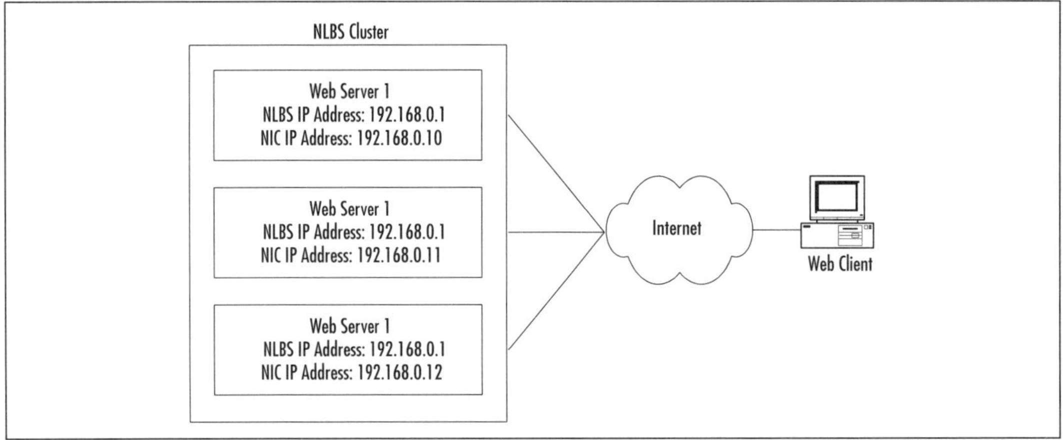

NLBS can be used to increase availability as well as scalability. It is easy to incrementally increase availability and scalability by adding a server. Just like Cluster Service, NLBS can be used for rolling upgrades. These are useful when you want to update a Web page. You can take a single server offline to update the files without rushing. Then start that server and move on to another one.

NLBS works by distributing inbound client traffic between servers. Each NLBS server uses the same virtual IP address, but only one of the servers responds to a client request. The NLBS partitions traffic between the servers. In Figure 11.8, four servers are shown. When a request comes in, only one of the servers will respond.

Figure 11.8 A Network Load-Balanced Cluster

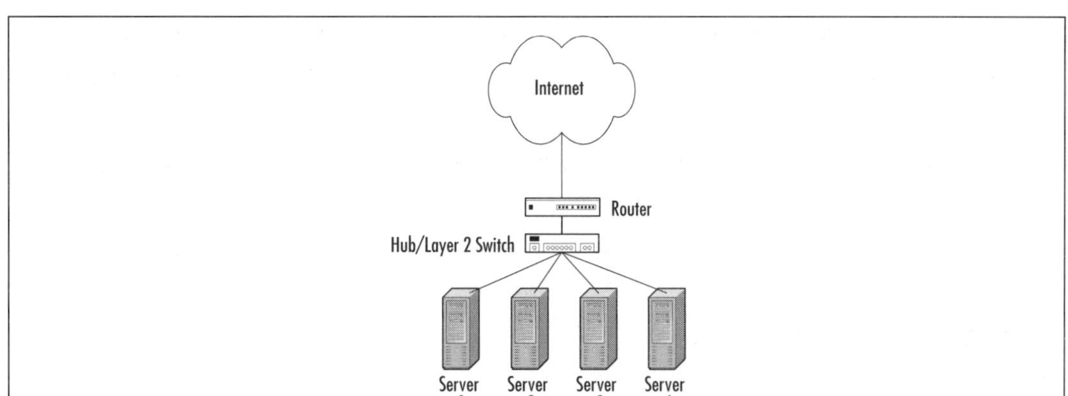

Each server sends out heartbeat messages about once per second. If a heartbeat message is not received from a server in a given period of time, the server is assumed to have failed, the convergence process starts, and the server is taken out of the cluster.

In our example, let's say that Server3 crashes. Since Server3 stops sending heartbeat messages, the other servers know it is offline. They automatically take Server3 out of the cluster when the failure is detected (see Figure 11.9). This happens within 10 seconds.

Figure 11.9 A Cluster Node Failure

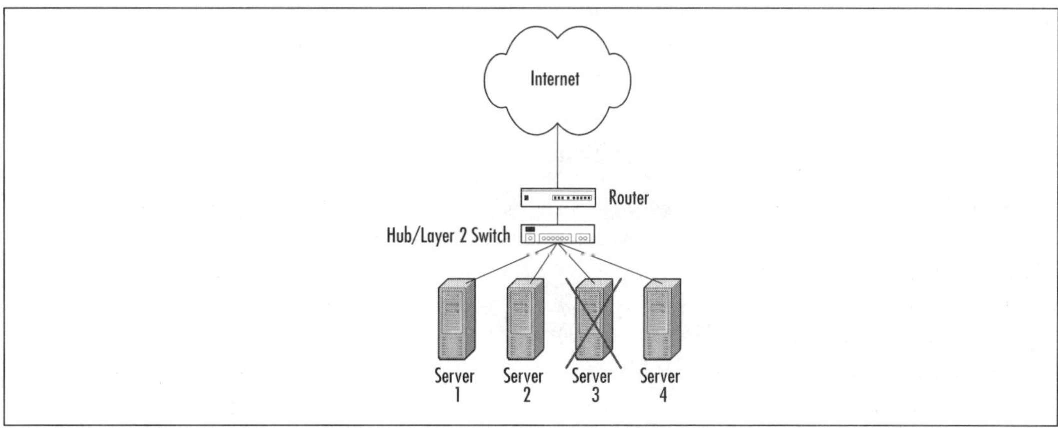

If our cluster starts receiving more requests than it can handle, it is easy to add a server. Simply configure a new server the same way you configured the old server and place it on the network. If you have a Web farm made up of four servers and you find that user requests are taking too much time, you can add another server to take some of the load (see Figure 11.10). To accomplish this task, you need to configure the new server with the same NLBS settings as the other servers in the cluster. Then configure the Web services like the other servers in the cluster and copy the Web pages to it.

Figure 11.10 Adding a New Server to the Cluster

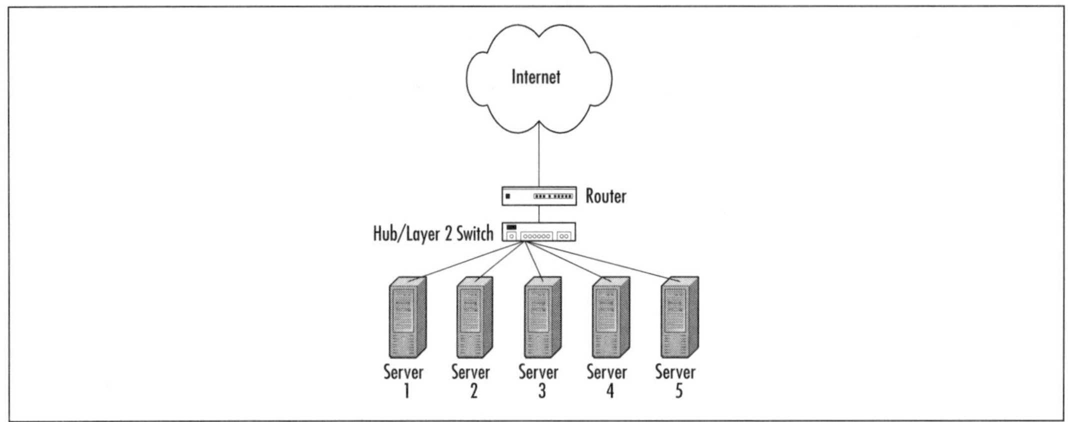

NLBS uses port rules to determine which servers respond to what traffic. You can set only the highest-priority server to respond to requests, or you can set the percentage of traffic each server should respond to. When you have multiple hosts responding to client requests, this setup is referred to as *multiple-host load balancing*. If only the highest-priority host responds to requests, this method is called *single-host load balancing*. Single-host load balancing provides only high availability, not load balancing.

If you have multiple-host load balancing, you can set the client affinity. There are three types of client affinity:

- **No client affinity** Each request by a single client can be handled by a different server. This maximizes the load-balancing features of NLBS but is impractical for certain situations.

- **Single-client affinity** Ensures that one server will always respond to a particular client, based on the source IP address of the request. This is necessary when client sessions are used, such as when a client is accessing a Terminal Server session or a VPN session.

- **Class C affinity** Sends all requests from a particular class C IP address to a single server.

Figure 11.11 shows the configuration of port rules on NLBS. You can see that affinity can be None, Single, or Class C. There is another option for *load weight*, which is the amount of traffic the server should handle relative to the other servers in the cluster. Load weight can be any number from 1 to 100, or it can be set to *equal*. Since nodes may join and leave the cluster, it is not necessary for the percentages to add up to 100. The percentage of requests to which the server responds is the total of all the servers' percentages divided by the local number.

Figure 11.11 Configuring NLBS Parameters

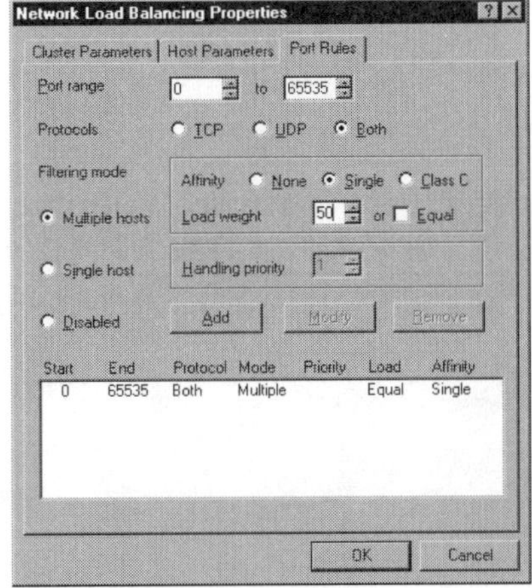

Advanced Exchange Clustering

Now that you know the basics of how Exchange 2000 can be clustered, let's discuss some advanced clustering topics. Exchange 2000 now allows you to form *Active/Active clusters*, which allow you to run Exchange services on both nodes of a cluster and, if a server fails, the surviving server will be able to run both Exchange virtual servers. Active/Active clusters allow you to utilize both machines in a cluster so that you don't have one server sitting idle most of the time.

This section also talks about Windows 2000 Datacenter Server. Since Datacenter Server allows four-way clusters, we'll discuss the ways in which a four-way cluster compares to a two-way cluster and the advantages of four-way clusters. We'll also discuss various ways you can configure your cluster hardware on Datacenter Server for maximum performance and reliability.

Active/Active Clusters

Before Exchange 2000, you could have Exchange on the same cluster as another clustered service, but you couldn't have two Exchange virtual servers on the same cluster. (You could have an Exchange virtual server and a file/print virtual server on the same cluster. This concept was diagrammed in Figure 11.2).

Because Exchange 2000 can now have multiple storage groups and multiple protocol virtual servers, you can now implement Active/Active Exchange servers. Active/Active Exchange clusters have multiple virtual servers that both run Exchange services at the same time. As you can see in Figure 11.12, both Cluster1 and Cluster2 are running Exchange 2000. In Figure 11.13, the Cluster1 server has failed, and its services have moved to Cluster2.

Figure 11.12 Active/Active Cluster Before a Failure

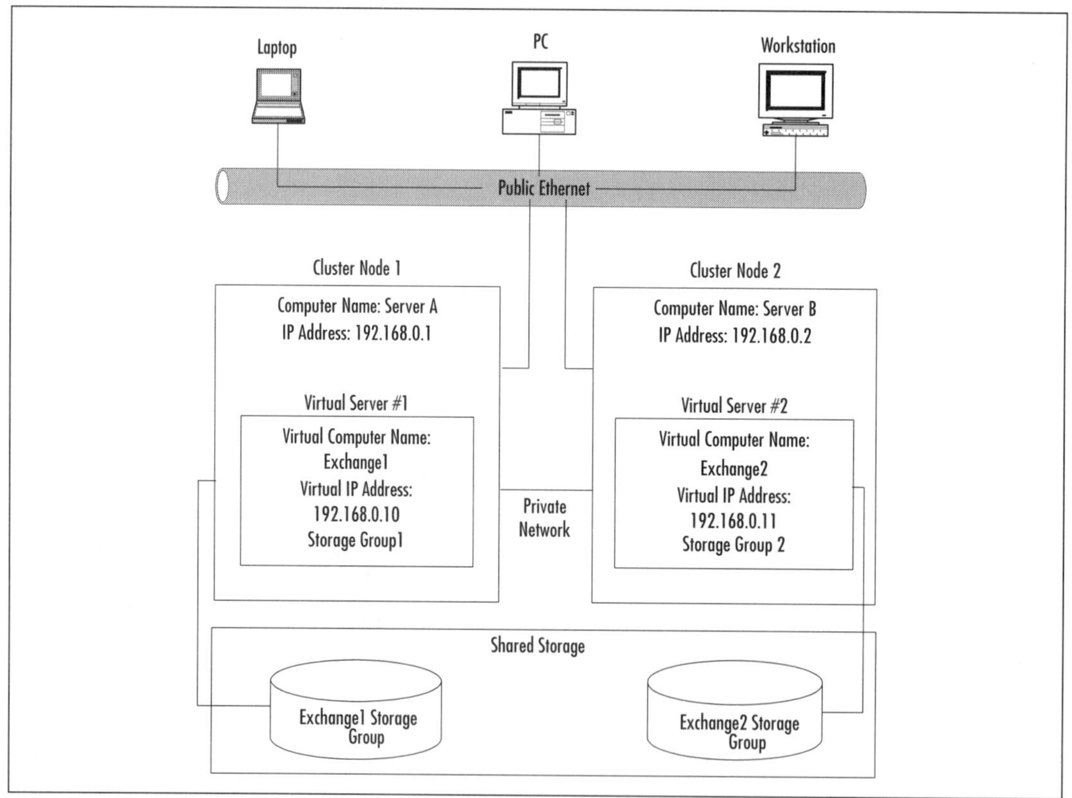

Figure 11.13 Active/Active Exchange Cluster After Failure

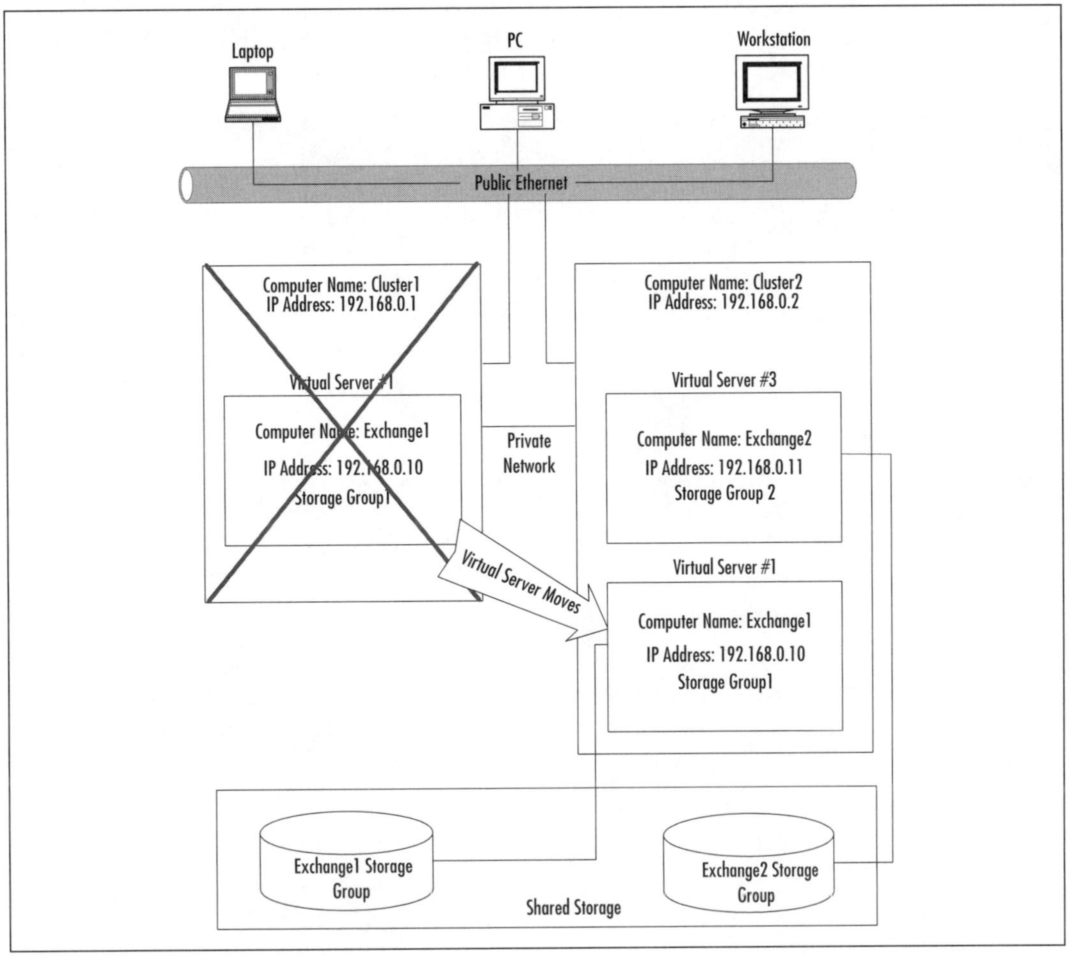

Because both servers are actively serving clients at the same time, you do not have a server that is sitting idle until a failure, but you have to be careful that you don't overload the surviving node of the cluster after a failure. You also have to make sure that you don't try to run more than four storage groups on a single server. We'll talk about capacity planning in the Planning Your Exchange Cluster section of this chapter.

Active/Active versus Active/Passive Services

Certain Exchange services are capable of Active/Active configuration, and some are not. The following services can be Active/Active:

- SA
- IS
- POP3
- IMAP4
- SMTP
- HTTP
- Full-text indexing

Some services can only be Active/Passive clustered, meaning that it can be installed on only one of the nodes in a cluster. These are:

- The Message Transfer Agent (MTA) service can be installed on multiple nodes in the cluster, but even during a failure, only one instance of the MTA is started on a given server. The single MTA service instance is able to handle multiple virtual servers.

- Only one public folder instance can run on a cluster. To Active/Active cluster Exchange, you need to delete the public folder instances on all but one of the servers.

- The Chat service is also capable of being clustered, but it can run only Active/Passive.

Some Exchange services cannot be clustered at all. These are:

- Network News Transfer Protocol (NNTP)
- Key Management Service (KMS)
- Instant Messaging

Datacenter Server

Microsoft Windows 2000 Datacenter Server is definitely Microsoft's most powerful operating system. It can support up to 32 processors, 64 gigabytes of memory, and most important, at least to our discussion here, up to four-way clusters.

With two-way clusters, you essentially have 50 percent of your hardware sitting idle if you don't want performance to degrade in the event one fails. In Figures 11.14 and 11.15, you can see an Exchange server CPU utilization before and after one of the servers fails. Because neither server is using more than half its utilization, CPU utilization after the failure does not exceed 100 percent.

Figure 11.14 An Active/Active Exchange Cluster Before a Failure

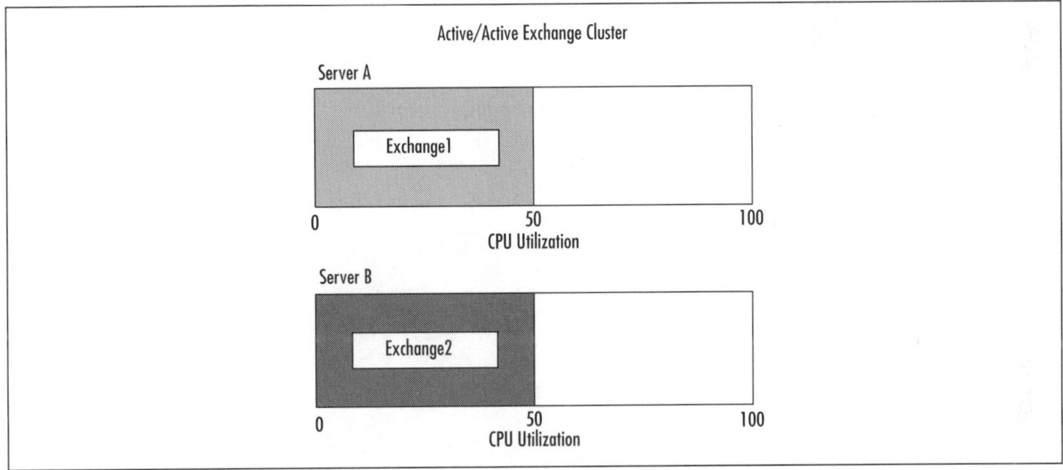

Figure 11.15 An Active/Active Exchange Cluster After a Failure

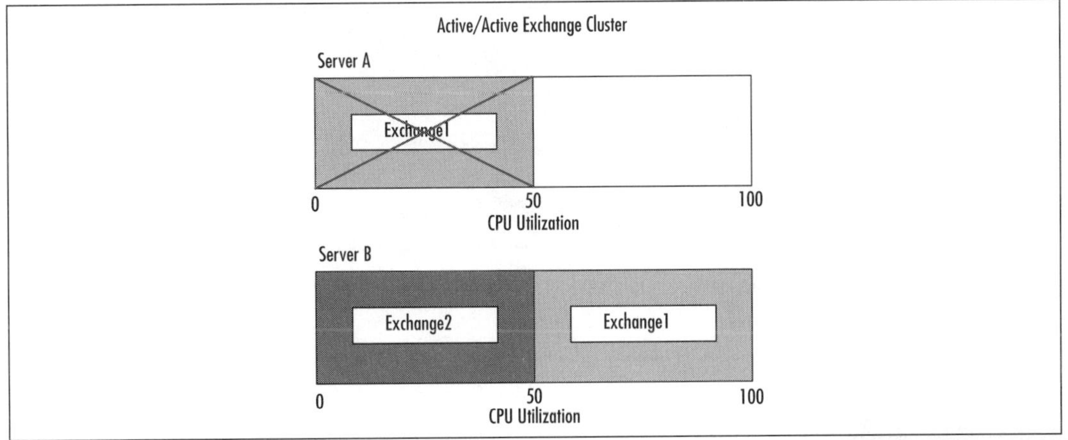

Because Datacenter Server can have up to four servers in the cluster, each machine can be up to 75 percent utilized. However, since you cannot split up a virtual server, you need to be careful how your virtual servers fail over. For example, you have four servers in a cluster, each with a single virtual server using 75 percent of the CPU on the server. If one of the servers fails, the virtual server has to move to another machine. That machine will have two virtual servers that each want 75 percent of the CPU utilization.

Datacenter Server requires using Fibre Channel connections for the shared storage area. Fibre Channel is similar to SCSI, but it uses fiber optic cable instead of copper cable to transfer information. Fibre Channel can use a Fibre Channel hub or switch (similar to a network hub or switch) to connect multiple devices. Fibre Channel is also significantly faster than SCSI interfaces. Advanced cluster configurations (see Figure 11.16) can have redundant Fibre Channel switches and redundant Fibre Channel controllers for increased reliability.

Figure 11.16 An Advanced Cluster Configuration

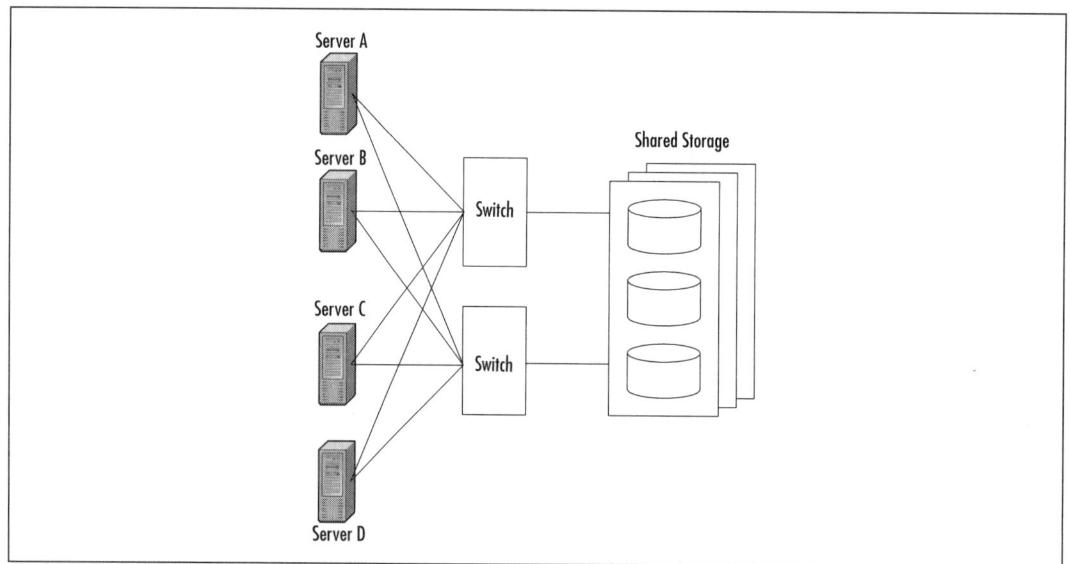

NOTE

Exchange 2000 requires Exchange 2000 Service Pack 1 to run on Datacenter Server.

Planning Your Exchange Cluster

When you are trying to determine if you should cluster your Exchange servers, you need to know the advantages and disadvantages of clustering. You also need to know the failures clustering can protect against and the failures it can't. This section discusses these issues.

You need to plan for various issues when building an Exchange 2000 cluster. Capacity planning is critical when you are building clusters. Because one server might have to do the work of two in the event of failure, it is important to plan how much a server should be utilized. Once you've done this planning, of course, you need to monitor the servers to make sure that they are not exceeding the capacity you've planned for.

Because of the limit of four storage groups running on a server, it is important to know what will happen to the storage groups in case a server fails. If you are running a simple two-node cluster, obviously you can't have more than a total of four storage groups on the servers.

We also look at some of the tools available to help you manage your cluster. If your Exchange server crashed and the virtual server moved over to another node in your network, it would continue to function. If you weren't monitoring the status of the cluster, you might not notice that the server was sitting at a blue screen.

When to Use Clustering

The obvious factor deciding the question of when to use clustering is, of course, availability. Clustering allows Exchange to remain available through all sorts of failures, including hardware failures such as motherboard, CPU, memory, and power supply failures as well as software failures such as blue screens and system freezes.

However, clustering can do more than just provide high availability. The other big advantage to clustering is referred to as a *rolling upgrade*. Rolling upgrades allow you to upgrade your servers one at a time, with no (significant) downtime. For instance, you can add memory or install Windows 2000 or Exchange 2000 service packs with minimal downtime. You can't, however, defragment an Exchange database. More on this issue in just a moment.

Rolling upgrades are done by following these steps:

1. Move the virtual server to another node in the cluster.

2. Perform the upgrade (add the memory, CPU, service pack, etc.).

3. Move the virtual server back to the original server.

This process can be repeated for each node in the cluster. Some organizations implement clusters only for performing upgrades and maintenance. Because users perceive no outage, upgrades do not necessarily have to be performed late at night or on weekends.

As we said before, you can also use NLBS to cluster your front-end servers for redundancy and load balancing, but you can't use NLBS to cluster your information store. This is because only one storage group can have a copy of a particular user's mailbox. You can still use NLBS to increase the performance and reliability of your Exchange system, though. Since you can use NLBS to cluster your front-end servers, you can have a cluster of machines handling users accessing their mailboxes through the Web or IMAP4/POP3 access. Since Secure Sockets Layer (SSL) encryption takes a great deal of CPU time to decrypt, it might be worthwhile to spread that load across multiple servers and get the added advantage of high availability. However, you can't use NLBS to make the information store highly available or load balanced, because each server would have to access the same information store, and it is not possible to replicate an information store.

When Not to Use Clustering

Since cluster uses a shared storage, Exchange stores the databases on the shared store. As we've gone over in previous chapters, there are many Exchange services to start up Exchange, and they are dependent on each other for initializing.

Database Corruption

If a failure occurs, the second system takes over the storage area and starts the services on that server. Therefore, if a database becomes corrupted on one server, neither server will be able to start the database. For this reason, clustering Exchange cannot protect against corrupted databases. If you were hoping to recover from corrupted databases, clustering will not help you.

Service Startup Time

If you can't tolerate a few minutes of downtime to fail the services over to the other server, don't use clustering. Remember that when an Exchange server crashes, it needs to check the consistency of its databases and replay the uncommitted log files, starting at the last checkpoint. This means that when you're in the biggest hurry to get the Exchange services back up, it is going to take the most time. This is another reason that you might not want to cluster your Exchange servers.

Load Balancing Information Stores

Since only one server is able to access a storage area at a time, you can't load-balance Exchange information stores using clustering. You can, however, configure both servers with their own storage group in an Active/Active cluster. This is done by installing Exchange on more than one node in a cluster and adding a storage group to each node in the cluster.

Database Maintenance

With a clustered server, you can add bring down one node and still run Exchange on a second node. This feature allows you to install service packs or add memory or CPUs. However, you can't do offline maintenance of the database (such as defragmentation or consistency checks) since only one process may access a database at a time. Any database maintenance must be performed while the Exchange server databases are dismounted. Ideally, this task would be done during a scheduled downtime.

Extra Work

Finally, increased administrative tasks are associated with clustering servers. Now you have two or more machines that you have to maintain, not just one. You have to monitor all servers in the cluster to make sure they are all working correctly. Remember that because of the high availability, you might not realize that there is a problem with one of the servers. If one server fails, you will essentially be running in a nonclustered state. You should use some sort of monitoring to make sure that, if a server fails, you know about it as soon as possible.

Capacity Planning

When planning your cluster, you need to be sure to include capacity planning. Two nodes in a cluster might hum along just fine until a server fails. The remaining server must now run all the resource groups from both nodes and is completely overloaded and unusable. For example, say that you have an Active/Active Exchange cluster using two identical servers, and each server is running at 80 percent CPU capacity. If one server fails, the load of both virtual servers will exceed the capacity of the remaining server, and the server will bog down. This situation will result in reduced performance, increased response times, and, in extreme cases, the system might be so overburdened as to be unusable or crash. This, of course, is contrary to the reason you installed a cluster in the first place.

When doing capacity planning on a cluster, you need to determine if the performance of the cluster during a failure is as important as normal operations. If it is important, you should not burden the servers in your two-way cluster more than 50 percent. However, you might decide that slower response times are acceptable during a failure. In this case, you might be willing to allow each node to exceed 50 percent utilization. As we can see in Figures 11.17 and 11.18, if both servers are using 75 percent of the CPU and one server fails, the other will obviously not be able to run at 150 percent. This situation will result in slower performance and, in extreme situations, the server will stop responding.

Figure 11.17 Two Servers Each Using 75 Percent of the CPU

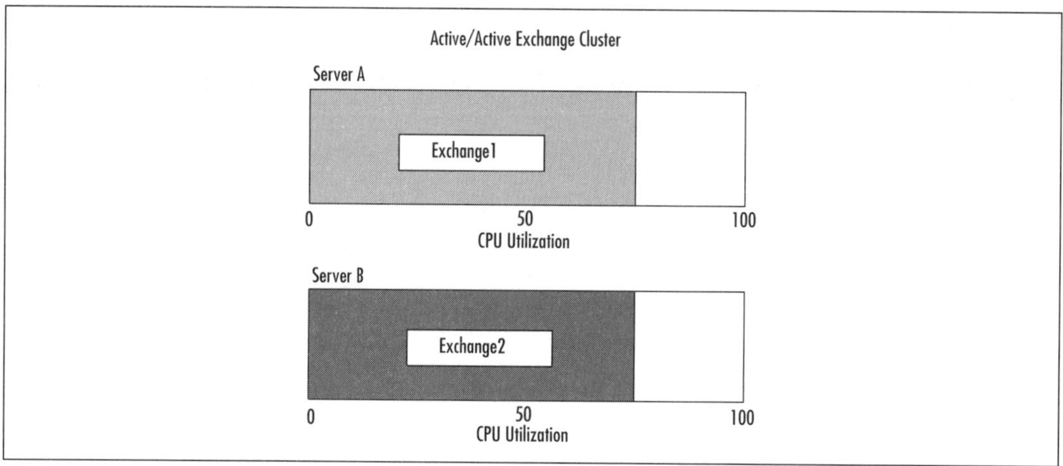

Figure 11.18 Two Servers Using 75 Percent of the CPU After One Server Crashed

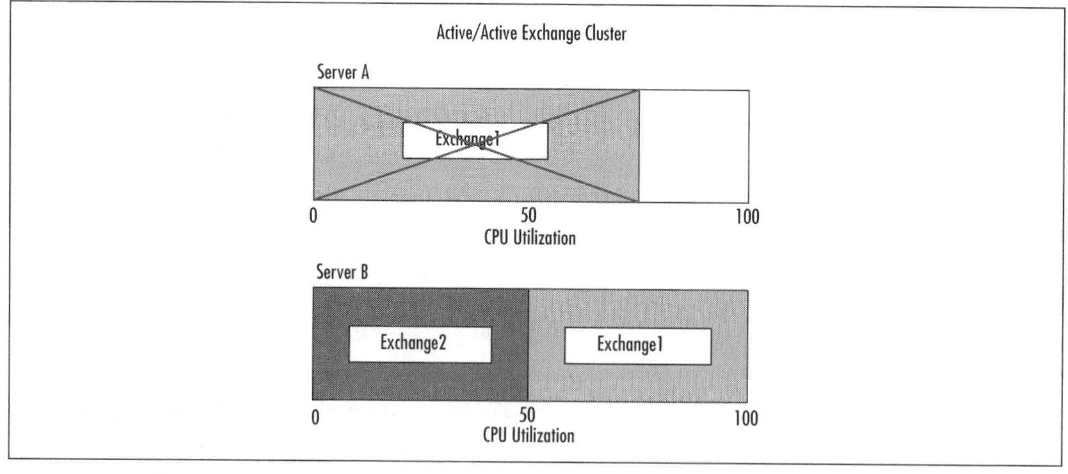

Exceed Storage Group Limit During Failure

Because an Exchange 2000 server can run up to four storage groups at a time, you need to plan your cluster so that you don't try to start more than four storage groups on a server. For example, you could put two storage groups on each node of a two-way cluster, or three on one and a single storage group on the other. That way, if one server failed, the other server in the cluster would be running all four storage groups. In the example shown in Figure 11.19, two Active/Active Exchange servers are each running two storage groups. When Server B fails, both storage groups move to Server A.

Figure 11.19 Storage Groups Move from One Active/Active Exchange Server to the Other

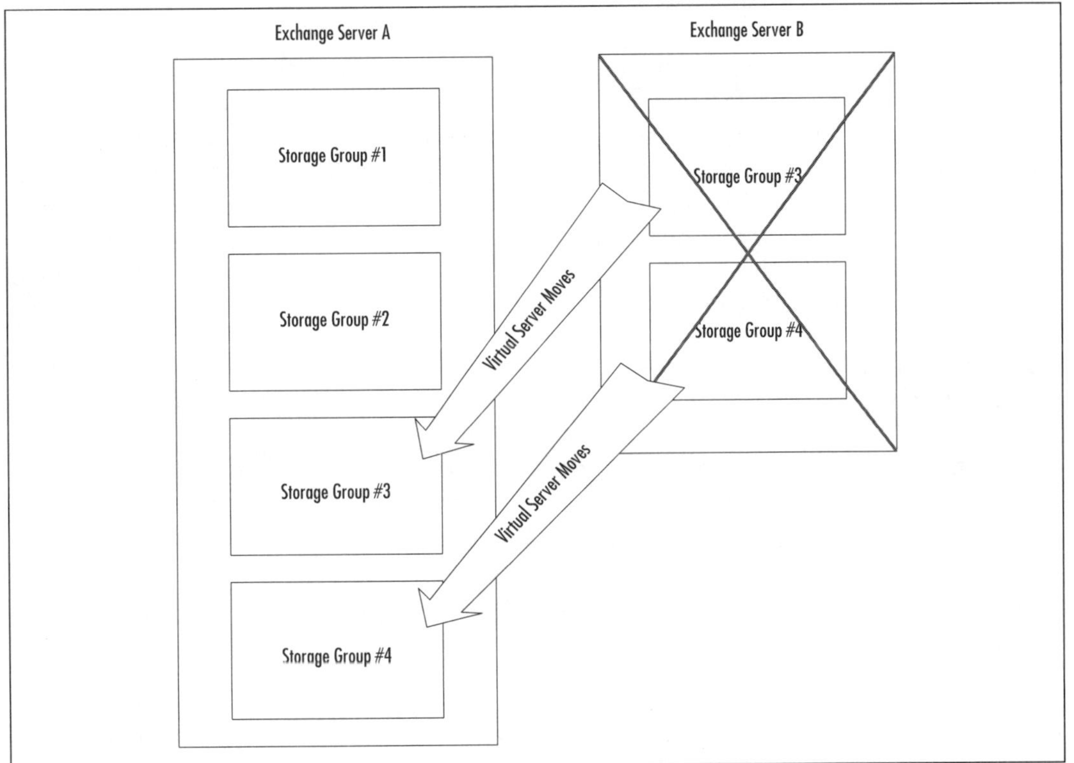

If you are using Datacenter Server and have a four-way cluster, you need to decide how many failures you need to protect against. If you are expecting only one failure at a time, you can put up to two storage groups on each server. Then when one fails, the two groups will move to another server. If you design the cluster this way, you must make sure that you configure the Exchange virtual servers so that one server does not try to start more than four storage groups if you have two servers fail.

The Failback Option

If the server that originally ran the service comes back online, you may choose to have the virtual server *failback* to the server that is the "preferred owner" of the resource group. Failback allows a virtual server to move back to the node it was on before a failure. The option to failback resource groups is selectable by resource group.

Failback is a good option when a single server will be exceeding capacity during a failure. If failback is set and the failed server comes back online, services will automatically move back to the preferred server. The problem with failback is that during the process, services are taken offline, just as they were in the original failover. If you don't want any more downtime than necessary, leave the failback option off. For example, if a server in your clustered node experiences a crash at 8:00 in the morning, resources will be transferred over to the working second server. Then let's say the crashed server is repaired by 1:00 PM. If you have failback configured, the newly fixed server will be asking for its services back at 1:00 PM, which can cause more downtime during the transfer. If you'd rather wait until 6:00 PM to move the services yourself, you need to leave failback off.

Using Cluster Utilities

This section lists a few utilities you can use to monitor and maintain your clusters. As we said before, it is important to monitor your system to ensure that it is functioning properly. There's not much point in having a cluster if one of the servers "blue-screens" and no one notices until the other server crashes. In addition, it is recommended that you use the Cluster Verification utility to ensure that the cluster has been configured properly. It's better to find out that it wasn't installed correctly before you put the cluster into production use. Take a look at the following terms related to cluster utilities:

- **Cluster Administrator** This is the best utility to look at the status of your Cluster Service cluster. It shows which server is running particular virtual servers, and it allows you to start and stop services or move virtual servers between servers.

- **WLBS** Used to determine the status and configure NLBS clusters remotely. This utility comes with Windows 2000 Advanced Server.

- **Cluster Verification** This utility ensures that a two-node cluster is configured properly. It can be found in the Windows 2000 Server Resource Kit or downloaded from the Microsoft Web site.

Installing an Exchange Cluster

This section shows how to build an Exchange 2000 cluster. Of course, before you can build an Exchange 2000 cluster, you need to be able to build a Windows 2000 cluster. We describe the steps required to build a cluster from Windows 2000 Advanced Server or Datacenter Server. Next we describe how to install Exchange 2000 onto that cluster. We also describe how to upgrade your existing Exchange 5.5 cluster to an Exchange 2000 cluster. Finally, we lay out the steps necessary to install an NLBS cluster.

Building a New Windows 2000 Cluster

Before you can install Exchange 2000 on a cluster, you first need to build the Windows 2000 cluster. Here we cover the basics of how to install and configure a cluster. Make sure that when you install Exchange 2000, you are using the same account you used to install the Cluster Service. This account must be a member of the Domain Admins group and the Built-in/Administrators group. Do the following:

1. Configure your hardware. Of course, this needs to be done on the Microsoft Hardware Compatibility List (HCL). The HCL can be found online at www.microsoft.com/hcl. It is best to configure the various hardware components exactly the same way (using the same slots for each device in each machine). Doing so makes configuration easier and ensures that there are no compatibility problems.

   Each server needs the following:

   - A hard drive controller for a boot drive. This drive is generally an internal drive used to hold the operating system.

   - A separate hard drive controller (SCSI or Fibre Channel) for the shared disks. This device must be in addition to the boot drive adapter and appropriate connection cables. For example, Adaptec's 2940U2W card has an external connector that you can use.

   - Two network interface cards (recommended).

In addition to each server, you also need:

   - A shared disk storage array that is able to connect to multiple computers. Make sure that both servers can see all the drives in the array (you can usually do this in the BIOS setup of the drive controller). Compaq makes the 4200 series data storage enclosure that holds up to 14 drives.

2. Turn off the shared storage area. Install Windows 2000 Advanced Server or Datacenter Server on both nodes of the cluster, but do not install the Cluster Service. The two servers can be installed at the same time. If you are using Datacenter Server, you need to use the installation media provided by your hardware vendor.

3. Configure networking components on both nodes. Again, the shared storage unit should still be powered off during this step. Configure the private cluster LAN interfaces and the public LAN interfaces. You should rename the interfaces *Private Connection* and *Public Connection* or something else that tells you which interface is which. Obviously, the public addresses need to conform to your LAN. The private connection IP addresses should be a subnet that is not in use on your network. For example, if you use 10.X.X.X on your public network, you should configure the private connections with 192.168.0.X.

4. Configure the shared disks from the first node in the cluster. This step needs to be done while only one node of the cluster is powered on. To make sure that the first node will be able to see the shared storage properly, turn off all the nodes in the cluster. Then power on the shared storage, then the first node. Then do the following steps:

   - Create the quorum disk. The disk needs only 50 megabytes (MB). If you are using a RAID array, you can simply create a small partition for the quorum disk.

   - Configure the shared disks. You can break these up if you will be doing Active/Active clustering. The disks need to be formatted as NTFS, and they cannot be dynamic disks. Dynamic disks are new to Windows 2000 and can be dynamically reconfigured. However, they can't be used with Cluster Service.

5. Install the Cluster Service on the first node. This is done with Add/Remove Windows Components. Select the Cluster Service, and follow the prompts. We've included the steps as follows, but you will be asked to provide the following information:

   - Confirmation that you have read and understood the HCL

   - The name of the cluster

   - The cluster service account username and password

   - The disks that the cluster will access

   - The location of the quorum disk

- The network configurations and whether they will be for the public or private network

- The IP address of the cluster

a. On Node #1, select Add/Remove Programs |Add/Remove Windows Components | Cluster Service.

b. Decide if you want to create or join a cluster, as shown in Figure 11.20. You will create a new cluster in this scenario.

Figure 11.20 Creating or Joining a Cluster

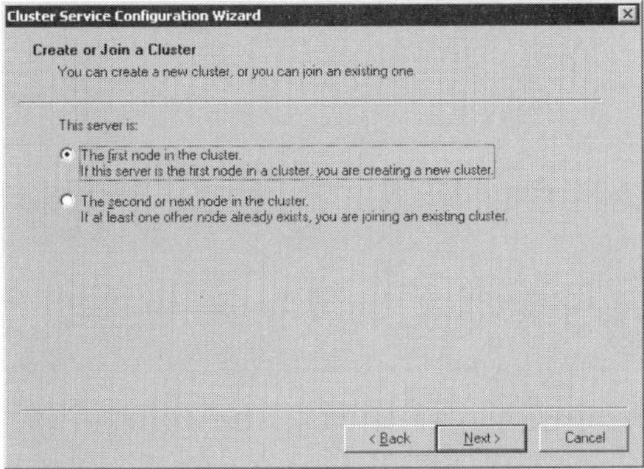

c. When the system prompts you for the cluster name, enter the name for your Windows 2000 cluster. We are calling ours Cluster1, as you can see in Figure 11.21.

Figure 11.21 Naming Your Cluster

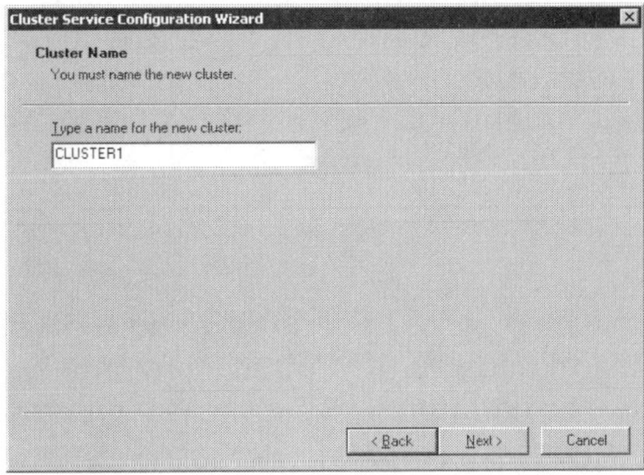

d. You are prompted for the name and password of your clustering service account. We are calling ours cluster_svc, with password cluster_svc, as you can see in Figure 11.22.

Figure 11.22 Cluster Service Account and Password

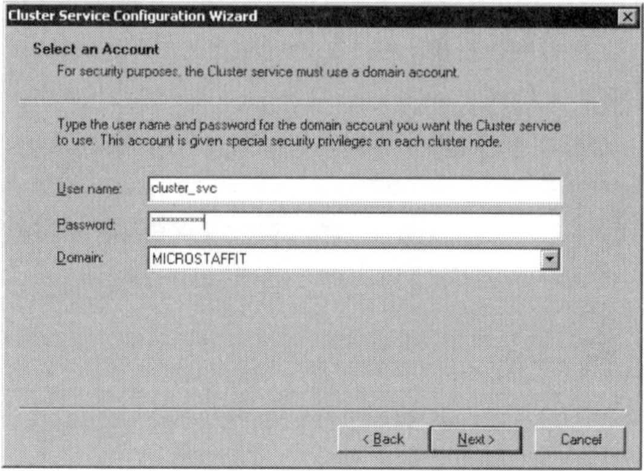

WARNING

Account permissions are crucial. The account that you used in ForestPrep should also be the account that you want the clustering service to use. It should also be the account that you log on to when you install Exchange. If you did not plan for this, you may get errors during the beginning of the Exchange install, such as: "The component 'Microsoft Exchange Messaging and Collaboration Services' cannot be assigned the action 'Install' because Active Directory has not replicated all the necessary permissions for the deleted items container. Please wait until replication completes before running setup." This error means that you have permissions problems. Either run the Exchange Administration Delegation Wizard to give the cluster service account permissions over the Exchange organization, or hand craft the permissions in Active Directory Users and Computers.

e. Next, you're asked to add or remove disks that you want clustering to manage. If you have any internal drives appearing in the right-hand pane, select them and choose Remove to put them back to the other side. See Figure 11.23.

Figure 11.23 Configure Disks for Cluster Management

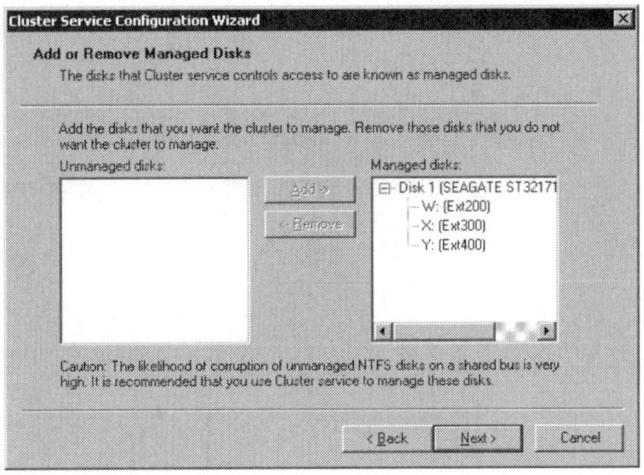

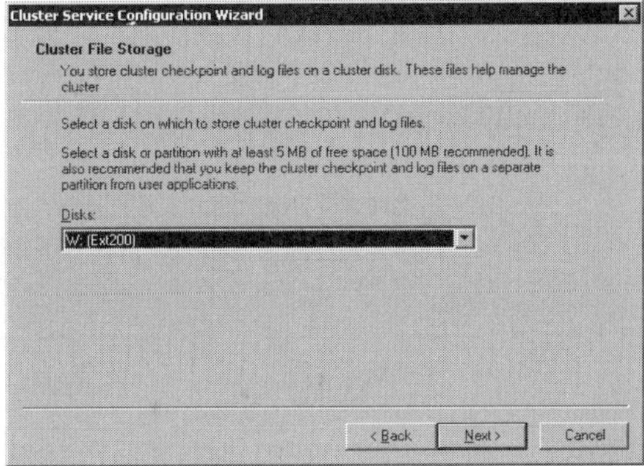

f. You should place your quorum on a separate physical external drive. We have only one physical external drive, so we put the quorum on the W: drive, as you can see in Figure 11.24.

Figure 11.24 Assigning the Cluster Quorum

g. You are given information and a warning about using private and public networks on the same physical LAN card. Then you are presented with the network connections menu. Normally you would not have only one NIC in your server, you would have two—one for public network and one for the private heartbeat. See Figure 11.25 for instructions on selecting your networking setup. You can see that it pulled in information on our default local area connection with our IP address ending in .178.

Figure 11.25 Configuring Your Public and Private Network

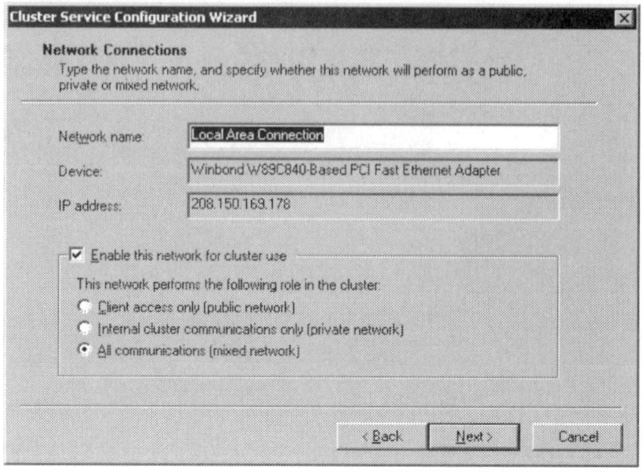

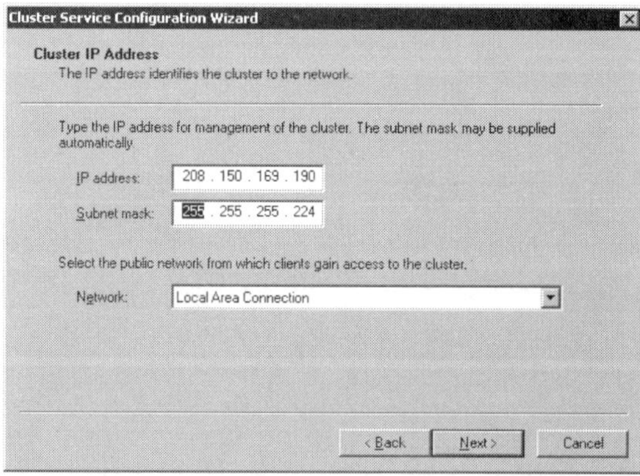

h. Next you are prompted for the unique IP address that will be for your cluster alone. We assigned an address ending in .190. The subnet mask was completed by the menu, as you can see in Figure 11.26.

When the install is finished, go to your second node, and turn it on. Configure the Cluster Service on the service (or second) node. The install is very similar. We include our steps here:

Figure 11.26 Cluster Unique IP Address

6. To install the Cluster Service on the second node:

a. For Node #2: select Add/Remove Programs |Add/Remove Windows Components | Cluster Service.

b. Decide if you want to create or join a cluster, as shown in Figure 11.27. In this case, join the cluster you just created.

Figure 11.27 Joining the Cluster

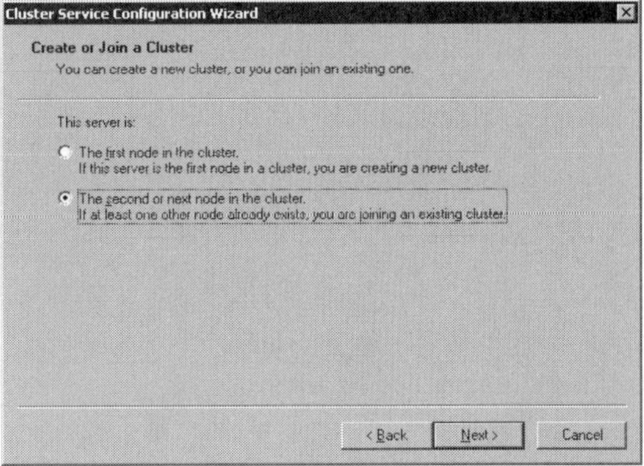

c. When the system prompts you for the cluster name, put in the name for your Windows 2000 cluster, Cluster1. You should *not* have to select "Connect to cluster as." Simply select next, as shown in Figure 11.28.

Figure 11.28 Defining the Cluster Name

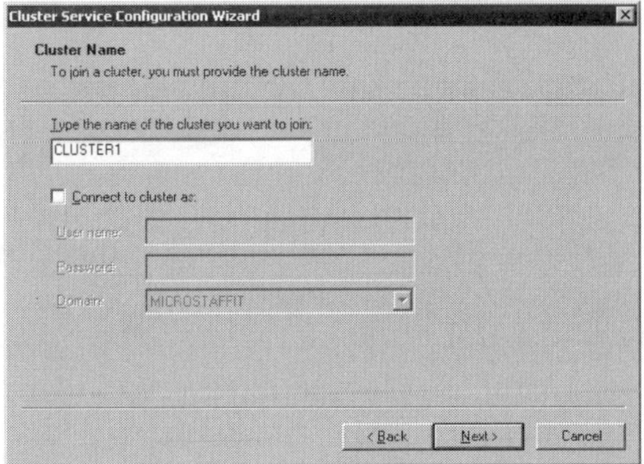

d. Next you are prompted for the password of your clustering service account. You should see the account and domain name prepopulated. Simply type in the password, as shown in Figure 11.29.

e. The rest of the install should go smoothly.

Figure 11.29 Cluster Service Password

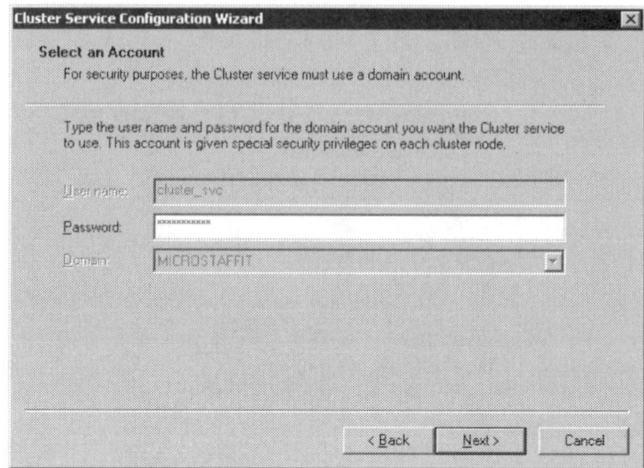

> **TIP**
>
> During installation of a two-node cluster, even if you will use a crossover cable to connect the servers on the private cluster LAN, put both connections on a hub during installation. That way, the Cluster Service will see the NIC as connected and you will be able to configure it during the Cluster Service installation. Otherwise, you might not be able to configure the network correctly until after you bring up the second server.

7. Test the installation. You can now open the Cluster Administrator and see the virtual server created by default. You can move this service between the two nodes by right-clicking the resource group and selecting Move. In Figure 11.30, you can see that we have two physical nodes (two servers) called Cancer and Aries, and they are both up. Figure 11.31 shows that the cluster resources for Cluster Group are up and online on the server called Cancer.

8. If you are installing Datacenter Server, you can add more nodes at this time. These are done the same way as the second node, described previously.

During the installation of the first node, the Cluster Service automatically created several important things. The most important is the cluster group. This is a virtual server that the Cluster Service uses to manage the cluster. It is important that you don't add any services to this group. You can connect to this server from the network and see what happens when you move the virtual server between nodes. Try pulling out a power plug or removing the LAN on the private network and see the result.

Figure 11.30 A Working Pair of Nodes in a Cluster

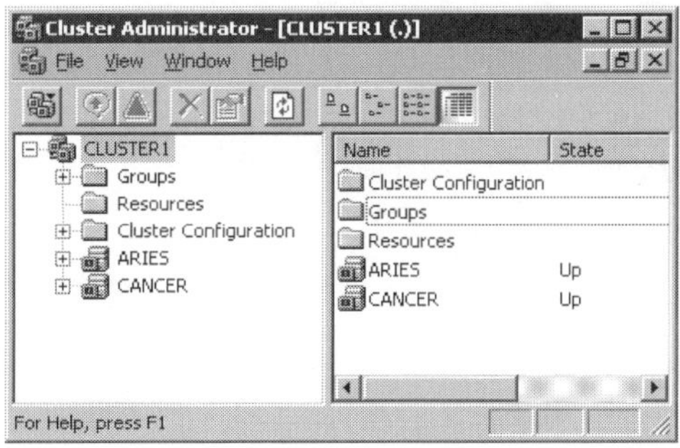

Figure 11.31 A Working Cluster Online on the Physical Node Cancer

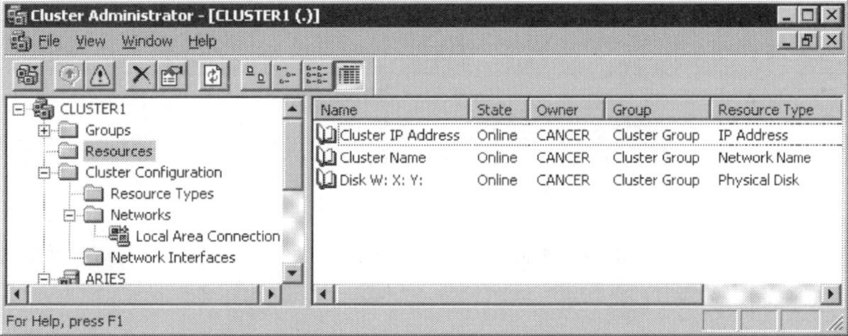

Installing Exchange 2000 on a Cluster

After you have your Windows 2000 cluster running, you are ready to install Exchange 2000. Make sure you have everything ready for Exchange, such as having both NNTP and SMTP installed on both systems.

If this is not the first Exchange 2000 server in the organization, make sure that the account is a granted the Exchange Full Administrator privilege. If you will be running the ForestPrep portion of the installation, make sure that the account is a member of Domain Admins, Schema Admins, and Enterprise Admins.

If you will be installing an Active/Active cluster (see Figure 11.32), both virtual servers need their own shared storage areas. Make sure these areas are configured before you start installing Exchange.

Now you're ready to start installing Exchange 2000. You must complete the installation on the first node before you can start on the other node. Make sure that you install Exchange the same way on both nodes. For example, install the same components on both nodes, use the same drive letters and directories for the Installable File System for both nodes, and so

Figure 11.32 An Active/Active Exchange Server

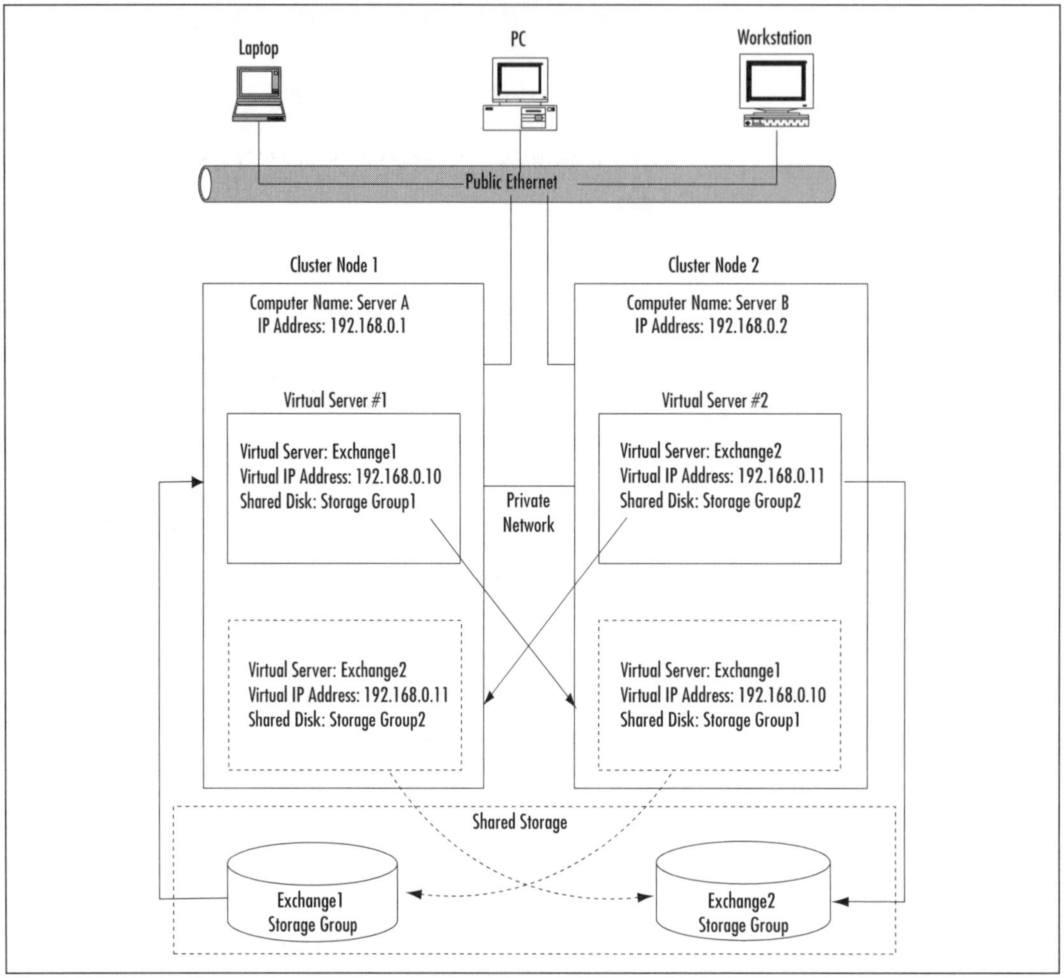

on. Follow these installation steps for an Exchange installation on Nodes 1 and 2:

1. Make sure you are logged on with the same account that you ran ForestPrep in and defined the clustering service to use.

2. Install Exchange 2000 from the CD, selecting i386\setup.exe.

3. Choose the options that you want. We chose the Typical installation. For the install path, use the default C:\program files\ exchsrvr\ (see Figure 11.33).

Figure 11.33 Installing Exchange for a Clustered Node

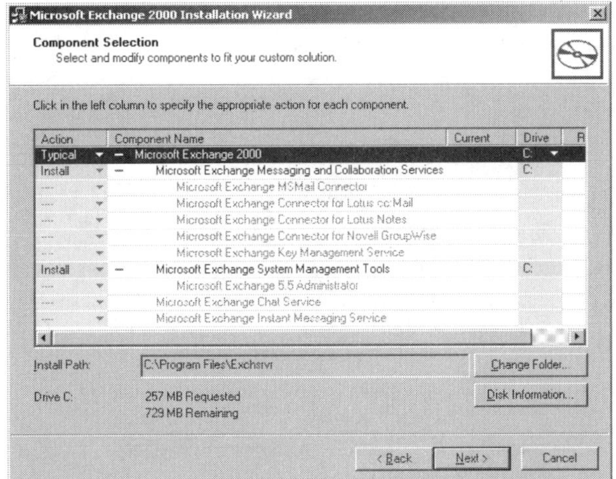

4. After the installation begins, Setup tells you that it will install the cluster-aware version of Microsoft Exchange. When it is finished, install Exchange on the second node by completing the steps in this section.

5. Make sure you are logged on with the same account that you ran ForestPrep in and defined the clustering service to use.

6. Choose the options that you want. We chose Typical. For the install path, use the default C:\program files\exchsrvr\.

7. After the installation begins, Setup tells you that it will install the cluster-aware version of Microsoft Exchange. When it is finished, it prompts you to reboot the server.

Next you must create an Exchange virtual server group for each instance of Exchange you will run. (Microsoft recommends that you do not use the default cluster group to run Exchange.) We will create the virtual server by creating a Resource Group and adding the following:

- An IP address resource

- A cluster name resource

- A cluster disk resource

- An Exchange System Attendant resource

Once the System Attendant is added, the rest of the services will be added to the Cluster Manager.

First of all, let's take a look at what has been added to Cluster Administrator as a result of the Exchange install. Figure 11.34 indicates that more Resource Types have been added that are Exchange specific.

Figure 11.34 Exchange-Specific Resource Types in Cluster Administrator

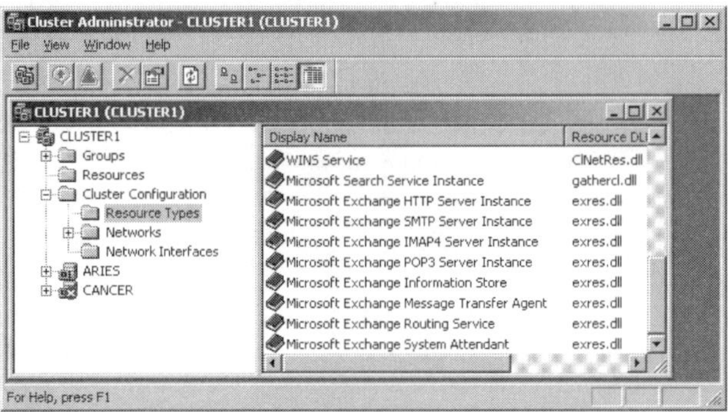

To create the Exchange Virtual Server Group, complete the following steps:

1. In Cluster Administrator, right-click the groups container and create a new group. Within that group, you can right-click and create the new resources: IP address, cluster name, and disk resources. Verify that they can fail over between the two nodes before moving to Step 2.

NOTE

Microsoft recommends that you have a unique group created that has its own IP address, server name, and Storage Group. They do not recommend that you put a virtual resource (such as the Exchange Virtual Server) on the same drive as the quorom drive. However, in the scenario created for this book, we have just one external drive, so we are using the first cluster group created, under Groups, called "Cluster Group."

2. To create the Exchange System Attendant resource, highlight your Exchange Group in the left-hand pane; and you should see your three resources on the right, as in Figure 11.35.

Figure 11.35 Exchange Group with Resources before Creating Exchange Resources

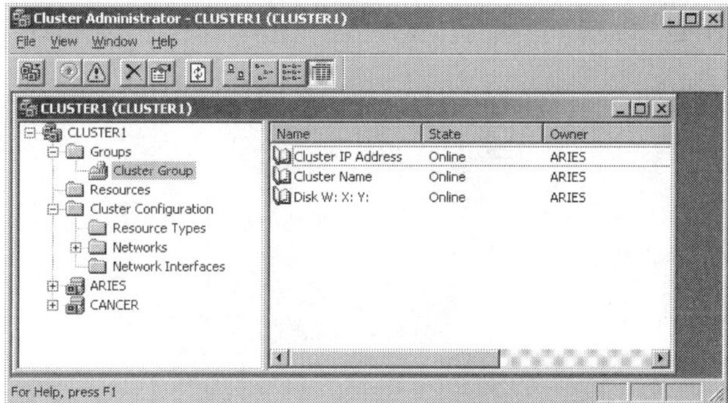

3. Put your mouse in the right pane, right-click, and select New | Resource, and select the Microsoft Exchange System Attendant resource. Complete the resource information, as shown in Figure 11.36. Click Next.

Figure 11.36 Exchange System Attendant Resource

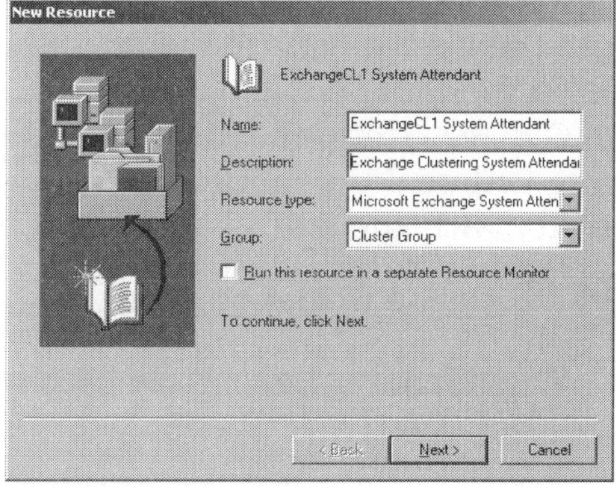

4. Select the possible owners of this resource. These are the physical servers that it will run on. We choose Aries and Cancer, our two Clustering nodes. Click Next.

5. Select the resources that have to be brought online before the Exchange System attendant. Here is where you select the resources that you defined in the Exchange Group earlier. Highlight the resources on the left hand pane, select Add as shown in Figure 11.37, and the resources should then be placed on the right hand side of the form. (Note that you do not have to include

the IP address, but normally you would want that resource to be associated with your Exchange server.) Click Next.

Figure 11.37 Dependencies That Must Be Brought Online First

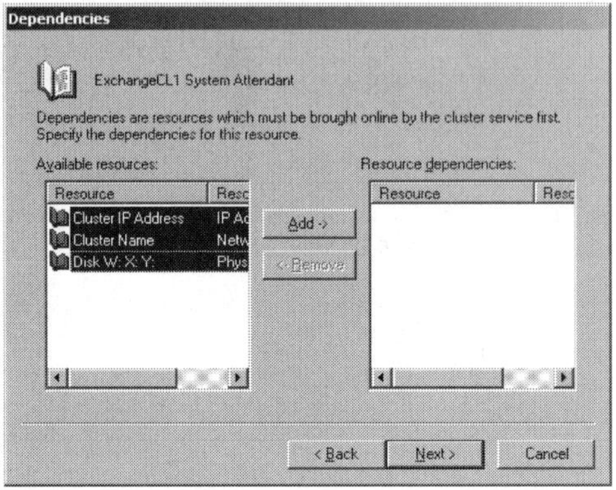

6. You are asked to enter the path for the data directory. This is the point where you identify on the external storage where the Exchange data will go. We will select w:\exchsrvr. You would select the appropriate disk drive that is in your Exchange Storage Group. You should then get a pop-up window that says Cluster Resource "… System Attendant" created successfully. Now, highlight the Exchange Cluster Group in the left hand pane, right-click, and select Bring Online. You should then see your Cluster Administrator with the status as in Figure 11.38.

Figure 11.38 Online Exchange Cluster

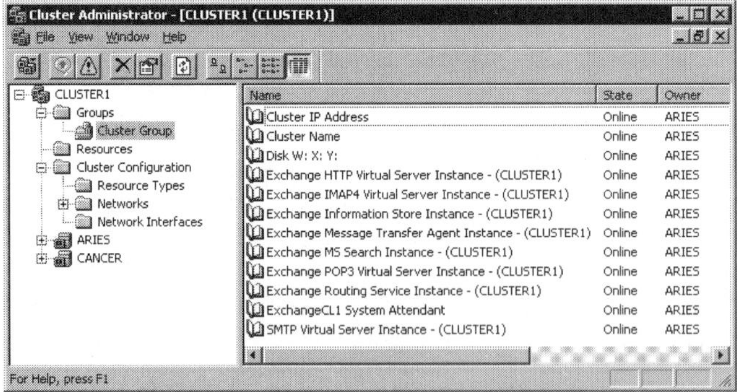

7. To verify that you have clustered Exchange, run Exchange System Manager. Instead of your node names of the two physical servers, you should see the clustered server name. As you can see in

Figure 11.39, the System Manager indicates we have an Exchange server called Cluster1.

Figure 11.39 Clustered Exchange Server as Seen in Exchange System Manager

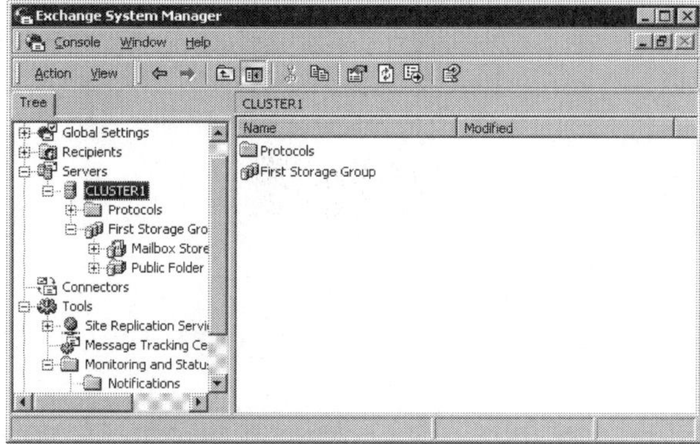

8. Now, to verify that failover works, go into Cluster Administrator, right-click your cluster group, and select Move Group. This moves the Exchange Virtual Server in our example from Aries to Cancer. So, as you can see in Figure 11.40, the Exchange Virtual Server has been moved to run on Cancer. Compare this with the previous Cluster Administrator figure (Figure 11.38) to note the difference.

Figure 11.40 Clustered Exchange Server as Seen in Exchange System Manager

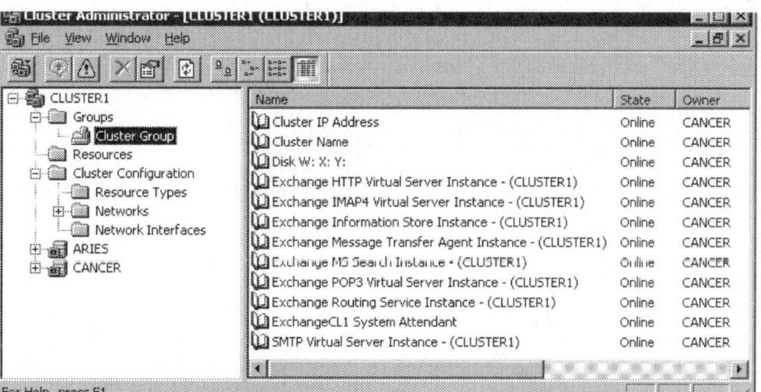

How to Upgrade from an Exchange 5.5 Cluster

If you have an existing Exchange 5.5 server running on a Windows NT Server Enterprise Edition cluster and want to upgrade to Exchange 2000 on a Windows 2000 Advanced Server cluster, you can choose from two basic methods. The first and most obvious is to migrate all your users on the cluster server to a different server in the same site. Then upgrade the cluster server to Windows 2000, install Exchange 2000, and move the users back to the new clustered Windows 2000/Exchange 2000 server. This is probably the best solution for most organizations.

Although the previous option is recommended, there is a way to migrate the server to Exchange 2000. First, you need to upgrade to Windows 2000 Advanced Server. This can be done one machine at a time in order to minimize downtime, using a rolling upgrade. To upgrade to Windows 2000:

1. Make sure that you have at least one good backup of the server.

2. Move all resource groups to one machine.

3. Run the Windows 2000 Upgrade on the machine with no resource groups.

4. Move all resource groups to the recently upgraded machine.

5. Run the Windows 2000 Upgrade on the other machine.

6. Move the resource groups back to their preferred server.

Since Active Directory is required for Exchange 2000, you also need to upgrade to Active Directory if you haven't already done so. Furthermore, you should run the Active Directory Connector to add all your users to AD.

Once the cluster has been migrated to Windows 2000, you can upgrade to Exchange 2000. Make sure that you have at least Exchange Service Pack 3 installed. Perform the following procedures:

1. Make sure that you have a full backup of your servers.

2. Take the Exchange resource group offline.

3. Go to your shared cluster drive used by Exchange and rename the Mdbdata directory to something else (such as mdbdata5.5).

4. Remove Exchange 5.5 from both nodes using the Setup program. Make sure that you don't delete the server from the site. To do this, run the Exchange 5.5 Setup program, and select Remove All. Do this on both servers.

5. Install Exchange 2000 on the first node. Use the same method described in the previous section. Make sure that you use the same drive and folder you were using with Exchange 5.5. This process makes the schema changes to the Active Directory forest if that has not already been done. After installing Exchange Server on the first node, restart that node.

6. Install Exchange 2000 on the second node. Use the method described in the previous section. Make sure that you use the same drive and folder you were using with Exchange 5.5 and that you select the same components as on the first server. You need to select the same drive for the Installable File System that you chose for the first system. After installing Exchange Server on the second node, restart that node.

7. Open Cluster Administrator, and in the same cluster group that was used for Exchange 5.5, add a Microsoft Exchange System Attendant resource. This is done by right-clicking the Exchange resource group, clicking New, then clicking Resource. Enter a name for the resource, and in the Resource Type box, click the Microsoft Exchange System Attendant option. Make sure that you select the correct resource group in which to put the System Attendant. Add dependencies for the network name, and for the Data Directory, make sure that the directory is on the shared drive. Make sure that this directory is empty.

8. Copy the Priv.EDB and Pub.EDB files from the directory you renamed to the Exchsrvr\Mdbdata5.5 directory, and rename these files Priv1.EDB and Pub1.EDB.

9. Bring the resource group online in Cluster Administrator.

There are some requirements to perform this method:

- The new Exchange 2000 cluster can't be the first Exchange 2000 server in the Exchange 5.5 site. You must either upgrade a non-clustered Exchange 5.5 server to Exchange 2000 or build a temporary Exchange 2000 server.

- The new Exchange 2000 cluster cannot be a bridgehead to an Exchange 5.5 site. You must move any directory replication connectors to another server before you upgrade.

- The Exchange 5.5 cluster cannot be the first server in the site. You must move the system folders (Free/Busy connector, Organizational Forms, and offline address book) to another server in the site.

You cannot upgrade a nonclustered Exchange 5.5 server to an Exchange 2000 cluster. You must build the cluster, then migrate mailboxes to it.

How to Install and Configure the Network Load Balancing Service

Installation of the NLBS is fairly straightforward. To work, all servers need to be on the same network segment. To configure NLBS on two or more machines:

1. Install NLBS. This is done through Network and Dial-up Connections, which you can open by right-clicking Network Neighborhood and clicking Properties. Click Install, Service, and Add. Click Network Load Balancing.

2. Configure NLBS. This is done by right-clicking an adapter and clicking Properties. Click the NLBS component, and click Properties. Configure the IP address for the cluster, and add an IP address for the individual machine. This IP address will be used to manage the individual machine.

3. Configure the filtering mode. Filtering mode lets you select the option that only the server with the highest priority gets traffic (when you don't need high availability) or the option to distribute the load.

4. Set client affinity. Setting client affinity instructs the cluster to use a single node to service a client.

Once you have NLBS installed, you can configure Exchange 2000 to be a front-end server. This is done by installing Exchange and selecting the appropriate components. Then, in the Exchange Service Manager, you can set the server to be a front-end-only server.

Troubleshooting

In this section we describe some of the areas that can cause administrators trouble if they are not careful. As we said earlier, no amount of clustering will help prevent database corruption. Later we describe how to recover a lost or corrupted quorum drive and how to stop cluster resources without initiating a failover.

Database Corruption

As we said before, if your databases become corrupted, no amount of clustering will help you. If database corruption occurs, you need to fix the databases or restore from backup.

To restore from backup, you need to locate a backup and run your backup software. Dismount the corrupted database, and then select the database to be restored and restore it. We discussed backups and restores of Exchange databases in more depth in Chapter 10. To attempt to fix a corrupted database, you need to use the Eseutil utility. This is done by going to a command prompt and typing:

```
Eseutil /p databasefile
```

Chapter 12 discusses how to use the Eseutil utility to repair Exchange databases.

Quorum Drive Failure

Problems can result if the quorum log file becomes lost or corrupted. The first way to recover from this situation is to restore the quorum log from backup. This file, stored on the quorum drive in an MSCS directory, is called quolog.log.

If you can't restore the quorum log from backup, you can recreate it by doing the following:

1. At a command prompt in the C:\winnt\cluster directory, type **clussvc -debug –resetquorumlog**.
2. Stop the Cluster Service.
3. Restart the Cluster Service.

These steps start the Cluster Service on the machine on which they are performed. Then, as other nodes are brought online, the nodes update the quorum log with current information.

Accidentally Stopping an Exchange Service

At some point, you are likely to accidentally stop an Exchange service using either the command prompt or through the service's Control Panel. You will then notice that all the other Exchange services are stopping, even though they are not dependent on the service you stopped. This is because the Resource Monitor DLL noticed that one of the Exchange services was stopped and decided to attempt to restart the services on another node in the cluster.

To make sure that this doesn't happen, always use the Cluster Administrator to stop or restart services. If you use the Cluster Administrator for these tasks, the Resource DLL will know that the service was stopped on purpose and will not initiate a failure.

Summary

In this chapter, we discussed the two different types of clustering in Windows 2000: Cluster Service and Network Load Balancing Service. Cluster Service uses shared storage architecture to allow multiple servers to access a common storage area. If one of the nodes in a cluster fails, another server is able to access that area of shared storage and start the servers. Windows 2000 Advanced Server supports two-way clusters, and Datacenter Server supports up to four-way clusters. NLBS is used to distribute client requests across multiple servers. This is ideal for Web servers but can also be used for Terminal Servers and VPN servers. Using NLBS to cluster your Outlook Web Access is an excellent way to reduce the load on your Exchange database servers.

Additional hardware and software are required to support a cluster server. You need external drive space that can be shared by multiple servers. Each server needs two drive controllers, and multiple NICs are strongly recommended. Since Windows 2000 Server does not support clustering, you need Advanced Server or Datacenter Server.

We discussed how to install each of these services and how to install Exchange 2000 to utilize each of these services for availability and load balancing. When designing your Exchange cluster, you need to do some capacity planning to make sure that you are not overloading a server if there is a failure.

Cluster Service uses various components to function. Shared storage is the most important; it is used to move applications between servers. A dedicated network between the cluster nodes is used so that the nodes of the cluster know if a node fails. A quorum drive on the shared storage is used in case the network fails, so that the servers can continue functioning if the private network fails.

As we said a number of times throughout the chapter, Cluster Service cannot protect against a corrupted database. If you get a corrupted database on an Exchange cluster, you need to restore the database from backup or attempt to fix the database with Eseutil. Before you start ordering the hardware for your Exchange cluster, you must be sure that you are implementing a cluster for the right reason. After some consideration, you might find that it's not worth the additional cost in hardware, software, and administration.

FAQs

Visit **www.syngress.com/solutions** to have your questions about this chapter answered by the author.

Q: How does NLBS determine which server should reply to a request?

A: The algorithm used lets each server determine which server will handle the request. Since all servers use the same algorithm, they can all come to the same conclusion independently. The server that is selected is based on the client's IP address, port number, and other factors.

Q: I set my HTTP to use SSL only, and now my services fail over repeatedly. What's wrong?

A: The cluster server tests various conditions to make sure that all Exchange services are running properly. One of the things it tests are the connections to the various protocols—HTTP, IMAP4, and POP3. If you set any of these protocols to SSL only, the cluster server cannot connect properly and therefore assumes that the protocol isn't working. It tries to move the services to another server, but no other servers will be able to work properly. Make sure that you don't force SSL only on any of these protocols on a cluster server.

Q: I restored a cluster database from a backup, then tried to run the eseutil /cc command, but it returned an error message. How do I start the recovery process?

A: At a command prompt, type **set cluster_network_name=*clustername***, where *clustername* is the network name used by the cluster.

Q: I uninstalled Exchange, but the Exchange Organization still exists, even though it was the last server. How do I remove the organization?

A: The only way to remove the Organization is to install another non-clustered Exchange server, then remove it.

Basic Monitoring and Troubleshooting Methodology

Solutions in this chapter:

- **Basic Troubleshooting Methodology for Exchange 2000**
- **Message Stores and Storage Groups**
- **Message Flow and Routing**

Introduction

Usually technical books devote the very beginning of their content to architecture. However, we decided to place the Exchange architecture discussion closer to those people who care about it: the support analysts. Do you need to know *everything* about how Exchange is architected? Most Exchange administrators don't have to know about *every* feature in Exchange 2000. Not all of you are going to implement Exchange Conference Server, multiple public folder trees, ASP servicing, clustering, and instant messaging.

When you take a look at Exchange 2000 and compare it with Exchange 5.5, you are basically taking on the comparative task of learning a new operating system. Exchange 2000 is immense. The developers had a saying that Exchange is so big that it can't fit into three heads; double that and make it six heads for Exchange 2000.

A Troubleshooting Case Study

Our company recently got a phone call from a client with a problematic Exchange server. We had been working with the client the week before, and now something was wrong with Internet e-mail. Exchange is a critical part of their business process; the company's 200 users need it for e-mail for internal workflow projects and to work with clients and vendors—and especially for marketing communications. Now their Exchange server simply wasn't working at 100 percent, and they knew we had encouraged them to contact us before a small problem became larger. Here's how the situation played out:

- Once on site, we wrote down their problem and what they thought happened. Simple Mail Transfer Protocol (SMTP) Internet mail was coming in to the Exchange Server, but in batches. E-mail was being sent out to the Internet, and the queues were good and empty, but the e-mail wasn't being received on the other end—so where was the e-mail, and what was going on?

- We looked at all the events in the event log. There was nothing in the system log of importance, and there was nothing of importance in the application log concerning the network. It was unclear to the support team what had happened.

Continued

- The event viewer showed that the system had not been shut down or rebooted. Only the Internet e-mail wasn't working. By knowing the basic architecture, we then knew that it had nothing to do with the Message Transfer Agent (MTA), the Information Stores, and other internal components—only connections *out*. What things can go wrong with Internet mail? What type of components interface with SMTP services?

- We checked the network and pinged the gateway and the Domain Name System (DNS) servers. They were fine. We then did tracert to various systems. They appeared to be working normally.

- Next, we looked at the calendar and figured out which day it had been that people started noticing the problems with their e-mails. We called the networking support team and asked about any DNS changes. They said that they had made changes a few days before, but the local Exchange team had implemented the changes appropriately and had tested fine.

- We talked to the network team some more, and after a few phone calls back and forth, it turned out that the DNS information in all the client's DNS servers had not replicated out, and there were DNS records still pointing to nonexisting servers. So, based on some DNS servers having correct data, e-mail from the Internet was being routed correctly on some occasions. However, when the incorrect DNS servers were being consulted, errors occurred. Once all the DNS servers were configured completely, e-mail started routing correctly.

This was a very basic problem that could have gotten worse by using the wrong tools or by jumping into connector property pages and changing values. The key to Exchange troubleshooting is to go slowly, consider all the variables, and start ruling out nonvariables.

The reason this chapter focuses on the basics of Exchange 2000 architecture and basic troubleshooting is this: When it *really* gets complex, you will probably end up reinstalling Windows 2000 and Exchange 2000 and doing a full restore. If you are a member of a support staff, you know you simply don't have the luxury of troubleshooting for days on end. You must get the system back up in some form so that people can be productive.

So, one way to be an effective Exchange administrator, trainer, support analyst, or developer is to understand the architecture of Exchange. You cannot be hesitant about gaining this understanding. You must learn the architecture, try to diagram it yourself, question the flows, read white papers, study Microsoft TechNet, and e-mail Exchange newsgroups your questions, until you finally understand it. The only thing more important than knowing which components are affected is to know which components are *not* affected.

This chapter discusses the *basic* storage architecture of Exchange, then reviews how messages flow within an Exchange server, how they flow between two Exchange servers in a Routing Group, and how messages are routed otherwise. After each section, we review troubleshooting methodology and tools. You need to be able to list on your fingers the tools that are essential to troubleshooting. Then try these tools on working (nonproduction) systems so that you feel comfortable.

Basic Troubleshooting Methodology for Exchange 2000

For readers new to Windows 2000 or Exchange, we first go over basic troubleshooting methodology and tools. One key to working with Exchange 2000 is waiting for the configuration changes to replicate. You need to understand how to start and stop services, read the event log, and start diagnostic logging.

Wait and Refresh

Waiting and refreshing are good ideas when you are working with Exchange 5.5 and Exchange 2000. When working on Exchange servers, always take your time for changes to be made and replicated throughout the area affected. Many times we have seen people charge into making changes on an Exchange server when the best choice would have been to wait. Furthermore, now that you are using Active Directory as a part of Exchange, you will rely on other servers in the network to commit changes and then replicate them. As for *refreshing*, we are talking about refreshing your screen in the Microsoft Management Console (MMC). Whenever you make changes to a snap-in to the MMC, such as Exchange System Manager, remember to refresh your screens. We have found that going in and out of the MMC is sometimes required.

Know Your Services

Exchange services running on your server are based on what is installed on your system. The services' abbreviations are shown in the second column in Tables 12.1 and 12.2. Spend some time starting and stopping the services to understand which service must be started first, which second, and so on. By understanding service dependencies, you can bring the services up one by one for troubleshooting.

Table 12.1 Basic Exchange Services

Basic Services	Abbreviation
Microsoft Exchange System Attendant	MSExchangeSA
Microsoft Exchange Information Store	MSExchangeIS
Microsoft Exchange POP3	Pop3svc
Microsoft Exchange IMAP4	Imap4svc
Microsoft Exchange MTA	MsExchangeMTA
SMTP Routing Engine and Transport	MSExchangeTransport

Table 12.2 Optional Exchange Services

Optional Services	Abbreviation
Microsoft Exchange Event	MSExchangeES
Microsoft Exchange Site Replication Service	MSExchangeSRS
Microsoft Mail	MSExchangeMSMI
Microsoft Exchange Schedule Plus Free/Busy	MSExchangeFB
Microsoft Exchange Directory Synchronization	MSExchangeDX
Microsoft Exchange Address List	MSExchangeAL
MAPI Address Book Proxy Service	MSExchange NSPI Proxy
MAPI Address Book Referral Service	MSExchangeRFR Interface
Lotus Notes GroupWise	LME-GWISE
Lotus Notes	LME-NOTES
Lotus cc:Mail	MSExchangeCCMC
Microsoft Exchange Router for Novell GroupWise	MSExchangeGWRtr
Microsoft Exchange Conferencing	MSExchangeCONF
Microsoft Exchange H.323 Bridge	MSExchangeH323
Microsoft Exchange T.120 MCU	MSExchangeT120

Many system administrators prefer to use the command-line interface when they work on Windows 2000 and Exchange 2000 systems. By running **net start <abbreviation>** or **net stop <abbreviation>**, where *abbreviation* is the service abbreviation in Tables 12.1 and 12.2, you can start and stop these services. **Net start** by itself shows you that services are up and running.

You will also see these service names in the registry. Look at HKEY_LOCAL_MACHINE\SYSTEM\CurrentControlSet\Services. You will see the abbreviated names from the second column if the service or feature is installed. A third place you will see these service abbreviations is in the logging sections described later in this section. Finally, you will see these service abbreviations in some form in the Event Viewer Log under the source column.

Exchange Installable File System (ExIFS)

Exchange has a hidden service installed on your server. You will not be able to see it in the services applet or in the command line net start. As previously discussed in this book, the Exchange Installable File System (ExIFS) exposes Exchange 2000 information stores to the file system. Exchange 2000 automatically creates an M: drive on the local Exchange server that allows you to share the mailbox or public folder that is the root level of the default public folder tree, the root level of all mailboxes, and a domain folder for each accessible domain. Previously, in Exchange 5.5, clients could access data in the stores via Messaging Application Program Interface (MAPI), Lightweight Directory Access Protocol (LDAP), Network News Transport Protocol (NNTP), HyperText Transfer Protocol (HTTP), Post Office Protocol v3 (POP3), and Internet Message Access Protocol v4 (IMAP4) clients. Exchange 2000 clients can now use Explorer, My Computer, or other file access applications and tools to open, read, write, and save data on the Exchange Server information stores.

ExIFS is the hidden service for the Installable File System. It must be started for some of the Exchange services to start. For example, in the registry, go to HKEY_LOCAL_MACHINE\SYSTEM\CurrentControlSet\Services\MSExchangeIS. In the DependOnService value you will see that to be started, the Information Store depends on the services EXIFS, IISADMIN, and MSExchangeSA.

In terms of troubleshooting, you normally should *not* have to start or stop this service. (Frankly, you should be worried if you have to.) If you are having problems accessing the Information Store, first run **net stop exifs** to see if ExIFS is running. If it is running, it will prompt you to stop other services, so you know that is not your problem. Enter **n** to not stop this and the other services. If ExIFS is *not* running, take a look at the error

Continued

log to see if you can clue in on why this has stopped. It is recommended that you run the following from the command line:

- subst m: /d (deletes the substituted virtual directory m:)
- **execute net start exifs**

The ExIFS service should start up. Then remember to start your other Exchange services. If the ExIFS service does not start up, check to see if users are connected to the m: drive. From the command line, run:

- **net session** (and see who is connected)
- **net session /delete** (deletes all open sessions)

Try to start ExIFS again. Note that this sidebar is to help you troubleshoot only. Do not start and stop ExIFS otherwise. Look to the Web for any late-breaking news on this service.

Event Viewer Logs

Take the time daily to review the Windows 2000 system and application event logs. Select Start | Run | eventvwr. Understand what your event logs look like when your environment is working. Figure 12.1 is a snapshot of our Exchange Server for a few hours.

In Figure 12.1, you can see that the Exchange server is running garbage collection and is performing defragmentation processes on the multiple stores within the three storage groups defined on this Exchange server. The default defrag time is 1:00 AM.

How did we know that? You can see that the MSExchangeIS service was the source of many of the events in Figure 12.1. You should walk through the events and keep track of "good" (informational) events and "bad" (warning or error) events. Once you understand the factors that represent a good event, you can run monitoring software to alert you to events that do or do not occur.

When you are having problems with Exchange, walk through the Event Viewer and look up the Source, Category, and Event information in Microsoft TechNet. This practice will help you understand if this is, first, a known problem, and second, how you might be able to resolve it.

Figure 12.1 MS Exchange Server Event Log

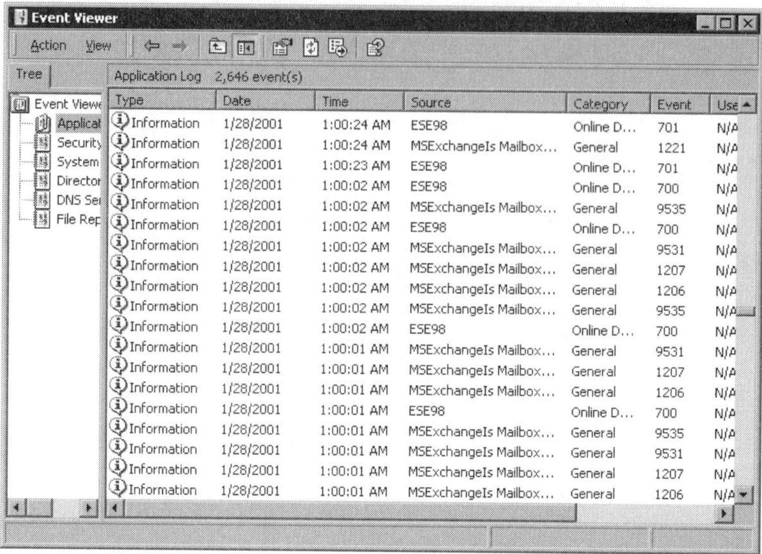

Diagnostic Logging

Another basic troubleshooting step is to turn on diagnostic logging on an Exchange component. To follow up with the previous proactive step, you can set diagnostic logging on some of your Exchange objects to Medium or Maximum. Then observe the event log for what occurs when your system is working. Save these logs for a later comparison. If possible, in Microsoft TechNet or Microsoft Knowledge Base articles, research the logging settings and how they are used.

For instance, in Exchange System Manager, as shown in Figure 12.2, we select Servers | Server1 | Server1 Properties | Diagnostics Logging. We can then choose an object on which we want to start logging diagnostic information. Here we have selected Maximum logging for the Information Store Mailbox Logons. Now we can observe in Event Viewer that a user has logged on to our Exchange server in a specific storage group on a specific store. (These terms are explained in the Storage Group Architecture section in this chapter.) You would normally leave all diagnostic logging at level None. This setting would have the least impact on your system. When you are experiencing problems, turn the suspect object's logging level to Medium or Maximum to observe process flow.

Figure 12.2 MS Exchange Diagnostics Logging

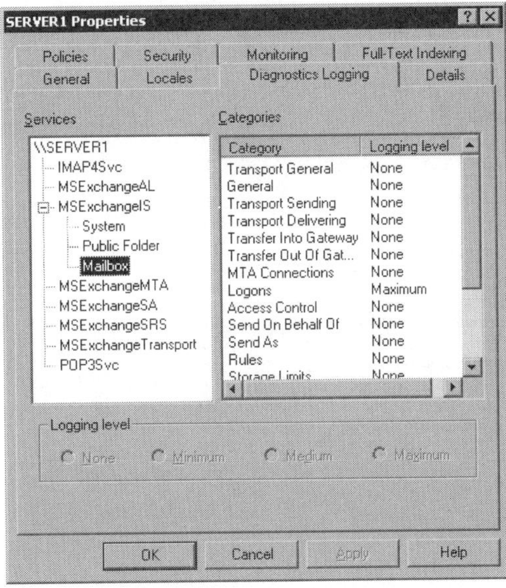

Monitoring Services and Objects

In Exchange System Manager | Tools | Monitoring and Status, you can get a quick status of your main Exchange components. Figure 12.3 indicates that a disk we are monitoring has entered a warning state, but the connectors are OK and available. Let's look at how we set this up as well as review the meaning of the status.

Figure 12.3 View of MasterMMC Console

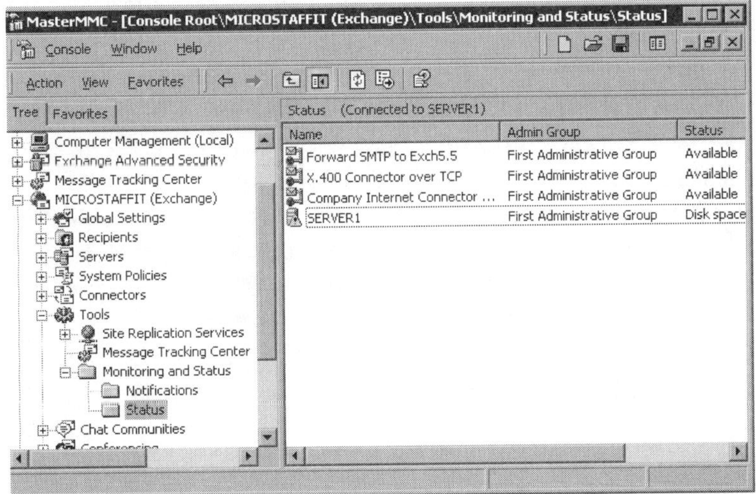

In the Status right-hand pane in Figure 12.3, you see a list of configured connectors and servers. The status of these objects is either available
or unreachable. It is possible to drill down more into server objects. You
can select the Server object in the right-hand pane of Figure 12.3 and
right-click Properties. You will see a quick status of the Server objects that
you are monitoring. In Figure 12.4, you will see that we have configured
one resource, *Free space*, and we have configured a set of Microsoft
Exchange Services.

Figure 12.4 Server1 Properties Showing Monitoring Status

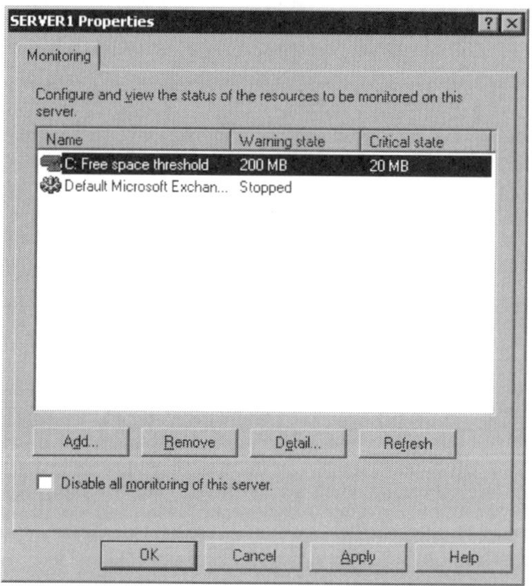

To monitor Server objects, double-click the item labeled Default
Exchange Services; you will see something like Figure 12.5. These are the
default Exchange Services on your system. You can add more services to
monitor by selecting the Add button. The State shown in the figure is
Running. A service is either *Running* or *Not Running*.

Notice in Figure 12.4 that there is a little yellow triangle with an excla-
mation mark (!) on the Disk object. This is telling us that we have entered
the warning state configured for disk space. In this example, we are monitoring disk space on the C: drive on our test system, which is holding all
our Exchange objects. We set up the configuration to have the monitor
enter a warning state when there is less than 500 MB on our C: drive and
to enter a critical state when there is less than 100 MB. The "!" indicator
on the left icon in Figure 12.4 shows that our Exchange server has entered
the warning state.

Figure 12.5 Default MS Exchange Services

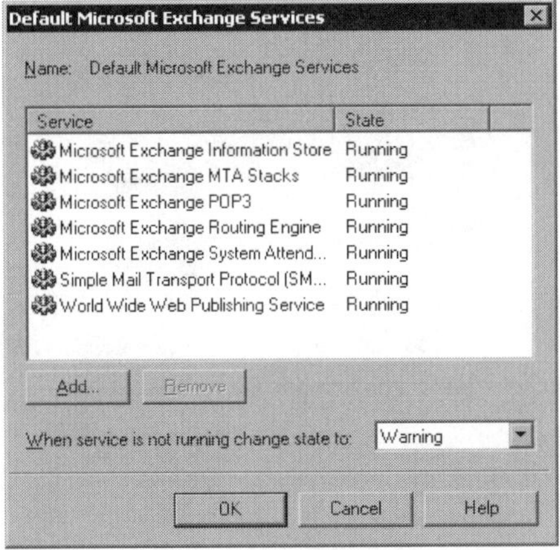

Free disk space is just one object you can monitor on a server. In Figure 12.4, in the Monitoring page, you would select Add to add more objects to monitor. You can monitor:

- Available virtual memory
- CPU utilization
- Free disk space
- SMTP queue growth
- Windows 2000 service
- X.400 queue growth

The Help button is very thorough in explaining these objects. Key to configuring these monitored objects is understanding what a good value is; then you configure for an abnormal value. If you select the Notifications icon in Figure 12.5, you can configure how you want to be notified when any of the noted resources enter a warning or critical state.

In Figure 12.6, we elected to notify user1 and user2 when any of the objects entered the warning state. We specified server1 as the server to monitor and the server that should e-mail us the notification. Normally, you would specify a different e-mail server to notify you, not the one you are monitoring. (This is because if you want the monitored server to send you an e-mail and the server goes down—you won't get the message!) Set up a series of monitoring configurations to ensure that you are not relying on what could be a down system to send you an notification e-mail.

Figure 12.6 Configuring the Notification for Warning and Critical States

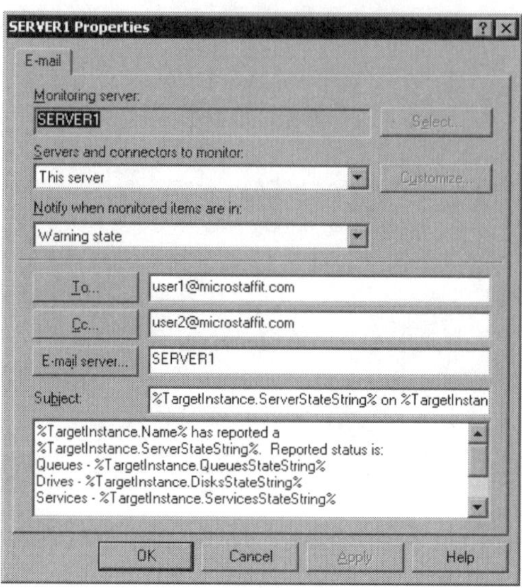

When you receive the notification e-mail, it appears as shown in Figure 12.7. This message is not very informative, but it tells you that the Drives object has entered a warning state. You should remember that *Drives* means low disk space.

Figure 12.7 Notification E-Mail

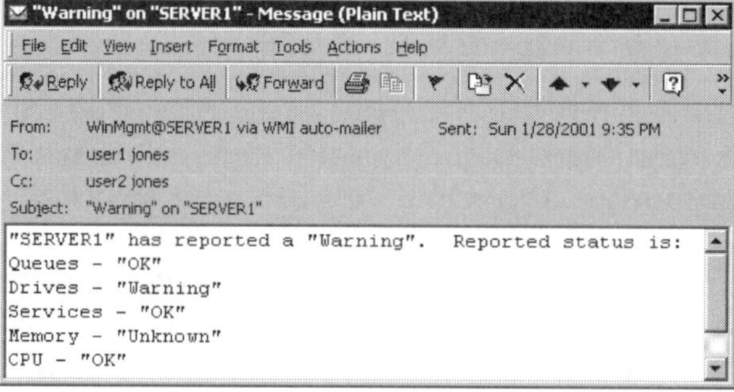

For readers who are familiar with legacy Exchange, this tool is very similar to the Link Monitors and Server Monitors. A key difference is that in Exchange 2000, these monitors do not have to be started or stopped. They run continuously.

Message Stores and Storage Groups

First let's discuss Information Stores, transaction logs, storage groups, and public folder trees; then we go over a methodology and a few tools on fixing problems with these components.

Message Stores and Storage Group Architecture

The first basic lesson is how the stores, log files, and storage groups are arranged. These components have the highest probability of causing a down Exchange server. As you can see from Figure 12.8, the default installation of Exchange 2000 places in the path c:\Program Files\exchsrvr\ MDBDATA the basic databases and log files for your Exchange Server.

Figure 12.8 Exchange 2000 Default Objects for c:\Program Files\exchsrvr\MDBDATA

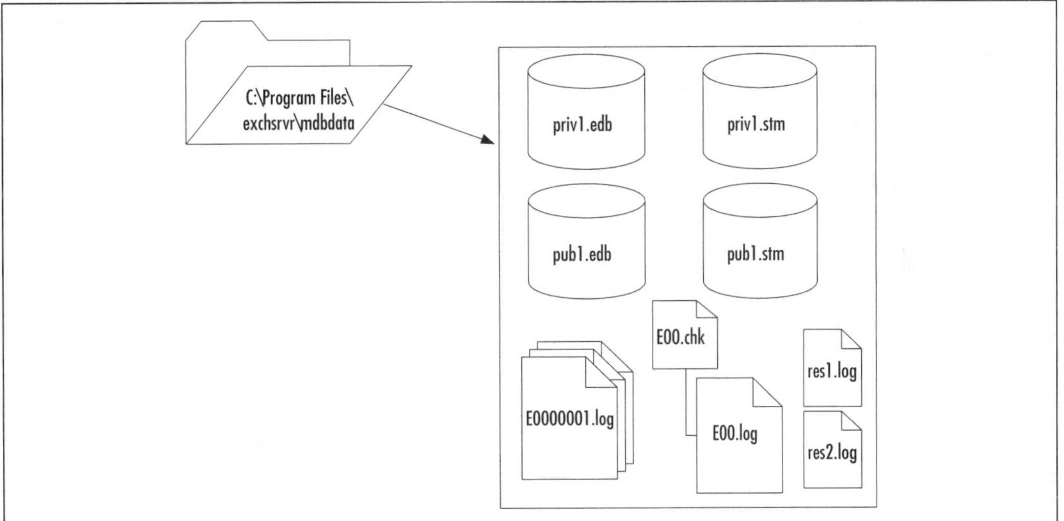

Information Stores

Previously, in Exchange 5.5, messages were kept in database files called priv.edb and pub.edb. Priv.edb contains private, personal, and individual e-mail that normally has a user account associated with the mailbox. Pub.edb contains public information that is secured by the administrator, who defines which user or groups of users can view the data. In Exchange 2000, these two files are now called priv1.edb and pub1.edb (by default).

The concept of single-instance store (SIS) applies, in that a message is stored once, and the database has pointers to the mailboxes that reference that message.

So, Exchange 2000 still includes the priv1.edb, but it also has a companion file, priv1.stm. Priv1.edb files contain rich-text format (RTF) messages. A priv1.stm file contains non-RTF messages and information. The .stm suffix comes from the word *streaming* and is utilized for containing Internet Multipurpose Internet Mail Extension (MIME) data. Typical .stm data is audio, video, and any streaming MIME data.

Transaction Logs

Note that the private and public databases are not complete without the inclusion of transaction logs. The transaction logs function basically the same as in legacy Exchange. You have one active transaction log and then multiple sequentially numbered transaction logs that contain past Exchange database transactions. (Refer to Chapter 10 for more information on the use of transaction logs.)

For those of you new to Exchange, it is important to understand that Exchange uses *write-ahead* log files with the Exchange databases. *Write-ahead* means that before a transaction is committed to the database, it is first written sequentially to the log file. Once the transaction is completely written to the log file, only then will it be applied to the Exchange database.

For example, when an information store operation is performed in Exchange, it is first committed to the transaction log file E00.log on disk. All operations must be complete and committed to the transaction log before it will be applied to the corresponding database. Operations are committed in sequence in the transaction log file, and the file E00.chk tracks the point in the log file of the last committed transaction. When the transaction log file is full (5 MB is the limit), the full E00.log file is renamed E0000001.log, and subsequent operations are then committed to a new E00.log file. The Exchange server sequentially numbers the renamed log files to ensure that the operations are saved in the correct order. The next saved log file would be E0000002.log, and so on. When Exchange is performing a recovery sequence or when services are starting up and the .chk file indicates that there are outstanding transactions to be applied, Exchange's Extensible Storage Engine (ESE) proceeds to apply any outstanding transactions from the log files to the appropriate Exchange databases (*.edb, *.stm). In Exchange, transactions are *atomic operations*. This means two things: First, only when the transactions are committed to the database are they noted in the transaction log as being committed, and second, if the transaction(s) were not committed completely, any incomplete transactions would be rolled back.

Reserve Logs

You will see in Figure 12.8 that there are two files named res1.log and res2.log. These are reserve files that have a size of 5 MB each. You will see these in Microsoft Explorer as 5,120 KB. If you delete them, the Exchange system will recreate them the next time the services restart. Try it. When the Exchange server is logging away and creating sequential transaction log after transaction log, at some point, if a backup is not performed and if circular logging is disabled, you will run out of space on the logical disk. Remember that Exchange is dependent on disk storage for two things: to save messages in the information stores (.edb, .stm) and to create transaction logs that will hold all operations before they are committed to the databases. When Exchange notices that there is no more disk space, it flushes its data to the two reserve files and then shuts down the Exchange system. At that point, it is up to the system administrator to perform a backup (which removes transaction logs at the end) or add more disk space for Exchange to restart.

Proactive Monitoring

Never allow your server to run out of disk space and cause your Exchange server to stop. This is one problem that is possible to avoid. Think of this situation as the equivalent of running out of gas in your car. *Always* run proactive monitoring applications that can alert you via e-mail or via a pager that your servers are running low on disk space. Personal digital assistants (PDAs) such as Palm Pilots are great for administrators working on a large campus. If you can't purchase proactive monitoring applications, do one of the following:

- Configure Exchange 2000 Server Monitor for Free Disk Space.

- Configure Windows 2000 Performance Monitor Log and Alerts and set an alert to monitor the necessary logical drives. This is more resource-intensive and should not be a normal configuration.

Storage Groups and Multiple Message Stores

Now that you understand the basic components of the default Exchange system, let's move on. Remember, legacy Exchange 5.5 had one private and public information store per Exchange server. Exchange 2000 now allows multiple stores per Exchange server. They are grouped in an object called a *storage group*; you can have up to four storage groups per server, with a maximum of five databases per storage group, so you could theoretically have 20 databases per server.

In addition, each storage group has its own instance of the ESE. The Extensible Storage Engine ensures that all databases within a storage group are consistent; within a storage group, there is one set of transaction logs. Operations within a transaction log can apply to any of the databases defined in the storage group.

Figure 12.9 shows an example of multiple storage groups and stores. On the left is the first storage group that was installed with Exchange. It contains three different pairs of databases (private data, public data, and company infrastructure data). The middle storage group is the corporate storage group, CorpSG. It contains just one pair of databases. The storage group on the right, MarketingSG, has two pairs of database (Marketing and MarketingFax). Table 12.3 contains more details on these storage groups.

Figure 12.9 Multiple Storage Groups and Stores

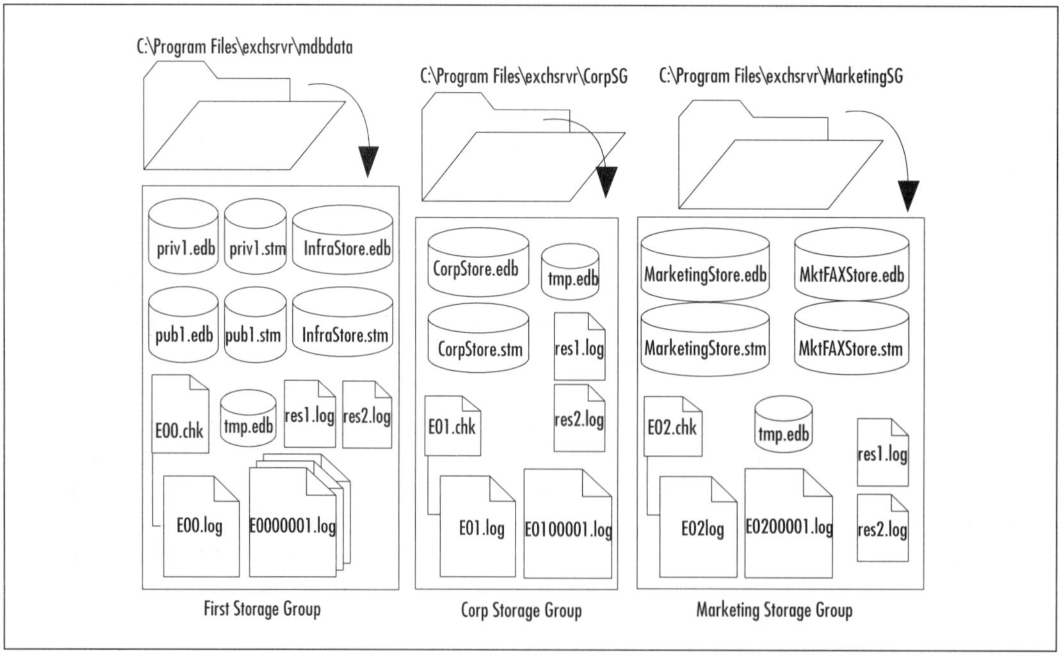

NOTE

When first researching Exchange 2000, articles noted that the ESE architecture actually allows for 16 storage groups. They also noted that there were six stores per storage group, but that ESE reserved the 16th storage group for itself for internal operations (restore). If you had 16 storage groups, you would end up having 96 stores on a server. This was impractical from performance and resources standpoints. The current version of Exchange 2000 is limited to four storage groups of five stores, which would end up maximizing one server with 20 stores.

You would utilize storage groups and multiple databases for ease of administration, flexibility in configuration, and optimizing your backup and recovery strategies. Furthermore, it is possible to configure a unique set of policies for each storage group. Therefore, we might put more restrictive policies on the first storage group and then loosen up requirements on Corporate and Marketing. You might want to have four information stores with a maximum file size of 50 GB each, rather than one information store at 200 GB. This would allow faster restores if just one database became corrupted. (Note that if a drive fails and all the stores are on that drive, they would all have to be restored.)

Another reason for multiple stores becomes apparent when you are performing maintenance operations: You would have to take only one set of users down at a time. As an ASP, you might want to create storage groups based on the companies you are hosting as well. Administering these servers and securing the environment will be much easier with a clear delineation between storage groups. Also within the storage groups, you might want to differentiate your users among databases. You could decide to place key personnel on one Exchange store priv1.edb and the rest of the company on store priv2.edb. You could back up the priv1.edb full of executive users nightly and loosen storage limits. (Choose Properties in the Storage Group Store in Exchange System Manager). You could place more limits on the priv2.edb database (which contains basic users) and back it up with a different backup strategy—say, once every two days.

Also key to the storage group concept is that you affiliate one transaction log with one storage group, not one per database! Remember, a family of transaction logs contains the active transaction log (E00.log), past sequentially numbered transaction logs (E0000001.log, E000000x.log, and so on), and the res.logs (res1.log, res2.log) in that same folder path. So, if you had one storage group with five Exchange databases, you would have only one transaction log family. If you had three storage groups, each group would have its own family of transaction logs that would be specifically applied to it. As an example, we've created three storage groups on our Exchange server. We have one storage group each for the users in Corporate Headquarters, Marketing, and the rest of the company. See Table 12.3 for details of these components.

Table 12.3 Multiple Storage Groups and Stores with Associated Transaction Logs

Storage Group Name	First Storage Group	CorpSG	MarketingSG
Use	First/Default Storage Group. Everyone not in Corporate or Marketing.	Everyone reporting to Corporate Office.	Everyone reporting to Marketing.
Stores	Mailbox Store Public Folder Store Infrastructure Store	CorpStore	MarketingStore MktFAXStore
Storage Group Folder Path and Files	C:\Program Files \exchsrvr\MDBDATA	C:\Program Files \exchsrvr\CorpSG	C:\Program Files \exchsrvr\ MarketingSG
Private Stores	Priv1.edb Priv1.stm InfraStore.edb InfraStore.stm	CorpStore.edb CorpStore.stm	MarketingStore .edb MarketingStore .stm MktFAXStore .edb MktFAXStore .stm
Public Stores	Pub1.edb Pub1.stm		
Transaction Log Path and Names	E00.log E0000001.log E0000002.log	E01.log E0100001.log	E02.log E0200001.log E0200002.log
Other Files	Res1.log Res2.log Tmp.edb E00.chk	Res1.log Res2.log Tmp.edb E01.chk	Res1.log Res2.log Tmp.edb Eo2.chk

You can see that we have two private stores within both the default First storage group and the MarketingSG. The CorpSG storage group has one private information store. There is only one public information store on the Exchange server, and this is the default public store for all the other private information stores. For the storage groups with multiple stores, notice that we do not have a set of transaction logs per store. So any transactions for both the MarketingStore and the MktFAXStore will be committed to the E02.log file. Then the transactions will be applied to the individual stores as appropriate. Further note that in the First storage group, we have two private sets and one public set of stores. All transactions for these stores will be committed to the same log family.

Multiple Public Folder Trees

Legacy Exchange allowed only one public information store per server. Public stores contain messaging content that can be exposed to the entire Exchange organization. Remember, user mailboxes are stored in the priv1.edb file, and the users that typically own the mailbox are the only viewers. Public folders are stored in the pub1.edb file and are created with the intent of sharing all their data to all Exchange users. The Exchange 5.5 design and the default installation of Exchange 2000 installs one public information store. This is known as the equivalent of having one *public folder tree*. However, Exchange 2000 allows the creation of multiple public folder trees that can be secured and exposed in finer detail. You might want to have the default public folder tree designated for most of your organization's public information, and you can then create a second public folder tree that will be populated with information just for one department—for example, human resources or marketing.

A caveat to secondary and multiple public folder trees is that not every messaging client can view these extra public folder trees. More specifically, the *first* and commonly named default public folder tree is visible to clients using MAPI, IMAP, and Web-based Distributed Authoring and Versioning (webDAV) protocols. Any *additional* public folder trees will not be visible to MAPI clients, such as Outlook. You access these additional public folder trees by Outlook Web Access (OWA) or ExIFS (i.e., a browser or by a Win32-compliant application such as Microsoft Office 2000).

Problems with Databases, Storage Groups, and Public Folder Trees

In comparison with legacy Exchange servers, Exchange 2000 servers can give you higher fault tolerance due, first, to enhancements in Exchange 2000, and second, to the fact that it is running on Windows 2000. However, with regard to troubleshooting, corrupted databases have been a common problem in Exchange in the past. Database corruption can occur:

- When your server is shut down with no warning
- When you have SCSI bus errors
- When you have hardware errors
- When the operating system "hiccups"
- When you move users

Your task is to fix the database and then determine why the corruption happened. Here we address the methodology (the logic plus use of tools such as Isinteg and Eseutil) that will help you resolve these problems.

> **TIP**
>
> When you are running a large number of executables out of the c:\Program Files\Exchsrvr\bin folder, take the time to append this path to your Environment Variable in Control Panel | System. It saves you time in typing.

Isinteg

Isinteg is a utility that scans the information stores for inconsistencies. We've run Isinteg against the databases when the Information Store Service would not start. Check your event log to see if you can determine if running Isinteg would be useful. Sometimes the Event Viewer can give you advice on what to do next.

Isinteg has changed a bit since Exchange 5.5; it now allows for the inclusion of multiple storage groups and stores. There are many tests you can run against your information stores; Isinteg checks folders, messages, access control lists, private mailboxes, public newsfeeds, reference counts on messages, attachments, and more.

First, make sure that you have a valid backup of your data. Next, you will have to dismount the information store that you plan to scan. Go to the command line and run **isinteg**; you will see many types of tests. The great feature of Isinteg is that it can run in "safe mode." You can run Isinteg solely to investigate if you do have problems, and you do not have to worry about Isinteg fixing your system automatically. The default option is to check for problems. You must specify the Fix option to check *and* fix your problems. To run all the tests in check mode, use the following command sequence:

```
Isinteg –s servername –test alltests
```

Isinteg will check the Exchange configuration of the server and return a list of all the information stores you can check, as shown in Figure 12.10. You can see in Figure 12.10 that the Marketing Store #5 is offline. You can run Isinteg only against offline stores, so we select 5, an offline Marketing Store.

Figure 12.10 Execution of the Isinteg Command

```
C:\WINNT\System32\cmd.exe - isinteg -s server1 -test alltests
    2      Online          InfraStore
    3      Online          Mailbox Store (SERVER1)
    4      Online          Public Folder Store (SERVER1)
Storage Group Name: MarketingSG
    5      Online          MarketingStore
    6      Online          MktFAXStore
Enter a number to select a database or press Return to exit.


C:\>isinteg -s server1 -test alltests
Databases for server server1:
Only databases marked as Offline can be checked

Index  Status          Database-Name
Storage Group Name: CorpSG
    1      Online          CorpStore
Storage Group Name: First Storage Group
    2      Online          InfraStore
    3      Online          Mailbox Store (SERVER1)
    4      Online          Public Folder Store (SERVER1)
Storage Group Name: MarketingSG
    5      Offline         MarketingStore
    6      Online          MktFAXStore
Enter a number to select a database or press Return to exit.
```

Isinteg runs for a while (depending on the size of your store) and logs its report to a saved file; see the following output:

```
Started: 01/06/01 02:04:28

Server name: SERVER1.microstaffit.com

Database name: MarketingSG\MarketingStore

Output log: isinteg.pri

Check mode: check only

Options: -log -RefDbLoc -Test testFldRcv testFldSub testMsgRef
testMsgSoftRef testAttachRef testACLListRef testACLItemRef
testNewsfeedRef testFolder testDelFolder testMessage testAttach
testMailbox testReceiveFld testACLList testACLItem testOofHist
testPerUser testGlobal testDlvrTo testSearchQ testTimedEvents
testMoreFld testTombstone testNewsfeed testSearch testDumpsterProps
testAllTests testEnd


Starting test 1 of 18, 'Search Folder Links'

. Time: 0h:0m:0s

Starting test 2 of 18, 'Global'

, number of rows = 1. Time: 0h:0m:0s
```

```
Starting test 3 of 18, 'Delivered To'
. Time: 0h:0m:0s
Starting test 4 of 18, 'Repl Schedule'
. Time: 0h:0m:0s
Starting test 5 of 18, 'Timed Events'
. Time: 0h:0m:0s
Starting test 6 of 18, 'reference table construction'
. Time: 0h:0m:0s
Starting test 7 of 18, 'Folder'
, number of rows = 82. Time: 0h:0m:0s
Starting test 8 of 18, 'Deleted Messages'
. Time: 0h:0m:0s
Starting test 9 of 18, 'Message'
, number of rows = 448. Time: 0h:0m:0s
Starting test 10 of 18, 'Attachment'
, number of rows = 580. Time: 0h:0m:0s
Starting test 11 of 18, 'Mailbox'
, number of rows = 4. Time: 0h:0m:0s
Starting test 12 of 18, 'Sites'
, number of rows = 13. Time: 0h:0m:0s
Starting test 13 of 18, 'Categories'
. Time: 0h:0m:0s
Starting test 14 of 18, 'Per-User Read'
. Time: 0h:0m:0s
Starting test 15 of 18, 'special folders'
. Time: 0h:0m:0s
Starting test 16 of 18, 'Message Tombstone'
. Time: 0h:0m:0s
Starting test 17 of 18, 'Folder Tombstone'
. Time: 0h:0m:0s
Starting test 18 of 18, 'reference count verification'
. Time: 0h:0m:0s
The Information Store has been shut down clean.
Hence disabling the Row Count/Dumpster Count test.
```

```
Specify -test rowcounts (or) -test dumpsterref explicitly to run this
test
```

```
. . . . . SUMMARY . . . . .
Total number of tests : 18

Total number of warnings : 0

Total number of errors : 0

Total number of fixes : 0

Total time : 0h:0m:2s
```

The output shows that we ran 18 tests, and we had 0 warnings and errors. You can see that such feedback will give you some insight into the consistency of the databases in your Exchange server. If you see any problems with your tests, you can run the test again with the Fix option, as follows:

```
Isinteg –s servername –fix test alltests
```

Note that Isinteg fails when you have more than five storage groups. That should not be a problem, because Exchange 2000 (currently) will not let you create more than four storage groups per server.

Eseutil

Eseutil.exe should be run with caution against your production servers. Eseutil analyzes the information stores on your Exchange server and can perform various corrective and sometimes destructive operations. It operates at a lower level than Isinteg and, depending on the option used, can defragment your database, compact it, and repair it, but it can also delete corrupted pages instead of saving them. With the exception of the /d option, which assists in defragmentation and compaction, and the /g option, which performs a read-only integrity check, Eseutil should not be run against a production system unless your previous troubleshooting has led you to believe that you have a corrupted database. Microsoft documentation indicates that you should be in contact with Microsoft technical support *before* you begin using this utility. This tool is normally not used for maintenance; it is intended for use when you are in trouble.

By running **eseutil.exe /?** on the command line, you can get a good hint as to how to run Eseutil, as Figure 12.11 shows.

The information store databases are automatically defragmented at 2:00 AM by default. This process, known as *online defragmentation*, throws away any data that is not being used. To reclaim lost space and reduce the size of your database, you would have to dismount the Exchange stores so

Figure 12.11 Execution of the Eseutil Command

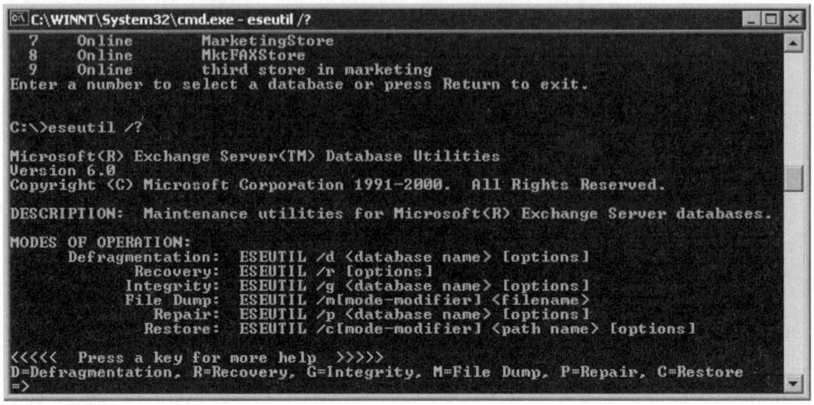

that you can run Eseutil and perform an offline defragmentation. It should not be necessary to perform this defragmentation as part of your normal maintenance routine. If required, dismount the necessary stores and then run eseutil.exe with the /d option. All the defragmentation options are shown in Figure 12.12.

Figure 12.12 Execution of Eseutil with the /d Option Specified

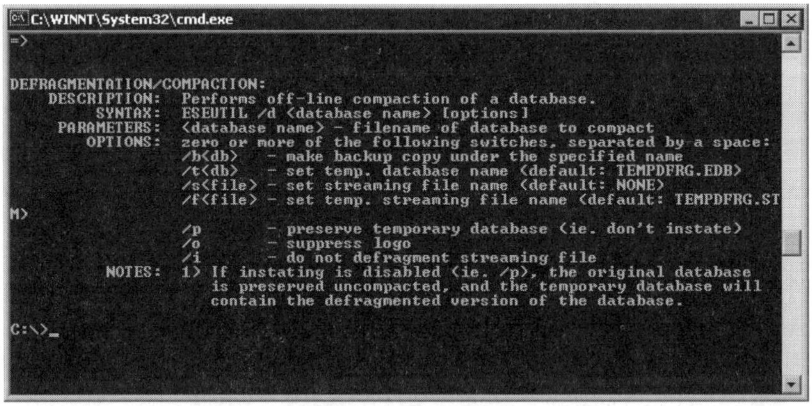

Eseutil /d filename requires enough disk space to contain two temporary files that have the same amount of disk space as the databases you are analyzing. Microsoft advises against selecting a network drive for these temporary files, because doing so will slow your defragmentation. If you are concerned about the health of your databases and would like to know if the defragmentation not only works but improves your situation, run eseutil /d with the /p option. This command will create the temporary files but will not overwrite your original ones. Take a look at Figure 12.13 for a typical output of eseutil /d.

Figure 12.13 Typical Output of the Eseutil Command

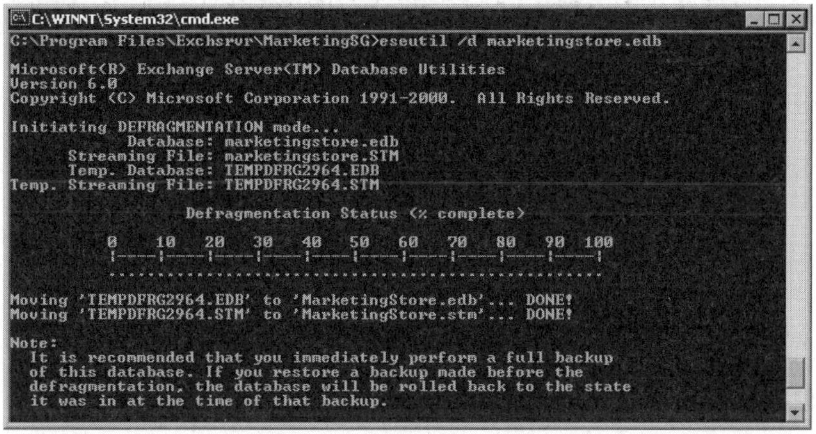

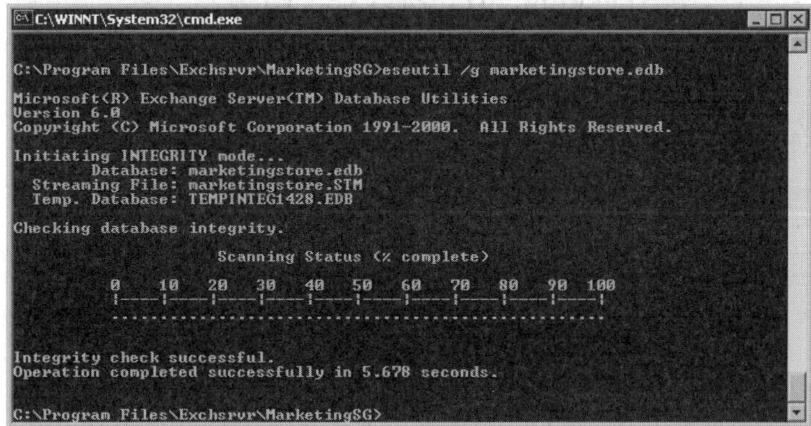

For an integrity check, running eseutil /g should be fine. This is a read-only operation, and you should look at the output log file to understand the integrity of your database. This log file ends with .integ.raw and is saved under the corresponding storage group of the store you are examining. Figure 12.14 shows the eseutil /g command running against one of the stores in a storage group.

Figure 12.14 Execution of the Eseutil /g Command

Eseutil /r performs a recovery of your databases. Eseutil /p performs a repair. It is important that you are working with Microsoft Product Support Services (PSS) when performing these last two options. Again, these should be used when you know you have a good backup, you are prepared to restore the backup, and you are comfortable with the knowledge that you could lose any transactions that occurred between the backup and the present time. The /r option works on recovering the database, and the /p option works to repair damaged databases. We have seen Eseutil work successfully at many live sites on corrupted databases, but we had to be very careful. It is crucial not to start cycling your server up and down in an attempt to bring your database up. Put all services on manual as soon as you can, then stop all services. Ensure that your event log indicates that the error lies in your information stores, not at a lower-level dependency. If you cannot work with Microsoft PSS, do some research on Microsoft TechNet to see if there is a comparable known problem.

Checklist and Guidelines for Repairing Corrupted Databases and Storage

Follow these guidelines as you work to repair corrupted databases and storage:

- Ensure that you have a good backup readily available.

- Ensure that, at a minimum, you have the necessary software to reinstall not only Exchange but also Windows 2000, drivers for SCSI or RAID controllers, tape peripherals, and network drivers.

- Run WinRoute against your Exchange server and save to a file on another server. (More on this practice later in the chapter.)

- If you have the disk space, save a complete duplicate copy of the databases and log files with which you will be working.

Message Flow and Routing

Now that you understand more clearly how data is stored in Exchange, let's go over how the messages flow within an Exchange server, between Exchange servers in your Routing Group, and between an Exchange server and another messaging system (Exchange or non-Exchange). We then review methodology and tools on troubleshooting message flow and routing problems.

Message Flow and Routing Architecture

This section does not review the way a client accesses its e-mail; it reviews the way messaging systems transfer messages to their final destination (client access is not the concern). Some white papers break message flow and routing into two categories; others break them into multiple categories. Here, we discuss message flow as it relates to the components that it uses to arrive at its final destination:

- **Local delivery** You send an e-mail message that is being delivered to your colleague in the office down the hall. The two of you are on the same Exchange server. The message does not leave that physical Exchange server; it simply has pointers moving around internally.

- **SMTP delivery** You send an e-mail message that is being delivered to three colleagues. One person is in your routing group, one is in a different routing group, and one has a basic Internet account based on SMTP.

- **X.400 delivery** Think of this as the legacy Exchange 5.5 MTA delivery. You send an e-mail message that is being delivered to three colleagues. One is on a legacy Exchange 5.5 system that is using a site connector over X.400, one is on a foreign (non-SMTP) e-mail system, and the other is in a different Exchange routing group. These messages end up taking the same route—via the X.400 connector.

Delivering a Message Within the Same Server

We assume that the users in this example Figure 12.15 are using Outlook 2000 and Exchange 2000. User1 sends a message to his colleague, User2. These two users are on the same Exchange 2000 server:

1. User1 creates a message and clicks Send.

2. User1 sees the message leave his Outbox and appear in his Sent box. The information store submits the message to the Exchange store driver.

3. The Exchange store driver processes the message and submits a portion of the header called the *mail message object* through the Exchange Interprocess Communication (EXIPC) to the Internet Information Service (IIS). EXIPC is an interface between the Exchange information store and IIS. An important point to remember is that it is a mail message object that traverses IIS, not the entire message.

Figure 12.15 Internal Messaging Transfer on an Exchange Server

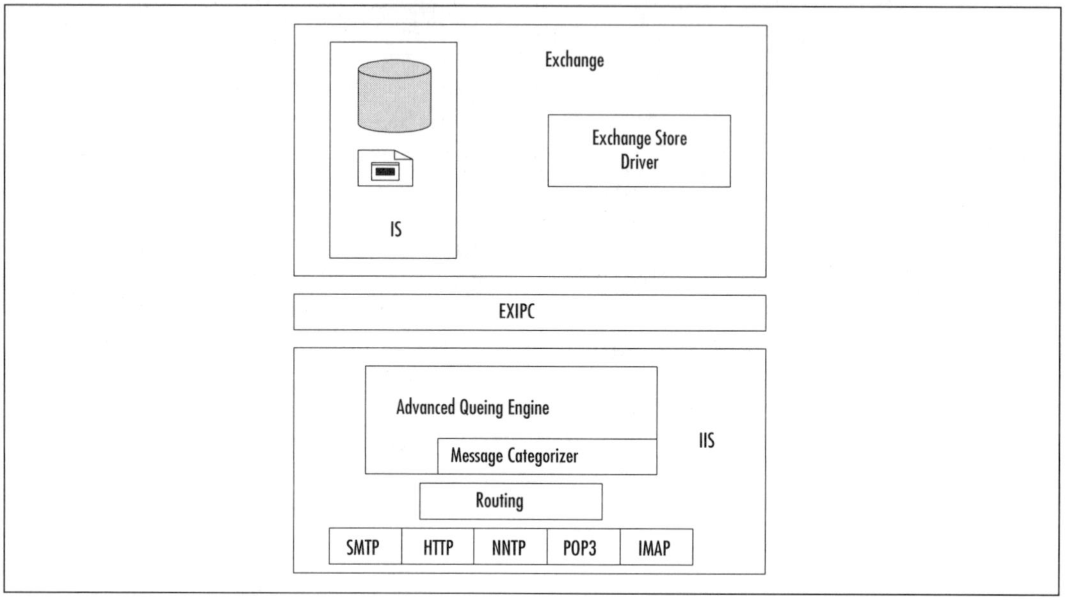

4. The Advanced Queuing Engine within IIS receives the mail message object.

5. The Message Categorizer examines the mail message object, looks at the sender and recipient names, checks against all the limits the administrators might have placed on everyone, and then continues processing if everything is OK. The Categorizer expands distribution lists and bifurcates the mail message object into two copies if necessary—one for RTF recipients and one for MIME recipients.

6. The Message Categorizer determines if the message is to stay local on the server, if it is to go out using SMTP, or if it will be delivered another way.

7. Because this is a message being delivered to a user on the same server, the Message Categorizer indicates that it is local and tells the Routing Engine the destination. The Advanced Queuing Engine then places the mail message object in a temporary holding queue, ready to be sent out.

8. The Routing Engine determines how to route the message (which is simple in this case) and gives this information back to the mail message object waiting in the holding queue.

9. The Exchange Store Driver processes the mail message object but doesn't create a second message. It creates a pointer from the original message to User2's mailbox. The message appears in User2's Inbox.

Delivering a Message Within the Same Routing Group

When a message leaves an Exchange 2000 server and is destined for an Exchange 2000 server in the same routing group, it will be transferred via SMTP from the originating server to the recipient's Exchange 2000 server. When a message leaves an Exchange 2000 server and is destined for an Exchange 5.5 server in the same routing group or site, it will be transferred via remote procedure calls (RPCs) from the originating server to the recipient's Exchange 5.5 server. (The same is true in the other direction.)

We assume that the users in this example are using Outlook 2000 and Exchange 2000. User1 sends a message to her colleague, User3. These two users are on different Exchange 2000 servers but in the same Exchange routing group. The process is as follows:

1. User1 creates a message and clicks Send.

2. User1 sees it leave her Outbox and appear in her Sent box. The information store submits a mail message object to the Exchange Store driver.

3. The Exchange Store driver processes the mail message object and submits it through EXIPC to IIS.

4. The Advanced Queuing Engine receives the mail message object.

5. The Message Categorizer examines the mail message object, looks at the names of the sender and recipients, checks against all the limits the administrators might have placed on everyone, and then continues processing if everything is OK. The Categorizer expands distribution lists and bifurcates the mail message object into two copies if necessary—one for RTF recipients and one for MIME recipients

6. The Message Categorizer will determine if the message is to stay local on the server, if it is to go out using SMTP, or if it will be delivered another way.

7. Remember, in this scenario, this message is being delivered to a user off the server but within the same routing group. SMTP will

be used if it is an Exchange 2000 destination; RPC will be used if it has an Exchange 5.5 destination.

8. For the Exchange 5.5 recipient (see Figure 12.16):

    a. The Message Categorizer indicates it is for the legacy Exchange 5.5 system using RPC. It tells the Routing Engine the destination, and the Advanced Queuing Engine then places the mail message object in a temporary holding queue ready to be sent out.

    b. The Routing Engine's rule for processing legacy systems is to pretend it is destined for the local server. It determines how to route the message and gives this information back to the mail message object waiting in the holding queue. The Advanced queuing message submits the message to MTS-OUT on the Exchange Store.

    c. The Exchange 2000 Message Transfer Agent processes the waiting message and sends it via RPCs to the legacy system's MTA.

Figure 12.16 Messaging Transfer Within a Routing Group, Exchange 2000 to Exchange 5.5

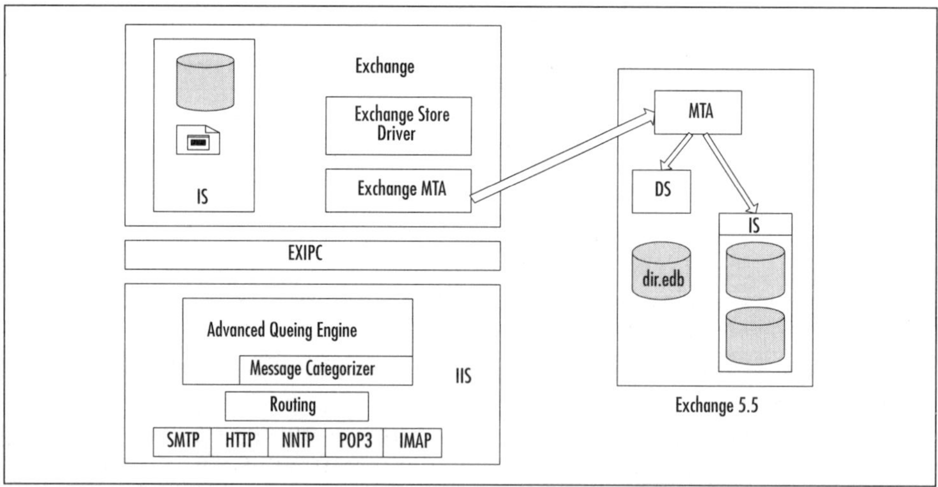

9. For the Exchange 2000 recipient (see Figure 12.17):

    a. The Message Categorizer indicates that it is SMTP message and tells the Routing Engine the destination. The Advanced Queuing Engine then places the mail message object in a temporary holding queue ready to be sent out.

b. The Routing Engine determines how to route the message and gives this information back to the mail message object waiting in the holding queue. If it is SMTP, the mail message object is combined with the message body from the store driver and the message is transferred directly to the SMTP port 25 on the target Exchange 2000 server.

Figure 12.17 Messaging Transfer Within a Routing Group, Exchange 2000 to Exchange 2000

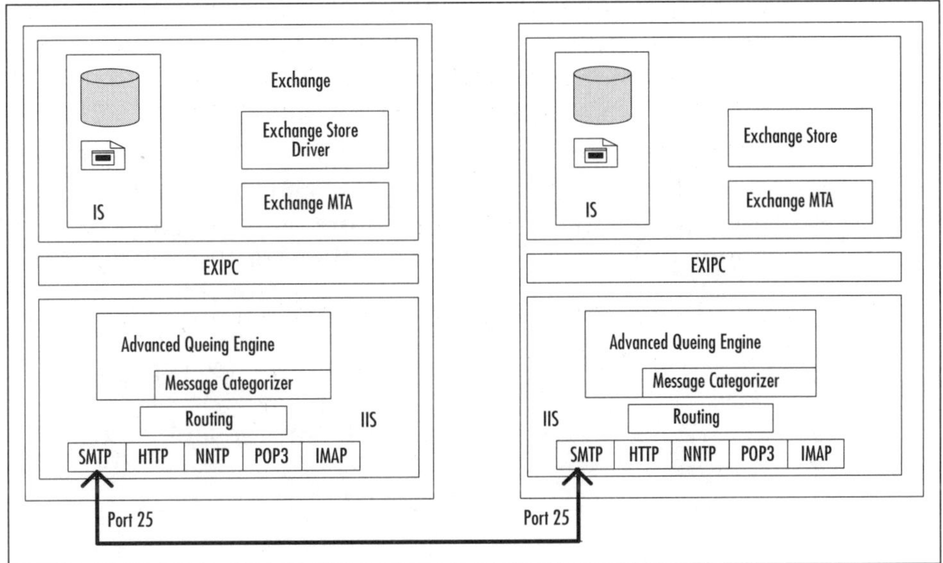

Delivering a Message to a Different Routing Group

If your message is to be delivered outside your routing group to another routing group or to a foreign e-mail system, it requires an additional step. Before the message leaves your Exchange server, the Routing Engine consults the link state table and chooses a connector mechanism. The link state table is similar to the Exchange GateWay Address Routing Table (GWART) in legacy Exchange. When you use the WinRoute tool that is explained at the end of this chapter, it shows you how to view the link state table:

1. User1 creates a message and clicks Send.

2. User1 sees it leave his Outbox and appear in his Sent box. The information store submits a mail message object to the Exchange Store driver.

3. The Exchange Store driver processes the message and submits it through EXIPC to IIS.

4. The Advanced Queuing Engine receives the mail message object.

5. The Message Categorizer examines the message, looks at the names of the senders and recipients, checks against all the limits the administrators might have placed on everyone, and then continues processing if everything is OK. The Categorizer expands distribution lists and bifurcates the mail message object into two copies if necessary—one for RTF recipients and one for MIME recipients.

6. The Message Categorizer determines if the message is to stay local on the server, if it is to go out using SMTP, or if it will be delivered another way. If the message is being delivered to a user within the Exchange organization but in another routing group, Active Directory will be consulted for routing group information.

7. The link state table will be checked for the correct route or path to take, whether SMTP or X.400 (see Figure 12.18).

Figure 12.18 Messaging Transfer Using the Link State Table to a Connector

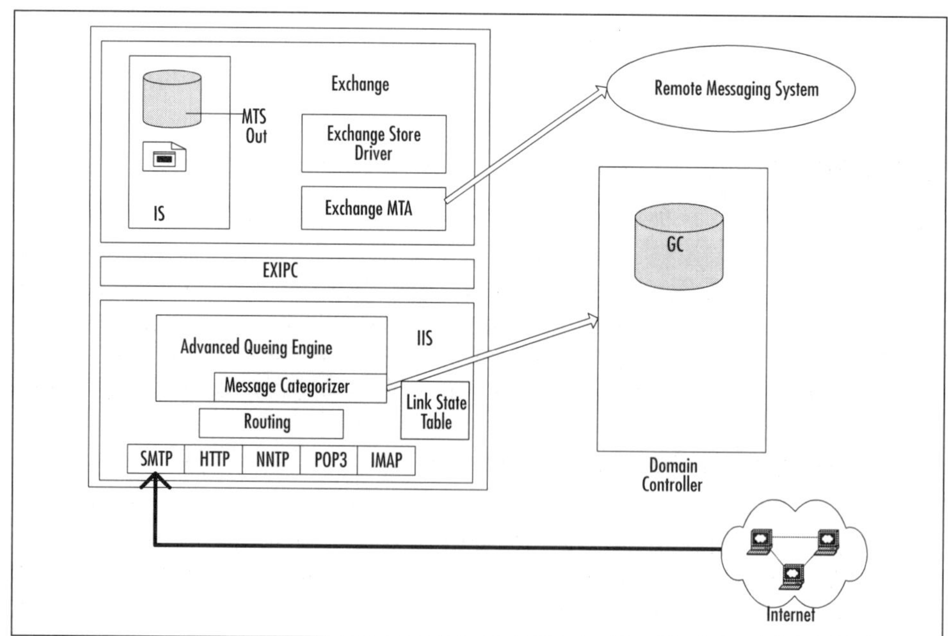

8. If the message takes the SMTP path:

    a. The Message Categorizer indicates that the message is destined for SMTP and tells the Routing Engine the destination. The Advanced Queuing Engine then places the mail message object in a temporary holding queue ready to be sent out.

    b. The Routing Engine determines how to route the message (based on information from the link state table) and gives this information back to the mail message object waiting in the holding queue. The server takes the message off the holding queue and transfers it directly to the SMTP port 25 on the target system. If you have a bridgehead server, the originating server does not transfer to the target system, but instead hands it off to the bridgehead to perform the work.

9. If the message takes the X.400 path:

    a. The Message Categorizer indicates that the message is destined for the X.400 connector. It tells the Routing Engine the destination, and the Advanced Queuing Engine then places the message in a temporary holding queue ready to be sent out.

    b. The Routing Engine determines how to route the message (based on information from the link state table) and gives this information back to the mail message object waiting in the holding queue. The Advanced queuing message submits the message to MTS-OUT on the Exchange Store.

    c. The Exchange 2000 MTA processes the waiting message and sends it to the remote messaging system.

Problems with Message Flow and Routing

Now that we have reviewed message flow with respect to routing, it is time to think about what message flow means with respect to troubleshooting. When you're working on a problem, sometimes it is just as important to know what you *don't* have to look at as what you do. Here we review some of the common tools and methodology in resolving message flow problems, such as the Message Tracking Center, Winroute, and Viewing Queues.

Message Tracking Center

One of the basic problems you will encounter as an administrator is that of a message not being delivered. Where did it stop and why? Was it the network? The remote system? Something with our routing? So the question then becomes: Where in the process did the message transfer fail? One alternative is to enable message tracking on your Exchange server. This creates a daily log of all messages entering and leaving your Exchange server. You turn on message tracking in Exchange System Manager by bringing up your server Properties and configuring the General tab as shown in Figure 12.19.

Figure 12.19 Enabling Message Tracking, Subject Logging, and Display

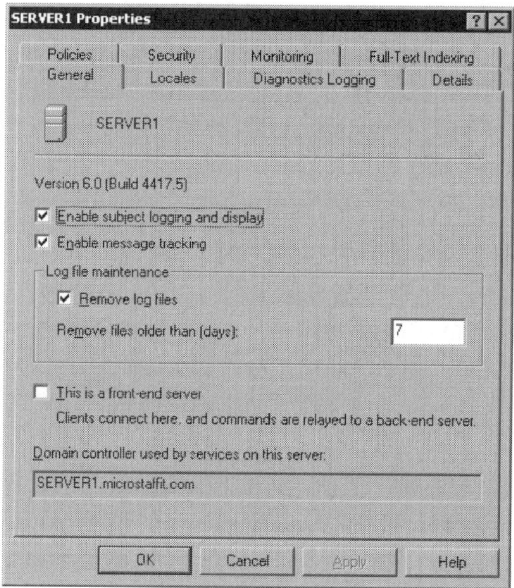

By default, the log files are saved under c:\Program Files\exchsrvr\ servername.log\ and are shared as \\servername\servername.log. They are numbered sequentially per day.

To begin tracking messages, you add the Message Tracking Center snap-in to the MMC. Right-click the Message Tracking Center and select Track Message. You are immediately given a three-tabbed search window to configure, as shown in Figure 12.20. As you can see, we searched for any messages sent from user2 jones on SERVER1. We selected the past two days under the Date & Time tab. By selecting Find Now, we managed to find seven messages that had been sent in the past two days. The search could take a while. Furthermore, we found that in the Message Tracking Center, we had to exit and restart the program to make the search work correctly. The new search did not work every time.

By highlighting a message and selecting Message Tracking, we can see the detail of user2's message, as shown in Figure 12.21.

Figure 12.20 Message Tracking Center

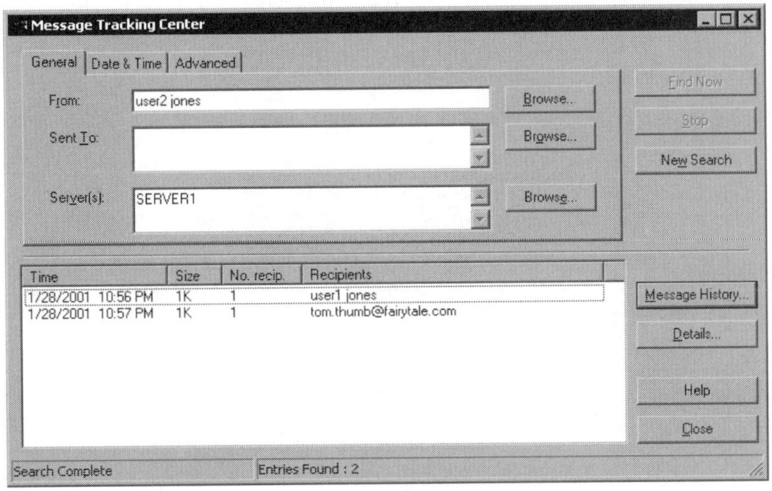

Figure 12.21 Message History Local Delivery

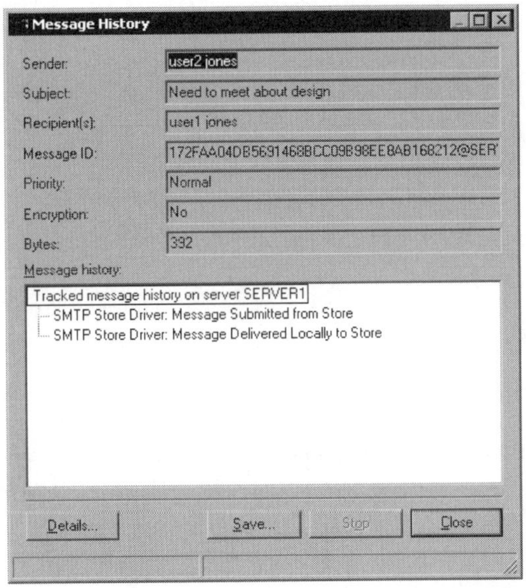

You can see more details on each of these history entries by high-lighting and selecting Details. Figure 12.21 shows a message being delivered locally. Figure 12.22 shows a message being delivered via SMTP.

You will use the Message Tracking Center when you are trying to determine what happened to a message. Some times recipients say they never got a message, so you'll need to see if you can trace what happened between your Exchange server and the message destination. Other times, you might have a problem with your interim components, and this tool will assist you in seeing which component is working.

Figure 12.22 Message History SMTP External Delivery

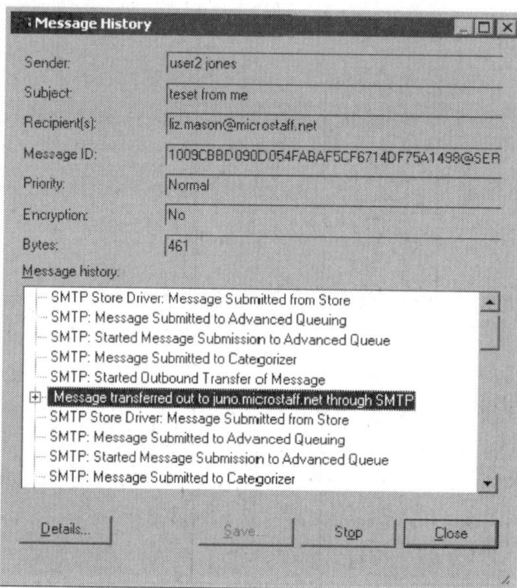

You will also use the Message Tracking Center in conjunction with the other tools reviewed in the following sections, such as WinRoute and viewing Queues.

Queues Viewer

Another way to monitor the Exchange components is to look at the queues holding messages going in and out of your Exchange server. In Exchange System Manager | Server | Protocols, you can select the protocol of your choice and look at the queues. In Figure 12.23, we show you the queue status of SMTP.

Queue Explanations

The columns in the queue states are fairly simple to understand:

Connection state This state relates to the connection on the server. *Ready* indicates that the connection is ready to be utilized but is waiting idle. *Active* indicates that it is actively being used. *Retry* indicates that the connection did not succeed, and it is

Figure 12.23 Queue View of SMTP

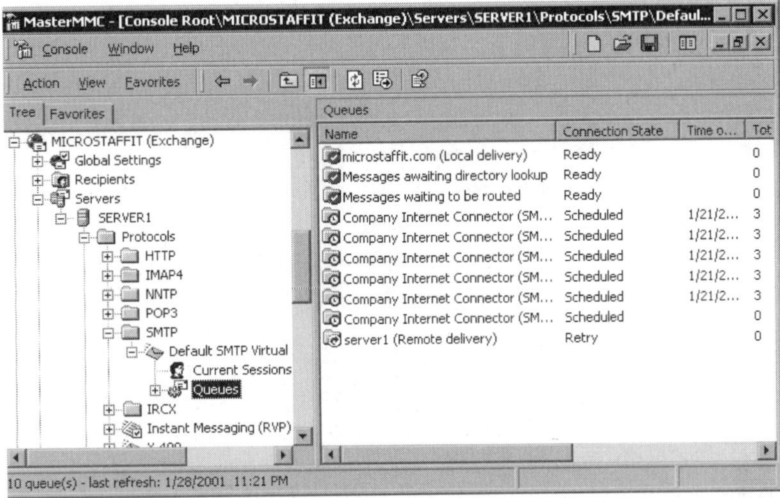

waiting to retry. *Scheduled* indicates that the connection is not continuous but is waiting for the next scheduled time to connect. *Frozen* indicates that you or someone has frozen the queue, and the messages are waiting to be routed. Messages can still enter the queue if the routing categorizer is up. *Remote* is indicated when a queue is holding messages for an SMTP client. The only way the messages can leave the queue is for an Enhanced Turn (ETRN) command or an older TURN command. If the connection indicates Remote, it is waiting for a TURN or an ETRN.

Time of submission of oldest message This is the time or date of the oldest message submitted to that queue.

Total number of messages

Total message size (KB) This is the total size of all messages in the queue.

Time of next connection retry When a queue is scheduled, this is when it will retry next. Remember, you can force a connection by right-clicking a queue and selecting Force Connection.

Queue Actions

You can select a queue name and, by right-clicking, can run a couple of different tasks. If you want to delete one or many messages in the queue, highlight them and then delete them. If user3 sent a 50 MB attachment to a distribution list that used a scheduled connector that has poor bandwidth, you might decide to delete the message so the other messages could go through. You have the option to send a message back to the originator informing him or her that the message was not delivered (NDR). Reasons that you would not send an NDR might be that you are troubleshooting and have restored old messages from a backup. You would not want to send NDRs back to the originators because that would confuse them into thinking their original message did not get sent.

Another task is to force a connection to start. You could have an Internet or X.400 connection that is scheduled to connect every four hours. It is possible to force it to start and connect with this tool. This is helpful when you are trying to manually walk a message through the system.

You can list the messages in the queue by selecting the task to enumerate. Enumerating 100 messages will list the first 100, and enumerating all the messages will list all the messages in your queue. Once you enumerate them, you could decide to freeze them. Freezing them prevents them from leaving the queue. So, if you had a 50 MB message, you could freeze it and later unfreeze it when you wanted to have it sent. It is best to freeze messages before deleting them. If you didn't freeze them, one or two of the messages could end up being delivered before the delete action was processed. Take a look at the Custom Filter option. By creating a filter specifying messages of specific criteria (user1 to user2, and so on), examining queues can be more manageable.

Local Delivery Queue

If messages are stuck in the local delivery queue, it most likely means that there are problems with the information store components or the information store service. Recall that Exchange 2000 network protocols are not in the Web Storage System. These were pulled out and put into IIS. Therefore, one would assume that if there is a problem in local delivery, network protocols are not involved.

Check to see that the Information Service is running.

Check that the event log has no application errors.

Think about stopping the information store service and then restarting it. Then observe the application event log to see if there are any warnings or errors that pertain to the start-up.

Messages Awaiting Directory Queue

When you have messages awaiting directory lookup, they are having AD resolution problems accessing a domain controller. This would be more a networking and Active Directory problem.

Check to see that you can connect to a domain controller.

Ask to see if anything was changed pertaining to Active Directory around the time that the messages started appearing in this queue.

Messages Waiting to Be Routed

You could have messages waiting to be routed for one of many reasons. There could be a problem with accessing the link state table, or there could be something wrong with the Routing Engine. Enumerate the messages in the queue and look at their properties.

Other Queues

You might have other queues, as shown in Figure 12.24. Note the queues that have a clock on the folder icon, which shows that they have a scheduled connection time. If you freeze these queues and enumerate them, you can see when the messages were submitted, to whom they are going, and so on.

Figure 12.24 SMTP Virtual Server Queues

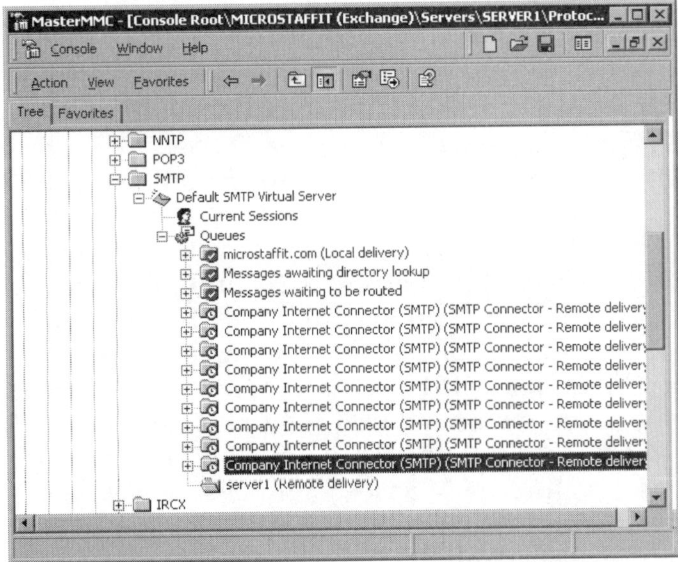

Figure 12.25 shows the sender's and recipient's names and the priority. The Details tab shows when the message was sent, when the Exchange server received it, and when the message expires.

Figure 12.25 Properties of Frozen Message in SMTP Virtual Server Queues

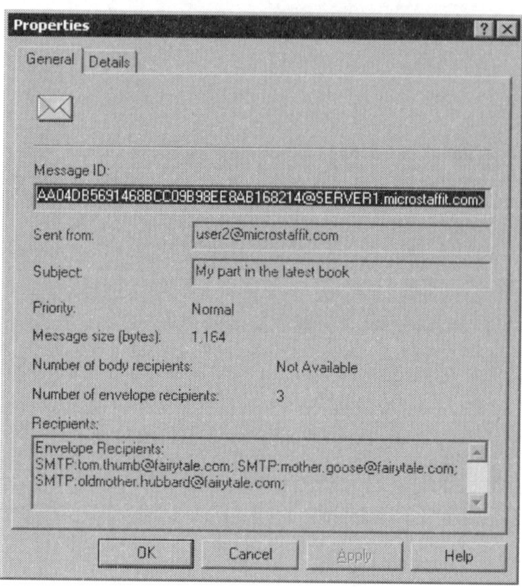

Protocol Logging

When you are having trouble understanding what is occurring with message flow, routing, or possibly accessing the Exchange server itself, you can always turn on protocol logging. Protocol logging that could be helpful to you is HTTP, SMTP, and NNTP. If you had OWA clients that were having difficulties using their browsers to get to their mailboxes, HTTP protocol logging would help you understand at what point in the client/server connection it is failing. As for SMTP, this logging will help you understand handshake problems in SMTP. For users reading newsgroups, the NNTP protocol logging will log the sessions attempted by these users.

For SMTP or NNTP protocols, go into Exchange System Manager | Servers | Protocols, and select the protocol SMTP or NNTP. Select the virtual server(s) that you want to monitor, and right-click Properties. Figure 12.26 is for SMTP Properties. Select the Enable Logging check box.

For HTTP, go into Internet Services Manager, select your server, and right-click. Once there, expand the protocol, and right-click Properties on the Default Web site. The Web Site tab looks very similar to the SMTP/NNTP in Figure 12.26. Select the Enable Logging check box.

Next, select the log format that you want and choose Properties, as shown in Figure 12.27.

Figure 12.26 Snapshot of Default SMTP Virtual Server Properties

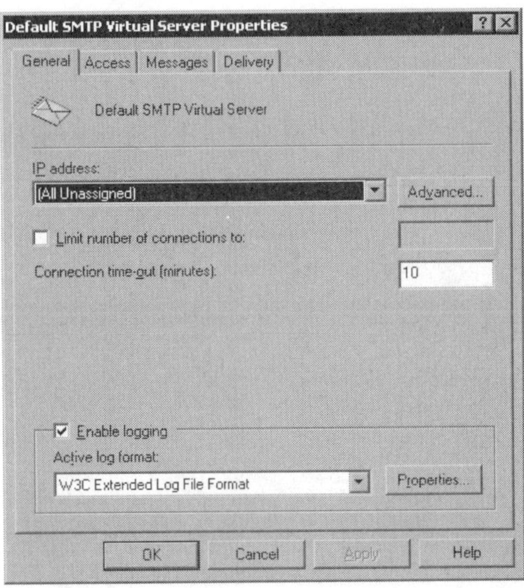

Figure 12.27 View of General Properties in Default SMTP Virtual Server

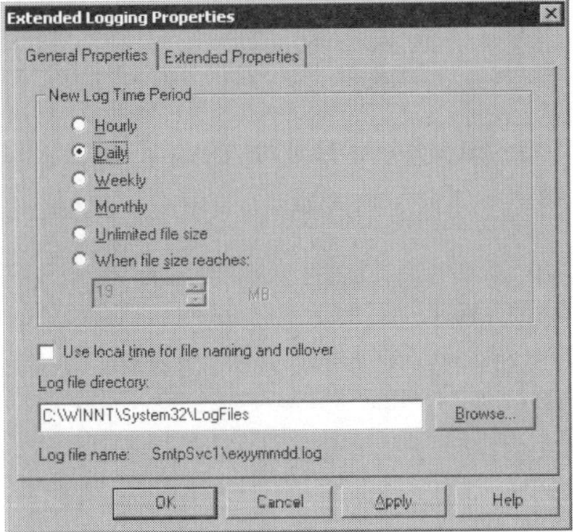

Most log files are kept under %sysetemroot%\system32\logfiles, but you could choose to place them on a separate physical disk. When you are configuring Exchange server and log files, make sure to pay attention to performance issues that can occur with the random access of data (in the Exchange .edb files) and sequential access of data (in various log files). We encourage you to select the local time for file naming and rollover if you have a small organization. The default is to use Greenwich Mean Time

(GMT), which really helps when you are debugging problems that involve network connections over different time zones. It is a bit disconcerting at first, but you do get used to it. Use the weekly log file as a general rule unless all your system administrators agree to another time frame.

The Extended Properties tab, as shown in Figure 12.28, lets you choose all the necessary information for debugging. The properties shown in the figure are a good start.

Figure 12.28 View of Extended Logging Properties

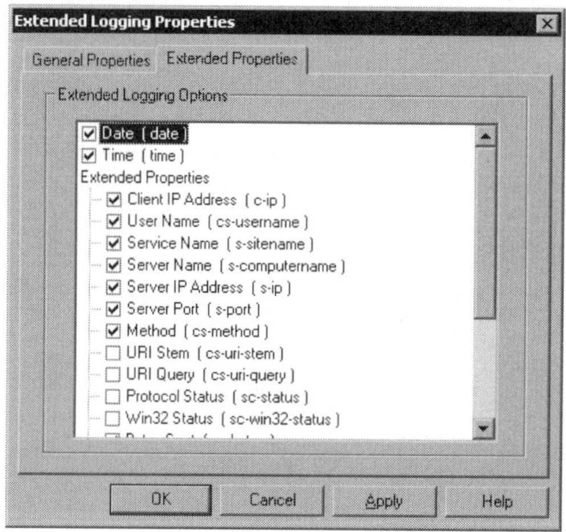

The following is an example of SMTP protocol logging output:

```
#Software: Microsoft Internet Information Services 5.0
#Version: 1.0
#Date: 2001-01-06 20:31:30
#Fields: date time c-ip cs-username s-sitename s-computername s-ip s-port cs-method sc-bytes cs-bytes
2001-01-06 20:37:49 - OutboundConnectionResponse SMTPSVC1 SERVER1 - 25 - 96 0
2001-01-06 20:37:49 june.microstaff.net OutboundConnectionCommand SMTPSVC1 SERVER1 - 25 EHLO 4 0
2001-01-06 20:37:49 june.microstaff.net OutboundConnectionResponse SMTPSVC1 SERVER1 - 25 - 39 0
2001-01-06 20:37:49 june.microstaff.net OutboundConnectionCommand SMTPSVC1 SERVER1 - 25 MAIL 4 0
2001-01-06 20:37:49 june.microstaff.net OutboundConnectionResponse SMTPSVC1 SERVER1 - 25 - 43 0
```

WinRoute

WinRoute is available on the Exchange 2000 resource kit and on Microsoft Developer Network (MSDN)'s BackOffice Server Test Platform CD. WinRoute is a tool that connects to port 691 on your Exchange server. This port is used because link state information is passed between servers within a routing group using port 691. So, by connecting to port 691, WinRoute latches on to the information table data and extracts it into a more user-friendly viewer. This is helpful when you are trying to determine the status of the connectors as seen by the server to which you are connected. You can save the link table to a file for reference when performing routing configurations or when planning. It is a great help when trying to restore an Exchange server that hosts connectors. By having a printout or diagram of the routing table, you will be able to see how you had it configured before you made changes.

When you run WinRoute, the first thing it does is give you a pop-up menu to select the server name to which you are going to connect, as shown in Figure 12.29. You could decide to edit some of the binding options, but you don't have to.

Figure 12.29 WinRoute Log-On Screen

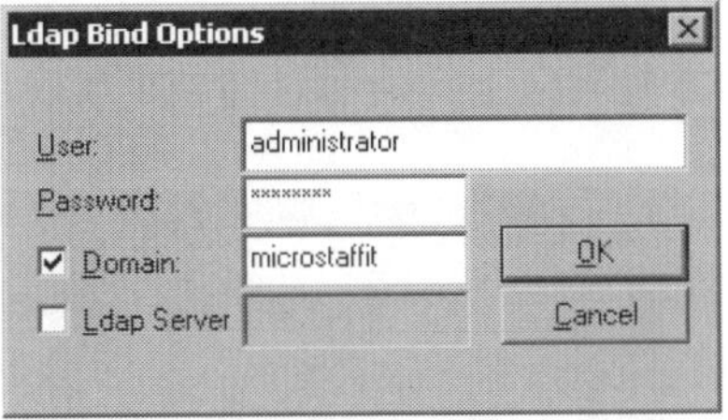

The WinRoute window has three panes to it; it tells you the routes within your Exchange organization (see Figure 12.30).

Here you can see that we have two connectors defined for SMTP. The Company Internet connector (SMTP) has a cost of 1, which means it will be used more often than the connector named Forward SMTP to Exchange 5.5. The highlighted data in the lower third pane corresponds to the highlighted value in the upper pane. Although you can see this information in the Exchange System Manager, WinRoute gives you the ability to check all the routing information of the organization within one quick tool. If you start walking through the data, you will be able to see all the routing information for the organization. The good news is that you don't have to interpret it yourself. Try this one right now on your server to see what we mean.

Figure 12.30 WinRoute Console

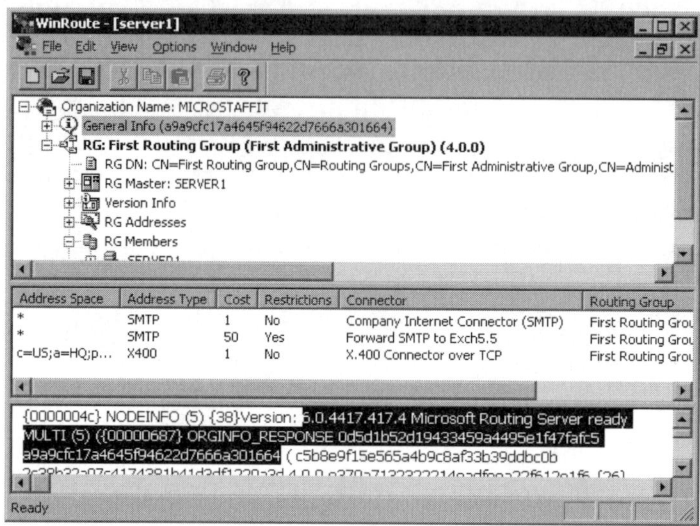

By selecting Options ? Get Statistics, you will be able to get a quick snapshot of the objects in your Exchange organization, as shown in Figure 12.31 on our test Exchange server.

Figure 12.31 WinRoute Statistics on Link State Table

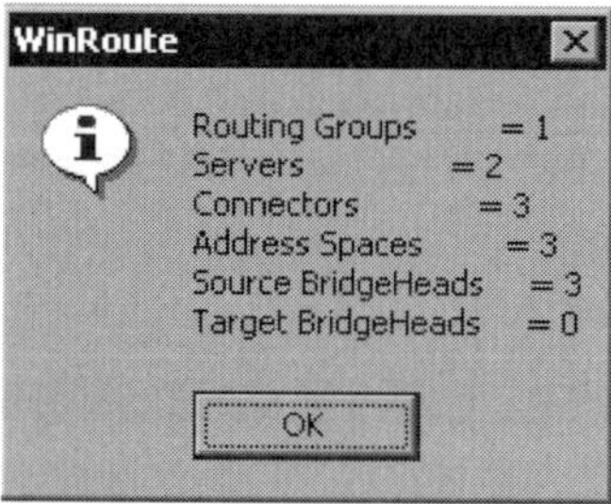

Message Flow Guidelines

The following pointers are guidelines, or pointers, to think about when troubleshooting. They are not "rules" *per se*, because troubleshooting situations in Exchange 2000 are still being discovered, but they are a good start for working out a problem situation.

When you troubleshoot and fix an Exchange problem, spend some time after the fix creating a diagram of the components that were affected. This will help you understand the message flow and key components for the next time you have an Exchange problem.

Message Flow Guideline 1

Always have a good understanding of what the network administrator is doing with DNS servers, DNS records, and the like. Many times we've been on site to determine why mail is:

- Going out but not coming in

- Coming in but not going out

- Not coming in *or* going out

when it was all working the day before. If you can rule out your own team of Exchange administrators, think "networking." If you have outsourced part or all your networking management, call to see if DNS has been worked on in the past day or two. Ask them if *anything* has changed. Check all the networking components that *might* be involved in the message flow.

Message Flow Guideline 2

If a message is being sent to a local user (the originator and recipient are on the same Exchange server) and the message does not appear in the recipient's mailbox, you should not have to worry about SMTP, X.400, MTAs, or such. Look in the local event viewer log to see if there are any problems with the Information Store, ExIFS.

Message Flow Guideline 3

If a message is being sent to a legacy Exchange 5.5 user within the same routing group or site, you shouldn't have to worry about SMTP. You should investigate at the RPC level (Run RPC Ping, etc.).

Message Flow Guideline 4

When a client sends a nonlocal message (to a recipient not on the Exchange server) and he or she gets an *immediate* response saying that the message is not deliverable, then you, the administrator, can start to suspect that *if* the message is addressed correctly, there is something wrong with how the message is *routed*. You know that message flow requires that a message sits in a queue, is assigned routing information, and is routed and delivered. If a message is leaving the server, a route to leave this server must be found. Routing is assisted by a "lookup" in the Active Directory, the link state table, and/or DNS. Most times a "lookup" will find the final destination quickly. (This assumes that all connections arc up, working, and always on.) If it doesn't find a route, it will be returned to the user. So, you need to determine why the route could not be found. Usually routing problems are easier to fix than transport problems because they involve fewer variables.

For example, when we sent out the message shown in Figure 12.32, we sent it to [FAX:8037997342]. The *[address:data]* format says that we are sending it to address type FAX and the data for the fax is the phone number. Once we sent this message, we received an "Undeliverable" message from the system administrator in about 11 seconds. That was fairly immediate. Although the message in Figure 12.32 says "no transport provider was available for delivery," this can be translated as communicating that the message could not be routed to the destination known as the address type FAX.

Figure 12.32 Undeliverable Message: Route Not Available

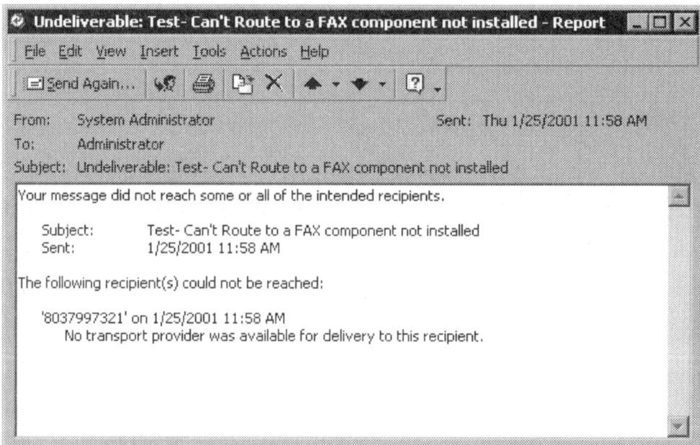

Message Flow Guideline 5

If a client sends a nonlocal message (to a recipient not on the Exchange server) and he or she doesn't get an immediate error, but they get an error *after a while*, the administrator could investigate how the messages are being *transported*—meaning that you assume it was assigned correct routing, but somehow the message isn't being delivered. If it is SMTP, run ping or tracert to see if you can reach the final destination. If it is using a transport that is scheduled, did someone change the schedule? Start thinking about how the message is transported out of the Exchange server, and then review all the ways that this transport can be affected or diagnosed.

Figure 12.33 shows an example of an error a user might see. We got this about two hours after we sent our problem message. (We had taken the network cable off the Exchange server, so it was not able to transmit the message. This caused the message delay.)

Figure 12.33 Delivery Status Notification Message: Message Delayed

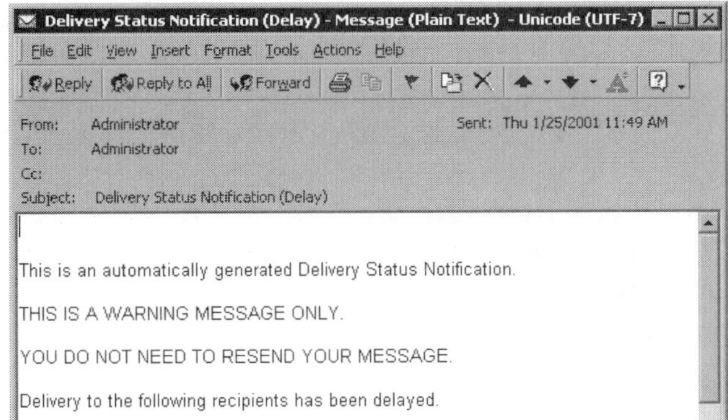

Message Flow Guideline 6

If a message is going out to a user who has an SMTP address, you shouldn't need to worry about troubleshooting X.400s or MTA components.

Message Flow Guideline 7

Subscribe to Microsoft TechNet and always refer to it before you start running tools that affect configuration. Check to see if TechNet has similar problems that match your symptoms—problems involving Active Directory, Windows 2000, and Exchange 2000.

When you have symptoms that lead you to believe that you are having problems with Active Directory components, make sure that you take your time determining when the problems started and what generic administrative tasks were occurring within your IT department. Microsoft provides tools such as ADSIEdit and LDP that let you edit Active Directory objects, but be careful with these. Make sure that you read up on what these tools do and how they work.

Active Directory Services Interface Editor (ADSIEdit) is a snap-in to the MMC that you can find on the Windows 2000 Advanced Server CD in the \support\Tools folder. This tool lets you see the Active Directory Schema and modify it. This is similar to using legacy Exchange Administrator in Raw mode. For instance, you might use ADSIEdit during the restore of an Exchange mailbox from backup. You will need to use this tool to find the LegacyExchangeDN value of the administrative group to which the Exchange database belongs. (There are nontroubleshooting reasons to use

ADSIEdit, such as modifying attributes, creating dynamic distributions lists based on an LDAP query, and more.)

LDP is a tool that you can find on the Windows 2000 Resource Kit or the Windows 2000 Server CD in the \support\Tools folder. This tool lets you perform LDAP searches and modifications against Active Directory. You could use this tool if ADSIEdit did not provide the LDAP information that you required.

Please note that you should be very careful in making Active Directory modifications. Such changes can cause permanent damage to your Active Directory environment.

Summary

Storage architecture and routing changed tremendously from legacy Exchange 5.5 to Exchange 2000. The introduction of multiple stores and multiple storage groups have made administration and backup easier. However, the new architecture makes troubleshooting and restoring data more complex. It is important that you experiment with repairing and restoring the multiple stores in storage groups on test systems so that you feel comfortable with the new environment. The integration of Active Directory as well as the ubiquitous presence of SMTP throughout Exchange 2000 has made the configuring of Exchange and its connectors simpler. On the other hand, SMTP has moved from Exchange to IIS, and the directory service is in Active Directory. It is important that you master these building blocks, because they have a tremendous impact on the replication of organizational data and the routing of messages within Exchange.

The keys to troubleshooting are patience and experience. Make sure that you read as many white papers on architecture, message flow, and routing as you can. Employ proactive monitoring tools to prevent servers from becoming starved for resources and thirsty for network bandwidth. Exchange 2000 has many tools and features to help you monitor and maintain your environment. Keep your eyes open for new troubleshooting tips. Make sure that you have access to Microsoft TechNet, and spend time each month reviewing new features or tricks on Exchange.

FAQs

FAQs Visit **www.syngress.com/solutions** to have your questions about this chapter answered by the author.

Q: When should I use Isinteg?

A: You can use Isinteg when the information store will not start. Isinteg scans the information stores for inconsistencies. It is fairly harmless without the Fix option—when you use the Fix option with a test, it has the potential to fix and harm your system, but it is much safer than Eseutil.

Q: When should I use Eseutil?

A: With the exception of the /d option, which assists in defragmentation and compaction, and the /g option, which performs a read-only integrity check, you should use Eseutil as little as possible, under supervision from Microsoft, and when you have readily available backup media in case of problems.

Q: Users say that they never got my message. How can I find out if a message was delivered to a specific user?

A: Enable message tracking, and select Subject and Date listing. You will be able to search all messaging logs for sent and received messages using the Message Tracking Center.

Q: What are res.logs in the database folders?

A: They are two files that reserve 5 MB space each for Exchange in case the logical drive fills up. When the space is gone on the logical drive, Exchange flushes any operations to these two files and then shuts down.

TCP and UDP Ports

Table A.1 Use of TCP and UDP Ports in Windows 2000 and Exchange 2000

Port	TCP/UDP	Service	Windows 2000	Exchange 2000
25	TCP	Simple Mail Transfer Protocol (SMTP)		✓
42	TCP	WINS Replication	✓	
47	TCP	Generic routing encapsulation (GRE) for Point-to-Point Tunneling Protocol (PPTP)	✓	
53	TCP	Domain Name System (DNS)	✓	
53	UDP	DNS Name Resolution	✓	
67	UDP	Dynamic Host Configuration Protocol (DHCP) Lease (Bootstrap Protocol, or BOOTP)	✓	
68	UDP	DHCP Lease	✓	
80	TCP	Hypertext Transfer Protocol (HTTP)		✓
88	UDP	Kerberos	✓	
102	TCP	Mail Transfer Agent (MTA) (x.400 over TCP/IP)		✓
110	TCP	Post Office Protocol v3 (POP3)		✓
119	TCP	Network News Transport Protocol (NNTP)		✓
135	TCP	Location Service: remote-procedure call (RPC), RPC EP Mapper, WINS Manager, DHCP Manager, Distributed Transaction Coordinator, or DTC)	✓	✓
137	TCP	WINS Registration	✓	
137	UDP	Network Basic Input/Output System (NetBIOS) Name Service	✓	
138	UDP	NetBIOS Datagram Service	✓	
139	TCP	NetBIOS Session Service	✓	
143	TCP	Internet Message Access Protocol (IMAP)		✓
389	TCP/ UDP	Lightweight Directory Access Protocol (LDAP)	✓	✓

Continued

Table A.1 Continued

Port	TCP/UDP	Service	Windows 2000	Exchange 2000
443	TCP	HTTP (Secure Sockets Layer, or SSL)		✓
465	TCP	SMTP (SSL)		✓
500	TCP/ UDP	Internet Security Association and Key Management Protocol (ISAKMP)/Oakley negotiation traffic (IPSec)	✓	
522	TCP	User Location Store	✓	
563	TCP	NNTP (SSL)		✓
636	TCP/ UDP	LDAP (over Transport Layer Security protocol (TLS)/SSL)	✓	✓
750	TCP	Kerberos Authentication	✓	
750	UDP	Kerberos Authentication	✓	
751	TCP	Kerberos Authentication	✓	
751	UDP	Kerberos Authentication	✓	
752	UDP	Kerberos Password Server	✓	
753	UDP	Kerberos User Registration Server	✓	
754	TCP	Kerberos Slave Propagation	✓	
888	TCP	Logon and Environment Passing	✓	
993	TCP	IMAP4 (SSL)		✓
995	TCP	POP3 (SSL)		✓
1109	TCP	POP with Kerberos	✓	
1720	TCP	h.323 Call Setup		✓
1723	TCP	Point-to-Point Tunneling Protocol (PPTP) Control Channel (IP Protocol 47 – GRE)	✓	
1731	TCP	Audio Call Control		✓
2053	TCP	Kerberos de-multiplexor	✓	
2105	TCP	Kerberos encrypted rlogin	✓	
2980	TCP	Instant Messaging Service		✓
3268		Global Catalog	✓	

Continued

Table A.1 Continued

Port	TCP/UDP	Service	Windows 2000	Exchange 2000
3269		Global Catalog	✓	
3389	TCP	Terminal Services	✓	
Dynamic	TCP	Directory Replication	✓	
Dynamic	TCP	h.323 Call Control		✓
Dynamic	UDP	h.323 Call (RTP over UDP)		✓

Physical Networking and VPN Protocol Details

Physical Networking

Connecting a client computer to the same LAN that links to the Exchange Server is a configuration with the least likely interruption to service due to a physical problem. LANs are typically constructed of reliable wiring and few points of failure. There are several common types of LANs that you will encounter. Each of these is specified by a physical and data-link layer protocol combination (Layers 1 and 2 of the OSI reference model):

- Ethernet

- Token Ring

- Fiber Distributed Data Interface (FDDI)

Ethernet is, by far, the most common type of LAN. The basic Ethernet specification requires a logical bus topology that can run on a physical topology of either a bus or star, except in the case of 10BaseFL, which uses a point-to-point topology. A *physical bus* is simply a length of cabling to which each node is attached. A *physical star* has a hub or switch in the center attached to each node by a separate cable, as shown in Figure B.1. Network nodes contend for access to the network at any time using an access method called *carrier sense multiple access/collision detect* (CSMA/CD). A collision occurs when two nodes contend for access to the wire at the same time. Ethernet, which is the Institute of Electrical and Electronics Engineers (IEEE) 802.3 specification, resolves collisions by allowing each node to re-transmit after a random period of waiting time. There are several versions of Ethernet, detailed in Table B.1.

Figure B.1 Physical Star Topology

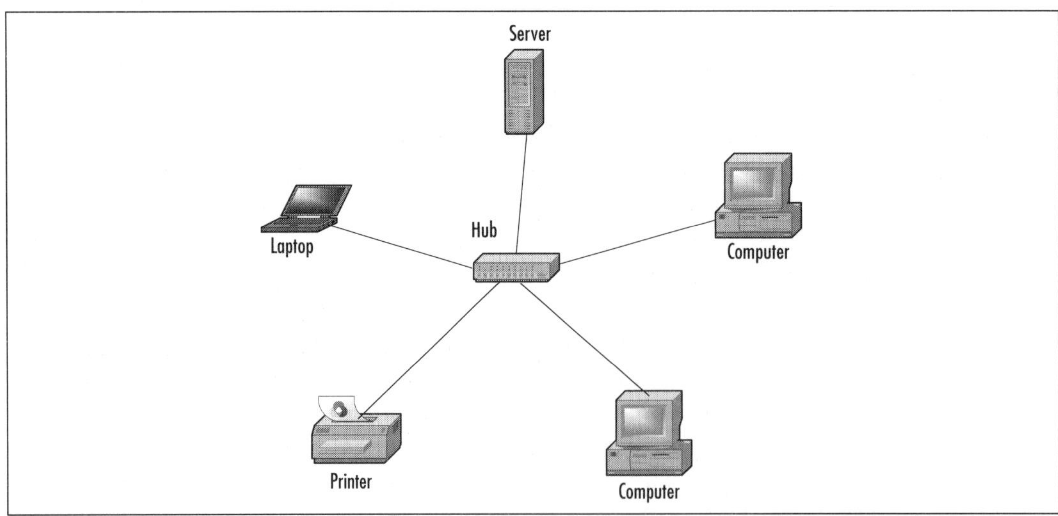

Table B.1 Ethernet Specifications

Ethernet Specification	Speed	Cable Type	Maximum Length of Cable Segment	Physical Topology
10BaseT	10 Mbps	Copper unshielded twisted pair, Cat5	100 feet	Star
10Base5	10 Mbps	Thick 50 ohm coaxial	500 feet	Bus
10Base2	10 Mbps	Thin 50 ohm coaxial	185 feet	Bus
10BaseFL	10 Mbps	Fiber optic	2000 feet	Point-to-Point
100BaseTX	100 Mbps	Copper unshielded twisted pair, Cat5	100 feet	Star
100BaseFX	100 Mbps	2 stranded fiber optic	400 meters	Star
100BaseT4	100 Mbps	Copper unshielded twisted pair, Cat3, Cat4 or Cat5	100 feet	Star

Token Ring was originally developed by IBM and then became the IEEE 802.5 specification. It specifies a logical ring topology that can run on either a physical ring or star topology. A physical ring topology is a group of network nodes that are connected in serial fashion, with the last connected to the first, in a circle. Token Ring uses a token passing media access method. A network node must be handed a specially formatted frame called a *token* in order to be granted access to the network. Token Ring networks originally used copper shielded twisted pair wiring, but later included Cat5 copper unshielded twisted pair wiring. Token Ring networks transmit at a speed of 4 Mbps or 16 Mbps.

FDDI is somewhat unusual to run into, but with the increased demand for bandwidth, it is becoming more common. American National Standards Institute (ANSI) X3T9.5 specifies FDDI. This method is both a physical and logical ring topology, although it uses a physical dual ring architecture for redundancy in case of a ring failure. FDDI runs at a speed of 100 Mbps and uses token passing, much like Token Ring.

Types of Connections via Remote Access Servers

Remote Access Servers (RAS) provide dial-up connections to the enterprise network, or intranet. Dial-up connections can use the following types of connections:

- Analog

- Digital Subscriber Line (DSL)

- Integrated Services Digital Network (ISDN)

Analog

Analog connections use either the Serial Line Internet Protocol (SLIP) or the Point-to-Point Protocol (PPP) over standard telephone lines and modems. Both SLIP and PPP define methods of transmitting IP packets. PPP can also transmit Internetwork Packet Exchange (IPX) and AppleTalk also.

Dial-up connections to an enterprise network can be cost effective for remote users or, in some cases, for remote sites. This is largely due to the prevalence and availability of the telephone network. Many organizations configure a dial-up connection as a backup link in case a WAN link fails, for that matter.

The main drawbacks to analog connections are the slowness of the link (56 Kbps or slower), the large amount of overhead (each byte is checked for errors, as opposed to entire packets on a network link), and the expense of long-distance or 800-number charges if a local number is not available.

SLIP is the older of the two protocols, having originated on UNIX systems. It is required for those UNIX systems that cannot support PPP. If you have a UNIX remote access server that only supports SLIP, then all the client workstations that connect to that server must be configured with SLIP. However, if you have a UNIX client workstation that only supports SLIP, then you can configure your Remote Access Server to support both SLIP and PPP, then allow other workstations to use PPP. Aside from supporting multiple protocols, PPP supports basic compression and encryption, so it is a much more desirable protocol to use.

Both PPP and SLIP are available in Windows 2000 for connecting to networks. The default dial-up connection in Windows 2000 is configured with PPP, due to its prevalence and preferred usage in Windows 2000 remote access servers. This procedure assumes that you have already installed a modem on your computer. To configure an analog connection on a Windows 2000 computer:

1. Right-click My Network Places.

2. Select Properties. The Network and Dial-up Connections window will appear.

3. Double-click the Make New Connection icon. The wizard will start.

4. Click Next.

5. Select Dial-up to Private Network and click Next. This dialog is shown in Figure B.2.

6. Type in the phone number and check the box if you prefer using the dialing rules. Click Next.

7. Select whether this connection is for all users, or for the current logged in user. Click Next.

8. Type a name for the connection and click Finish. The connection will show up in the Network and Dial-up Connections window. This is, by default, a PPP connection at this point, so if you needed a PPP connection you may stop here.

9. Right-click your new connection and select Properties.

10. Click the Networking tab.

11. Click the drop-down arrow for the box entitled, "Type of dial-up server I am calling:" and select SLIP: Unix Connection.

12. Click OK to finish.

Figure B.2 Configuring a Dial-up Connection on Windows 2000

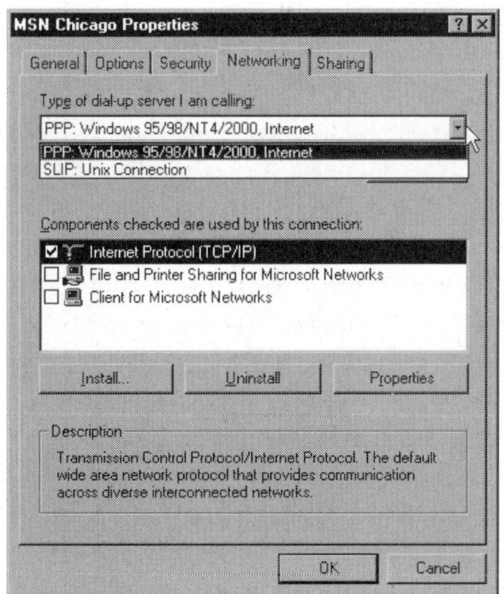

DSL

Digital Subscriber Line (DSL) technology utilizes the same twisted-pair copper wires that telephones use for high-bandwidth data transmissions. xDSL describes different types of DSL technology, such as Very-high-data-rate Digital Subscriber Line (VDSL) and Asymmetric Digital Subscriber Line (ADSL). Because xDSL services provide dedicated point-to-point connections over the last mile (the twisted pair copper wiring on the telephone company's local loop) with minimal changes to the service provider's network, it draws significant attention as a new technology.

VDSL technology depends on the upcoming technology of Fiber To The Neighborhood (FTTN) in which fiber optic media is installed to reach optical network units that feed large buildings and neighborhoods. From the optical network units, short drops of copper wiring service the building and the neighborhood. This is where VDSL comes in. Because fiber optic media provides services for the majority of the distance, vastly increased speeds are available on the copper media. The speeds are dependent upon the length of the wiring. Over short distances of 1,000 feet, downloads may be as fast as 50 to 55 Mbps, while a 4,000 feet distance would enable about 13 Mbps download speed.

VDSL is currently being defined and discussed and is not ready for implementation except with a small number of preliminary products. It is likely that VDSL will incorporate slower upload speeds using echo cancellation except in the shortest distances where it may be only slightly slower or equivalent to the download speed. VDSL is clearly an appropriate technology for an enterprise network to use in connecting to the Internet.

ADSL provides high-speed data transmission over standard telephone wiring, enabling telephone companies to realize more profits from their existing copper infrastructure. The term *asymmetric* refers to the fact that the upstream and downstream transmission rates are different. ADSL offers up to 9 Mbps downloading capability and up to 640 Kbps uploading capability. Note the usage of "*up to.*" ADSL speeds vary based on the quality of the copper wire and distance to service provider's network.

ADSL's asymmetric speed system matches the usage of users who tend to consume Internet media, downloading HTML Web pages along with multimedia components, and who tend to upload much smaller data amounts in the form of e-mail and small file transfers. ADSL is not as appropriate for businesses that transmit equal amounts of data to and from the Internet. Nor is it appropriate for an Internet Web server since a Web server tends to upload data to users through the Internet rather than download from them.

ADSL does not digitize the voice line. Instead, ADSL transmits standard analog voice service. Whereas the voice service uses a dial-up number, the data service doesn't. A portion of the analog line's bandwidth that is not utilized by voice transmission is used for data. This enables a simultaneous voice and data transmission. A splitter is placed on the telephone jack to filter out ADSL signaling and ensure the quality of the line.

ADSL equipment divides the available bandwidth of the telephone line using one of the following methods:

- **Frequency division multiplexing (FDM)** FDM assigns one frequency band for upstream data and another band for downstream data. The downstream path is divided using time division multiplexing (TDM) into high and low speed channels. The upstream path is divided using TDM into corresponding low speed channels so that each upstream and downstream channel is a pair.

- **Echo cancellation** Echo cancellation assigns the upstream band to overlap the downstream band, then separates the bands with a local mechanism that is also used in V.32 and V.34 modems.

Regardless of how the bandwidth is divided, ADSL dedicates a 4 kHz region for the telephone voice service.

In order to use a Windows 2000 computer with an ADSL line, you need a special DSL adapter. You first install the DSL adapter physically into the computer, and then when the computer powers online, you install the drivers so that the adapter is recognized as a network adapter. The connection is then displayed in Network and Dial-up Connections, which is found in the Control Panel.

Many corporations will be looking into DSL for their telecommuters. DSL will provide a high-speed connection for them, making telecommuters more productive with network applications. When users install DSL in their homes, they will need filters for their telephone jacks to work appropriately. These filters enable the voice traffic to flow through to the telephone without data interrupting it.

ISDN

The Integrated Systems Digital Network (ISDN) is often referred to as the *I Still Don't Know* acronym. The reason for this sarcastic description is based on the fact that ISDN was not immediately available or was not widely used even though it was broadly discussed. ISDN was an exciting option for remote access when it was introduced since it provided increased bandwidth, reduced latency, faster call establishment, and less noise interference with the signal when you compare it to a standard dial-up connection. What prevented it from becoming immediately popular was its price and availability.

ISDN is a digital call switching service that is provided in two forms:

- Basic Rate Interface (BRI)
- Primary Rate Interface (PRI)

Both types of interfaces are available in most areas where legacy analog PSTN equipment has been updated with digital equipment. The new digital switches can support both ISDN and plain old telephone service (POTS).

BRI provides two B (bearer) channels and one D (data) channel. The B channels provide 64 Kbps bandwidth each and are used for bearer services (voice or data) while the D channel at 16 Kbps is used for signaling and control. The D channel is used for building, maintaining, and releasing the bearer service connections over the B channels. BRI's bandwidth is therefore 128 Kbps over the B channels. BRI can be provided over legacy analog phone service local loops. ISDN local loop length is limited to approximately 18,000 feet.

PRI provides 23 B channels at 64 Kbps and 1 D channel at 64 Kbps. The B channels still provide bearer services while the D channel provides signaling and control in the same way as it does for BRI. PRI services are provided over T1 lines. PRI's bandwidth is 1.472 Mbps over those 23 B channels. (In Europe and across the Pacific Rim, PRI services are provided over E1 leased lines with 30 64Kbps B channels and a single 64Kbps D channel.)

The components used in ISDN networks include several types:

- **Terminal Adapter (TA)** An adapter that is used with legacy equipment or non-ISDN-capable equipment in order to connect to the ISDN network—used for BRI-rates.

- **Terminal Equipment Type 1 (TE1)** A device that can connect directly to an ISDN network and has ISDN capabilities built in.

- **Terminal Equipment Type 2 (TE2)** A device that requires a TA to connect to the ISDN network.

- **Network Termination Type 1 (NT1)** A device which sends and receives signals to the service provider's ISDN switch.

- **Network Termination Type 2 (NT2)** A device that concentrates ISDN switching services at the client's site. NT2 devices connect to NT1 devices in order to access the service provider's ISDN network.

- **Local Exchange (LE)** An ISDN switch providing both switching and termination services for ISDN traffic, located at the service provider's network.

It is possible to have TA and TE1 devices with NT2 devices built in, or with both NT1 and NT2 devices built in. It is common in Europe to only have a built-in NT2 device since service providers provide NT1 services. In the United States, however, both NT1 and NT2 devices are required. When configuring ISDN routing, each TE1, TE2, NT1, or NT2 device must be configured with the correct type of LE switch.

When a connection between two hosts over an ISDN B channel link is created, it is encapsulated in PPP (Point-to-Point Protocol), HDLC, X.25, or V.120 protocols. Both ISDN routers must be configured with the same encapsulation in order for data to transmit properly. The majority of ISDN implementations encapsulate with PPP. D channels use Link Access Procedure on the D channel (LAPD) for signaling between terminal equipment and the ISDN switch. Within a service provider's ISDN network, the ISDN switches use Signaling System 7 (SS7) protocol.

ISDN operates at the physical, data-link, and network layers of the OSI protocol reference model. The LE provides clocking for the physical layer's synchronous bitstream of ISDN data. Data-link layer addressing assigns a unique physical address called a terminal endpoint identifier (TEI) to each ISDN interface. At the network layer, ISDN services on each device are assigned logical addresses.

When either a TE1 or TE2 comes online, it requests a TEI from the service provider's LE. The LE assigns a unique TEI for traffic identification. The switch assigns a Service Profile Identifier (SPID), a logical address, to each B channel. The SPID is used like a telephone number to build the circuit connection between ISDN devices. A Service Access Point Identifier (SAPI) is assigned to each separate service performed by the ISDN device. SAPIs are used to prioritize data.

Windows 2000 uses an ISDN line the same way that it uses a modem and analog line. It is considered a dial-up network connection and is configured in the Network and Dial-up Connections icon found in Control Panel. You can implement a complex advanced routing system using Windows 2000 and multiple ISDN adapters with multiple dialing profiles and multilink PPP (a system in which multiple PPP links are added to create a higher bandwidth connection overall).

The first thing you need to do is install the ISDN interface adapter into the computer. Then, you need to power up the computer so that the ISDN ports are detected by the hardware detection mechanism within Windows 2000. You will use the Device Manager to configure the switch type for the ISDN adapter. To access the Device Manager, right-click on My Computer and select Properties from the pull-down menu. Then click the Hardware tab and click the Device Manager button. A Windows 2000 computer needs to know what ISDN switch (LE) the ISDN adapter is connecting to. The

AT&T 5ESS (ATT), the National ISDN-1 (NI-1), and Northern Telecom (NTI) switches are all common options. Once the switch is identified, use the following instructions to configure the ISDN connection:

1. Right-click on My Network Places.
2. Select Properties. The Network and Dial-up Connections window will appear.
3. Right-click on the connection that uses the ISDN device.
4. Select Properties from the pull-down menu.
5. Click the ISDN device in the Connect using box on the General tab.
6. Click Configure.
7. Select the line type or check the box whether to negotiate the line type.
8. Click OK to exit.

VPN Protocol Details

This section provides some supporting technical information on three VPN protocols, Internet Protocol Security (IPSec), Point-to-Point Tunneling Protocol (PPTP), and Layer 2 Tunneling Protocol (L2TP).

IPSec

Internet Protocol Security (IPSec) is a set of VPN protocols that creates tunnels between devices, provides authentication mechanism, and enables confidentiality of data. IPSec includes the following components:

- IPSec tunnels use the Authentication Header (AH) protocol to encapsulate the original IP packet in another IP packet with a new IP header—the AH header. AH can authenticate the data source, but the AH header does not provide data confidentiality.

- IPSec tunnels use the Encapsulating Security Payload (ESP) protocol to provide data confidentiality by encrypting the original IP packet and attaching an ESP header with an IP header, plus an ESP trailer. ESP also enables data source authentication through an authenticator, but that authenticator can be turned off by setting it to null.

IPSec tunnels may use AH with ESP, or ESP alone, to provide a fully confidential tunnel. Two components are used for encryption within IPSec: a cipher and a secret key. The cipher is an algorithm that converts data to an encrypted form. The cipher uses the secret key to decrypt the data. IPSec supports Data Encryption Standard (DES) and Triple Data Encryption Standard (3DES). In DES, a single secret key is used to encrypt data and to decrypt it. In 3DES, there are three secret keys used. The first key is used to encrypt. The second key is used to partially decrypt. The third key is used to encrypt again. IPSec encryption is applied to packets at Layer 3, the network layer in the OSI reference model.

PPTP

The Point-to-Point Tunneling Protocol (PPTP) provides a method of tunneling PPP frames within IP datagrams to connect securely over the Internet. Microsoft developed PPTP to create, maintain, and terminate tunnels using encapsulated PPP frames. PPTP helped form the basis for L2TP.

Many legacy NT networks may be using PPTP as the VPN system. When upgrading to Windows 2000, it can be tempting to simply leave the existing PPTP system in place. However, it is recommended that an upgrade of the PPTP system to L2TP is considered, at the very least, because of L2TP's superior security features.

PPTP uses TCP port 1723, so you should make certain your firewall will not filter that port out. PPTP Control Connection packets provide PPTP tunnel maintenance. PPTP packets provide tunneled data. The PPTP frame is encapsulated with a Generic Routing Encapsulation (GRE) header. Some Internet service providers configure their routers to filter out GRE packets because they use GRE packets for routing information. This can cause PPTP tunneled data to not be forwarded across the Internet, but can be remedied by removing the GRE filters or changing to L2TP.

To create a PPTP connection, you start in the Network and Dial-up Connections dialog box found in the Control Panel. Or you may right-click on My Network Places and select Properties from the pull-down menu.

1. Double-click the Make New Connection icon.

2. Click Next.

3. Select Connect to a private network through the Internet.

4. Click Next.

5. You can select an existing dial-up connection, or if you are already connected to the Internet, select "Do not dial the initial connection."

6. Click Next.

7. Type in the IP address or hostname of the PPTP server.

8. Click Next.

9. Select whether this is a connection to be made available for all users or just for the currently logged in user.

10. Click Next.

11. Type a name for the connection.

12. Click Finish.

L2TP

The Layer 2 Tunneling Protocol (L2TP) is an Internet Engineering Task Force (IETF) standard that extends the Point-to-Point Protocol (PPP). L2TP supports multiple protocols, due to its PPP relation, as well as private IP addressing over the Internet. L2TP can be used with remote access infrastructure, including modems, ISDN and DSL technology. Two components of the L2TP tunnel are:

- **L2TP access concentrator (LAC)** A device to which a client connects directly as a network access server. From here, PPP frames are tunneled to the L2TP network server (LNS).

- **L2TP Network Server (LNS)** The server at the end of the L2TP tunnel that accepts L2TP/PPP frames and passes them to higher layer protocols.

L2TP creates the concept of the virtual access interface. This concept provides that each client connecting via L2TP is assigned an instance of a virtual interface, which is unique on the server. A virtual template interface can be created for the basis of all virtual access interfaces, providing common configurations (as well as preventing human errors). The LAC exchanges PPP messages with remote users, while exchanging L2TP requests and responses with the LNS at the other side of each L2TP tunnel created with a virtual access interface for the remote users. Connecting via L2TP follows a short sequence of actions:

1. A remote user dials up to ISP and creates a PPP connection with the ISP's LAC.

2. LAC partially authenticates the remote user with CHAP or PAP. The LAC determines if the user can be connected to the LNS and if so, does so.

3. The LAC authenticates the LNS and vice versa. Then a tunnel is created.

4. The L2TP session is initiated for the remote user between the LAC and LNS.

5. The LAC forwards the CHAP or PAP information to the LNS, which forwards it directly to the virtual access interface for the session. If the information is correct, the session negotiation is completed and the session is established. If incorrect, the remote user is disconnected.

To ensure that the packets transmitted using L2TP are encrypted and secure, L2TP tunneled data is processed through a series of headers. When a header is processed, it is read for its information, acted on and then dropped off the packet, and discarded much like the pieces of a rocket ship being dropped off after their part in blasting a rocket into the atmosphere is finished. An L2TP server receiving an L2TP packet will process the data-link header and trailer first. The IP header is processed next. Then the IPSec ESP Auth trailer is processed for authentication of the IPSec ESP header and remaining data. The IPSec ESP header is processed next, and the encrypted packet data is decrypted. The UDP header is processed and the L2TP header is reviewed for the Tunnel ID and Call ID to specify the L2TP tunnel. Then the PPP header is processed to access the remaining data and process it at the upper protocol layers.

L2TP uses User Datagram Protocol (UDP) to send packets of tunneled data as well as tunnel maintenance control. Windows 2000 clients are L2TP compliant, and do not require the LAC to create the L2TP tunnel on their behalves. Instead each client creates the L2TP tunnel by interacting directly with the LNS. Both the Windows 2000 L2TP client and a Windows 2000 L2TP server (LNS) use UDP port 1701, although the server can be configured to use another port as well. Make certain that your firewall does not filter out this port or you will have problems using L2TP in your environment.

To create an L2TP VPN connection in Windows 2000, you begin with the Network and Dial-up Connections dialog box found in the Control Panel. You can also access this dialog box by right-clicking the My Network Places icon on the desktop and selecting Properties from the pull-down menu.

1. Double-click the Make New Connection icon and click Next.

2. Select Connect to a private network through the Internet and click Next.

3. You can select an existing dial-up connection, or if you are already connected to the Internet, select "Do not dial the initial connection." Click Next.

4. Type in the IP address or hostname of the LNS and click Next.

5. Select whether this is a connection to be made available for all users or just for the currently logged in user. Click Next.

6. Type a name for the connection.

7. Click Finish.

To ensure that this connection will only connect to L2TP servers, you can configure the connection's properties. Right-click the new icon in the Network and Dial-up Connections window and select Properties from the pull-down menu. Click the Networking tab. Drop down the box for "Type of VPN Server I am calling" and select Layer-2 Tunneling Protocol (L2TP). You may need to change the authentication settings for the connection if your organization has not implemented the defaults. In order to do so,

1. Click the Security tab.

2. Select the Advanced (Custom Settings) button.

3. Click the Settings button.

4. Make your changes and click OK when complete.

Index

N

NTBackup, 434, 441, 455
  package, 456
  usage, 461, 471. *See also* Exchange
    2000
NTDS, 78
NTDSUTIL, 41
NTFS. *See* NT File System
NTLM. *See* NT LAN Manager

O

O. *See* Organization
Object class, 118
Object Linking and Embedding
    Database (OLE DB), 2.5 support,
    21
Objects. *See* Mail-enabled recipient
    objects
  permission, 285
Office 2000, 244
  applications, 10
Office Developer Tools 2000, 3
Office (Microsoft), usage. *See* Exchange
    store access
Offline address book server. *See*
    Exchange 2000
Offline address lists
  creation, 187–188
  editing/removal, 189
  management, 187–190
  rebuilding, 189–190
Offline backups, 438
Offline defragmentation, 546
Offline logon, 140
Offline storage files, usage, 272–273
Offload SSL processing, 406
OLE DB. *See* Object Linking and
    Embedding Database
On-demand content conversion, 14

Online address lists
  client permissions, setting, 186–187
  management, 182–187
Online backups, 438
Online defragmentation, 545
Open System Interconnection (OSI)
    Reference Model, 104, 225, 578,
    587
Operating system, problems, 542
Operations Support Systems/Business
    Support Systems (OSS/BSS), 404
  services, 407
.OPS file, 248
.org (domain name), 43
Organization name, 284
Organization (O), 269
  moving, 321
  units, securing, 414–416
Organizational Unit (OU), 5, 37, 45,
    269, 300, 401. *See also* Top-level
    OU
  creation, 413
  descriptive name, 65
  hierarchy, 65
  plan, 82
  synchronization, 301
  tree, 61
    structure, 36–37
  usage, 65–66, 153
OSI. *See* Open System Interconnection
OSS/BSS. *See* Operations Support
    Systems/Business Support
    Systems
.OST files, 240–241, 341
OU. *See* Organizational Unit
Outbound SMTP server, 421
Outbox, 272
Outer firewall, 404–405
Outlook, 17

The Global Knowledge Advantage

Global Knowledge has a global delivery system for its products and services. The company has 28 subsidiaries, and offers its programs through a total of 60+ locations. No other vendor can provide consistent services across a geographic area this large. Global Knowledge is the largest independent information technology education provider, offering programs on a variety of platforms. This enables our multi-platform and multi-national customers to obtain all of their programs from a single vendor. The company has developed the unique CompetusTM Framework software tool and methodology which can quickly reconfigure courseware to the proficiency level of a student on an interactive basis. Combined with self-paced and on-line programs, this technology can reduce the time required for training by prescribing content in only the deficient skills areas. The company has fully automated every aspect of the education process, from registration and follow-up, to "just-in-time" production of courseware. Global Knowledge through its Enterprise Services Consultancy, can customize programs and products to suit the needs of an individual customer.

Global Knowledge Classroom Education Programs

The backbone of our delivery options is classroom-based education. Our modern, well-equipped facilities staffed with the finest instructors offer programs in a wide variety of information technology topics, many of which lead to professional certifications.

Custom Learning Solutions

This delivery option has been created for companies and governments that value customized learning solutions. For them, our consultancy-based approach of developing targeted education solutions is most effective at helping them meet specific objectives.

Self-Paced and Multimedia Products

This delivery option offers self-paced program titles in interactive CD-ROM, videotape and audio tape programs. In addition, we offer custom development of interactive multimedia courseware to customers and partners. Call us at 1-888-427-4228.

Electronic Delivery of Training

Our network-based training service delivers efficient competency-based, interactive training via the World Wide Web and organizational intranets. This leading-edge delivery option provides a custom learning path and "just-in-time" training for maximum convenience to students.

Global Knowledge Courses Available

Microsoft

- Windows 2000 Deployment Strategies
- Introduction to Directory Services
- Windows 2000 Client Administration
- Windows 2000 Server
- Windows 2000 Update
- MCSE Bootcamp
- Microsoft Networking Essentials
- Windows NT 4.0 Workstation
- Windows NT 4.0 Server
- Windows NT Troubleshooting
- Windows NT 4.0 Security
- Windows 2000 Security
- Introduction to Microsoft Web Tools

Management Skills

- Project Management for IT Professionals
- Microsoft Project Workshop
- Management Skills for IT Professionals

Network Fundamentals

- Understanding Computer Networks
- Telecommunications Fundamentals I
- Telecommunications Fundamentals II
- Understanding Networking Fundamentals
- Upgrading and Repairing PCs
- DOS/Windows A+ Preparation
- Network Cabling Systems

WAN Networking and Telephony

- Building Broadband Networks
- Frame Relay Internetworking
- Converging Voice and Data Networks
- Introduction to Voice Over IP
- Understanding Digital Subscriber Line (xDSL)

Internetworking

- ATM Essentials
- ATM Internetworking
- ATM Troubleshooting
- Understanding Networking Protocols
- Internetworking Routers and Switches
- Network Troubleshooting
- Internetworking with TCP/IP
- Troubleshooting TCP/IP Networks
- Network Management
- Network Security Administration
- Virtual Private Networks
- Storage Area Networks
- Cisco OSPF Design and Configuration
- Cisco Border Gateway Protocol (BGP) Configuration

Web Site Management and Development

- Advanced Web Site Design
- Introduction to XML
- Building a Web Site
- Introduction to JavaScript
- Web Development Fundamentals
- Introduction to Web Databases

PERL, UNIX, and Linux

- PERL Scripting
- PERL with CGI for the Web
- UNIX Level I
- UNIX Level II
- Introduction to Linux for New Users
- Linux Installation, Configuration, and Maintenance

Authorized Vendor Training

Red Hat

- Introduction to Red Hat Linux
- Red Hat Linux Systems Administration
- Red Hat Linux Network and Security Administration
- RHCE Rapid Track Certification

Cisco Systems

- Interconnecting Cisco Network Devices
- Advanced Cisco Router Configuration
- Installation and Maintenance of Cisco Routers
- Cisco Internetwork Troubleshooting
- Designing Cisco Networks
- Cisco Internetwork Design
- Configuring Cisco Catalyst Switches
- Cisco Campus ATM Solutions
- Cisco Voice Over Frame Relay, ATM, and IP
- Configuring for Selsius IP Phones
- Building Cisco Remote Access Networks
- Managing Cisco Network Security
- Cisco Enterprise Management Solutions

Nortel Networks

- Nortel Networks Accelerated Router Configuration
- Nortel Networks Advanced IP Routing
- Nortel Networks WAN Protocols
- Nortel Networks Frame Switching
- Nortel Networks Accelar 1000 Comprehensive Configuration
- Nortel Networks Centillion Switching
- Network Management with Optivity for Windows

Oracle Training

- Introduction to Oracle8 and PL/SQL
- Oracle8 Database Administration

Custom Corporate Network Training

Train on Cutting Edge Technology

We can bring the best in skill-based training to your facility to create a real-world hands-on training experience. Global Knowledge has invested millions of dollars in network hardware and software to train our students on the same equipment they will work with on the job. Our relationships with vendors allow us to incorporate the latest equipment and platforms into your on-site labs.

Maximize Your Training Budget

Global Knowledge provides experienced instructors, comprehensive course materials, and all the networking equipment needed to deliver high quality training. You provide the students; we provide the knowledge.

Avoid Travel Expenses

On-site courses allow you to schedule technical training at your convenience, saving time, expense, and the opportunity cost of travel away from the workplace.

Discuss Confidential Topics

Private on-site training permits the open discussion of sensitive issues such as security, access, and network design. We can work with your existing network's proprietary files while demonstrating the latest technologies.

Customize Course Content

Global Knowledge can tailor your courses to include the technologies and the topics which have the greatest impact on your business. We can complement your internal training efforts or provide a total solution to your training needs.

Corporate Pass

The Corporate Pass Discount Program rewards our best network training customers with preferred pricing on public courses, discounts on multimedia training packages, and an array of career planning services.

Global Knowledge Training Lifecycle

Supporting the Dynamic and Specialized Training Requirements of Information Technology Professionals

- Define Profile
- Assess Skills
- Design Training
- Deliver Training
- Test Knowledge
- Update Profile
- Use New Skills

Global Knowledge

Global Knowledge programs are developed and presented by industry professionals with "real-world" experience. Designed to help professionals meet today's
interconnectivity and interoperability challenges, most of our programs feature
hands-on labs that incorporate state-of-the-art communication components and
equipment.

ON-SITE TEAM TRAINING

Bring Global Knowledge's powerful training programs to your company. At Global
Knowledge, we will custom design courses to meet your specific network requirements. Call (919)-461-8686 for more information.

YOUR GUARANTEE

Global Knowledge believes its courses offer the best possible training in this field.
If during the first day you are not satisfied and wish to withdraw from the course,
simply notify the instructor, return all course materials and receive a 100%
refund.

REGISTRATION INFORMATION

In the US:
call: (888) 762–4442
fax: (919) 469–7070
visit our website:
www.globalknowledge.com

Syngress Publishing's Sweepstake Terms

OFFICIAL RULES - NO PURCHASE NECESSARY

1) TIMING
The contest (the "Contest") begins March 1, 2001 at 9:00 a.m. EST and ends
November 30, 2001 at 11:59 p.m. EST (the "Entry Period"). You must enter the
contest during the Entry Period.

2) THE PRIZES
Three (3) prizes will be awarded: (a) a Sony DVD Player ("1st Prize"); (b) a Palm
Pilot V ("2nd Prize"); and (c) a Rio MP3 Player ("3rd Prize"). One of each prize will
be awarded. The approximate retail value of the three prizes is as follows: (a) the
Sony DVD Player is approximately $595; (b) the Palm Pilot V is approximately
$399; and (c) the Rio MP3 Player is approximately $299.

Sponsors make no warranty, guaranty or representation of any kind concerning
any prize. Prize values are subject to change.

3) ELIGIBILITY REQUIREMENTS
No purchase is necessary. Contest is void in Puerto Rico, and where prohibited by
law. Employees of Syngress Publishing, Inc. (the "Sponsor") and their affiliates,
subsidiaries, officers, agents or any other person or entity directly associated with
the contest (the "Contest Entities") and the immediate family members and/or persons living in the same household as such persons are not eligible to enter the
Contest.

This contest is open only to people that meet the following requirements:

- legal residents of the United States

- Must be at least 21 years of age or older at the time of winning

- Must own a major credit card

4) HOW TO ENTER: No purchase is necessary to enter. Contestants can
enter by mail (see below) or may enter on the Syngress website located at:
www.syngress.com/sweepstake.html. ONLY ONE ENTRY PER PERSON OR E-MAIL
ADDRESS PER HOUSEHOLD WILL BE ACCEPTED.

No purchase is necessary to enter. To enter by mail, print your name, address,
daytime telephone number, email address and age. Mail this in a hand-addressed
envelope to: **Syngress Publishing Contest, Syngress Publishing, Inc., 800
Hingham Street, Rockland, MA 02370**. All mail entries must be postmarked
before November 15, 2001.

Sponsor assumes no responsibility for lost, late, or misdirected entries or for any
computer, online, telephone, or human error or technical malfunctions that may
occur. Incomplete mail entries are void. All entries become the property of Sponsor
and will not be returned.

If a prize notification or prize is returned to Sponsor or its fulfillment companies as undeliverable for any reason, it will be awarded to an alternate. If necessary, due to unavailability, a prize of equal or great value will be awarded at the discretion of the Sponsor. Prizes are not transferable, assignable or redeemable for cash.

By entering the Contest on the Sponsor Internet site, you may occasionally receive promotion announcements from Sponsor through e-mail. If you no longer wish to receive these e-mails, you may cease your participation in such promotions by sending an e-mail to promotions@syngress.com with your First Name, Last Name, and your e-mail address.

5) WINNER SELECTION/DEADLINE DATES: Random drawings will be conducted by the Sponsor from among all eligible entries. Odds of winning the prize depend on the number of eligible entries received. The first drawing will be for the winner of the 1st Prize, then a drawing will be held from all remaining eligible entries for the winner of the 2nd Prize and finally a drawing will be held from all remaining eligible entries for the winner of the 3rd Prize. These drawings will occur on December 1, 2001, at the offices of Syngress Publishing, Inc., 800 Hingham Street, Rockland, MA 02370. The decisions by the Sponsor shall be final and binding in all respects.

6) GENERAL CONDITIONS: Contest entrants agree to be bound by the terms of these official rules. The laws of the Commonwealth of Massachusetts and the United States govern this Contest, and the state and federal courts located in Suffolk and Middlesex Counties in the Commonwealth of Massachusetts shall be the sole jurisdiction for any disputes related to the Contest. All federal, state, and local laws and regulations apply. Winners will be notified via e-mail and/or U.S. Mail within two (2) weeks of prize drawing. Winners will be required to execute and return an Affidavit of Eligibility and Release of Liability and where legal, Publicity Release within 14 days following the date of issuance of notification. Non-compliance within this time period or return of any prize/prize notification as undeliverable may result in disqualification and selection of an alternate winner. Acceptance of prize constitutes permission for Sponsor to use winner's name and likeness for advertising and promotional purposes without additional compensation unless prohibited by law. BY ENTERING, PARTICIPANTS RELEASE AND HOLD HARMLESS SYNGRESS PUBLISHING, INC., AND ITS RESPECTIVE PARENT CORPORATIONS, SUBSIDIARIES, AFFILIATES, DIRECTORS, OFFICERS, PRIZE SUPPLIERS, EMPLOYEES AND AGENTS FROM ANY AND ALL LIABILITY OR ANY INJURIES, LOSS OR DAMAGE OF ANY KIND ARISING FROM OR IN CONNECTION WITH THE CONTEST OR ACCEPTANCE OR USE OF THE PRIZES WON.

7) INTERNET: If for any reason this contest is not capable of running as planned due to infection by computer virus, bugs, tampering, unauthorized intervention, fraud, technical failures, or any other causes beyond the control of the Sponsor which corrupt or affect the administration, security, fairness, integrity, or proper conduct of this contest, the Sponsor reserves the right, at its sole discretion, to disqualify any individual who tampers with the entry process, and to cancel, terminate, modify, or suspend the online portion of the contest. The Sponsor assumes no responsibility for any error, omission, interruption, deletion, defect, delay in operation or transmission, communications line failure, theft or destruction or unauthorized access to, or alteration of, entries. Sponsor is not responsible for any problems or technical malfunction of any telephone network or telephone lines, computer on-line systems, servers, or providers, computer equipment, software, failure of any e-mail or entry to be received by Sponsor on account of technical problems, human error or traffic congestion on the Internet or at any Web site, or any combination thereof, including any injury or damage to participant's or any other person's computer relating to or resulting from participation in the Contest or downloading any materials in the Contest. CAUTION: ANY ATTEMPT TO DELIBERATELY DAMAGE ANY WEB SITE OR UNDERMINE THE LEGITIMATE OPERATION OF THE CONTEST IS A VIOLATION OF CRIMINAL AND CIVIL LAWS AND SHOULD SUCH AN ATTEMPT BE MADE, SPONSOR RESERVES THE RIGHT TO SEEK DAMAGES OR OTHER REMEDIES FROM ANY SUCH PERSON (S) RESPONSIBLE FOR THE ATTEMPT TO THE FULLEST EXTENT PERMITTED BY LAW. In the event of a dispute as to the identity of a winner based on an e-mail address, the winning entry will be declared made by the authorized account holder of the e-mail address submitted at time of entry. "Authorized account holder" is defined as the natural person who is assigned to an e-mail address by an Internet access provider, on-line service provider, or other organization (e.g., business, educational, institution, etc.) that is responsible for assigning e-mail addresses for the domain associated with the submitted e-mail address.

8) WHO WON: Winners who enter on the web site will be notified by e-mail and winners who had entered via mail will be notified by mail. The winners will also be posted on our web site. Alternatively, to receive the names of the winners please send a self addressed stamped envelope to: Syngress Publishing Contest, care of Syngress Publishing, Inc., 800 Hingham Street, Rockland, MA 02370.

The Sponsor of this sweepstakes is Syngress Publishing, Inc., 800 Hingham Street, Rockland, MA 02370.